The Archaeology of Ancient North America

This volume surveys the archaeology of native North Americans from their arrival on the continent 15,000 years ago up to contact with European colonizers. Offering rich descriptions of monumental structures, domestic architecture, vibrant objects, and spiritual forces, Tim Pauketat and Ken Sassaman show how indigenous people shaped both their history and North America's many varied environments. They place the student in the past as they trace how Native Americans dealt with challenges such as climate change, the rise of social hierarchies and political power, and ethnic conflict. Written in a clear and engaging style with a compelling narrative, *The Archaeology of Ancient North America* presents the grand historical themes and intimate stories of ancient Americans in full, living color.

- Includes a rich illustration program of 295 images, all reproduced in full color.
- Narrates the experiences of Native America in humanistic terms by emphasizing the culture and history of the people who settled the North American continent.
- Links the text with online computer applications and web sites.

Timothy R. Pauketat is Director of the Illinois State Archaeological Survey and professor of anthropology and medieval studies at the University of Illinois, Urbana-Champaign. He is the author or editor of more than a dozen books, with research interests that span the Americas.

Kenneth E. Sassaman is the Hyatt and Cici Brown Professor of Florida Archaeology at the University of Florida. His research centers on the culture history of ancient hunter-gatherers of the Archaic period (ca. 11,000–3,000 years ago).

Both Sassaman and Pauketat are previous winners of the Southeastern Archaeological Conference's C. B. Moore Award in Southeastern Archaeology.

The Archaeology of Ancient North America

Timothy R. Pauketat
University of Illinois

Kenneth E. Sassaman
University of Florida

CAMBRIDGE
UNIVERSITY PRESS

CAMBRIDGE
UNIVERSITY PRESS

Shaftesbury Road, Cambridge CB2 8EA, United Kingdom

One Liberty Plaza, 20th Floor, New York, NY 10006, USA

477 Williamstown Road, Port Melbourne, VIC 3207, Australia

314–321, 3rd Floor, Plot 3, Splendor Forum, Jasola District Centre, New Delhi – 110025, India

103 Penang Road, #05–06/07, Visioncrest Commercial, Singapore 238467

Cambridge University Press is part of Cambridge University Press & Assessment, a department of the University of Cambridge.

We share the University's mission to contribute to society through the pursuit of education, learning and research at the highest international levels of excellence.

www.cambridge.org
Information on this title: www.cambridge.org/9780521762496

DOI: 10.1017/9781139019439

First published 2020 (version 2, August 2022)

Printed in the United Kingdom by TJ Books Limited, Padstow Cornwall

A catalogue record for this publication is available from the British Library

Library of Congress Cataloging-in-Publication data
Names: Pauketat, Timothy R., author. | Sassaman, Kenneth E., author.
Title: The archaeology of ancient North America / Timothy R. Pauketat, Kenneth E. Sassaman.
Description: Cambridge ; New York, NY : Cambridge University Press, [2019] | Includes bibliographical references and index.
Identifiers: LCCN 2019015911 | ISBN 9780521762496
Subjects: LCSH: Indians of North America – Antiquities. | Paleo-Indians – North America. | Indians of North America – Social life and customs. | Human ecology – North America. | North America – Antiquities.
Classification: LCC E77.9 P38 2019 | DDC 970.004/97–dc23
LC record available at https://lccn.loc.gov/2019015911

ISBN 978-0-521-76249-6 Hardback
ISBN 978-0-521-74627-4 Paperback

Contents

Figures

Tables

Sidebars

Acknowledgements

Many people, organizations, and institutions assisted us in the preparation of this book. Ross Hassig, Stephen Lekson, Michael Mathiowetz, Randall McGuire, and Christine VanPool read drafts of various chapters or supplied information and opinions essential to the writing of those chapters. Patricia Crown, Paul Fish, Suzanne Fish, Lynn Gamble, Michael Glassow, Gerardo Gutierrez, Steve Lekson, Chip Wills, and Greg Wilson led excursions or accompanied us on a number of field trips to a variety of places featured in this book. We have collaborated with and bounced ideas off Susan Alt, David Anderson, Danielle Benden, Meggan Blessing, Ernie Boszhardt, Thomas Emerson, Don Holly, Asa Randall, and many others during this volume's compilation.

Aspects of our own research projects, supported by the National Science Foundation, the National Endowment for the Humanities, the Hyatt and Cici Brown Endowment for Florida Archaeology, and the John Templeton Foundation, have spilled on to the pages of this book. A generous subvention from the Brown Endowment, in fact, is the reason that we have color on the following pages! The Departments of Anthropology at the Universities of Florida and Illinois, along with the Illinois State Archaeological Survey (ISAS), provided general support during the years in which we researched and drafted the text. The Amerind Foundation, in Dragoon, Arizona, provided a home and research support while one of us (Tim) was drafting chapters in 2012: a special thanks to former director, John Ware. He and Eric Kaldahl, at the Amerind, allowed us into their curation areas to photograph or film several cultural objects that appear in this book. Many other institutions, museums, and individuals provided additional help with the objects, sites, maps, and photographs featured in this book and are listed in the figure credits: we thank them all.

We are also grateful to the wonderful staff of Cambridge University Press (CUP), especially Beatrice Rehl, who saw this project through from start to finish with limitless patience. She bought into our premise for writing this particular book, which was that "college professors and general book sellers desperately need a book that not only covers ancient North America, but also brings some life to the topic, conveys the thrill and satisfaction of archaeological discovery, highlights the human emotions and controversies behind archaeology, and works through the complex research problems to find the higher purposes of studying North America's past" (original prospectus submitted to CUP). If we have succeeded, it is in large part due to the emotional support from our wonderful partners over the years. Thanks Susan and Meggan.

Of course, any shortcomings doubtless stem from our own emotional and intellectual excesses and inadequacies, and not those of CUP or anyone else acknowledged above. We loved writing this book, and believe fervently that archaeology has much to teach all people about our collective past, present, and future. We hope that you find such lessons on the pages that follow.

Preface: Rebooting North American Archaeology

Understanding the archaeology of any continent is an ambitious goal, whether you are a student, an interested nonspecialist, or a professional archaeologist. After all, the scope of the subject is but a few continental steps away from the history of the world (see Locator Map). Unfortunately, learning about the archaeology of native North America from a book, such as this, over the course of some manageable period – say, a few months – still entails glossing over many details about people, places, and things. Certainly, this book necessarily focuses on those aspects of the past that we think most important. These are the ones that shed light on the human experience, generally, and its causal relationships to human history. As you will see, this leads us to foreground particular sites and research projects, to follow particular archaeological narratives as they develop, to accentuate certain kinds of historical relationships (and not others), and to generalize.

Few authors feel comfortable with generalizing at continental scales. The reasons include the humbling recognition, unavoidable as an archaeologist, that the more one knows about any archaeological subject, the more one understands how little one actually knows. Sometimes this is the case regardless of scale. For instance, few of us can fully appreciate the big historical implications of momentous occasions that affect thousands, whether those events are weather-related, such as El Niño rains, or large-scale ritual spectacles held in villages or pueblos. Similarly, there exist many unknowns about sensory experience and its causal power – what specific people might be induced to feel or do given, say, the flavors of foods, the spectacular visual qualities of ritual gatherings and celestial phenomena, or the colors, textures, and designs of particular objects. Archaeologists have only recently begun to think seriously about how the embodied experience of movement through space, and hence the qualities of specific spaces or experiences, affect our humanity, shape our identities, or afford certain futures (see especially Chapters 5, 8–11, and 14–15). There are so many unknowns.

But these are all reasons to do archaeology. Understanding the causal linkages between sense, movement, design, and history is to some degree possible through an archaeology of the Native American, American Indian, or First Nations past. Such lessons, of course, may be of immediate concern to living descendants, whose heritage, identity,

Atlantic Ocean

Greenland

Newfoundland

Puerto Rico

Hispaniola

Lake Ontario

Lake Erie

Florida

Cuba

Lake Huron

Hudson Bay

Lake Superior

Lake Michigan

Yucatan
Peninsula

Canada

Gulf of Mexico

United States

Mexico

Pacific Ocean

Alaska

Vancouver
Island

California

Bala
California

Aleutian Islands

N

Elevation (meters)

High: 5930

Low: -76

0   500   1,000   2,000 km

USGS EROS Center. 2007.
North American Elevation 1-Kilometer Resolution. 3rd ed. National Atlas of the US. Reston, VA.

Projection: Lambert Azimuthal Equal Area
This poster was created on February 28, 2012

and sovereignty are at stake. A good deal of respect and deference needs to be brought to the table of any study of the North American past. This is important also because North American archaeology's lessons are relevant to non-Indian peoples everywhere, who stand to benefit from knowing who, what, where, how, and why changes of all kinds happened in the past, are happening now, and will happen in our collective future.

Of course, bear in mind that in archaeology, as in history, there are no absolute truths. People are not mere matter that might be contained in a test tube or placed on a laboratory table and evaluated using the laws of physics or chemistry. Instead, history and heritage, both of which are rooted in the stuff – the artifacts, features, landscapes, etc. – that archaeologists deal in everyday, are always subject to negotiation. In fact, archaeological remains are very much the media of human imagination (or lack thereof), which is always reckoned with respect to the past and, from there, the things and places that comprise that past. This is why the news is filled with stories of pipelines threatening sacred sites, illicit diggers stealing pots, tourists and ranchers defacing rock art, and developers bulldozing whole village sites. This is why from time to time American Indians dispute interpretations that adversely affect their own narratives.

We, your authors, are not immune. Any First Nations, American Indian, Yupik, Iñupiat, or other native person reading this book might rightfully disagree with certain of our claims to knowledge and, thus, choose to narrate the past differently. Certainly, other archaeologists predisposed to think differently than us will dispute some of our inferences. That is as it should be. We do not claim to know everything or to speak for everybody. Our tack is to approach the human past with a good deal of intellectual and historical humility.

However, we do fervently believe that North American archaeology holds key insights into some important historical issues that matter for us all today. First and foremost among these is the manner in which we understand the mediation of human history, if not humanity generally. Who or what causes this or that, and where, when, how, and why?

Our commitment to asking such questions and the weight we give to media, to various other agents of change, and to narratives make our book unlike all previous textbooks on North American archaeology – and there are a few (Fagan 2005; Neusius and Gross 2014; Snow 2010). Previous authors with ideas founded in older theories of cultural and societal change wrote almost all of these earlier works. The sources of change recognized by them often seem to be (1) gradual and long term, (2) external to the human experience, and (3) local and ahistorical (i.e., one region's or period's people seem unaffected by their neighbors or their ancestors). For many, climate change and population growth were the explanations for everything. What people did – and how they related to other phenomena, places, and things – mattered very little. Actual people – or their things and constructions – were but passive reflections of the times.

This strikes us as more than intolerably colonial. Few North Americans today, native or nonnative, would ever accept such ahistorical explanations of our own world. And yet, from these earlier viewpoints, societies and their institutions were the units of change, treated as if they evolved slowly through time in ways that shaped the docile bodies of human beings.

Of course, fetishizing society in such ways deemphasizes, if unintentionally, the immediate relevance of the North American past to the present (see Chapter 2). It does this by implying that pre-Columbian peoples were not the makers of history (see Chapter 9) but natural organisms, members of bio-social populations who were bound by putatively conservative cultures and subject in turn to immutable rules and norms. Culture and cultural materials were understood to be not active and malleable interlocutors of history but instead passive reflections of slow-moving, organismic, societal adaptations. Artifacts were, thus, either functional items that served some societal purpose or superfluous nonfunctional ritual objects. Nonhuman beings, substances, forces, and phenomena – even those that people may have recognized as integral to their humanity – are especially marginal to such social-evolutionary visions of the past. This is why so few of these earlier archaeologists questioned the use of the word "prehistoric" to describe pre-contact North Americans (but see Lightfoot 1995).

All such treatments of the indigenous peoples of North America, past or present, are highly problematic, if only owing to the colonial history of North America (see Chapter 3). All archaeology needs to work toward maximizing the roles and voices of American Indian people – past and present. Any archaeology that denies an American Indian cultural logic to the North American past risks colonizing that past with its own biases. This is because pre-Columbian North America was unequivocally not (not, not) a place populated by modern individuals whose goals were to maximize caloric intake and minimize energy expenditures or who merely functioned as cogs in some mechanistic society (see Chapter 1's juxtapositioning of John Muir and Henry Ford). It is time to abandon such twentieth-century views and reboot North American archaeology.

Perhaps the place to begin is with the continent itself. And so, in Chapter 1, we use Google Earth to fly over it, hoping to transcend some of the traditional "culture area" divisions of the continent – the Plains, the Southwest, the Northwest Coast, the Eastern Woodlands – rooted in earlier beliefs that indigenous Americans populated societies that developed by adapting to environments (subject in turn to climate change and population growth). Admittedly, we do not fully abandon the subcontinental divisions, but we do shape our chapters around issues, with some chapters very intentionally comparing one region's history with another's.

The histories of which we speak are not, of course, written. Instead, histories are lived. They include the larger material-cultural constructions of people who relate to and through the forces, matter, and beings of their worlds. Histories result in altered configurations of people, places, things, substances, and phenomena that then, in turn, impinge on (not determine) future relationships.

Defined in this way, there were no prehistoric people. Moreover, there was an element of reading and writing in all people's historical constructions. That is, pre-Columbian people wrote their histories in the land and through objects. For example, certain "medicine bundles" contained a series of mnemonic objects that would be opened and read much like a scroll (see Chapters 3, 8, 10, and 11). One might call this oral history, but let us be clear: it was based on knowledge *recorded* via an ordered assemblage of things, much as written language is an ordered assemblage of abstract characters. Many cultural objects and even entire landscapes had similar mnemonic power to call to mind relationships, historical and otherwise – prayer sticks, sacred pipes, peace medals, decorated pots, designed architectural spaces, aligned mounds, geometric earthworks.

Hence, North American archaeological history is not reliant on identifying prominent, usually European, human actors – the Juan Cabrillos and Francisco Coronados of their time – or on reading their texts. Both human actors and texts do embody the sorts of historical relationships about which we speak, of course, but both can also mask the actual relationships that we need to explain. Instead, the histories of which we speak were contingent on understanding relationships that happened, and that always necessarily happen, through material, spatial, and corporeal media over time. These were historical contingencies that played out at local, regional, subcontinental, and, sometimes, even continental scales. We cannot ignore the Pacific Coast's relationship deep into the continent's interior, or the Southwest's historical impacts on the Mississippi Valley, and vice versa. If left to our own devices, we would not ignore north and west Mexico, or pretend that Mesoamerica had no impacts north of the US–Mexico border. It did.

Questions of Time and History

This brings us to the question of time in relation to history. As we repeat in Chapter 9, history in the western sense of the term would seem predicated on linear time, and on the recognition that linear time can be segmented into periods or eras. It also considers time to be objective and irreversible, unfolding at a constant rate. But history in the sense we use it in this book is not beholden to a linear narrative nor is it dependent on the actual events that fill time. It is, rather, what people make of the past, however that may be conceived. And it can unfold at different rates, depending on the kinds and qualities of experiences and relationships at play.

Certainly, we do base this book's narratives around chronological dates, and for ease of understanding we primarily use Gregorian calendar years BCE (Before Common Era) or CE (Common Era), as opposed to years BP (Before Present), BC (Before Christ), or AD (*Anno Domini*, Latin for "in the year of our lord"). In a few instances we retain calibrated BP date ranges (cal BP) in order to remind archaeologists who prefer them where we are in time. Generally speaking, all dates used in this book are based either on dendrochronology (tree rings), especially in the US Southwest/northwestern Mexico, or on radiocarbon assays. The latter are measurements of the amount of radioactive carbon within some archaeologically recovered organic substance. Of course, because the amount of radioactive carbon in the atmosphere fluctuated in the past, archaeologists calibrate the radiocarbon date against some other standard, such as tree rings, in order to derive a calendar year estimate. We use calibrated dates and date ranges, though such estimates are seldom perfectly synchronized and are subject to change in the future.

It should be pointed out that even calendar years can be deceptive for reasons explained earlier. That is, history is not an absolute unfolding of time at a constant rate. In fact, it is well established – in part through Einstein's Theory of Relativity – that time speeds up and slows down relative to the contexts of its unfolding. Thus, archaeologists often speak of the temporality of some context, event, material assemblage, or landscape, by which they mean its temporal dimension or implications – what time felt like in that situation (Gosden 1994; Ingold 2000). A dark cave or monumental landscape has a distinctive temporality. It slows time down. So might a stark landscape (Chapters 4 and 8) or a big sky (Chapter 11). On the other hand, increasingly congested and cluttered fields of action, especially those filled with many small things, speed up one's sense of time passing (consider Chapters 14–15).

Hence, you might also conclude that history-making, in the way we describe it above, necessarily happened at different rates and scales. Long periods of apparent stasis (early Holocene foragers?) versus short bursts of change (early Mississippian?) might deceptively appear as if they were based solely in the presence or absence of great history-making people. But the contrasts might also be telling us that there were fundamental dissimilarities in the fields of social experience between epochs that, in turn, produced the people who ostensibly made the difference (Robb and Pauketat 2013). Transitions between such epochs, exemplified by the early mounding of the American Southeast (Chapter 9), the differences between the early and late Puebloan worlds (Chapter 14), or more obviously the era of Native–European "contacts" (Chapter 3), are even more critical for us to understand. So too does it become imperative to rethink the environment and climate change. Something like the ocean then becomes an actor in the worlds of people, and sea-level rise a historical factor central to human history (Chapter 5). So might weather events, such as those stemming from, say, the Neoglacial or the medieval warming (Chapters 6 and 10).

How to Read this Book

Because we reject simplistic cause-and-effect scenarios, where the environment might be said to cause cultural adaptations along with the histories of people generally, or where simple societies are thought to "evolve" into more complex ones, there are a number of ways to read this book. Chapter 1 is not a straightforward environmental summary, but one that builds a bit of history and your own experience into it – thanks to Google Earth. Chapter 2 delves more into the social history of people, past and present. Then Chapter 3 covers what some other authors would relegate to the last chapter – historic-era "contacts" and "colonialism." Given such beginnings, we could imagine some readers simply skipping to Chapter 4 in order to get to the meat of the book – the first people in the continent. Some might also choose to skip to specific research foci or areas of the continent, and this is yet possible despite our best attempts to break out of both the evolutionary approach to the past (foragers versus sedentary food producers) and the culture-area approach to the past. You can still find most of the late Pleistocene and early Holocene material in Chapters 4 and 5, much of the rest of the hunter-gatherer archaeology in Chapters 6 through 9, and most of the text on agricultural or "complex" societies in Chapters 10–15. Similarly, most of the information on the Arctic is found in Chapter 8; the lion's share of our text on the West is contained in three chapters (6, 11, and 13); the Southwest is largely covered in two chapters (14 and 15); and the Eastern Woodlands is spread primarily across four chapters (7, 9, 10, and 12).

But skipping the first three chapters might lead you to miss one of our big historical points: the past happened historically, and history is not a one-dimensional or simple-linear evolutionary process. In fact, history is to some extent always constructed in the present, based on the past, for the future. Likewise, the histories of some so-called culture areas most certainly and consequentially impinged on the histories of others. For such reasons, which we harp on now and again in chapters to come, we sometimes begin chapters with a later historical vignette. In the case of Chapter 9, we reverse the chronological order of the chapter entirely. In other cases, we reference time and again the causal relationships between the people, places, and things in otherwise separate chapters.

The causal elephant in the room, in fact, is Mesoamerica and the Caribbean. There is no legitimate reason whatsoever to believe that today's US–Mexico border, or the 150 km (90 mi) between the Florida Keys and Cuba, was much of a barrier at all in the past; there is also no reason to overlook the fact that west, central, and northern Mexican connections with people and places north of the Rio Grande were likely critical to the specific historical developments in the north. Specific cultural practices, gods, or religious movements likely have their genesis to the south. Yet even we, owing to the scale of the project before you and the realities of publishing in the twenty-first century, could not include a chapter on Mesoamerica and the Caribbean.

That is unfortunate since there are some startling parallel developments between Mesoamerica, the Southwest/Northwest, the Southeast, Midwest, and even Plains. Some such parallels – as with the big historical changes between California, Illinois, and New Mexico around 900 CE – surely have other explanations: the Medieval Climatic Anomaly, for instance, must figure prominently. Then again, our current reboot of North American archaeology, by rejecting old-fashioned notions of ahistorical development that have been far too dependent on prime movers (climate change and population among them), ends by reconsidering all of the causal factors of the North American past, including climate change, in a new way (sometimes called "post-humanist" or "new materialist" [see Chapters 1 and 16; Harris and Cippola 2017]). Our new-ancient history of North America and North Americans does not necessarily seek to strictly delimit human social history from culture, or from the landscape or the history of other things and phenomena: weather, nonhuman organisms, celestial objects, and other seemingly inanimate but powerful, locomotive forces. This tack, we hope, broadens the story of the continent and, we believe, enhances the relevance of the North American past in the present for the future.

1 Envisioning North America

John Muir had a religious experience in the Yosemite Valley of California (Figure 1.1). After several years of college coursework in Wisconsin, Muir fled to Canada in 1863 with his brother to evade the Civil War draft, returning a few years later to work as a sawyer in Indiana, only to have his eye pierced in a work-related accident. Regaining his sight after six weeks of confinement in a dark room, Muir set out on a 1,000-mile hike from Indiana to Florida, where he intended to gain passage to South America to continue his journey, but instead succumbed to malaria on the Gulf coast and diverted his path to New York via boat, where he boarded a train to California.

Muir arrived in the Yosemite Valley in 1868 to see what he had until then only read about. Recounted in his book *First Summer in the Sierra* (1911), Muir observed what he called the "grandest of all

Fig 1.1 Panoramic view of the Yosemite Valley of California, one of the many spectacular vistas that inspired John Muir to devote his life to environmental preservation. Yosemite Valley in the summer with El Capitan, Half Dome, and Bridalveil falls in the background. Johan Viirok photo, 2011/Wikimedia.

special temples of Nature." Steep, sheer cliffs, cascading waterfalls, and shadowy vistas stirred his deepest emotions, reaffirming his belief in the divinity of nature. Muir was a devote Christian and thus predisposed to viewing nature as the work of God. And yet, he took divinity beyond common belief by bringing the supernatural – the divine – down to earth, so to speak. Without rejecting biblical doctrine, Muir went further, to suggest that earthly things were themselves spiritual, transcendent of the physical limits of nature. For Muir and those who influenced his thinking – notably Henry David Thoreau and Ralph Waldo Emerson – going to the mountains was like going to church.

Living as he did in the age of frontier expansion, Muir had good reason to believe that his "church" was in danger. He was particularly concerned about overgrazing of grassland in Yosemite and authored articles for popular magazines denouncing any land-use practices that would impact what he considered "pristine" land. Muir's many writings inspired others to join his crusade to preserve nature. He successfully petitioned the US Congress to pass the National Parks Bill in 1890, establishing Yosemite and Sequoia National Parks. Two years later he co-founded the Sierra Club, an environmental advocacy group with more than 1.3 million members today. His many other contributions to wilderness preservation are unparalleled in US history, and memorials to his life can be found in national parks, in the names of mountains and trails, and in a commemorative day in California (April 21).

As influential as Muir was in establishing the preservation movement in the USA, he was bound to encounter opposition from individuals, agencies, and governments seeking a foothold in the economic opportunities of a burgeoning nation. Adversity in this respect sometimes came from unsuspected sources. In 1896 Muir established a relationship with Gifford Pinchot, who nine years later would become the first chief of the US Forest Service. Pinchot was a leader in the *conservation* movement, an approach to nature that promoted sustainable use of resources for the benefit of people. His perspective ran counter to the *preservation* movement, championed by Muir, which held that wilderness should be set aside from any human use other than visitation. Both men criticized reckless exploitation of natural resources, but Pinchot's approach was far more utilitarian than Muir's, being responsive to the nation's growing demand for timber and fuel.

Born on a farm near Detroit in the same year that Muir fled to Canada was the son of William and Mary Ford. Growing up to become one of America's greatest industrialists, Henry Ford died 83 years later with enormous wealth, power, and renown. He is credited with building an automobile industry that fundamentally changed not only the way products were made, but also how they were marketed and consumed. Ford was a gifted innovator of production, perfecting an assembly line approach to reduce costs while increasing output (Figure 1.2). He wanted to create products, like the Model T automobile, that everyday people could afford, and he ensured that hope for his own laborers by paying them higher-than-average wages. He even created a franchise system to establish dealerships across first the country, then the world. In Ford's vision, peace and prosperity came from consumerism, an economy and society of robust purchasing and consuming, driven, theoretically, by the free choice of buyers in an open market (Figure 1.2).

The way Ford envisioned nature was very different than the way Muir viewed nature. We will grant that Ford may have been just as awestruck as Muir by nature's wonders, such as the waterfalls of

Fig 1.2 Workers in Highland Park, Michigan pull together magnetos and flywheels for 1913 Ford autos at the first moving assembly line. Wikimedia.

the Sierra. However, Ford devoted much of his life to transforming nature (or tapping into its potential) through technology, including the tools used to make vehicles (the transformation of matter and energy), and the vehicles themselves, tools for people to move farther and faster than their biology allowed, thus saving time and personal energy for other pursuits. Ford was a Christian, but he rarely made public statements with regard to religion. It is hardly controversial to suggest, nonetheless, that he felt comfortable with the idea that God granted dominion over nature to humans who were faithful and righteous, as well as the notion that people were directed from above to go forth and prosper. The mid-eighteenth-century notion that came to be known as *Manifest Destiny* was informed by these same beliefs, a mandate to expand out and subdue nature (including, by mid-eighteenth-century logic, Indians) for the sake of God and Country (Figure 1.3). In Aldous Huxley's 1932 classic, *Brave New World*, society is organized by the principles of Fordism, and the years are dated AF (or *Anno Ford*), in the Year of Our Ford. In a *Brave New World*, capitalism and piety had morphed into one.

Wrapped up in the growth and prosperity of their fledgling nation, nonnative American people attributed their motives to godly causes, and enabled their actions through a variety of technological

Fig 1.3 The 1872 painting by John Gast, *Spirit of the Frontier*, is a visual allegory of Manifest Destiny, the doctrine of progress for a fledgling nation. The mythical goddess Columbia leads her people westward with innovations like the railroad and telegraph, displacing, along the way, indigenous people and the bison of their homeland. Wikimedia.

innovations: the steam engine, railroad, revolver pistol, barbed wire, cotton gin, telegraph, sewing machine, and, later, the motorcar, among others. It is not difficult, from a modern, western perspective, to look back over the recent history of North America and be awestruck by the "progress" technology enabled. And it follows that we tend to ascribe a great deal of explanatory power to technology in our narratives about social and cultural change. For the German intellectual Karl Marx, technology reveals a human's relationship to nature, but also to other humans (through labor arrangements and class relations), and to the ideas that motivate or suppress action. So influential was Marx in shaping western thinking about technology that his theory came to be a central theme in anthropological understanding of cultural variation and change. The ethnographer Julian Steward (1955), for instance, developed the concept of *Culture Core* to describe the technological articulation between humans and the environment among nonwestern people, using as examples the Shoshone Indians of the Great Basin. For Steward, the entirety of Shoshone culture could be explained as Core, with them devoting most of their time, energy, and thought to the pursuit of food.

Confronting an archaeological record dominated by tools and the by-products of their manufacture and use, students of the ancient past in North America found utility in Steward's manner of thinking. Through stratigraphic excavations that revealed changes in technology over time, archaeologists began to assemble a narrative with themes familiar to western history. The notion of *progress* crept in as histories of innovations such as groundstone, pottery, and irrigation were portrayed as *improvements* over less efficient or effective antecedents. Only rarely was a change in technology seen as energetically neutral or inconsequential. The trouble with thinking such as this is that the technology itself becomes the agent of change, as in the computer HAL in *2001: A Space Odyssey*, or Skynet's AI network in the *Terminator* movies.

Social scientists refer to the tendency to imbue technology with powers it does not actually have as *technological fetishism* (i.e., the worship of technology). This is hardly a conscious decision in most cases, but rather an example of the human tendency to simplify complex phenomena, in this case explanations for change. To fetishize technology is to endow technology with the power to solve problems: grow economies, save time, cure disease, and the like. Surely the technologies are real, and they can be compared with alternatives to measure relative costs, benefits, efficiencies, and capacities. But there is little in those metrics that helps to understand how technological change relates to culture change. We may assume that a more efficient technology, if made available, would quickly be adopted and used, but in the particular historical context in which the innovation arises, its adoption and use is contingent on factors beyond energetic efficiency. The slow, bumpy road to electric cars in North America attests to the contingencies of the internal combustion market Ford and others created.

Technological fetishism and Manifest Destiny go hand in hand in the logic of western progress, and archaeological narratives have been influenced by these concepts. It is the narrative of technological dominion over nature in the future that Muir feared the most. Technology in this sense was not merely the way humans ensured their survival, but also the means by which they grew immensely in scale and complexity. It follows that a preoccupation with technology has structured our view of nature in general, and let us think of the North American past as *prehistory*, where "primitives," thought to lack the capacity to overcome nature's constraints, were simply slaves to nature, nothing more than a Culture Core. Underpinned by racist logic since at least the Middle Ages, this view of the primitive made it hard for western observers to see anything progressive in the archaeological record of North America, or, if they did, to attribute progress to the achievements of men like Henry Ford. Even when great technological innovations were recognized, fetishism would hold the tools themselves responsible.

Ironically, North American archaeology has entered a new era of theorizing about the past in which objects, places, and nonhuman organisms are endowed with spirits and powers, the ability to evoke or prevent actions on the part of humans. Called *post-humanism* by some theorists (Wolfe 2009), this novel thinking has a counterpart in activism which strives to remove humans from the top of the Great Chain of Being, suggesting they have no inherent right to destroy nature or set themselves above it (Harris and Cipolla 2017). The philosophy is consistent with John Muir's thinking, as it is with native North Americans who find spirituality in all manner of being. And it runs counter to the dominant themes of western philosophy since the Enlightenment and continuing through the time of Ford, in which technological change, as a measure of progress, explains everything.

If Muir was too romantic and Ford too ambitious, then Pinchot strikes a pragmatic middle ground. All people in all times and places have practical needs that must be met. In some theories of change, the process of meeting these needs is invisible and participants are dupes in a selective process about which they know nothing. In other theories, change comes from people bouncing into each other and sharing ideas. Such encounters are certainly the source of something new, but if followed to its logical conclusion, this process tends to subdue cultural diversity, as we are witnessing today through globalization. And yet in other theories, interactions produce novel results, increase cultural diversity, and thus enhance resiliency in the face of change. In these settings, human imagination and creativity abound, and technologies are conscripted into service far beyond their intended purposes.

Our theoretical tendency in writing this book is to allow multivocal histories to emerge from the juxtaposition of different ways of thinking, including nonwestern thought. We have our own biases, which will no doubt show, but we also recognize that different ways of seeing the world – as in the contrast between Muir and Ford – produce new forms of knowledge. In this sense, we turn now to an overview of the physical aspects of North America salient to a variety of theoretical approaches in archaeology.

Getting to Know a Continent

Few individuals get to know North America by traveling about the entire continent, although extraordinary people like John Muir have always existed and always will. The rest of us know about the landscapes of North America from description and imagery, such as paintings, photographs, and especially film, television, and the Internet. Maps of course figure prominently in our representation of geography. Most maps are two-dimensional projections of three-dimensional space and are thus never entirely realistic. In addition, maps are constructed at varying scales, from different perspectives, and with select features, such as ground cover, topography, bodies of water, or buildings and roads. In this sense maps vary with intent or purpose. Maps are also static, unlike films, and cannot effectively capture motion in real time.

Modern technology opens up perspectives on geography that no paper map can supply. Regular users of the Internet are familiar with Google Earth, a virtual globe created by superimposing digital satellite imagery and aerial photography to project interactive coverage of the earth's surface (Figure 1.4). Introduced in 2005, Google Earth is available free of charge for noncommercial users, like university students. If you can, go to a computer, tablet, or smartphone now and open Google Earth. In the latest (2020) version, the globe appears in full form against a dark but starry backdrop and rotates slowly in a counterclockwise direction, true to form. In an earlier iteration, Google Earth automatically rotated the globe so that North America was front and center. As you zoomed in on this older version the borders and names of US states emerged. As you zoomed in farther, the roads and buildings of Kansas appeared and ultimately the town of Lawrence, home to the University of Kansas and its Jayhawks. Given its geographic centrality in Google Earth, one might assume that Lawrence sits at the center of the continent, but that is not exactly the case, at least not by most calculations. If defined as all land north of South America, North America has a center point somewhere in North Dakota. The specific location depends, of course, on the boundaries

Fig 1.4 The North American continent as seen in the digital satellite imagery of Google Earth.

Fig 1.5 Postcard from the 1930s of the monument emplaced at the purported geographical center of North America in Rugby, North Dakota. Wikimedia.

one recognizes. In fact, North Dakotans have feuded over claims to geographic centrality since 1932, when citizens in the town of Rugby erected a 21 foot tall obelisk to mark the spot (Figure 1.5). Townspeople in nearby Orrin and Balta have ever since raised objections, as their towns are closer to the center than is Rugby, by some calculations. By yet other calculations, the continental midpoint is actually a small slough outside town (it too the recipient of a monument of piled stone that was later flooded).

Lawrence, Kansas no longer assumes geographic centrality in Google Earth, but it will do as a starting point for touring the continent. At about 260 m (853 ft) above mean sea level (amsl), Lawrence, Kansas is a little more than one-third the average elevation in North America (720 m [2362 ft] amsl). We will both ascend and descend in elevation as we traverse the virtual continent, starting off in what was Shawnee reservation land before the Kansas territory was opened for settlement in 1854.

Head North

We begin by expanding our perspective. But first select the "Everything" option in the "Map Style" of the pulldown menu of Google Earth to display borders and other landmarks for our journey. Next type "Lawrence, Kansas" into the search engine and you will be taken to our starting point. Now, zoom out until town and county borders disappear, but you still see state borders and names. Now simply key the "up" arrow to move north across the landscape, toward Canada and the Arctic Circle. You will first ascend the Missouri River, passing over Omaha and the southern Iowa Drift Plain with its rolling tallgrass plains of wind-blown silt (loess) and glacial till. Central Iowa marks the southern extent of Ice Age glaciers when humans arrived in the midcontinent some 14,000 years ago (it was even farther south during the last glacial maximum, roughly 21,000 years ago). The landscape from this point northward was therefore uninhabitable until glacial ice receded over the ensuing millennia. As it had done in previous eras, ice receded as the climate warmed to expose not simply land, but a landscape of moraines, drumlins, glacial lakes, and outwash plains such as the one in southern Iowa.

Travel a bit farther north in Google Earth and you will enter the state of Minnesota, where glacial lakes and moraines abound. You will also notice a second major river coming into view from the east, on which the city of Minneapolis lies. This of course is the great Mississippi River, North America's largest drainage system. The upper portion of the river is an entrenched, multi-channel river with many bars and islands. As we will see later, 4,000 km (2,500 mi) to the south the river empties into the Gulf of Mexico in flat, swampy terrain vastly different than the postglacial landscape to the north. The Mississippi River not only connects these very different places, it is responsible for much of the difference. Silt and clay from once-glaciated land has eroded over the millennia and been transported by the river from northern glacial plains to southern floodplains, levees, and related features, feeding some of the most productive farmland in the world. Some of this displaced sediment eventually made its way to the mouth of the river, the Mississippi Delta, home to New Orleans.

As you move into south-central Canada you will notice to the west a series of large, elongated lakes. The largest of them is Lake Winnipeg, a 24,500 km^2 (9,500 mi^2) freshwater body that is among the remnants of a glacial lake known to geologists as Lake Agassiz (Figure 1.6). When it formed from meltwater at the end of the Ice Age, Lake Agassiz held more water than is contained in all the lakes of the world today. It of course has since been drained considerably, with much of its water escaping through waterways heading north, but some into the Mississippi River via the ancestor of one of its tributaries, the Minnesota River. A postglacial process known as *isostatic rebound* (the rise of land that was depressed under the weight of glaciers) is partly to blame for the draining of Lake Agassiz, and, as we will see later, other changes in northern terrain that affected patterns of human settlement. Off the view of Google Earth to the east are the Great Lakes, a series of five interconnected lakes that today comprise the largest body of freshwater in the world. Like Lakes Winnipeg, Manitoba, and numerous other glacial lakes, the Great Lakes formed from meltwater but they filled more slowly and in deeper basins (more than 400 m [~1,300 ft] in Lake Superior) than most others,

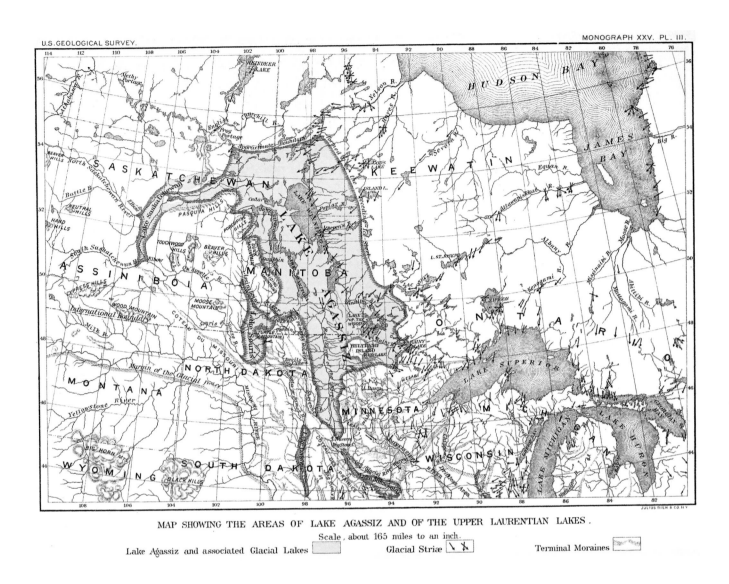

U.S.GEOLOGICAL SURVEY.   MONOGRAPH XXV. PL. III.

MAP SHOWING THE AREAS OF LAKE AGASSIZ AND OF THE UPPER LAURENTIAN LAKES.
Scale, about 165 miles to an inch.

Lake Agassiz and associated Glacial Lakes   Glacial Striæ   Terminal Moraines

Fig 1.6 The projected extent of Lake Agassiz by nineteenth-century geologist Warren Upham. At its maximum extent during the last Ice Age, Lake Agassiz was larger than all five modern Great Lakes combined. Wikimedia.

creating a dynamic situation of advancing shorelines for the earliest settlers. In Chapter 4 we feature some ongoing underwater archaeology at sites of early settlement on the now-flooded shoreline of Lake Superior.

Relatively small lakes known as "kettles" dominate the landscape of central Canada as you travel farther north, but eventually you arrive at a massive body of water along the eastern margin of your view. This is Hudson Bay, a saltwater embayment encompassing 1,230,000 km² (470,000 mi²), the second largest bay in the world. Classified by geographers as part of the North Atlantic Ocean, Hudson Bay actually occupies the interface between the Arctic and Atlantic oceans. According to most geologists, the shape and size of the bay goes back to the very formation of North America (Figure 1.7). In fact, the broad region of ancient rock that encircles Hudson Bay is the currently exposed nucleus of the continent, part of what geologists refer to as a *craton*, specifically the Laurentia craton. Consisting of highly eroded volcanic rock at the surface, the Canadian Shield is that portion of Laurentia most affected by glaciation (notably, scraped down to bare rock). It is the exposed core of North America, part of a mountain-forming event (the Trans-Hudson orogeny) dating some 1.8–2 billion years ago. When it was young the Canadian Shield consisted of sharp mountain peaks up to 12,000 m (39,000 ft) tall, with much volcanic activity. Average elevation today in the Canadian Shield is only about 40 m higher than that of much of Kansas, owing to the long, gradual processes of erosion and deposition that have subdued the marked relief of a young continent.

Although its geological origin is attributed to continent-forming processes far older than the last glaciation, the basin enclosing Hudson Bay has had a major role in more recent, transformative environmental changes. It was the growth center for the major ice sheet of the last (Wisconsin) glaciation, known as the Laurentide ice sheet. At up to two miles thick at its peak, the Laurentide ice sheet covered nearly all of Canada and much of the northern United States. As we will

Fig 1.7 An *Inukshuk* on the shore of Hudson Bay. For the Inuit who constructed them, *Inukshuk* were stone landmarks or monuments, in this case in human-like form. Those along the modern shoreline of Hudson Bay bear witness to changes in climate and water levels. A major center of glacial expansion during the last Ice Age, Hudson Bay continues to register the consequences of climate change, now in a regime of accelerated warming. Wikimedia.

see in Chapter 5, the melting of Ice Age glaciers not only affected the landscape in ways we have noted already, but it also changed global air circulation, the salinity of near-shore ocean waters, and, of course, sea level.

Travel one final leg northward in Google Earth from Hudson Bay and you will begin to see frozen lakes, ice sheets, and other indications of high-latitude terrain. Coastal waters appear (Beaufort Sea to the west, the Gulf of Bothia to the east), interspersed with islands and shaped by crenulated shorelines. You soon cross the Northwest Passage, connecting Baffin Bay to the east with the Arctic Ocean to the west. At this point stop and zoom out until Greenland emerges in the upper right (northeast) corner of your view. You are now looking at North American land (plus Greenland) encompassed by the Arctic Circle, the southern extremity of the polar day and polar night (once-a-year days of 24-hour sunlight and 24-hour darkness). As we will see in Chapter 8, Arctic conditions were never a deterrent to human settlement in North America, although they certainly pushed people to the edge of survival in some cases. We will also see that for eleventh-century Norsemen who attempted to colonize North America by way of Greenland, Arctic conditions of the Little Ice Age were too much to bear.

Head West

Re-center your view in Google Earth by entering "Lawrence, Kansas" into the search engine. Then zoom out like before, until the county borders disappear. Pressing the "left" arrow key at this point takes you west, across the Great Plains and toward the Rockies, Sierras, and Pacific Ocean.

The first thing you may notice moving west through Kansas is the change in color and texture of the terrain just past Wichita. This is the eastern margin of the Great Plains, an immense swath of grasslands that stretches from the Rio Grande to Canada. The province is divided by geographers into many subdivisions, a few distinguished by geological uplift, such as the Black Hills to the north of your view, in South Dakota and Wyoming, and the central uplift of Texas, to the south. The entire province is technically the western margin of the Interior Plains, which extends eastward to the Appalachian Plateau. Ultimately, the relative flatness of the Interior Plains is owed to the fact that for half a billion years (570–70 million years ago [mya]) it was covered by a shallow sea. Thousands of feet of sediment accumulated on the sea floor, burying the underlying bedrock. Slow uplift of the continent after 70 mya drained the region and led to not only rock formations like the Black Hills and Central Texas Uplift, but also, after about 10 mya, a long period of downcutting by rivers and streams that sculpted much of the terrain. This carved-out landscape becomes quite apparent in Google Earth as you move farther west out of Kansas and into Colorado. You are looking down on the High Plains and Colorado Piedmont, where channels of the Arkansas River (to the south) and Platte River (to the north) remove water and sediment from elevated land.

Another feature besides topography that distinguishes the Great Plains from its eastern counterpart in the lowlands is its vegetation (Figure 1.8). Before modern plows were pulled through the province, prairie grasses blanketed the landscape. In areas of favorable conditions, grasslands supported enormous herds of grazing animals, notably the American bison (*Bison bison*), a major resource for the peoples of Chapters 5 and 14. Grasslands have occupied the Great Plains for thousands of years because trees generally cannot, at least not outside the margins of watercourses. This is especially the case in the High Plains, where rainfall is low and droughts frequent. The eastern margin of the Plains sees more rainfall, hence richer grasslands,

Fig 1.8 A view south of Laramie, Wyoming, across the short grass prairie of the northern Great Plains, which once supported enormous herds of bison. Carol M. Highsmith photo/Library of Congress Prints and Photographs Division.

including patches of tallgrass prairie like we crossed on our virtual trip north through Iowa.

As we move farther west, across Colorado, we see why the western margin of the Great Plains is so dry: mountains, big mountains. The peaks you see are those of the Rocky Mountains, many more than 4,000 m (13,123 ft) amsl. As part of the greater North American Cordillera, the Rockies contribute to what climatologists call a *rainshadow effect*. As warm, moist air masses pass over mountain ranges they rise, and when they rise they lose pressure, and with it temperature. Moisture condenses as the air cools, leading to rainfall on the windward side of the mountains, a process known technically as orographic precipitation. Depleted of water, air masses moving over mountains are dry, essentially casting a shadow of aridity on the leeward side of mountains. With respect to the Rockies and the cordillera of which they are a part, moist air from the Pacific does not often make it past the continental divide (which you are viewing in western Colorado), leaving a rainshadow across the adjacent, western margin of the Great Plains.

The Rockies mark the edge of a cordillera that also includes the Pacific Coast Mountain and the Sierra Nevada ranges, each running generally north to south. Between these major ranges are basins and plateaus. You are crossing over the northern reaches of one of two major plateaus in the cordillera as you advance west into Utah. Home to ancestral Pueblo people, as well as others, the Colorado Plateau is a massive province of generally undeformed but uplifted rock averaging about 1,830 m (6,000 ft) amsl. Much of the sharp topographic relief of the plateau is owed to erosion by the Colorado River and its tributaries, which drain the entire province. You are looking at the main channel of the Colorado River in the southeast corner of Utah. If you follow the river south into Arizona, you will see a place where the channel turns west. This is the Grand Canyon, an iconic feature of the Colorado Plateau (Figure 1.9). With cuts as deep as 610 m (2,000 ft), the Grand Canyon exposes the thick sedimentary layers of one of the most tectonically stable regions in North America. For a landscape shaped so much by water, the plateau is actually pretty dry. Much like the rainshadow effect of the Rockies, the plateau is blocked from moist Pacific air by mountains to the west. Precipitation varies across the province, however, with better-watered areas supporting forests of pine, fir, and spruce. As we will see in Chapter 10, the semi-arid

Fig 1.9 The Grand Canyon in Arizona and the Colorado River that made it possible. Slow, gradual processes like the downcutting of rivers exemplify the uniformitarian principle that archaeologists borrowed from geology (see the section entitled "Space, Time, and Change" below). Wikimedia.

climate of the plateau posed formidable challenges to early farming communities.

A prominent feature on the north side of your view is Great Salt Lake of northwest Utah. The lake is situated in the northeast corner of the Basin and Range province, which borders the Colorado Plateau to the east and extends north to the Columbia Plateau and south into Mexico. Its western boundary is marked by the fault scarp of the Sierra Nevada mountains, which creates another rainshadow effect and thus arid climate throughout much of the province. Great Salt Lake is a remnant of a Pleistocene lake known to geologists as Lake Bonneville. At its peak size near the end of the Ice Age, Lake Bonneville was nearly as large as Lake Michigan is today. About 14,500 years ago a large portion of the lake was released through a pass and the ensuing drier and warmer climate dried up much of the remaining portions. Great Salt Lake is today the largest surviving remnant; it is, in fact, the largest saltwater lake in the western hemisphere. Because the lake has no outlet, its high salinity (higher than seawater) is owed to evaporation of mineral-rich water delivered from the surrounding basin by three major rivers and several streams.

The portion of the Basin and Range province encompassed today by western Utah and nearly all of Nevada is known as the Great Basin. Advance a little farther west in Google Earth and you will see terrain in southern Nevada that resembles, as nineteenth-century geologist

Clarence Dutton put it, "an army of caterpillars marching toward Mexico." These are the north–south trending fault-block mountain ranges that are attributed by most geologists to tectonic forces at the contact between oceanic and continental plates. In this situation, the intervening valleys are structural, not erosional (as in the Colorado Plateau). As we will see in Chapter 6, the varied topography of the province – pluvial flats and seasonal lakes in the valleys, upsloping alluvial fans that merge into piedmont, and mountain fault blocks with steep fronts and gentle backslopes – offered good opportunities for humans to relocate seasonally and make effective use of diverse settings.

Travel slightly farther west to the edge of the Great Basin and you will see the Sierra Nevadas, home to the Yosemite Valley that captured John Muir's imagination. Consisting of granite that was uplifted starting about 4 million years ago, the Sierras have peaks as high as, even higher than, the Rockies (at 4,421 m [14,505 ft] amsl, Mount Whitney in the Sierras is the highest elevation in the contiguous USA). Alpine lakes like Lake Tahoe and the deep valleys of Yosemite are among the consequences of glaciation during the early Pleistocene. Today, abundant snowfall along the eastern (windward) margin of the Sierras melts in the spring and feeds the headwaters of the Sacramento and San Joaquin rivers, situated in the intermontane valley of central California, that generally green, flat terrain in Google Earth between Sacramento and Bakersfield.

The Pacific Ocean beckons as we reach the end of our western leg. First we cross one more range of mountains, further testimony to a tectonic history involving compression, subduction, and volcanism at the contact between the oceanic and continental plates. Ocean trenches are associated with convergences between plates, as seen in the steep shorelines and shelves along the Pacific coast. Proliferating under these conditions are extensive kelp forests and the many species up the food chain that were important to humans as early as the late Pleistocene (Erlandson et al. 2007). To the south of your coastal view in Google Earth are the Channel Islands of the Santa Barbara area. Connected as a single island during the late Pleistocene, the Channel Islands would later figure prominently in the history of the Chumash, one of North America's nonagricultural complex societies, as discussed in Chapter 12. Other complex hunter-gatherer societies benefiting from an abundance of Pacific resources populated the coast from northern California to Alaska (see Chapters 7 and 12).

Head East

Bring Google Earth back to Lawrence, zoom out again, then key the "right" arrow to head east toward the Appalachian Mountains and Atlantic coast. Your path forward eastward is marked conveniently by the Missouri River. With headwaters in the Rocky Mountains of western Montana, the Missouri is the longest river in North America. Just as the Missouri River was a major conduit of western expansion during the nineteenth century, it was a route of both westward *and* eastward migration at various times in the ancient past.

As you follow the Missouri River across the state with the same name, you follow a physiographic seam between the once-glaciated terrain of outwash plains to the north and the Ozark Plateau of the Interior Highlands to the south. The Missouri River, in fact, parallels the southernmost margin of glacial advance during the Late Glacial Maximum, some 20,000 years ago. We have already encountered glacial plains in our excursion north, but the Interior Highlands are something different. The province is an uplifted and contorted, then dissected, plateau of Paleozoic age (542–251 mya) marine deposits. In contrast, the St. Francois Mountains of southeast Missouri were formed by igneous activities dating about 1.5 billion years ago, and their modern surface exposures are among the oldest in North America. The mountains are located in that dark green (wooded) area of your Google Earth view of southeast Missouri. Natural lead (galena) and other minerals from the St. Francois figured prominently in regional exchange going back millennia in eastern North America (see Chapter 8).

A short trip eastward brings you to the confluence of the Missouri and Mississippi rivers, just north of St. Louis (Figure 1.10). This is the north end of the American Bottom, a 450 km^2 (175 mi^2) portion of the Mississippi River floodplain extending from Alton, Illinois (where the river bends to the west, north of its confluence with the Missouri) to the Kaskaskia River of southern Illinois, about 100 km (62 mi) distant, as the crow flies. The American Bottom lies between two fingers of the Ozark Plateau, just south of the Pleistocene glacial advance. After flowing through the limestone-constricted valley north of Alton, the river opens into a broad, open plain of softer substrate, where water slows, the river meanders, and alluvial sediment is deposited through flooding to form some of the most productive farmland

Fig 1.10 The confluence of the Missouri and Mississippi rivers marks the northern end of the American Bottom, some of North America's most productive farmland. Note the mixing of muddy water of the Missouri River on the left with the clearer water of the Mississippi River on the right. View facing north. Courtesy of Dawn M. Lamm, US Army Corps of Engineers.

in North America. It was in this uniquely productive area that corn farmers of the eleventh century established settlements housing thousands of people and the economic, religious, and political institutions to support them. Featured in Chapter 10, the Mississippian societies of the past millennium, denizens of Cahokia, east of St. Louis, as well as scores of other mound centers in the eastern USA, were among the continent's most populous and elaborate societies.

About 200 km downriver from St. Louis (to the south of your view), you will see the confluence of another major river, the Ohio. Just as the Missouri River runs from the western continental divide of the Rockies to the Mississippi River, the Ohio runs to the same river from the eastern divide of the Appalachians in western Pennsylvania. At 1,575 km (979 mi) in length, the Ohio River is only two-fifths the size of the Missouri, but it is actually the largest tributary, by volume, of the Mississippi River. Its greater volume is due largely to the relatively wet climate of the eastern USA, but equally important is the physiography of its complex basin. In addition to draining a 1,000 km (621 mi) long expanse of the Appalachian Plateau, the Ohio River drainage encompasses most of the Interior Low Plateau, a province that extends from northern Alabama to southern Illinois. Major rivers such as the Wabash, Green, Cumberland, and Tennessee all drain into the Ohio.

Looking over the lower reach of the Ohio River valley you will see the interdigitation between glacial till plains to the north and the unglaciated portions of the Interior Low Plateau to the south. This province to the south is essentially uplifted limestone and other sedimentary rock, currently with "upland" elevations in the range of 340–430 m (1,100–1,400 ft) amsl. Because it is soluble in water, limestone is subject to rapid erosion, and, having been exposed to water flows (both surface and underground) for some 300 million years, the province is highly weathered. Indeed, the so-called Nashville Basin, to the south in your view, was once a high dome of limestone. It is now a bowl-shaped depression, surrounded by an upland rim of more resistant sedimentary rock, including cherts and other fine-grained siliceous materials that were important to ancient tool makers. Nashville sits at the northwest edge of the basin, so if you look east of Nashville in Google Earth you will see a dark green arc, the wooded terrain of an inward sloping escarpment. The erosion of limestone across other portions of the Interior Low Plateau has created a diverse *karstic* landscape of sinks, caves, and rockshelters, features of great import to ancient people (Chapter 13).

Continue east on your virtual journey through the Low Plateau into the Bluegrass region of eastern Kentucky (Lexington lies at its center), and then upwards, into the Cumberland Plateau, the southern expanse of the greater Appalachian Plateau. This is a dissected plateau of sandstone and other sedimentary rock with relief rising eastward in Kentucky to more than 750 m (2,460 ft) amsl. The broad dissected plateau to the north of your view into West Virginia, southern Ohio, and western Pennsylvania is known as the Alleghany Plateau, but it is contiguous with the Cumberland Plateau and of similar geological makeup.

The Appalachian Mountains proper appear just to the east of the plateaus in eastern Tennessee and follow the boundary separating West Virginia from Virginia. The Appalachians are ancient mountains, first forming at about 480 mya when North America and Africa were still connected. The folded and thrusted belts of sedimentary and volcanic rocks attest to the deformation of plate tectonics. Peaks of the young Appalachians were as high as the Rockies, but an advanced level of weathering has reduced the average elevations to about 910 m (3,000 ft) (the highest peak, Mount Mitchell in North Carolina, is 2,037 m [6,684 ft] amsl). The wave-like pattern of terrain you see in Google Earth is the folded belts of the Appalachians: the Ridge and Valley province on the west side, and the Blue Ridge province on the east.

These belts run parallel to the Atlantic coast from Alabama to New York; the northern extension of the Appalachians into New England and southeast Canada differs from the ranges to the south for a variety of reasons, notably being immediately adjacent to the modern coastline. South of the Hudson River in New York, the Appalachians are fully enclosed by dissected plateaus, and, on the Atlantic side, by the Coastal Plain. The plateau you see to the east of the Blue Ridge is known as the Piedmont. Essentially the remnant of highly eroded mountain chains, the Piedmont extends the length of the southern Appalachians, widening from north to south, and with elevations ranging from 50 to 250 m (164–820 ft) amsl. The Piedmont ends at the Fall Line: the contact between the hard-rock geology of the mountains and the unconsolidated marine sediments of the Coastal Plain. The Fall Line in Google Earth is evident at the point moving eastward where rivers become sinuous and wetlands appear. As the name implies, the Fall Line is marked by shoals and low waterfalls in rivers flowing out of the Piedmont. Many modern cities of the eastern United States lie at the confluence on the Fall Line and such rivers, being the farthest large watercraft can travel upriver without the aid of locks, dams, or artificial channels. Fall Line locations also figured significantly in the siting of major encampments and villages of the ancient past.

Perhaps the most conspicuous features of the Atlantic coastline as you end the eastbound leg of our tour are the large bay to the north and the cape of sand enclosing embayments to the south. The former feature is the Chesapeake Bay, the largest estuary in the United States (Figure 1.11). Estuarine environments are places where fresh and salt water mix to create marine habitat of enormous economic value to humans: hundreds of species of fish, shellfish, and crab, among other fauna. The bay is essentially a drowned river valley – in this case the Susquehanna – meaning that it is where the river flowed before the sea level rose after the Ice Age. The embayments to the south of the Chesapeake in your view are likewise drowned river valleys, but in these cases enclosed by an outer bank to create a massive lagoon, or sound (Pamlico Sound, in your view to the south, is the largest sound of the US east coast). The easternmost point of the outer bank is Cape Hatteras, the point where two major currents of the Atlantic collide, creating turbulent waters and expansive sandbar formations.

Fig 1.11 Aerial view of the Chesapeake Bay with Bay Bridge in the background, connecting the Maryland capital city, Annapolis, with its eastern shore in Queen Anne County. Carol M. Highsmith photo/Library of Congress Prints and Photographs Division.

One last feature of the eastern seaboard bears mentioning. You will notice off the shore the contact between light and dark blue waters, roughly 40 km east of Cape Hatteras, and 120 km east of the mouth of the Chesapeake Bay. This is the edge of the continental shelf, basically the underwater extension of the continental landmass. Much of this shelf was exposed during the late Pleistocene when humans arrived, at a time when water levels were about 80 m lower than today. The shelf is broad along much of the Atlantic seaboard, and especially in the Gulf of Mexico. The continental margin, seen here at the contact of the two shades of blue, is where the low-sloping shelf drops off steeply. None of the land east of this margin would have been available for human occupation at any time in the human past, but virtually all of the shelf may have been occupied in the late Pleistocene, and thereafter increasingly landward as water levels rose in the postglacial era. The situation along the Pacific rim, as noted earlier, is altogether different, with comparatively little land exposed during the Ice Age and thus little land flooded afterwards.

Head South

Take one final return trip to Lawrence, Kansas and zoom out, and then key the "down" arrow. Moving southward you immediately encounter again the Interior Highlands, specifically the Ozark Mountains. When you saw the Ozarks earlier, heading east, you crossed the St. Francois

Mountains, an ancient, intrusive volcanic formation surrounded by an uplifted, dissected plateau of limestone and dolomite. Moving south out of Lawrence you skirt the limestone margin of the Ozarks known as the Springfield Plateau (it is that crenulated topography you see in the southeast corner of Kansas and continuing on to Tulsa, to the south). Springs, caves, and sinkholes abound throughout the Springfield Plateau.

Advance a short distance south and you will see the southwestern margin of the Ozarks, marked prominently by the Boston Mountains, seen in the dark green, wooded area of northwest Arkansas and east Oklahoma. These are the highest mountains in the province, with peaks over 780 m (2,560 ft) separated by deep valleys. Following the southern margin of the Bostons is the Arkansas River, a major tributary of the Mississippi River. (Tulsa, Oklahoma and Little Rock, Arkansas both sit on the Arkansas River.) With headwaters in the Rockies of Colorado, the Arkansas River crosses several physiographic provinces and is a major drainage basin of the southern Plains.

On the south side of the Arkansas River is the last significant topographic relief of this southbound trip. Here lie the Ouachita Mountains, sandwiching the Arkansas River with the Boston Mountains to the north (Figure 1.12). The Ouachitas were once part of the Appalachians and are thus folded mountains; like the Ridge and Valley you crossed over earlier, the Ouachitas have a distinctive sinuous pattern when viewed from above. Unlike most other mountains in North America, the Ouachitas trend east–west, owing to tectonic

Fig 1.12 Autumn in the Ouachita Mountains of Arkansas. Once part of the Appalachians, the Ouachitas were sources of minerals like quartz crystals that factored prominently in the trade and ritual practices of ancient Native Americans. Tammo Photo, 2011/ Wikimedia.

activity about 300 mya, when the Gulf coastline ran through central Arkansas. They are also distinct in lacking the volcanism and metamorphosis seen in the Appalachians, contributing to an unusual mineralogical inventory, notably large quartz crystals, prized by humans both now and long ago.

Another major tributary river of the Mississippi forms the border between Oklahoma and Texas. This is the Red River, which takes a sharp turn south in Arkansas, dropping into Louisiana. The southernmost drainage of the Great Plains, the Red River crosses arid lands of north Texas and southern Oklahoma; in fact, water flow north of the state boundary is intermittent, drying up completely during drought, which can be frequent.

As you have traveled south making note of physiography to the east side of your view, you also passed along the southeast margin of the Central Lowlands, and beyond that the Great Plains. The prairie and grasslands on the west side of your view continue much farther south, into central Texas. However, your trail now leaves the Plains proper as you enter northeast Texas and head toward modern-day Dallas. That city is situated on the northwest edge of the Blackland Belt, a grassland and savannah perpetuated for millennia by frequent fire and grazing bison herds. To the east and south of the Blacklands, continuing on to the Gulf coast, is the broad Coastal Plain of Texas and Louisiana. Before continuing on to the coast, make note of the unusual landscape west of Austin. This is the Central Texas Uplift, or Llano Uplift, a roughly circular dome of Precambrian granite and associated volcanic rock. Rimmed by limestone ridges, the uplift lies in the eastern margin of the much larger Edwards Plateau, a limestone formation containing chert and related rocks of economic value to ancient tool makers.

The Gulf coast has already appeared at the bottom of your screen, and as you proceed a little farther south you will see multiple embayments along an arcuate coastline. Also evident at this point is the broad, submerged shelf of the Gulf. Overall, we can attribute the physiography of the Gulf to plate tectonic activity some 300 million years ago, but also to the loading of sediment from rivers draining the continent, particularly the Mississippi River. As a generally enclosed ocean basin, the Gulf of Mexico has only a narrow connection to the Atlantic Ocean and Caribbean Sea, and thus has a low tidal range. Almost half of the basin is shallow water of the continental shelf, and over time, as sea levels have fluctuated within an overall rising regime, the low-relief terrain of the shelf has been subject to large-scale change. The peninsula of Florida, for instance, is now only about half as broad as it was when humans entered North America.

It stands to reason that generally shallow and calm Gulf waters were not much of an impediment to people with watercraft. So, as you move southward along the western margin of the Gulf, you can see how it would be possible to follow the coastline along the submerged shelf and arrive eventually in Mexico, then eastward into Belize and the Yucatan peninsula, just off to the east of your view (White 2005). The continental shelf narrows as we traverse the western margin of the Gulf, but it widens again to the east, as you approach Cuba (Figure 1.13).

At this point, without traveling any farther south, zoom out until you see the entire Gulf of Mexico, all of Central America, the isthmus of Panama, northern South America, the Caribbean islands, and the southern United States. From this perspective you get a good sense that North America links up in multiple pathways of both earth and water to Central and South America. Over the years, archaeologists have speculated on the cultural and historical connections across the Gulf, through Mexico, and along the Caribbean island chain. Aside from well-known connections between Mesoamerica and north-western Mexico or the American Southwest (see Chapters 14–15), linkages between Central and South America, the Caribbean, and the

Fig 1.13 The southernmost land in the continental USA is Key West, Florida, a mere 93 miles (150 km) from Havana, Cuba, across the Gulf Stream water of the Florida Straits. Todd Feit photo/Wikimedia.

continental USA remain speculative. Mid-twentieth-century efforts to document connections through similarities in material culture (e.g., Ford 1969) were met with skepticism, and through today there is no "smoking gun" evidence that people routinely crossed the Gulf by boat, not even the 150 km (93 mi) passage of the Straits of Florida separating northeast Cuba from the Florida Keys. Granted, this is the throughway of the Gulf Stream, a swift and dangerous current to cross in small boats. There are, however, other ways to cross Gulf water, and even the passage between Cuba and Florida may have been occasionally calm as winds and currents shifted with climate change (Cooper 2013). Irrespective of currents and their dangers, we know that the Calusa of southwest Florida made the passage routinely during the sixteenth century. Bear in mind that when humans first arrived in the western hemisphere, the Gulf of Mexico was only half its size, basically the basin marked by dark blue (deeper water) in your Google Earth image. Passage between the now-submerged portions of the Yucatan peninsula and peninsular Florida (by way of Cuba, or not) was likely feasible in small watercraft.

Space, Time, and Change

We will end our Google Earth tour by noting how much of North America we have yet to visit. Indeed, by limiting our trip to the cardinal directions emanating from Lawrence, Kansas, we missed much of the four corners of the continent: the Alaskan peninsula and Northwest Coast; Baja and the desert Southwest; Florida and the South Atlantic Slope; and the maritime provinces of New England and eastern Canada. Other many noteworthy features of the continent escaped our attention too, but we will return repeatedly to the physical landscape in our journey through the human past in chapters to come. We have seen enough already to know that North America is an incredibly diverse continent, and we will see even more diversity as we follow the human story through 14,000+ years of dwelling.

The long sweep of human history in North America parallels the geological history of the continent when viewed through the lens of natural science. A defining principle in our understanding of the geology of North America is the concept of *uniformitarianism*. First formulated by Scottish naturalists in the eighteenth century and made popular by geologist Charles Lyell in 1830, uniformitarianism is the belief that the natural laws and processes we can see operating in the world today have always operated in the past. The same applies to rates of change observed in the recent past. Thus, the slow but incessant downcutting of a river through sedimentary rock explains the formation of geologic features such as the Grand Canyon, if given enough time – in this case at least 17 million years. Applied uncritically to North American archaeology, uniformitarianism leads to the equivocal proposition that nothing in the past is without a modern analog, and, if change is always slow and gradual, we have had relatively little time (~14,000 years) for change to occur. In the Short Chronology assumed for native North Americans through the 1920s (see Chapter 2), there was not enough time for "primitives" to have "evolved" into "civilizations."

Uniformitarianism was first proposed in opposition to *catastrophism*, the theory that geologic change occurred episodically and catastrophically, with long periods of stability between events of rapid change. Floods, earthquakes, and volcanic eruptions certainly fit this bill, as do the more spectacular and potentially global-scale effects of extraterrestrial impacts, like the asteroid strike that is proposed, but still unproven, to have impacted the Canadian Shield about 12,800 years ago (Firestone et al. 2007) and led to the *Younger Dryas stadial* of the late Pleistocene, and with it the extinction of many of the Ice Age creatures of North America. Scientists critical of the asteroid theory agree that the Younger Dryas was a rapid change in global climate, but they point to a process involving the collapse of the North American ice sheets. Gradual as the melting of glaciers may have been in the late Pleistocene, the rapid reversal in temperature that is the Younger Dryas signifies a tipping point in the complex relationship between atmospheric moisture, temperature, and circulation.

Geologists and other natural scientists no longer hold to the gradualist dictum of uniformitarianism, and instead accept that rapid, "catastrophic" events punctuated the past (Figure 1.14). The same is true of archaeologists who have come to grips with evidence for eventful, revolutionary changes in the human past. Sometimes rapid changes in environment and culture were in lockstep, and sometimes changes in culture erupted from encounters between people of distinct backgrounds and experiences. Clearly the two were not always independent, as we can imagine that encounters involving the migration of people from a homeland impacted by rapid environmental

Fig 1.14 Mount St. Helens in Washington erupting in 1980 to remind us of the periodic and often catastrophic events of nature that punctuate long-term processes of environmental change. Culture history has its moments of rapid change too. Wikimedia.

change (e.g., drought, flooding, river channel switching) can ultimately be traced to "natural" processes. Either way, ensuing cultural changes were themselves rapid in many cases, contradicting the gradualist logic that significant change requires significant time.

There is one other parallel between geology and culture that bears mentioning. Just as our short review of the surface geology of North America reveals how long-term processes and long-ago events are encased in the morphology and composition of the landscape, histories of lives lived long ago are encoded in the cultural traditions and practices of native North Americans. Acknowledging events, both natural and cultural, as significant forces of change eliminates the need to document continuity in process, even as it recognizes that all change is contingent on what already exists, or what came before. In our journey through ancient North America we will be reminded again and again of the complex interplay between tradition and innovation, between pasts and futures. When we see cases of technological ingenuity and innovation, we may be persuaded to think of Henry Ford. But we also find examples of human societies that reflect a keen sense of stewardship over the land, as in the beliefs of John Muir. Perhaps both comparisons are somewhat persuasive, but we like to think that Native American experiences in North America, before Europeans arrived, are best understood on their own terms. Granted, we generally do not know how people thought about their own experiences, but that is why we do archaeology: to investigate the unknown, not to simply recapitulate what we already think we might know. In the next chapter we'll take a look at changes in the way North American archaeology has been practiced since Europeans and others established themselves as late arrivals.

2 A Social History of North American Archaeologists and Native Americans

Who doesn't like archaeology? Everyone enjoys finding something interesting, and most people have some interest in the past. This may be enough to understand why archaeology is so popular. Indeed, archaeology has a public cachet like few other professions. Ordinary people who visit our digs or come hear our talks comment on their longstanding dream of being an archaeologist. "How very lucky," they sometimes say, "to get paid to play in the dirt."

Archaeology is certainly different from most other professions. And yet, like most other professions, archaeology's popular profile deviates somewhat from the reality of everyday practice. Many archaeologists spend most of their time in front of a computer: analyzing data, writing reports, articles, and books – like this one – or preparing for class or some other lecture. Sure, real archaeologists do real fieldwork, too. Both of us have ongoing field projects in the USA and members of the public sometimes join in alongside students and paid staff. These volunteers generally know that the popular perception of archaeology does not square with their long, hot days hunched over a screen pulling small bits of animal bone from a matrix of earth. Indeed, the popular image of archaeology is a bit more glamorous, or at least more intriguing. It is the image of travel and adventure, of exploration and discovery. It is the image of a machete-wielding, brow-sweating crusader who would sacrifice life and limb for the next great find. It is the image of … *Indiana Jones*?

It is hard to deny or escape the influence of Indiana Jones (Figure 2.1). Journalists covering archaeology stories often invoke his image with quips about snakes, whips, and Nazis. The soundtrack to the movie resonates on cell phones of would-be archaeologists. Rides at theme parks hurl adventure-seekers through a virtual world of tombs, mummies, and spirits. And the ghost of Indy appears every Halloween in the form of fedora-wearing revelers.

Fig 2.1 Indiana Jones was more of an antiquarian than an archaeologist. He was more interested in obtaining objects than in investigating the context of objects to make inferences about the past lives of people. Getty Image.

Archaeologists today have a love–hate relationship with Indiana Jones. The image Hollywood has created around this character lifts public support for archaeology because, if for no other reason, it makes people feel good. However, archaeologists find themselves frequently pointing out the flaws of an Indiana Jones-approach to archaeology. Like others of his time, Indy was after objects. He collected objects for the sake of building museum collections, and these museums were housed in elite institutions, such as Harvard, and funded by wealthy benefactors. The information potential of the objects was second to the objects themselves, resulting in limited concern for the context and association of artifacts. This is not an inaccurate portrayal of the situation back in the nineteenth and early twentieth century, but the profession has since come a long way from its roots in *antiquarianism*.

Not Indy-like since the Mid-Twentieth Century

In the Indiana Jones movies Harrison Ford plays the part of an antiquarian, which means he has a preoccupation with objects from the past. The term is most often associated with those who sought out particularly valuable objects, not necessarily for their monetary worth, but because of their uniqueness or rarity of form, and, for the more progressively minded, for their historical significance. The term antiquarian has long been used in a pejorative sense, to signify someone fixed on obscure and arcane details of history (through objects) to the exclusion of broader, more abstract inquiry. Much of the recent past of American archaeology has been distancing itself from its antiquarian beginnings. In some respects, the push away from antiquarianism was deliberate, as archaeologists set out in the twentieth century to address broad themes of history and anthropology. And in other respects, the waning credibility of antiquarianism followed broader trends in society and culture. And yet, because antiquarianism lives on in Hollywood, it endures in the popular imagination.

The Mound-builder Myth

Another enduring myth of the American imagination is the notion that the many earthen mounds of North America were built by people other than the ancestors of native North Americans. This myth took root in the early years of western colonial expansion and persisted in both academic and public circles until the late nineteenth century. Even today some fringe thinkers would deny an Indian hand in the construction of mounds (www.history.com/shows/ancient-aliens). With hindsight, we refer to this falsehood as the "Mound-builder Myth," and it bears historical significance for benchmarking changes in public perception about Indians (Figure 2.2). Unable to accept that contemporary Indians could build monuments of earth, nineteenth-century thinkers buoyed popular imagination about a host of alternative candidates: one of the Lost Tribes of Israel, an extinct race of giants, and the Welsh among them. Dissociating Indians from their earthworks made it easier for frontiersmen to expropriate land they believed to be unimproved by native people or their ancestors. Scholars of the day woefully underestimated the depth of Indian history in North America (see "Short Chronology", p. 50), leading them to assume that too little time had passed for civilization to take hold.

Fig 2.2 Nineteenth-century antiquarian William Pidgeon was among the many prolific writers who promoted the idea that a lost race of people built the mounds of the New World long before Indians arrived. In his 1858 book, *Traditions of Dee-Coo-Dah and Antiquarian Researches,* he included this illustration of an ancient American Battle-Mound, depicting an epic struggle between the mound-builders and marauding Indians (www.ohiohistory.org).

ANCIENT AMERICAN BATTLE-MOUND.

A lost mound-builder people, many imagined, must have been killed off by the ancestors of modern Indians (Squier and Davis 1848). They looked to the great civilizations of the world for the roots of America's mound-builders, and eventually a few would look to the cosmos for an extraterrestrial source.

All the while, evidence that ancestors of the Indians built and used mounds was tucked away in the recesses of history. Spanish conquistador Hernando de Soto witnessed firsthand the occupation of mound complexes in the mid-sixteenth-century American Southeast (in Florida, Georgia, South Carolina, and more). A few decades later the French painter Jacques Le Moyne gave us a glimpse of a mourning ceremony surrounding a small burial mound in a village. And some two centuries later Thomas Jefferson would conduct the very first scientific investigation of a mound near his home at Monticello, seeing enough to rule out a lost race of people and to give due consideration to the ancestors of local Indians (see www.monticello.org/site/research-and-collections/jeffersons-excavation-indian-burial-mound).

Archaeology Finds its Purpose

Jefferson is sometimes credited with being the Father of American Archaeology because his purpose in digging into a mound was to collect information, not merely objects. In 1780 he embarked on answering a survey issued by the French government that included questions about the Indians of Virginia. In his *Notes on the State of Virginia*, Jefferson (1787) provided a trove of information on late eighteenth-century tribes, but he also did what no one had before: excavate into the earth for the express purpose of answering a question. In the end, he may not have been able to draw any direct links between the mound he dug and the native people of Virginia, but Jefferson could see in the way the Indians interacted with the mound that it was meaningful to them. It was, after all, filled with the skeletal remains of hundreds of people.

Jefferson deserves credit too for giving archaeology a purpose beyond problem solving. In seeking material evidence to answer a question that could not be solved with literary sources, he was opening the potential for archaeology to become a *historical* science. In his time, and through the mid-twentieth century, histories were written by select individuals, generally those with access to wealth and power. Archaeology offered a way to expand the purview of history for people with neither literary traditions, nor the wealth and power to practice them if they did. Nonetheless, the narratives of North American archaeology, until recently, have been dominated by nonnative voices, notably those of privilege, starting with Jefferson.

Circumstances have changed over the past century such that archaeology has become increasingly self-critical and socially responsible, and with it multivocal. Broad disagreements exist among those who view archaeological inquiry through different theoretical lenses, but room has opened up for alternative voices, notably those of native people, but also those silenced before the civil rights and the feminist movements raised public consciousness about the biases of history and science. Archaeology has both mirrored and refracted these influences. In the sections that follow we take a look at the major social trends that affected and were affected by the practice of archaeology in North America since the late nineteenth century, when the US government began its enduring influence in the writing of native history.

A Social History of North American Archaeology since the Nineteenth Century

If the early history of North American archaeology is the history of antiquarianism, then its history since the early nineteenth century is one of government intervention. In a variety of legislative, judicial, and executive actions, the federal governments of the USA and Canada, as well as their respective state and provincial governments, have intervened in the practice of archaeology, both positively and negatively. Laws protecting archaeological sites and objects, dating to the early twentieth century, are obvious examples of positive interventions, but less evident yet equally important actions involve laws and regulations concerning education, social welfare, and infrastructure, among other topics. Thus, a social history of archaeology in North America cannot possibly be written without considering how governmental actions have affected society more broadly. Arguably, it all started with busting the Mound-builder Myth 140 years ago.

The Federal Mythbusters

In 1881, only five years after the Battle at Little Big Horn, Congress passed a bill to fund the Smithsonian Institution to investigate mounds for evidence of their origins, and thus put the Mound-builder Myth to rest once and for all. The century that had passed since Jefferson received the French questionnaire transformed entirely the cultural landscape of native North America. Under his presidency in 1803, the United States purchased from France the territory of Louisiana, which ran from the delta of the Mississippi River up through the northern Plains just beyond the present-day Canadian border, doubling the size of the United States. The following year Lewis and Clark began their ascent of the Missouri River, and the USA began a long, deliberate effort to remove or at least control native people in its relentless expansion westward.

Jefferson actually favored the acculturation approach advocated by George Washington, which allowed Indians to maintain homeland so long as they adopted "civil" behavior, namely a lawful, sedentary, and productive lifestyle. But one of his eventual successors disagreed. As a military general, Andrew Jackson instigated war with the Creek Nation in 1813 to force it to cede 14 million acres of land in Georgia and Alabama. When he became president 16 years later Jackson introduced a bill to Congress to remove all Indians east of the Mississippi. Signed into law on May 28, 1830, the *Indian Removal Act* ushered in a decade of forced ejection of the Five Civilized Tribes of the Southeast – Creek, Cherokee, Choctaw, Chickasaw, and Seminole. Thousands of natives died along what came to be known as the *Trail of Tears* (Figure 2.3). Ensuing decades across the entire nation saw a repetition of treaties written and violated, battles waged and won and lost, and entire cultures and peoples erased. In popular narrative, it is a history that culminated in the centennial year of the nation (1876), when General George Custer and 250 soldiers misjudged the numbers and resolve of Sioux warriors under the leadership of Sitting Bull and Crazy Horse and all but 40 of Custer's men were killed. Underlying all such events of this dark history was the desire of those in power to remove Indians from places of economic and political value, relocate them to places of little consequence (usually arid land with poor soils and limited

Fig 2.3 This 1942 painting by Robert Lindneux commemorates the suffering of Cherokee people on the *Trail of Tears* of forced removal. An estimated 4,000 of the 15,000 Cherokee died of hunger, disease, and exhaustion en route to Oklahoma (www.peoplesworld.org).

forest, and away from major arteries), regulate their mobility (even for seasonal hunts), and restrict access to government and its citizenry. As with the Battle of Little Big Horn, violence erupted often, and in many places, but usually for similar reasons – to defend homeland and autonomy.

By the time Congress issued $5,000 per year to the Smithsonian Institution to investigate mounds, native people and their earthworks had long been separated from one another, both literally through removal and genocide, and figuratively in the sense of lost history and identity. Cyrus Thomas, the man charged with solving the Mound-builder Myth, did what he could with written records, but it ultimately came down to doing what Jefferson had, only now on a massive scale. Thomas hired a cadre of field men to survey and excavate mounds. Based on observations of mound stratigraphy and careful comparisons of mortuary treatment and grave goods, Thomas (1894) was able to prove, once and for all, that ancestors of historic-era Indians built the mounds. It is noteworthy that Thomas, like most of his colleagues, initially bought into the myth. We can be grateful that he was open-minded enough to allow the data to convince him he was wrong.

How ironic and unfortunate, then, that after the Mound-builder Myth was busted, landowners with mounds on their property increasingly leveled them to make way for more farmland or pasture land. If not the work of some mysterious, long-lost people, but instead the work of ancestors of Indians they did not hold in high regard, mounds were merely a nuisance to them, something to erase from the landscape. It is a racist sentiment that persists today in thankfully smaller circles.

Democratizing the Academy

As public perception of Indian history was influenced by federal interventions, those who would study Indian history expanded through legislative edict too. In the midst of the Civil War, Abraham Lincoln signed into law the Morrill Act of 1862, the act establishing land-grant colleges across states of the union including, after the war, southern states. The original intent of the Morrill Act was to establish institutions for teaching agriculture and the "mechanical" arts (the nineteenth-century term for engineering), as well as military training, but it did not exclude classical studies and natural sciences, a truly *liberal arts* education (Figure 2.4).

Fig 2.4 Iowa State University (ISU) was the first to take the opportunity of the Morrill Act of 1862 and offer higher education to anyone regardless of class, race, or gender. Morrill Hall was opened at ISU in 1891 to commemorate the Vermont senator who sponsored the bill. Library of Congress, Prints and Photographs Division, IOWA, 85-AMES, 3-2.

Under the act, states were granted 30,000 acres of federal land to build colleges. Guided primarily by an agricultural mission, land-grant colleges arose in rural areas of states, often far from urban centers. Areas with no existing infrastructure for higher education now housed colleges, and for the first time people living far from urban centers could pursue degrees without leaving their home states. The bill was eventually extended to every state and territory in the nation, even those created after 1862. Both of our (Pauketat's and Sassaman's) universities are land-grant institutions, the University of Illinois designated in 1867, and the University of Florida in 1884. Both started as agricultural colleges but have evolved into two of the nation's largest and most diverse universities, both with large anthropology programs and plenty of archaeology. We do not imagine that archaeology was taught in the classrooms of Illinois or Florida in the late nineteenth century, but the Morrill Act not only opened up opportunities for higher education to a broader citizenry than ever before, it also laid the foundation for liberal arts programs and inter-disciplinary research, including archaeological investigations. The Morrill Act ensured that archaeology would eventually exist outside the halls of Harvard, Yale, and other Ivy League schools.

Eighty years after the Morrill Act was signed into law, a second federal initiative was enacted to create educational opportunities for American soldiers returning from duty during World War II. The Servicemen's Readjustment Act of 1944, known commonly as the GI Bill, introduced benefits to returning veterans that included funding for college, as well as low-interest mortgages and unemployment compensation (Figure 2.5). The program was wildly successful and is credited by some economic historians as having staved off another Great Depression (Olson 1973:600). By the time the program ended 12 years later, some 2.2 million returning servicemen had used the GI Bill to attend college. Similar federal programs were offered to millions of veterans of the Korean and Vietnam wars, and extended in 1966 to those serving during times of peace.

The number of veterans who pursued college education far exceeded expectations in the early years of the GI Bill, overwhelming schools and creating a huge demand for professors and other educators. Throughout the early years politicians and university presidents debated the wisdom of opening opportunity for higher education to all veterans, with some suggesting that only those whose education

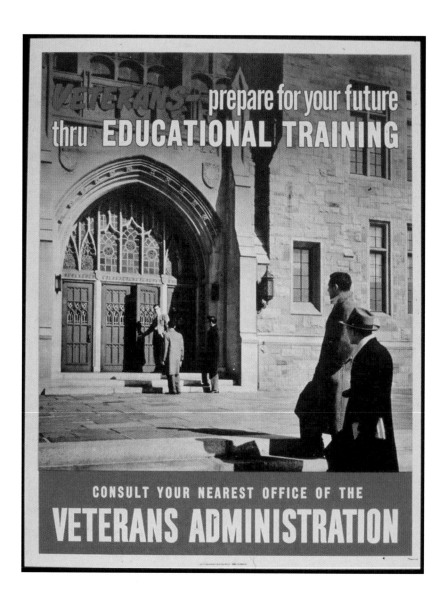

Fig 2.5 The GI Bill of 1944 offered opportunities for service men and women to attend colleges and universities and pursue careers of their choice. Some chose archaeology and that helped to democratize a profession that was hitherto dominated by graduates of Ivy League schools. Office for Emergency Management. Office of War Information. Domestic Operations Branch. Bureau of Special Services.

was interrupted by the war be eligible and others arguing that only those seeking the most promising career paths be funded. But after all the debate, American lawmakers endorsed a program that would be described by Northwestern University President Franklyn D. Snyder as "the greatest experiment in democratic education the world has ever seen" (quoted in Olson 1973:606). The first generation of beneficiaries included a few who would go on to become professional archaeologists, and a later generation would include one of the leaders in public archaeology, Thomas F. King, whose college career began after serving in the Navy in the 1960s (https://archaeology channel.org/video-guide/video-interviews/1771-our-unprotected-heritage-an-interview-with-tom-king). The GI Bill in its modern

Sidebar 2.1 Democratizing higher education beyond the GI Bill

When Congress enacted the GI Bill in 1944 their intent was clearly economic. Nonetheless, some advocates of the bill wanted to simply reward veterans for their service to the country, and they likewise saw education as an investment in long-term futures. As one might guess, the vast majority (more than 97 percent) of those attending college on the bill after World War II were men, although some 65,000 women took advantage of the opportunity too. The same gender disparity characterized archaeology and most professions requiring college degrees in the immediate post-war era. Only after confronting growing public intolerance of gender inequalities in the 1960s did legislators enact laws prohibiting discrimination against women. Parallel developments in the civil rights of racial and ethnic minorities, disabled people, and other disadvantaged groups created opportunities never before available. Still, professional archaeologists in North America today remain mostly white, if not also mostly men. The gender ratio has improved considerably but few people of color pursue archaeology professionally. With access to higher education perhaps never better, limited participation of students of African, Asian, and Latin American heritage goes beyond access. It involves issues as vast as practical concerns (is employment in archaeology assured?) to cultural proclivities (does archaeology have any value?). Native American participation in archaeology is especially wanting for a profession devoted to the study of indigenous people. Organizations such as the Society for American Archaeology offer scholarship funds to Native American students for field training in archaeology, a small but important step in greater indigenous participation in a profession that has grown less exclusive and more diverse with each generation.

incarnation is far different from the original, but it still enables veterans to pursue an education they might not otherwise be able to afford.

New Deal Archaeology

The Morrill Act of 1863 and the GI Bill of 1944 went far in democratizing the academy, and with it the profession of archaeology. However, the US government had a more direct impact on the practice of archaeology in its efforts to stave off economic failure and catapult the nation into the second half of the twentieth century. In the throes of the Great Depression in the early 1930s, President Franklin D. Roosevelt worked with Congress to enact a series of economic programs to relieve unemployment, recover the economy, and reform a financial system that fostered the Stock Market crash of 1929. The political landscape of the United States was restructured in the process, with Democrats achieving the majority and Republicans split over government intervention, with half viewing the relief programs, known collectively as the "New Deal," as an deterrent to growth in the free market, much as conservatives today opposed the economic stimulus proposals of the Democrats under President Barack Obama in 2009. Among the New Deal initiatives were "shovel-ready" projects to not only put people to work immediately but, in the process, improve infrastructure in places of underdevelopment, such as the Deep South, where the average family had no electricity, no running water, and no indoor plumbing. Being literally "shovel-ready," government-funded archaeologists factored significantly in New Deal projects nationwide (Figure 2.6).

The impact of New Deal programs on the practice of archaeology is hard to exaggerate (Fagette 1996; Means 2013). Most of the government-funded work took place in southern states (see Lyon 1996 for a thorough account of New Deal archaeology in the South), but it also extended across much of the country. Southern states were targeted for both practical and economic reasons: work could be conducted virtually year-round, and rural populations in the region were especially impoverished. Projects to build infrastructure in the South, most notably reservoirs, thus served the dual purpose of offering employment while implementing improvements that would grow the economy and improve the quality of life. As with federal programs today, the Works Progress Administration (WPA) initiatives were not welcomed by all state leaders; South Carolina, for instance, withdrew from New Deal programs after first embracing

Fig 2.6 This 1935 excavation at the Macon North Plateau site in Georgia was among the many New Deal archaeology projects that revolutionized knowledge about the ancient Southeast while providing immediate economic relief to the unemployed of the Great Depression. (newdealarchaeology.files.wordpress.com)

them (Hayes 2001), and no federal funds were used on archaeological projects there.

When New Deal programs began in the 1930s, few professional archaeologists were available to supervise work crews and early projects were at times chaotic, the operations haphazard. States eventually developed their own organizations to run projects while some WPA programs, such as the Tennessee Valley Authority (TVA), developed their own administration. William S. Webb, a professor of physics at the University of Kentucky, was selected as the first Director of TVA Archaeology. Lacking formal training in archaeology, Webb drew criticism from some professionals, and his excavation techniques, by some accounts, were substandard. However, Webb had the passion and leadership skills to organize dozens of massive excavations in advance of reservoir construction, and the many reports he and his co-workers issued remain valuable today as the only knowledge of sites long-since flooded (Lyon 1996). By the late 1930s, New Deal projects involved scores of professional archaeologists, many trained at the University of Chicago under Professor Fay-Cooper Cole, a student of Franz Boas (see section on culture history below).

Behind the scenes of New Deal archaeology were hundreds, even thousands, of laborers whose on-the-job training compensated for their lack of formal education. On some projects, laborers were divided into "shovel men," "trowel men," and "wheelbarrow men," and there was a hierarchy of foremen working at varying pay scales. Stark divisions along lines of gender and race were evident in most projects. Women, for instance, were generally excluded from fieldwork and instead relegated to the labs, where they washed, sorted, and cataloged artifacts. However, at several projects in the South, African-American women labored in the field, where they were expected to wear dresses (Figure 2.7; see also Claassen 1993). One of the very few women able to supervise a New Deal excavation was Harriet Smith, a University of Chicago graduate who led the excavation of a mound at Cahokia in Illinois after four years of persuading male bureaucrats she could handle the job (Sullivan et al. 2011:76).

The impact of New Deal archaeology on institutions of education and government was substantial, as it was for American society in general. Many museums and university departments were initiated to

Fig 2.7 African-American women excavating at Irene Mound in Georgia in December 1937 (georgiaencyclopedia.org).

meet the growing demand for professional training and to deal with the enormous amount of material and information that was collected on New Deal digs. An entire generation of professional archaeologists cut their teeth on New Deal projects. The National Park Service and Smithsonian Institution had to reorganize their operations to accommodate vast numbers of projects and personnel. Founded in 1934, the Society for American Archaeology (today with more than 7,000 members) was in part an outgrowth of New Deal work, with its first meeting devoted almost exclusively to the results of federally funded projects. The methods and techniques of archaeological field and lab work, as well as reporting, were greatly improved, even standardized. The sheer volume of work done is mind-boggling, even by today's standards, and although some projects were not adequately reported, repositories across the country house collections that form the core of our understanding of culture history in much of North America. Because New Deal programs involved people of vast background and interest, projects served to raise public awareness of archaeology and indigenous culture history. Never again would a development project be implemented in the USA without some measure of public concern for historic preservation. (For further information, see

www.newdealarchaeology.com,http://archaeologychannel.org/
video-guide/kentucky-videos/952-wpa-archaeology-legacy-of-an-
era and http://diglib.lib.utk.edu/wpa, the last including photographs
taken by Works Progress Administra-tion workers.)

Perhaps most importantly, New Deal archaeology wedded the
interests of historic preservation with the economic reality of growth
and development. In the aftermath of the Depression and then World
War II, the US economy and its population burgeoned, much like it
did after the Civil War. Growth in wealth and people, the expansion
of a middle class moving into suburban single-family homes, and
the development of infrastructure to connect people and places outside of cities all had impacts on America's archaeological resources.
Understandably, as growth continued, encounters with archaeological remains increased, much as they did with colonial expansion
westward. In this era of unbridled expansion, the federal government
intervened with laws to protect archaeological sites from destruction.
The 1966 National Historic Preservation Act is perhaps the most
influential of them all, intended to give archaeologists and others the
chance to evaluate the impact of development on historical resources.
It was the kind of compromise between preservation and "progress"
that Pinchot championed and John Muir resisted (see Chapter 1). A
progressive "Great Society," someone like President Lyndon Johnson
might have said, was one that honored its past as it moved toward
a better future. A parallel development occurred in environmental
protection with the passage of bills like the National Environmental
Protection Act of 1969.

Federal legislation written in the 1960s left an indelible mark on
the practice of archaeology today. Bills such as the National Historic
Preservation Act mandated when and how archaeology would be done
on federal lands and federally funded or permitted projects; it established the administrative apparatus that would be used to implement
archaeological review; and it created the criteria by which historical
value would be measured. From this arose what we have called for
decades *cultural resource management*, or CRM for short. Also known
generically as "contract archaeology" in both Canada and the USA,
CRM has grown to become the dominant mode of archaeological
practice today.

Sidebar 2.2 Laws on the books

In Mexico, an 1897 federal law declared pre-Columbian monuments to be the property of the Republic of Mexico and another law in 1972 declared all pre-Columbian artifacts to be the cultural patrimony of the Republic. Such is not the case in the United States and Canada, where sites, ruins, and earthen monuments may be owned by private citizens. Federal laws affecting archaeology in the United States go back to the early twentieth century and involve more than a dozen major statutes. Canada's federal laws are not nearly as old or as numerous, but the various provinces and territories of Canada have promulgated their own statutes since the mid-twentieth century. US states and municipalities likewise impose their own statutes, although any action involving federal funding or permitting invokes federal laws, notably the National Historic Preservation Act of 1966 and its amendments. A list of the major laws "on the books" gives you a sense of the regulatory character of North American archaeology.

United States

- *Antiquities Act of 1906* provides for the protection of historic, prehistoric, and scientific features located on federal lands; authorizes the President to designate National Monuments; and authorizes the Secretaries of the Interior, Agriculture, and Defense to issue permits for archaeological investigations on lands under their control.
- *National Park Service Act of 1916* establishes the National Park Service as the agency to manage federal parks.
- *Historic Sites Act of 1935* establishes national policy on preservation of historic sites, buildings, and objects, establishing within the National Park Service, the Historic Sites Survey, the Historic American Building Survey, the Historic American Engineering Record, and the National Historic Landmarks Program.
- *Reservoir Salvage Act of 1960* provides for the recovery of historical and archaeological resources that might be lost or destroyed in the construction of dams and reservoirs.

- *National Historic Preservation Act of 1966*, as amended, establishes a comprehensive program for the preservation of historic and archaeological properties including creation of the National Register of Historic Places, State Historic Preservation Offices, and the Section 106 Review Process.
- *National Environmental Policy Act of 1969* requires federal agencies to employ a systematic and interdisciplinary approach that incorporates the natural and social sciences in any planning and decision-making that may impact the environment.
- *Archaeological and Historic Preservation Act of 1974* amends the 1960 Reservoir Salvage Act by providing for the preservation of significant scientific, prehistoric, historic, and archaeological materials and data that might be lost or destroyed by any federally funded activity that is associated with the construction of a dam or reservoir.
- *American Indian Religious Freedom Act of 1978* states that it is a policy of the United States to protect and preserve for American Indians their inherent right of freedom to believe, express, and exercise the traditional religions, including access to sites, use and possession of sacred objects, and the freedom to worship through ceremonial and traditional rites.
- *Archaeological Resources Protection Act of 1979* requires permits for the excavation or removal of archaeological resources on federal lands and sets penalties for violators.
- *Native American Graves Protection and Repatriation Act of 1990* gives control of Native American human remains, funerary objects, sacred objects, and objects of cultural patrimony that are discovered on federal land to federally recognized American Indian tribes or Native Hawaiian organizations. The law also requires agencies and museums that receive federal funding to repatriate such remains and objects.

Canada

- *Historic Sites and Monuments Board* formed in 1919.
- *Cultural Property Export and Import Act of 1985* deals with the export from Canada of cultural property and the import into Canada of cultural property illegally exported from foreign states.
- *Canadian Environmental Assessment Act of 1992* requires federal departments to conduct environmental assessments for proposed projects where the federal government is the proponent or where the project involves federal funding, permits, or licensing.
- Major provincial/territorial archaeological statutes include *Cultural Property Act of Quebec* (1972), *Ontario Heritage Act* (1975), *Heritage Property Act of Saskatchewan* (1980), and about a dozen other statutes that give provincial governments the power to preserve heritage through protection, mitigation, and enforcement.

For more information:

- Federal Historic Preservation Laws: The Official Compilation of United States Cultural Heritage Statutes, 2006 Edition: https://www.nps.gov/subjects/historicpreservation/upload/NPS_FHPL_book_online.pdf.
- National Trust for Historic Preservation has a compendium of key laws: www.preservationnation.org/information-center/law-and-policy/legal-resources/understanding-preservation-law/federal-law/#.UMZvTqyjfB0.
- In Canada, Parks Canada has an online publication on archaeological law entitled *Unearthing the Law: Archaeological Legislation on Lands in Canada*: https://www.pc.gc.ca/en/docs/r/pfa-fap/index.

Cultural Resource Management

One could argue that CRM began with the Mound-builder Mythbusters (see above), insofar as it was a federal directive. But CRM is far more than government-mandated archaeology. It is a complex set of laws and regulations that are repeatedly updated and expanded. It is the apparatus of regulatory oversight that involves countless government agents. It is an ongoing negotiation among a variety of stakeholders involved in actions that impact the land and its resources. And it is an industry of expertise that employs the vast majority of people who can honestly claim that they make a living as a professional archaeologist.

Not everyone can practice CRM archaeology, although it takes only a field school or equivalent experience to break into the business as a field technician. More formal training and higher education is needed to ascend the ranks. For instance, to obtain government contracts and the permits necessary to implement field investigations, an individual has to hold a graduate degree. It follows that CRM in its earliest incarnation was exclusively a university-based enterprise. Having been deeply involved with the New Deal programs of the Depression, state universities in the South were especially poised to take up the new round of government-mandated work, this time codifed in laws not subject to contingencies of unemployment or economic growth, but instead a sustained commitment to stewardship of the archaeological record.

Beginning in the late 1960s, large CRM programs flourished at the universities of Alabama, Tennessee, and South Carolina, among others. Universities offered the needed combination of infrastructure (labs), intellectual capacity (professors), and labor (students) to pull off large projects, plus they operated the resources for their own replication, namely the training of future archaeologists through both coursework and real-world experience. The downside to university CRM programs was that technical staff (again, students) were transient, "managers" had to balance the demands and calendars of academic and contractual obligations, and the intellectual culture of higher education sometimes was at odds with the more practical concerns of preservation and development. It was not unusual for archaeology outfits at universities to default on government contracts in the early decades of CRM. Government officials became as frustrated with "pointy-headed academics" who failed at "practical" matters like managing budgets and meeting deadlines, as academic archaeologists were with agency officials interested in meeting only the letter, but not the spirit, of CRM law.

Today, few universities host large CRM programs like those of the 1960s and '70s, and the ones that have flourished tend to be quasi-independent programs with staff dedicated to the acquisition and execution of contracts (Figure 2.8). The best of the best are predicated on strong and lasting relationships with one or more government agencies, such as those charged with defense, energy, and transportation (see https://isas.illinois.edu). They seem to have struck a good balance between research and stewardship, enabling development to proceed as needed while pursuing research agendas that inform the interpretation of archaeological remains and, by extension, address the criteria of significance built into federal and state law (see below).

No matter the quality and effectiveness of university-based CRM outfits, the demand for CRM work far exceeded the resource capacity of universities to supply services. Thus, in the reality of supply-and-demand economics, private-sector CRM emerged by the 1990s as the leading employer of professional archaeologists. Many large corporations long involved in environmental impact assessments were able to bring archaeological consulting into their existing

Fig 2.8 Large-scale excavations of Cahokia's East St. Louis Precinct by the Illinois State Archaeological Survey, 2013. Courtesy of Illinois State Archaeological Survey.

missions. Otherwise, entrepreneurs hung their shingles, starting up scores of small operations, some growing to become quite large and lucrative. Not all owners and operators of private CRM forms hold graduate degrees in archaeology or related fields, but all such firms have to have degree-holding personnel to be awarded government contracts: it's the law. Thus, private-sector archaeology is populated by Ph.D. and Masters degree holders, some of whom sought CRM employment from the start, and attended programs catering to the demand, while others took up CRM careers after abandoning hopes for a secure job in academia, an increasingly difficult goal to reach.

Many CRM firms do consistently good work, even those whose primary mission is to turn a profit. But for all the exemplary work, the business of CRM is beset with a variety of problems, some tied to lack of better regulation and an ethos of profit that sometimes challenges ethics. As in any endeavor, many problems come down to particular individuals, those with inadequate training and thus misguided actions. The business is not licensed and regulated the way law and medicine are. Professional organizations such as the Register of Professional Archaeologists (www.rpanet.org) serve to promote ethical and legal practice, but they do not have regulatory authority, nor are all government agencies and other sponsors of CRM willing to impose restrictions on the "free market," although many do. The state-run offices of historic preservation and state archaeologists, both mandated by federal law, often keep track of the performance of CRM firms and individuals, offering in some cases their advice to agencies on the quality of work one can expect from a given firm. They are forbidden by law to restrict access to the market and thus, in the open competition of contract bids, firms that can do the most for the least are often the winners. One can easily imagine how a competitive market such as this leads sometimes to corruption and bad practice, all in the interest of profit margins and sustained success.

In recent years some private-sector firms have promoted an archaeology that prioritizes research and conservation ahead of business. Naturally, these are not-for-profit outfits, such as *Archaeology Southwest* (formerly the *Institute for Desert Research*) (www.archaeol ogysouthwest.org), which involves far more than investigating sites and areas impacted by modern development. Professional staff at Archaeology Southwest conduct research through competitive grants, as well as contracts; host a variety of public outreach events and publish a popular magazine; sponsor field schools; and purchase properties and obtain conservation easements, much like the Archaeological Conservancy (https://www.archaeologicalconservancy.org), to preserve important sites and landscapes. In a sense, outfits like Archaeology Southwest are the ideal balance between the practical and philosophical aspects of historic preservation. They may not solve all the problems of a CRM culture, the legacies of which in both academia and private industries include some dark moments, but they do offer an innovative alternative to either of these other approaches.

Recent legislation in both the USA and Canada turns on the growing political clout of Native Americans and First Nations in reasserting their authority in matters affecting indigenous heritage and quality of life. In the USA, the Native American Graves Protection and Repatriation Act of 1990 had an immediate impact on archaeology and related fields, while in Canada, heritage issues among First Nations are secondary to enduring impoverishment and the struggle for autonomy. It was not until 1960 that First Nations people received the right to vote (some 40 years later than in the USA), and as recently as 1969 government officials tried to abolish the Indian Act of 1867 – which established a reservation system and criteria for tribal or band membership (amended in 1985 to allow First Nations people to define their own membership rules) – and assimilate Indians as an ethnic minority with no special privileges. Implicated in such efforts are the rights of First Nations people to maintain control over land earmarked for hydroelectric dams or mining, threats that persist today.

Recognition by federal governments for greater self-determination by Indians in matters of heritage is changing the way archaeology is practiced in North America. It raises questions long ignored, such as: Who has the authority to do archaeology? What purpose does it serve? And who, if anyone, owns the past? At the heart of these questions is the contradiction between those whose past is being investigated and those who promulgate historical preservation legislation. Sure, it is hardly controversial for the US government to impose its will on the preservation of, say, the Brooklyn Bridge, but does it have the right and responsibility to preserve or excavate an aboriginal mound or habitation site?

We will return to these very important questions at the close of this chapter, after we take a look at the social history of being Indian in North America. But before that we need to consider the rationale used by government to determine whether any particular historical or archaeological resource is worth preserving. The answer is embedded in the criteria used to nominate such resources to the National Register of Historic Places (NRHP), itself a legislative edict. The Register was created in 1966 with passage of the National Historic Preservation Act and it is essentially a list of the districts, buildings, sites, places, and objects deemed worthy of preservation.

There are tax incentives available to encourage private citizens and corporations to nominate their properties to the Register, but of greater relevance to archaeology is its criteria for eligibility, the way archaeologists determine whether a resource is "significant" enough to warrant what is referred to as "mitigation" in the face of a potential threat, such as the construction of a road, dam, or bridge, for example, or even the harvest of timber wood in a national forest. Resources of obvious significance to Euro-Americans were acknowledged and preserved long before the Register was created. As you might expect, these were resources associated with "big" persons and events, like Jefferson's Monticello, Civil War battlefields, or any place George Washington slept. Properties associated with important "events" or "persons" are eligible for inclusion in the Register under Criteria A and B, and another criterion (C) covers distinctive architectural characteristics, like one of Frank Lloyd Wright's creations.

It is Criterion D that matters most to archaeologists practicing CRM. Under this criterion, a property is eligible for the Register if it has yielded, or is likely to yield, *information* important to history (including that of preliterate periods sometimes called "prehistory"). The operative word here is *information*. Unlike the other criteria, which hinge on the objective reality of particular places, persons, and events, Criterion D asks archaeologists to make arguments of significance based on the potential to advance or improve our knowledge about the past. This invokes the pool of knowledge archaeologists have about the past, the potential they imagine for expanding that knowledge, and, by extension, how approaches to archaeological practice have changed over the years. We thus turn briefly to a review of the major shifts in archaeological practice from the time we stopped treating the past as an assemblage of things to be harvested and deposited in museums and started to treat it as a source of histories yet to be written.

Culture History Reigns

The explosion of new observations at archaeological sites across the USA dating to the WPA era was akin to exploring a new land. For the first time, archaeologists and their publics were confronting the fact that native peoples had histories and expressions far beyond the imagination. Before 1927, when a Folsom spearpoint was found embedded in the ribs of an Ice Age bison, scholars believed that Indians had occupied North America for only about 4,000 years. Known as the "Short Chronology," this wrongheaded assumption was as much a cultural bias about the limited diversity and complexity of indigenous people as it was a lack of systematic investigation. WPA projects included the excavation of deeply stratified sites such as shell middens and rockshelters, with profiles several meters tall serving as testimony to long-term histories, and changes in artifact types and other evidence testifying further to major shifts in cultural traditions and economic activity. The Folsom find more than doubled the span of history thought possible, from 4,000 to at least 10,000 years, given that the species of bison that fell victim to a spear-wielding hunter became extinct at the end of the Ice Age (Figure 2.9).

Stratigraphic excavations documenting long-term sequences of culture history were actually mastered in North

Fig 2.9 The 1927 discovery of a spearpoint between the ribs of an Ice Age bison at the Folsom site in New Mexico more than doubled the time native people were believed to have inhabited North America. History now had much more time on its side. © Denver Museum of Natural History.

Sidebar 2.3 Short goes long out on the range

In the spring of 1927 Jesse D. Figgins, Director of the Colorado Museum of Natural History, traveled to the Smithsonian Institution in Washington, DC to show resident scientists what had been found at a site in New Mexico. Among those Figgins met were Aleš Hrdlička and William Henry Holmes, staunch critics of any claim for human antiquity in the Americas. They were happy to see the beautifully made spearpoints Figgins had brought from a site known as Folsom, but neither gentleman was convinced that they were made by Ice Age people. Like so many other claims for human antiquity in the Americas, the Folsom site lacked definitive evidence for the age of the artifacts. Hrdlička advised Figgins to keep digging until he found unassailable proof. In an age predating radiocarbon dating, such proof would have to come from the stratigraphic association between the spearpoints and material of known age.

George McJunkin knew the site was old. He was the African-American cowboy who found bison bones at Folsom in 1908. Born in 1851 to slave parents in Texas, McJunkin traveled to New Mexico at the age of 17 to become a ranch hand. He taught himself to read, speak Spanish, and play music. He also developed a keen sense of history and nature as he worked on several ranches throughout the Southwest. While working at Crowfoot Ranch in 1908, McJunkin spotted some bison bones eroding out of an arroyo. Being familiar with modern bison, McJunkin suspected that the eroding specimens were from an extinct species. Others had made similar claims about Ice Age deposits, but no one had found a direct association between bison bones and artifacts, leaving Hrdlička and Holmes skeptical about the antiquity of New World humans.

McJunkin shared the discovery of bison bones with others, but the site was not investigated professionally until 1926, four years after his death, and even then for the purpose of collecting only bone. The potential for spearpoints may have been imagined by various parties involved, but no one, not even Figgins, anticipated what was to come. By July of that year the first spearpoint was discovered in the bone bed they had excavated, but, to Figgins' disappointment, it was not found *in situ*, meaning a direct association between artifact and bison bone was not observed. Figgins instructed the crew to be especially watchful for additional finds, but by the end of the field season, only one other spearpoint was found, again not *in situ*.

It was thus with great uncertainty about the age of the spearpoints that Figgins visited Hrdlička, Holmes, and other scientists at the Smithsonian the following spring. Mindful of the advice Hrdlička offered, Figgins directed his crew to resume excavations at Folsom with even greater care, and on August 29, 1927 his foreman reported the discovery of a spearpoint in direct association with a bison rib. Telegrams were sent to the Smithsonian and elsewhere to call in the experts to view the evidence themselves. Hrdlička sent Frank Roberts in his stead, and a few days later he was joined by A. V. Kidder, then of the Carnegie Institute of Washington. All who viewed the association between spearpoint and rib agreed that the two were contemporaneous. Additional associations were found, and ensuing geological work by leading experts established that the bone deposit was either late Pleistocene or early Holocene in age (i.e., at least ~10,000 years old). Here then, finally, was unassailable proof of the antiquity of humans in the Americas.

As for Hrdlička and Holmes, they would never endorse the Folsom find, but could no longer categorically deny that humans had arrived in the New World well before 4,000 years ago. Skeptics are good for science inasmuch as they hold practitioners to the highest reasonable standards of proof. Still, one has to imagine that part of the skepticism over the antiquity of humans by these scientists and fellow citizens was influenced by the same misconceptions about Native Americans that denied them any hand in the construction of mounds. (Most of the information for this sidebar was taken from the excellent account of the Folsom site by David J. Meltzer [2006], who also reports on his own, modern investigations.)

America well before the Depression and its New Deal archaeology (Figure 2.10). Alfred V. Kidder of Harvard University began excavations at Pecos Pueblo in 1915 and over more than a decade he revealed

Fig 2.10 Excavations into deeply stratified middens, mounds, river floodplains, and caves starting in the late nineteenth century provided the framework for histories through the sequences of cultural and environmental change registered in successive layers and the things they contained. Top: excavations of the thick midden on the east side of the Pecos Pueblo in New Mexico by A. V. Kidder began in 1915. National Park Service Photo (www.nps.gov/peco/learn/historyculture/alfred-vincent-kidder.htm). Bottom: excavations into the 18-ft high western side of the Emeryville Shell Mound by Max Uhle, 1902. Wikimedia.

a 2,000-year-long sequence of occupation among the Ancestral Pueblo of New Mexico. He was preceded by Max Uhle, the German archaeologist who led excavations of the Emeryville Shell Mound on San Francisco Bay, and before then the explorations of Clarence B. Moore, Jefferies Wyman, and other wealthy and/or well-placed northerners. But before the acceptance of greater time depth for native history – catapulted into public consciousness by the Folsom discovery – stratigraphic sequences were underappreciated. With more time came the potential for more change, and thus greater diversity. For the archaeological historian operating long before the age of radiometric dating, stratigraphy became a measure of time, and the sequence of changes, the figurative chapters of indigenous history (see Lyman and O'Brien 1999 for a cogent history of stratigraphic excavations in North America).

Exceptionally productive and innovative archaeologists of the early twentieth century, such as A. V. Kidder, were classically trained, generally in the Ivy League schools of the Northeast. They were predisposed to view stratigraphy as the record of human history, and thus more inclined to imagine deep time in the deep profiles they observed. At the same time, in the museums and universities of North America, discontent was growing over the enduring biases of the Short Chronology, most notably the evolutionary model that propped it up. Franz Boas, known in some circles as the "Father of American Anthropology," was critical of the late nineteenth-century approach to anthropology known today as *cultural evolutionism.* Ever since the Enlightenment of the seventeenth and eighteenth centuries, Europeans and, later, Euro-Americans speculated that societies passed through stages of increasing development or improvement, enabled by the application of rational thought and technology. In the 1877 classic *Ancient Societies,* American anthropologist Lewis Henry Morgan divided human history into three stages of development: Savagery, Barbarism, and Civilization. The evolution of society from lower to upper stages of development was believed by Morgan and his followers to follow a linear path from primitive to advanced, each change attended by progressively sophisticated innovations such as fire, pottery making, plant and animal domestication, metal working, and writing. It was believed that over time all societies would evolve through this sequence, and thus the absence of many of the attributes of "Civilization" among Native Americans meant that not enough time had passed for societies to evolve. In this view, native history in

Fig 2.11 Franz Boas began a celebrated career in ethnography in the 1880s on Baffin Island in Canada, where he studied the impact of environment on Inuit migrations. His perspectives on human variation and change inspired the culture-historical paradigm of Americanist archaeology (www.franz-boas.de).

the Americas was short and its societies still at lower stages of evolution.

Boas and his students were critical of knowledge claims about social evolution based on the existence of a handful of attributes, as well as the idea that all societies passed through the same evolutionary sequence as if their fates were pre-determined. They pointed out that any theory that presup-poses a progression of culture leading to a stage likened to modern Europe was *ethnocentric*. Boas argued further that the model of cultural evolution wrongfully presupposed the outcome; erroneously assumed that societies were bounded and distinct; and that it unjustifiably reduced social varia-tion to a series of proxy variables. He instead championed an inductive, empirical approach to anthropology that involved fieldwork geared toward the study of actual experience and actual context (Figure 2.11). Boas believed that, in any given population, biology, language, and culture were autono-mous, and that cultural forms often cross social bounda-ries, diffusing to become a source of change. Histories had to be written from the particulars of actual human experi-ence (and understood in their own terms, a concept known widely as *cultural relativism*, the opposite of ethnocentrism), and not presupposed by a model that equates time with progress. In an influential history of theory in American anthropology, Marvin Harris (1968) dubbed Boas' approach *historical particularism*.

The influence of Boas in American archaeology became manifested in an approach known as *culture history*, or cul-tural-historical archaeology. Many archaeologists today would consider themselves cultural historians (see below), but culture history of the early to mid-twentieth century aimed to define societies of distinct ethnic and cultural iden-tity on the basis of material traits alone, namely artifacts. It emphasized the geographic variation in cultures and attrib-uted such variation to diffusion, migration, and related his-torical events. Culture history actually has a deeper legacy in Europe, having originated in Germany, where applications sometimes served nationalistic political agendas, the most egregious example being the Nazi efforts to assert Aryan supremacy through archaeological contrivances (Trigger 2007:240–241). Otherwise, culture history was generally regarded as an inductive approach to the past, where data were allowed to "speak for themselves," without prejudice arising from extant models or political agendas.

As might be expected, a culture-historical approach to archaeology became preoccupied with artifact typology and comparative analyses. As noted, stratigraphy lent itself to the making of culture history much in the way that strata and index fossils allow paleontologists to reconstruct natural history. Archaeology also developed other methods for inferring time in the absence of stratigraphy, such as *seriation*, a relative dating method based on the assumption that change in material culture within a cultural tradition was slow and gradual (Figure 2.12). Radiometric dating would later add absolute chronology to culture histories constructed from relative dating methods, revealing, in some cases, weaknesses in culture-historical methods.

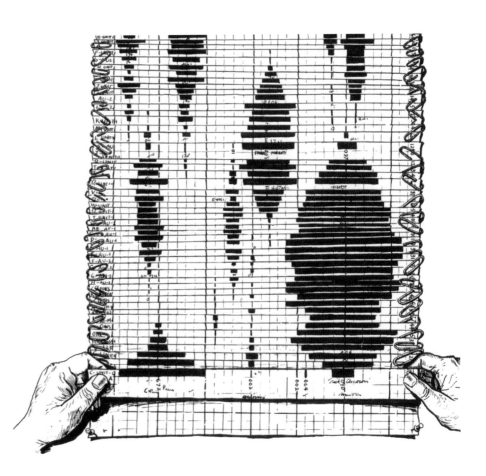

Fig 2.12 A seriation graph constructed by archaeologist James A. Ford from strips of paper that express the relative frequency of potsherds by type from surface collections from the Lower Mississippi Valley (Ford 1962: figure 8).

Rise of Science, Return of Evolution

In 1942, in the heyday of cultural-historical archaeology, a newly minted Harvard Ph.D. enlisted in the US Marines and was deployed to Europe, where he was wounded and captured behind enemy lines, being held prisoner by the Germans until the end of the war. Three years later Walter W. Taylor would publish his doctoral dissertation, *A Study in Archaeology* (1948), arguably one of the most influential books of the profession. In *A Study*, Taylor derided the cultural-historical approach for being merely descriptive, proposing in its place an integrative, "conjunctive" approach to archaeology that would go beyond artifact chronologies to incorporate the study of diet, settlement pattern, technology, ritual, and other dimensions of cultural variation. Taylor called for a deliberately scientific approach to archaeology, one that offered potential to not merely describe what happened in the past but also explain *why* it happened. His hope was to achieve a more holistic, anthropological archaeology, one that could use the tools of science to more fully understand the complexities of culture.

Taylor was about ten years ahead of the times, and his work was largely ignored or vilified for being overly critical of stalwart culture historians such as A. V. Kidder (Hudson 2008). By the late 1960s, however, much of what Taylor proposed for archaeology came to fruition in the guise of *processual* archaeology. As formulated by Lewis R. Binford (1962), processual archaeology applied the methods of scientific inquiry to the development of generalizable, law-like knowledge about human variation and change. In the time of Sputnik, the space age, and the cold war, big science was coming into its own, leading to changes in technology so rapid and so influential that virtually all peoples' lives were affected, for better or worse. Archaeology under leaders like Binford offered hope that knowledge about the human condition would find application in the real world, to become applicable in inferring causes from observed outcomes, and hence *explain*, not just describe, variation and change (Figure 2.13).

An archaeology so conceived needed a unified body of theory to draw on for its deductive method, and that largely fell to the natural sciences. By the 1940s, natural selection theory as conceived by Darwin had been wedded to newfound knowledge in genetics and population biology to form what was called the *new* or *modern synthesis* (Huxley

Fig 2.13 Lewis Binford (right) with Johnny Rulland in Alaska in 1999. Binford studied Nunamuit hunting practices to observe the relationship between behavior and material output among practicing hunters in order to build generalizable models of hunting behavior in the ancient past, a method known as *ethnoarchaeology*. Courtesy of James H. Barker.

1942). Well before this development influenced archaeology, anthropologist Julian Steward (1955) assembled the makings of *cultural ecology*, an approach emphasizing the relationships between humans and their environments. A student of Boas' first student, Alfred Kroeber, Steward would reintroduce anthropology to generalizing, evolutionary approaches to culture change, while also allowing that evolution was multilinear, meaning that it was context-specific and subject to historical particulars.

Shortly later, in a direct denouncement of Boasian particularism, anthropologist Leslie White (1959) would resuscitate some of the tenets of late nineteenth-century cultural evolutionism to advance a *neoevolutionary* theory of cultural variation and change. Attributing cultural change to the ability of a society to harness increasingly greater amounts of energy, White revived the core logic of progressive, unilineal evolution. One of his students, Elman Service (1962), would contribute a new typology of social evolution (band, tribes, chiefdoms, states) that has endured to this day, if now only rhetorically. By formalizing the logic of evolution in energetic terms, White also laid some of the groundwork for microeconomic approaches to behavioral and evolutionary ecology, as well as the cybernetic and systems theoretics that were popular in the 1970s. In the context of ecological and evolutionary approaches, archaeologists increasingly collaborated with colleagues in fields spanning the natural, physical, and social sciences. Specialties in zooarchaeology, paleoethnobotany, palynology, dendrochronology, ceramic engineering, malacology, and geoarchaeology, to name a few, all flourished with the rise of scientific archaeology, as Walter Taylor had hoped.

Field training in archaeology became much more formalized and rigorous in the dawn of processualism. At a field school run by Paul S. Martin at sites in the Southwest, students were charged with developing hypotheses that would inform the methods of sampling, excavation, and analysis (Chazin and Nash 2013). Students were encouraged to think big with hypotheses of broad significance. This was a major change for Martin and his field schools, which for years were structured by questions of culture history, not culture process. He viewed the scientific method as liberating for his students, for they got to choose what it was they wanted to learn, and not only fill-in-the-blanks of a cryptic culture history, or, worse, simply do the bidding of their professor.

Loss of Innocence

As liberating as science may be, in the absence of good judgment, it can also be dangerous, as countless stories of "mad scientists" like Dr. Frankenstein attest. In the shortened history of archaeological thinking outlined above, it may appear that science was pitted against history, or perhaps humanism. This is unfortunate because all of the practitioners involved were scientists inasmuch as they based their knowledge claims on observable phenomena. Boas was an adamant empiricist, eschewing the overgeneralizations and reductionism of totalizing logic in favor of detailed descriptions of actual experience. He understood clearly how damaging generalizable knowledge claims can be when taken out of context, or conscripted for political purposes, as in the racial typologies Boas stridently resisted (Gravlee et al. 2003).

As processual archaeology came into its own in the 1970s, skepticism about science and government began to foment in a variety of social movements ranging from environmentalism to human rights to legal reforms. The Vietnam War, Watergate, the Iranian hostage crisis, and a nuclear accident at Three Mile Island are among the events of the 1970s that kindled doubts over the future of American society. In this context a variety of mostly European scholars in the arts,

Fig 2.14 Debate over the cultural value of Confederate monuments like this one in Union, West Virginia exemplifies the political nature of competing knowledge claims. Proponents for leaving monuments in place point to respect for fallen soldiers fighting over state's rights; opponents point to the enduring racism attending the contest of slavery even well beyond the Civil War and emancipation. Wikimedia.

humanities, and eventually the social sciences began to articulate ideas that were critical of scientific or objective efforts to explain reality. *Postmodernism*, as it came to be known, posited that all knowledge claims are social constructs; that there is no absolute truth, only relative truths; and that knowledge ought to be evaluated not for its "truthfulness," but rather for its intended purposes and unintended consequences. In other words, postmodernism rejected totalizing knowledge claims (e.g., all x are y; every x does y) and promoted critical self-reflection about the role of knowledge in reproducing and changing society (Figure 2.14).

Since the 1980s, any approach to archaeology that does not fit the models of processualism or culture history has been labeled *postprocessual*, the profession's equivalent to postmodernism. Even modern variations on culture history are put in this camp, if, for instance, one is willing to allow that any historical narrative is one of several alternatives. In fact, a wide array of approaches to archaeology since the 1960s get lumped in too. Other innovations exist on the edges of modern practice. In all such cases, the methods employed are empirical; they do not involve conjurers, crystal balls, or oracles. There is nothing magical about them. They are, instead, often deeply contextual, dependent on the details of actual human experience and its meaning, and not always rejecting generalizations, but careful to not allow such knowledge claims to reproduce themselves outside the bounds of experience. In short, postprocessual archaeologists are scientists too, just not beholden to objectivity and absolute truth.

Critical self-reflection in anthropology also led to the loss of innocence over the colonialist mentality that structured western thought since at least the sixteenth century. Evolutionary models that posited "primitive" and "advanced" forms of humanity were called out for their racist overtones, as was androcentric thinking on the origins of modern humans, agriculture, and the state. Classic works in ethnography were deconstructed and recast as the tools of imperialism, while the presumed exceptionalism of modernity was exposed as a rhetorical ploy to keep "savages" in their slot

Sidebar 2.4 Theories and theorizing

You might think that you can ignore theories or theorizing in archaeology. After all, isn't it just about digging in the dirt? Or, isn't a theory just somebody else's contrived guess about the past? As commonly used, a "theory" is sometimes confused with "hypothesis" or, worse, any crazy speculative idea or opinion you could imagine: what's your theory about the origins of the first Americans? But that is not how archaeologists, or many scientists, use the word theory. For them, theory is not the same as a testable hypothesis. In fact, a theory is much broader and richer than that. It consists of an entire set of established facts, assumptions, deep-seated principles, working models, and speculative assertions related to how one might explain something in the past. It is never simply true or false, but is a robust body of knowledge and ideas that guide research. It is always changing as we learn more, and hence we tend to stress *theorizing* over theories. In archaeology, various teams of researchers – or even entire traditions or schools of thought – work in concert on various theories. Importantly, each group or each theory is founded on principles (such as the physical "laws" of thermodynamics and gravity, or such as the understanding of how human cognition works, how people behave [or misbehave], or how

social experience variously engenders cultural identities or motivates action).

Different principled (theoretical) approaches to understanding have been given different names by philosophers and archaeologists. For example, structuralism is the belief that human cognition (mental structures) conveys culture and motivates action. Phenomenology is very different, and holds the opposite – that experience of the world itself is what produces predispositions to act in the minds of people. Neomarxism comes down in between, depending on the variety espoused. Some are very much like theorists who once identified as engaged in "agency theory" or "practice theory" (McGuire 1992, 2008; Ortner 1984). More recently, archaeologists have moved to recognize the importance of nonhuman agency or the powerful qualities and effects of materials, objects, substances, or phenomena on people. Labeled variously post-humanism, new materialism, and symmetrical approaches (see also Chapter 1), advocates theorize about "animistic" ontologies (see Chapter 8) or the relationships between people and the nonhuman realm (Bennett 2010; Hodder 2011; Webmoor 2007). Who or what was the cause of some consequence?

(Trouillot 1991). Postmodernism made it difficult, nearly impossible, to practice science as usual.

In the changes attending such an intellectual upheaval, archaeology survives, even thrives, as the only means to know what human experiences were like before they were written about, literally, in ways we can understand. But that puts archaeology in the difficult position of inferring meaning from the mute traces of human experience. For the longest time, archaeologists have looked to the present to make inferences about the past based on the principle of uniformitarianism. Under the critical scrutiny of postmodernism, archaeologists became loath to transplant our views of modernity on to the ancient past, all the while sensitive that the category "premodern" was itself a form of subjugation. Indeed, the particular events of encounter, displacement, diaspora, and ethnocide in the context of European colonization were unparalleled in scope and consequence. However, encounters among people of vastly different histories took place in North America long before Europeans arrived, so how unique, in fact, was modernity (Cobb 2005)?

There are newer theoretical approaches in archaeology that "decenter" human agency and strategies in the past and elevate non-human or even nonorganic historical cause-and-effect (Harris and Cippola 2017). Certainly, there is much that archaeologists do not know and some say will never know. But for many, it is the questions we ask that limit inquiry more than do the objective conditions of the archaeological record. When questions aim to develop generalizable knowledge (e.g., understanding of cross-cultural comparisons), they converge on formalized themes or models and ways to investigate them. When questions are more particular (e.g., understanding of situated human experience), they diverge into an unending array of particular times, places, and persons. In this open space between subjectivity and objectivity, between fiction and nonfiction, we begin to hear alternative voices in archaeological discourse, and through them, novel perspectives.

Native Americans as Objects, Subjects, Agents

Just as Hollywood promotes an image of archaeology in the form of Indiana Jones, a variety of stereotypic characters have come to be associated with Native American culture and history. Among them is Iron Eyes Cody, an icon of the ecology movement of the 1960s and 1970s. He was the make-believe Indian who, in a variety of public service announcements (PSAs) for the "Keep America Beautiful" campaign, reminded us of the ills of litter and pollution. In the most memorable commercial (www.youtube.com/watch?v=j7OHG7tHrNM), Iron Eyes paddles his way in a birch-bark canoe through what at first appears to be wilderness but quickly changes into an embayment of floating trash, industrial waste, and dead fish. As he makes landfall and ascends a litter-strewn bank to a roadway, the narrator intones in a deep, dark voice: "Some people have a deep, abiding respect for the natural beauty that was once this country. And some people don't.

Fig 2.15 Italian-American actor Espera Oscar de Corti with President Jimmy Carter at the White House, April 1978. As Iron Eyes Cody, de Corti made a career out of playing Indian. US National Archives and Records Administration/Wikimedia.

People start pollution, people can stop it." With cars speeding by, the camera turns to Iron Eyes as a bag filled with litter, tossed from a car window, lands at his feet. He turns to the camera as it pans in on his face, and we see falling, from his right eye, a single, mournful tear.

Would it surprise you to know that Iron Eyes Cody was an Italian American, not an Indian? Maybe not (Figure 2.15). We have come to expect the incredible from popular media, and most of us know not to accept things at face value. The Keep America Beautiful campaign was well-meaning. It hoped in 1970, with the making of this and other PSAs, to motivate people to stop littering and clean up the country. It successfully conscripted the image of Iron Eyes Cody as a consummate ecologist, a representative of native sensibilities to maintain harmony with nature, to treat it, as the ad states, with respect. It mattered little to the producers of the PSA that Iron Eyes was not an Indian, so long as he could play the part. In what historian Philip Joseph Deloria (1999) calls "Playing Indian," non-Indian Americans have long acted out their fantasies about what it means to be "Indian" in order to achieve various goals, or to promote various identities. Never mind that indigenous people at various times in the ancient past may have transgressed the "balance of nature" by acting in ways that had unforeseen, negative consequences (Krech 2000), the notion of an "ecological Indian" endures in the popular imagination.

Indians have been objectified by non-Indians for a variety of purposes, and for every image that is portrayed, a backlash of criticism ensues. The appropriateness of using Native American mascots in sports, for instance, has been hotly debated in the USA and Canada since the 1960s. For every person who would argue that Indian mascots perpetuate negative stereotypes, another would suggest that mascots embody respect and honor for native people. With increasing resolve and authority, native people are taking back control of their images and their histories, recently with help from federal or state/provincial governments, as in the passage of the Native American Graves Protection and Repatriation Act (NAGPRA). It is no surprise that the changes we see of late are predicated on a long history of government interventions that produced only negative consequences for Indians, and with it, justifiable resistance.

Organized Resistance

Ironically, another actor playing the part of an Italian American would help bring to public attention a growing resistance movement among Indians in the early 1970s. For his portrayal of Vito Corleone in the film *The Godfather*, Marlon Brando won an Academy Award for Best Actor. Brando boycotted the awards ceremony, sending in his place Sacheen Littlefeather, an Apache Indian rights activist, to express objection to the stereotypic depiction of American Indians in film and television (https://www.youtube.com/watch?v=2QUacU014yU). In addition, Littlefeather conveyed Brando's support for the ongoing occupation of Wounded Knee, South Dakota by members of the American Indian Movement (AIM). On February 27, 1973, some 200 Oglala Sioux and followers of AIM seized the town of Wounded Knee, located on the Pine Ridge Indian Reservation, and occupied it for 73 days as the US Marshals Service, FBI agents, and other authorities cordoned off the area. The siege followed a failed attempt at impeaching a corrupt tribal president, but its larger purpose was to protest the failure of the US government to fulfill treaties with Indians, a complaint that goes back to the very first treaties of a fledgling nation in the 1770s.

Leading the protest at Wounded Knee was Russell C. Means, an Oglala Sioux who rose to national attention in 1970 by commandeering the *Mayflower* ship replica in Plymouth, Massachusetts on Thanksgiving Day. He later organized a prayer vigil atop the presidential heads of Mount Rushmore, and in 1972 led a cross-country caravan to Washington, DC to occupy the Bureau of Indian Affairs (BIA) in protest of centuries-long broken treaties. In dramatic, occasionally violent protests that brought attention to the ongoing plight of native people, Means was perhaps the best-known Indian since Sitting Bull and Crazy Horse, chiefs who led their people in battles of the Great Sioux War of 1876.

Both sides in the Wounded Knee siege were armed and shooting was frequent. Two of the Indian protestors were shot and killed, and an FBI agent was paralyzed by a gunshot and later died. Buildings in the town were irreparably damaged by fire, and by the time the

Fig 2.16 AIM leaders Russell Means (left) and Dennis Banks holding a press conference in May 1973 to announce settlement with the US government after a 71-day siege of Wounded Knee in South Dakota. Getty Image.

stand-off was over, the small community was in shambles. Means and another AIM leader, Dennis Banks, were indicted on charges related to the siege, but their cases were dismissed owing to prosecutorial misconduct (Figure 2.16).

Means and his followers chose the Wounded Knee site for good reason. On December 29, 1890, at that very site, some 150 Indian men, women, and children were massacred by soldiers of the 7th Cavalry Regiment; another 50 or more were wounded, and 31 soldiers also died, many from "friendly fire" (Figure 2.17). In the years leading up to this incident, the US government had tightened its noose around the neck of Lakota people. White hunters had driven to near-extinction the bison herds that Plains Indians depended on for centuries. Treaties to prevent encroachment on tribal lands by miners and settlers were not honored (in fact, they were actively undermined), and reservation conditions worsened with each passing year. In this atmosphere of mistrust and unrest, a Paiute prophet by the name of *Wovoka* appeared in the Great Basin with hope for rebirth. In the Lakota version of what came to be known as the *Ghost Dance* religion, a Christ-like messiah would fall to earth in the form of an Indian and lead his people to the upper world as white men disappeared from native land and bison returned in abundance. The people and their ancestors would then return to a renewed land to live in

Sidebar 2.5 Russell C. Means: a complicated man

Russell Means died on October 22, 2012 at the age of 72. Diagnosed with cancer in 2011, he eschewed biomedicine in favor of native, herbal remedies. He built a career resisting the imposition of dominant culture while also pursuing opportunities for acting in Hollywood productions like *The Last of the Mohicans* (1992). He was a complicated man, rife with contradictions. He was both hero and villain, the sort of person you could love as much as hate. Means succeeded in mobilizing the image of the Indian warrior to good effect, but he was also criticized for being an unapologetic self-promoter.

He was addicted to drugs and alcohol as a young man, arrested for clashes with the law, tried for abetting a murder, and imprisoned for rioting. He was stabbed once and shot several times. Means attended four colleges but never earned a degree. In his twenties he worked as a janitor, dance instructor, and cowboy. Later in life he mounted hapless campaigns for the governorship of New Mexico and presidency of the United States. In the latter he lost the Libertarian Party nomination to Ron Paul, the Texas Congressman.

In the bigger picture of Native American history, it is the much-publicized activism of Russell Means that best defines his life. As an emerging leader in AIM, Means led a theatrical raid of the *Mayflower* replica, a prayer vigil atop Mount Rushmore, a cross-country caravan to deliver demands to the BIA in Washington, a 73-day siege of Wounded Knee, and a gathering at Little Big Horn on the centennial anniversary of Custer's Last Stand. He traveled to Nicaragua in the mid-1980s to support Miskito Indians threatened by the Sandinista government.

Means "retired" from AIM in 1988 after years of feuding with its leadership. Many of them disowned him, accusing him of opportunism and selfishness. A year later he reported to Congress on what he perceived to be rampant corruption in tribal governments and federal programs assisting Indians. It was, after all, the corruption of a tribal president that prompted Means and colleagues to lay siege to Wounded Knee in 1973.

Fig 2.17 Cemetery at Wounded Knee on the Pine Ridge Indian Reservation of South Dakota, where approximately 150 victims of the December 29, 1890 massacre are buried. More recent interments of military veterans of Lakota heritage encircle the fenced area of the massacre victims. Kenneth E. Sassaman photo, 2012.

Fig 2.18 Frederic Remington illustration (1890) of the Ghost Dance of the Oglala Lakota at Pine Ridge. Wikimedia.

peace. All this would come to pass by performing the Ghost Dance, a large ritual gathering that frightened government officials and white settlers, motivating military action. One BIA agent ridiculed the paranoia and warned that trouble would surely ensue if US troops were deployed to thwart what he considered to be a harmless religious rite (Figure 2.18).

The BIA agent was right, but it wasn't the dance as much as the growing discontent that warranted concern. In February of 1890, the federal government broke a treaty with the Sioux by dividing into five small reservations tribal land that encompassed much of the state of South Dakota. The BIA tried to compensate for the change by deploying white farmers to teach the Sioux how to grow crops, not taking into account the utterly inadequate soils and unforgiving climate of the reservations. By the end of the first growing season it was clear that people would starve, as farming was a bust and the government had cut in half the food rations it provided to offset the loss of bison.

Hunkpapa Sioux leader Sitting Bull was considered by the federal government to be the ring leader behind the Ghost Dance and so on December 15, 1890 he was arrested at his home on the Standing Rock reservation and soon after shot in a skirmish of resistance that left him dead along with several of his people. Afterwards, about 200 members of the Hunkpapa fled Standing Rock to join Chief Spotted Elk on the Cheyenne River reservation to the south. A few days later Spotted Elk and his people, along with several dozen Hunkpapa, left the Cheyenne River reservation to seek refuge with Red Cloud and his people at Pine Ridge. On December 28 Spotted Elk's party of about 350 people, including 120 women and children,

Sidebar 2.6 Visiting Wounded Knee

You can visit the mass grave site at Wounded Knee, on the Pine Ridge Reservation in South Dakota, but be prepared for a sobering experience. The historical details of the massacre are enough to soften even the hardest of souls, and the larger context of injustices against American Indians is enough to raise doubts in even the most patriotic of citizen. But all of that pales in comparison to the material reality of the site. Striding a small hilltop overlooking a barren landscape is a small, fenced compound. At the entrance are two masonry pillars connected above by a simple metal arch adorned with a cross. At the opposite end of the fenced area is a small, gabled building, also with a simple cross. On one side of the fenced area is a marble monument with the names of those who were killed on December 29, 1890, and then buried in a mass grave three days later by strangers. Visitors can enter the fenced area, walk its confined perimeter, and read carefully the names inscribed in stone. Grass grows freely over the area, but two well-worn paths attest to frequent visitation. Offerings of "medicines" are evident in strands of colorful cloth tied to the fence.

Surrounding the fenced area are the marked graves of individuals who died more recently, and under different circumstances. Included are veterans of international conflicts in Vietnam and the Middle East, as well as other members of the community, men, women, and children alike. Some graves are marked with a simple wooden cross inscribed with only a name, while others have headstones similar to those one finds in just about any cemetery in the USA. Either way, graves outside the fenced compound tend to be marked in their entirety, not just at the head. The individuality and attention to detail seen in the more recent burials stands in sharp contrast to the impersonal and anonymous character of the mass grave. The distinction is heightened by the fence separating the two areas.

Unthinking, insensitive visitors to Wounded Knee are liable to comment on the dilapidated look and feel of the place. It certainly is no Arlington Cemetery, nor should it be. Tourists who can set aside their desire for a sanitized experience may find something of deeper value, namely an understanding of how past events like the Wounded Knee massacre remain instrumental in Indian identity. The gravesite runs counter to American sensibilities about the look and feel of a National Historic Landmark because the Oglala Sioux have kept the US government from imposing its will, notably in the allocation of funding for capital improvements. The Sioux also refused US funds for land reclamation after the courts determined that sacred land surrounding Mount Rushmore was indeed wrongly expropriated, and they refused federal assistance for the construction of the *Crazy Horse Memorial* (http://crazyhorsememorial.org), which Chief Henry Standing Bear commissioned in 1948. Offers of reparation for transgressions wrought long ago are consistently rebuffed, especially when they are tied to the sites and rites of remembering the past. The take-away message for the thoughtful visitor is one of self-determination and cultural autonomy, the very attributes most of us take for granted but many American Indians hold foremost in their thoughts and actions.

was intercepted by the 7th Cavalry and escorted to Wounded Knee Creek, where they made camp. The following morning, before dawn, hundreds of cavalrymen surrounded the camp and set up four rapid-fire Hotchkiss guns. The Indians were ordered to surrender their weapons, and as they complied, one member of the group, who was allegedly deaf and incapable of understanding the order, discharged his rifle in a scuffle. A chaotic battle ensued, and one hour later, at least 150 and as many as 300 Indians lay dead. Left frozen on the ground after a three-day blizzard, the dead were gathered by military operatives and placed in a mass grave at the top of a hill overlooking the encampment. The site of the massacre and the mass grave is today a National Historic Landmark, one of the nation's most tragic monuments.

The 1890 massacre at Wounded Knee is one of countless incidences of violence stemming from broken treaties and power plays on the part of the US government. And the 1973 occupation of Wounded Knee was one of countless acts of resistance by Indians to government impositions and atrocities tracing as far back as the sixteenth century. In the best-selling book *Bury My Heart at Wounded Knee*, author Dee Brown (1970) describes the late nineteenth-century history of forced displacement, genocide, and warfare ostensibly from an Indian point of view, although he was not Indian. Appearing at about the same time, the book *Custer Died for Your Sins: An Indian Manifesto* (1969) was critical of the work of churches, governments, and even anthropologists to help Native Americans, calling instead for Indians to take control of their own destiny. Its author, the late Vine Deloria, Jr. (1933–2005), was Standing Rock Sioux, Professor of Political Science at the University of Arizona (1978–1990), and father of historian Philip J. Deloria, whom we introduced earlier. *Custer Died for Your Sins* was indeed a manifesto for Indian activism, catalyzing a nascent American Indian Movement that would jolt people from complacency and awaken them to the injustices and atrocities that had mounted over centuries of colonial rule.

American Indian Movement

Founded in 1968, the American Indian Movement (AIM) is an activist organization whose initial purpose was to address growing concerns for the Native American community in Minneapolis, but it quickly grew into a nationwide movement. A short history of the organization on its website (www.aimovement.org) says that AIM has been around informally for 500 years, meaning that Indians have long banded together to maintain sovereignty and dignity since their first encounters with Europeans. The formalization of AIM in 1968 was one of several organizational efforts to raise consciousness about the enduring injustices of subjugation and discrimination.

One of AIM's most ambitious efforts came in October 1972 when members traveled to Washington, DC to present the Bureau of Indian Affairs a 20-point list of demands, including the abolition of the BIA. Most of the demands centered on treaties and their violations, as well as representation in government and the restoration of more than 100 million acres of land.

Among the acreage in question was the area of the Black Hills around Mount Rushmore. A year earlier, AIM members occupied for a few days land above the heads of US presidents to remind people of the Treaty of Fort Laramie, which created the Great Sioux Reservation in 1868. When gold was discovered in the Black Hills in 1874, thousands of prospectors converged on new towns like Deadwood to stake claims. Crossing into Indian land without authority, prospectors were routinely attacked by the Sioux. The US Army struggled to keep miners out of Indian Territory, but with only limited effect. In May 1875, a Sioux delegation traveled to Washington to meet with President Ulysses Grant and other officials, but was unable to persuade them to honor the treaty. Instead, Grant offered the Sioux $25,000 for the land if they relocated to Indian reservations in Oklahoma. Refusing the offer, the Sioux delegation returned to the Black Hills to a constituency increasingly determined to fight for their land.

After a bloody year of conflict in 1876, punctuated by the Battle of Little Bighorn, the US government seized control over the Black Hills and created five smaller reservations on which to relocate the Sioux. More than a century later, the Sioux Nation won a battle in the US Supreme Court when it was acknowledged that the taking of property required compensation. The court upheld an award of $15.5 million for the market value of the land in 1877, plus 103 years of interest at 5 percent, an additional $105 million. The Sioux refused the money and insisted instead that the land be returned to them.

The unclaimed funds continue to accrue interest in an account held by the BIA. In recent years a debate has risen over the refusal to accept the money, with at least one group, alleged to be backed by 5,000 tribal members, willing to accept it. Some fear retribution from tribal leaders who continue to reject the offer. With at least one prominent member of the Pine Ridge community stating that those "who agree to take the money would be giving up their identities as Indians" (Brokaw 2009), their fears may be warranted.

The Black Hills case underscores the difficulty of negotiating settlements for transgressions and injustices enacted long ago. So much has changed, including what it means to be an Indian (see below). Even AIM has had difficulty maintaining a unified sense of purpose since its founding 50 years ago. In 1993 it split into two factions, mostly due to disagreements over centralized, authoritative control, something deemed by one faction contrary to indigenous politics and the original philosophy of AIM.

Assimilation and Acculturation

Whether by coercion, persuasion, stratagem, or indifference, American Indians since the time of first European contact have been the subjects of western assimilation and acculturation (see Chapter 3). Long before the US government began its formal campaign to "Americanize" Indians, Spanish missions in the Americas sought to convert Indians to Christianity in order to pursue their own colonial interests, including preventing other European powers from gaining a foothold in the New World. Of course, the Dutch, French, and British had other ideas, and they too sought to Christianize natives in alternative ways, such as the Praying Towns of New England Puritans or the French Jesuits' efforts in Canada to add Christianity to Indian beliefs without replacing them. No matter the approach, the logic of Christianization was "based on Lockean Enlightenment notions of the perfectibility of even lowly forms of man" (Castille 1996:744). The racism of this sentiment is quite obvious, but embedded within it was a European androcentrism that made the experience especially devastating for women.

The US government became involved with assimilation efforts through civic means. George Washington was the first to propose the cultural transformation of Indians through education, arguing that in a land of immigrants, a standard set of cultural values would unite people in common cause. Perhaps mindful that the Indians got here first, Washington believed that once they were educated as United States citizens, Indians could merge traditional ways with modern practices, living peacefully among others in society. Accommodations such as this were off the table after the so-called Indian Wars of the late nineteenth century, when the government began to outlaw certain native ceremonies.

Efforts at Indian acculturation were bolstered by church-backed citizens groups, mostly Protestants, who took up the charge as God's work, much like their colonial forebears. By 1865 the US government entered into contracts with various missionary groups to operate Indian schools for teaching English, civics, and even practical skills like farming. These efforts were often established on reservation land and were, in some cases, such as those headed by Quakers, successful in balancing assimilation with native sensibilities.

Before the end of the nineteenth century, Indian schools expanded to locations outside reservations. The Carlisle Indian Boarding School in Pennsylvania was the first to open and became a model for schools elsewhere (Figure 2.19). Its founder, Richard Henry Pratt, had served in the Civil War, commanding Native Americans who were enlisted as scouts for the 10th Cavalry. He was later in charge of Indian prisoners held in St. Augustine, Florida, where he established opportunities for education using volunteer teachers. So successful was the effort, in Pratt's view, that he lobbied Congress to establish schools for the express purpose of educating Indians. In 1879 the Carlisle School opened its doors to a group of Lakota youth. Pratt recruited his first class by persuading Lakota elders that the reason the white man was able to take their land was because he was educated.

The legacy of Carlisle and the other Indian schools is a mix of paternalism and controversy. More than 12,000 students from 140 tribes passed through the school, some gaining an education that improved their lives and those of their families. But only 8 percent graduated. Many more fled, and hundreds died while at school, many from infectious disease such as tuberculosis. Students were beaten, confined, or put to hard labor for using native language. They were required to take English names, dress like "Americans," and follow a military regimen. Pratt believed that to achieve full assimilation, Indians had to be uprooted from their traditions and beliefs and immersed fully in the culture and practice of "mainstream" America. He was known to

Fig 2.19 Students assembled at the Carlisle Indian
Industrial Boarding School (1879–1918), in Carlisle,
Pennsylvania. Wikimedia.

say, "Kill the Indian in him, but save the man." Because of his extreme
views on assimilation, Pratt was forced to retire as superintendent in
1904. Carlisle remained open for another 14 years.

With a history of forced assimilation lasting some 400 years, Native
Americans and First Nations people struggle to define themselves as a
people. Of course, indigenous people are as diverse today as they ever
were, rendering foolish any blanket statement about how "Indians"
think or act. At the same time, in the context of colonial hegemony,
genocide, forced displacement, and assimilation, the aboriginal people of North America are united in contradistinction to the west.
This is not to say that all Indians agree on who they are, how they fit
into society at large, or what their goals moving forward ought to be.
Like all people in all times, differences of perspective and value exist
among Indians today, despite efforts on the part of some outsiders to
erase diversity.

Authenticity, Autonomy, and Self-Determination

Negotiating Indian identity has been, and continues to be, both a legal and moral imperative. Left for non-Indians to decide, Indian identity is usually simplified. As we have seen, the non-Indians in this history have operated through legal mandate and the exercise of force to define "Indian" in terms that are self-serving. It follows that the definition of "Indian" has changed with changing agendas (Castille 1996). For a young US Congress, which operated under Constitutional right to "interact" with tribes, land transfer through treaty was the driving motive, and for that only chiefs mattered. With reservation systems of the late 1800s, land allocation became the issue and with it the need to identify "authentic" Indians (generally "¼ blood"). By the 1960s, a land-based focus gave way to broader criteria and cultural reform, and with emphasis on economic and political sovereignty. Most recently, and with growing autonomy, Indian tribes are pursuing new opportunities for the future, in some cases drawing on newfound wealth to reinvent themselves, although poverty persists in other cases, on many reservations, with uncertain futures. We can add to the array of modern identities the growing population of "generic" Indians, as well as the "supratribal" consciousness of New Age people. Such "wannabe" Indians do not belong to a particular tribe or even have any Indian heritage at all – or if they do, their tribal affiliation or heritage is not regarded as "legitimate" – but they tend to aspire to Indian philosophies and back Indian causes.

So who actually is Indian today? If we follow the lead of history, we would appeal to the courts for an answer. If we step aside and ask Indians who is Indian, we presume to know who to ask. Right, wrong, or indifferent, the US government still intervenes in matters of Indian identity. The 2010 census in the United States reports 2.9 million people as Native American, with another 2.3 million as mixed Native American and other. *Federally recognized tribe* is the legal term for a group recognized by the BIA as legitimate recipients of the resources and services they administer. The designation has also proven necessary for bringing land claims against the USA.

In the 1970s a balance was struck between the dependency aspects of federal recognition and the right to self-determination. The Indian Self-Determination and Education Assistance Act (ISDEAA) of 1975 authorized the government to enter into contracts with and provide grants to tribes, who then had the authority to administer the funds themselves. This was a considerable improvement over earlier legislation. The Indian Reorganization Act of 1934 was an early step in the creation of tribal self-governance, but tribal actions were still subject to BIA review. The 1950s witnessed renewed efforts for Native American assimilation, and, in the process, to terminate tribes. More than a hundred tribes lost federal recognition under the rationale that their members were better off as "regular" US citizens.

The ISDEAA reversed a 30-year effort by the federal government under its misguided termination policy to renege on treaty obligations to Indian tribes. Years of protest and lobbying by groups like AIM and the broader civil rights community helped usher in this change. The Indian Civil Rights Act of 1968, which extended the Bill of Rights to tribes, was likewise an outcome of activism. President Richard Nixon threw his support behind these and other initiatives to turn US policy on Indian affairs toward greater self-determination.

No matter the change in federal policy, the BIA still finds it necessary to establish criteria for tribal identity. Among the criteria it issued in 1978 are demonstrable Indian descent, community continuity, and political authority, often difficult to substantiate and always a painstaking process to pursue, taking most tribes years to complete. As of January 2018, some 567 tribes have federal recognition, with more than 1.7 million members. Several hundred other tribes are seeking recognition, some more actively than others.

Federal recognition gives not only access to certain government resources, and the freedom to allocate them, but also the freedom to exercise economic opportunities not available to non-Indians, such as gaming operations, which have grown since the passage of the Indian Gaming Regulatory Act of 1988 to a multi-billion-dollar-a-year industry. The outcome for some tribes has been positive, for others not so much. The Seminole of Florida and Pequot of Connecticut, for instance, have parlayed gambling revenue into thriving cultural enterprises that include museums of culture and history and a full-time staff of archaeologists, historians, and other scholars to handle heritage issues (Figure 2.20).

This then delivers us to the questions posed earlier in this chapter about the right to do archaeology, to write about the past. With the legislative, economic, and political capacity to write their own histories, why do Indian tribes need archaeologists, or at least non-Indian

Fig 2.20 The Mashantucket Pequot Museum and Research Center in Connecticut. As stated on the museum's website: "the Pequot Museum is committed to transforming how indigenous culture and peoples are represented to accurately portray a next generation Native narrative that gives greater understanding to the evolution of a new Native voice." The Pequot have successfully taken up opportunities in the free market to reassert authority in the telling of their own history. Wikimedia.

archaeologists? "We have been the objects of scientific investigations and publications for far too long, and it is our intent to become people once again, not specimens" (Deloria 1992:595).

As we have seen, the histories of archaeology and Native Americans are vastly different, even as they intersect in the common interests of Indian pasts. The sentiment expressed above by Vine Deloria is an apt response to objectifying and totalizing approaches to native histories in the Americas (see also Watkins 2012). But archaeology has always been, and is even more so now, interested in allowing the particulars of human experience to structure the narratives of the past. These experiences are incredibly interesting in their own right, as we hope to show in this book, and should not be glossed as generalized knowledge. Embracing this sentiment, archaeologists may find greater willingness on the part of Native Americans to collaborate (Dongoske et al. 1997). At a minimum, we can operate, as archaeologists, with the resolve that native perspectives on their own past are salient to *any* understanding of their past, especially as that knowledge is mobilized in the cultural and political arenas of modern life.

As objects of archaeological inquiry and subjects of government control, Native Americans have been and continue to be victimized. However, the indigenous people of North America have always been agents too, exercising resistance to the imposition of will, writing their own histories, and determining their own futures, even if by terms they themselves did not choose. It was the historic preservation movement, for instance, that opened up legal space for the implementation of laws such as NAGPRA, which privileges Native American religious freedoms over academic or governmental prerogatives. In turn, the direct, collaborative involvement of native peoples has given archaeology new vitality and purpose (Colwell-Chanthaphonh and Ferguson 2008; Dongoske et al. 2000; Echo-Hawk 2000; Kerber 2006; Nicolas 2010; Silliman 2008). Some non-Indian archaeologists express doubt or concern over the legitimacy of native views of the past (e.g., McGhee 2008; Snow 2010), but we, like many of our colleagues, invite the dialogue (see papers in the April 2010 issue of *American Antiquity*). The dialectic that comes from alternative points of view and different experiences is, after all, the raw material of change, as we will see in the next chapter.

3 Contact, Colonialism, and Convergence

Contact – the very idea is problematic. After all, what isn't a contact? Any moment in which two people, two nonhuman beings, and even two inert things meet each other would seem to qualify. But which contacts are "culture contacts," as in the meeting of unrelated people (or the creations of those people)? Arguably, both sides of any contact are cultured in some fashion, so perhaps interpersonal contacts are always, in some sense, culture contacts, which arguably should extend to one's encounters with the cultural objects or constructed places of others. Thus, contact was a question for everybody from culture historians to post-processualists (see Chapter 2) even as it is a question for so-called "new materialists" (see Chapter 16).

One might argue that all of the answers to the questions posed above depend on one's definitions – and archaeologists, by definition, love to define things. Perhaps we should limit ourselves to the "first meetings" between natives, as opposed to later colonial period contacts and relationships (Dickason and McNab 2009:62). But the problem remains as to when first meetings cease being first and become sustained relationships, colonial or otherwise. Are relationships just a bunch of repeated encounters, as when one seeks to contact and communicate with a friend or relative? If so, how many times do two people, or peoples and their associated configurations of things and spaces, have to meet to have a relationship? And when do relationships become colonial, which by definition involves appropriations of physical resources, lands, labor, and souls (Loren 2007)?

Archaeologists' definitions of things such as culture contacts and colonial relations come from previously studied historical examples, and the more we know the more we change our definitions. So perhaps, since we are at the beginning of a chapter on North American contact and colonialism, we should not yet answer the questions posed above. Let's consider some examples from that period of history – the sixteenth through nineteenth centuries CE – when people from different parts of the world and with distinct histories converged in North America. To do this, we need not begin at the beginning, whenever that was. Indeed, the history of contact and colonialism is all around us still. Let us pick a moment.

Contact in North America

Owing in equal parts to the truly ancient history of native North America, and also to the designations applied to them by Europeans, a map of the native ethnic territories and language groups within a century of "first contact" looks something like that in Figure 3.1. The Plains and Southwest/Northwest Mexico include populations speaking a variety of Uto-Aztecan languages, linking them to peoples in Mesoamerica, and Athapaskan languages, derived ultimately from mother cultures in Canada. California shows a myriad of languages, some restricted to single valleys, telling of the geographic barriers that enabled social and linguistic isolation. The coastal languages up the Northwest Coast into Alaska show something similar, but with the coastal waterways allowing for interactions and migrations, producing a patchwork appearance. The Plains and Eastern Woodlands reveal something very different, an open geography that facilitated the homogenizing of speech if not also the formation of larger political territories, punctuated by the occasional language isolate, results of large-scale migrations that extend back to the peopling of the continent (Sassaman 2010).

By 1693, the Spanish had reconquered New Mexico, reclaiming what they had lost when the southwestern Pueblos, led by a charismatic religious leader named Popé, had revolted 13 years earlier. Coordinating their attacks using knotted cords to count down the days, Puebloan rebels had mounted a surprise attack against Spanish settlements on August 10, 1680. They killed up to 400 Spaniards and mestizo settlers and burned churches. Another 2,000 colonists fled, initially to the provincial Spanish capital at Santa Fe and then, after three days of bitter fighting there, south along El Camino Real (the Royal Road) to present-day El Paso and Ciudad Juárez. Some of the people of Isleta Pueblo joined them in their migration south. During the thirteen-year interim, the Puebloan people reestablished control over their own lands, religious practices, and fates (Preucel 2002). But the Spanish returned, led by Don Diego de Vargas in 1692, and

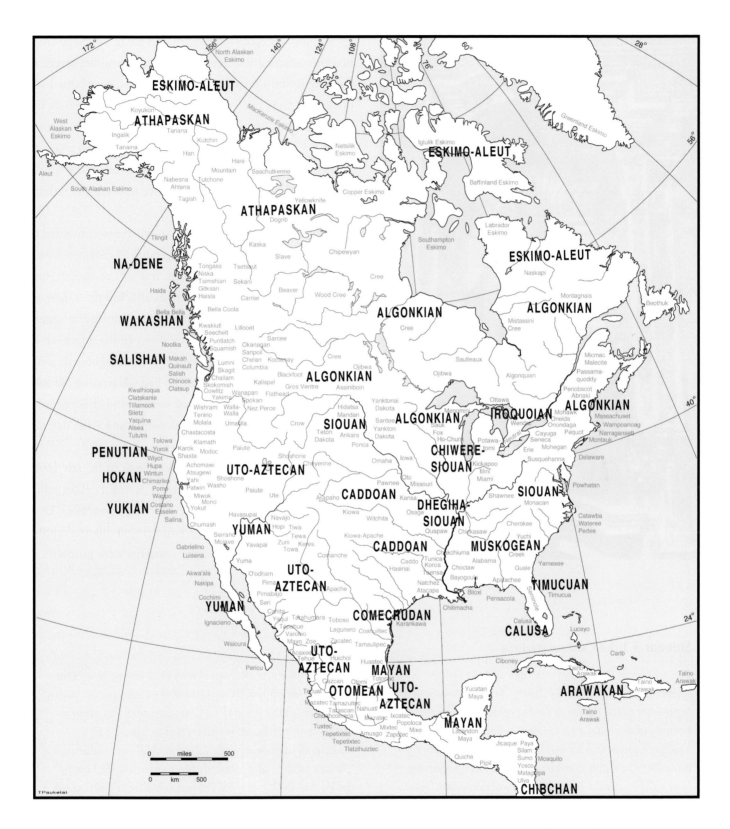

Fig 3.1 Map of native American nations, tribes, language groups, and ethnicities in the sixteenth century CE. Timothy R. Pauketat map, 2019.

Fig 3.2 La Conquistadora, St. Peter's Basilica, Santa Fe, New Mexico. Timothy R. Pauketat photo, 2013.

"peacefully" renegotiated reentry into Santa Fe. Diego credited this peaceful reconquest to a carved wooden image of the Virgin Mary, later dubbed *La Conquistadora* (Our Lady of Conquering Love) and today also known euphemistically as Our Lady of Peace, to which he had prayed before reentry (Figure 3.2). Of course, while Diego was away on a trip to Mexico in 1693, Puebloan factions reassumed control over the city, and Diego used military force to crush the Indians upon his return, slaying hundreds.

Skirmishes and attempted native rebellions continued to 1700, producing factions of indigenous Christian converts and traditionalists. In that year at one of the largest Hopi pueblos, Awat'ovi, the traditionalists attacked the converted Hopi, who had received envoys from the Spanish and sought to reestablish the mission church there. In the attack, all of the male converts within Awat'ovi were slaughtered, some burned alive inside kivas where they had taken refuge (Brooks 2016). Afterwards, the converted women and children were redistributed to other Hopi settlements and Awat'ovi was abandoned.

From their point of view, the Spaniards in the late 1690s were bringing Christ to the tribute-paying Pueblos while keeping them safe from raids by Apaches, Comanches, Utes, and Navajos, who took Puebloan women and children captive. Of course, the Spaniards' larger concerns were geopolitical.

Sidebar 3.1 La Conquistadora

The reentry of Don Diego de Vargas and the Spanish is celebrated today in Santa Fe during the second week of September as the *Fiestas de Santa Fe*, kicked off by the burning of Zozobra, a 15 m (50 ft) tall marionette puppet. The more important icon of the week-long celebration, however, is La Conquistadora (Our Lady of Conquering Love), the 75 cm (30 in) tall carved wooden statue (also called a "bulto") of the Virgin Mary to which Diego de Vargas had pleaded his case. She is paraded down San Francisco Street in Santa Fe dressed in one of the outfits from her extensive wardrobe. Known before 1692 variously as "Our Lady of Assumption," "Our Lady of the Conception," and "Our Lady of the Rosary," La Conquistadora was probably carved in the early 1600s and carried to Santa Fe by a Franciscan missionary in 1625, a powerful embodiment of Christ's mother who interceded in human affairs. During the Pueblo Revolt of 1680, she was saved from destruction and hidden away. Today, she is kept in a side chapel of the St. Francis Basilica. Her garments are changed depending on the occasion (www.traditioninaction.org/religious/a008rp.htm).

By the late 1690s, the French were probing westward from their colonies along the Mississippi River, seeking to extend New France's trade relations into the Plains, Southwest, and Mexico. In 1719, word came to the Governor of New Mexico in Santa Fe, Antonio Valverde y Cosio, that the French incursions were to be curtailed. Spain was at war with France, and so Valverde sent an expedition of some 560 men – most of whom were Puebloan Indians – out into what is today Kansas. They returned with evidence of French activity but no military results. The next year, Governor Valverde sent another fighting force of just over a hundred mounted royal Spanish and Puebloan soldiers from Santa Fe under the command of his lieutenant, Governor Villasur. The Villasur expedition traveled almost 800 miles (1,300 km) into the Great Plains until they reached the confluence of the Loup and Platte rivers, near present-day Columbus, Nebraska. There, they encountered a large band of Pawnee and Oto Indians on the move. They were accompanied, Villasur's men thought, by at least one French trader (Chavez 1994).

Unfortunately for them, Villasur did not suspect that the Pawnee, Oto, and French would attack early the next morning, but they did, catching the Spanish and Puebloan force by surprise. The battle that ensued was later painted on to a large hide, perhaps by indigenous painters in a Santa Fe workshop, and hung inside a Santa Fe residence. In this "Segesser II" hide painting, Pawnee and Oto warriors are shown chopping, slashing, and impaling the Villasur force (Chavez 1994; Hotz 1970). These Plains Indians wore little more than colorful body paint, moccasins, leg garters, and padded cloth headbands into battle, the latter to protect themselves from blows to the head. In such fashion, they killed 48 of the enemy, many cut down in a final hopeless last stand (Hotz 1970).

In important ways, the events swirling around Santa Fe leading up to the Villasur encounter and its subsequent commemoration on a hide wall-hanging epitomize colonial-era encounters between native North Americans and Europeans or Euro-Americans. Consider these points:

(1) The distances involved were great. Plains and Great Basin Apaches, Comanches, Utes, and Navajos raided into the Southwest, and had done so without horses before the Spanish arrival. Lines of communication and long-distance travel were extensive.

(2) There were no passive victims. Pueblo communities carried out a successful rebellion and the Pawnee-Oto were proactive partners in an increasingly global trade network.

(3) Native organizations and gender relations were elaborate – calendrical, communal, military, and religious.

(4) Each encounter mattered over the long term, violent or peaceful, as did the narratives of such encounters. Contacts are moments when people relate to and affect each other, not to mention the places and things entangled in the moment of engagement. Such moments can change the course of history.

(5) Even the narratives of such encounters had effects, as in the Segesser painting (a pictorial narrative) or La Conquistadora (a narrative in wood). The painting hung in a building, was viewed daily and treasured for centuries, and is today exhibited in the Palace of the Governors, part of the New Mexico History Museum in Santa Fe. The carving of the Virgin Mary survived the Pueblo Revolt and now resides in St. Francis Basilica in Santa Fe where it continues to engage people and their pasts.

If such points are correct, then we all need to think much more about who or what were consequential players in the past and why. Because such causes and effects, presumably, also matter for our own future. So, let us examine other contacts of various sorts to see if observations such as these hold up.

Norse Contacts: 1000–1300s CE

The sagas of the Norse, Christianized descendants of northern Europe's Vikings of the late eighth into the eleventh century CE told of a short-lived colony in a place called Vinland. This was the culmination of an expansion of the Viking people, agricultural Scandinavians who, beginning in the late 700s, climbed aboard ships and commenced great free-for-all plunders of various European ports, ships, and settlements. More than likely, this expansion was both a direct consequence of, and a sort of resistance to, Charlemagne's Carolingian Empire in central Europe. It also may have been an indirect result of an economic slowdown in trans-European trade. The time was ripe for the Viking approach to European relations.

Thus, lacking a centralized imperial base, Viking looters and mercenaries from various petty kingdoms raided along Europe's west coast, into the Mediterranean and as far south and east as Baghdad, the capital of the Islamic empire. Here they left their calling cards, carved runestones and graffiti that told of their great deeds. They colonized Iceland and Greenland, far to the west, established trade relationships with non-Viking Europeans and west Asians, and left behind colonial occupations in cities that changed the course of European history: Kiev, Constantinople, Dublin, Paris. They were organized into "corporate" communities, where related extended families lived together in longhouses and participated in processing the booty derived from raiding, and where great prestige was conferred on successful warriors and leaders. In death, Viking souls would make their way to Valhalla in their ships, which were actually used as coffins for burials of the prestigious dead.

The colonization of Greenland provided the launch pad for further explorations west, and led to the Norse discovery of North America (Figure 3.3). As recounted in Icelandic sagas, Leif Ericson and a couple dozen or more men sailed to a land beyond Greenland, previously sighted by an Icelander who had been blown off course during his voyage to Greenland. Sailing south to find the land a decade or two later, Leif and his brother Thorvald founded in the early 1000s a settlement in what he called Vinland. Known originally as Leifsburdir (or Leif's booths), its description corresponds to the only known Norse colony in America, an archaeological site known as L'Anse aux Meadows, located on the northern tip of Newfoundland (Figure 3.4). L'Anse aux Meadows consists of eight wood-frame peat-covered homes, three workshops, and a blacksmith's forge, all similar to contemporary buildings known in Greenland and Iceland (Dickason and McNab 2009).

Norse colonists seem never to have reached the interior of the continent, despite runestones reported in Minnesota and Oklahoma, famous forgeries (named the Kensington Stone and the Heavener Stone) produced by Scandinavian immigrants during the nineteenth century (Feder 2014). According to the sagas, subsequent Norse colonists in Vinland attempted to trade with people they called "Skraelings" – the now-extinct Algonkian-speaking Beothuk and Dorset Eskimo – who had large eyes, broad faces, and tangled hair (Kunz and Sigurosson 2008). Such attempts led to misunderstandings and violence, with the deaths of Eskimo and Norse men. The Norse colony was withdrawn shortly thereafter, although sporadic trade

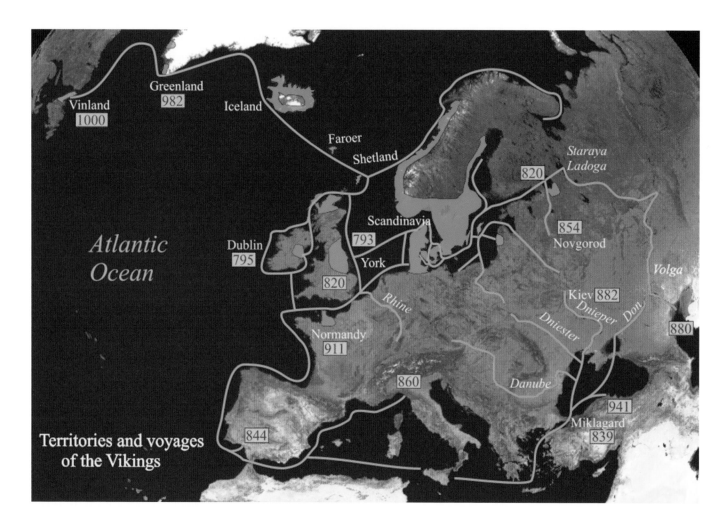

Fig 3.3 Map showing the itineraries of the Vikings in the first millennium CE. Wikimedia.

continued between the Norse of Greenland and a "Thule-Eskimo" population, originally from farther west. The Thule people would eventually occupy Greenland, trading and warring with the Norse, before that colony was also given up as the temperatures dipped at the beginning of the Little Ice Age (1450–1850 CE). The Norse episode over, no other European contacts with native North America are known until the arrival of Christopher Columbus.

Conquests: 1492–1600 CE

The history of New Spain began with the arrival of Columbus on the shores of San Salvador, Bahamas, on October 12, 1492 (Figure 3.5). On that first trip, Columbus and his men established the first European settlement in Hispaniola (modern-day Haiti and the Dominican Republic). On a second return trip from Spain in 1493,

Fig 3.4 L'Anse aux Meadows site reconstruction. Dylan Kereluk photo/Wikimedia.

the Spanish encounters with native Carib, Taíno, and Arawak peoples began to sour, and frequently turned violent. Eventually, these native groups would be erased from history, as clashes, enslavements, and European diseases such as smallpox and measles took their toll (Hunter 2011).

In the meantime, other Spaniards – almost all men, since women were often not allowed to travel to the New World – sought military fame, landholdings, and wealth in North America, as they would have in Spain at the time. Indeed, they had just reconquered Spain in 1492, removing the Moors or forcing them into servitude. A veteran of that *Reconquista*, Juan Ponce de Leon, accompanied Columbus on his second journey to the New World and won fame and landholdings in Hispaniola, where he was also involved in a massacre of the Taínos and the establishment of gold-mining and farming *encomiendas* (a native-labor allocation system organized by the Spanish Crown). Local Indians and captives from afar were made to pay tribute to Ponce de Leon and other Spanish elites, or made to work for them. At the time, Spanish slaving ships routinely raided the Bahamas and Florida to capture and enslave indigenous men and women. The natives did not take this lying down, and the Caribs, for instance, actively raided Spanish settlements into the early sixteenth century.

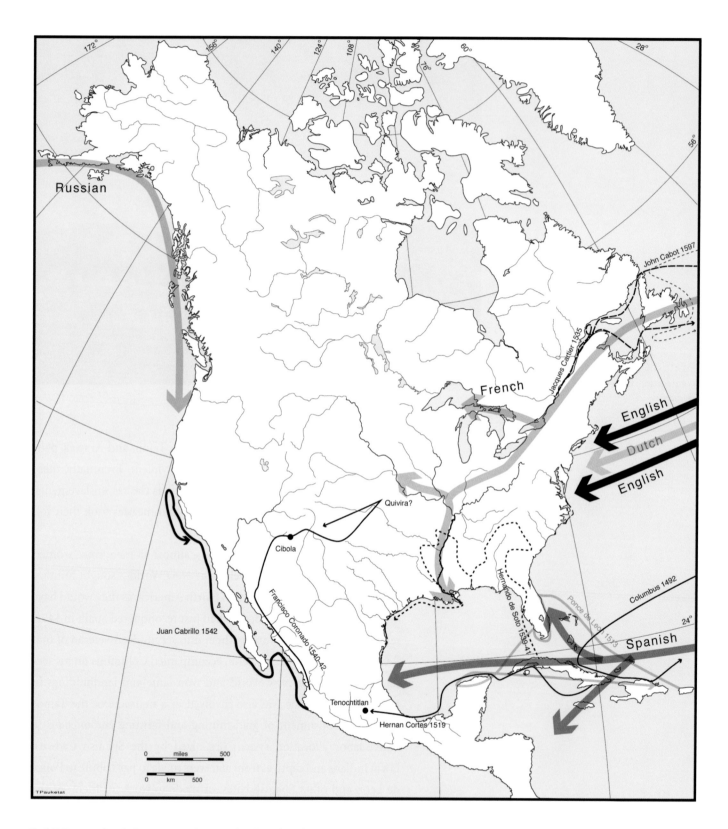

Fig 3.5 Routes of early European explorers and major colonial incursions into North America. Timothy R. Pauketat map.

From Ponce de Leon to Cortés

In 1513, Ponce de Leon led an expedition to the North American mainland with three ships and a couple hundred men. He was not seeking a fountain of youth, a myth created after his death. Rather, he was seeking gold and an expansion of his landholdings. On April 2, he dropped anchor along the western side of the peninsula, which he named *La Florida*, presumably for the flowery country discovered during the Easter season of flowers (Fuson 2000). His encounters with the native people there were violent, as were those of most subsequent Spanish entradas: Alonso Alvarez de Piñeda in 1519, Pánfilo de Narváez in 1527, Hernando de Soto in 1539–1543, Francisco Vázquez de Coronado y Luján in 1540–1541, Tristán de Luna y Arellano in 1559–1560, and others (Clayton et al. 1993). The results certainly had long-term effects on the native Floridians, with European viruses the most active agents of change, spreading from coastal populations along well-traveled routes and social lines of communication into the interior. Viral infections devastated Indian communities. Untold numbers died.

The entradas into southeastern North America were costly in another way for the conquistadors: Ponce de Leon died of a poison arrow shot into his leg on a second return journey to Florida in 1521; Hernando de Soto lost half of his men, and himself died of fever along the Mississippi River in 1542; Pánfilo de Narváez and some 300 men lost their lives along the coastal Southeast, with only four men surviving by traveling across Texas and into the Southwest and northwestern Mexico. Coronado went bankrupt.

But the cost paid for the European discovery of the New World was no greater than that paid by the people of central Mexico (Castillo 2008). Not long after Leon's initial expedition to Florida, the great empire of the Mexica (pronounced *Mĕ-shē'-ka*), better known as the Aztecs, with its fabulous island capital in the Valley of Mexico, would fall to another conquistador through an unlikely series of events (Figure 3.6). Hernán Cortés was the leader of this expedition, which proceeded in 1519 (despite the previous year's attempts by his superior, the Governor of Cuba, Diego Velázquez, to recall the expedition after it had begun). With some 15 mounted soldiers, 500 Spanish fighting men, and 15 cannon, the expedition proceeded toward the great fabled city of the Aztec, Tenochtitlan (pronounced *tĕ-nōsh-tēt'-län*, today's

Mexico City). Cortés was ruthless, massacring hundreds (possibly thousands) of nobles in the city of Cholula en route to Tenochtitlan. He was also cunning. Along the road to Tenochtitlan, he allied himself with non-Aztec native cities which sought to be liberated from Aztec domination and was given hundreds of human porters and perhaps one to two thousand Indian warriors. Once in the Valley of Mexico, the king of the Aztecs, today known as Montezuma (the younger), unwisely allowed Cortés and his men entry into the city center. Cortés placed the king under house arrest and, shortly thereafter, left the city with his second-in-command – Pedro de Alvarado – in charge, having heard in the spring of 1520 that the Governor of Cuba was sending an army to stop Cortés in his mission to conquer the Aztecs (more than likely, the Governor imagined that this would make Cortés too powerful). Some 900 Spaniards, led by the red-haired Pánfilo de Narváez, had been sent to subdue Cortés. But Cortés, with only a couple hundred soldiers at his disposal, defeated Narváez and persuaded Narváez's men to join him. They all returned to Tenochtitlan, now a reinforced army of hundreds of Spaniards and a thousand or more indigenous warriors (Hassig 2006).

Meanwhile, in Cortés' absence, his second-in-command back in Tenochtitlan (perhaps under his orders) had massacred thousands

Fig 3.6 Aztec capital city of Tenochtitlan, by Diego Rivera. Wikimedia.

of weaponless residents during a city-wide ceremony. And, with that, the Aztecs had had enough. Cortés was allowed back in to the city, but its people rose up and attacked the Spaniards. The Aztecs decimated Cortés' army as it fled the city, killing at least 850 of his men, and possibly all of his allied Indian troops. Cortés himself almost perished while fleeing the island city via a causeway that cut across Lake Texcoco. Had that happened, world history would have been different.

One might think the attempted conquest should have ended there. But it didn't. The Aztec capital and its imperial hold on outlying subject cities had been shaken, and the empire was in political turmoil. In that context, Cortés returned from the coast in 1521, now officially empowered by Spain to take Tenochtitlan. His army of Indians and reinforcements from Cuba choked off the city with a blockade of ships and soldiers, and brought Tenochtitlan to its knees. The city fell and Cortés took over its administration (Hassig 2006).

Of course, all of this was but the beginning of the actual transformation of the Aztec Empire into colonial Mexico. After all, what had Cortés and his indigenous military allies actually accomplished? They had eliminated the political superstructure of the vast Aztec nation. But the everyday lives of the Aztec people had not changed. They believed in Aztec gods and their daily rhythms were set by an Aztec calendar and traditional agricultural practices. The real conquest of the hearts, minds, and backs of the central Mexican Indian peoples began afterward, with the Cortés government and the Catholic church forcing Indian laborers to (1) demolish the great monuments of Tenochtitlan and its allied cities and (2) adopt Christianity. Demolition was a physical act that could not be easily forgotten, much less overlooked, and Christian conversion was also a new physical and temporal experience that had long-lasting practical consequences (see "Missionization and the Colonial Project," below). To achieve this overall historic change, one more physical transformation would put the nail in the Aztec coffin. Beginning in 1519, waves of European diseases washed over Mesoamerica. Through the rest of the sixteenth century, as much as 90 percent of the indigenous population of central Mexico would die, most from smallpox and typhus (Storey 2012). Given estimates of the indigenous population of central Mexico in the millions, the loss was nothing less than disastrous. The final conquest of Mexico, that is, was a demographic calamity (Hassig 1985).

At the same time, a new hybrid population was being born: the mestizos – children born of native women and Spanish men. So rapid was the replacement of purely indigenous people with mestizos that one must imagine each Spaniard – again almost all men who had left their wives back in Spain – having routine sex with many dozens of indigenous concubines, slaves, and rape victims. By 1700, mestizos had largely replaced the American Indians in the former Mesoamerica and the Spanish territories to the north, with many complications for the identity politics of the time (Loren 2000).

From Soto to Coronado, Cabrillo, and Oñate

Similar calamities were experienced by the indigenous peoples of the American Southeast and Southwest, also on the heels of penetrations by conquistadors. The most significant in the Southeast was that of Hernando de Soto (Clayton et al. 1993). A veteran of the conquest of the Inca in 1533, Soto's search for wealth and power brought him and upwards of 700 young men-at-arms, along with a couple hundred horses and hundreds of heads of livestock, to the coast of Florida. Fewer than half of the men would survive.

In May of 1539, landing somewhere near the spot where Leon had dropped anchor, the Hernando de Soto expedition intended to traverse all of the interior of the Southeast. Over the next four years, the expedition would travel from the peninsula of Florida, up through Georgia and the Carolinas, across Tennessee, Alabama, and Mississippi, into Arkansas, Texas, and Louisiana, and then back to Mexico City. They would penetrate the very heart of a southeastern civilization composed of the people of several language families that archaeologists term the "Mississippians" (Chapter 10). And in Soto's army's wake, European smallpox and measles would run rampant, spreading in densely populated towns and provinces and killing thousands in each locality. Eventually, the population of the Eastern Woodlands of North America, likely several million, was reduced to tens of thousands.

Hernando de Soto would not have known, and might not have cared, about the future costs of his expedition. Moving up through the towns and villages of the Timucuan agriculturalists, the first great Mississippian province that the expedition encountered was that of the Apalachee, in the Florida panhandle. The expedition spent its first winter at the Apalachee capital of Anhaica, a town later used by

Spanish missionaries to bring European religion to the continent. Later, Hernando de Soto would encounter in Georgia and South Carolina the great polities called Coosa and Cofitachequi, among others, each with hereditary leaders or rulers who governed thousands of people, including the territories of subordinated vassals. Sensing the threat embodied by the intruders, each of the leaders attempted to move the expedition along and out of their political territory. The female ruler of Cofitachequi famously promised more riches in her neighbor's domain, a ploy that worked to get the Europeans out of her lands. In each of the capital towns, each built two or three days' walk distant from the last, the Spanish noted that religious temples and elite housing were built atop rectangular earthen platforms or pyramids. Most towns were fortified, and the Indians treated the Spaniards much like they treated other visiting native dignitaries or powerful enemies.

In southern Alabama, Soto was assaulted by the warriors of the Mabila province, ruled by an Indian king named Tuscaloosa, who lived in a large fortified Mississippian capital town (Figure 3.7). The Spanish countered in a day-long battle that saw 200 Spaniards, some 50 horses, and at least 2,000 Indian warriors killed (Clayton et al. 1993). The Spaniards burned the capital town of Mabila (after

Fig 3.7 Hernando de Soto and his men burn Mabila, after a surprise attack by Chief Tuscaloosa and his people, 1540 CE. Illustration by Herb Roe. Wikimedia.

which Mobile, Alabama is named) and should have gone to the coast to be resupplied by ships from Cuba. But Hernando de Soto didn't go there, perhaps aware that the loss of a third of his army would have been a disgrace worthy of recall. Instead, he went north and wintered in Mississippi. There, another group, possibly ancestors of the Chickasaw, attacked the expedition after Soto had made demands of them. The Spanish army suffered another 40 dead. In the spring of 1541, the expedition and all of its animals crossed the Mississippi River in boats that they built. Once across, they encountered more centralized Mississippian provinces, sometimes called "chiefdoms" by archaeologists (see Chapter 10).

The people of one province, Casqui, famously used Hernando de Soto's advancing force to help themselves militarily. The Spaniards, greeted happily by the Casqui, baptized some of the natives and even raised a great wooden cross atop the earthen pyramid of the capital town, now called the Parkin site (Morse and Morse 1983:309). The cross, the base of which has since been rediscovered, was just less than a meter in diameter and so tall that it reportedly took a hundred men to lift it into place (www.archaeologicalconservancy.org/arkansas-archaeologists-find-remains-de-sotos-cross). The Spaniards assumed that they had converted the Casqui to Catholicism.

Parkin was a compact, heavily fortified town and the endemic warring of the region had been so severe for so long that few locals lived outside the walls for fear of attack. Today, the archaeological site appears similar to a Mesopotamian tell, with the debris of everyday life accumulating as organic sediments a meter high within the palisade walls. Under such conditions, the victorious citizens of Casqui might have happily raised a supposed Christian cross, especially since they probably understood it in their own terms: both upright wooden posts (often emplaced atop pyramids) and crosses happened to be cosmic symbols in the Mississippian world. Perhaps the Casquians thought that they had converted the Spaniards.

In any case, Hernando de Soto and his army proceeded to the next province of Pacaha, the traditional enemy of the Casqui. The Pacahans fled in advance, and the Casqui raided and looted the empty town, their primary goal being to defile their adversary's ancestral temple. They took the sacred bones from the Pacahan temple, threw them on the ground, and trampled on them. Hernando de Soto later negotiated a truce between the two sides and moved on.

Afterwards, the expedition traveled into present-day western Arkansas or eastern Oklahoma, where Soto skirmished with the Tula, likely a Mississippianized group of Caddo Indians. And by this time, having lost upwards of half of its men and most of its horses, the fatigued force made its way back to the Mississippi River, where Hernando de Soto died of fever. Initially choosing to return to Mexico overland through Texas, the expedition was unable to sustain itself in the dry, sparsely populated area. It returned to the Mississippi River, and built brigantines by melting down iron for nails and cutting trees for lumber. After the winter and spring floods, the Spaniards launched the boats into the river and paddled down the Mississippi in 1543. Along the way, they passed through a series of Mississippian provinces; the warriors of each group harassed the bedraggled Spanish force, packing great dugout canoes full of archers and boatsmen who attempted to pick off the Spaniards one by one. Nearly a dozen Spaniards were impaled by arrows and bled out or fell into the murky Mississippi. After almost two months, the men who remained had passed into the Gulf of Mexico and, sailing southward along the coast, reached a Spanish colonial town and were taken back to Mexico City.

Perhaps the Hernando de Soto expedition might not have turned out so poorly had they been able to connect up with the Coronado expedition, which was passing through Kansas when the Soto force was only a few hundred miles to the southeast in western Arkansas. Francisco Vázquez de Coronado y Luján had organized an expedition into northwest Mexico and the American Southwest a year after Hernando de Soto had departed, Coronado's intent being to find the seven golden "cities of Cíbola," reported by a Spanish friar the year before (Bolton 1990). Eager to find these cities, Coronado and his 300 or so mostly mounted Spaniards, nearly a thousand Mesoamerican warriors, a number of African and American Indian slaves, and a herd of cattle traveled north into present-day Arizona and New Mexico until they arrived in the land of the Zuni. Their pueblos were the so-called cities of gold, but there was little wealth of the sort Coronado had imagined. Thus, he broke the expedition into a series of smaller expeditions, one of which entered the country of the Hopi – reportedly at war with the Zuni – and reached the Grand Canyon, while another traveled to the east and encountered the Rio Grande pueblos. Both at Zuni and in the Rio Grande country, Coronado's men forced their way into the towns, killing hundreds of Puebloans. Not finding what he had expected, Coronado moved north to find and conquer another fabled civilization called Quivira, described by a captured Pawnee man from the Plains, likely an itinerant trader, nicknamed "El Turco" or, in English, "The Turk" (Bolton 1990).

Traveling through present-day Texas, the expedition was amazed by great herds of bison on the southern Plains along with the nomadic bison-hunting Apache. Coronado then encountered the likely ancestors of the sedentary, agricultural Wichita in southern Kansas, people who spoke a Caddo-family language similar to The Turk. From interactions and translated discussions with the Wichita, Coronado came to believe that The Turk had been misdirecting them in their quest for Quivira. After torturing and enchaining the Pawnee guide, Coronado took a small mounted reconnaissance contingent north into central Kansas. There he seems to have encountered the ancestral Pawnee but, not having found a civilization, executed The Turk and began his return to Mexico in the spring of 1542 (Figure 3.8). Had he remained on his eastern course and passed to the southeast through Oklahoma, Coronado might have met the Mississippianized Caddo near the ancient site of Spiro, 300 miles (500 km) away on the Arkansas River, and eventually crossed paths with Hernando de Soto. Moreover, had he continued 350–400 miles (550–650 km) downriver from and to the east of his Kansas location, he would have reached the long-abandoned Mississippian city of Cahokia, a midcontinental civilization easily the size and grandeur of the legendary Quivira (see Wedel 1994). Of course, it had been abandoned for 200 years (see Chapter 10).

On his return trip, Coronado followed a segment of the long-established Indian trail between the East and Southwest, later known as the Santa Fe Trail (later Route 66, and today Interstate 40), perhaps engraving his name at Autograph Rock, in the Oklahoma panhandle. He convalesced in New Mexico after an injury, but departed in April 1542, leaving two friars behind to proselytize the Pueblos.

In the meantime, Juan Rodríguez Cabrillo and his three ships were sailing northward up the West Coast from Mexico. Cabrillo had been in the army of Hernán Cortés in 1519 that helped to conquer the Aztecs. Afterwards, he had garnered fame and fortune as a conquistador in the years leading up to his California expedition. Then, through a series of unlikely events, Cabrillo had assumed the task of exploring the land that would come to be called California in 1542. He was also

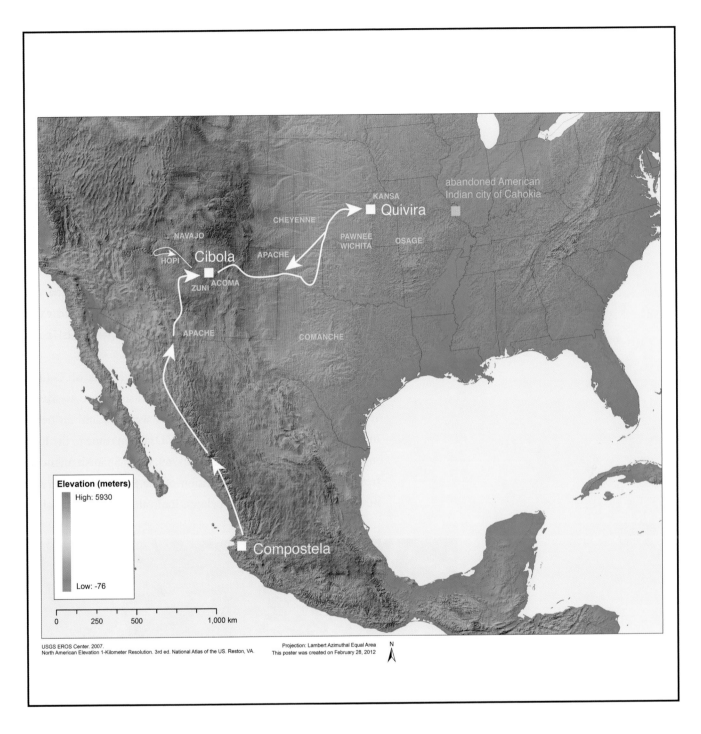

Fig 3.8 The Coronado expedition, 1540–1542.

hoping to locate the fabled cities of Cíbola (Wagner 1941). He may
even have been expecting to encounter Coronado somewhere along
the coast, though unbeknownst to Cabrillo, Coronado was already on
his way back from the Southwest. Finally, Cabrillo may also have been

attempting to find the mouth of the Rio Grande (incorrectly believed by him to flow north).

Sailing northward to and beyond the Channel Islands, Cabrillo and his men witnessed the complex maritime lifestyle of the Chumash and other Hokan- and Penutian-speaking coastal populations who lived in villages or small "towns" atop shell mounds in pole-and-thatch houses (Figure 3.9). These native ocean-going hunter-fishers traveled between islands and coasts in impressive plank canoes and, accordingly, were doubtless intrigued by the arrival of Cabrillo's large plank ships. They were inquisitive and, by and large, peaceful and friendly. That said, Cabrillo and his men kidnapped several Indians, adults and adolescents, and skirmished with some locals. During one such skirmish, Cabrillo fell on rocks and broke an arm. The wound became gangrenous and the infamous conquistador and explorer of coastal California died before leaving the Channel Islands (see Chapter 13).

Subsequent expeditions into the coastal regions of California, Oregon, Washington, British Columbia, and southeast Alaska in the seventeenth and early eighteenth century were few and far between, one such stop being made by Sir Francis Drake en route to the Far East in 1579. This periodicity changed in 1769, when Spanish missionaries from Mexico initiated the extension of the Spanish mission system north to San Francisco (see below). Radical social change followed.

Fig 3.9 Reconstructed Chumash Indian houses at the Chumash Indian Museum, Thousand Oaks, California. Timothy R. Pauketat photo, 2016.

Similar sustained native–European contacts did not begin along the Northwest Coast until 1788, with the arrival of James Cook's trading expedition to British Columbia. Shortly thereafter, Meriwether Lewis and William Clark arrived to spend the winter of 1805–1806 on the Oregon coast.

Long before this time, the Spanish had effectively colonized the greater Southwest, thanks to a group of colonizers from Mexico City in 1598 in search of gold and souls, led by Don Juan de Oñate. A few years after that date, in 1601, Oñate, like Coronado, had also led an expedition to find Quivira. He and more than one hundred men-at-arms, a similar number of indigenous warriors and porters, a dozen priests, and more than three hundred horses and mules traveled back into Oklahoma and Kansas. There he encountered warring groups of Plains Village societies, unwittingly becoming part of a battle of hundreds of combatants. Not that this failed expedition deterred him from others even as the conquistador era was drawing to a close. Oñate, who would inscribe his name at El Morro National Monument en route to the Gulf of Mexico a few years later, was the last of a dying breed (www.nps.gov/elmo/index.htm).

Return of the Vikings: 1496–1607 CE

Northern European people, particularly the French and English, heirs to the seafaring ways of the Vikings (some genetically linked to them), returned to northeastern North America at the end of the fifteenth century (Figure 3.5). The first was an Italian, Giovanni Caboto – a.k.a. John Cabot (Hunter 2011). The king of England, Henry VII, commissioned Cabot to locate this New World of Columbus', about which word had spread rapidly in Europe. Cabot reached it in 1497 – technically rediscovering the North American mainland at Newfoundland – and, unlike the Spanish, with little native contact. But he did report locating the great cod fisheries off the coast of Newfoundland, a detail that immediately attracted fishermen from the coastal areas of western Europe. Subsequently in 1508, John Cabot's son, Sebastian, sailed in the direction of Hudson Bay, seeking a northwest passage around North America to the Orient. Years later, in the 1570s, Sir Martin Frobisher attempted to find an Arctic passage and encountered the Thule Eskimo, now called the Inuit, and brought the first of several captives back to England. Eventually abandoning that route, the Englishman Sir Francis Drake – deemed a pirate by the Spanish Crown – sailed around the Americas and landed on the coast of California in 1579, claiming it for Queen Elizabeth I. On this trip, he followed Ferdinand Magellan's 1520 discovery of the Strait of Magellan.

More significant in terms of native contact were the voyages in 1534 and 1535 of the French explorer Jacques Cartier, who was also seeking the northwest passage (Stephens 1890). Cartier located the Gulf of St. Lawrence and the mouth of the St. Lawrence River in what later came to be called Canada after a local word for "village." Like Hernando de Soto, he also planted a cross in the new territory, though Cartier claimed it for France. In 1535, he and his three ships sailed upriver, slaughtering many (now-extinct) great auks and trading with local Mi'kmaq (a.k.a. Micmac) peoples, Algonkian-speaking forager-farmers who lived in small-scale settlements. The company anchored at a village, now present-day Quebec City, and took their small ship upriver to a large town of St. Lawrence Iroquoian forager-farmers, under present-day Montreal. Upon reaching the town, Hochelaga, they were greeted by a thousand men, women, and children. Cartier and his men describe a dense settlement of 50 longhouses – each some 38 m long – surrounded by a 12 m (40 ft) high palisade wall with one entrance. The Iroquois world was one of embattled towns, which Cartier more fully realized in 1541 after he founded the settlement of Charlesbourg-Royal.

The people of Hochelaga would be dispersed after Cartier's visit and before Samuel de Champlain arrived in 1603, one of many mini-diasporas subsequently folded into the village confederacies of Wendat and their enemies to the south: the Mohawks, Onondagas, Oneidas, Senecas, and Cayugas unified as the Haudenosaunee (or Iroquois) Confederacy (see Chapter 12). Each of the latter were made up of some 20,000–30,000 persons before being ravaged by European diseases in the seventeenth century (Birch and Williamson 2013; Williamson 2012). To the northeast and northwest, the Algonkian-speaking Beothuk of Newfoundland fared even worse. The Beothuk, with a population of perhaps 1,000 people, were being actively exterminated during these centuries, the last known pure-blood descendant dying in 1829. On the other hand, the Montagnais-Naskapi (or Innu) – Algonkian-speaking enemies of the Iroquois – prospered through their trade with the French.

Fig 3.10 Powhatan, or Wahunsenacawh, in his chambers. Wikimedia.

French colonies were attempted in the southeastern part of the continent, including a colony of Huguenots (persecuted Protestants from France) near Jacksonville, Florida in 1564. But these lands were contested by Spain and the colony was attacked and burned by the Spaniards, who had founded what is now the oldest continuously occupied town in North America, St. Augustine, in 1565. Later colonies in the St. Lawrence area fared better, with the early 1600s seeing a host of Acadian settlements in Quebec. At the same time, English settlers had founded the first permanent colony in Virginia, at Jamestown.

In 1607, a hundred English colonists built this fortified village on the banks of the Powhatan – now James – River (Kelso 2006). That they did this in the midst of a powerful, hierarchical Indian polity or chiefdom, called Tsenacomacoh, made for legendary encounters between historical characters known to many: the ruler Powhatan (a.k.a. Wahunsenacawh), his elite daughter Pocahontas, the colonial leader Captain John Smith, whose life she saved, and her later tobacco-entrepreneur husband, John Rolfe (Figure 3.10). Sitting in the Chesapeake Bay, the history of the contact between Indians and Europeans here ties directly into the political history of the United States and its capital city in Washington, DC (see Chapter 12).

Powhatan's domain subsumed a series of vassal provinces composed of multiple Algonkian, Siouan, and Iroquoian ethnic groups – quite possibly the organized diversity being the *raison d'être* of Tsenacomacoh. It now appears that this diversity was routinely organized at great feasts hosted by Wahunsenacawh and his district administrators, called *weroances*, at fortified residences. Wahunsenacawh's own home at Werowocomoco was an embanked enclosure set apart from the villages of his dominion, as excavations by archaeologist Martin Gallivan (2012) and colleagues have shown.

It also seems likely that the Jamestown colony was allowed to exist within the Powhatan territory because, initially, it served the interests of Wahunsenacawh. It served the interests of its colonists less well, with most of the 500 initial and replacement colonists, including non-English European settlers and African servants, dying in the first five years. Many perished of disease and others starved, leading some to raid Indian food stores and usurp native farmlands. A war began a couple years after the founding of Jamestown that saw massacres of natives, the burning of cornfields, and, eventually, the capture of Pocahontas, who later married the Englishman Rolfe and moved to England. The successor and brother of Wahunsenacawh attempted to destroy the Jamestown colony in 1622 and again in 1644. Hundreds died, but the attempts failed. Instead, the great Powhatan province was decimated and eventually disappeared.

Missionization and the Colonial Project: From the 1500s on

The history of English colonial relations with indigenous people was, of course, markedly different from that of the French and Spanish, particularly to the extent that the latter "missionized" local native populations. Much of this began at the end of the conquistador phase of European colonization of North America, with its direct and devastating impacts. Spanish weaponry, for instance, had brought about the deaths of thousands of people. European-borne diseases had killed or would soon kill millions through the sixteenth and seventeenth centuries, an early if largely unintentional form of biological warfare. And this biological conflict and demographic calamity was intensified during the mission period, accompanied in some cases by great tears in the cultural fabric of native tribes and nations and, in others, by the accommodation and subordination of native cultural practices within a new, Euro-centric, Christianizing cultural hegemony.

The materiality – which is to say the material dimension – of the native–colonizer relations forged at specific sites across the continent is unmistakable and essential to appreciating what and how changes were occurring. For starters, wherever European missionaries went to spread the tenets of their religion in the sixteenth through nineteenth centuries, they brought along their European-ness. By this we mean the manufactured products of civilization as opposed to – a missionary might have noted – the trappings of the primitive. Not that this was bad for Native Americans, many of whom used access to such goods to bolster their traditional positions of authority. For instance,

Europeans living in 16th- and 17th-century Spanish Florida were drawn into the local dynamics of indigenous chiefdoms, bolstering and reinforcing the political power of traditional Indian leaders. Hereditary chiefs retained considerable internal autonomy over secular matters and ruled using traditional lines of authority ... In the process, the paramount chiefs of Spanish Florida not only created a new market for their agricultural surplus but also gained access to new tools and technologies to improve their yield. The caciques converted their surpluses into Spanish goods (cloth, tools, beads, and the like) and received tribute from both the Spanish and their own people.

(Thomas 2012:44–45)

Of course, as mission life dragged on, such economic relations were undercut, sometimes intentionally by the Crown and the church. Christianity was not just a set of abstract beliefs about the death and resurrection of a god-made-human, it was a lived reality complete with ceremonial garb, sacred texts, silver and bejeweled drinking containers, carved icons, candles, church bells, individualized relationships with deities, and distinct manners and taboos attached to the most fundamental aspects of humanity: eating, drinking, growing crops, speaking, or having sex. For many indigenous peoples, the world was a more fluid and less-hierarchical arena of human and nonhuman agents and spirits, where dreams were extensions of one's spirit and shamans might intercede between the unseen powers of the cosmos. This did not square with the church. What one did when and how needed to be strictly regulated, or so the priests, monks, and friars believed, especially in churches and around mission settlements. This meant regulating the bodies of laborers, which in turn denied native lords their own controls over the populace.

Such idealized bodily controls are no more evident than in a series of famous *casta* paintings that projected racial categories on to members of society who would have otherwise experienced more open and transracial realities, where Indians, mestizos, Europeans, and Africans mixed relatively freely (Figure 3.11). At the Los Adaes settlement in Louisiana, along the frontier with Spanish Texas, more than half of the inhabitants in the early 1700s were of mixed blood. Such familial conditions worried European religious authorities who called for discipline (Loren 2000). For instance, the early seventeenth-century

Fig 3.11 Casta painting showing family of diverse background, ca. 1763. Wikimedia.

French Jesuit missionaries in Quebec approached their loose-living Wyandot (i.e., Huron) and Montagnais subjects with rigid hierarchical practices, imposing a strict moral code in part through the formal spatial configurations of mission buildings and an insistence on native conversion to sedentary, literate lifestyles.

Although pale versions of great Gothic cathedrals in France, mission churches were formal and symmetrical constructions that were designed to impart European cosmic order and hierarchical social order via the experiential aspects of interior spaces and exterior form (think, steeple). The Spanish mission buildings in the borderlands from Florida west to Santa Fe and on into California were elaborate and imposing (Figure 3.12). They were built to impress upon the supplicant's mind his or her relationship to heaven and earth, often oriented cardinally or to a seasonal sunrise, with sunlight shining through a clearstory window, striking the altar at the appropriate season. Horizontally, their layout was configured as a virtual cruciform, with the movement of people necessarily being up through the nave along the vertical axis of a cross toward the top, or altar, and then expanding near the front of the nave to form the horizontal cross-member. In the Southwest, adobe mission churches and conventos, the homes of friars and monks, were formally sited with respect to the seasons, a practice understood by the astronomically sophisticated Puebloan natives, who were of course also the labor force who built the monumental religious buildings.

The indigenous people of the borderlands were largely sedentary if not hierarchically organized, from the Mississippians of the Southeast to the Pueblos of the Southwest and the Chumash of southern California. They were valued largely for their organized tribute-paying potential and labor power. Tribute demands were made through the established native hierarchy, while labor was extracted and converted into wealth by the Crown via *encomiendas*, labor grants made to various soldiers and officials (tantamount to slave labor). Labor value was further realized through a strategy the Spanish called "reduction" – the

Fig 3.12 Gran Quivira mission church (background) and pueblo (foreground), New Mexico. Timothy R. Pauketat photo, 2009.

Sidebar 3.2 The formal symmetry of mission churches

In Google Earth, search for "Quarai Ruins, NM" or "Pecos National Historical Park, NM" to see the sixteenth-century ruins of cruciform Puebloan mission churches. Type in "Mission San Xavier del Bac, AZ" to see the extant Tohono O'odham mission church. Compare these with Saint Peter's Basilica in the middle of "Vatican City" in Rome.

relocation and concentration of Indians to specific locations – most notably to missions.

Of course, because of their added power to convert natives and array them under a Euro-centric economy, mission buildings and missionaries – and indeed the entire mission complex – were subject to attack by both indigenous and European adversaries. Certainly the Jesuit missions of the Northeast were caught up in the rapidly changing geopolitics of the day involving the French, English, Dutch, Iroquois, and Algonkians violently playing one off the other (Figure 3.13). Of the various seventeenth-century missions in the St. Lawrence region, most ultimately failed or were destroyed, with that at Port Royal, Nova Scotia, for example, attacked and burned by the English colonists of Virginia in 1613. A later mission to the Wyandot, at Sainte-Marie,

Fig 3.13 Map of New France, 1657, by Francesco Buiseppe Bressani. Toronto Public Library (www.torontopubliclibrary.ca/detail.jsp?R=DC-BR-912-17-B67).

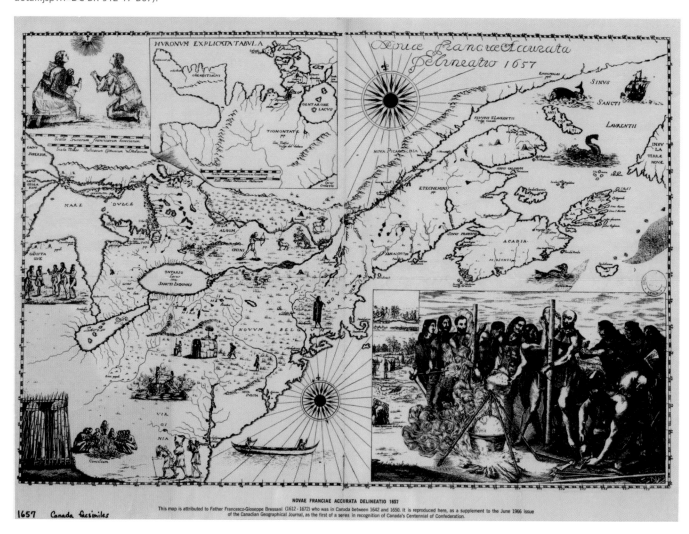

Sidebar 3.3 Long-distance raids and captive-taking

Captive-taking was a traditional practice of many indigenous North Americans, with captive women and children often being adopted into their new communities. Many eastern tribes took white captives, treating them as they would native counterparts. Iroquoian groups, among others, might sacrifice some male captives. As the European-supported fur trade expanded in the seventeenth century, the long arm of the Iroquois reached well into the Midwest. During the so-called Beaver Wars in the 1640s and '50s, the Dutch- and English-backed Iroquois raided the French-backed Algonkian groups from Hudson Bay to the Illinois Country. People fleeing the deadly Iroquois, including the people who called themselves the Illini, abandoned the state of Michigan. By 1680, the Iroquois even raided the Illini living near Starved Rock on the Illinois River, more than 500 miles (800 km) from New York State. Recorded by the Frenchman on the scene, Henri de Tonti, the 500 or more Iroquois, with guns, pursued the 1,000-plus fleeing Illini to the river's confluence with the Mississippi. There the aggressors captured some 700 women and children, killing and burning half at the stake and marching the rest on foot – tethered together with leather halters – back to the Iroquois homeland.

was burned by the Iroquois, who were, in the mid-seventeenth century, being armed by the Dutch. Its priests were "martyred" – killed by native warriors and then canonized as saints by the Catholic church. Today, Sainte-Marie-among-the-Huron is a National Historic Site of Canada.

In California, mission construction began later than elsewhere. The Spanish and later Mexican governments funded 21 Franciscan, Dominican, and Jesuit missions between 1769 and 1834, in part to counter the movement of Russians colonizing southward – their most important settlement being the multi-ethnic Russian-American outpost of Fort Ross (Lightfoot et al. 1998). The results of the California missionizing process were extreme. The conversions of both Indian beliefs and the native landscape – with indigenous populations plummeting through disease and outright manslaughter, and with cattle denuding the natural vegetation – were simultaneous and dramatic (Silliman 2005). In the face of such unsettling change, native people were forced into patron–client arrangements within missions and, later, secular versions of the missions called "ranchos" (Silliman 2004). Presidios, or fortified outposts of the Crown, provided the military backing for the entire enterprise. In southern California, the Chumash had been lured into missions or rounded up by the church, which sought to Christianize the natives by scheduling their time and enforcing work requirements (Figure 3.14). The friars saw themselves and the church as the patriarchical head of the new society, with the natives being the simple children who required re-education (a

Fig 3.14 Santa Barbara mission lavanderia basin for washing clothes, fed by an aqueduct system, with a sculpted sandstone mountain lion torso-and-head spout carved by Chumash artisans in 1808. Timothy R. Pauketat photo, 2015.

perspective that yet seeps through in the official literature of active mission churches). Later ranchos in California assumed control over some of the former church lands and labor forces, ostensibly releasing Indians from their serfdom, but most Indians had no choice. The "people released from missions" often "had no families or territories to return to" (Silliman 2012:238).

And yet, against all odds, the ideals of the colonizers had to sometimes bend to the wills of native peoples across the borderlands and missions of North America. Californian Indians proactively reasserted their identities and beliefs by rejecting some European technologies which were, after all, cultural knowhow (Silliman 2004). At Rancho Petaluma, near present-day San Francisco, chipped-stone arrowheads actually surge in frequency later in time, as if native men made a point (literally) of engaging in traditional hunting practices to remain Indian. Likewise, the Chumash of southern California were quite selective in their adoption of metal tools that might otherwise be deemed as more efficient than stone tools. In the Southwest, Puebloan kivas, traditional ceremonial buildings, were sometimes included in the grounds of the church. Likewise, at the Mission San Luis in the capital of the Apalachee – first visited by Pánfilo de Narváez – in Florida's

Fig 3.15 Watercolor of San Luis de Talimali mission in Tallahassee, Florida, ca. 1633. Wikimedia.

panhandle, a native council house "fronted the main mission plaza, symbolizing in architecture the ongoing negotiations between native and Franciscan belief systems" (Thomas 2012:45). Where possible, the indigenous people of the missions asserted their own identities and wills – and some might say subverted the church – through architectural, technological, food-gathering, culinary, and even native-religious practices (Figure 3.15).

Movements in the American Period: 1783–1973 and 1990 CE

In various times and places, resistance to European and Euro-American colonialism by indigenous people took on the cast of a culture war. And such cultural resistance frequently transformed into actual military action. This is especially true of the "American colonial period" beginning in 1783 with the end of the American Revolutionary War and continuing, in some ways, to today. During that time, there were scores of significant social, religious, and political "movements" that sought nothing less than a halt to the expansion of the United States of America. Conceived in the simplest of terms, such movements were aggregations of people from diverse backgrounds who followed and promoted a person – a prophet or a visionary – or an idea that was, almost inextricably, embodied by a person, place, practice, or thing. Such movements were composed of meaningful, emotional experiences, which is the reason why they developed a following in the first place (Wallace 1956).

Prophetic movements, sometimes called revitalizations or nativistic cults, were not new in the American period, and in fact likely have an ancient history in North America. Some have noted that many indigenous North American people possessed "visionary" cultures, engrained practices that saw people seeking dreams or apparitions of spirits, ancestors, and other beings that might guide them in their lives. A routine "rite of passage" for many young men was the "vision quest," a period of isolation in a rock shelter or remote location where the individual sought the apparition of his spirit guide, the being who would guide him through the rest of his life. Such cultures, in turn, are based on "relational ontologies" – subconscious ways or "theories" of being (the ontological part) imparted through experience whereby people come to understand themselves as strands in a web of human and nonhuman relationships (see Chapter 8). Sometimes the relational-ontological perspective is termed "animism," which encompasses those cultural and religious practices that recognize other places, things, substances, or phenomena to have spirits and, at some times and in some places, to be alive.

Of course, neither relational ontologies nor animism are necessary for movements to occur. Social, religious, and political movements are known the world over, and happened as part of the founding moments of world religions as led by Christ, Mohammed, and Buddha, among others. A movement is simply that which *moves* people to achieve some larger historical end. In colonial America, native movements were often the source of organized resistance to colonial powers even where indigenous leaders and governing councils existed. And those organizations changed history.

Thus, the great Iroquoian leader Hiawatha was himself a successful pan-tribal spokesman and a great spiritual leader who is credited with peacefully organizing the Five Nation Iroquois League, or Haudenosaunee, in the 1600s (composed of the Mohawks, Oneidas, Onondagas, Senecas, and Cayugas). This was in turn the basis of a powerful confederacy that governed Iroquois economic and military actions in the 1700s. Likewise, the Lenni Lenape (i.e., Delaware) prophet Neolin had a vision of returning to a pre-British world that began in the 1760s with rejecting western practices, alcohol consumption, and Christianity. Whereas Hiawatha's movement was embodied by the wampum belt, Neolin's followers were given carved prayer sticks that were to be used to commune with the spirit world. His religious movement was the basis of a rebellion fomented by Pontiac against the British from 1763 to 1766 (Dixon 2005).

With the Americans taking over control of what they called the Northwest Territories (now the American Midwest) by 1783, the native people who remained were placed under significant political

Fig 3.16 Tenskwatawa, the Shawnee prophet, by Charles Bird King, ca. 1820. Wikimedia.

and economic pressure. While Great Britain was still in control of Canada to the north, a Shawnee prophet named Tenskwatawa emerged in 1805 to preach abstinence from alcohol, a return to the old ways, and a removal of whites from their lands (Figure 3.16). Having had a vision, similar to Neolin and others, sent from the "Master of Life," the Shawnee prophet's influence grew, with pilgrims making journeys from other parts of the Territories to the religious centers that he founded, first at Greenville, Ohio and later at Prophetstown, Indiana, to hear his words or handle strands of beans that enabled conversion to the prophet's revitalized religion. With the help of his famous brother, Tecumseh, Tenskwatawa's prophetic movement became a political movement to unify the disparate Indian tribes of the Midwest and South into an Indian nation. Only with the destruction of Prophetstown by future-president William Henry Harrison and the death of Tecumseh at American hands during the War of 1812 did this pan-tribal national movement fade (Sugden 1997). Shawnee people today yet revere the prophet, however, as one who fought for indigeneity itself and who ensured the continuity of Shawnee traditions (Jones 2004). A similar historical legacy accompanied other movements, most powerfully in the form of the Ghost Dance, a pan-tribal movement led by a Piute prophet named Wovoka, who envisioned a Messiah who would rid the world of white settlers and restore native peoples to their lands and bison herds to the Plains. As discussed in Chapter 2, the site was selected in 1973 by the American Indian Movement for a protest against US treaty violations, led by activists Dennis Banks and Russell Means, raising non-Indian awareness of native rights and the plight of reservation life in the twentieth century. That awareness, and the increasingly powerful voices of indigenous leaders in the late twentieth century, led to the success of another movement – NAGPRA – although not technically a prophetic or religious one.

Convergences: The Past and Future in People, Places, and Things

To be sure, movements are not abstract notions, but are made up of actual people, places, and things in motion. Hiawatha had his wampum belts, Neolin his prayer sticks, Tenskwatawa his strands of beans, Wovoka his Ghost Dance shirts, and even NAGPRA had its "touchstones" – the bones and artifacts of the past itself. Great gatherings of people and big ideas gave all momentum. Ceremonial grounds and capital towns were the sites where people handled the ritual objects or wore the ceremonial garb and moved in concert with the supernatural powers at large. These objects and grounds were the media of encounters, resistant or collaborative, with other people and powers.

Of course, there were hundreds of prophets and as many movements in the colonial era alone, some profound and large scale, like Wovoka's Ghost Dance or NAGPRA, and others hardly noticeable, virtual lone voices crying in the wilderness. The Europeans and Euro-Americans dismissed their followers as delusional, led by fanatics and hucksters, as if they were somehow unlike their own western religions. But if we boil them (and their western counterparts) down to their raw essences, what are they? They are people attempting to rebalance their unbalanced worlds. For many Native Americans, this was an everyday affair. They lived in worlds where the course of events seems caused in part by powers outside their control, where the spirits of the dead may yet reside in places on earth, where animal, plant, and human life is coupled together, or where one might commune with the gods through special substances, with special objects, in special places. Things, substances, and places might have powers and – coordinated or personified by a human being – so too might people.

Take the example of the Plains Indian peace pipe (or "calumet"). The pipe did more than symbolize a belief – it was belief in action. The pipe bowl was a feminine form, made from stone or fired clay from the earth. It was kept separate from the pipe stem, a masculine part, in a sacred pipe bundle and, usually, on an altar in a sacred building. Smoking the pipe involved first putting the two pieces together, which is to say recreating the fundamental relationships of the universe. Then, the burning tobacco opened a portal between worlds – the cosmic dimension of the deities and the earthbound world of people, the substance itself being burned and fundamentally transformed from

Fig 3.17 Lakota priest Slow Bull holding the calumet pipe in prayer. Edward S. Curtis, Library of Congress, Washington, DC. Wikimedia.

living, organic substance to ash and smoke, the latter inhaled by the living human being and exhaled into the sky. The act was powerful. It was an act of contact (Figure 3.17).

This is why European things and technologies had such a huge historical impact in native circles. They were a testament to the powers coordinated or understood in moments by individuals, some on behalf of his or her people. The power and fundamentally religious qualities of such things were both understood and misunderstood by colonial administrations, from the pre-American Europeans to George Washington. Washington, for instance, sought to strategically manipulate indigenous groups and obtain treaty concessions by, among other things, handing out "peace medals" to traditional leaders. Meriwether Lewis and William Clark did the same, as instructed by President Thomas Jefferson, all along their trek up the Missouri, across the Rockies and Plateau, and down the Columbia River to the Pacific Ocean. To the native leaders, the medal served as a physical instantiation of their power. The practice of producing and consuming peace medals continued throughout the eighteenth and nineteenth centuries until the end of Benjamin Harrison's term in 1893 (note, his grandfather, William Henry Harrison, had sacked and burned Prophetstown). The image on the back of Harrison's medal captures the irony of the relations between white America and native America, with the white settler centrally positioned alongside an Indian chief and above a crossed peace pipe and tomahawk (Figure 3.18). The production, gifting, and display of the medals were power-laden material acts of contact that, in turn, idealized a colonial relationship.

Peace medals had historical effects, although not always the ones desired by one side of the cultural exchange or the other. And those effects – colonial and otherwise – linger. Any object owes its magic or

Fig 3.18 Replica of the Benjamin Harrison peace medal. Timothy R. Pauketat collection and photo, 2018.

ability to "enchant" people to its entanglement in the complicated histories of people and their cultural worlds in contact moving alongside others through landscapes rich with histories shared, contested, or misunderstood (Gell 1992). Such contacts – the fundamentals of how people, places, and things relate to one another – are not restricted to first meetings or even to a four-century period. AIM and NAGPRA, among other things, should clearly demonstrate that contact and colonialism are here with us now, still. The happenings of the first encounters certainly help us better understand the processes of history and the particulars of who we are and where we find ourselves today.

The lessons we should remember?

First, as first noted with the Villasur expedition, the fields of human experience in native North America were wide open. Distances were not viewed as insurmountable barriers to movements. Long-distance journeys were more than possible, they were commonplace. Group migrations were the response to political and military threats. Prophets attracted distant pilgrims and the word of powerful religious ceremonies spread far and wide. As archaeologist Steve Lekson

Sidebar 3.4 In the news, 2008

SPALDING, Idaho (AP) – From the rolling Clearwater Valley to New York City's concrete canyonlands, a silver medal that may have been given to a Nez Perce Indian chief by Lewis and Clark in 1806 has made an improbable journey. Its provenance isn't ironclad, but some historians believe this Jefferson Peace Medal minted in Philadelphia went up the Missouri River in a pirogue, was buried in an Indian grave, later plundered by Northern Pacific Railroad workers, and eventually landed with Edward Dean Adams, the New York financier and J. P. Morgan contemporary. Long considered stolen, it surfaced around 2002 in the American Museum of Natural History's South American collection. Allen Pinkham, a distant nephew of Cut Nose, the chief believed to have received the medal, is now pushing for its return to Idaho. Pinkham sees it as a step in correcting two centuries of injustices since the "extremely

hungry and much fatigued" adventurers – Lewis's and Clark's own words and spelling – tromped into his great-great-great-great uncle's village and changed the tribe's world forever. "When we quit stealing from one another, then we become one people," he told The Associated Press. "This is also part of that recovery." Historians say the medal with President Thomas Jefferson's image on one side and hands clasped in friendship on the other … bore witness to Manifest Destiny in action: the opening of the frontier, the laying of the rails, Edward Adams' Wall Street – in short, America's rise to power, and Indians' fall from it. "It's this portal to all these stories," said Mike Venso, a former Idaho journalist now living in St. Louis who helped trace the medal to museum storage at New York City. "That's the magic of this object."

(www.lewisandclarktrail.com/legacy/peacemedals.htm)

(1999) has noted with regard to long-distance communication in pre-Columbian America: "Everybody knew everything all of the time."

Second, there were no passive victims. Pueblo communities carried out a successful rebellion. Indigenous allies of Hernán Cortés are largely responsible for the military success against the Aztecs. The Pawnee-Oto who attacked Villasur and the aggressive members of the Haudenosaunee were proactive partners in an increasingly global trade network. The ancestral Chickasaw drove out Hernando de Soto. The Turk may have stalled or even fooled Coronado. And a concerted organization of Native Americans, whether via the remains of their ancestors or a claim to a Jeffersonian peace medal, can rebalance or "de-colonize" relationships. These are movements in the present about the past. They happen through continued encounters and contacts, many generations removed from the initial ones between Puebloans, Mesoamericans, Mississippians, Californians, Iroquoians, Algonkians, etc. and those who came from Europe, Asia, and Africa.

Each encounter mattered over the long term, violent or peaceful. The calamitous depopulations associated with the "conquests" of Hernán Cortés, Hernando de Soto, and Francisco Vázquez de Coronado and the missionizing of native groups forced radical realignments of native society and led, if indirectly, to rebellions, confederacies, and new identities. The convergence of events and people in the Powhatan region shaped the political culture of the early United States. The enslavements and appropriations of native labor and material goods enabled globalizing developments and capital accumulations to an extent difficult to measure today, but that have defined world history in recent centuries.

So too did the media and narratives – the physical and experiential legacies – of such encounters matter, and continue to matter: hide paintings, crosses raised in new lands, mission churches, a paraded wooden carving, bells calling laborers to work, peace medals, fake Viking runestones. All are cultural. Some are colonial. None is exceptional in kind, as these comprise the processes of human history, even if the specific North American histories that they define were entirely unique.

4 Ancient Immigrants

As told to anthropologist John Swanton by Creek Indian Jackson Lewis in 1910, *A'tcik hǎ'ta* was the original name of the Hitchiti people of Georgia, and *hitchiti* was the Muskogee (Creek) word meaning "to see." These ancestors came to be known as those who went *to see* the place where the sun appeared each morning. As Lewis remembered it:

They (A'tcik hǎ'ta) came from a place where the sea was narrow and frozen over. Crossing across the ice they traveled from place to place toward the east until they reached the Atlantic Ocean. They traveled to see from where the sun came.

(Swanton 1922:72)

Aside from its stated motive for migrating, this account of Hitchiti origins bears resemblance to one of the origins "stories" archaeologists like to tell. Since about the middle part of the last century, archaeologists have generally agreed that humans entered North America via a land bridge that connected Siberia with Alaska during the late Pleistocene (Ice Age), when sea levels were down (Figure 4.1). Opinions differ on what happened next, but the leading idea is that people migrated southward and then eastward, quickly, after reaching unglaciated terrain. Until recently, archaeologists have agreed that the land on to which this wave of migration spread was previously unoccupied by humans, an open "wilderness" of enormous proportions.

Evidence for the rapid movement of immigrants across the continent is seen in a series of distinctive stone tool types. Most notable among them are lance-shaped stone implements that were flaked on both sides (making them *bifaces*), tapered at one end (making them *points*), and flaked lengthwise from the base on both sides (making them *fluted*). Found in 1932 with the bones of now-extinct Ice Age creatures such as mammoth, camel, and horse at the Blackwater Draw site near Clovis, New Mexico, fluted points would eventually be found at thousands of other locations across the entire continental USA, as well as northern Mexico (Anderson et al. 2010). The definitive fluted

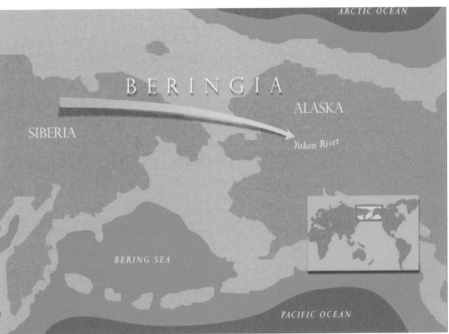

Fig 4.1 When the sea level was down during the last Ice Age, Siberia was connected to the Alaskan peninsula to form what is known as Beringia, or the Bering Land Bridge. Until recently, archaeologists agreed that North America was colonized by people crossing the land bridge. Genetics research confirms that ancestors of native North Americans came to this continent from Asia, but the specific route or routes they took are a matter of great debate. Top: Courtesy of Julia McMahon (artist) and Diana Yates, University of Illinois. Bottom: Getty Image.

point type would come to be known as *Clovis*, and Clovis people (those who made and used these points) came to be known as the first successful colonists of North America. Today's exacting chronology places the Clovis period in the three-century range of 11,200–10,900 BCE (Waters and Stafford 2007). Colonization would appear to have been quick, if only the story were true.

As new discoveries are made and long-accepted ideas like the Short Chronology (see Chapter 2) are abandoned, new narratives are written. As we review below, archaeological knowledge of the Clovis experience in North America is actually quite robust, an outcome of research that has remained lively and productive since it began in the

1930s. However, the plausibility of longstanding assumptions about Clovis has waned in recent years. Many, perhaps most, specialists now agree that bearers of Clovis culture were not the first to colonize North America, only the most successful and most visible, archaeologically speaking. Also questioned is the notion that Clovis people originated in the northwest part of the continent and then quickly made their way south and east, in the fashion of the Hitchiti migration story. If Clovis was not the first, but instead descended from some yet-to-be-identified ancestry of immigrants, then Clovis may have originated in the south, or in the east, and then spread as a people and culture in a westerly direction (Beck and Jones 2010), traveling "to see" where the sun *set* each night, as it were.

If more than one immigrant population made it to the continent from different points of origin and with no recent biological or cultural history linking them, then stories of the "peopling" of North America may not sound all that much different from the narratives of "contact" featured in the last chapter. Indeed, migrating into a land occupied by unknown "others" is a fundamentally different experience than migrating into an unoccupied "wilderness." In the Hitchiti origin story told by Lewis, encounters with others were common. The eventual arrival of Europeans figures prominently, but notable too were encounters with strangers who "emerged from the navel of the earth somewhere out west near the Rocky Mountains." They were said to be warlike, these Muskogee interlopers, so some of the Hitchiti befriended them, eventually becoming one people who "allied somewhere in Florida" (Swanton 1922:73).

As we saw in Chapter 3, the interplay between indigene and immigrant, between those emplaced and those displaced, has historically defined the contours of cultural affiliation, alliance, and animosity. One could quibble over the "accuracy" of the Hitchiti origins story, but its relevance lies less in its details than in its general sense that people of distinct language and culture, and ultimately different origins, converged to beget a new people. Anthropologists refer to this process as *ethnogenesis*, and it explains how cultural diversity and novel forms of expression come not from *isolation*, as in the biological process of speciation, but rather from *interaction*. It may have been just as likely, under different circumstances, that the ancestral Hitchiti and Creek never allied in places like Florida, but instead repelled one another, or created distance between them. Either way, their alternate fates would have been structured by the events of encounter that punctuated their respective histories.

Now, for the conditions of encounter and ethnogenesis to factor into any origins story for native North America, archaeologists have to establish the existence of two or more peoples on the landscape who would have mutually regarded each other as the "other." The *Clovis First* model described briefly above is also, by default, the *Clovis Only* model, for it anticipates no cultural counterparts of distinct ancestry. We will review in this chapter the evidence that makes Clovis unlikely to be the first humans to inhabit North America, nor the only people to occupy the continent at the end of the Ice Age. If and how Clovis people interacted with "others" – biologically, socially, culturally – is of pressing concern to both science and modern society because of its implications for the ancestry of Native American and First Nations people. Indeed, origins stories are as much about defining identity in the present as they are about making sense of the ancient past.

The data we need to address origins and patterns of descent are pretty basic but hardly self-evident. The timing, geographic point of origin, and route of migration of people into North America are among the most basic questions. However, the usual archaeological evidence (e.g., artifacts like stone, bone, and ivory tools) is not always

Sidebar 4.1 On the origins of origins

Humans of western disposition are preoccupied with "origins": the beginning of the universe and earth, the genesis of life, and the onset of humanity. Revolutions weigh on the mind too, with a great deal of thought given to game-changing innovations like fire, pottery, and agriculture. This fascination with origins and revolutions is a part of an imagination that structures the nature of archaeological research, as well as public perception.

The British archaeologist Clive Gamble (2007) has wryly suggested that archaeologists were put on this earth to explain origins. Indeed, it is the search for the oldest (fill in the blank) that motivates much archaeological work. It is certainly what the public has come to expect of archaeology. However, as Gamble shows, origins are often illusionary, an imposed benchmark for change that separates time into

"before" and "after" moments of consequence. Origins objectify imagined events as causes for change, reducing processes that play out over long stretches of time into pivotal moments. It follows that time between points of origins is flattened into timelessness, changelessness.

Origins are also about identity, about asserting claims to beginnings, and with it the exclusive privileges of "first dibs." To be sure, Paleoindian research has a colonial nationalist bent to it: the rugged frontiersmen of the Ice Age, conquering big beasts, overcoming adversity, venturing off into uncharted territory. It is hardly coincidental that this sounds a lot like the colonization of America by Europeans, and in this regard, Paleoindians have been conscripted by Euro-Americans as their own ancestors.

insightful because it is not always well dated, or, if well dated, it is not always conducive to large-scale pattern recognition – that is, seeing the bigger picture. We have to guard against assuming that a given artifact type, such as the fluted Clovis point, represents the existence of a particular group of related and like-minded people, as if the point itself were a person and the similarities of all such "persons" were due to genetic relatedness.

As we will see, genetics actually figures prominently in our current understanding of the timing, origins, and descent of the early immigrants. Data on the genetic makeup of modern native people provide the basis for projecting how long ago and from where native ancestors split off from a parent population. The short answer, which we elaborate later, is that this took place somewhere in northeast Asia at least 24,000 years ago. It is true that aside from Inuit and Athabaskan people – whose ancestors came to North America much later – modern Indians in North America do not express the level of genetic diversity to suggest multiple lines of ancestry tracing to vastly different times and/or different places of origin. Still, combined with occasional data on *ancient DNA* (aDNA) – which reveals genetic diversity no longer present – some modern genetics data cannot be explained by a single founding population that went on to become the ancestral lineage of all living native people.

Another sort of biological variation thickens the plot. Although they comprise but a small sample of ancient immigrants, the skeletal remains of several individuals dating to as much as 11,000 years ago simply do not fit within the range of morphological variation seen in modern populations. Prominent among them are the remains of Kennewick Man, a 9,300-year-old individual with cranial features akin to modern Polynesians but unlike modern Native Americans (Figure 4.2). Discoveries such as this confound a direct line of descent between "original" people and those of the present, suggesting perhaps that only one of multiple immigrant populations survived to beget modern Indians. However, recent DNA analysis of Kennewick Man's bone tissue shows him to be an ancestor of modern native North American people (Rasmussen et al. 2015). Legal disputes among scientists, the US government, and the Umatilla tribe of Washington over the patrimony of Kennewick Man underscore the importance of the matter to both modern native identities and the interests of scientists to study ancient remains (Thomas 2001).

Fig 4.2 Facial reconstruction of what Kennewick Man may have looked like. Model by StudioEIS. Photo by Grant Delin.

Sidebar 4.2 Kennewick Man and cultural diversity

Eroding from the bank of the Columbia River in July 1996 were the skeletal remains of an individual who came to be known as Kennewick Man. The remains were delivered to archaeologist James Chatters, who, upon first glance, assumed they belonged to an early Euro-American settler. Indeed, the facial features of this individual looked nothing like those of ancestral and descendant Native Americans. However, Euro-American attribution was precluded by the considerable age of the bones. A radiocarbon age estimate placed this individual in the ninth millennium before present, clearly someone of indigenous heritage. Chatters also found another indication of great antiquity: embedded in the pelvis of Kennewick Man was a portion of a stone projectile point. Evidently Kennewick Man was the victim of interpersonal violence, or possibly a hunting accident?

The stone projectile in Kennewick Man resembles a Cascade point, while his physical characteristics deviate markedly from those of the descendants of those who made this technology, members of the Old Cordilleran tradition. This is not to say that Kennewick Man was not an ancestor of modern native people, for DNA analysis indicates that he was (Rasmussen et al. 2015). What the archaeological record indicates is that the cultural, if not biological, diversity of early people in the region was considerable and that aside from genetic affinity, people of

distinct cultural traditions were challenged to work out their differences, much like modern societies. In the early history of the Interior Plateau, this may have meant the displacement of indigenous groups by newcomers. Chatters and colleagues (2012), for instance, argue that eastbound people of the Old Cordilleran tradition outcompeted the last people of the Western Stemmed tradition.

Population movements north from the Great Basin and Columbia Plateau had to await the receding of the ice of the late Pleistocene. The history of sustained settlement in the Canadian Plateau picks up about 8,000 years ago, although judging from occasional scatters of stone tools of the Old Cordilleran and older traditions, brief incursions north and east happened much earlier. Sustained settlement began with the long-lived Nesikep tradition. Subdivided into three successive but overlapping phases (Early Nesikep [8,000–6,000 BP], Lochnore [6,500–4,000 BP], and Lehman [6,000–4,500 BP]) on the basis of stone tool types, the Nesikep tradition is characterized by generalized foraging. Small family groups moved frequently to maintain a broad-based diet that included deer, elk, bear, beaver, marmot, muskrat, ducks, fish, mollusks, and a variety of plants (Prentiss and Kuijt 2012:39). Evidence for permanent housing, storage, or social privilege is lacking.

When added up, archaeological, genetic, and skeletal data on the peopling of North America paint a more complicated picture than imagined only two decades ago (Goebel et al. 2008). We do not know with certainty when the first Americans arrived, where they originated, and by what route they traveled. We can be fairly certain that there was more than one immigrant population involved, even if one or more of them did not survive in sufficient numbers to show up in the biological profile of modern people and thus did not interact biologically with those who did. Of course, this would not preclude other types of interaction that inflected the course of history and so the story involves more than biological descent.

We continue our look into origins with what is known best, namely Clovis. We then take a look at archaeological evidence for so-called "pre-Clovis" occupations, which include presumed Clovis ancestors as well as "others." Growing evidence for the existence of people other than those who made and used Clovis points enables alternative hypotheses for the timing and route of multiple migrations into the continent, along with clues for the sorts of interactions that took place among people of various biological and cultural lineages. We conclude the chapter by considering how archaeological data square with data on genetics, skeletal morphology, and even language. Despite the efforts of scientists to reconcile apparently contradictory data (e.g., Auerbach 2010), the only thing that seems certain at this time is that Clovis was not alone.

Clovis

The material record of Clovis experiences in North America is what old-school culture historians called a *horizon style*: something that "occupied a great deal of space but very little time" (Willey and Philips 1958:32). Indeed, fluted Clovis points were deposited across most of the unglaciated portions of North America in the late Pleistocene, and they were made and used over a relatively short period (archaeologically speaking). Other attributes besides fluted points help to define Clovis, but these tend to fail as horizon markers in comparing regional expressions, or trends over time. Fluted points themselves express a great deal of interregional variation in form and technology (Morrow and Morrow 1999), and some researchers are loath to apply the Clovis moniker to anything outside a limited range of forms (e.g., Collins 1999; Haynes 2002). So we start by asking how archaeologists define Clovis and then look at its distribution across space and time.

How Do We Recognize Clovis?

The defining attribute of the Clovis horizon is its namesake fluted point (Figure 4.3). This is a bifacially flaked stone implement thought to have been the tip of the weapon with which people dispatched large game (see below, "Did Clovis People Routinely Kill and Consume Megafauna?"). Fluting refers to the process of striking a flake from

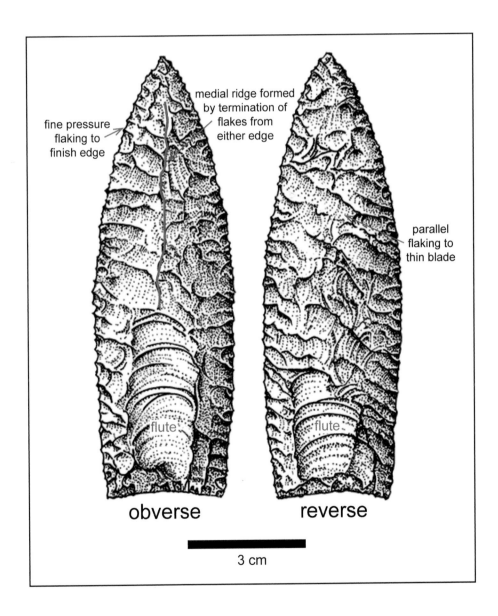

fine pressure flaking to finish edge

medial ridge formed by termination of flakes from either edge

parallel flaking to thin blade

flute

flute

obverse   reverse

3 cm

Fig 4.3 Two views of a Clovis point, showing distinctive features, such as the flutes, that distinguish this Paleoindian technological tradition from others. Kenneth E. Sassaman image.

the base of the blade toward the tip. The resulting scar left after the flake was removed resembles the grooving you see on fluted glass. Typically executed on both faces of Clovis points, about one-third or more along the length, fluting was unique to North America; none of the Old World Paleolithic traditions that involved bifacial tool technology had fluted points. Although the intended function of fluting is uncertain, that it facilitated the attachment of points to foreshafts (for use as projectiles or at least thrusting spears) seems highly plausible. No matter its actual purpose, fluting is so distinctive that it makes for a powerful horizon marker.

On the other hand, fluting was not exclusive to the Clovis horizon in North America. Later, presumably descendant traditions such as Folsom, Cumberland, Redstone, Gainey, and Bull Brook involved the fluting of points, some not much different from those of Clovis. In making sense out of the diversity of late Pleistocene fluted points, archaeologists look to not only the subtleties of form, but also manufacturing techniques. By most definitions, Clovis points have parallel to slightly expanding blade margins, a concave, ground-edged base, and were made using an overshot flaking technique (known in French as *outré passé*) before being fluted. This technique resulted in flake scars that extended across the entire face of the blade, *perpendicular* to its length (while flutes run *parallel*), and it appears to be the oldest thinning technique of the fluted point traditions, making Clovis the original.

Of course, there is more to the Clovis archaeological record than fluted points. Other flaked stone items include bifacial knives and preforms, unifacial scrapers, gravers, and blades, along with cores for producing flakes and blades. Organic media such as bone, antler, and ivory were used to make points, beveled rods (projectiles or foreshafts), awls, anvils, wrenches, and even needles. Organic artifacts are preserved only in unusual circumstances, like the submerged sites of Florida, and thus do not work terribly well as horizon markers. Conversely, stone implements are well preserved under most conditions, but beyond a suite of unifacial tools that are pervasive (and persist well after Clovis), tool classes other than fluted points have more limited distribution. Large blades and blade cores, for instance, are common to the southern Plains and parts of the Southeast, but not elsewhere (Collins 1999). In another example, the "caching" of stone tools (see below) extended from the Northwest into the southern Plains, but not into the Southeast, where Clovis points abound.

Across the entire continent, Clovis points were typically made from microcrystalline, fine-grained rocks such as chert, flint, agate, chalcedony, crystal quartz, and obsidian. The technique of fluting, as well as the pressure flaking executed along the blade margins of Clovis points, demanded high-quality raw material. Because high-quality material is not found everywhere – it is in fact absent in portions of the continent – Clovis tool makers routinely moved stone (as tools, raw material, or both) over hundreds of kilometers. Whether non-local stone arrived at places of deposition by the movement of individuals and groups or by trade between groups (Meltzer 1989a), the geographic range of Clovis activities was indeed vast.

Where was Clovis?

Clovis points are widespread, attesting to rapid and pervasive colonization of those portions of North America that were unglaciated during the final centuries of the Ice Age, basically the continental USA and the adjoining portions of the borderlands of Canada and Mexico. Clovis points are scarce to nonexistent in Alaska and the corridor linking Alaska with the lower USA that was believed to be free of ice and available for southward passage after global temperatures began to rise. The limited number of Clovis points in the very region long believed to be the entry point into North America is a nagging problem, as is the lack of a clear predecessor in Siberia, the presumed point of departure (Goebel 2004). These regions were inhabited by humans long before and through the Clovis era, but definitive ancestry for Clovis evades recognition.

The rapid dissemination of Clovis points across the USA suggests to some archaeologists that people colonized the continent in a "wave of advance," moving west to east, across an unoccupied, pristine landscape (e.g., Kelly and Todd 1988). They would have moved frequently, employing a specialized, portable technology to effectively dispatch and process game, notably megafauna. They would not have spent much time in any given location, instead following migratory game species. The idea that Clovis people contributed to the extinction of megafauna by hunting them aggressively ("The Overkill Hypothesis"; Martin 1973) is supported by this "wave of advance" model.

Recent study of the distribution of Clovis points provides alternative hypotheses. For instance, Clovis points are often clustered in strategic localities on the landscape, such as the confluence of rivers, along physiographic boundaries, and, not surprisingly, permanent sources of freshwater, a scarce resource in much of late Pleistocene North America. David Anderson (1996) sees this as the outcome of a process of colonization that involved "staging areas" for the growth and spread of Clovis populations. In this sense, Clovis people mapped on to favorable locations in the landscape and then persisted in the use of such locations over generations as they expanded out through population growth. Places like the middle Tennessee River valley of northern Alabama – in which numerous Clovis points have been found at sites along the river – was one such staging area.

At the scale of the entire continent, Clovis points are far more numerous east than west of the Mississippi River (Figure 4.4). In fact, the majority of Clovis points in the Paleoindian Database of the Americas (PIDBA) were found in the East. PIDBA is an online interactive database of Paleoindian points maintained by David Anderson at the University of Tennessee (http://pidba.utk.edu). Containing information on thousands of Clovis points and other point types, PIDBA is tied into a geographic information system (GIS) that enables map projections of find spots, as well as spatial analyses (Anderson et al. 2010). Because so many of the points in PIDBA came from the collections of private citizens, who generally collect near places of residence and in locations of land alteration, its spatial projections are biased toward the most heavily populated and disturbed parts of North America (Shott 2005). Moreover, the diversity of fluted point types in the eastern USA exceeds that of the West, making ascriptions to the Clovis type problematic in the East. Nonetheless, the density of fluted points in the East is so high and the diversity so great as to suggest that Clovis originated east of the Mississippi and may have persisted in its descendant fluted-point traditions much later than those of the West.

When was Clovis?

In a review of all radiocarbon age estimates for Clovis points, Michael Waters and Thomas Stafford (2007) concluded that Clovis history spanned a three-century period from 11,200 to 10,900 BCE. Nearly all reliable estimates come from sites in the Southwest and Plains, and most of these in association with the remains of late Pleistocene megafauna (Figure 4.5).

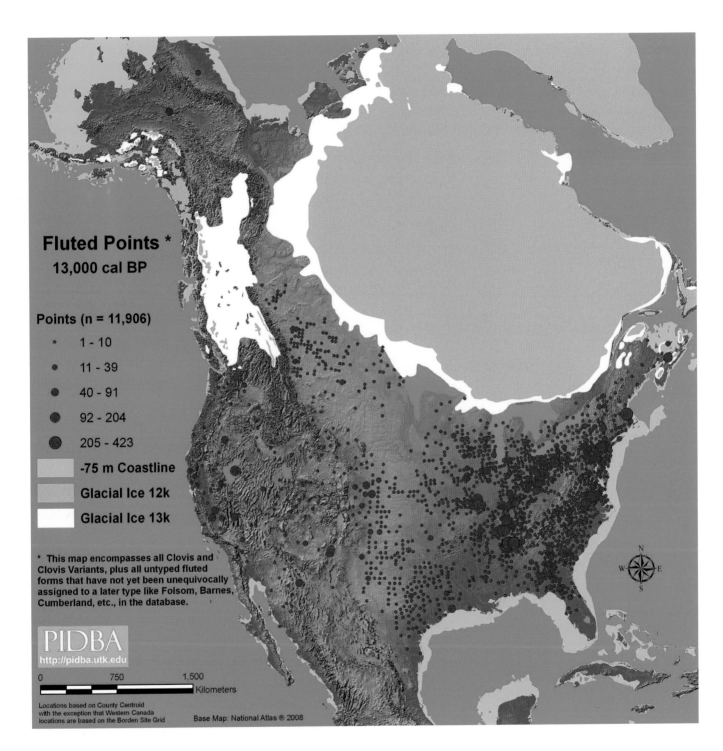

Fluted Points *

13,000 cal BP

Points (n = 11,906)

·   1 - 10

●   11 - 39

●   40 - 91

●   92 - 204

●   205 - 423

     -75 m Coastline

     Glacial Ice 12k

     Glacial Ice 13k

* This map encompasses all Clovis and Clovis Variants, plus all untyped fluted forms that have not yet been unequivocally assigned to a later type like Folsom, Barnes, Cumberland, etc., in the database.

PIDBA
http://pidba.utk.edu

0   750   1,500
                   Kilometers

Locations based on County Centroid
with the exception that Western Canada
locations are based on the Borden Site Grid   Base Map: National Atlas ® 2008

Fig 4.4 The Paleoindian Database of the Americas, maintained by David Anderson and colleagues at the University of Tennessee, enables some first-order assessment of the continental-scale distribution of diagnostic Paleoindian points, such as Clovis. Courtesy of David G. Anderson.

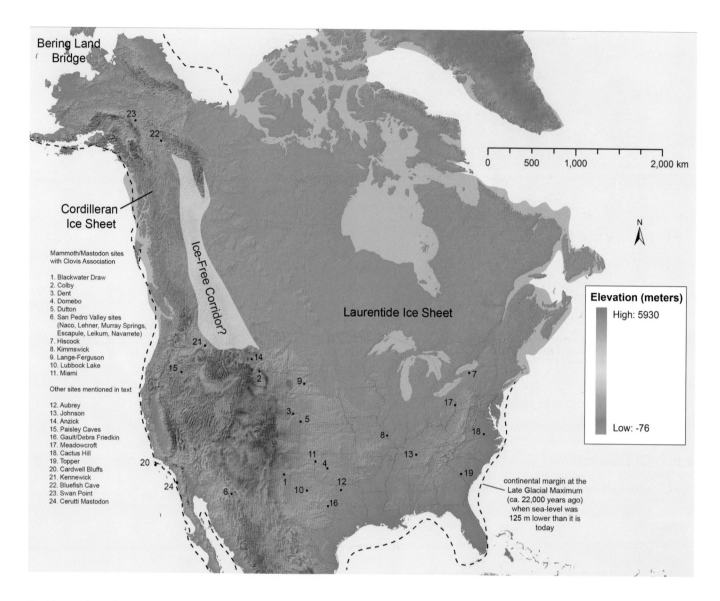

Fig 4.5 Locations of select Clovis and other Paleoindian sites in North America, showing in particular locations of sites with Clovis points in association with the remains of mammoth or mastodon.

Because sites with Clovis points in the East are not well dated, we do not know if they fall within this three-century span. If people making Clovis points arrived in the East from the West, as long presumed, then sites with Clovis points in the East are expected to be the youngest in age, postdating the heyday of southwestern and Plains Clovis. Contributing to this logic is the limited association of eastern Clovis points with the remains of megafauna, most of which went extinct at about 10,900 BCE (see below). Of course, the degree to which Clovis people relied on megafauna is itself a matter of intense debate (Figure 4.6). If we allow that they did not live by megafauna alone, and thus do not assume that most eastern fluted points postdate the extinction of these creatures, Clovis may some day be found

Fig 4.6 "A pre-historic mammoth hunt" as depicted in the 1876 book *A Popular History of the United States* by William Cullen Bryant and Sydney Howard Gay. Wikimedia.

to predate 11,200 BCE in the East. As it now stands, two good candidates are the Aubrey site in Texas, estimated to date to 11,200 BCE, and the Johnson site in Tennessee, possibly dating back to 12,000 BCE. Some archaeologists have good reason to dismiss these earlier dates, but given how few reliable age estimates there are for the region, those predating the accepted time range for Clovis are particularly provocative. As plausible as it may be, a southeastern origin for Clovis is yet to find consensus among archaeologists.

We would expect the oldest Clovis sites to be in the northwestern part of the continent if the tradition and its people had moved into the lower 48 states from Alaska along the so-called Ice Free Corridor. This had been the expectation since Clovis was first discovered in New Mexico in the early 1930s, but evidence to support this scenario has never materialized. The Ice Free Corridor was a seam of unglaciated land between the two major ice sheets covering northern North America in the late Pleistocene: the Laurentide to the east and the Cordilleran to the west. These sheets converged at the continental divide of the northern Rocky Mountains, at times coalescing into one continuous ice sheet, at other times (when warmer) receding to

Sidebar 4.3 Breaking the ice

Imagine yourself as part of a small group crossing on foot a land bridge connecting your homeland in Siberia to an unknown land in Alaska, and beyond. The Bering Sea that separates these lands today would have to fall some 100 meters for this "bridge" to emerge. That is precisely what happened several times during the last Ice Age, when much of the globe's moisture was locked up in glaciers. At the last glacial maximum, some 22,000 years ago, sea levels were 125 m below present levels and the "bridge" connecting Asia with North America about 1,600 km wide. As conditions allowed, plants and animals colonized this emerging, new land, with some crossing over from Asia and others crossing from the opposite direction. Humans are believed to be among those making the eastbound journey for the first time.

If you were part of that very first group you were entering a world never before seen, a truly novel experience. What motivated you and your companions is anyone's guess. You may have been persuaded to follow familiar game in its migrations eastward. Perhaps you experienced diminished returns on traditional living and sought new opportunity. Maybe groups that your people had gotten along with for generations were no longer cooperating and you decided to flee rather than fight. Or you could have been following the Hitchiti way and traveled to see where the sun emerged each day. Whatever it was that drove you and yours to migrate east, the cold reality of the Ice Age set in about mid-way through Alaska, when you encountered a wall of ice extending far into the sky. With no break in the wall, no passageway through it, you may have tried to go around, but that would have been an extraordinarily long detour.

You could instead have waited until it warmed enough for an opening in the ice, an "Ice Free Corridor" connecting unglaciated parts of the Alaskan peninsula with ice-free land at lower latitude (roughly the Canadian–Montana border).

Such a corridor would eventually appear, between the two major ice sheets, on the eastern margin of the northern Rockies. But it would have been a long wait for you and your descendants, many thousands of years, before that was possible. Crossing the glaciers before there was an opening may have been not impossible, but highly unlikely given their 2,500 km expanse.

The few Pleistocene archaeological and paleontological sites known from the corridor region are generally late, postdating 12,000 years ago. Recent geological evidence suggests that there was no passage south of the eastern margin of the Rockies until after about 14,000 years ago, and it opened earliest in the south, suggesting that movement into the region by humans and animals came from the midcontinent, not Alaska or northwest Canada.

Timing is everything. Had an Ice Free Corridor been available for passage southward at 21,000, 18,000, or even 15,000 years ago, the history of North America would have been vastly different. Because clear passage was not likely available until Clovis times, we should not expect that the direct ancestors of Clovis people colonized the unglaciated parts of North America from the north. An alternative route must have been used, most likely the Pacific coast. As we discuss elsewhere in this chapter, the use of boats is implicated in a coastal migration, and that opens up the possibility that humans did not have to wait for a land bridge to form before crossing from Asia into North America. By the same token, the disappearance of the land bridge at the end of the Ice Age did not preclude movement across the Chukchi and Bering seas by boat. A NOAA animation of the gradual flooding of Beringia gives some perspective on the limits to foot travel in such a dynamic landscape of water, ice, and disappearing land (https://commons.wikimedia.org/wiki/File:Beringia_land_bridge-noaagov.gif).

expose land available for plant and animal colonization, as well as human migration. The corridor apparently was not open until just before or even after the beginning of the Clovis era (Mandryx et al. 2001), making it unlikely that Clovis ancestors traveled this route (but see Dawe and Kornfeld [2017] and Potter et al. [2017] for plausible alternatives in the interior).

Clovis Ancestors?

Clovis points are rare in Alaska, as they are in the region of the Ice Free Corridor. If ice sheets prevented people from moving south through Canada until after Clovis appeared in the Plains and American Southwest, then we may want to look elsewhere for the ancestors of Clovis. Obviously, the people who made Clovis points had ancestors, no matter where the tell-tale fluted point tradition originated. Alaska cannot be ruled out entirely just because passage southward by land was blocked by ice; Clovis ancestors may have occupied unglaciated Alaska for generations and then made their way down the Pacific coastline, as opportunities arose.

There have been a few hints of Clovis ancestry at sites in Siberia and Alaska, although none is fully convincing. A 25,000-year-old tool complex documented at Ust-Kova in Siberia, for example, includes (unfluted) bifaces, scrapers, gravers, and other forms with parallels in Clovis (Goebel et al. 1991), but from a highly disturbed context. Moreover, a presumed candidate for Clovis ancestry, the Ushki site in western Siberia, is now known to postdate the beginning of Clovis by a few centuries (Goebel et al. 2003), leaving the region with no clear progenitor.

The Nenana complex of northeast Alaska likewise includes a variety of tools with resemblance to Clovis assemblages from the American Southwest (Goebel et al. 1991), but it is only a century or two older than Clovis and is succeeded at some sites by assemblages of the Denali complex, which bear little affinity to Clovis. At some sites in the region, Nenana assemblages overlie Denali assemblages, and at most sites they are either coeval or postdate the Clovis horizon (Bever 2006).

Lacking strong evidence for Clovis ancestry in Siberia, Alaska, and the greater Northwest, and the growing possibility that Clovis actually arose from ancestors in the southern Plains or Southeast, it stands to reason that some archaeologists would look east, not west, to map the route of immigration. To be sure, Dennis Stanford and Bruce Bradley (2012) have proposed that people of the Solutrean tradition of western Europe made their way via watercraft along the edge of the pack ice of the north Atlantic Ocean, eventually arriving in eastern North America. The heyday of the Solutrean period in France and Spain dates from 21,000 to 17,000 years ago, nearly four millennia before Clovis. Still, Stanford and Bradley find reason to believe Solutrean immigrants were the ultimate ancestors of Clovis people.

The *Solutrean Hypothesis*, as it has come to be known, is based on proposed similarities in technologies, such as overshot flaking on bifaces, unifacial scrapers, and beveled ivory rods. Stanford and Bradley see evidence for transitional forms between Solutrean and Clovis at sites in Pennsylvania, Virginia, and Florida believed to date from 15,000–13,000 BCE.

Few archaeologists accept the Solutrean Hypothesis as plausible (Meltzer 2009; Straus 2000), although it has garnered support outside the profession. The similarities between Solutrean and Clovis technology, many have noted, could very well be independent, parallel developments. Critics have also pointed to discrepancies in chronology, the implausibility of canoe travel in the north Atlantic, and the lack of other Solutrean traits in Clovis culture, particularly the artistic tradition expressed most famously in cave paintings of Europe. Indeed, it is curious that Clovis people did not seem to ever make use of caves (Walthall 1998), let alone paint imagery on cave walls. The more popular embrace of a hypothesis shunned by many professional archaeologists hints at a perverse form of nationalism that attributes native ancestry to a European lineage.

Did Clovis People Routinely Kill and Consume Megafauna?

The archaeological record from around 11,000 rcybp [~13,000 cal BP or 11,050 BCE] in North America *is not ambiguous in indicating that megamammal-hunting was practiced*. An exceptionally high number of mammoth and mastodon killsites in North America is a signal about Clovis foraging that should astonish us with its implications. (Haynes 2002:818; italics original, calibrated age estimate and BCE date added)

The remains of mammoth or mastodon are found in association with Clovis points at 16 sites in North America, all but one west of the Mississippi River (Table 4.1). Another five sites with mastodon remains but lacking Clovis points are found east of the Mississippi, and one additional mammoth find in Wyoming lacks Clovis points but is of Clovis age. Several additional sites of mammoth and mastodon bone with presumptive butchering cut marks but lacking direct association with stone tools are scattered across the USA, and a couple of sites have produced stone tools with blood residues of mammoth, as well as smaller game (Haynes 2002:179). Considering that the vast

Table 4.1 Clovis sites with definitive or probable association with the remains of mammoth or mastodon, with notes on other animal and plant remains recovered (after Haynes 2002: tables 2.3 and 5.1).

Site	State	Mammoth/mastodon	Other animal remains
Blackwater Locality 1	New Mexico	8 mammoths	bison, horse, camel, paleolama, peccary, carnivores, rodents, box turtle
Colby	Wyoming	7 mammoths	pronghorn, camel, bison, ass, hare
Dent	Colorado	15 mammoths	
Domebo	Oklahoma	1 mammoth	
Dutton	Colorado	1 mammoth	
Escapule	Arizona	1 mammoth	horse
Hiscock	New York	1 mastodon	caribou, stag-moose, California condor, grebe, small unidentified mammal
Kimmswick	Missouri	2 mastodons	micromammals (mostly rodents)
Lange-Ferguson	North Dakota	2 mammoths	
Lehner	Arizona	13 mammoths	horse, camel, bison, micromammals, other taxa
Leikum	Arizona	2 mammoths	
Lubbock Lake	Texas	2(?) mammoths	
Miami	Texas	5 mammoths	
Murray Springs	Arizona	2 mammoths	horse, camel, bison, micromammals, other taxa
Naco	Arizona	1 mammoth	bison
Navarette	Arizona	1 mammoth	

majority of thousands of Clovis finds in North America lack any associated food remains or residues, the inventory of megamammals (the largest group of megafauna) with unequivocal Clovis association is hardly "exceptionally high," at least not in relative terms. Without a doubt, people who wielded weapons and knives fitted with Clovis points at least occasionally dispatched and consumed megafauna. But did they do so routinely? Was Clovis technology, settlement, and society structured primarily around the hunting of large prey? And, if so, did Clovis hunters contribute to the extinction of megafauna?

The degree to which Clovis people hunted megafauna is a matter of intense debate. Because Clovis became known to the world in the discovery of fluted points with eight mammoths at Blackwater Draw, the default position, going back to the 1930s, is that Clovis people were big-game hunters. Every interpretation and artistic impression of Clovis life for decades was predicated on the unquestioned assumption that mammoth, mastodon, and other megamammals were hunted routinely.

As data on Clovis accumulated and archaeologists turned a critical eye toward its interpretation, a variety of issues demanded attention. Many have to do with *taphonomy*, the process by which living creatures are transformed into fossilized remains. The term is applied more broadly in archaeology to refer to processes of assemblage formation, the way things accumulate and are changed in archaeological contexts. A variety of biological and physical agents affect the condition and position of material remains, from the time they are deposited on or in the ground to the time they are unearthed and collected, which, in the case of Clovis, is about 13,000 years. It is a wonder that anything other than the toughest stone survived the ravages of weather, soil and water chemistry, animal gnawing, freezing, thawing, erosion, and transport, among other agents, including humans. As much as we may hope that the archaeological record is an unbiased record of what was deposited by humans thousands of years ago, Pompeii-like conditions in archaeology are exceedingly rare.

Very little bone has survived at terrestrial Clovis sites. Given the massive size and density of the bones of mammoth, it is hardly surprising that they would be preserved better than, say, the bones of fish, and thus they are more conspicuous, even if not the most frequent remains deposited at a site. But under most conditions, even mammoth bone needs to be buried to survive millennia, eventually subject to the mineralization that makes it a fossil (note that bone recovered from archaeological sites in North America is generally still organic, given its relatively young age compared with, say, dinosaur bone, which is entirely fossilized).

Gary Haynes (2002:199) has summarized the pros and cons of hunting megamammals during Clovis times. The nutritional advantage is obvious. Not only does your average-sized mammoth provide lots of protein, fats, and other nutrients, it is potentially storable for future use. Of course, meat packages were so enormous that some may have been wasted. Similarly, as a source of sharable food, mammoths provided opportunities for gaining prestige through giving, although this had the potential for tension and conflict. Cooperative hunting would have fostered social cohesion, but it may have added costs to big-game hunting that lessened its advantage over foraging alone or in smaller groups.

Targeting big game at the end of the Ice Age may have been the optimal strategy, if, that is, the landscape lacked many alternatives (Haynes 2002:215–228). However, foraging models that rank megamammals at the head of an optimal diet assume that Clovis people were the first humans to arrive in North America (e.g., Waguespack and Surovell 2003), an increasingly untenable assumption.

On balance, Haynes suggests that Clovis hunters may have been opportunistic in their killing and consumption of mammoth (in the West), and less so of mastodon (in the East). These creatures were vulnerable to extinction at the end of the Ice Age, so many of the kills were likely culled from diminished, weakened, and increasingly circumscribed populations. This may help to explain why mammoth and mastodon kills in North America tend to date to the last few centuries of the Pleistocene, and why Clovis, as a cultural horizon, was so short-lived. It follows that the hunting of megamammals was distinctively Clovis, and that those aspects of Clovis culture best known to archaeologists (e.g., fluted points, beveled ivory rods, scrapers) are primarily about killing, processing, and consuming big game. It may very well have been the case that Clovis hunters participated in only an occasional mammoth hunt but spent the rest of their lives talking about it.

Younger Dryas Cooling, Megafauna Extinctions, and a Clovis Comet?

At 10,850 BCE, the otherwise warming climate of the late Pleistocene reversed abruptly into a multi-century period of cold and dry climate known colloquially as the "Big Freeze." This was the onset of the Younger Dryas stadial, and it marks both the extinction of many species of Pleistocene fauna and the end of the Clovis tradition, as archaeologists know it. The cause of the reversal in global warming is attributed to the collapse of the North American ice sheets, which then rerouted tropical water circulation southward and possibly pushed the jet stream northward. Alternatively, some scientists have postulated that the earth was impacted by a comet or asteroid at 10,950 BCE (12,900 cal BP), which caused widespread fires and a clouding of the atmosphere that dampened solar radiation and thus dropped temperatures (Firestone et al. 2007). This theory is contested by many scientists and much of the evidence for some sort of impact has been discounted (Figure 4.7).

Clovis Caches

At some 25 locations across the American West Clovis people emplaced assemblages of remarkable artifacts in the ground, at places apart from kill sites or camps. Known to archaeologists as "caches," such deposits include the typical fluted points, although some are exceptionally large and exquisite. Other cached items include ovate bifaces or biface preforms, beveled ivory rods, and large flakes. Some of the caches include items that appear to have been used or to have been intended to be used, while those with "hypertrophic" items are generally regarded as ritual deposits. One such cache from the Anzick

Fig 4.7 Asa Randall pointing to the so-called "Black Mat" exposed in an arroyo at the Murray Springs Clovis site in Arizona. Kenneth E. Sassaman photo, 2008.

Sidebar 4.4 Murray Springs and the Black Mat

Murray Springs is a Clovis site complex in the San Pedro Valley of southeast Arizona. Sites of the complex include a mammoth kill, a bison kill, and a hunting camp, all buried by 2.5 m of alluvium. Bone and stone artifacts were exposed by an arroyo that cut through the sediment, prompting excavations in the 1960s by C. Vance Haynes and students of the University of Arizona (Haynes and Huckell 2007).

Immediately above the Clovis layer at Murray Springs is a thin stratum of dark sediment that has come to be known as the "Black Mat." Proponents of the Clovis comet theory argue that the Black Mat is a charred, carbon-rich layer of soil that formed from widespread scorching of the earth. This deposit is purported to contain nanodiamonds, metallic microspherules, iridium dust, and other constituents attributed to an extraterrestrial source. Black Mats have been observed above Clovis layers at dozens of sites in North America, as well as nonarchaeological deposits in Mexico, Europe, the Middle East, and elsewhere.

Many scientists, Haynes (2008) among them, have raised doubts about the extraterrestrial cause for the Black Mat. At Murray Springs and elsewhere, the deposit is actually an algal mat that formed under processes typical of wetland environments, notably shallow marshlands. Most of the microscopic particles thought to come from an impact event and widespread burning are found in a variety of wetlands across the globe. Although the Younger Dryas was a period of generally colder and drier climate, water tables rose in places like southeast Arizona thanks to decreased evaporation.

The exact timing of formation of Black Mats is not certain at all sites, but these deposits apparently coincide with the disappearance of all Pleistocene megafauna except bison. The extinction of Ice Age creatures has long been regarded as gradual (Grayson and Meltzer 2002), perhaps the unintended consequence of prodigious Clovis hunters (Martin 1973). However, the extinctions of mammoths, mastodons, horses, camels, dire wolves, American lions, short-faced bears, sloths, and tapirs came at once, and quickly, at the onset of the Younger Dryas, 12,900 years ago. Clovis is thought by some to have become extinct too. Insofar as Clovis culture was centered on the hunting of Ice Age creatures, this goes without saying. However, as we will see in Chapter 5, Clovis people left descendants, so humans did not succumb to the cold of the Younger Dryas nor did the demise of Ice Age creatures drive humans into starvation and extinction. To be sure, something abrupt happened at 12,900 years ago. Evidence for an impact event is not yet secure although the theory is still on the table, but no matter the cause of the Younger Dryas, it did not kill off humans. It just changed the way they made a living.

Murray Springs is on land of the Bureau of Land Management and open to the public. Go see it for yourself (https://www.blm.gov/visit/murray-springs-clovis-site).

site in Montana appears to have been associated with a human burial (Figure 4.8).

Caches were likely emplaced in the ground for various reasons. Those described by David Kilby (2013) as "utilitarian" presumably served as a sort of insurance policy against failure away from home. That is, caches of tools and raw material were stashed in remote locations of hunting and other activities that removed Clovis people from places where they could replace tools at their leisure, generally at home and near sources of toolstone. In contrast, those containing hypertrophic forms are restricted to the Northwest and the northern Rockies and include raw materials quarried from locations to

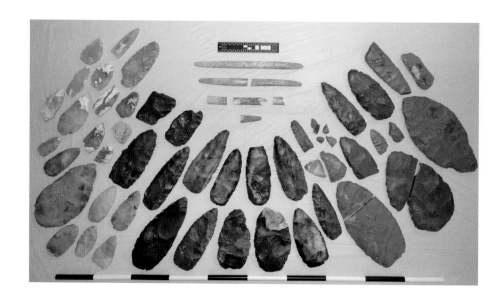

Fig 4.8 The Anzick Clovis cache from Montana included a variety of bifaces, other stone items, and a few organic artifacts, all covered in red ochre and associated with the remains of a two-year-old child. Courtesy of S. Stockton White V.

the south and east. If Clovis people were routinely moving into these areas to hunt or perform other activities involving bifaces, we might expect more kill sites and camp sites in the greater region. However, Clovis points and Clovis sites are actually not all that common in the region, suggesting that caches with elaborate artifacts (some smeared with red ochre, a pervasive ritual substance later in time) truly were nonutilitarian (Deller et al. 2009). As we will see below, the intermountain west was home to a population whose relationship to Clovis people remains to be determined. Perhaps caches like those in Washington, Montana, and Colorado include deposits that were intended to mediate the social relationships between distinct groups of people, much as they seem to have been during later periods of North American archaeology in the Southeast (Sassaman 2010).

Pre-Clovis, Non-Clovis, and Other Puzzles

Recent discoveries at sites across the western hemisphere make it difficult to recognize the bearers of Clovis culture as the first to populate North America. Two different sorts of discoveries are challenging the Clovis-First model. Foremost are assemblages of stone tools and associated remains that predate the Clovis era, sometimes by only a few centuries, in other cases possibly by millennia. Some of these recent finds attest to possible Clovis ancestry, while others are so different as to suggest that people of distinct tradition and ancestry colonized North America. The second type of discovery consists of sites with assemblages that date to the Clovis era, or even slightly later, but with no apparent affinity to Clovis culture. These include sites along the Pacific coasts of North and South America with evidence for full-blown maritime economies. Coupled with evidence for pre-Clovis sites in proximity to the Pacific coast, these maritime occupations attest to colonization of the Americas via watercraft. How Clovis related to coastal dwellers is anyone's guess, but no matter the relationship, Clovis people were not likely alone and not likely the first in North America.

What Makes Something Pre-Clovis?

Claims for anything that deviates from doctrine invite skepticism and scrutiny. As claims for pre-Clovis finds grew in frequency in the 1970s and '80s, some prominent archaeologists laid out the criteria that would have to be met for such finds to be considered legitimate (e.g., Dincauze 1984; Meltzer 1989b). Any claim for pre-Clovis would have to consist of materials:

(1) of *bona fide* human manufacture (e.g., stone tools) and/or modification (e.g., cut bone) found *in situ*;
(2) in a stratum below a stratum containing Clovis artifacts;
(3) dated independently to an age greater than Clovis.

Virtually no claims passed this test through the end of the twentieth century, and today only a handful do. Because the criteria involve stratigraphic relationships between Clovis and purported predecessors, sites lacking Clovis components are usually met with the toughest skepticism. As we see in summaries of recent discoveries below, sites with components greater than 13,150 years of age but lacking overlying Clovis components are among the more compelling candidates for pre-Clovis occupations of the Americas.

Pre-Clovis Sites in North and South America

The inventory of sites with archaeological remains predating the Clovis era is sparse but growing. Twenty-five years ago the list was woefully sparse; 50 years ago it was virtually blank, notwithstanding outlandish claims that succumbed to critical scrutiny (Meltzer 2009). Today we have varying levels of confidence in several sites in North and South America with evidence of human occupations predating 11,200 BCE, the onset of Clovis.

Cerutti Mastodon Site, California

One of the most recent and controversial discoveries consists of the fragmentary remains of a single mastodon associated with alleged hammerstones and anvils of human manufacture estimated to date to 130,000 years ago (Holen et al. 2017). If this is indeed an archaeological site and not simply the location of a "natural" death of a mastodon, it would push the peopling of the New World back to the emergence of fully modern humans in the Old World. A similar claim came from work at Calico Hills in California headed by famed paleoanthropologist Louis Leakey. Vance Haynes (1973) determined that the alleged stone tools at Calico Hills were "geofacts," not artifacts, meaning that they formed under natural conditions, such as the impact of rocks on other rocks as they were transported by gravity or other agents. The same assessment is leveled against the Cerutti Mastodon hammers and anvils, but we include this find in our list of possible pre-Clovis sites because the research is ongoing and may one day, against received wisdom, be substantiated.

Bluefish Cave, Yukon, Canada

Excavated in the 1970s and 1980s by Jacques Cinq-Mars, Bluefish Cave produced allegedly human-worked mammoth bone dated to about 28,000 years ago, during the Late Glacial Maximum. New AMS assays on cut bone corroborate this early age, if a little later at ca. 24,000 years ago (Bourgeon et al. 2017). Bluefish Cave may not only represent the truly oldest known archaeological site to date in North America, its age supports the so-called Beringian Standstill Hypothesis, which suggests that a genetically isolated population from Asia persisted in Beringia for thousands of years before dispersing into lower North and South America after the Ice Age. This of course says nothing about the relationship of this Standstill population to Clovis, which remains poorly represented in Alaska and the Yukon.

Swan Point, Alaska

In the Tanana River valley of east-central Alaska, a shallow site with worked mammoth tusk and artifacts of undisputed human manufacture appears to date to as early as 14,500 years ago (Holmes 2001). Because the site is so shallow (<1 m), associations between artifacts,

Fig 4.9 Dennis Jenkins at the entrance to Paisley Cave in Oregon, one of the more convincing pre-Clovis sites in North America. Odell Cross photo/*Daily Mail*.

bone, and dated charcoal are sometimes ambiguous, and there are overlying components at the site dating as late as the historic era. The site is regarded as the oldest in Alaska and the only evidence for mammoth hunting in the state. No Clovis artifacts have been recovered from Swan Point. The microblade artifacts in the earliest component at the site show affinity to the Dyuktai culture of late Pleistocene Siberia. We should note that nothing resembling Dyuktai has ever been found in the lower 48 states of the USA or farther south.

Paisley Caves, Oregon

A complex of four caves in the northern Great Basin of south-central Oregon includes deep strata with fossilized feces that have been dated to about 14,000 years ago (Figure 4.9). Human DNA has been detected in the paleofeces, and critics who suspected the samples were contaminated have been silenced by an ever-growing inventory of securely dated artifacts and bone of Ice Age fauna. In 2012 the lead investigator, Dennis Jenkins of the University of Oregon, announced the discovery of Western Stemmed bifaces in a stratum slightly older than Clovis (Jenkins et al. 2012). See the section below on the Western Pluvial Lakes tradition for the implications of this find for ancestry distinctively apart from Clovis.

Fig 4.10 Inside Meadowcroft Rockshelter, after excavations started in 1973 by James Adovasio. The entrance to the site was later secured to enable visitation and to protect it from damage. Meadowcroft Rockshelter is recognized as a Pennsylvania Commonwealth Treasure and is an official project of Save America's Treasures. Sue Ruth photo/Wikimedia.

Debra L. Friedkin, Texas

Although the site is shallow, the presence of an overlying Clovis stratum at the Debra L. Friedkin site in central Texas secures a pre-Clovis age for the deeper assemblage. Here, a tool complex named after Buttermilk Creek has been dated to as much as 15,500 years ago (Waters et al. 2011). Recovered in careful excavation from a 20 cm thick layer beneath a Clovis stratum were thousands of flakes and more than fifty flaked stone tools. Certain aspects of the assemblage – such as the blades, blade cores, lance-shape biface preforms, and a few overshot flakes – offer tantalizing hints of the Clovis tradition to come. Despite the lack of fluting, the Buttermilk Creek Complex is perhaps the best candidate for Clovis ancestry in North America. Sites with artifact assemblages beneath Clovis strata in Virginia, South Carolina, Florida, and elsewhere in the East add to the inventory of possible ancestry, but the connection to Clovis is not always apparent.

Meadowcroft Rockshelter, Pennsylvania

The much-maligned pre-Clovis evidence from Meadowcroft Rockshelter in southwestern Pennsylvania has been somewhat vindicated by discoveries elsewhere (Figure 4.10). Since the 1970s, when James Adovasio and colleagues announced pre-Clovis remains at the base of 4 m of stratified deposits, critics have pointed out potential issues with radiometric dating and disturbance. Indeed, it is odd that deposits dated from 16,000 to 19,000 years ago do not contain the remains of extinct Ice Age creatures, only those of species that survived into the modern era. Moreover, some have claimed that artifacts found in the basal stratum resemble later types, and Clovis is absent from overlaying layers (recall that Clovis people appear to have avoided caves and rockshelters). Nonetheless, with growing evidence for pre-Clovis occupations elsewhere in North America, Meadowcroft garners wider acceptance today than it did in the 1970s.

Cactus Hill, Virginia

Occupying a sand dune overlooking the Nottoway River in southeastern Virgina, Cactus Hill contains a stratum with unfluted bifacial tools and other artifacts that are estimated to be roughly 15,000–17,000 years old. Clovis-like artifacts have been recovered from a stratum only several centimeters above the deeper layer. Some archaeologists believe that pentagonal-shaped bifaces from below have ancestral affinity to Clovis. Accompanying the bifaces were blades and blade cores, but none of the unifaces of the Clovis tradition. None of the faunal remains from the pre-Clovis level were those of extinct Ice Age species. Because Cactus Hill is such a shallow, open-air site, like Swan Point, the potential for mixing and other disturbances is great. Still, as with Meadowcroft, the mounting evidence for pre-Clovis occupations elsewhere helps to secure the site's legitimacy.

Topper, South Carolina

On a raised terrace overlooking the Savannah River in South Carolina is a deeply buried site that Albert Goodyear and colleagues have been investigating for more than twenty years (Figure 4.11). The Topper

Fig 4.11 Ongoing excavations at the Topper site in South Carolina. Through 2012 the public was invited to join field expeditions to the site led by Albert Goodyear. The corporate landowner of Topper constructed a pavilion over the excavation to protect it from the elements. Courtesy of Derek T. Anderson.

site contains a Clovis component in sands buried some 1.4 m below the present-day surface, and another 2 m deeper are two possible pre-Clovis components. The younger of the two is estimated to date to more than 14,000 BCE and consists of chert artifacts from a core and microlithic industry. The older of the two is some 4 m below the Clovis layer and consists of chert and charcoal of questionable human agency dating to ~50,000 years ago. Analysis of the pre-Clovis components has begun to appear in print, but some archaeologists reserve judgment on the veracity of the finds, at least the oldest component.

Monte Verde, Chile

Erosion caused by logging in southern Chile in 1975 exposed the bones of a mastodon and other archaeological evidence of human occupation dating 14,800 BP, a millennium earlier than Clovis. Excavations at Monte Verde led by Tom Dillehay (1997) would in time uncover a remarkable assemblage of artifacts and features, all nicely preserved in a peaty bog that formed shortly after the site was abandoned. Evidence for hearths, parts of a tent-like structure, and diverse plant and animal remains, including a slab of mastodon meat, attest to occupation by a group estimated by Dillehay to number some 20 to 30 people. As might be expected, Monte Verde invited skepticism when its age was announced. In 1997, at the invitation of Dillehay, a group of 12 leading archaeologists – some of the toughest skeptics among them – traveled to the site to see the evidence themselves (Meltzer et al. 1997). The endorsement of this group bolstered growing support for a pre-Clovis presence in the Americas, one that was sufficiently distinct from Clovis to warrant consideration of separate migrations. At about 60 km from the Pacific coast and with nine species of marine algae, Monte Verde was likely established by maritime people (Dillehay et al. 2008).

Monte Verde is arguably the strongest case for something older than Clovis, but it is also powerful testament to a Pacific coastal migration. Had the ancestors of the inhabitants of Monte Verde moved into the Americas on foot, across the Bering Land Bridge, they would not have been able to continue south by land because the Ice Free Corridor was not yet open (cf. Dawe and Kornfeld 2017; Potter et al. 2017). A coastal route southward would appear necessary if the peopling of the Americas predates 12,000 BCE. And if immigration could have been accomplished only by boat, the availability of a Land Bridge and an

Ice Free Corridor is inconsequential. Were the first immigrants of the Americas, as Knut Fladmark (1979) long ago speculated, a sea-faring people?

Maritime Migration

There is now ample evidence that people inhabited the Pacific coast of North and South America by the time of Clovis, and we can also be fairly certain that these coastal people were distinct from Clovis, at least culturally. Found in recent decades at sites along the entire Pacific coast, from Alaska to Peru, are the residues of maritime adaptations: fish and shellfish, seabirds, and saltwater plants. Remains of watercraft this old are elusive, but the occupation of certain islands would not have been possible without boats because they were, as the term "island" implies, detached from the mainland, even with sea level down more than 100 m. Likewise, there were stretches of the coast that would have been difficult, if not impossible, to traverse on foot.

Monte Verde gives us a good idea how early a Pacific migration event occurred (>12,850 BCE), but its counterparts on the coast, from north to south, are either coeval with or postdate Clovis. The problem is sea-level rise and submergence of the oldest coastal sites. Having risen rapidly since the Late Glacial Maximum of 20,000 years ago, the Pacific Ocean transgressed across low-lying terrain, including large portions of south-central Beringia, the presumed entry point of immigration. Of course, much of the Pacific rim consists of steep terrain, where rising sea flooded less land compared with, say, the gulf coastal plain of the American Southeast. Locations of inhabitable land adjacent to steep offshore slopes are thus good places to locate early sites. Jon Erlandson and colleagues from the University of Oregon have done just that on the northern Channel Islands of southern California, where several sites have been dated to 13,000–11,300 cal BP, or 11,050–9350 BCE (Erlandson et al. 2008). During the Late Glacial Maximum, the northern Channel Islands were joined together as a single land mass known as *Santarosae*, but it was still separated by water from the mainland, some 8 km to the east (Figure 4.12). Even though the oldest coastal sites were apparently submerged as sea level rose and Santarosae was divided into four separate islands, terrestrial sites of late Pleistocene age are preserved today in locations that offered freshwater and supplies of stone to coastal dwellers. Marine shell middens accumulated at one site complex known as Cardwell

Bluffs, where Paleoindians quarried and modified nodules of chert (Erlandson et al. 2011). Stemmed and barbed projectile points and "crescents" made from this chert – unlike anything Clovis – compare favorably with tools of the Western Stemmed tradition at places like Paisley Caves. Sites on Santa Rosa Island with these same artifact types include the remains of geese, seabirds, fish, and sea mammals.

Together with other early maritime sites along the Pacific rim, the northern Channel Island record attests to well-established and diversified marine adaptations by the end of the Pleistocene. Under the Clovis-First model, coastal occupations in North America were believed to be a consequence of populations that expanded out of the interior of the continent, a sort of last resort after exhausting the supply of terrestrial game such as mammoth and mastodon. Coupled with

Fig 4.12 Santa Cruz Island off the coast of Santa Barbara, California has been the subject of recent archaeological investigations into early maritime communities who likely colonized North America by boat. Carol M. Highsmith photo/Wikimedia.

Fig 4.13 Kelp forest tank, Monterey Bay Aquarium, California. Kelp forests along the Pacific coast supported rich marine biomes that early colonists would have been able to depend on as they migrated south. Jon Erlandson refers to this route as the "kelp highway" of immigration. Wikimedia.

this assumption was the unfounded belief that the coastline of the Alaskan peninsula and the northern Northwest Coast was too glaciated to allow safe passage southward along the coast, whether by foot or by boat. However, new evidence shows that the now-submerged outer coasts of these areas were deglaciated by about 14,000 BCE, and that they supported a combination of marine and terrestrial resources useful to humans.

Not only was it possible for people to migrate southward along the coast after 14,000 BCE, the ecological conditions of this time may have provided strong incentive to do so. The inducement, according to Erlandson and colleagues (2007), was the widespread distribution of productive kelp forests around the nearshore margins of the north Pacific. Kelp forests are the keystone of a complex web of organisms with potential value to humans, such as seals, sea otters, fish, shellfish, and seabirds (Figure 4.13). Paralleling the coast for hundreds of miles, kelp forests would have been something of an ecological corridor for sea-faring people, a literal "kelp highway" of immigration (Erlandson et al. 2007). And even though the northern reaches of the highway may have been frozen for most of the year, kelp is quite capable of surviving seasonal ice cover. The linear nature of the nearshore habitat underpinned by kelp would have encouraged the rapid migration of maritime people southward from the north Pacific.

Groups of people migrating southward along the Pacific rim had opportunity and motivation to move into the interior of the continent, especially after reaching the more temperate climate of lower latitudes. As we noted for the Channel Islands, freshwater and toolstone are among the resources early coastal immigrants sought in locations away from the shoreline. In locations farther north, people apparently followed food into the interior. The large rivers of the Northwest Coast and northern California supported runs of anadromous fish, such as salmon, which migrate upriver each year to spawn. Salmon would later become the economic foundation for some of the most complex hunter-gatherer societies of North America (see Chapter 13).

That spawning salmon would have coaxed humans into the interior reaches of the Pacific west is a hypothesis worthy of serious consideration (Erlandson and Braje 2012:152). Awaiting humans deep in some interior areas were networks of lakes and marshlands where oases of aquatic and terrestrial fauna and plants flourished. The so-called Western Pluvial Lakes tradition of the Columbia Plateau and Great Basin regions exemplifies this sort of adaptation and we now suspect with considerable confidence that people of this tradition trace their ancestry to the Pacific coast.

Western Pluvial Lakes Tradition

The best candidate for Paleoindian ancestry distinct from Clovis is seen in the Western Pluvial Lakes tradition (WPLT) of the Columbia Plateau and Great Basin. One of the diagnostic artifacts of the tradition is the Western Stemmed point, once believed to be a spin-off of Clovis technology. As noted earlier, Western Stemmed points at the base of Paisley Cave in Oregon actually predate the Clovis era by many centuries. Granted, absolute age estimates for Clovis in the far West are wanting, but even circumstantial evidence for its precedence is lacking. What is more, some sites in northeast Asia contain assemblages of stemmed points that bear resemblance to those of the WPLT (Goebel et al. 2003). Although none of these is definitely pre-Clovis in age, they support a coastal route of immigration. Stemmed points of the northern Channel Islands of California, along with flaked stone crescents similar to those of the WPLT (Figure 4.14), date back to at least Clovis times, while earlier occurrences along the coast have presumably been either flooded or eroded by rising seas. Notably, one of the varieties of stemmed points from the Channel Islands, the so-called Channel Island Barbed point, bears strong affinity to the "tanged" points of the Incipient Jomon period of Japan, dating to 13,550–11,850 BCE (see also Erlandson and Braje 2012:154).

The geographic gaps between the locations of stemmed points of Asia, the Northwest Coast, and Channel Islands may prove to be the outcome of inundated coastlines, and we may never know whether coastal sites with stemmed points and crescents predate the oldest interior sites of the WPLT, currently dated in excess of 14,000 years ago. No matter, the preponderance of evidence suggests that groups bearing stemmed points traveled to North America by boats along the Pacific rim and quickly found their way into the interior Columbia

Fig 4.14 Artifacts from an early site on Santa Rosa Island, California, including tanged points and crescents that bear affinity to artifacts of the Western Pluvial Lakes tradition. Courtesy of Jon Erlandson.

Plateau and Great Basin, most likely by paddling up rivers. After establishing themselves in the region, people of the WPLT may have come into contact with the bearers of Clovis culture, who must have traveled west into the region from the Plains (Beck and Jones 2010). The cultural and biological differences between people archaeologists know as the WPLT and Clovis traditions are as unknown to us as is the outcome of their interactions, if any. On these matters, the data on genetics, language, and skeletal morphology are in occasional contradiction.

Genes and Persons

To this point we have focused all of our attention on archaeological data, mostly stone tools, animal remains, and radiocarbon ages. Whereas this is fitting given the subject matter of this book, there are other sorts of evidence that bear on our understanding of the peopling of North America. Genetics provide a provocative source of new data, but they come generally from the living, not the dead. Not only do the genes of living native descendants provide clues to the biological diversity of founding populations, they are also the basis for inferring how long ago and from where these immigrants arrived.

A second body of biological evidence – the morphology of human skulls and other skeletal elements – cannot pinpoint the time and place of immigration, but it shows more variation than the genetics data do, suggesting multiple events and sources of migration (Figure 4.15). Add to this mix of biological data something patently cultural, namely language. Mirroring much of the genetics data, historical linguistics projects limited diversity and a 20,000+ year root for modern Amerindian languages.

The results of research in genetics, skeletal morphology, language, and archaeology are not simply hard to reconcile, they are completely contradictory in many cases. A quick review of some of the major results illustrates the point (see Morrow [2017] for summary of results since 2016). Although interpretations vary, geneticists generally agree that the major ancestral line leading to modern Indians arrived in Beringia in a major wave of immigration sometime between 20,000 and 40,000 years ago. Recall that terrestrial passage southward would not have been possible before about 12,000 BCE, presumably halting mass movement (unless by boat!) for thousands of years, more than 20,000 years by some estimates. Geneticists speculate that a founding population remained in Beringia before moving farther east and

Fig 4.15 Modern genetics data suggest that the ancestors of all Native Americans, excluding Inuit, who came later, entered North America in a single migration no earlier than 23,000 years ago. Data on skeletal morphometrics and material culture are hard to reconcile with the results of genetics research. G. Mülzel artwork/Wikimedia.

south. In proposing the Beringian Incubator or Standstill model (see Kemp and Schurr 2010), geneticists see a long period of waiting for people of limited genetic diversity. The consequence of one subsequent immigration is seen in modern genomes, but apparently from

Sidebar 4.5 American Neanderthals?

The cavemen in the Geico commercials of the late 2000s played the part of Neanderthals, the butt of modern jokes about evolutionary laggards. The humor in the Geico commercials is in the irony of "evolutionary laggards" living and acting the part of metrosexual men: polished, stylish, even sensitive. They are meant to look like "us" to make the point that switching one's insurance to Geico is so simple that "even a caveman can do it."

For many decades paleoanthropologists have argued that Neanderthals were a different species than modern humans. Although members of the two species lived in relatively close proximity to one another in various regions of the Old World some 45,000–40,000 years BP, and ultimately had a common ancestor in Africa before splitting into two branches, they did not interbreed sufficiently to leave a definitive biological marker (i.e., genetic) in modern populations. In this scenario, Neanderthals went extinct, leaving no descendants and contributing nothing to the biological makeup of modern people. Neanderthals persist only, as it goes, in television and film as dim-witted dolts, insufficiently cultured to make it beyond the Stone Age.

Those who made the case that Neanderthals went extinct and left no descendants rested their case mostly on the analysis of modern DNA, which traces the origins of the modern human lineage to Africa after the time Neanderthal ancestors left the continent and migrated north. The "Out of Africa" theory, as it came to be known, posits no role for Neanderthals in the genetic history of humans, because the reconstructions of lineages traced to Africa do not show any significant "foreign" input.

Critics of the Out of Africa theory point to the range of morphological variation in fossil human skeletons from sites across the globe and argue that lines of descent can be traced well past the emergence of fully modern humans in Africa to include lineages in southeast Asia, the Middle East,

Europe, and elsewhere. In what came to be known as the Multiregional Hypothesis, fully modern humans emerged in different parts of the world at roughly the same time and then continued to migrate and interbreed along the way to diminish genetic diversity over time. To this way of thinking, Neanderthals were among our ancestors. The evidence comes from bone, not extrapolated from the genetic profiles of modern people.

Ancient DNA, of course, gets us back to the actual persons involved in this biological saga. Not surprisingly, DNA is not routinely preserved in bone tissue tens of thousands of years old, most of which has fossilized. Recent advances in the science of ancient DNA has enabled for the first time the detection of subtle genetic markers that not only place Neanderthals in the line leading to humans, but also enable us to measure the amount of Neanderthal DNA carried by people today, which is admittedly minute but there nonetheless. With this startling new evidence, some of the staunchest critics of the Multiregional Hypothesis have capitulated, sometimes in highly public fashion. On November 15, 2012, renowned paleoanthropologist Chris Stringer appeared on *The Colbert Report* to admit he was wrong about Neanderthals.

What does any of this have to do with North American archaeology? Well, the pre-Clovis people of North America have a bit of a Neanderthal complex going on. They are acknowledged as existing but not yet given much credit for contributing to the lineages of native North America. Clovis is still it. And as was the case with Neanderthals, the genetics of North American ancestry excludes much variation and generally points to one place of origin, but the morphology of what few skeletons we have says otherwise. We will likely find out some day soon that multiple biological and cultural groups contributed to the lineages of native North America. American Neanderthals indeed.

the same parent population (Kemp and Schurr 2010). Genetic variation among extant populations is attributed to a history of genetic drift (i.e., change due to the sampling biases of small populations) against an overall backdrop of marked similarity.

Similarities stop when we compare certain ancient skeletal remains with the morphology of later and modern native people. Craniometric analyses (i.e., measurements of the skull) in recent years show that at least two distinct populations inhabited the Americas by the early Holocene. The earlier of the two consists of individuals with long, narrow crania and prognathous faces; the latter population has short, round crania, and flat faces. Referred to generally as "Paleoamericans," individuals of this former group have posed something of a dilemma for archaeologists because they bear little resemblance to either modern Amerindians or the northeast Asiatic populations of presumed common ancestry, like the latter population. As we noted earlier in this chapter, Kennewick Man brought this puzzle into the public eye, but he is not alone in representing a branch of ancestry that, like Neanderthals, geneticists might expect to have gone extinct without contributing to modern populations (see Rasmussen et al. 2015). Some analysts attribute differences between the two to microevolution since colonization, while others envision multiple founding migrations from distinct source populations (see Anderson 2010).

In comparing the data of genetics and craniometrics, two caveats must be borne in mind. First, the genetics data account for only those biological lineages leading to living people. They do not record the existence of people of distinct genetic composition who never produced offspring with individuals in lineages descending to living people. Some of the individuals who do not seem to fit the range of craniometric variation among recent populations may have been among people who did not interact reproductively with Amerindian ancestors, even if they came into contact and interacted culturally.

The second caveat is that the oldest "Paleoamericans" known to us from skeletal remains are several thousand years younger than the immigration event projected by genetics data. Is it possible that a Paleoamerican subgroup split off from an ancestral line and soon after went extinct? If the root cause of the variation is genetic drift, as the geneticists suggest, and not a separate-source immigration, then specific instances of drift operated to differentially distribute existing variations in the founding population, as well as any that arose in the interim. Multiple "splintering" events are implicated, each entailing a subset of the full range of variation in the founding population.

Arguably, the skeletal variation of ancient Native Americans reflects migration history and the microevolution of geographic diversity (Jantz et al. 2010). Considering that people throughout North American history moved around a lot, under all sorts of sociocultural circumstances, one of the most defining features of the biological history of humans has been, and continues to be, gene flow. Jantz et al. (2010) describe morphological variations that do not square with a straightforward ecogeographic model in which all humans in the New World passed through the "cold filter" of Beringia. Rather, their analysis reveals trends for *cormic indices* (ratio of the sitting height to total height) indicative of both arctic- and tropical-adapted bodies, supporting the case for multiple migrations early on, at least one following a maritime route that delivered humans to South America no later than the late Pleistocene, as archaeological data suggest.

Coupled with data from bone chemistry, morphological variations in early human postcranial bone suggest that coastal and interior plateau groups can be discriminated due to microevolutionary adaptations to diverse niches of the Northwest Coast and Plateau (Cybulski 2010). Models have been developed to account for subregional variation such as this, linking in some cases morphometric and archaeological data (e.g., Chatters et al. 2012), in others introducing new evidence for low-frequency haplotypes among populations from the Northwest Coast to Peru (Perego et al. 2009). No doubt future work in both genetics and skeletal biology will continue to clarify that the peopling of North and South America entailed multiple migrations and probably multiple points of origin.

Conclusion

Both the biological and cultural diversity of late Pleistocene people in the Americas is too great to be accounted for by a single wave of migration from a single ancestral source (Faught 2008). Now that archaeologists have come to grips with the existence of people not only earlier but *other* than Clovis (but see Fiedel [2017] for a recent defense of the Clovis-First [and -Only] model based on the genome of the Anzick burial), they have their work cut out to define and explain the diversity. Which of the various pre-Clovis people were true ancestors to Clovis, and which, if any, became extinct to the point that they left no biological trace among modern people? As the science of ancient DNA improves, and if it is applied to ancient tissue more broadly, we may find that ancient lineages extrapolated from the genetics of modern people alone reveal only the broadest of biological histories. The picture is clearly more complicated than modern samples and methods reveal.

Despite the limits of our data, we can imagine a history where one or more indigenous peoples existed in North America before a distinctive culture, Clovis, arose and swept the land rapidly. It is a process that was repeatedly played out in ancient times before it became manifest in the modern era we know from written history, when multiple cultural and biological stems converged in flashes of change, sometimes violent, but also peacefully, despite cultural differences. We know from cross-cultural observations that it does not take all that much time for distinctiveness to contribute bits and pieces of tradition and innovation to cultural expressions the anthropologist Levi-Strauss called *bricolage*, products of ethnogenesis. Biologically, of course, variation is obliterated with interbreeding, or what geneticists call gene flow. So, by the time we get to, say, the early Holocene of ~10,000 years ago, cultural and biological expressions look much different than simply the persistence of one and the failure of the other, or even a blending of traits. In a scenario of two vastly different peoples occupying North America, people not only had to deal with living off a land that was rapidly changing, they had to deal with others whose views on moving forward may have been different.

The sea was it. At least some, maybe most, or even all of the first immigrants arrived in the Americas by watercraft. That they made their way inland at various places along the Pacific coast is perhaps not at all surprising, because they indeed had traveled far already. But moving to the interior, from the coast, involved more than traversing more space. Why coastal dwellers moved eastward, into terrain of a type with which they had limited or no experience, is uncertain. It seems reasonable that some moved to the interior by way of rivers, after anadromous fish, perhaps (Erlandson and Braje 2012). Or conditions on the coast may have occasionally soured, coaxing people to seek alternatives landward (Surovell 2003). And then again, some may have simply wanted to see the place from where the sun came. No matter the reason for keeping on the move, by the time early coastal dwellers of the Pacific rim reached the Rocky Mountains they confronted the *Others*, people of Clovis ancestry. Surely these people had common ancestors and shared culture at some point back in time, but at this point in time, under these conditions, the differences outweighed the similarities and we thus see the makings of all sorts of innovation and change.

It is under these conditions of encounter that we must consider the parallel fervor of environmental change. The Younger Dryas interrupted for a few centuries a trend toward warmer global temperatures that ended the Ice Age. With warmer climate came higher seas, raging rivers, and emergent lakes, as glaciers melted. The coastline was especially vulnerable to rapid warming and so we must consider, as we do in the next chapter, that the experiences of people at the end of the Ice Age, moving landward as sea rose quickly, may not look all that different from our own near-term futures.

5 Sea Change, See Change

Full fathom five thy father lies:
Of his bones are coral made:
Those are pearls that were his eyes:
Nothing of him that doth fade
But doth suffer a sea-change
Into something rich and strange.

Ariel's song, *The Tempest*, William Shakespeare, 1610

Four centuries after Shakespeare introduced the term *sea-change* to describe profound change caused by the sea – literally, the watery transformation of Ferdinand's father's body – modern speakers of English use the term to refer broadly to change caused by all sorts of agents, humans among them. An interesting convergence between Shakespeare's intent and modern meanings of *sea change* (the term is no longer hyphenated) is found in current discourse about global warming. Climate prognosticators warn of dramatic, sudden change in our near future: increased frequency and severity of storms, droughts, and floods; animal and plant extinctions; salinization of freshwater; and loss of coastal land and habitat from sea-level rise. Because nearly 40 percent of North Americans today live on or near the coast, projections for rising oceans are of particular concern (Figure 5.1). If we take extreme projections at face value (up to 6 m this century [Nicholls et al. 2005]), sea change will come in Shakespearian fashion – the watery transformation of vast coastlines and the social bodies that inhabit and work them.

To the extent that we are the agents of our own sea change – notably the atmospheric spike in greenhouse gases caused by industrialization – we ought to have the will, if not also the capacity, to avert disaster. Of course, climate change is actually nothing new. Since the end of the last Ice Age, average global temperatures have warmed by about 7 degrees Celsius (~12.5 degrees Fahrenheit), much of it coming early in

Fig 5.1 The last house of Holland Island, Maryland, home to 360 people before rising sea inundated the land. This photo was taken in October 2009; the house fell into the bay one year later. Wikimedia.

the postglacial era, and some of it coming in spikes of rapid warming, as in the past century or two. And for every spike in warming there have been episodes of cooling that reversed climate trends, such as the Younger Dryas of the late Pleistocene (Chapter 4) or the Little Ice Age of the last millennium (Fagan 2001). Paleoclimatologists understand many of the myriad forces of nature that affect global climate, among them precessional cycles of the earth's orbit, sunspots, asteroid strikes, and volcanic eruptions. Humans, of course, are not implicated in any such causes. Certainly, agents of "natural" change, like the sea, operated long before the first human looked up at the sky and wondered if it would ever rain again.

Notwithstanding the first farmers of 10,000 years ago who cleared forests and tilled soil in the Middle East to upset the "natural" balance of atmospheric gases (e.g., Ruddiman 2005), climate change caused by direct human agency – what is known as *anthropogenic* change – is most often portrayed as a uniquely modern thing. Intergovernmental panels in fact make a distinction between climate *change* and climate *variability*, the former of truly anthropogenic cause, specifically the spike in carbon dioxide emissions from the combustion of fossil fuels. Ancient human impacts on climate and environment are recognized worldwide (e.g., Redman 1999), but they are most often portrayed as localized, perhaps regional, and never global in scale. The climate fluctuations these ancient people endured are presumed to be those of nature, not culture, so it is often said that the ancients lived by fate alone, neither to blame for climate change nor held responsible for mitigating its consequences. As with Ferdinand's father, sea change for the ancients would appear, under this logic, to be beyond human control.

In this chapter we are not so much interested in challenging the exceptionalism of anthropogenic change in the postindustrial era; we focus instead on the relationship between the experience and the expectation of change through time. In this respect, ancient North Americans and modern people have more in common than you might imagine. For instance, humans have not experienced the rate of climate change projected for the near-term future (i.e., the next century or two) since the end of the Ice Age. Assuming that humans 12,000 years ago were paying attention to the changes around them, it stands to reason that they would come to expect change to continue, perhaps even have a good sense of its direction and pace. With experience as a guide, would not the futures of these ancient people be somewhat self-determined, not merely fateful?

It takes more than a leap of faith to accept that ancient people took fate into their own hands. If we hope to go beyond the rhetoric of today's climate change debate, it will take hard evidence. In this chapter we take a look at the archaeological evidence for *sea changes* in the ancient past that were stimulated by abrupt climate change. A key factor in our review of these cases is the rate and magnitude of change. As noted earlier, climate variation common to a range of fluctuations at the scale of human experience is not change per se, merely variation. These sorts of fluctuations are the stuff of annual rounds, storage, surplus production, exchange networks, and other means by which nonwestern people deal with cyclical changes in temperature, precipitation, and the availability of animal and plant resources. It is also the stuff of ecological theory that explains particular ways of making a living as adaptations to particular environmental conditions (Binford 2001). From an ecological standpoint, environmental changes that come slowly and in small increments enable populations to adapt. Change that comes fast and furious catches people often by surprise, unless, that is, fast change was nothing new.

Our emphasis on the experience of change is aptly captured by another turn of the phrase *sea change*. To the extent that people *see* change, *experience* change, they have the capacity to anticipate change in the future, and perhaps even affect its outcome. Without a meaningful connection to the past, futures may indeed be fateful, as in the aphorism of Spanish-American George Santayana (1863–1952): "Those who cannot remember the past are condemned to repeat it." Unfortunately, Santayana, like so many other western philosophers, viewed the capacity to connect past and futures as uniquely modern, an outcome of the Enlightenment and other European cultural movements to break from "traditional" living and promote scientific reasoning and rational logic to explain and thus control nature. Henry Ford and the industry he fostered were beneficiaries of this logic, and now the same industry that helped to "free" humans from the fatefulness of nature is being held responsible for climate change not experienced since the time this logic was emplaced (see Chapter 1).

Take away the agency of the ancients and we take away a vast body of human experience dealing with change. Sure, the material reality of life in North America today is hardly comparable to that of, say, 8,000 years ago. But are we justified in assuming that ancient people simply bent to the will of climate change because they lacked the writing systems and historical databases of modern societies? Was traditional living to the ancients simply the way things had to be done, held unawares in the mind and thus blindly reproduced through practice, or was it instead a treasure trove of potential alternatives for intervening and determining one's own fate?

These are lofty questions for an introduction to North American archaeology, but they must be asked if we are to think about the past as something more than a chronicle of extinct, premodern experience. As we review some of North America's case material on the experiences of climate change, starting with life just after the Ice Age, three caveats discussed in Sidebar 5.1 are worth bearing in mind.

The Pleistocene–Holocene Transition

If change is constant, then what is a transition? In the change known to archaeologists as the Pleistocene–Holocene transition, the transition qualifies as a sea change (Figure 5.2). It marked the end of the

Sidebar 5.1 Cultural baggage

The people who first set foot in North America carried with them histories encoded in possessions, legends, knowhow, genealogies, rituals, and landscapes, among other dimensions of culture. They had ideas about what was edible, where to camp, how often to move, who was eligible to mate, how to heal a wound, what to do with the dead, and every other decision, mundane or profound, that affected one's future. It is hard to dispute these assertions, but you will not find much discussion in archaeological literature on the cultural dispositions of first peoples. The tendency instead is to reduce the decision-making of ancient hunter-gatherers to the microeconomics of energy budgets as they affected reproductive fitness, in the logic of behavioral ecology. Unfortunately, such a theory of culture centered on the material realities of surviving and reproducing biologically is not concerned with (1) cultural diversity, (2) unintended consequences, and (3) Romer's Rule.

For starters, that people in general survived under such dramatic climatic change is testament to the diversity of cultural practices, even at this early time. The same applies to every other people who confronted new circumstances not previously experienced, including Europeans and others who arrived late to the continent. Even mundane practices that escape consciousness can produce surprising results. No one set out to engineer domesticated grain in North America, or elsewhere, but the process got started with the day-to-day gathering of plant foods by hunter-gatherers well

back in the Archaic. Likewise, no one set out to raise global temperatures; it resulted, instead, from actions believed inconsequential to climate. Similarly perhaps, the first fishlike creatures to leave water and traverse land some 370 million years ago did not intend to become amphibians; they were simply trying to get to the next pond when the one they were in began to shrink. Of course, intentions had nothing to do with it. Through the process of natural selection scripted so well by Darwin, those members of a fish population capable of moving and surviving temporarily on land would have survived and reproduced more often than those challenged with life out of water under conditions of shrinking habitat, in this case, drying-up ponds. Through time, the population evolves toward greater numbers of land-crossing organisms. Bear in mind that all this change takes place with no purpose other than trying to maintain the status quo. This principle is known in evolutionary biology as Romer's Rule, and it explains how substantial change might come about as organisms strive to not change. We hasten to add that humans, of course, do many (but not all) things with purpose and resolve, and can draw on experiences other than their own to plan futures. We note as well that humans often strive to keep things as they are and thus draw on "tradition" as the rationale for action. And even though tradition is hardly equivalent to the hard-wired genetics of our ambitious amphibians, it too has the capacity to be the raw material for change.

Ice Age and the beginning of the recent (Holocene) period, if you consider 11,500 years "recent." In geological terms, it is the current warm period and thus, technically, an interglacial period. In point of fact the transition marked dramatic changes in not only global temperature, but also precipitation and airflow patterns, ocean currents, river dynamics, soil development, vegetation and animal distributions, and much more. The extinction of megafauna already noted was followed, after the Younger Dryas (after 9550 BCE), by an overall reduction in biodiversity and the environmental patchiness that supported it (Graham and Lundelius 1994). Under warmer

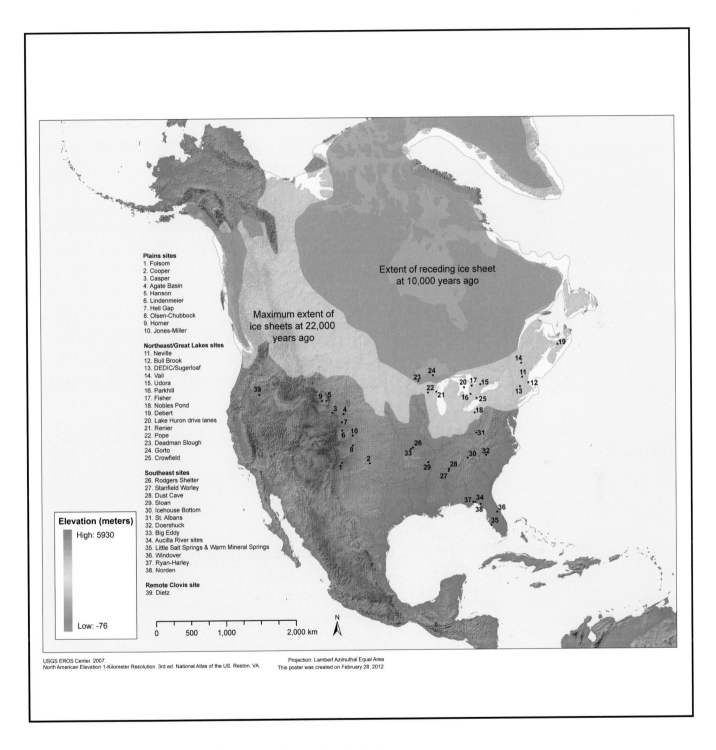

Fig 5.2 Locations of late Paleoindian sites in North America mentioned in text.

conditions vast biomes like the Great Plains became established, enabling rapid expansion of modern bison populations and the humans who increasingly hunted them. New land to the north was exposed as glaciers melted and receded, and old land to the south was submerged as the sea level rose. Many such changes came fast and they were truly transformative of the landscape, its biota, and its rhythms. Geologist Russell Graham thinks that much of this took place in as little as 40 years.

Here we focus on a few especially marked changes and their consequence for the distribution and disposition of early Holocene communities (Table 5.1). We will start with the Great Plains, where bison hunting was intensified with the expansion of grasslands and persisted through European contact. We will then take a look at developments along the receding glacial front to see how caribou hunting became a communal pursuit involving infrastructure and planning not unlike that on the Plains. Next we consider changes to the rivers and forests of the midcontinent and Eastern Woodlands that enticed communities to reduce their range of movements and, in some cases, assert connections to places that some archaeologists read as territorialism. And finally, we arrive at the front of transgressive sea, where coastal populations experienced such rapid sea-level rise that they must have repeatedly relocated landward, even within a lifetime.

Grassland and Bison Boom

Bison was the one type of Pleistocene megafauna that survived the Younger Dryas stadial and went on to proliferate across much of North America at a breakneck pace. Granted, some species of Ice Age bison did not make it to the Holocene. Those that went extinct (essentially replaced by new, descendant species) were generally more mega- than the modern species (*Bison bison*). Still, modern bison are the largest terrestrial mammals in North America, measuring 2–3.5 m long, and 1.5–1.9 m tall, and weighing between 1,000 and 2,000 pounds (Figure 5.3). And whatever modern bison gave up in size they made up for in numbers. Imagine a landscape of open grassland, reaching off to the horizon as far as the eye can see, populated by a sea of creatures the size of minivans, too many to count. That was the situation before bison hunting became a commercial operation

Table 5.1 Chronological highlights of Pleistocene–Holocene transitional cultures (after Chapdelaine 2012; Holliday 2000; Anderson and Sassaman 2012).

Year cal BP	Archaeological period	Cultural patterns
13,150–12,850	Clovis	Fluted points, mobile settlement, late Pleistocene megafauna hunting, continental in scope
12,800–11,900	Folsom	Fluted points, mobile settlement, Younger Dryas bison hunting, Great Plains
12,000–8000	Plano traditions	Unfluted lanceolate points with parallel flaking; bison hunting
	Regional variants of Plano:	
12,000–11,500	Agate Basin	
12,000–10,700	Hell Gap	
11,900–10,600	Alberta	
10,600–10,000	Cody	Scottsbluff and Eden points, Cody knife
12,900–12,500	Gainey/Barnes	Great Lakes fluted points with strong Clovis affinity, caribou hunting
12,900–12,500	Bull Brook/Debert	New England fluted points with strong Clovis affinity, caribou hunting
12,500–11,900	Parkhill	Northern Great Lakes, Ontario fluted points
12,450–11,500	Dalton	Unfluted lanceolate points with lateral resharpening (knives), adzes, cemeteries
11,800–10,800	Side-notched	Big Sandy, Bolen, and related side-notched points with lateral resharpening (knives)
10,800–10,000	Corner-notched	Kirk and related corner-notched points with lateral resharpening (knives)
uncertain	Suwannee/Simpson	Florida unfluted, waisted, and fishtailed lanceolate points; associated with Pleistocene fauna, but dating uncertain; possibly coeval with Clovis or even older

Fig 5.3 American bison in Hayden Valley, Yellowstone National Park, September 2011. Wikimedia.

in the nineteenth century. It is estimated that more than 60 million bison populated North America before Europeans arrived. By 1890 their numbers had dwindled to an estimated 750. They may have survived the Ice Age, but bison almost did not survive early Euro-American history.

We are in this chapter, of course, interested in the situation well before then, when the Younger Dryas stadial kicked off quickly at about 12,800 years ago, and then just as quickly ended several centuries later, when climate really started to warm up without significant, long-term reversals. Bison eat grass, along with other low-lying vegetation, in prairie, steppe, and even woodland habitats. The grasslands that eventually covered the Plains from Canada to Texas were especially conducive to large, migratory herds. With the extinction of other grazers and browsers, such as mammoth and mastodon, bison expanded into the largely uncontested niche of the emergent postglacial Plains. With established traditions of big-game hunting in place for at least 3,000 years, Plains communities of the early Holocene appear to have been poised for something even bigger.

Folsom Bison Hunters

You will remember that the Folsom discovery in the 1920s recounted in Chapter 2 shattered the Short Chronology of native North America. The archaeological record of Folsom history since that discovery has grown in leaps and bounds. Much of it, like the first find, reflects a lifestyle involving the dispatching of bison. And it was a lifestyle that persisted with variations for millennia. Shifts in resource orientation, movement, and alliance – many of them stimulated by climate change – are marked by subtle, but meaningful, variations in projectile point style.

Folsom points, like Clovis, are fluted and thus distinctive in form (Figure 5.4). In proportion to the total length of points, Folsom flutes are longer than those of Clovis. They are purportedly difficult to replicate (Waguespack 2012:93), apparently because the flute extends nearly the full length of the point. No matter the differences, archaeologists agree that Folsom technology descended from Clovis. Not only are they both fluted-point technologies, but other elements of the flaked stone industry (e.g., end scrapers, burins) of Clovis times persisted through Folsom times. The Folsom period is dated to 10,850–9950 BCE (Waguespack 2012:92–93), and thus coincides with the Younger Dryas.

As with Clovis, we know more about the kill sites than about the habitation sites of Folsom people, but in some cases the details of kill sites are remarkable. For instance, coupled with new field investigations, recent analysis of the Folsom type site assemblage by David Meltzer (2006) paints a vivid picture of bison hunting 12,000 years ago. The assemblage of bison bone at Folsom consists of 32 individuals. The age profile and condition of the remains suggest that this was a single kill event that took place most likely in the fall. Meltzer finds

Fig 5.4 A sample of Folsom points from the Folsom site. Found in 1926, the two broken points on the left were the first to be found; the two on the right were found after excavations were completed. Unlike the point found associated with the bison ribs (see Chapter 2, Figure 2.9), none of those in this figure was found *in situ*. Courtesy of David J. Meltzer.

5 cm

no evidence for habitation at the site, but instead is able to infer from the types of stone used that the hunters likely passed through present-day Colorado. The pattern of butchering at the site suggests that hunters removed both meat and bone from the kill site, presumably for transport back to sites of residence.

The location of kill sites depended perhaps more on the availability of natural features for trapping bison, such as the arroyos at Folsom or the Cooper site in Oklahoma (Bement 1999), than it did on proximity to residential sites. Other natural "traps" included parabolic sand dunes like those at the Caspar site in Wyoming (Frison 1974). Enhancements to natural features, such as wooden fences or corrals, improved hunting success and indicate an investment in facilities for long-term, repeated use. Eventually, as we will see later (Chapter 11), entire landscapes were engineered with cairns, drive lanes, and other facilities that may have alleviated the need to find suitable natural features for bison traps. Irrespective of facilities – natural or artificial – when a large number of bison were taken, Folsom hunters would relocate their entire communities to the source of meat and take advantage of the freezing winter for on-site storage, as they did at Agate Basin in Wyoming (Frison and Stanford 1982). The number of bison killed varied from site to site, with larger kills likely involving communal hunting parties, a practice that evidently increased over time (Figure 5.5). Folsom kill sites with the remains of the extinct species of bison (*Bison antiquus* and *Bison occidentalis*) usually contain fewer than 15 individuals (Waguespack 2012:93).

Definite evidence for Folsom habitation is rare. Three hard-packed areas at the Hanson site in the Bighorn Basin of central Wyoming may be the remnants of circular lodges (Frison and Bradley 1980). A diverse assemblage of animal bone (mountain sheep, deer, marmot, rabbit, as well as bison), along with plant remains, attests to subsistence activities beyond bison hunting. The multicomponent Lindenmeier site in Colorado is arguably the best example of a Folsom encampment, even without evidence for structures. The volume and variety of tools recovered from Lindenmeier bespeaks of activities other than hunting and butchering, notably hide processing (Wilmsen 1974). Arguably, limited evidence for habitation structures at Folsom sites is not unexpected of people who relocated frequently and traversed great distances between residences, and houses may well have been simple framed structures that were covered with bison hides.

Fig 5.5 Alfred Jacob Miller's artistic impression of bison hunting by horseback-riding Plains Indians, ca. 1858–1860. Although Miller is not likely to have witnessed this particular hunt and likely exaggerated its scale, the use of natural features like this cliff enabled hunters to take many bison at once. Wikimedia.

As with Clovis, Folsom tool assemblages contain raw materials from quarries hundreds of kilometers away. The range of settlement mobility was vast, no doubt in sync with equally vast bison migrations. But also important to Folsom communities was their connection to groups distributed widely across the Plains, and beyond. Folsom points are found at sites across the entire mid-section of the North American continent, from Texas to southern Canada, and from the Rockies to the Ozarks. Isolated Folsom points show up in places even farther afield, all the way to the Atlantic seaboard. Given that other populations coeval with Folsom occupied land outside the Plains, interactions between Folsom communities and their neighbors are not unexpected. Unfortunately, direct evidence for interactions eludes us. Sites with combinations of Folsom points and other, contemporaneous forms known from the East, such as Dalton (see below), have been documented on the eastern margins of the Plains (Wyckoff and Bartlett 1995), but we cannot be sure members of these respective populations met face to face. Given the rapidly changing landscape of Folsom times, it seems reasonable to assume that

Sidebar 5.2 Ethnicity and ecology: making difference work

In a classic piece of ethnographic research, Norwegian anthropologist Fredrik Barth (1969) documented the relationship between ecological and ethnic diversity in the Swat Valley of northwest Pakistan, on the fringe of the Himalayas. At the time of his fieldwork in the 1950s, the region was inhabited by three distinct ethnic groups: sedentary farmers known as Pathans, transhumant herders and part-time farmers known as Kohistanis, and nomadic herders known as the Gujar. Intensive farming was only possible in the lowlands of the valley, so Pathans occupied permanent villages at low elevation. Limits to their settlement were determined by the seasonal threshold of farming two crops a year (mostly corn and millet), which was determined mostly by elevation: the higher in elevation, the shorter the growing season. The Kohistanis, in contrast, were able to get by with a shorter growing season because they supplemented farming with herding (sheep, goats, cattle, water buffalo), and could thus occupy land at higher elevation. The scale of their operations was small compared with that of the Pathans, but transhumance gave them the edge in an environment for which the Pathans were ill-equipped. The third ethnic group in the region, the Gujar, moved between these two extremes, running herds in upland pastures of Kohistani territory and moving into lowlands of Pathan territory when snowfall precluded grazing.

It would thus appear that the Swat region accommodated ethnic diversity because each of the three groups occupied different habitats or different niches, much like species of plants and animals that co-occur in a given location. There was a time when anthropologists attributed all cultural diversity to ecological variations such as this, as in the Culture Area Concept championed in the USA by Alfred Kroeber (1939), among others. Barth's study, however, took this logic one step further. The history of interactions among ethnic groups of the Swat region has as much to do with shaping the contours of difference as it did with ecology. Through the mid-twentieth century the Kohistanis were repeatedly pushed northward (and upward) by the Pathan. Moving into higher elevations precluded intensive agriculture, but with the addition of herding they were able to maintain a modicum of autonomy, or at least did not have to be under the thumb of the Pathans. As for the Pathans,

their aggression against Kohistanis left them without a cheap source of farm labor, a niche that eventually was filled by free-ranging Gujars. When not working at lowland farms, Gujar herders took advantage of grazing land that was outside the reach of Kohistanis, who now divided their time between farming and herding. All seemed to fall into place, but not because each of these groups kept to themselves or had little history of interaction. Rather, the ethnic divisions among them had more to do with the consequences of interactions than with ecology.

Now, apply this same logic to the cultural diversity of late Pleistocene North America. We might expect, without even thinking, that the grassland adaptations of Folsom people arose and flourished apart from the deciduous woodlands adaptations of the Dalton people, or the boreal forests adaptations of Great Lakes communities, simply because they did not overlap. But of course these ecological zones were undergoing rapid change at this time, shifting in distribution and structure. And, of course, people, like the mobile prey they sought, moved as well, and not always in lockstep with shifting biomes. If we then look at the interface between grasslands and woodlands in the American heartland, for instance, we find not a sharp fixed boundary, but rather a crenulated, ever-changing one. Over the course of Folsom times, for instance, grasslands migrated eastward, as climate warmed. This was the moving front of the long grass prairie (recall from Chapter 1 the rainshadow effects of grassland ecology east of the Rockies), some of the most productive grassland in the world. As they interdigitated with the forests of the Eastern Woodlands, grasslands paved the way for bison migrations eastward and with them people. Contacts between Folsom people and their neighbors seem inevitable, and they may have taken any number of forms, including avoidance. But they could also have opened up possibilities for collaboration and symbiosis. Indeed, under such rapidly changing ecological conditions, diversification would have been beneficial. Thus, part of what we observe in the archaeological record of the Pleistocene–Holocene transition was the assertion and maintenance of ethnic diversity as an insurance plan against failure that pooled risk across a number of groups with different, yet complementary ecological niches.

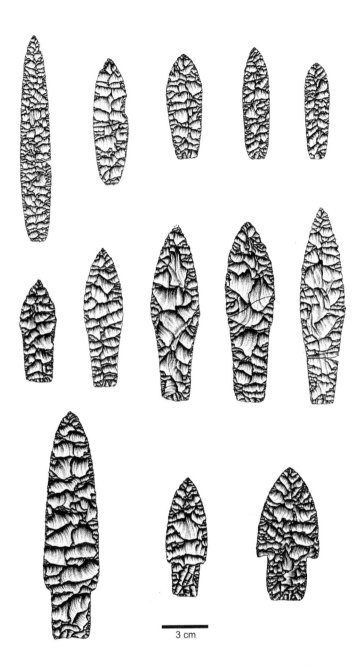

3 cm

Fig 5.6 Middle Paleoindian Plano point types from sites in the Great Plains of Wyoming. Top row: Agate Basin points from the Agate Basin site and vicinity; middle row: Hell Gap points from the Casper site; bottom row: Alberta points from the Hudson-Meng and Agate Basin sites. Images by Connie Robinson adapted from Kornfeld et al. 2010, figures 2.33–2.35. Used with permission of Marcel Kornfeld and George Frison.

encounters along time-transgressive fronts – like the Plains–Woodland border of the present-day Ozarks – were inevitable, even if infrequent.

Places like Lindenmeier show that Folsom communities returned repeatedly to preferred homes and bases. Places like this no doubt carried both the history of prior use for every group that occupied it, but perhaps also a sense of value or identity that connected people to places. We will see below with late Paleoindian traditions of the Eastern Woodlands that places clearly carried the weight of heritage for both the living, and the dead.

Plano Traditions

After about 12,000 years ago, as the Folsom tradition waned, a series of technological traditions involving unfluted lanceolate points appeared on the Great Plains as bison hunting continued within an overall milieu of growing cultural diversity (Figure 5.6). The Hell Gap site in eastern Wyoming encapsulates much of this diversity (Larson et al. 2009). In addition to artifacts of Clovis and Folsom affinity, assemblages from Hell Gap include examples of unfluted lanceolate type such as Agate Basin, Hell Gap, Alberta, Frederick, Lusk, Midland, and the Cody complex, all part of the widespread Plano tradition. Agate Basin and Hell Gap are the oldest among them, perhaps even overlapping with Folsom at the end of its time. The others fall more-or-less into sequence, with considerable overlap, although dates for certain varieties are not plentiful and stratified sequences like those of Hell Gap rare. The place apparently attracted people for millennia, and circular arrangements of postholes attest to tipi-like structures of presumably domestic purpose. By the early Holocene, residents of Hell Gap deposited the remains of a variety of game besides bison, plus small mammals, fish, birds, and berries.

Bison continued to be a significant, if not the main, source of food throughout Plano times. In fact, intensity of bison hunting would appear to have increased given the scale of some Plano bone beds. At the Olsen-Chubbuck site in Colorado,

Fig 5.7 The bony remains of a single kill event of almost 200 bison at the Olsen-Chubbuck site in Colorado was exposed in the late 1950s by Joe Ben Wheat. In this case, bison were driven into a dry gulch (arroyo), where most were butchered in place (Wheat 1972).

for instance, a single kill event involved nearly 200 bison (Figure 5.7). This Cody complex site was excavated in the late 1950s by Joe Ben Wheat (1972) of the University of Colorado. His work revealed a thick bed of bison bone stretching along about 50 m of the bottom of an old arroyo, or dry gulch. Based on the distribution and condition of the bone bed, Wheat was able to infer that the bison were stampeded into the arroyo from the north, where hunters were positioned upwind. As they dropped into the trap, the first bison were crushed by those that followed behind, leaving skeletons with contorted spines. So many bison were piled on top of one another that the hunters were either unable or unwilling to harvest the entire kill. A bottom layer of 13 bison went completely untouched, and an overlying layer of many more were only partially butchered. Still, an estimated 50,000 pounds of meat was taken from the kill, far more than could be consumed by a small band of people (<25) before it spoiled, even if half were converted to jerky and eaten over ensuing months. Given the demographic composition of the bison at Olsen-Chubbuck, an entire herd was driven into the gulch, and the presence of 16 newborn calves suggested that the kill took place in late May or early June. Later analysis of tooth eruption placed the kill in late summer or early fall (Kornfeld et al. 2010:243). Among the 27 projectile points in the bone bed were Scottsbluff and Eden types, both part of the Cody complex.

The kill at Olsen-Chubbuck portends the sort of cooperative or communal hunting that would later become an institution of certain Plains societies. Given its relatively early timing in the year, this particular event may not have been in preparation for winter but instead a gathering of people for social reasons, when grasslands flourished and bison began to aggregate into herds numbering in the thousands by late summer. Other Cody complex kills provide better glimpses into winter preparation. The Horner site in Wyoming (Todd 1983), for instance, is a late fall or early winter kill of about 70 bison in a shallow gulch. A wooden corral may have been emplaced above the gulch to facilitate the drive. A similar facility is suggested for the Hell Gap-age Jones-Miller site in Colorado (Stanford 1978). Storage in winter was made simple by freezing temperatures.

Climate clearly affected the distribution and productivity of grasslands in the Plains and with it the size and health of bison herds. Worsening climate also affected the size of bison themselves. A well-documented trend toward smaller bison in the mid-Holocene – thought by some researchers to register the effects of overexploitation – is now firmly tied to decreased precipitation after about 8,000 years ago (Hill et al. 2008). This change effectively marked the end of the Plano period on the Plains, and a time of increased diversity in diet, technology, and lifestyle. The postglacial trend of warmer climate had reached its apogee at about this time, challenging human populations that were used to cold weather to find alternatives locally, or to move farther north.

Terra Nova

In June 2013, Alaska was experiencing a heatwave, with highs in the mid-80s across most of the state and skies so sunny (and 18 hours long) that people were advised by the media to use sunscreen. The extreme conditions of those particular days is a microcosm of days yet to come, according to climate scientists. The most obvious consequence for the Arctic is melting ice, along with melting permafrost, which is more-or-less permanently frozen soil (Figure 5.8). Alaska and arctic Canada have plenty of both, but they are receding in many

Fig 5.8 Melting permafrost leads to mass wasting of the coastline of Alaska. Wikimedia.

locations, giving way to new land, much as happened at a rapid pace at the end of the Ice Age. But with gains of inhabitable land that were formerly covered by ice comes loss of land that is structurally dependent on ice. Coastal Alaska is especially vulnerable to land loss because many villages depend on frozen soil and ice to blunt the erosion of rivers and the sea. And even in places where land is neither lost nor gained over time, sustaining human settlement will be difficult because of melting snow and ice. For instance, the Sacramento and San Joaquin valleys of California, which supply a large fraction of America's table vegetables, are increasingly short of water in the late summer because snow in the adjacent Sierra Nevada mountains (which supplies water to the valleys) melts too quickly in the spring.

In late glacial times along the northern Plains a rapidly changing landscape of glacial lakes and meltwater streams in open spruce parkland was fronted to the north by a receding ice sheet. Surface finds of Clovis points in the southern part of this region attest to parties moving into the emerging new terrain as it became available. Descendant fluted-point traditions known in the region as Gainey and Barnes, along with Folsom, involved expansion of people farther north over time, seemingly in lockstep with emerging new land. The absence of evidence for long-term habitation in the region may be testimony to the transient nature of this rapidly changing landscape or a consequence of harsh preservation conditions. As the deciduous forests to the south migrated northward to replace pine, which in turn replaced

Sidebar 5.3 America's latest climate refugees?

In May 2013 *The Guardian* newspaper published an in-depth feature on the challenge of climate change for residents of Newtok, Alaska. Their town is disappearing in the Bering Sea, expected to be completely under water soon. Mostly native Alaskans, the people of Newtok were dubbed "America's First Climate Refugees" by *The Guardian*, although the problem goes far beyond Newtok. More than 180 other Alaskan villages are under threat of flooding and erosion. Countless other coastal communities in the ancient past experienced similar futures.

The Ninglick River that flows past Newtok on either side of the peninsula on which it sits is eating away at the shoreline by as much as 100 feet/year, a rate that has accelerated with melting permafrost and diminished sea ice protection. A study by the US Army Corps of Engineers concluded that seawalls or other protective measures would not mitigate the impact of global warming, and thus the residents must plan for relocation.

The villagers selected a new site about 9 miles (16 km) away, at higher elevation. Relocating the town is estimated to cost about $130 million, but the relocation efforts of its ~350 residents are barely underway thanks to internal politics and uncertainty about government funding. As of 2019 a community center and several houses have been constructed at the new town of Mertarvick. Complete abandonment of Newtok is expected by 2023.

spruce parkland to the north, conditions grew better for sustained settlement. By 10,000 years ago tall-grass prairie expanded across present-day Iowa and Minnesota, accommodating the eastward spread of bison and the Plano-related communities that targeted bison (Gibbon 2012:330–331). Groups adapted to either deciduous forests or boreal forests were thus interdigitated, at times, by Plains communities.

The situation in the Northeast was similar, although here mountains had a large role in the spread of postglacial vegetation. At the Late Glacial Maximum of ~20,000 years ago, New England was under a mile-thick glacier (the southern reach of the Laurentide Ice Sheet). Tundra vegetation persisted until about 14,000 years ago in southern New England, and another two millennia in northern New England and southeast Canada. As the glacier receded after Clovis times, spruce forests colonized newly opened terrain, followed by jack pine, white pine, and hemlock. Deciduous forests began to gain a foothold after about 9,500 years ago, but mostly in lowland terrain, while higher elevations continued to be dominated by conifers. This differentiation between lowland and upland sites persisted through the middle Holocene, with beech eventually becoming abundant in the uplands.

The land between New England and the northern Plains is dominated today by the Great Lakes. As we discussed in Chapter 1, postglacial lakes in North America were often much larger than they are today. You may recall that Lake Winnipeg in central Canada was the former Lake Agassiz, which held more water when it formed at the end of the Ice Age than is contained in all the world's lakes today. Or recall that Lake Bonneville of the Great Basin was several times larger than its modern counterpart, Great Salt Lake, before it was partially drained about 14,500 years ago when it overflowed a natural dam. In the case of some of the Great Lakes, natural dams and isostatic rebound kept water from completely filling the deep basins formed by glacial scouring. Thus, some of the lakeside terrain emerging from receding ice was only later flooded, well after humans colonized it. As we will see shortly, now-submerged land of Lake Huron was targeted by hunters who followed their Plains neighbors in engineering a landscape to enhance hunting success.

The game of choice for Paleoindian hunters of the receding glacial front was caribou (*Rangifer* spp.). A variety of species and subspecies of this large ungulate can be divided into barren-ground caribou, which inhabit tundra, and woodland caribou, which inhabit boreal forest (Figure 5.9). Both are migratory, although certain subspecies of woodland caribou do not migrate far and form relatively small aggregate populations. Other woodland species and the barren-ground caribou, however, form large herds for lengthy migrations to feeding grounds in summer and winter. Like other communities of animals and the plants on which they depended, caribou of distinct ecological niches adjusted to time-transgression climate changes with changes in the scale, direction, and timing of seasonal moves. Humans must have been challenged to stay abreast of the changes.

The fluted-point traditions of the Northeast and Great Lakes regions attest to a continuing commitment to large-scale, communal hunts. The Bull Brook site in Massachusetts is perhaps the best example of a large aggregation site of Paleoindian age. Consisting of 36 discrete clusters of more than 40,000 artifacts arranged in an oval measuring 170 by 135 m, Bull Brook was salvaged from destruction in the 1950s by private citizens. For decades thereafter archaeologists debated whether Bull Brook was the result of a single, large-scale aggregation of people, or the amalgam of multiple, small-scale occupations by small groups. Recent study of the collection and records (thankfully donated to the Peabody Essex Museum in Salem) by Brian Robinson and colleagues (2009) makes a very convincing case for large-scale aggregation.

Fig 5.9 Barren-ground caribou (*Rangifer tarandus groenlandicus*) of Alaska. Wikimedia.

Bull Brook goes beyond the evidence for hunting to show us something about the social workings of cooperation (Figure 5.10). Robinson and colleagues (2009) interpret the site as the staging ground for communal caribou hunting. Ninety-five percent of the stone artifacts from Bull Brook come from sources at least 200 to 450 km away, and from multiple directions. The pattern of cluster distribution is decidedly oval, with differences among clusters indicative of specialized spaces and activities. Most notably, clusters dominated by bifaces are concentrated in the south and inner part of the oval, and clusters dominated by scrapers encircle the entire oval around its outside perimeter. The biface production activities presumably relate to hunting preparation, and the scrapers, used in hide working, are the residues of domestic activities, perhaps gearing up for the winter with hides essential for both clothing and housing. The artifact and activity patterns may reflect gender differences, based on analogues with arctic cultures (Robinson et al. 2009:440). Especially noteworthy is the concentration of flakes of fluting in the central area of the oval, suggesting that this signature step in the production of fluted points was ritualized, perhaps part of hunting magic.

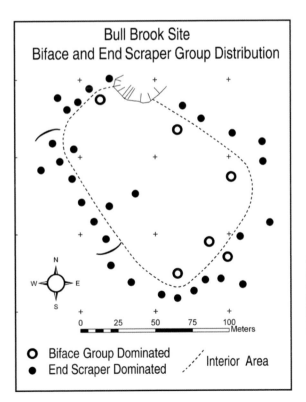

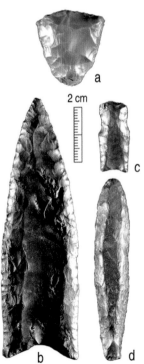

Fig 5.10 Clusters of fluted points, end scrapers, and other tools at the Bull Brook site north of Boston, Massachusetts are arrayed in an oval area the size of two football fields. Brian Robinson interprets this site as a highly structured aggregation settlement, possibly associated with a fall/winter caribou hunt (Robinson et al. 2009).

The Bull Brook site is indicative of the first of a series of post-Clovis fluted-point phases in the greater Northeast (Curran 1999; Ellis and Deller 1997), estimated to date to 10,950–10,550 BCE, right on the heels of Clovis and coeval with the Younger Dryas. By the later end of the Younger Dryas, continental glaciers had receded enough to open up much of the Northeast, and Bull Brook was some 300 km south of the boundary separating receding tundra from expanding forests. Sea level was still down at 55 m lower than present, exposing land now inundated, but meltwater had filled the St. Lawrence Basin and what would eventually become the Great Lakes, making present-day New England and southeast Canada a massive peninsula, much like an inverted Florida, but in this case with a wall of ice to the northwest. This must have been an extremely dynamic environment, with ice, land, water, and migratory herds in a perpetual state of change.

Bull Brook may be the best example of a regional gathering of cooperative hunters and their families in the New England area, but other northern sites likewise attest to large-scale occupation by Paleoindian communities. These include DEDIC/Sugarloaf in Massachusetts (Chilton et al. 2005); Vail in Maine (Gramly 1982); Udora (Storck and Spiess 1994), Parkhill (Ellis and Deller 2000), and Fisher (Storck 1997) in Ontario; Nobles Pond in Ohio (Seeman 1994); and Debert in Nova Scotia (MacDonald 1968), the northeasterly-most fluted-point site in North America. These sites include at least 8 (Vail) and as many as 36 (Debert) artifact clusters indicative of households or similar coresidential units. Bull Brook shows better than any that many such units aggregated, and when they did their encampments were highly structured, thus planned. Ellis and Deller (2000) venture that some of these large sites were used only once or twice, and not over many generations. Ironically, as big and as structured as they were, these were not long-term settlements. This perhaps was the nature of a rapidly changing landscape, but it nonetheless attests to an advanced level of social integration among otherwise dispersed and mobile communities.

Part of the record of northern hunters is now inundated by the waters of modern lakes and seas. For instance, deep beneath the waters of Lake Huron is a now-submerged causeway that linked central Ontario with northern Michigan during the late Pleistocene and early Holocene. Between about 9550 and 6050 BCE, lake levels were as much as 100 m below the present level of about ~176 m amsl. Scientists at the University of Michigan have deployed side-scan sonar and remotely operated underwater vehicles to map archaeological evidence for the use of the causeway for caribou hunting (O'Shea and Meadows 2009). They have found remarkable evidence for rock alignments reminiscent of caribou drive lanes used in the historic era in Canada (Figure 5.11). The alignments follow the contours of the now-flooded surface, taking advantage of valleys and slopes that

Fig 5.11 A now submerged causeway on the floor of Lake Huron (top) was a migration route of caribou that was modified by early hunters to create drive lanes like the ones seen from the air (middle) and on the ground (bottom) at Victoria Island in northern Canada. Lake Huron map courtesy of John O'Shea. Photos of Victoria Island drive lanes courtesy of Jack W. Brink.

would have guided caribou migration. Clusters of especially large boulders are interpreted by John O'Shea and colleagues (2014) as possible hunting blinds. Other signals in the sonar data are thought to represent some sort of hunting structure, one quite large, although it seems unlikely that this location would have supported large groups of people for extended periods of time, given, that is, the unfavorable conditions of winter. O'Shea and colleagues (2014) conclude that only small, transient hunting parties were involved, although clearly a great deal of effort was expended in fabricating the infrastructure of driving caribou, thus the location must have been, or at least intended to have been, used repeatedly over an extended period.

Our knowledge of northern fluted-point and Plano traditions beyond the hunting of caribou is limited, but burials and artifact caches provide a small glimpse into ritual life. The oldest-known human burial in the Great Lakes region is a cremation of an adolescent male at the Renier site in northern Wisconsin (Mason and Irwin 1960). Burned with the corpse were 10 Plano points made from a raw material from southwest Wisconsin. Somewhat later examples of burned biface caches (but lacking bone) in the region include Pope in east-central Wisconsin (Ritzenthaler 1972), Deadman Slough in northwestern Wisconsin (Meinholz and Kuehn 1996), and Gorto in the Upper Peninsula of Michigan (Buckmaster and Paquette 1988). An earlier example is suggested at the Crowfield site near London, Ontario (Deller and Ellis 1984), where some 4,500 burned fragments from an estimated 182+ tools include parts of 30 fluted points (Figure 5.12). The 1.5 m in diameter, 20 cm deep cluster of fragments at Crowfield most likely came from a cremation pit (Deller et al. 2009). As we will now see with developments of late Paleoindian societies of the Mississippi River valley to the south, cemeteries, caches, and elaborate material culture appear to have played a key role in establishing the boundaries and alliances of ever-shifting communities of the postglacial era.

Rivers and Forests

The American Southeast was not covered in ice when humans arrived in the late Pleistocene, but parts of it were substantially different than they are today. For example, boreal spruce forests like those of central

0cm   5cm

Fig 5.12 Some of the heat-fractured fluted points from the Crowfield site west of London, Ontario. Two specimens at the lower right are preforms. Courtesy of Christopher J. Ellis and D. Brian Deller.

Canada existed as far south as Memphis, Tennessee when people first arrived. Climate was actually quite variable across the region during the waning centuries of the Ice Age, making it hard to generalize beyond a given locality. The Younger Dryas, in fact, may have only dampened, but not suspended, environmental changes already afoot. Still, by the end of this multicentury reversal, when warming climate ensued without major interruption, the Southeast underwent rapid transitions in forest cover, rainfall patterns, river dynamics, and sea level. The Southeast was perhaps never a bad place to make a living, but by the time the Holocene came around, after 11,500 years ago (cal BP), it was becoming even more livable for all manner of plants, animals, and people. Rivers and deciduous forests were key assets.

Although parts of the Southeast may have been relatively invulnerable to changes attending the Younger Dryas of 10,850–9550 BCE (12,800–11,500 cal BP), major portions of the region apparently saw declining populations in the first few centuries of the interval (Anderson et al. 2011). Of course, radiocarbon assays for fluted-point finds in the Southeast are insufficient to indicate when Clovis began and ended in the region (see Chapter 4), while a variety of other fluted-point types, such as Cumberland and Redstone, are known for parts of the region, but are just as poorly dated as Clovis.

What appears to be a retrenchment of growing population from ~10,850 to 10,450 BCE (12,800–12,400 cal BP) may be merely a blind spot in our archaeological visibility. When the record of occupation again becomes evident, after about 12,500 years ago (cal BP), the Southeast was home to the most pervasive archaeological culture since Clovis. Known today as *Dalton*, this Central Mississippi River valley tradition would eventually spread across the region from Missouri to Texas and from Virginia to north Florida, essentially across the entire Southeast. Once thought to coincide with the first millennium of the Holocene, Dalton culture actually dates to the last two-thirds of the Younger Dryas, ~10,500–9550 BCE (Goodyear 1982). It overlaps with and is succeeded by a series of related cultures sharing side- and corner-notched biface technology. Clovis, Dalton, and the notched-point traditions used the same unifacial technology, notably formal end scrapers, presumably hide-working tools. The technological affinity to Clovis seems obvious, but these later traditions in the Southeast in fact entail a number of cultural innovations. Attending many cultural developments were changes in rivers, wetlands, and deciduous forests that improved the availability of plants and animals of value to humans. We will first take a look at what makes something uniquely Dalton, and then follow with a brief look at the side- and corner-notched traditions.

Dalton

Distinctive land-use practices, mortuary ritual, and stone tool technology separate Dalton from what came before. Starting with hafted bifaces, we see in Dalton the first sustained use of a resharpening technique that often left a beveled cross-section and occasionally serrations, like a steak knife. Clovis and its affines were resharpened from the tip down, evidently maintaining the penetration function of the point in its use as a projectile. Many, perhaps most, Dalton points were drafted into projectile uses too, but the pattern of lateral resharpening shows an emphasis on cutting, not penetration. No matter the function, Dalton points must have been hafted to a handle or shaft that was sufficiently long and heavy to make it difficult to resharpen the edges of tools bifacially. To keep an edge symmetrical in cross-section one has to remove flakes from both sides of a biface. An unhafted tool can be flipped end over end to achieve this effect, but a hafted tool with the handle turned away from the user is awkward to re-edge for lack of grip. The solution, for Dalton tool users, was to rotate the hafted tool around the long axis of the handle (and biface), resulting in an asymmetrical, beveled cross-section (Figure 5.13). Further evidence for this resharpening technique can be seen in the "shoulders" of Dalton points, the point above which

Fig 5.13 Dalton points from the Brand site in Arkansas in various stages of reduction. Top row: preform stage; second row: initial stage; third row: advanced stage; bottom row: final stage (Goodyear 1974:27).

5 cm

blades were exposed outside the handle and thus subject to retouch while hafted. The result is a distinctive sort of biface, one that has affinity to the basal thinning and shape of a likely Clovis ancestor, but novel elements, like lateral resharpening, beveled cross-sections, and shoulders. Incidentally, archaeologist Sam McGahey (1996) notes that the orientation of beveling varies with the handedness of the tool user. Not only is he able to detect right- and left-handed users, and verify the numerical dominance of the former, but he can also infer possible home ranges of communities with different proportions of right- and left-handed tool users.

Some have argued that bevels were added to make points spin in flight (e.g., Lipo et al. 2012), and if so, beveling was an addition to existing lanceolate projectile technology. However, lateral retouch on Dalton points sometimes goes to extremes, producing narrow needle-like points that some classify today as "drills." Such drills certainly were not suited to flight. So, rather than assign a singular or specialized function to all Dalton "points," we might consider instead that the technology was designed to serve multiple functions (points, knives, drills) as it was systematically re-edged along lateral margins, with each stage along the way providing rather specific use options. It was a sophisticated technology that continued to depend on high-quality raw material, as Clovis did, but with patterns of toolstone procurement that suggest that land-use patterns had become restricted to subregions (Koldehoff and Walthall 2004), making the deployment of technology more predictable and strategic. As we will see shortly, bifaces had value to Dalton people, perhaps much like Clovis, that went beyond the logistics of hunting.

Continuing with Dalton in the tradition of Clovis is the uniface technology that includes formalized hafted end scrapers, among other types. Again, the formalized components of unifacial technology reveal more than a need for hide scraping. They were "overdesigned," so to speak, for the mass production of hides, largely to prepare for freezing winters. The need for tailored winter clothing – which we see in the bone needles of Paleoindian toolkits – must have been accentuated during the Younger Dryas (Osborn 2014). It stands to reason, as well, that overwintering continued to be a challenge in the early Holocene with increases in latitude and altitude. Indeed, the formalized end scraper technology of Clovis derivation persisted latest (~6550 BCE) in the north and along the Appalachian Mountains.

The technology would not appear again in any significant fashion in the Southeast until the eighteenth-century Chickasaw repurposed it for the deer skin trade (Johnson 1997).

Early Dalton people may have encountered a few laggards of Ice Age extinction, and they likely encountered bison, elk, and perhaps woodland caribou occasionally. But the Dalton tradition spans the later end of the Younger Dryas, well after its abrupt onset and mass extinctions. By this time the Central Mississippi River valley supported oak-hickory forest, habitat conducive to the propagation of white-tailed deer (*Odocoileus virginianus*). Dalton is known to archaeologists as a deer-hunting tradition, not because they did not take animals besides deer, for they did (Walker 2007), but because the biface and uniface technology and land-use practices of Dalton communities conform to the ecology and geography of white-tailed deer. Unlike bison and caribou, white-tailed deer do not aggregate in large herds and migrate between seasonal feeding grounds. Sure, they move about their range and aggregate in small groups in winter, especially to the north, but they do not cover the geography of their distant ungulate cousins. Put simply, deer hunters and their families did not have to relocate as often as bison and caribou hunters did, at least not to hunt. Bear in mind that white-tailed deer existed in North America long before the end of the Ice Age, and were able to adapt to boreal forests of the time, as they do today in Canada, where they are quite large. Taking bison, caribou, and even mammoth over white-tailed deer was therefore sometimes a matter of choice, as well as availability, and it required a different strategy of hunting, and different tools (Goodyear 1974). Once deciduous forests began to expand up the Mississippi River valley in the late Pleistocene, deer habitat grew and with it a greater human reliance on this smaller but less-risky game. Oak forests provided for deer not only cover from predators but sources of acorns for fall forage. Where forests met river courses along terraces and floodplains, conditions for the propagation of white-tailed deer could not have been better.

Watercraft for traveling along rivers and streams are not known for Dalton times, but components of woodworking technology hint at the use of dug-out canoes. Dalton adzes are perhaps the oldest flaked stone woodworking tools in North America, and are especially prevalent at sites in the Central Mississippi Valley. Microscopic charcoal in the bits of some Dalton adzes may have gotten embedded from chopping at the charred wood of logs that were hollowed out by fire for making canoes (Yerkes and Gaertner 1997), just as ethnohistoric canoe-makers in the region did. Dalton adzes may have just as often been used for constructing houses and related domestic facilities. Unfortunately, like the canoes, Dalton houses have never been found.

Other aspects of Dalton culture point to a number of changes besides flaked stone technology that signal a break from Clovis. For instance, Brad Koldehoff and John Walthall (2004) document a southerly shift from Clovis to Dalton in the orientation and scale of toolstone displacement in the Mississippi Valley, suggesting a realignment of regional populations in an overall regime of shrinking settlement range. Koldehoff and Walthall view this shift as the "settling in" of Dalton people into more-or-less fixed ranges. At the same time we find the first use of caves and rockshelters in the region (Walthall 1998). The basal components of cave and rockshelter layers in the Ozarks (e.g., Rodgers Shelter) and parts of the Midsouth (e.g., Stanfield Worley) contain Dalton assemblages, but never Clovis points (Figure 5.14). Walthall (1998) attributes this emergent new practice to fall deer hunting, although thanks to the heightened preservation of organic matter in caves and shelters, we know that Dalton people deposited the bones of animals besides deer, as well as plants. At Dust Cave in Alabama, for instance, Dalton occupants regularly took migratory waterfowl (Walker 2007).

Fig 5.14 Russell Cave in Alabama is one of many caves and rockshelters that contain deeply stratified archaeological deposits (https://www.nps.gov/ruca/index.htm) with Dalton-period components at the base. Carol M. Highsmith photo/Wikimedia.

Use of caves and rockshelters by Dalton communities takes us well outside the Central Mississippi Valley. By the late Younger Dryas, Dalton, as a distinctive biface tradition, spread across most of the Southeast, where different nomenclature is used to describe local variations: Colbert, Greenbrier, Hardaway, Nuckells, and San Patrice. Dalton points and affines show up occasionally in the Northeast and upper Midwest, but they are rare, as they are in peninsular Florida. Still, the expanse of Dalton in the Southeast and lower Midwest is vast, exceeded by only Clovis. And although land-use changes from Clovis to Dalton times are poorly known outside the Central Mississippi Valley, we might expect circumscription of groups either within segments of river valleys or in territories that crosscut valleys within physiographic provinces. The subregional diversity of Dalton-like points alludes to a growing "territoriality" or similar sociogeographic distinctions.

If the land-use patterns of Dalton groups signify an emerging territorialism, then the Central Mississippi Valley was the mother of all territories. It was in this region that the oldest cemetery in North America was established at the Sloan site. Excavated by Dan Morse in 1974, Sloan in northeast Arkansas consisted of 29 clusters of more than 430 Dalton artifacts in an area about 12 x 12 m in plan (Morse 1997). The artifacts included a full range of Dalton flaked-stone tools: points, biface preforms, scrapers, and adzes, along with hammers, abraders, cobble tools, and a few lumps of hematite. These are the same sorts of items one might find at any Dalton site, but at Sloan they were associated with more than 200 bone fragments. Preservation was poor, making it difficult to identify the bone, but most were classified as "unquestionably human," and none was identified definitely as nonhuman. The clusters of artifacts and bone are interpreted by Morse as human burials, an estimated 28–30 individuals, young and old alike.

Although most of the artifacts from Sloan may not have been made for burial with the deceased, most were in pristine condition, with unused or freshly resharpened edges (Yerkes and Gaertner 1997:69–71). Moreover, more than two dozen of the 146 Dalton points from the site were far bigger than the others, apparently made and deposited for expressly ritual purposes (Figure 5.15). Classified as "Large Daltons" by Morse (1997:17–18), these hypertrophic forms occasionally assume extreme proportions. All but two from Sloan were made

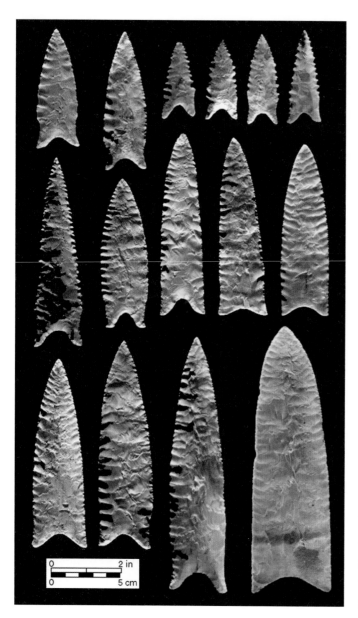

Fig 5.15 Dalton points from the Sloan mortuary site in Arkansas. (Sassaman 2010:100, with images provided courtesy of Dan Morse and Bruce Bradley).

from nonlocal raw material, and only a few showed signs of use. Similarly large varieties of Dalton points – sometimes referred to as "Sloan Daltons" – have been found at more than 30 other sites in the Central Mississippi Valley. Measuring up to 38 cm long, oversized Daltons are often cached together; at least six caches of up to nine points each have been documented in the southern half of the region (Walthall and Koldehoff 1998:260). Oversized Daltons were not routinely broken or burned in these caches, nor at Sloan, which contrasts with the destruction of ritual bifaces among late Paleoindian traditions of the north (e.g., at Crowfield [Deller and Ellis 1984]).

Do cemeteries like Sloan necessarily signal a measure of territoriality, as Charles and Buikstra (1983) suggested for later, mound-building people, or do they instead signal a means to integrate people who were distributed across many "territories"? The distribution of oversized Dalton points would suggest the latter. These items were displaced far from sources of raw material, suggesting that individuals traveled far outside habitual use areas to acquire "exotic" stones, or that they at least passed such items along routes of travel, notably the Mississippi River. Described by Walthall and Koldehoff as the "Cult of the Long Blade," regional interaction in Dalton times may have served the need to reduce the risks of rapidly changing environments, uniting dispersed groups through shared ritual, but ultimately enabling people to move across "territories" in times of need, perhaps even facilitating marriages of individuals from widely separated communities. If so, we should not expect, necessarily, that the individuals interred at Sloan were born and raised in the local area. Increasingly, archaeologists are finding that early cemeteries in the Southeast contain both local and nonlocal people (e.g., Quinn et al. 2008). Thus, rather than thinking of cemeteries as the territorial markers of distinct communities, they instead seem to have served as places of gathering for diverse people, or perhaps the locus of ritual for networks spanning vast areas. It is worth noting that the Sloan site is located on a relict Pleistocene dune, distant from any known Dalton encampment.

Places of gathering may have been needed to maintain sufficient social connections during times of small populations and rapid change. As described by David Anderson:

Such gatherings are assumed to have continued to occur throughout all of later prehistory in the region, at least until people began to live in larger, permanent communities. These aggregation events would have been critical for forming and maintaining social and kinship/mating networks, exchanging information about resources and conditions over large areas (including the locations of other people), and reinforcing social ties through feasting, ceremony and ritual, perhaps incorporating specialized crafting, such as the manufacture and caching of challenging stone implements.

(Anderson and Sassaman 2012:52)

We may thus be witnessing in the late Pleistocene of the Central Mississippi Valley the appearance of interaction networks that defined the contours of cultural identity and affiliation. And this may not have been restricted to populations that shared broadly similar technologies and economies; indeed, the practical value in establishing ties to others is to diversify one's portfolio, to offset the risk of failure with alternatives to standard practice. It follows that Dalton appears so distinctive to us not because it was isolated from its counterparts to the west and north, but because difference was asserted in order to render unambiguous the relationships of people spread out over half a continent.

Side- and Corner-Notched Traditions

A few centuries before Dalton disappeared from the landscape, at the beginning of the Holocene some 11,500 years ago (9550 BCE), tool makers in the Southeast introduced the innovation of notching the basal margins of bifaces to enable more robust hafting of points to handles or foreshafts. The tradition of lateral resharpening seen in Dalton continued in what can be glossed as the Side-Notched and Corner-Notched traditions of the Eastern Woodlands (Figure 5.16). Side-notching is the older of the traditions, beginning as early as 8850 BCE (Sherwood et al. 2004). A variety of type names have been used to account for subregional variants of side-notched (e.g., Big Sandy, Kessel, Bolen, Taylor, Hardaway) and corner-notched (e.g., Kirk, Palmer, Charleston, Stillwell) forms, a measure perhaps of increased cultural diversity over Dalton. Despite the diversity, the side- and

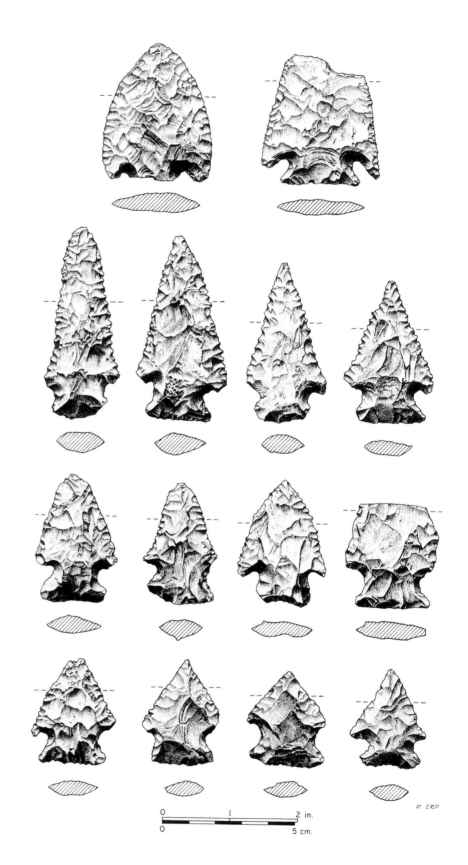

Fig 5.16 Kirk Corner-Notched biface in various stages of resharpening from the Lewis-East site in South Carolina. Darby Erd drawing (Sassaman et al. 2002:48).

corner-notched traditions share a common technological repertoire with roots in the Dalton bifacial and unifacial toolkits. Like Dalton, these related traditions maintained a diverse diet that included the hunting of white-tailed deer within generally temperate forest conditions. Collectively they extend beyond the reach of Dalton to include the Mid-Atlantic, Northeast, and upper Midwest, as well as peninsular Florida. Bear in mind that the coastal record of these early Holocene traditions, like those that came before, is now inundated along the Gulf and much of the Atlantic coast, as well as now-infilled lakes and wetlands.

Many of the same cave and rockshelter sites with Dalton components at the bottom have overlying strata containing side- and corner-notched points. These contexts have been key to providing a glimpse into the organic aspects of early Holocene life, notably food remains, and they have been incredibly valuable in establishing the sequence of cultural changes. We can add to these sites the many deeply stratified alluvial sites of the Southeast, Midwest, and Northeast (e.g., Icehouse Bottom, St. Albans, Doershuk, Big Eddy, Neville) that provide good contexts for the relative order of changes. Emphasis on the big riverine and cave sites has biased our perception of early Holocene land-use, which evidently diversified with time, as climate ameliorated and vegetation zones assumed more-or-less modern configuration.

Much recent research on the notched-point traditions has turned on analyses of stylistic and technological variations in tool design and the integration of assemblage data into models of regional settlement organization. The former approach aims to reconstruct the boundaries of habitual use areas or territories, which are believed to have shrunk over time as population grew and "settled in" to particular areas. Independent work by Kara Bridgman Sweeney (2013) and David Thulman (2006) attests to ranges among users of side-notched points that extend across a number of drainages and interfluves of the lower Southeast. At this time, at least three ranges encompassed present-day South Carolina, Georgia, and Florida, with a major boundary between the Atlantic and Gulf-draining river valleys, diagonally cutting through south Georgia. Raw material preferences appear to map on to these ranges, although the marine cherts of the South Atlantic Slope are not as readily distinguished as raw material to the north and west. That side-notched groups shared a broad repertoire of stone technology speaks to not only common ancestry but sustained inter-action among them. The gathering places of Dalton times are not evident in the record of early Holocene living, nor are there as many items of obvious ritual significance as seen in Dalton.

A more detailed reconstruction of land-use for the Kirk Corner-Notched horizon of the South Atlantic Slope was proffered by David Anderson and Glen Hanson (1988) from their work in the Savannah River valley of Georgia and South Carolina (Figure 5.17). The valley crosscuts three physiographic provinces: the Appalachians, Piedmont, and Coastal Plain. Reconciling the differences in Kirk tool assemblages across these provinces, Anderson and Hanson proposed that bands of people moved with the seasons – from cold-weather settlements in the upcountry to warm-season settlement in the lowcountry, includ-ing presumably the coast – to take advantage of food resources as they became available. It was during autumn, they surmised, that groups

Fig 5.17 Model of Early Archaic regional settlement ranges in the South Atlantic Slope (left) and seasonal settlement organization in the Savannah River valley of Georgia and South Carolina (right) (Anderson and Hanson 1988).

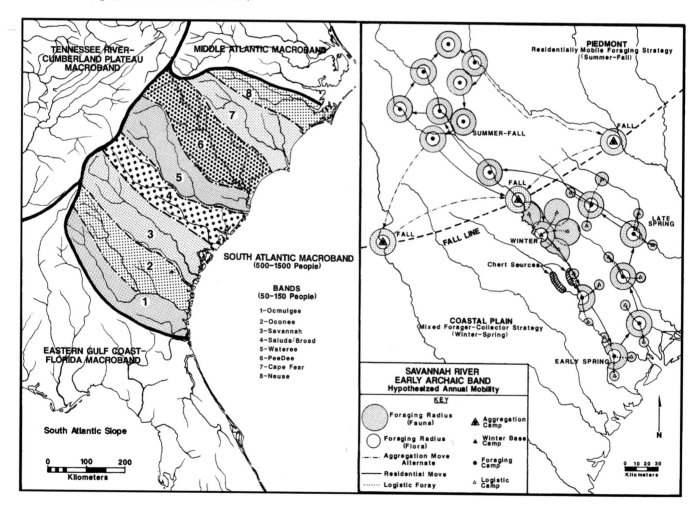

aggregated in the Fall Zone between the up- and lowcountry, places not only of marked ecological diversity but conducive to cross-river movements because of the "falls" or shoals of its unique physiography. Thus, Anderson and Hanson model both the organizational structure of annual mobility, as well as the means by which groups in separate ranges (drainages) interacted. Alternatively, Daniel (1998) interprets the same data to suggest that the annual ranges of bands crosscut river valleys, centering their "territories" not on drainages but rather on sources of high-quality toolstone. This lithic-centric perspective is a reasonable alternative, but it fails to take into account variables other than toolstone procurement.

The early Holocene record of settlement in the Southeast consists of a larger number of artifacts and sites than is known from before, and arguably a better sense of the structure and organization of regional settlement. However, again, it is truncated geographically by seas, lakes, and wetlands that rose and filled at the end of the Ice Age at a rate that has since been unmatched. We now take up the challenge of summarizing this waterworld of rapid change.

Water Rising

Among the more dramatic environmental changes of the Pleistocene–Holocene transition was rise in sea level. Since the Late Glacial Maximum of ~22,000 years ago, sea level has risen ~120 m. Much of this occurred in the first several centuries of documented human presence in North America (ca. 12,000–11,000 BCE), and by Clovis times (11,000 BCE), sea level had risen ~60 m. Another 20 m of water would be added over the ensuing millennium. Myriad other inputs of water enhanced increasingly wetter conditions across much of the continent. The warming of postglacial North America resulted in major reconfigurations in the distribution and flow of both surface water and groundwater, and with them changes in the distribution and integration of people.

Of course, sea-level change was hardly uniform across the continent, let alone the globe. *Relative* sea-level change is the more effective measure, as it takes into account the elevation of water relative to land. In places where land rises along with water, rising water is less consequential than in places where land is either stable or actually subsiding.

Several forces explain uplift of land – from volcanic activity to deltaic aggradation – but common across the glaciated portions of North America was the force of isostatic rebound: literally the rebounding of land that had been depressed by the weight of glacial ice. Sites in Alaska and the Northeast register the outpacing of water by rebounding land, which, when combined with sediment build-up from coastal erosion, can actually prograde land seaward (e.g., Cape Espenberg; Darwent et al. 2013). Rebound can affect shorelines far from glaciated terrain, but generally the farther south we go the less countervailing forces outpace rising water. For instance, the likely summer feeding grounds for caribou that were hunted by residents of Bull Brook in Massachusetts 11,000 years ago are now under ~50 m of water (Robinson et al. 2009).

Of all the coastlines of North America, none has lost more inhabitable land since the Ice Age than the Gulf coast of the Southeast, and more specifically the Gulf coast of Florida (Figure 5.18). During Clovis

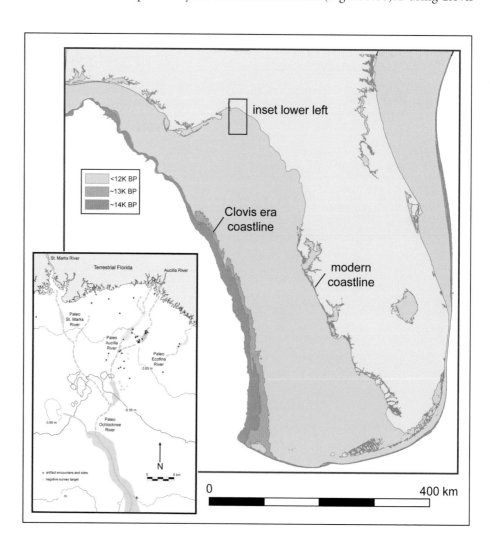

Fig 5.18 Gulf coastal sites predating ca. 4,500 years ago are now underwater. Strategies to locate underwater sites include following the now-submerged channels of paleorivers (inset map), and traveling to the Clovis shoreline to seek potential targets with sonar and other remote sensing technology. Figure adapted from images courtesy of Michael Faught.

times the coast was as much as 250 km west of its current position. Put another way, the Florida peninsula at 13,000 years ago was twice as broad as it is today. Most of the loss came from the Gulf side, where the underlying limestone platform assumes a gentle downward slope. Raise water levels on a gentle slope and lots of land is flooded; lower water and lots of land is exposed. Contrast this with the relatively steep coastlines of the Pacific, where water can rise without significant land loss. Adding to the severity of Florida's vulnerability to rising sea is the porosity of its underlying limestone. Pushed up from sinks, vents, and other openings of a karstic terrain, freshwater perched above saltwater turned a virtual desert in late Ice Age Florida into a world of countless springs, swamps, sloughs, and lagoons by 8,000 years ago. The Everglades would begin to take shape shortly afterwards.

Beneath Gulf Waters

So the archaeological record of some of the most severe changes of the Pleistocene–Holocene transition is mostly underwater in Florida. Being inundated does not make the record inaccessible, but locating sites under tens of meters of water is not easy. Recent efforts to locate evidence for Paleoindian activity on the now-submerged continental shelf involved using remote sensing to locate likely targets, followed by various recovery efforts, including use of an airlift dredge (Adovasio and Hemmings 2011); evidence for a human presence was not detected in waters 40–100 m deep. More success has been made starting from the known channels of Gulf-coast rivers and working outward into the Gulf. Michael Faught (2004a, 2004b) has documented several sites in water less than 5 m deep along the Paleo Aucilla River and adjacent channels. These are no older than the early Holocene, however. Deposits of Paleoindian age are well documented in flooded sinkholes of the extant Aucilla River, where David Webb (2006) and his team uncovered not only Paleoindian artifacts, but also the remains of Ice Age fauna, notably ivory that was modified into beveled rods and other items (Hemmings 2004).

Deep Sinks

The Aucilla River sinks remind us that the effects of postglacial warming in Florida involved far more than a retreating Gulf coast. Groundwater levels rose quickly, flooding low-lying terrain, channels and lagoons, and sinkholes of great depth. Especially deep sinks in the

Sarasota area of south Florida show that Paleoindians engaged with sinks even when water levels were far below the surface (Figure 5.19). The near-surface sink at Little Salt Springs is 61 m deep and overflowing today, but when humans first visited, >12,000 years ago, water was down at least 27 m (Clausen et al. 1979). A ledge at this depth enabled access to the water, provided one climbed down the 27 m sink to reach it. Below the ledge is a much deeper cavern, from which groundwater emanates under pressure. Human skeletal remains and

Fig 5.19 Florida sinkholes like Little Salt Spring near Sarasota were oases of water and aquatic resources in the otherwise dry habitat of the late Pleistocene. Investigations at Little Salt Spring warranted the cover of *Science* in 1979 (Steve Daniels artwork; Clausen et al. 1979).

artifacts have been recovered from throughout the sink. Hundreds more burials were located in the wetlands surrounding the sinkhole. These are believed to date a good bit later, from about 9,000–6,000 years ago, when burial in water was common (see below). By this time the sink had completely filled and began to spill over. The nearby Warm Mineral Springs offers evidence that purposeful burial underwater goes back to at least 9550 BCE in Florida (Clausen et al. 1975), initiated at a time when water was low (−14 m here) and scarce, and then growing in frequency as water rose to the surface. Paleoindian settlement in Florida has long been understood as tethered to sources of potable water, such as deep sinks like Little Salt and Warm Mineral that tapped into groundwater too deep and under too little pressure to make its way to the surface (Dunbar 1991; Thulman 2009). It follows that sinks would gather cultural significance rather quickly, not simply because of the obvious practical value, but also because of their sheer awesomeness, like Mayan cenotes. As the need to tether settlement to sources of freshwater waned in the early Holocene, these places continued to gather people and things, only now in a ritualized manner that connected the water and the dead, and, we assume, their past.

Pond Burials

Several other mortuary ponds have been documented across the Florida peninsula. The best known is Windover, near Cape Canaveral. Salvaged from peat-mining in the 1980s by a team led by Glen Doran (2002) were 168 individuals. Occurring in clusters and marked by wooden stakes, the burials dated mostly from 6100 to 5900 BCE. The anoxic conditions of the burials resulted in unusually good preservation of organic matter, including fiber matting, wooden artifacts, and even human brain tissue. Whether people resided in the vicinity of Windover over the time it was used for human interment is not known. Still, the spatial arrangement of burials does not appear to have been haphazard or random, but instead planned and maintained, much like Sloan.

Pond cemeteries in Florida ceased to operate after about 6,000 years ago, when the first mortuary mounds were constructed. The transformation from pond to mound burials coincided with a significant reduction in the rate of sea-level rise and related changes in water levels (Sassaman 2012). It is curious that the practice of human burial in a medium (water) that was in short supply would cease after that medium became plentiful. The answer, no doubt, goes well beyond the mundane to involve cosmology and other aspects of belief that helped people cope with change. It seems likely, too, that the shift from burial in the watery underworld of ponds to the earthy "upper" world of mounds coincided with the realignment of communities across the landscape (Randall and Sassaman 2010).

But who were the people who practiced pond burials and what was their relationship to the late Pleistocene communities of Florida? Hafted bifaces and other artifacts from Windover show apparent ancestry to the Mount Taylor tradition of 5400–2600 BCE, whose history we will take up in Chapter 9, in our discussion of ancient monuments. But that is looking forward, to the transition to shell and sand mounds. Looking back, Windover has no immediate antecedent with credible archaeological documentation. If we skip back two millennia to Little Salt and Warm Mineral Springs, human remains are associated with various side-notched forms (e.g., Greenbrier, Bolen) that bridge the Pleistocene–Holocene transition, as noted earlier. We have already traced these various threads of ancestry through Dalton, but recall that Dalton is poorly represented in Florida. Its likely counterpart in Florida is found in the Suwannee and Simpson traditions.

Suwannee and Simpson

Paleoindian hafted bifaces with waisted or recurvate (fishtail-like) lateral margins are relatively unique to Florida and Coastal Plain Georgia, and into the southern portion of South Carolina. The type names *Suwannee* and *Simpson* are the most commonly applied by regional specialists, the latter being the exceptionally recurvate variety (Figure 5.20). Other types are known, and recent efforts to sort out this variability into meaningful time-space units have enjoyed some success (Dunbar 2006; Thulman 2006). James Dunbar has demonstrated Clovis ancestry for Suwannee/Simpson in the occurrence of "waisted" Clovis points, and proffers that Suwannee/Simpson occupies the post-Clovis horizon of Dalton times (Dunbar 2006:408). However, Suwannee points have been found in association with Pleistocene fauna at the Ryan-Harley and Norder sites in Florida, meaning that Suwannee is more than 12,800 years (cal BP) old – at 10,850 BCE coeval with Clovis – or that some Ice Age creatures

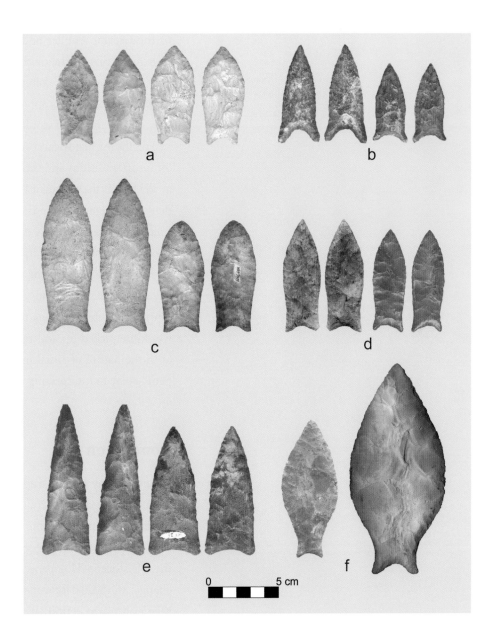

Fig 5.20 Simpson and Suwannee points from Florida, including variants of Suwannee and a counterpart of Clovis affinity. With the exception of two Simpson points at lower right, all other points are shown in both obverse and reverse perspectives. Individual photos courtesy of James S. Dunbar and David Thulman.

survived later in the region than elsewhere in North America (Dunbar and Vojnovski 2007).

Push the Florida types back a millennium or two before Dalton and we have possibly a third or fourth addition to the cultural diversity of late Pleistocene North America. It has not escaped attention that the recurvate forms of Florida, including the waisted Clovis, bear resemblance to some of the fishtail varieties of late Pleistocene South America. The Gulf of Mexico would have been at least 80 m lower at this time, and the shoreline of Florida considerably closer to the land of the Greater Antilles and Yucatan peninsula. Might some groups have made this journey, either way, linking, through a relatively short time but great space, colonists of the Pacific who made it to South America before Clovis appeared as a distinctive North American tradition? The answer, it would seem, lies beneath the sea.

Finally, the historical connection between people of the Suwannee/Simpson traditions and those who later practiced pond burials is not at all clear. If the bodies at Little Salt and Warm Mineral Springs were deliberately emplaced in the sink at ca. 11,500 years ago (cal BP), the precedent was set and we are left to trace the genealogy of this practice going forward. That may be tough and the answer may never be known. Some see a major disjuncture at about 9,000 years ago (cal BP, or 7050 BCE), perhaps abandonment of large tracts of peninsular Florida (Faught and Waggoner 2012). That practices like pond burials would be picked up and reinvented for new purposes goes to show both the nature of ritual in dealing with change, and the active role people play in interpreting their own past.

Conclusion

Whatever may have disrupted the flow of history in Florida about 8,500 years ago reverberated across much of the continent, as did many more climate events and the social movements that reckoned with them. Indeed, there would be many more sea changes beyond the Pleistocene–Holocene transition, many tied to major climate change: the Mid-Holocene Climatic Optimum, the Neoglacial, the Medieval Warm Period, the Little Ice Age, the Anthropocene. The first major one to inflect the course of human history is indeed worthy of extended discussion because it was so extreme that it sets the upper limit for what we can expect in the future. Sure, it was experienced by small populations of hunters and gatherers whose mobility and resourcefulness were useful in thwarting change. But it also put people in motion across a landscape, the extant ecological and cultural diversity of which was too great to preclude encounters with other people and other ways of living. Under conditions of rapid change, maximizing diversity must have been a good thing.

Beyond diversifying, what are the lessons here for dealing with change? Primarily, places of cultural value were critical resources for anchoring dispersed and mobile populations to networks of interaction and cooperation. As we have seen, these can be places activated by communal efforts (bison drives), shared infrastructure (drive lanes), overwintering (caves/rockshelters), cemeteries (Sloan), and even portals into the underworld (sinkholes). These can be, but do not have to be, places of residence. Rather, they were places of gathering, where people who were dispersed for all or part of the year spent time together. Sure, the communal hunt or similar public activity was part of it (*if* you could hunt), but greater value came from the social

Sidebar 5.4 Places to meet not always great places to dwell, but who cares?

A site in southeast Oregon known as Dietz is among the largest, if not *the* largest, fluted-point sites west of the Mississippi River (Pinson 2011). Located in the northern Great Basin, Dietz consists of a series of artifact clusters spread out across ~70 hectares (170+ acres). Seventy-five whole and broken fluted points were among the clusters, as were a few dozen preforms, channel flakes (indicative of fluting on site), and associated by-products of manufacture. Finished fluted points at Dietz bear strong affinity to classic Clovis points, which suggests the assemblage predates the Younger Dryas interval (Pinson 2011).

Although most of the activity at Dietz took place before the sea change that was the Younger Dryas, conditions were hardly ideal. Geoarchaeologist Ariane Pinson, who led a research team in the Dietz Basin from 1993 to 2001, concludes that the site was not such a great place to hunt, let alone dwell. A late glacial lake at the site dried up before people of Clovis affiliation came on the scene. Other locations two to three days distant would have provided resource-rich wetland habitat, but Dietz was a dried-up basin, perhaps "one of the most game-poor spots in the region" (Pinson 2011:297).

So, if not a resource-rich location capable of supporting intensive settlement, what attracted people to Dietz? All of the fluted points found at Dietz were made from obsidian, but from sources stretching in all directions, with the most frequently sought source 120 km to the south (Pinson 2011:291). This ring-like pattern of raw material procurement suggests that people traveled to Dietz from many points of origin: north, south, east, and west. But the paucity of water and food resources makes it unlikely that people aggregated there from all locations at once. Rather, Dietz might be thought of as a crossroads of sorts, a place of articulation between well-watered resource patches spread far and wide and the communities of people who moved among them.

Although the Dietz assemblage predates the global extinction of megamammals like mammoth, direct associations between Ice Age creatures and people are not known for the northern Great Basin. Clovis faunal assemblages in the region instead show remarkably modern fauna (Grayson 2011). Apparently, the transition to a postglacial way of life did not have to await the Younger Dryas. Routine movements from place to place would have enabled not only a diverse subsistence regime, but also opportunities for interaction with widely distributed groups, perhaps even with members of the Western Stemmed tradition, whose calling cards were also left at Dietz and are now known to be coeval with, if not also predate, Clovis (see Chapter 4).

In contemplating the significance of a place like Dietz, we are reminded of the gathering of Burning Man in the desert of Nevada. Hardly conducive to long-term settlement, this hot, dry location now attracts more than 70,000 persons each year. After two weeks of revelry, creativity, and socializing, participants return to their respective places of dwelling and their usual lives, but certainly, for many, Burning Man endures through the year as a reason for being.

capital and knowledge one gained from being part of something big. Practical and ritual knowledge flowed through these channels far more effectively than through individual, face-to-face contacts, which no doubt were much more common than big gatherings. How else do we explain the rapidity with which change spread?

In seeing places as network hubs, rather than corporate centers, we are compelled to ask different questions about dealing with environmental change, ones that are expressly social. If so, we need to step back in the next chapter to examine what anthropologists have long believed to be the social baseline for indigenous people of North America. Our journey will take us first to a place that underwent a perverse sort of sea change: the disappearance of a sea and its transformation into arid land.

6 Gender, Kinship, and the Commune
The Great Basin and Greater Western Archaic

In the opening line of their book *The Creation of Inequality* (2012), archaeologists Kent Flannery and Joyce Marcus declare that "we were all born equal." Their intent in this book is to outline the evolution of complex societies worldwide, a process that carried people away from a presumed egalitarian starting point and toward "civilization" and its institutions of inequality, such as slavery, poverty, and class. It is true that slavery, poverty, and class were unfamiliar to the oldest societies of the human lineage, but were people of these societies truly born equal? Were there no cultural values associated with the biological distinction between males and females? What about differences in age, or the skills of crafting, foraging, or even storytelling? Did inherited differences in capacities for strength and agility not matter? Were genetic differences in disease immunity or reproductive fertility inconsequential?

We think that Flannery and Marcus would agree that people are not born equal in the biological sense, and the goal of their book is to explain the creation of *social* inequality, a patently cultural and historical process. But is not social *equality* also created under particular historical and cultural circumstances? Sure, and the French Revolution is a classic case in point. Beset by the entrenched inequalities of monarchies and churches, revolutionaries in 1790s France commandeered the future with a mandate for liberty and equality. They were forced into action by the material conditions of oppressive rule, and they drew inspiration from philosophers like Jean-Jacques Rousseau, who in the middle part of the eighteenth century authored many highly influential texts on society and politics (Figure 6.1).

Rousseau's 1755 book *Discourse on Inequality* questioned the longstanding notion that social differences were authorized by "natural" law: that some people were meant to be slaves or peasants, and others the privileged. To make his case, Rousseau made a distinction between natural or physical inequality, on the one hand, and moral

Fig 6.1 The storming of the Bastille on July 14, 1789, as depicted by Jean-Pierre Houël. A symbol of the abuses of the monarchy, the Bastille fell to become a flashpoint of the French Revolution. Wikimedia.

and political inequality on the other. The former type subsumes those biological attributes noted above – age, sex, strength, agility, fertility – and is the basis for physical differences among all people. The latter is a matter of convention, the assertion of power by some over others, all traced to differences in access to wealth. This conversion to "civil" society, following Rousseau, resides in human dominion over nature, the establishment of property rights, and in the apparatus of law and government to enforce such rights.

Rousseau persuades us that there is nothing "natural" about social inequality. But what then is "natural," if anything, about human society? The answer to that question has preoccupied theorists for centuries, with the general consensus being that egalitarian societies preceded societies with institutionalized inequalities, such as the state. However, opinions differ on whether egalitarianism is inherent to small-scale, "primitive" society, or a matter of historical contingency. Rousseau himself broke rank from his contemporaries in seeing "natural man" as an agent of free will, able to perceive differences among his fellow humans and to mitigate their potential for inequality. He fell short of seeing the equality of "natural man" as political strategy or ideology, as in the mandate of the French Revolution to assert and protect liberty, equality, and fraternity. Still, there remains the implication that humans would "naturally" tend toward equality, whether by choice or not, and this way of thinking helped to "naturalize" the French Revolution.

In romanticizing primitive society as the antithesis of monarchy, Rousseau, like others since, introduced a few assumptions that have not held up to modern scrutiny. Foremost is the notion that "natural man" was also "isolated man," living largely in solitude. It goes without saying that an ethos of equality is not hard to maintain in a society of one. But it also goes without saying that society cannot exist apart from social relationships, and for that you need more people. Minimally, social relationships underpinning sexual reproduction are required, although things like families, bands, and lineages (i.e., kinship) are not inevitable to a sexually reproducing species, but instead are created by social convention. Here then we understand that even natural man is civil in the sense of having social commitments, but even now, with a society large enough to self-replicate, the assumption of *isolation* remains, in this case isolated from civilization by virtue of its primitiveness.

This is the very logic that led anthropologists in the 1950s and 1960s to remote, isolated parts of the world to document what Alan Barnard (2004:5) calls the last vestiges of natural man. These were the hunter-gatherer or forager societies of Africa, Australia, South America, and the Arctic – people who appeared at the time to be isolated from the rest of the world and, because of that, still primitive, still egalitarian. The hope was that we could learn about the essential qualities of society by studying these vestiges of a premodern world (Figure 6.2).

It turns out these assumptions were flawed. It turns out that many of the so-called primitives of the world were actually historical consequences of expanding states, in some cases victims of political oppression, not unlike European victims of the French monarchy and the church. Their apparent remoteness in places like the deserts of southern Africa was in some cases imposed, in others chosen. Above all, the presumed "natural" qualities of their society proved to be asserted as a form of resistance, or as a matter of autonomy. Egalitarianism in these cases was created, not just lived. It existed not in spite of the state, but because of it. Archaeologists would later suggest that similar outcomes emerged from social inequalities long before the rise of states.

Fig 6.2 Ethnographic hunter-gatherers, such as the Hadza people of Tanzania, were assumed to represent humans in a state of nature. Later work undermined these claims by showing how connected and impacted people like the Hadza are by the globalization of state-level societies. Wikimedia.

Having lost faith in the existence of evolutionary holdovers to our primitive beginnings, anthropologists turned to the historical circumstances, like those of the French Revolution, that led to major social change. In this respect, ancient, small-scale societies, like those of the ethnographic present, can be viewed in brighter light, one that illuminates not only the inner workings of egalitarianism, but also how societies such as these arise in opposition to inequality. The tendency in archaeology is to look first to the material conditions that make social equality an adaptive or sustainable choice. In a way, this puts us firmly on a natural sciences footing, as we come to understand the constraints and opportunities of living off the land. But we will see that that is not enough to explain all variations on a hunter-gatherer theme, which run the gamut from the mobile bands of the Great Basin to the fully sedentary and hierarchical "house societies" of the Northwest Coast (see Chapter 13). But no matter the scale of society or the degree of inequality, each grouping that we can describe as a "people" garners its identity not only from its relationship to nature, but from its relationship, historically, to all those other people of its past and present.

Archaeology has a huge role to play in documenting societal variation that existed in the absence of the state (which is not to say in the absence of inequality). It is clear that the archaeological inventory of North American societies that can be glossed as "hunter-gatherers" far outstrips the range of variation among indigenous societies at European contact. So, as we take a look at some of the many hunter-gatherer societies of ancient North America, consider that the following attributes, which crop up in various times and places, confound the simplistic sense of "natural man" that makes modern society appear so different.

(1) *Place-making.* We have already seen, in the previous chapter, that places in the landscape of those who colonized North America became not only physical anchors for recurring practice, and sources of material resources, but imbued with significance that connected people and places across time. This is not the dominion over nature that Rousseau imaged about civil society, but nonetheless a measure of cultural value and thus a source of social power.

(2) *Infrastructure.* We have also already seen examples of landscape engineering among caribou and bison hunters of the late Pleistocene, and will see plenty more as we survey Holocene North America. Infrastructure involving long-term investments verges on the concepts of property that shaped Rousseau's thinking, as it entails myriad social obligations in its construction, skilled use, and inheritance. It equates with property, even when configured as communal. Anthropologist James Woodburn (1982) would consider an economy like this to be "delayed return" in the sense that it enchains people over time, even generations, in order to reap the long-term benefit of their labor. Societies dependent on agriculture, for example, have delayed-return economies. This contrasts with what Woodburn calls "immediate-return" economies, which involve the daily pursuit of subsistence, without much social impingement, and come closest to Rousseau's natural man.

(3) *Architecture.* Society is materialized in the buildings it builds and occupies, and it is among the infrastructure that connects people across generations. Evidence for structures of any sort has evaded discussion to this point for lack of good evidence, even though we have places like Bull Brook that hosted large social gatherings. Houses eventually present themselves in varied form, some

suggestive of ritual or public use, anticipating the social distinctions of later history. Community formations become evident to us too, and we see traces of social difference that bespeak extralocal connections.

(4) *Gender-specific technology*. The sexual division of labor has long been considered one of those "natural" attributes of primitive society, something often attributed to the biological and social imperatives of motherhood. When gender-specific technologies become institutions of practice, we find reason to suspect that gender itself becomes a major dimension of social difference, far beyond those of biology. Convergences of place, infrastructure, and gendered practice may have been among the more powerful forces of social change. Likewise, gender relations were particularly vulnerable to transformation through encounters with Europeans and Christians, whose sensibilities expected women to be subservient.

(5) *Long-distance exchange*. We can debate whether exotic materials at a given archaeological site arrived indirectly, through exchange, or directly, via procurement or immigration. Either way they signify connections to other places, and other persons. We have already seen enough to know that both people and things were moving about the continent at scales that necessarily crosscut social boundaries, local and extralocal. We are driven to consider how connections afar influenced identity and difference across different social contexts.

(6) *Migrations in and out*. An enduring narrative of North American archaeology is the one that depicts populations through time settling in to become increasingly stationary, eventually "packing" into regions and localities that become more-or-less fixed as territories and homelands. Evidence to the contrary continues to mount. Throughout the entire sequence of native North American history people moved in and out of places and regions, sometimes as part of massive realignments of populations, sometimes as individuals and small communities. Either way migrations put people with little to no prior experience into contact with one another, creating the potential for cultural differences between newcomers and indigenous people to become politicized.

Our goal in this chapter and the next is to showcase variation among hunter-gatherers of ancient North America from a social perspective, and with a critical eye toward the presumed equality that comes from living off the land. Explaining *diversity*, as opposed to norms or similarities in hunter-gatherer lifeways, has been the tactic of modern inquiry (e.g., Kelly 1995), but much of this research begins and ends with diversity attributed to environmental variations, such as the availability of plant foods or seasonal changes in temperature (e.g., Binford 2001). No one can deny these variables are critical to understanding the distribution and organization of people across the landscape. But are they enough? Do they explain all aspects of hunter-gatherer culture and society? Let's see if this is the case with the penultimate North American version of "natural man," the hunter-gatherer societies of the Great Basin (Figure 6.3). In keeping with our stance that no native societies in North America existed in isolation, we also consider in this chapter the hunter-gatherers who occupied lands encircling the Great Basin, from mountains to deserts, and plateaus to plains.

The Great Basin

Given its peculiar physiographic qualities, the Great Basin fools us into seeing it as an isolated place, sequestered away from the rest of the continent. It is, after all, an inward-draining basin, enveloped by mountains, with no rivers running to the sea. And given its generally desert-like conditions, it would seem to be a great place to observe foragers in a marginal environment. In other words, it would be hard to find a better place in North America for studying "isolated man" and "natural man," the presumed core of humanity (Figure 6.4).

This was the logic of yesteryear, when Julian Steward studied Great Basin foragers and formulated a theory of culture that had at its "core" the manner by which humans adapted to their natural environment. Among the ethnographic foragers he studied, such as the Shoshone, Steward saw nothing but a *culture core*, that is, people whose technology, movements, social groupings, and even ideology were influenced strongly by the vicissitudes of nature, such as the spatial and temporal distribution of wild foods, or seasonal changes in precipitation and temperature. The study of *cultural ecology*, as Steward (1955) called

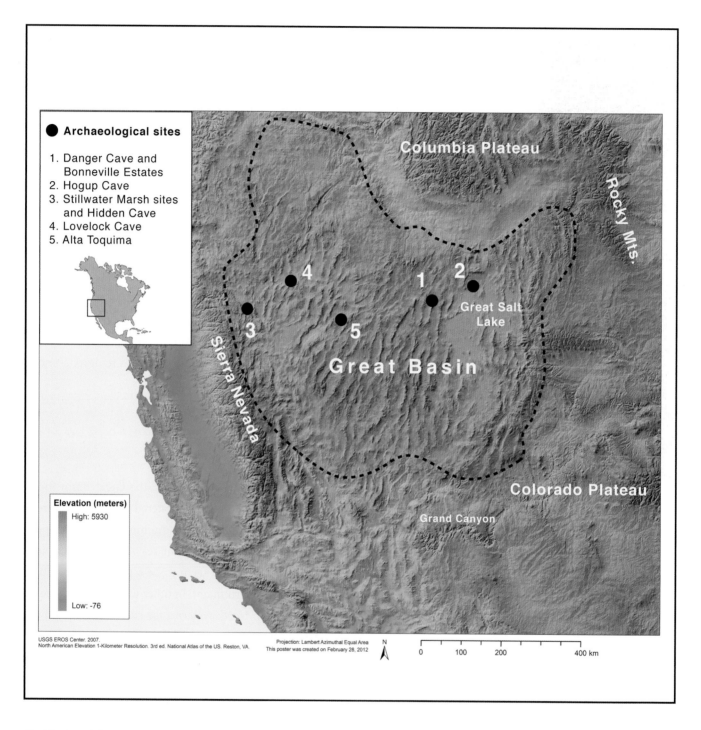

Fig 6.3 Map of the Great Basin and far West.

it, continues to shape the way archaeologists investigate ancient foragers, particularly in the emphasis he placed on the technology and techniques of the food quest.

In the decades since Steward's time, archaeology in the Great Basin has provided some of the best examples of ecological inquiry

Fig 6.4 After a spring storm in the Great Basin. Wikimedia.

on hunter-gatherer diversity worldwide (Simms et al. 2014). Modern study reveals more variation than ever imagined. With new discoveries and new perspectives on ancient foragers, the environment is now understood to be as cultural, historical, and political as any *built* environment (Simms 2008), hardly a matter of "nature" alone. Further, there is more to the Great Basin than its deserts. In fact, there are multiple smaller basins enclosed by the hydrographic Great Basin, most divided by the relief of mountain ranges oriented generally north–south, and differentiated by ecological regimes with distinct flora and fauna. Wetlands are now understood as places of enduring human value, invested as they were with facilities such as fish weirs. Caches in caves, hunting blinds, and drive lanes add to the repertoire of human enhancements to nature.

Confronting variation in Great Basin environment and culture means dealing with change too (Table 6.1). We review some of these

Table 6.1 Chronology of culture history and key developments in the Great Basin (after Fowler and Fowler 2008:xii; Simms 2008:142).

Years BP	Periods	Key cultural developments	Key environmental trends
3,000–500	Late Archaic	spread of bow and arrow; development of wetland settlement pattern; influx of Fremont farmers in central and eastern Utah	
4,000–200			climate cool and wet
7,000–3,000	Middle Archaic	increase in milling stones and use of coiled basketry; development of desert–mountain settlement; increased use of piñon nuts	
8,500–4,000			climate warm and dry; spread of piñon pine
9,000–7,000	Early Archaic	low elevation settlement; use of large side-notched projectile points	
12,000–8,500			climate warm and moist
11,500–9,000	Paleoarchaic	settlers of the early Holocene; use of large stemmed projectile points	
?–11,500	Paleoindian	colonists of terminal Pleistocene	

changes in the sections below, but first take a look at the Great Basin environment and its influence on archaeological understanding of indigenous hunter-gatherers. What we learn is that this is no longer Julian Steward's Great Basin.

Great Basin Environment and Archaeological Legacies

Being an inward draining basin, the Great Basin is true to its name, but that is only one way to look at it. More relevant to our understanding of human uses of the region are its north–south-trending mountain ranges and its intervening valleys. This is the "basin and range" physiography of the Great Basin (see Chapter 1), a province that extends well to the south into northern Mexico. Many of the ranges in the Great Basin exceed 3,000 m (10,000 feet) in elevation and the valleys about half that elevation in the center of the region and dropping off in all directions, especially to the south.

The juxtaposition between tall mountains and broad valleys is striking and defines the Great Basin as a landscape of *verticality*. The sharp relief of the ranges determines to a large extent the patterns of rainfall in the region, and, by extension, the distribution of certain plant and animal communities (Grayson 2011). Warm, moist air that travels from the Pacific into the Great Basin tends to drop most of its moisture on the western slopes of mountains as they rise with elevation, cool, and lose pressure. The Cascade Range and Sierra Nevada to the west capture much of this precipitation, but it also falls on ranges in the basin, especially in the western half. Snow that accumulates on mountain slopes in the winter melts to feed streams and lakes over the summer. Despite seasonal sources of water, the Great Basin is, on the whole, an arid environment.

Archaeologist-naturalist Donald Grayson (2011) has nicely summarized the relationship between verticality and vegetation in the Great Basin. He divides the region into two areas on the basis of plant distributions: the "low desert" of southern Nevada and southeastern California (home to the Mojave Desert), and the "high desert" to the north. The latter can be divided into zones based on elevation. Shrubs and herbs that thrive in hot, saline soils – most notably shadscale – populate the floors of many valleys. Up slope from valley floors is a zone dominated by sagebrush and grasses. Where mountain flanks meet valley floors trees start to appear. Species of juniper are most common below 2,000 m (6,600 ft), while piñon dominates at elevations above 2,200 m (7,200 ft). Piñon was an important food resource for Great Basin denizens, but its prevalence in the region is apparently a post-3000 BCE phenomenon. Upslope from the piñon–juniper zone of today vegetation returns to the assemblage of plants in the sagebrush–grass zone below. This "upper" sagebrush–grass zone extends to the tops of some mountains, but a second (alpine) tree zone consisting of pine, spruce, and fir occurs at elevations of 2,900–3,500 m (9,500–11,500 ft). Mountain peaks at higher elevation (up to ~4,400 m) support an alpine–tundra zone of herbaceous vegetation, but no trees.

Archaeological sites are found throughout all zones of elevation, from the valleys to the mountaintops. To the extent that vegetation zones shifted up and down over time, the distribution of sites relative to current zones cannot be read too literally. Habitation sites at the highest elevation, for instance, are relatively recent (Thomas 1982). Likewise, valley floors that were peppered with postglacial lakes in the early Holocene all but dried up during the mid-Holocene, precluding settlement that was common before and after. Occasional droughts during the past 2,500 years likewise hampered valley settlement, and perhaps encouraged more use of alpine locations (Bettinger 1999).

Great Basin archaeologists are well versed in the changes in environment that occurred over the course of the past 14,000 years and they expect, following the logic of cultural ecology, that archaeological evidence will mirror such changes. Conversely, long stretches of relative stability in environment might be expected to promote continuity in lifeways. One of the earliest systematic excavations in the region led Jesse D. Jennings (1957) to that very conclusion. At Danger Cave in western Utah, Jennings and his crew uncovered thousands of artifacts and plant and animal remains in three meters of strata, the oldest dating to about 10,000 years ago. Jennings surmised that inhabitants of Danger Cave were mobile and maintained a broad-spectrum diet over millennia of intermittent occupation. He likened this adaptation to Steward's characterization of Shoshone people in the early twentieth century: small family bands always on the move, with simple technology, in a perpetual search for food. Jennings himself found it "difficult to conceive of a life so directly and continuously focused on sheer survival." Dubbed by Jennings the "Desert Culture" and later renamed the "Desert Archaic," this dismal view of a hand-to-mouth existence has had enduring effects on research in the region, both positive and negative.

On the positive side, Jennings' view prompted others to muster data to the contrary. Immediate criticism came from those working in better-watered parts of the region, notably the western Great Basin, where sites adjacent to wetlands attest to less transient settlement than in the arid surroundings of Danger Cave. Others launched regional surveys to locate and test sites other than caves, some designed expressly to evaluate Steward's model of seasonal mobility (Thomas 1973). Further investigation of caves and rockshelters in the region showed some to be storage facilities for seasonal technology and food. Overall, work elsewhere underscored that Danger Cave was merely one type of site, even only one type of cave site, and that Great Basin lifeways varied not only over time but across the region.

The Desert Archaic concept survives in Great Basin archaeology, albeit with greater sensitivity to the diversity of lifeways that are encapsulated by this generalizing concept (Beck and Jones 2007). Regional specialists agree that Archaic communities were mobile, timing settlement moves to take advantage of seasonally available resources that spanned the entire vertical profile of the basin and range, from valley floors to mountaintops. But they also recognize that Archaic communities, at various times and in various places, made enhancements to the environment, from caching things in caves, to building fish weirs, to erecting drive lanes for hunting pronghorn and bighorn sheep. Even patterns of reoccupation reflect a more structured and predictable land-use pattern than implied by Steward's model of Shoshone settlement.

Moving People, Changing Environment

When we earlier visited the Great Basin, in Chapters 4 and 5, we were contemplating the relationship between the Western Stemmed and Clovis traditions, concluding that more than one wave of pioneers or colonists entered the region during the late Pleistocene, and they most likely came into contact with one another. It would thus appear, from this new vantage point, that the Great Basin was a multicultural landscape from the start. At the level of group membership and heritage, not all were born equal, even this early on. Thousands of years later an influx of people from southeastern California – speakers of Numic languages and ancestors of historic-era Shoshone, Northern Paiute, Ute, and Mono, among others – would again introduce cultural diversity from without (see section on "Numic Spread and Other Migrations" below).

The Pleistocene–Holocene transition made its mark in the Great Basin, as it did elsewhere, with developments in technology, land-use, and society accompanying emergent new landscapes, cultural as well as natural. Most notably on the "natural" side of things was erratic climate change. As archaeologist David Madson (1999:78) once quipped, "early Great Basin foragers were being whip-sawed from one climatic extreme to another, often within periods of less than a decade." By the time the dust settled on the transition, the Great Basin was wetter than it is today, and certainly much wetter than during the mid-Holocene (ca. 6500–2000 BCE), when average temperatures in the region spiked and annual rainfall tanked. Cooler and moister conditions returned after about 4,000 years ago, when populations burgeoned and diversified.

Paleoarchaic communities of 11,500–9,000 years ago and Early Archaic descendants of the ensuing two millennia took advantage of generally moist postglacial conditions by focusing settlement on the valley floors, in proximity to rivers and wetlands. Compared with later periods, population density remained low throughout this time and people were able to move about with little constraint. It seems unlikely that groups asserted territorial control over land and its resources, although repeated use of some sites suggests a growing level of commitment to place (Simms 2008). Fluidity in group membership – much like Steward observed with the Shoshone – afforded rapid adjustments to annual and seasonal variation in resource availability.

Diets expanded over the Paleoarchaic and Early Archaic periods to include resources that were up to this time scarce or simply too costly to use. Appearing in the basal levels of Danger Cave were fragments of milling stones, tools for processing small hard seeds from plants such as ricegrass, saltbush, blazing star, and pickleweed (Figure 6.5). Coupled with basketry, milling stones are among the hallmarks of these ancient people, and they signify an increased commitment to more labor-intensive foods. Humans cannot digest hard seeds without milling them into flour, and the nutritional value of seed flour is enhanced through wet cooking. Lacking pottery, Early Archaic chefs used baskets to cook seed flour and other ingredients with water. Baskets at first were twined and generally too loose to be watertight. Coiled baskets appear after about 9,000 years ago. The tighter construction enabled by coiling improved the water-holding capacity

Fig 6.5 Late Archaic mortar and pestle (left) and metate and mano (right) from the western Great Basin, used to process seeds. Photograph by Eugene M. Hattori, courtesy of Nevada State Museum, Carson City, Nevada, Nevada Department of Tourism and Cultural Affairs.

of baskets, which then served as containers for hot-rock cooking. Together, milling stones and coiled baskets signal the emergence of a broad-spectrum diet, one that included seasonal foods, like seeds, that could be stored for use over the winter.

Hunting remained important as the collection and storage of plant foods grew. Judging from the abundance of its bones in the oldest levels of caves, jackrabbit was standard fare. Lesser frequencies of mule deer, pronghorn, and sage grouse attest to options other than jackrabbit, and at caves close to wetlands – such as Danger, Hogup, and Booneville Estates – the bones of migratory waterfowl are not uncommon (Simms 2008:147). Fish bones and the seeds of marsh plants add further testimony to the generally wet conditions of the Early Archaic period.

After about 7,000 years ago wetlands of the Great Basin began to dry up. The region, indeed much of the globe, was entering an extended period of warming known variously as the Climatic Optimum, Hypsithermal, or Altithermal. The once-moist high desert of the northern Great Basin began to live up to its name. The Great Salt Lake nearly dried up entirely between 7,000 and 6,000 years ago. Although it expanded for a while thereafter, the lake regressed again at

Fig 6.6 Alice Steve, a Paiute woman, processes pine nuts with the use of a winnowing basket, ca. 1950s–1960s. Image UNRS-P1989-32–0345, Special Collections, University of Nevada, Reno Libraries.

about 5,300 years ago (Simms 2008:156). Many other bodies of water likewise shrank. Wetlands persisted in some areas, but at many sites, such as Danger Cave, the diminishing number of wetland species in Middle Archaic levels reflects increased aridity.

Until recently, Great Basin archaeologists viewed the mid-Holocene warm period as a challenge too tough for many populations to handle. Although few would suggest the region was abandoned, land-use and subsistence practices clearly were impacted. Overall we find a more dispersed pattern of settlement than in the earlier, moister period. The so-called "desert–mountain" settlement pattern of historic times began to take shape. This entailed seasonal movement between the valleys and the hills with apparently greater task differentiation than in prior millennia. Many sites were occupied for brief periods and for specific purposes, such as hunting pronghorn or netting jackrabbits. Ecological zones of verticality crept upwards in elevation, with shifting treelines and the sagebrush zones making way for encroaching piñon. Nuts of piñon pine became an increasingly important resource of the desert–mountain economy (Figure 6.6). Sites proliferated in the piñon–juniper belt of midrange elevations – generally between about 5,000 and 9,000 ft (1,525–2,745 m) amsl, depending on location. By the historic era, the piñon nut had become a staple, although the timing of its spread and adoption varied, with subregions like the Owens Valley of eastern California not seeing significant use of piñon nuts until after about 2,000 years ago.

The climate returned to wetter conditions after 3,000 years ago, during what some call the *Neoglacial* period. The wetland settlement pattern of the historic era emerged at this time. Going beyond the tethering of the Early Archaic, wetland settlement of the Late Archaic period (ca. 1000 BCE–1000 CE) now involved villages, some with earthlodges or pithouses. Seasonal mobility continued but some villages became places of large-scale gatherings, human burial, and investments of storage and food-collecting infrastructure. The Stillwater Marsh region of western Nevada was one such place. Human skeletons from Stillwater show that women were more likely anchored to villages than were men, whose limb bones reveal the wear and tear of frequent travel over steep terrain (Larson and Kelly 1995). Thus, land-use continued to involve movements into the mountains, but evidently by specialized work parties consisting mostly of men. Of course, women were instrumental in the procurement, storage, and processing of piñon nuts, which required forays into the uplands. As with the acorn economies of the Sierra Nevada to the west (see below), women had a primary role in the logistics of piñon harvesting, as well as the location and structure of piñon stores.

Building the Great Basin

Archaeologist Steven Simms (2008:152–153) views the Great Basin as a "built" environment. By this he means that the environment was enhanced by people to reduce risk and to intensify production. As he notes, many such improvements may not have been deliberate. For instance, milling stones accumulated over time at certain places and could be scavenged for reuse, thus reducing the technological costs of grinding seeds and nuts. Repeated use of particular locations in the landscape is itself indicative of structure imposed on the natural world. Material accumulations were no doubt accompanied by the sense of history that develops at places of enduring use.

Deliberate acts of enhancement are seen in the many caches of food and things left behind for later retrieval, or not. A *cache* is a stash, a type of storage, or in some cases offerings left behind, as with the Clovis caches of Chapter 4. We have already mentioned the storage of seeds and nuts. Great Basin denizens went far beyond food storage to cache all sorts of tools and raw materials, many of seasonal value. Cached at Lovelock Cave in west-central Nevada, for example, were 11 duck decoys made from bundled tule (Figure 6.7). Adorned with paint and feathers, the ca. 2,000-year-old decoys were remarkably detailed, and no doubt highly effective (Tuohy and Napton 1986). Some caves in western Nevada apparently were dedicated to caching. One such example is Hidden Cave,

Fig 6.7 One of eleven 2,000-year-old duck decoys that were cached in baskets inside Lovelock Cave in Nevada. Braun Research Library Collection, Autry National Center, Los Angeles; LS. 3302/Wikimedia.

where David Hurst Thomas (1985) found caches of equipment, food, and medicines but little evidence for sustained occupation. Inasmuch as they were secluded, caches like this may signal social tensions. At the edge of the Stillwater area, Hidden Cave, like many others, served as a warehouse for seasonal equipment that was concealed in ways that suggest nonegalitarian social relations, a point we return to shortly. Beyond pragmatic concerns, ritual caches, like the bundles described in Chapters 3, 10, and 11, materialized connections among people, plants, animals, and otherworldly forces.

One could debate whether caches or accumulations of milling stones constitute a "built" environment, but there is no debating the infrastructure of hunting (Figure 6.8). Concentrated in northeast and west-central Nevada are scores of drive lanes and enclosures ("corrals") for hunting pronghorn (Hockett et al. 2013). These were mostly made from brush, and some of the more impressive were constructed from stacked rock. Long, arcuate drive lanes about 1 m tall converged into enclosures up to 600 m in diameter into which migrating pronghorn were driven, trapped, and then dispatched. A pair of enclosures in Utah consists of one open to the north to trap pronghorn migrating to lowlands in the fall, and the other open to the south to get them on the return spring migration (Simms 2008:153). Dozens of other variations existed, but they all signal large labor investments in technology and the coordinated efforts of large numbers of people. Infrastructure for hunting bighorn sheep was likewise constructed in the alpine reaches of the Great Basin (e.g., Thomas 1983).

Procuring lots of meat for the winter – like storing nuts and seeds – was a smart move, but the hunting enclosures were more than a fix for harsh weather. As just mentioned, some were designed for hunts in the spring. Bryan Hockett and colleagues (2013) have looked at the full array of enclosures and suggest they have less to do with feeding people per se than they do with integrating increasingly larger and diverse populations during the Late Archaic period and beyond. The social integration necessary to build and use enclosures effectively implies a level of alliance and

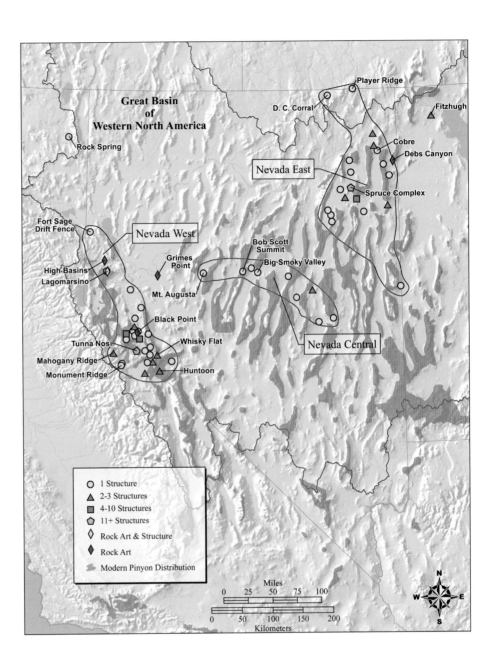

Fig 6.8 Locations of Great Basin hunting structures mapped by Bryan Hockett and colleagues (2013).

cooperation unexpected of small-scale autonomous communities. Certainly with more people in the landscape the potential for conflict and competition rose. Communal hunting, however, ameliorated differences among participating groups by pooling labor and meeting common needs, including those not directly related to subsistence, such as finding a suitable mate. In this sense it is worth noting that hunting enclosures are often associated with rock art. We may jump to the conclusion that rock art was simply hunting magic, but Hockett and colleagues suggest it may have served an instructional purpose.

Sidebar 6.1 Rocking the hunt

Rock art and hunting converged in a spectacular way on the southwest margins of the Great Basin, at a place known as the Coso Range, in southeastern California. Individual works of art in the Coso Range are estimated to number more than 100,000, the highest density of rock art in all of North America (Garfinkel 2006; Grant et al. 1968). These are *petroglyphs*, which are images created by pecking or carving rock, in this case the immense basalt flows of the Coso, whose dark, weathered surfaces, or desert varnish, were removed by pecking to expose the lighter-colored matrix. The majority of petroglyphs are stylized images of bighorn sheep and the hunters who dispatched them. It stands to reason that Coso art was a form of hunting magic, but Hildebrandt and McGuire (2002) go further to suggest that success in bighorn sheep hunting afforded male hunters advantage in attracting mates. Although it

is difficult to date precisely the production of Coso rock art, most of the hunt-related imagery seems to date to a period when bighorn sheep populations had succumbed to the intensity of hunting, after about 600 CE. Intensified rock art production in times of resource depression may have been an attempt to restore the sheep population (Garfinkel 2006; Garfinkel et al. 2009). Intent aside, it is not clear who actually produced all of this art. Was it the work of ritual specialists, or a more inclusive effort that included women as well as men, and involved objectives well beyond hunting bighorn sheep (Garfinkel and Austin 2011; Whitley 2000)? Judging from the density and diversity of Coso rock art, many different persons and objectives must have been involved. (For more on Coso rock art, see http://www.bradshawfoundation.com/coso/index.php.)

Indeed, people of diverse background and experience, and possibly different language, may have benefited from having visual teaching devices for sharing knowledge about communal hunts.

From Communal to Private?

With the construction and use of communal hunting facilities serving scores, if not hundreds, of people, we might expect that Great Basin communities confronted the possibility, if not likelihood, of institutionalized inequality. Were all people contributors to and beneficiaries of communal hunting? Were all those who participated in communal hunting equally knowledgeable and capable? Did organizing communal hunts require formal leadership? Who decided how to divide the meat and other products of hunts?

By the Late Archaic period some Great Basin communities – generally those of lowland villages – had become more numerous and complex, and they stood in contrast to those who maintained a more-or-less "traditional" lifestyle of high desert foraging. Notably, this change went far beyond villages and hunting infrastructure to involve all sorts of novel arrangements and technologies (Simms 2008:177–180), such as:

- increased food storage and intensified use of piñon by 2,000 years ago (Bettinger 1999);
- adoption of bow and arrow after 2,000 years ago (Bettinger and Eerkens 1999);
- adoption of pottery around 1,000 years ago in the western Great Basin (Eerkens and Lipo 2014);
- rise of big-game hunting as a form of prestige as early as 4,000 years ago (McGuire and Hildebrandt 2005);
- intensified rock art production after 3,000 years ago.

In the view of Robert Bettinger (1999), these and other changes of the Late Archaic period signal a shift from a communal or public sensibility about land and its resources to one of privatization and corporate ownership. Increased territorialism, kinship relationships that emphasized exclusion rather than inclusion, and competition over limited goods were among the impacts of this shift. Admittedly, none of this resulted in the institutions of inequality known for complex hunter-gatherers of the Northwest Coast or southwest Florida, but change in the Great Basin was headed in that direction starting in the Late Archaic period. How storage, pronghorn enclosures, fish weirs, bows and arrows, pottery, and rock art factored into rising social difference is a subject of enduring debate among regional specialists. Suffice it to say that things got more complex in the region, and not only because communities occupying lowland villages experienced the material conditions of intensification, but also because not all communities toed that line. For some, asserting equality in the face of rising inequality meant seeking refuge in remote parts of the region, much as the Mountain Shoshone of the Rockies did during the era of colonial expansion (Scheiber and Finley 2011). At 11,000 ft (3,355 m) amsl, sites in the Alta Toquima of south-central Nevada (Thomas 1982) went from bighorn hunting stations to seasonal villages after about 2,000 years ago. Were these the sites of people who thumbed their noses at lowland villages for following a trajectory of increased inequality?

Numic Spread and Other Migrations

Big changes in the organization of communities of the Great Basin or anywhere for that matter often invite explanations involving environmental change, in the spirit of Julian Steward. To be sure, the big changes we have covered to this point could not be understood without knowing how changes in precipitation and temperature affected the availability of food or the inhabitability of places on the landscape. However, we have also seen to this point that changes come about from interactions among people of different cultural disposition and that places become imbued with history and meaning that give them a gravitational pull irrespective of economic or ecological viability.

Arguably, from the late Pleistocene on, the Great Basin was home to more than one "people," and this goes well beyond the diversity expected of "*in situ* evolution" to include people who immigrated from elsewhere. Most notable among them is the spread of people who spoke Numic languages. As a branch of the Uto-Aztecan language family, Numic includes seven languages spoken by historic-era natives of the Great Basin, the southern Sierra Nevada, the Colorado Plateau, the Snake River Basin, and the southern Plains. Shoshone and Paiute are among the better-known Numic speakers of the Great Basin. The Western Mono of the Sierra Nevada were Numic speakers too, migrants from Nevada who arrived in California 600–300 years ago (Morgan 2010).

Research on the so-called "Numic spread" was initially preoccupied with the geographic origins of this branch and the timing of its split from the Uto-Aztecan trunk (e.g., Lamb 1958). When Robert Bettinger and Martin Baumhoff (1982) weighed in on the question more than 35 years ago, the Numic spread was considered an anomaly because it did not seem to be accompanied by major adaptive change in the Great Basin. It was also considered to be a late and rapid event resulting in the total replacement of pre-Numic by Numic people. Bettinger and Baumhoff corrected the first misconception by emphasizing the increasing role of seed processing and storage after 1,000 years ago, when Numic people were assumed to have spread north and east out of southern California, as Lamb (1958) predicted from linguistic data. This was an important advance in knowledge for it undermined the notion introduced by Julian Steward and propped up by Jesse Jennings that a basic Desert Culture persisted relatively unchanged since time immemorial. However, Bettinger and Baumhoff reinforced the second notion, namely that Numic people outcompeted indigenous foragers, who were more mobile and generalized than Numic-speaking interlopers.

Of course, language is not an adaptation and is thus subject to variations beyond foodways or mobility patterns. More recent perspectives on the Numic spread emphasize the complex relationships between language, society, economy, and power (e.g., Shaul 2014). Archaeologists cannot interrogate projectile points, basketry, or seed beaters for linguistic affiliation. What they can do, however, is embrace the premise that interactions among people of different linguistic and cultural heritage will result in novel outcomes, not merely the replacement of one by the other, no matter the inequity of power. Thus, Christopher Morgan (2010), in explaining the westernmost expression of Numic language in the southern Sierra Nevada, among the Mono, sees it as a process of negotiation with indigenous California people of different language and lifestyle. The acorn economy of the Mono is one expression of this *ethnogenetic* process, and it stands to reason that practices like acorn storage would vary in purpose and scale (Morgan 2012) and not refer to any particular level of cultural complexity or identity.

The spread of farming into the eastern Great Basin is another case in point. Corn farming appears in the region after about 2,000 years ago and is generally attributed to people who are thought to have immigrated from the American Southwest. The so-called Fremont cultures of the eastern Great Basin and western Colorado Plateau date from about 1,400 to 600 years ago (Madsen and Simms 1988). Their expansion north and west was evidently enabled by the Medieval Climatic Anomaly and their demise associated with the Little Ice Age (see Chapter 15). They indeed occupied a tenuous niche, one that could not expand much farther north or west, certainly not into the rainshadow of the Sierra Nevada.

As with the Numic spread, the expansion of Fremont culture into the Great Basin has been cast as an either-or proposition, in this case either the adoption of farming by indigenous foragers, or the wholesale replacement of indigenes by farmers. As Simms (2008:197) suggests, however, the real issue is the "nature of interaction between indigenes and immigrants during a time when a new culture was formed out of the interaction itself." This process of ethnogenesis is revealed in an archaeology of the Great Basin that does not treat its ancient people as isolated and their histories as static. Thus, let us consider in the balance of this chapter developments in land surrounding the Great Basin that ensured its history would not stand still, or alone.

Sierra Nevada and the High Desert of California

The western and eastern margins of the Great Basin are bracketed by mountains: the Rockies to the east and the Sierra Nevada range to the west. We last visited the Sierra Nevada in Chapter 1, recalling how John Muir was captivated by its picturesque vistas of waterfalls and lush vegetation. His experience was on the western slopes of the Sierra Nevada, the well-watered terrain that supports vast forests, including stands of black oak trees that produced the abundant acorns on which many native Californian peoples depended. Owing to the rainshadow effect described in Chapter 1, the eastern slopes of the Sierra Nevada, in contrast, were relatively dry and thus more Great Basin-like than their western counterparts in California. At the time of European contact, the eastern Sierra Nevada was occupied by Numic-speaking people (Northern Paiute and Owens Valley Paiute), along with one non-Numic group (Washo) whose history in the region likely predates the Numic spread. Conflict among these distinct people was not uncommon. Intermittent drought in the region no doubt contributed to intergroup tensions, leading some to seek refuge elsewhere, such as the Mono noted earlier, who resettled on the western slopes of the Sierras after allying with indigenous, non-Numic-speaking people.

The western slopes of the Sierra Nevada were densely occupied by a diversity of native people, all of whom followed the "California Pattern" (Arnold and Walsh 2010:13) of an acorn-intensive economy involving seasonal movements from the lower foothills in the winter to higher elevations in the summer. Until recently, this typical pattern was believed to have arrived late in the region, after mortar and pestle technology was innovated to process acorns (Arnold and Walsh 2010:82). There is now good evidence for acorn use as early as 5000 BCE, although long-term storage of acorns may not have become common until after 2000 BCE, if not much later. Increased reliance on acorn for winter stores, as well as for everyday use, likely impacted the organization of labor and distribution of groups in the region, leading to greater differentiation between both men and women and the ethnic groups to which they belonged (Figure 6.9).

Beyond acorn, lifeways in the foothills of the western Sierra Nevada turned on the availability of riparian habitat along watercourses draining central California: the Sacramento River to the north, and the San Joaquin River to the south. (In Chapter 13 we review the archaeology

Fig 6.9 Some of the bedrock mortars at Indian Grinding Stone State Historic Park in the Sierra Nevada Foothills of California. Carol M. Highsmith photo/Library of Congress Catalog (http://lccn.loc.gov/2013633763).

of these valleys and their delta, which hosted communities with relatively permanent villages and ranked social statuses.) Ethnographic tribes of the San Joaquin Valley had close affinity with, but were distinct from, foothill communities to the east (Hull 2007). Moving into more ancient time, evidence for ethnic differences between foothills and valley groups fades, and it seems likely that some groups made use of both subregions as they moved seasonally from high to low elevation (Arnold and Walsh 2010:91).

The origins of the classic "California Pattern" of seasonal movement up and down the western Sierra foothills remain uncertain. Archaeological chronology of the region is divided into Lower Archaic (8000–5500 BCE), Middle Archaic (5500–500 BCE), and Upper Archaic (500 BCE–1100 CE) periods. The Lower Archaic period is best represented by stone tools concentrated at sites around two lakes in the southern end of the valley, particularly Tulare Lake (Arnold and

Sidebar 6.2 Acorns, gender, power

Along the western slopes of the Sierras, at the headwaters of the San Joaquin River, a variety of native tribes in the historic era made good use of abundant oak trees in this relatively moist landscape. Like piñon, acorns from oak trees were collected in large quantities and stored for winter. As explained by archaeologist Thomas Jackson (1991), a reliance on acorn among certain California groups involved technology, planning, and organization that put women front and center in both the economy of everyday living and the politics of community affairs.

The logistics of acorn collecting were challenging. Some species of oak trees produce acorns yearly, some only every other year, and all are subject to boom and bust cycles. When acorns ripen they must be gathered quickly because creatures besides humans enjoy acorns too, and left on the ground they eventually spoil from moisture, mold, and insect infestation. The preferred species of acorns for the Western Mono was the black oak. At upland elevations of the western Sierras, where the Mono spent their summers, black oak was abundant. However, winter was spent at lower elevation, below the snow line. Acorn therefore had to be transported downslope, carried in burden baskets outfitted with tumplines (head bands for supporting the weight), apparently all by women.

Preparing acorn for eating was a laborious task. Unlike piñon, acorns cannot be eaten in a raw state, at least not in large quantities, because they contain lots of tannic acid, which makes them bitter and a bit toxic. So the tannins had to be removed. To accomplish this, the Western Mono, like others reliant on acorn, ground acorns into meal and then leached the meal with water in shallow sand basins. Each step in the process – from splitting open each acorn with a knife, to pounding kernels into meal, to leaching the meal with water – was repetitive and time-consuming. By one account it would take a day to process enough acorns to feed an average family for two to three days (Gayton 1948 in Jackson 1991:305). Even then the meal still had to be cooked, by a variety of means (as a gruel in water, baked into "pancakes"), all of which involved fire, cooking stones, and large quantities of fuel wood.

Technology for pounding acorn evolved from portable devices made of stone or wood to nonportable bedrock mortars, a change that occurred apparently less than 3,000 years ago. Bedrock mortars are essentially holes that have been pecked out of horizontal surface exposures of bedrock or large, flat-topped boulders. With the aid of a stone pestle, a load of acorns was emplaced in a mortar and then pounded into increasingly finer meal. The size and depth of mortars was once believed to be a function of age, with the deepest ones abandoned for being too deep. As Jackson notes, acorn meal would have cushioned the contact between pestle and mortar, so depth was not likely a function of use-life. Rather, mortars actually fall into one of three depth classes: shallow, medium, and deep. Ethnographic accounts suggest that mortars of increasing depth were used as the meal progressed from coarse to fine. Thus, mortars were made to certain specifications, and they were made to last.

There are literally thousands of bedrock mortars in the western Sierras, many occurring as isolated features or in groups of two or three. Some contain hundreds of mortars. Big assemblages are rare, but they are spaced evenly across the region and are associated with evidence for repeated, large-scale habitation and often in proximity to rock art. Locations with lots of mortars were not only strategically located to take advantage of abundant acorns, they became locations invested in the technology of mass processing and storage. Wooden granaries to hold unshelled acorns – occasionally built on stone platforms that remain archaeologically visible – were likewise major infrastructure.

Women's activities related to acorn storage structured much of the rest of Western Mono society. Because the locations of black oak groves, bedrock mortars, winter camps, granaries, and sources of water and fuel did not often coincide, a reliance on acorn imposed significant constraints on settlement. Women's decisions mediated these constraints, as did their significant investments in technology and labor. Bedrock mortars and granaries were described as the personal property of women in some accounts, and it stands to reason that rules governing access and inheritance were tied to women's identities and relations.

Walsh 2010:93–94). Before it was drained in modern times, Tulare Lake was among the largest freshwater bodies in North America. Faunal materials from once-lacustrine sites include shellfish, fish, and waterfowl, as well as deer bone, while evidence for plant use is scant. Sites in the adjacent foothills occasionally contain milling stones indicative of plant processing, but the age and cultural affiliation of these objects are ambiguous despite the occasional presence of Lower Archaic-age projectile points and crescents. It would appear that acorn-intensive economies were yet to develop (Arnold and Walsh 2010:94).

By about 3500 BCE, during the Middle Archaic period, evidence for plant processing, including acorns, grew more conspicuous. Mortars are common to foothill and valley sites alike, as are hunting weapons. Sites in the Delta region and elsewhere in the valley, however, contain more diverse assemblages of tools, along with ornaments and charms, which are rare at foothill sites. A likely explanation for these differences is that foothill sites were occupied only seasonally by groups that established more permanent use of the lowlands, a pattern known as Windmiller in the Delta region (Ragir 1972).

The ethnic and territorial distinctions among ethnographic tribes began to take form by the end of the Upper Archaic period. Site frequency actually drops over the previous period, but Upper Archaic sites tend to be larger and denser. They are also concentrated around water bodies, either the lakes and rivers of the valley or the tributaries of the foothills. Seasonal use of foothill locales continued unabated for many groups, but some sites of the western Sierras appear to have been perennial settlements, some with burial evidence for social ranking late in the period. Countering trends toward permanence, fluctuations in climate attending the Medieval Warm Period of ca. 800–1300 CE contributed to a cyclical pattern of abandonment and resettlement in the foothills (Arnold and Walsh 2010:97). Intergroup violence was also on the rise, and no doubt contributed to contests over identity and territory. Divergent alliances during this time are registered in the provenance of obsidian that was imported into the valley. Communities in the San Joaquin Valley obtained obsidian from east of the Sierra Nevada, including the Coso region, while those farther north in the valley tapped into more northern sources (Rosenthal et al. 2007).

The Coso connection in the valley takes us to the high desert of California and its Mojave Desert. Physiographically part of the Great

Basin, the Mohave is generally considered a distinctive culture area by archaeologists, and not only because it contains one of the hottest places on earth, Death Valley. It is also renowned as the lowest elevation in North America – 86 m below modern sea level – and only about 135 km from the highest elevation in the contiguous United States, Mt. Whitney, in the Sierra Nevada. Given its incredible physiographic qualities, the region warranted the ritual attention materialized by native people in media like the Coso petroglyphs (Figure 6.10).

Playa lakes of the once-moist Mohave Desert dried up progressively after the Ice Age, tethering human settlement of early Holocene age (Lake Mohave complex, 8000–6000 BCE) to ever-shifting shorelines, and occasionally springs. Over the ensuing mid-Holocene period (ca. 6000–3000 BCE), settlement expanded across the desert, often targeting springs that supported edible plant resources. The Pinto complex of 7000–3000 BCE registers an increase in milling stones presumably used to process seeds (Sutton et al. 2007). Continuing with a pattern established earlier, Pinto complex people hunted small

Fig 6.10 Petroglyphs of bighorn sheep in the Coso Range of California. Wikimedia.

game like rabbits and other rodents, took the occasional deer, and made opportunistic use of aquatic resources whenever available. Beads made from *Olivella* shell attest to connections with the Pacific coast.

Coeval with the early half of the Pinto complex was the Deadman Lake complex (7000–5000 BCE) of the southeastern Mojave Desert (Sutton et al. 2007). The Deadman Lake complex may have been merely a segment of the Pinto complex, but its communities may also have comprised a distinct ethnic group owing to their alliances with people of the Colorado Desert and Archaic Southwest (Chapter 15).

Occupation of the greater Mojave Desert waned over the millennium following the Pinto era, when mid-Holocene warming reached its heights. When conditions improved after 2000 BCE, occupation of the Mohave Desert paralleled developments in the Great Basin proper, with a boom in population at about 200 CE, when conditions were perhaps never wetter or cooler. This is when bow and arrow technology appeared in the region, as did large quantities of obsidian, much of it moving along trade connections elsewhere in California. With the onset of the Medieval Climatic Anomaly ca. 800 CE, settlement in the Mojave Desert shifted from permanent to seasonal water sources, and the obsidian trade waned. Despite limited settlement in the late pre-contact era, rock art locales like Coso continued to draw people to the desert, and ancestral Pueblo people mined turquoise to supply their ritual and aesthetic needs.

Rocky Mountains and High Plains

Bounding the Great Basin along its eastern margin are the Rocky Mountains, and beyond them the High Plains. The boundary demarcating the Rockies from the Plains is ambiguous in many places because of the extension of mountain ranges into grasslands. As with the Sierra Nevada range, the Rockies intercept moist air from the west, causing a rainshadow effect in the western High Plains, which in turn limits grasslands to the short-grass variety. The lack of rainfall and frost-free days – increasingly problematic as one moves farther north, into the northwest High Plains – limited the spread of farming. As with the Great Basin, this was the land of hunter-gatherers. Plant foods became important as the region's environments responded to the postglacial climate, but hunting large game remained a central pursuit. Bison, bighorn sheep, pronghorn, and deer were among the favored game.

We touched briefly on early hunters of the Rockies and Plains in Chapters 4 and 5. We did not, however, mention how common Clovis points are in the greater region, despite the limited number of mammoth kill sites, like those of the Southwest (Kornfeld et al. 2010:73). Sites with Clovis-like assemblages of the so-called Goshen complex contain mostly bison remains, as do subsequent Folsom assemblages (Larson et al. 2009). Like Clovis, Folsom points are widespread in the Rockies and Plains, even up to the timberline of the continental divide. The middle Paleoindian complexes known as Plano, as outlined in Chapter 5, continued in the Folsom tradition of bison hunting with lanceolate projectiles, but in these cases unfluted varieties.

Sites in the mountains and foothills of the Rockies suggest a hunting strategy distinct from that of the High Plains. At Mummy Cave in northwest Wyoming, a deeply stratified sequence spanning 9,000 years is dominated by the bones of bighorn sheep (Figure 6.11). Several other sites on the western slopes of the Bighorn Mountains in Wyoming substantiate this pattern (Kornfeld et al. 2010:97). The cultural and historical relationships between these sites and those of the Plains proper are uncertain.

Mummy Cave (Figure 6.12) and other stratified sites in the region register a shift from lanceolate to side-notched points at about 6000 BCE, the beginning of the Archaic period. Designs of hafted bifacial tools (points and knives) diversified over the ensuing millennia to include corner-notched, convex-based forms, and more. Once thought to be a time of limited occupation in the Rockies and High Plains, the Early Plains Archaic of ca. 6000–3000 BCE involved a variety of site types, including bison kill sites. In the northern Plains, the Head-Smashed-In site of Alberta contains a record of continuous bison jumping since Early Archaic times (Brink 2008).

The Middle Plains Archaic of ca. 3000–1000 BCE was ushered in by a cultural complex first defined at the McKean site of northeast Wyoming (Mulloy 1954). Judging from the

Fig 6.11 Bighorn sheep in the Rocky Mountain National Park, Colorado. Wikimedia.

Fig 6.12 Mummy Cave, Wyoming. Wikimedia.

number of sites across the region, the McKean complex of distinctive projectile points coincided with a substantial increase in population. Greater emphasis on plant processing is indicated by the marked increase in grinding slabs and manos. These trends continued into the Late Plains Archaic, after about 1000 BCE, with the addition of more frequent and larger communal bison hunts.

Mass kills of bison were nothing new on the Plains, but after 3,000 years ago, they became something of an institution. Climate change was clearly a major factor, but alone insufficient to explain this trend. As we noted in Chapter 5, the mid-Holocene climate from ca. 5500 to 3000 BCE was not terribly conducive to large and healthy bison herds. Even though conditions for bison improved quickly thereafter, McKean complex sites show only limited evidence for large-scale, systematic bison hunts (Kornfeld et al. 2010:254). Several centuries later, during the Late Plains Archaic, big hunts were on the rise.

The Late Plains Archaic began at 1000 BCE and ended 15 centuries later, at about 500 CE. The oldest sites of this period are concentrated in the northwest and northern Plains, and in the Powder River Basin of Montana and Wyoming, where a number of communal bison kill sites have been documented (Kornfeld et al. 2010:124–125). Such sites include bison jumps, like those of earlier times, as well as arroyo traps (e.g., Todd et al. 2001), some enhanced with lines of posts. By about 1 CE, the infrastructure of bison hunting included corrals built from wooden posts, along with traces of ritual structures (shamans' houses?) at locations in the northwest Plains (e.g., Frison 1971). These were among the sites of the so-called Besant culture, whose relationship to the development of complex bison hunting is picked back up in Chapter 11. For now it is worth noting the Besant cultural materials also bear some affinity to those of the Great Basin. Specifically, Besant coiled baskets found in caves in the Bighorn Mountains are strikingly similar to Fremont parching trays of comparable age in Nevada (see also Chapter 15). Beyond this, connections between Plains and Great Basin communities remain cryptic.

Infrastructure for capturing pronghorn and bighorn sheep is not uncommon in the High Plains and Rockies. The latter includes traps made from dead juniper, pine, and fir trees, which would of course be vulnerable to destruction from fire, as well as the usual attrition. Lines of stones mark drive lanes at timberline elevations, where sheep thrived in large numbers before recent disease and overhunting throttled them back. Converging drive lanes would have led sheep along steep slopes, where they were forced into catch pens and then clubbed to death (Kornfeld et al. 2010:305). It is not clear how far back in time such traps were used, but they were familiar tools of the so-called Shoshone Sheepeaters of the nineteenth century. Traps aside, capturing bighorn sheep with nets goes back to at least early Holocene times. A nearly 9,000-year-old net made from juniper bark was recovered from a limestone alcove in the Absaroka Mountains of northeast Wyoming (Frison et al. 1986). Stretched across a path of movement, the 50 m long net would have entangled sheep that were then dispatched with clubs. Not far from this location is Mummy Cave, where fragments of a similar net date to Late Archaic times. As noted earlier, bighorn sheep dominate the bones of game species throughout the 9,000-year sequence of Mummy Cave.

To this point the reader may think that Rockies and High Plains groups spent all of their time and effort on hunting large game. As with Clovis mammoth kills, bone beds of bison, mountain sheep, pronghorn, and deer bias our perception about the dietary role of large game. Inarguably, large game were of vital importance, and not only as a winter store. But High Plains and Rockies communities also subsisted on smaller mammals, notably rabbits and wood rats, as well as birds, fish, and a variety of plant foods, including seeds, roots, tubers, fruits, berries, greens, and the flesh of prickly pear cactus. Diets were thus diverse, adjusted with seasonal changes in availability and mediated by individual and group mobility.

The archaeological record of the Rockies and High Plains also provides some insight on the scale and integration of regional human populations. As might be expected from the foregoing discussion, regional populations were generally mobile and at times aggregated for communal hunts and other purposes. Sites with dense clusters of artifacts attest to places of intensive activity, although archaeologists are often not sure if a particular site was the locus of group aggregation or of repeated use by a small, independent community. Better evidence for the type, size, and contemporaneity of habitation structures would be useful in this regard, and the past few decades of research in the region have begun to answer the call.

Besides the rockshelters and caves of the Rockies and High Plains that provided ready-made protection from harsh weather, native people constructed and occupied semisubterranean pithouses (Larson 1997). These are generally shallow basin-shaped pits that were roofed with perishable materials (e.g., wood and hides) that have not survived. The floors of pithouses typically contain some postholes, hearths, and pits that are believed to be short-term storage facilities. Rabbits and other rodents dominate animal remains; occasional bony remains of larger game (bison, pronghorn, deer) remind us of the contribution of dried meat (pemmican) to the diet and that places of long-term habitation do not coincide with locations of communal hunting. Plant remains (e.g., bitterroot, prickly pear) are not uncommon in pithouses that contain groundstone tools.

Pithouses span nearly the entire history of High Plains dwelling, although most date to the end of the Early Plains Archaic, ca. 4500–3000 BCE (Kornfeld et al. 2010:392). They occur both in isolation and in groups of up to 13, although the bias of recovery looms large; none has been found from surface evidence alone but instead pithouses are often "discovered" in the course of land-alteration projects. One example of broad-scale excavation revealed five Early Archaic pithouses at the Split Rock Ranch site in central Wyoming (Eakin et al. 1997). The pits of these structures ranged from 2.8 to 5.5 m in diameter and they all contained multiple storage pits (Figure 6.13). Despite the obvious

Fig 6.13 Excavation of an Early Plains Archaic pithouse at the Split Rock Ranch site in central Wyoming showing pit features of at least two separate occupations. Courtesy of Dan Eakin.

advantage of semisubterranean living during cold weather, plant remains at Split Rock Ranch indicate occupation during the warm season. A somewhat later site in the Bighorn Basin, Spiro (not to be confused with the Spiro site of Oklahoma; see Chapter 10), contained nine pithouses with abundant internal hearths, earth ovens, and an abundance of fire-cracked rock, presumably indicative of winter dwelling. Considering the totality of tools, food remains, and features at Spiro, repeated, multi-seasonal use may be indicated over a portion of the Middle Plains Archaic period (Kornfeld et al. 2010:398).

Far more numerous than pithouses are rings of stone that were used to hold down covers to superstructures presumably made from wood (Figure 6.14). These are the "tipi rings" of the Plains and Rockies, and they number in the thousands. Evident on the surfaces of many landforms, tipi rings occur singularly or in clusters

Fig 6.14 Tipi rings in the Pryor Mountains of Montana. Wikimedia.

of dozens, even hundreds. They are nearly impossible to date except by association with diagnostic artifacts, and it is not often possible to determine how many tipis were occupied at a given time. We do know, from ethnohistoric sources, that Plains groups that gathered for communal hunts (or mustered for combat) erected scores of tipis in short order (see Chapter 11). Being relatively portable, the poles and hides that comprised the superstructure were taken away at the time of abandonment and the stones left behind in their more-or-less original position.

So ubiquitous are stone circles in the Plains and Rockies that they ought to draw more attention than they do as a source of data on group size and integration. In one study of stone circles with age estimates in Wyoming, Laura Scheiber (1993, in Kornfeld et al. 2010:401) found that Middle Archaic rings were smaller, less variable, and more widely spaced than later rings. One might infer from these observations alone that group size and integration increased since the Late Archaic period, when communal bison hunting intensified.

Other arrangements of stones in the Plains and Rockies attest to cultural landscapes of deep significance and value. The infrastructure of hunting already mentioned included stone cairns and drive lanes that were constructed and maintained for long-term use (see Chapter 11). Some alignments of cairns are located in places not conducive to animal drives and thus may have marked pathways of human travel. Moreover, isolated cairns also occur at points of elevation, perhaps to aid in wayfinding, or as an instrument of cosmology. Medicine wheels are another arrangement of emplaced stones, usually with a central cairn and radiating spokes, and signal astronomical or cosmological beliefs, which, like rock art, are ambiguous to modern observers but no doubt conveyed powerful meaning to those with personal connection (see Chapter 11).

Conclusion

The Great Basin and its surrounding regions were indeed a land of hunter-gatherers for virtually the entire sweep of North American history, or at least until the nineteenth century, when a Euro-American frontier encroached from the east. But was it the land of "natural man," as Julian Steward surmised from observing the victims of frontier expansion? If so, it must also have been the land of "natural woman," for, as we have seen, the practices of women were integral to the success of people living off wild resources alone. When we consider the mounting archaeological evidence for built environments in the Great Basin, Sierra Nevada, Mohave Desert, Rocky Mountains, and High Plains, it is difficult to separate the "natural" from the "cultural." Fifty years ago – owing to stubborn biases about the primitive nature of "natural man" – it would have been hard to imagine the scale of human modifications to the western landscape: miles of drive lanes, caches of tools and food, processing facilities for winter stores, pithouses, stone circles, and rock art. In their own way, ancient people bent nature to their needs, and oftentimes their needs went far beyond daily fare or even winter storage to encompass social networks stretching across vast geographies. The archaeological record of public-works projects, communal hunts, and shared artistic traditions shows that "natural man," and "woman," were no more isolated from others than he and she were the product of nature alone.

What we do not see in the archaeological record of the Great Basin and its adjoining regions of mountains, deserts, and plains is evidence for institutional inequalities that are familiar to persons of states. In the tradition of behavioral ecology that has shaped the way many archaeologists narrate human history in the region, enforced egalitarianism was adaptive: better to share with others, the logic goes, than to assume alone the risk that comes from living off a land with such drastic extremes of temperature and moisture. Pooling risk, in this case, enhanced resilience, increased flexibility. That's the way Steward saw it, and he was not wrong. At the same time, as we open up the scale of observation to compare communities across space and far back in time, we see greater diversity than was evident in the ethnographic moment of Steward's time. Archaeology in recent decades has transformed the way we view life in the western deserts and mountains of North America. Let us now take a new look at Archaic life east of the Mississippi River, where "natural man" has long been viewed as the beneficiary of broadleaf vegetation and wetland biomes, even as his (and her) communities have tended to be treated as discrete and isolated – which could not be farther from the truth.

7 Identity, Ethnicity, and Inequality
Holocene Hunter-Gatherers East of the Mississippi

In the last chapter our consideration of inequality revolved around differences between persons, particularly between men and women. In this chapter we expand the purview of inequality to the level of intergroup differences. Many social scientists refer to such differences as "ethnicity," which is often said to have two dimensions: (1) those values, qualities, or customs that serve to identify persons as members of a particular group, and (2) those values, qualities, or customs that constitute the identity of the "other." Ethnic differences may well trace to histories of geographic isolation between groups that eventually intersect in the course of migration, enslavement, or exploration. This is the stuff of "race" in the classic biological sense, although we are keenly aware that race, like ethnicity, is hardly an objective classification scheme in the context of power. One has to look no further than racial profiling today to substantiate this claim.

Ethnicity also has a hidden dimension that intersects with gender in many nonwestern cultures. The cultural distinction between two or more genders in any society can serve as metaphor for ethnic differences among groups. This is true partly because nonwestern kinship practices tend to be organized around unilineal descent, meaning that an individual at birth joins either his or her father's or mother's lineage, but not both. Practices such as these determine not only family membership but also eligibility for marriage; in most societies with unilineal descent, it is taboo to wed a person who is a member of your lineage. These sorts of distinctions get transposed over ethnicity when "traditional" life is disrupted by encounters with the "other" (see Chapters 3 and 4).

The changing contours of affiliation and ethnicity clearly turned on the coming and going of people from elsewhere. Let us now take a look at the hunter-gatherer history of eastern North America with a similar eye on ethnic process and the events that instigated change. As in the previous chapter, we will find that the tendency is to explain cultural difference and change in the East by looking to "nature," the purview of "natural man." Indeed, the diversity and dynamism of environments in eastern North America were powerful forces in their own right, but equally powerful were the historical forces that put diverse people into contact with one another routinely.

Eastern Woodlands Archaic

The Archaic period societies of eastern North America defy generalization. They ranged from small-scale mobile foragers to sedentary fishers to part-time gardeners. They included coastal dwellers, lake and river people, mountaineers, seal hunters, and those who mastered the bayous of the Deep South. Their histories span eight millennia (ca. 9500–1200 BCE) and change was common, compounding the cultural diversity that mapped on to different ecologies at any point in time (Table 7.1). In this section we will take a look at those Archaic societies that made their histories in the temperate environs of the Eastern Woodlands (Figure 7.1).

In the broad brush strokes of Eastern Archaic history, cultural diversity is seen as an outcome of regionalization, the inevitable niche-filling that occurred as populations grew in size and expanded into available spaces. Painted this way, the cause of diversity was not unlike biological speciation, the process of evolution that begins with geographical isolation of a splinter group from its parent population. Filling new niches, new environmental conditions, splinter groups diversified. The concept of marginality creeps in here too, as earlier splinters filled prime niches and later ones less productive niches. The colonization of the coasts was once believed to exemplify the latter (e.g., Osborn 1977). No one believes that now, but many regional specialists still expect all populations of the Eastern Archaic to have descended from their Paleoindian parent stock, specifically Clovis (see Chapters 4–5). They may accept the fact that more than one ancestral population existed in North America, but the implications of multiple ancestry for ensuing developments is rarely discussed (see Claassen [2015] and Sassaman [2010] for exceptions).

As we saw in Chapter 5, the immediate descendants of Clovis are evident in a variety of Early Archaic traditions in the East. Continuities in hide scraper technology and mortuary practices are most apparent. The greatest continuities are seen to the north, and in the Appalachian

Table 7.1 Chronological highlights of select Archaic cultural traditions.

Year cal BP	Historic period	Cultural patterns
8,500–3,000	Shell Mound Archaic	Variety of local traditions involving the intensive use of riverine sites in the lower Midwest and Midsouth, where freshwater shell, other faunal material, and artifacts accumulated, often with human and dog interments.
8,500–5,000	Morrow Mountain	Found at the very base of some Shell Mound Archaic sites. Later sites of the tradition distributed widely across the southern Appalachians and Piedmont. Sites tend to be small and ephemeral, with artifact assemblages dominated by expedient tools made from local raw materials.
6,500–5,500	Benton	Found at sites of the Shell Mound Archaic in the Middle Tennessee River valley, artifacts of Benton tradition are distributed across the Coastal Plain of Alabama and Mississippi. Oversized Benton points occasionally found in caches and/or burials.
5,350–4,700	Paris Island	Piedmont tradition of the Savannah River valley involving the manufacture and export of Southern Ovate bannerstones. Also innovated the use of soapstone for cooking slabs. Later centuries involved interaction with Stallings people downriver.
5,000–3,200	Stallings	Some of the oldest pottery in North America, associated with use of fresh- and saltwater shellfish in the greater Savannah River valley region. Later sites include circular settlements like the shell rings of the coast or the villages of the middle Savannah area.
4,700–4,200	Mill Branch	Descendant tradition of the Paris Island culture, involving oversized (hypertrophic) bannerstones and large bifaces of the Savannah River tradition. Interactions with people of Stallings culture led to outmigration to the Georgia Piedmont and the innovation of soapstone vessels.

Mountains, places that would have afforded refuge from the changes of postglacial warming. Recall that the Younger Dryas interrupted this trend, and perhaps enabled traditions like Dalton to flourish in

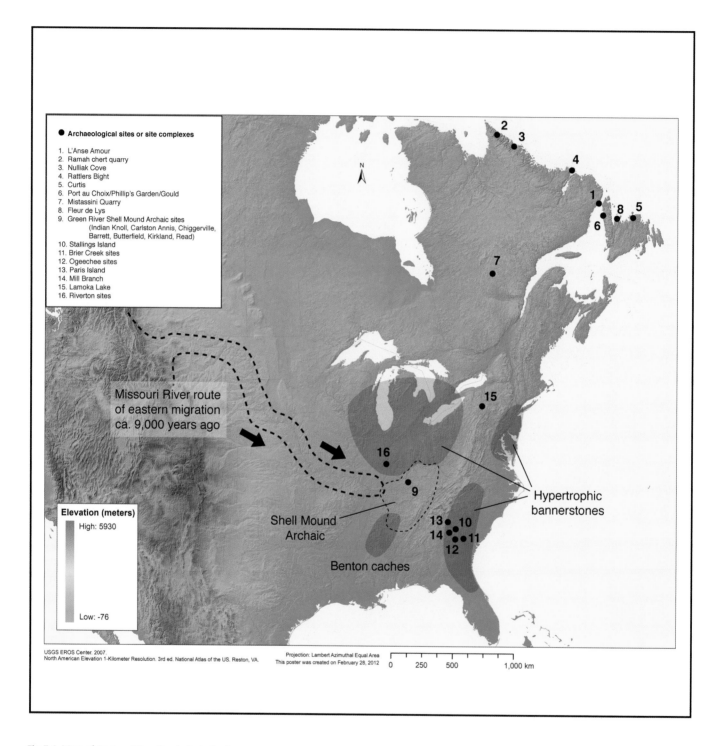

Fig 7.1 Map of Eastern Woodlands Archaic sites.

the south with vestiges of Clovis culture as it diversified with sub-regional variations that dovetailed into local ecologies.

The entangled processes of climate change and demographic realignments left something of a geographic void in the lower Midwest and Midsouth, between the Ohio and Tennessee rivers. In this void, after about 6500 BCE, appeared people with no apparent ancestry east of the Mississippi River. They began to occupy sites along major rivers, where they collected freshwater shellfish and deposited the remains in piles that sometimes grew to monumental proportions from long-term or repeated occupation. The technology, burial practices, and land-use practices of these early shellfishing people stand in sharp contrast to those who came before in the region. These people are known to archaeologists as the Shell Mound Archaic. Let us see how they were different and where they may have come from.

Shell Mound Archaic

Starting in the late seventh millennium BCE, and lasting for about 5,000 years, traditions of riverine living in the lower Midwest and Midsouth were made conspicuous by the accumulation of shell in mounds. The concept of a "Shell Mound Archaic" arose from Depression-era excavations of massive shell deposits in Kentucky, Tennessee, and northern Alabama, many led by Williams S. Webb (Figure 7.2; see Webb 1938, 1939, 1974; Webb and DeJarnette 1942). Then considered a more unitary cultural phenomenon than is believed today, the Shell Mound Archaic is still a useful term for discriminating populations of the region from those all around them, mindful that distant traditions of freshwater shellfishing – notably those of the St. Johns River

Fig 7.2 Excavation at the Bluff Creek site in Alabama, 1937 (Webb and DeJarnette 1942).

of northeast Florida – and their saltwater counterparts (on coasts of the Atlantic Ocean and Gulf of Mexico) were not necessarily related, and in most cases decidedly not (see Chapter 9).

Understanding how the Shell Mound Archaic marked a turn in Eastern Woodlands history means that we first consider its origins. Seen as an ecological phenomenon, the Shell Mound Archaic arose in the context of environmental changes that either improved the inhabitability of river valleys, diminished the capacity of interriverine landscapes to support people, or both (Brown and Vierra 1983). The operative agent in this case was the mid-Holocene Climatic Optimum, a period of relatively warm and dry climate that coincided with the onset of intensive shellfishing along major rivers. Whether the two developments are truly related in cause-and-effect fashion is a matter of perspective. And whether people were attracted to a burgeoning new opportunity or driven to use a resource (shellfish) and follow a lifestyle (tethered to riverine sites) that was against tradition, the unspoken assumption is that the Shell Mound Archaic people were of local ancestry. They simply changed, with the climate.

An alternative perspective on Shell Mound Archaic origins involves the immigration of people from the west (Sassaman 2010). According to this admittedly speculative model, in response to global warming some people of the Old Cordilleran tradition headed east across the Plateau, where they must have encountered descendants of the Western Stemmed tradition (Chatters et al. 2012), as we noted earlier. Continuing eastbound they would have crossed the continental divide and entered the headwaters of the Missouri River. Reversing Lewis and Clark's journey 8,500 years before it was launched, immigrants in canoes eventually arrived in the floodplain where the Missouri River dumps into the Mississippi (i.e., the American Bottom) and from there journeyed up the Ohio and Tennessee rivers, which may have appeared vacant and somewhat like home.

Evidence for the immigration of westerners into the Eastern Woodlands is circumstantial but worth considering. For starters, an ancestral line from Clovis to the Shell Mound Archaic finds no support in histories of land-use, technology, and mortuary practice. Given the discontinuities of practice, a population replacement seems likely, but in this case replacement after a period of regional abandonment by Clovis-descended groups. Land between the Ohio and Tennessee rivers was something of an open niche for newcomers.

A second line of evidence comes from comparisons of material culture and lifestyle, which was the method of early twentieth-century culture historians to trace migrations and cultural diffusion. At the base of the oldest Shell Mound Archaic sites in Tennessee are hafted bifaces with tapered stems (Dye 1996). Known as Morrow Mountain points (Coe 1964), these forms were a radical departure from the lineage of notched biface forms that followed Clovis (see Chapter 5), so much so that the archaeologist who defined the type looked to the far West for its source. To Joffre Coe (1964), the Morrow Mountain point and its culture at sites in North Carolina signaled a "site unit intrusion," essentially an immigration of people from afar.

Cultural affinities between the Morrow Mountain rudiments of the Shell Mound Archaic and the Cascade phase of the Old Cordilleran tradition are noteworthy. The leaf-shaped Cascade point and Morrow Mountain types are very similar in design and, again, sharply distinct from Clovis-derived technology. Other traits in common are edge-ground cobble tools, atlatl weights, and worked bone, and they both entailed a mobile, river-centric settlement pattern and diets that included freshwater shellfish.

Admittedly, differences between these far-flung traditions may outweigh the similarities. Nonetheless, by the time that the Shell Mound Archaic took shape in the Midsouth and lower Midwest, it had developed an identity that made it recognizably different from all that was around it, even as its people engaged "outsiders" through exchange and, at times, interpersonal conflict. Alternative ideas for the origins of the Shell Mound Archaic are highly consequential in the telling of North American history: on the one hand, we can attribute the Shell Mound Archaic to a set of enabling circumstances for people with long histories in the region, or, on the other hand, we can see it as a historical event of displacement and emplacement that put people of nonlocal language and culture in the ancestral land of others. The latter makes for a more vivid story.

Shell Mounds as Persistent Places

Sites of the Shell Mound Archaic include more than just shell mounds (Crothers 1999), and, indeed, they are not mounds in the sense of those constructions you will read about in Chapter 9. That is, shell mounds were not likely conceived of as monuments or with a particular end product in mind. They were, instead, places of enduring and repeated use, what Moore and Thompson (2012) call *persistent places*. As places people came back to for generations, sites of the Shell Mound Archaic accreted upwards and outwards, to become like mounds. At the same time, they gathered up people and history to become places of deep cultural value. The WPA archaeologists who did most of the digging into large shell mounds knew that these were places of intensive and long-term living. The layers of shell and earth contained vast assemblages of tools, food remains, and other residues of daily living. The shell preserved bone, antler, and other organic material by neutralizing acids in the soil, adding depth to an already diverse inventory of inorganic tools. Pits, ash lenses, clay floors, and hearths underscored the intensity of habitation. These may have been only seasonal occupations – abandoned for the uplands to avoid early spring floods – but they were repeated or persistent occupations.

Adding to the persistent nature of Shell Mound Archaic sites was the gravity of the deceased. Buried at many of the sites are scores, even hundreds, of humans, plus a large number of dogs. So prevalent were human burials at some sites that Cheryl Claassen (2010) surmises that they were primarily burial mounds, not habitation sites. An estimate for the total number of humans buried at Shell Mound Archaic sites reaches nearly 18,000 (Claassen 2010:107). And yet, human burials were distributed in and amongst the residues of other, seemingly mundane materials, leading some researchers to suggest that burial was incidental to everyday living (e.g., Milner and Jefferies 1998). Note that burial of the deceased amongst the living stands in sharp contrast to the dedicated cemeteries of Clovis, its descendants, and those we will discuss for the Eastern Subarctic, adding to the argument that the Shell Mound Archaic traces to origins elsewhere.

Claassen (2010) has looked into the details of Shell Mound Archaic burials and found clues about worldview and intergroup relations. Evidence for hostile relations is seen in instances of scalping, decapitation, embedded projectiles, fractured skulls, and even breaks to forearm bones from defending against blows with a club (see Smith [1996] for evidence from the lower Tennessee River, and Mensforth [2001, 2007] for evidence from the Green River). The rate of violent deaths varies across sites, but generally ranges from about 5 to 15 percent. To this tally Claassen adds individuals lacking bony evidence for violence but with mortuary treatments (e.g., group burials, burial on

Sidebar 7.1 Burials of the Shell Mound Archaic

The number of human burials at sites of the Shell Mound Archaic is staggering. In excess of 3,000 have been exhumed from sites in the Green River valley, more than a third from Indian Knoll alone (Haskins and Hermann 1996; Watson 2005). Other large mortuaries have been recovered from the shell-bearing sites of Carlson Annis, Chiggerville, Barrett, and Butterfield. Even sites with little or no shell sometimes have sizeable burial populations: 433 from Ward and 70 from Kirkland (Hensley 1994). Thus, the number of burials does not correlate with density or abundance of shell, eliminating the possibility that preservation of human bone depended on the acid-neutralizing capacity of mussel shell.

Green River burials are exclusively inhumations, mostly individuals who were tightly flexed in a fetal-like position. Minority treatments include semi-flexed, "seated," and rare extended burials. Cremations are completely absent from Green River sites and in a distinct minority at sites along the Tennessee River.

At sites with shell, burials can be under, in, or beside shell deposits. More than half of the Indian Knoll burials came from sand beneath the shell, into which round graves were dug. Burials in overlying shell were often emplaced in shallow depressions and then covered with shell. The percentage of burials below shell varies across sites, with the high at Indian Knoll contrasted with only 16 percent at Carlson Annis. At sites with discrete shell deposits, such as Read, burials were clustered in areas lacking shell (Milner and Jefferies 1998).

Multiple dimensions of variation in burial treatment hint at social inequalities, but most analysts have concluded that the Shell Mound Archaic were egalitarian people, lacking in institutions of difference. Based on grave accoutrements, this assessment is hardly controversial. Most individuals had unadorned graves. Only one-fourth were buried with some sort of artifact, usually shell beads. Atlatl weights (aka "bannerstones"), marine shell cups, turtleshell rattles, bone implements, and various stone tools were occasionally included in graves. Nonrandom patterning in the distribution of grave inclusions by age and sex is not evident beyond the disproportionate occurrence of shell beads with children (Claassen 1996).

Beyond grave accoutrements, cause of death and postmortem treatment hint at possible intercultural difference, as Claassen (2010) details. Graves with multiple individuals, embedded projectile points, and dismemberment (decapitation and removal of limbs) suggest that Green River denizens were occasionally engaged in conflict with others. Claassen further suggests that some unusual burials at the base of shell mounds were individuals who were sacrificed to consecrate a place of future ritual gathering. Were sacrificial victims captives?

Dogs add another dimension of possible difference (Morey 2010:168–176). Dogs were often treated like humans: tucked into round graves in flexed fashion, but never with grave goods. About half of all dogs at Green River sites were buried with people. The big exception is at the Read site, where dogs were buried in their own cemetery, 65 in all.

Decades-long research on the health and demography of Shell Mound Archaic skeletal populations has turned on contrasts with later period populations of farmers. In this respect Shell Mound Archaic people have been assumed to be more egalitarian than their agricultural counterparts, and because of that assumption, similarity and not difference is emphasized. The mortuary programs of the Shell Mound Archaic need to be interpreted in their own sociohistorical context, not used blithely as a benchmark for "primitive" living.

back, face-down, and twisted torsos) that tend to coincide with such evidence. Using these criteria, more than half of the individuals at some sites may have died violent deaths (Claassen 2010:122). This rate of lethal violence is remarkable for any population, but especially one believed to be egalitarian. We hasten to add, however, that many such deaths may have been ritualized, not merely a result of interpersonal conflict. This is precisely what Claassen envisions in the consecration of shell sites, as well as world renewal ceremonies and feasting events that involved human and other offerings at these "persistent places." Her ideas are controversial, to be sure, but Claassen rightfully puts the Shell Mound Archaic mortuary programs into proper regional context, which necessarily involves relations with people outside the area, those people "across the border."

Conflict and Peace on the Borders

As much as the landscape of Shell Mound Archaic people might be construed as dark and dangerous, we must also consider the flow of things and people across borders that hint at connections that were likely peaceful. Of course, conflict and peace-making may have been two sides of the same coin, as were difference and similarity. No doubt, negotiating cultural identities on borderlands was a tricky business.

We have already seen that instances of violent death are more than incidental, and they are especially frequent at sites in the Lower Ohio River valley, into which the Green River flows. The same goes for Archaic burials on the north side of the Ohio River (Schmidt et al. 2010), which are apparently those of people distinct from the Shell Mound Archaic. Judging from the distribution of certain classes of material culture, alliances among people on either side of the river appear to have been more common than were alliances that crossed the river. For instance, carved and engraved bone pins from sites north of the Ohio River valley express a variety of forms shared widely across a 500 km, east–west swath of the lower Midwest (Figure 7.3; see Jefferies 2004). These forms did not, however, cross into Kentucky and sites of the Shell Mound Archaic, which have produced only unadorned bone pins. Bannerstones and bifaces show similar trends for east–west similarity and north–south difference. One might expect that the Ohio River presented a challenge to cross-overs, but that was hardly the case with the Mississippi River, which did not deter cross-channel exchanges of bone pins or the idea of carving them (Jefferies 2004).

The southern borderlands appear to have been less violent, presumably more peaceful. Instances of traumatic death or trophy-taking are not so common at Shell Mound Archaic sites along the middle Tennessee River, which flows westbound across northern Alabama. Evidence for the movement of people and objects across the Coastal

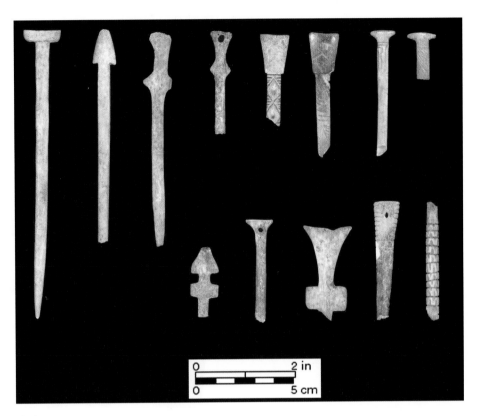

Fig 7.3 Carved and engraved bone pins from the Black Earth site in Illinois. Courtesy of Richard Jefferies and the Center for Archaeological Investigations, Southern Illinois University, Carbondale.

Plain of Alabama and Mississippi is more common. Much (most?) of the marine shell that ended up at Shell Mound Archaic sites derived from Gulf sources. It is hard to say how Gulf shell arrived in places like the Green River valley; Marquardt (1985) reasons it was diplomat-traders who traveled from Kentucky to broker deals, and that could very well have been the case. We also have evidence for caching objects at sites in the Coastal Plain that were made from materials acquired from northwest Alabama. The best examples are caches of Benton points and blades made from blue-gray Fort Payne chert (Johnson and Brookes 1989). Dating to the late Middle Archaic period (ca. 4000–3000 BCE), Benton caches have been documented at 13 locations along the Tombigbee River of Mississippi (Figure 7.4). They are also known from mortuary contexts in the Midsouth, where they sometimes accompany cremations and were themselves fractured by heat (e.g., Hofman 1985). Human remains are not usually found with caches farther to the south, although preservation conditions are not so good in contexts lacking shell. It is noteworthy that Benton caches bear affinity to the Clovis-descended ritual traditions of cremations, fire-damaged artifacts, and placement away from the living.

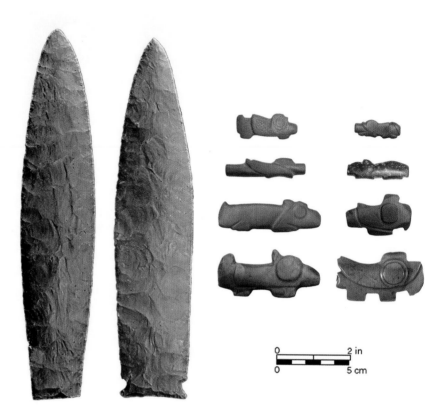

Fig 7.4 Examples of oversized Benton blades (left) and of zoomorphic beads that were produced in Mississippi and traded across the region (adapted from Anderson and Sassaman 2012:89 from images provided by Jay Johnson and Jessica Crawford).

Living Large

Another aspect of the Benton caching that bespeaks intercultural exchanges is the size of some of the bifaces. Like the oversized examples of Dalton points from Sloan (Chapter 5), Benton points sometimes assume large dimensions, up to 26 cm long in the caches documented by Johnson and Brooks (1989). They were also exquisitely crafted, true works of art. We might say they were "hypertrophic" or exaggerated in size, as well as form (Sassaman 2006). They were simply too big, too elaborate, to be mundane tools.

As components of ritual caches, hypertrophic Bentons, like Sloan Daltons, were operating as symbolic warrants, items with particular affordances, presumably about social or cultural identity. Hypertrophic bannerstones are another example of identity-making in regions of multiculturalism (Sassaman 2010:109–112). Traditions of hypertrophic bannerstones encircle the heartland of the Shell Mound Archaic, but do not penetrate it despite the fact the bannerstone (atlatl weight) technology had a Shell Mound Archaic pedigree

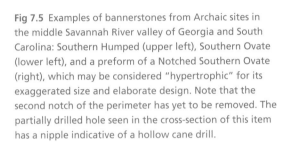

Fig 7.5 Examples of bannerstones from Archaic sites in the middle Savannah River valley of Georgia and South Carolina: Southern Humped (upper left), Southern Ovate (lower left), and a preform of a Notched Southern Ovate (right), which may be considered "hypertrophic" for its exaggerated size and elaborate design. Note that the second notch of the perimeter has yet to be removed. The partially drilled hole seen in the cross-section of this item has a nipple indicative of a hollow cane drill.

(Figure 7.5). It appears as if these elaborate material expressions signified intercultural exchange but defied assimilation. They are found at the seams of cultural difference. That is, each of these traditions involved people of at least two distinct ancestries, even people of different languages, who interacted in ways that caused at least some of them to exaggerate "tradition" through the production and distribution of symbols of identity blown out of proportion. It may have been one way to mediate conflict and difference. Another way was to hit the road.

Shell Mound Archaic Diaspora

If the distribution of Morrow Mountain points in the Eastern Woodlands is any indication, the hypothesized diaspora of Cascade phase people down the Missouri River did not stop at the heartland of the Shell Mound Archaic. Small sites with Morrow Mountain points are widely distributed across the Carolina and Georgia Piedmont, parts of the south Atlantic Coastal Plain, and north into the middle Atlantic region. A New England counterpart exists in the Stark Stemmed type (Dincauze 1976), found occasionally with bannerstones in Middle Archaic graves (Cross 1999). All of this was in place by the mid-sixth millennium BCE, coincident with or slightly later than the inception of shell-bearing sites in the lower Tennessee River valley, where Morrow Mountain points are found at the base of the oldest sites (Dye 1996). In some places, such as the Carolina and Georgia Piedmont, the Morrow Mountain tradition persisted for as much as 2,000 years, virtually unchanged. We will return to this long-lived tradition at the end of this section but first take a look at diasporic movements of later Shell Mound Archaic enclaves.

At least three instances of displacement and resettlement of Shell Mound Archaic people from the heartland can be inferred from archaeological sequences elsewhere in the East, as follows:

(1) Appearing at about 3000 BCE in the Savannah River valley that separates Georgia from South Carolina was an enclave of people whose stone tool technology bears affinity to Benton technology of the Midsouth. They may not have participated in caching practices like those already discussed, but they manufactured hafted bifaces for exchange and assumed a "middleman" brokerage role between coastal and Piedmont indigenes, much like those of the Midsouth, from where they presumably came (Sassaman 2006).

(2) In the Finger Lakes of western New York at about 2500 BCE communities of fishers appear with no precedence in the region. As part of the Lamoka Lake culture, these communities were regarded by William Ritchie (1969) as immigrants from the heartland of the Shell Mound Archaic. Paddling up the Ohio River to its headwaters would have put these people in proximity to the Finger Lakes. It also would have put them in the land of people of the Laurentian tradition, whose ancestry likely traces to Clovis. According to Ritchie (1969), interactions between Lamoka and Laurentian people begot a later phase known as Frontenac.

(3) After about 1800 BCE, people known to archaeologists as Riverton settled in the Wabash River valley of Illinois. The archaeologist who brought their history to light, Howard Winters (1969), knew that this tradition was without local ancestry, but he was reluctant to attribute them to the Shell Mound Archaic. The cultural diversity of the Wabash region before and during the Riverton era is not well known, but we have already noted differences between populations on either side of the Ohio River, and Riverton looks locally novel.

Space precludes a close examination of each of these diasporic events, so we will consider only one in greater detail – the oldest one – whose history is well established.

The Multicultural Genesis of Stallings Culture

When people of possible Benton ancestry appeared in the Savannah River valley around 3000 BCE they occupied an open niche between two extant populations, much as their ancestors had in the Midsouth three millennia earlier. Up the Savannah River, in the foothills or Piedmont of the region, were communities of the Paris Island culture, presumed descendants of Morrow Mountain ancestry. Down the Savannah River, in the Coastal Plain and on the coast, were communities of early Stallings culture, whose ancestry is unknown. The south Atlantic shoreline before about 2500 BCE had been inundated by rising sea, so we do not know what was happening on the coast at the time Benton descendants arrived in the region. Still, marine shell beads show up in the Piedmont at this time, and Piedmont soapstone made its way toward the coast, giving us reason to assume that alliances were already in place between widely separated groups along the river.

For at least part of the year Paris Island communities of the Piedmont occupied riverside settlements, where they built substantial in-ground post houses and accumulated considerable amounts of domestic refuse. Among the items left behind were perforated slabs of soapstone. Once believed to be weights for fishing nets (Claflin 1931), soapstone slabs were actually cooking stones, much like those used throughout North America in the age-old technique of "stone boiling." Heated in fires or coals, stones were transferred to containers to heat liquids contained in baskets, wooden vessels, or simply hide-lined pits. This was one way to cook liquid-based foods without having to place a vessel directly over fire, a necessary technique before the advent of pottery, a heat-resistant container.

In ethnohistoric and archaeological cases across the continent, stone boiling was the preferred means of extracting fat from nuts, bone, and fish, for preparing mush or porridge using acorns and other starchy substances, and for cooking any liquid-based food like soups and stews. In most cases, rocks used in this way did not last long from the stress of repeated heating and rapid cooling. Soapstone, however, is resistant to thermal shock and much more effective at absorbing and releasing heat than are quartz, granite, and other hard rocks. As discussed later in this chapter for the Eastern Subarctic, soapstone is easy to carve into innumerable shapes, including vessels. Eventually, soapstone vessel technology would come to the Southeast, but only after a long period of stone boiling with perforated soapstone slabs. The perforation of slabs enabled Archaic chefs to lift the stones from fire to vessel and back to fire with an antler tine or pointed stick.

Paris Island communities had ready access to soapstone in the Piedmont and they must have supplied coastal neighbors with the material, perhaps through Benton-descended middlemen. Soapstone slabs are not common at sites near the coast, although, again, the coastal record before about 2500 BCE was truncated by rising sea. After this time the residues of coastal living include sherds of the oldest pottery in the region, a ware known to archaeologists as Stallings fiber-tempered pottery (Sassaman 1993). Vessels of this tradition were simple open bowls made from local clay tempered with Spanish moss, hence the term "fiber-tempered." Upon firing, moss in the clay would carbonize and leave behind voids or fissures. The porosity of the pottery was not conducive to direct-heat cooking, but it made an excellent container for stone boiling, provided, that is, one had access to stone, which was quite rare on the coast and in the lower Coastal Plain.

With the advent of pottery, the potential for direct-heat cooking was in place. Remarkably, it would take another 1,000 years for this innovation to gain widespread acceptance. Trading partners up the Savannah River seem to have resisted any innovations in cooking, perhaps because of devotion to traditional technology. Coastal residents, however, must have perceived the advantages of innovations that lessened the need to import soapstone from Piedmont neighbors. It was, after all, a distant resource, one they could not acquire directly. Perhaps Benton-descended immigrants who implanted themselves between Piedmont and coastal groups were not great middlemen and instead disrupted the downriver flow of soapstone. Whatever the case may be, pottery took off quickly on the coast and would eventually find its way into the inventory of Late Archaic cookware in the interior even as it continued to be used as containers for stone boiling.

A few centuries after pottery appeared, groups from the low country began to make trips into the middle Savannah River area, where the fall line separates the Piedmont from the Coastal Plain, a province known as the Fall Zone. They were apparently interested in the mast resources of the area – acorn, walnut, and especially hickory – as well as the deer and turkey that relied on mast. None of these resources was prevalent in the low country, which was dominated by pine forests. Of course, coastal people had plenty of fish and shellfish to take, but it would have been difficult to live by those resources alone. Groups that made their way into the Fall Zone evidently harvested loads of nuts and acorns and stored them in large subterranean silos (i.e., big storage pits), presumably to tide them over the winter. But they did not stay in the Fall Zone year-round, at least not at first.

Another century or two later, by 2200 BCE, at least one community of Coastal Plain dwellers made the leap to full-time living in the Fall Zone. They may well have been the direct descendants of Benton immigrants, although more than likely the progeny of intermarriage between Piedmont and Coastal Plain residents. Two very different outcomes arose from this relocation up the river. First, a cultural revolution ensued from the coalescence of locals and newcomers (Sassaman 2006). Known to archaeologists as "Classic Stallings," this novel culture was marked by elaborately decorated pottery, a formalized mortuary program, circular villages, and ritual feasting. The namesake site for the culture, Stallings Island (Claflin 1931), in the Fall Zone, was the center of this development. The combination of thousands of soapstone cooking stones and thousands of fiber-tempered vessels at Stallings Island – none of which was used directly over fire, like they were on the coast – attests to an amalgam of traditional and innovative practices.

Not everyone in the upcountry was on board with this development, however. The Paris Island ancestry that was part of the Classic Stallings genesis bifurcated into two factions when early Stallings communities began to make seasonal use of the Fall Zone. A new culture known as Mill Branch appeared. Clearly descended from Paris Island stock, Mill Branch people eschewed the cultural revolution that was Classic Stallings and began to produce material culture to emphasize their difference. Most conspicuous were the hypertrophic bannerstones like those mentioned earlier. In fact, much of Mill Branch material culture involved elaborations on things traditional, as if to underscore the legacy of a culture that was threatened by change. Eventually they moved away, apparently to north-central Georgia, where they would begin to make soapstone vessels after about 2000 BCE. Centuries later, soapstone vessels hailing from this region would be among the trade goods of the Poverty Point culture of Louisiana (see Chapter 9). Mill Branch descendants would not give

up on regional alliances and exchange, but they rejected the developments of their homeland and sought alternatives elsewhere.

A Culture of Women

The cultural florescence that was Classic Stallings was more than just
a change in cooking technology or the permanence of settlement. It
was, arguably, a change in gender relations that elevated women to a
higher status than they may have experienced before. At a minimum,
the activities and prerogatives of women became more conspicuous with the growing inventory of pottery. Worldwide, in nonmar-
ket economies, women make and use pottery far more than do men
(Skibo and Schiffer 1995). We can add to that the tasks of shellfishing and mast processing, also under the purview of women in cases
worldwide.

Another, subtle aspect of Classic Stallings culture points to the centrality of women too. The dominant form of decoration of Classic
Stallings pottery is a style of punctation called "drag and jab" (see
Figure 7.6). These were intricate designs applied with a hand-held sty-
lus that was inserted into the exterior surface of wet clay at a low angle
to form a punctation, then pulled out, dragged along a line, reinserted, pulled out again, dragged some more, reinserted, and so on.
It is reminiscent of cursive writing in that it required precise motor
skill, and lots of practice. It follows that drag and jab punctation was
executed with the dominant hand. It also follows that one can infer
the handedness of the person decorating the pot if the orientation of
the pot at the time of decorating is known.

The orientation of punctations on hundreds of rim sherds from
sites of Classic Stallings culture reveal that 90 percent of the pottery was decorated by right-handed persons, the rest by southpaws
(Sassaman and Rudolphi 2001). This is not surprising given the
proportion of righties and lefties in many populations, including
those of modern North America. However, when broken down into
subregions of Classic Stallings culture, proportions of right- to left-
handed potters vary significantly. Because one's chance of being left-
handed is greatest if one's mother was left-handed, the nonrandom
distributions of handedness suggest that residence patterns of Stallings
potters ensured that daughters often remained in the villages of their
mothers, even after marriage. This is known to anthropologists as

Fig 7.6 Stallings drag and jab pottery sherds from sites in the middle Savannah River valley of Georgia and South Carolina.

postmarital residence, in this case matrilocal postmarital residence. This stands in contrast with patrilocal postmarital residence, which keeps related men together and is common among hunter-gatherers who rely on large game hunting, typically men's work.

If Classic Stallings culture was a culture of women, then Mill Branch culture increasingly became a culture of men. This is not to say that Stallings communities consisted only of women and Mill Branch

Sidebar 7.2 Handedness of Stallings pottery

Only about 10 percent of modern Americans are left-handed, but that's a good bit less than biology allows. It's culture that keeps left-handedness so low. Rates of left-handedness as high as 25 percent have been documented among people free of the constraints of modern living. It was not that long ago that parents and schoolteachers in the USA campaigned aggressively to convert southpaws to righties. Even without active conversion, the technologies of living in modern America, until recently, were biased against lefties. For instance, even though left-handed people are a distinct minority they account for the majority of chainsaw accidents because chainsaws are designed for right-handed use. Only recently have left-handed desks been made available in schoolrooms. An episode of *The Simpsons* showcased the plight of left-handed people in using things as simple as scissors or can openers. Since at least biblical times, being left-handed means being discriminated against.

Societies predating or avoiding Judeo-Christian and capitalist cultures are not so restrictive on hand dominance, but in none are left-handed people as numerous as their right-handed counterparts. Biological factors matter, although you will find no consensus about causes in the literature on handedness. Still, maternal influence is strong and thus we can model the potential for handedness in a given population if we know how many left-handed mothers we start with and how many of their daughters stay in the population to beget additional generations of related women. This is the logic of archaeologists who attempted in the 1960s to infer the postmarital residence patterns of Pueblo communities from the nonrandom distribution of pottery styles (Hill 1970; Longacre 1970). Their assumption was that daughters learned the craft from their mothers. Critics of this approach pointed out that young Pueblo women sometimes learned from their father's sisters, or even from totally unrelated women (Stanislawski 1978). Given the biological dimension of handedness, attributes that can be traced to hand dominance hold better potential for inferring postmarital residence patterns than does style alone.

The orientation of punctations on Stallings drag and jab pottery is one such attribute (Sassaman and Rudolphi 2001). Inferring the handedness of a potter who punctated a Stallings pot requires that we assume pots were routinely held in a particular position during the process of decorating surfaces. If the pot was oriented upright, with the opening to the top, punctations angled to the right would have been executed by a right-handed person and those oriented to the left by a left-handed person. Counted this way, 12.4 percent of the pots in a sample of 386 vessels were made by left-handed potters, not much higher than the rate of left-handedness in the general population of the USA today (Sassaman and Rudolphi 2001:419). However, Stallings drag and jab vessels from the middle Savannah River valley express nearly twice the rate of left-handedness, and those from the Brier Creek drainage to the south less than 3 percent. At 9.4 percent left-handed, pots from Ogeechee River sites, to the west, come closest to the regionwide rate. Individual assemblages of pots from each of the three subregions of Stallings settlement duplicate the results, lessening the chances that the patterning is random.

Sassaman and Rudolphi (2001) surmise that the nonrandom patterning of handedness evident in Stallings pottery was due to postmarital residence patterns that kept related women living together throughout their lifetimes. Following the rules of matrilocality, as it is known, men would have relocated to the villages of their brides upon marriage. The gender politics of these arrangements transcends the household to encompass a variety of social obligations and privileges between parents and in-laws. Matrilocality is not unheard of among forager societies, but patrilocality or ambilocality (wherein postmarital residence is flexible or changing) are more common (Kelly 1995). Given the apparent contradiction that Classic Stallings culture posed to the traditions of Piedmont indigenes, one has to question the long-term stability of any social arrangements predicated on asymmetry between the two main genders.

communities only of men, for that would be absurd. Rather, this speaks to structural principles of society that place greater or lesser emphasis on a particular gender. Group affiliation, marriage eligibility, inheritance, labor obligations, sharing, coresidency, and territoriality are all affected by gender relations. In that Mill Branch represents cultural resistance to a rising Classic Stallings culture, it was something of a gendered resistance. Hypertrophic bannerstones and knives, an emphasis on deer hunting, and seasonal forays into the mountains may have all been patently male things. This case in ancient gender politics goes to show that institutionalized social inequality can be grounded in the relations between men and women. Moreover, gender distinctions do not begin and end with the difference between men and women, but can be extrapolated outward to encompass larger social groupings, in this case those we might describe as ethnicity.

Resisting Inequality

The rules of inclusion in Classic Stallings culture were matched by rules of exclusion. Among the disaffected were factions of Mill Branch people who hit the road and headed to north-central Georgia. Their move may have resulted in greater autonomy than they experienced in the shadows of Stallings culture, but it was not long before they once again engaged neighbors in exchange, this time in soapstone vessels that wound up in places like Florida and Louisiana. Giving up the hustle and bustle of cosmopolitan life must have been hard.

For countless others not covered in any detail in this chapter, the assertion of autonomy and equality meant maintaining mobility. These were small-scale communities with little to carry. They used mobility, generalized reciprocity, and a variety of leveling mechanisms to forestall inequality. They rejected trends toward private property and territoriality. They avoided investments in place that would thwart freedom of movement, and they did not abide by rules of inclusion and exclusion because that limited options for social arrangements.

The Morrow Mountain people who did not stop in the Midsouth but instead kept moving east into the Carolinas and Georgia were among those who asserted autonomy. There were many others who did the same across the Eastern Woodlands, but you rarely hear about them because the material evidence of their lives is relatively sparse. They would have liked it that way. Like the peasants of revolutionary France, highly mobile hunter-gatherers of the Eastern Woodlands eschewed authority and power to create egalitarian societies of enduring character. This was not a natural state of affairs but instead political action. No one was born equal, but many of the less-conspicuous societies of the Eastern Woodlands were good at creating equals among equals.

Moving North

There is so much more to be written about the Archaic histories of eastern North America. We have yet to touch on the earliest mound-builders of the lower Mississippi Valley and Florida (see Chapter 9), and have not given due consideration to the numerous cave and rockshelter sites that lent Archaic histories a stratigraphic identity (e.g., Griffin 1974; Sherwood et al. 2004; Styles et al. 1983). The Great Lakes region has a history as deep as its bodies of water (Halsey 1999).

Space precludes a comprehensive review of Eastern Archaic histories, so we refer the interested reader to a number of regional summaries and compendia (Dent 1995; Emerson et al. 2009; Ritchie 1969; Sanger and Renouf 2006; Sassaman 2010). However, as we move north to explore the ancient hunter-gatherer traditions of the Subarctic and Arctic, we find it useful to consider how cultural distinctions mapped on to such distinctive ecologies. In so doing we must recall that the glacial margins of eastern North America extended well into the midcontinent at the time of human colonization. As glaciers receded north, plants, animals, and people took opportunity in newly available land. New bodies of water formed, others drained. Mosaics of habitat emerged and disappeared. Sustained settlement of parts of the Northeast may have awaited the spread of deciduous forests, but recent evidence for early human settlement in northern New England and Canada presents a more complicated picture, one involving entanglements between an ever-shifting Woodland front and indigenous people of the Eastern Canadian Subarctic.

Eastern Canadian Subarctic

North of the Eastern Woodlands, at much greater latitude, the cultural landscape of the Eastern Canadian Subarctic was inflected by the immigration of people from distant lands (Table 7.2). This happened

Table 7.2 Eastern Subarctic developments.

Years BP	Eskimo	Amerindian
8,500		Maritime Archaic
4,500	Pre-Dorset Paleoeskimo	
4,000		Susquehanna
3,500		Intermediate Indian
3,000	Groswater	
2,500	Dorset Paleoeskimo	
1,800		Late Pre-Contact Indian (aka Recent Indian)
900	Thule Eskimo	

repeatedly since about 3000 BCE, when Paleoeskimo people of Alaska began to migrate east across the Canadian Arctic (Friesen 2013). By the time they reached the north Atlantic coast, a few centuries later, they encountered Amerindian people who had migrated from the south, through New England. They were the ancient ancestors of various Algonkian people, such as the Beothuk of Newfoundland and the Innu of Labrador and eastern Quebec (Figure 7.7). Some of the descendants of these groups would also encounter, after 1200 CE, the Thule Eskimo, ancestors of the modern Inuit, who also migrated east from Alaska. Norse colonies on Greenland may have been an inducement for eastward migrations of the Thule, but this was also a period of warmer climate, an inducement for bowhead whales – which the Thule hunted – to migrate eastward across the Canadian Arctic archipelago. Around 1000 CE the Norse established a settlement on the northern tip of Newfoundland, at a place called L'Anse aux Meadows. The Dorset Paleoeskimo had already abandoned the area, possibly pushed out by early-arriving Thule. By the late fifteenth century CE the Norse would leave too, victims, it would appear, of the Little Ice Age (McGovern 1994), which made traditional farming nearly impossible (see Chapter 3). Native peoples of diverse heritage and identity persisted in the Eastern Canadian Subarctic to only later experience European colonists who would, this time around, bring irreversible change.

The impacts of European contact on native people of the Eastern Subarctic were dramatic. For two centuries, starting in the seventeenth century, the Innu were deeply involved in the fur trade, first

2.—MONTAGNAIS INDIANS (at Pointe Bleue.)

Fig 7.7 Innu people ca. 1889 at Pointe-Bleue on Lake Saint-John, Quebec. Ancestral Innu were among the indigenous communities of the boreal forest who became swept up in the French fur trade and Christianization in the seventeenth century. Wikimedia.

with the French, then with the British. A huge demand for beaver pelts in Europe stimulated an economy of trapping and trading that would alter irreparably the relationships native people had to the land and to one another. Propped up by European androcentrism, Innu men assumed roles in the new economy that were not available to women. Exacerbating this new gender distinction was the influence of Jesuit missionaries. Troubled by the autonomy and power women expressed in traditional ways, Jesuit priests worked to subordinate women with restrictions on divorce, sex, and travel, among other things. Innu men were squeezed: as much as they may have believed that their wives, sisters, and daughters were their equals, certain advantages accrued to men who complied with the new rules. Moreover, inequalities between neighboring groups arose from an emerging territorialism, pitting former allies against one another for access to land and its game. The territorialism that Frank Speck observed in the early twentieth century, it would seem, arose in the context of the fur trade and was not part of traditional Innu life, as Speck unwittingly assumed (Leacock 1954).

The anthropologist Eleanor Leacock (1954) is credited with exposing the limitations of an ethnohistoric perspective on the Innu. She rightfully corrected the written record by documenting changes to

Innu gender relations and society that were wrought by European contact. However, she could only imagine what life for Innu ancestors was like before contact because there were few archaeological data available. Like others of her time, Leacock assumed that pre-contact Innu were egalitarian and autonomous, and that their relationships with "others" was based on cooperation, not competition. It followed, in her mind, that territorialism was a foreign practice to the Innu. True, the fur trade shifted social relations for men away from the band and toward European traders, but was this the first time "traditional" life was challenged by change?

The culture of the ancestral Innu and other Eastern Subarctic people has generally been seen as "adaptation" to a pristine boreal forest environment – "natural man," to be sure (Holly 2013:12–13) – much like that of the Great Basin. Frank Speck was a student of Franz Boas and a contributor to salvage operations aimed at collecting data on indigenous people before they were entirely transformed by European colonists. Leacock made it clear that Speck was too late, but, again, in the absence of archaeological data, she and others could only imagine pre-contact life and their imaginations varied with perspective. From an ecological perspective, life in the boreal forests of the subarctic required mobility and flexibility. The forests actually contained few animal resources, many of which were available for only a brief time of the year. Although they were a major resource for many groups, migratory caribou were not terribly reliable. The deep snows of harsh winters were an impediment to travel for human and beast alike. Coastal resources were often abundant but likewise unreliable. Harp seals, for instance, made their way up and down the coast with changing seasons, but strong winds kept them offshore and out of reach of humans occasionally (Holly 2013:11). Annual variations in the distribution of pack ice and the flight of migratory birds added to the challenges.

Under such conditions we can expect limits to what people could do in the Eastern Subarctic. For the uncritical observer, such limits must have seemed too severe for much cultural development in the region. Sure, people were seen as highly adaptive to the boreal forests and coasts of the subarctic, but they were kept small in numbers and constantly on the move. This "imagined landscape of marginality," as archaeologist Don Holly (2013:16) calls it, was enough reason to flatten the history of subarctic people into a homogeneous lot of small-scale, mobile foragers, not unlike those of the Desert Culture of the Great Basin despite the vast differences in ecology.

To be sure, mobility was as much an asset to Eastern Subarctic foragers as it was to those of the Great Basin. Holly (2013:21–24) makes the point that the Eastern Subarctic is a place where food resources traveled too, far more than in the Great Basin. That does not mean that subarctic foragers could have waited around for food to arrive. That would have been the kiss of death. Rather, movement was the key to success, and not just the seasonal movements of a settlement system in equilibrium with its environment, but also entire relocations of people, abandonments, and emplacements, all of which had the potential to invite culture change through contact, coalescence, and, in some cases, avoidance. The ancient history of aboriginal life in the Eastern Subarctic is as much about the coming and going of other people as it is about the coming and going of herds of seals, flocks of birds, and herds of caribou.

Archaeologists working in the Eastern Canadian Subarctic have made great strides lately in mapping out the crossroads of cultural diversity that is this region's ancient history (see Holly [2013] for an insightful synthesis of these new findings). Regional specialists have long investigated the migrations of various peoples, and are now seeing how this played out beyond population replacements. Interactions among peoples of distinct heritage and culture led to heightened senses of tradition in some cases, and innovative practices in others. Alliances were forged among some and avoided among others. Occasionally, growing social inequalities within communities arose from dealing with the "outside" world (Holly 2005), not unlike those of European contact. Let's take a closer look at this turbulent history through the perspective of those who were the first to show up in the region from the west, people of Paleoeskimo traditions, and those they would encounter, people of the Maritime Archaic.

Paleoeskimos and the Maritime Archaic

At some point in the mid-third millennium BCE, a group of people from the Alaskan peninsula headed north and east across the Arctic. A few centuries later some of their descendants – people archaeologists refer to generically as "Paleoeskimo" – would arrive at the eastern margin of ice and land. Migrating south into the Eastern Subarctic

Fig 7.8 L'Anse Amour burial mound in Labrador, where a child was buried more than 8,000 years ago. Courtesy of Stephen Hull.

of present-day eastern Quebec, Labrador, and Newfoundland, Paleoeskimo people would encounter the artifacts, sites, and perhaps people of the Maritime Archaic tradition, which extended south into New England. Maritime Archaic people had made at least transient use of the region for millennia, leaving their mark at sites as far north as northern Labrador. Their mark must have grown more conspicuous to Paleoeskimos moving farther south, where coastal sites of Maritime Archaic communities hosted large aggregates of people. They may have also encountered the mortuary facilities of the Maritime Archaic, such as the stone-covered mound at L'Anse Amour in southern Labrador (Figure 7.8).

Maritime Archaic people were themselves immigrants to the region. From about 6500 BCE they made their way north, along the coast, where ice retreated quicker than in the interior high country. They fished coastal waters and hunted seals, walrus, other sea mammals, and birds most of the year, and moved into protected bays in the winter to hunt caribou and fish arctic char. The going must have been good. They reached the central Labrador coast by 5000 BCE, and northern Labrador 500 years later. It was there they encountered a source of fine-grained quartzite known today as Ramah chert.

Sidebar 7.3 L'Anse Amour: oldest Maritime Archaic burial

The oldest burial in Labrador comes from a site known as L'Anse Amour in the Strait of Belle Isle, just across the water from the northwest tip of Newfoundland (https://www.historicplaces.ca/en/rep-reg/place-lieu.aspx?id=14130). Dating back 8,300 years, this single burial consists of the remains of a juvenile in a slab-lined cist covered by boulders to form a mound 8 m in diameter (McGhee and Tuck 1975). Included in the grave were a variety of items: projectile points made from stone and bone, quartzite knives, an incised pendant, graphite pebbles covered in red ochre, a walrus tusk, a bird-bone whistle, and a caribou antler. The child was buried fully extended, with its head to the west and facing north. Evidence of habitation in the immediate area was not found.

L'Anse Amour gives us an early glimpse of a mortuary tradition that would flourish for millennia among Maritime Archaic communities. The tradition varied over time and across space, with boulder mounds common in the north and subterranean cemeteries common in the south, notably in coastal Maine (Robinson 2006). No matter the subregion, mortuary facilities of the tradition were sited away from the living, often at places of gathering for people who were otherwise dispersed across vast areas. By the time subterranean cemeteries arrived in the north

(ca. 4,500 years ago) – most famously at Port au Choix in Newfoundland (Tuck 1976) – Maritime Archaic communities were established as far north as northern Labrador, just ahead of the arrival of Paleoeskimos. From this point forward, mortuary facilities made conspicuous by piles of boulders may have been intended as claims to heritage in a multicultural landscape (Fitzhugh 2006).

But L'Anse Amour predates all that by millennia, during a period of frontier expansion into land never before seen by people. Those must have been incredibly anxious, even fearful times. Encasing the body of the child in a stony tomb may have been among the ways early pioneers dealt with all the uncertainty. Facing north, the child faces the direction of uncharted land, the great unknown. Considering the belief of ethnohistoric Innu, the child may have been "feared more than pitied" (Holly 2013:29; see also Wolff 2012), and thus contained under rock. The Innu were concerned that souls of the recently deceased would cause harm to the living if not contained and avoided. We may never know if the L'Anse Amour child was treated this way. Because Maritime Archaic burial practices would diversify over the millennia, the intent of this oldest burial was potentially different than those yet to come. Still, the dead were kept apart from the living throughout this history of mortuary practice.

Even though it was on the northern margin of this expanding settlement range, Ramah chert became a cultural hallmark. In the words of Holly (2013:33), "the discovery of Ramah by Maritime Archaic peoples was a defining moment in Eastern Subarctic history." Its pivotal role, however, was not technological, but social. Ramah chert would become a medium of exchange among communities distributed across hundreds of kilometers, as far south as southern New England. Regionwide circulation of Ramah chert coincided with a boom in settlement around 2500 BCE, when Paleoeskimos arrived. Growth in Maritime Archaic settlements actually unfolded over a long time, going from simple pithouses at 5000 BCE, to small rectangular above-ground houses a millennium later, to segmented longhouses up to 16 m long by 3500 BCE, and finally longhouses four times that size by the time Ramah chert exchange was in full swing (Figure 7.9). For the next millennium longhouses averaged 50 m and extended as much as 100 m in length, with up to 20 segments (presumed to be the domestic spaces of families sharing a house). They were also clustered at many sites. At Nulliak Cove in northern Labrador, for instance, at least 27 longhouses were constructed (Fitzhugh 2006).

Fig 7.9 Maritime Archaic longhouse at Aillik-2 in Labrador (adapted from Fitzhugh 1984:34, after Holly 2013:36).

Nulliak Cove was also the location of four boulder burial mounds, one with a red-ochre stained stone slab overlying sword-like bifaces made from Ramah chert (Rankin 2008). Rattlers Bight to the south contained two burial clusters with nine red-ochre stained burial pits and abundant Ramah tools (Fitzhugh 1978). Sheets of cut mica, non-local slate tools, copper pendants, and walrus tusks were also found among the graves at Rattlers Bight. Those at another cemetery in Newfoundland, Curtis, contained similar objects, including Ramah chert, but most were associated with only 3 of 15 graves (Holly 2013:37). The Port au Choix cemetery in Newfoundland amplifies the social distinctions of Maritime Archaic communities in its population of at least 117 individuals divided into three areas (Tuck 1976). Distributed unevenly across graves were objects like those listed above, plus an array of objects made from animal parts (needles, combs, beads, whistles), elaborate groundstone tools, and a dog burial, all coated in red ochre. One older male was buried with more than 200 great auk bills, four dozen beaver incisors, and an assortment of other objects made from bone and stone. Jelsma (2006) thinks that this individual may have been a shaman (see Chapter 8).

Maritime Archaic cemeteries and longhouses embody the inherent contradictions of social life in groups composed of people other than immediate kin. Inasmuch as they united multiple families under one roof, longhouses were communal houses. But they were segmented, and the segments possibly ranked. Cemeteries were communal facilities, but not ossuaries in which individuals were commingled. Certain individuals stood out as "special," and perhaps not everyone was eligible to be interred in these special places. The subsistence economy may have dictated that people cooperate; some of the targets of their diet required coordination of labor and knowhow. But there was more to it than that. Something we might call the ritual economy (Spielmann 2002) seems to have engendered competition for spiritual power, with access to Ramah chert, for example, conferring a huge advantage. We might aver that the acquisition and distribution of Ramah chert and other ritually charged substances was the basis for prestige that warranted special treatment in death.

Compounding the challenges of balancing cooperation with competition, descendant Maritime Archaic communities of the far north had to deal with Paleoeskimo interlopers after 2500 BCE. Some of the longhouses of this era are close to locations of early Paleoeskimo settlement (Fitzhugh 1984:21), inviting speculation that longhouses may have also served a defensive function. Similarly, the siting of burial mounds postdating 4,500 years ago in the north may well have been deliberate attempts to signal a Maritime Archaic birthright to land at the time of Paleoeskimo incursions (Rankin 2008).

We cannot be sure if Paleoeskimo and Maritime Archaic people actually came face to face, but it is hard to imagine they did not know of each other's existence, and that they did not have an opinion about it. The cultural construction of the "other" is a powerful tool of identity, sometimes a source of imitation, other times a thing to avoid, even abhor. In this case the outcome was clear: immigrating Paleoeskimo people and indigenous but frontier Maritime Archaic people do not seem to have interacted much. Perhaps they never truly met. Or maybe they did once, or twice, and that was enough. No matter, in only a few centuries after arriving Paleoeskimo people occupied all the northern land of their Maritime Archaic counterparts in what appears to be a total population replacement. How did that happen?

Paleoeskimos Take Center Stage

As Paleoeskimo people expanded farther south into land that was colonized so long ago by others, they could not have missed the obvious. Maritime Archaic predecessors left behind a conspicuous history. Confronting the residues of these indigenous people must have been common, but what they made of them was another matter altogether. Let's first consider the practical matter of making a living in subarctic land.

On this count early Paleoeskimos differed from Amerindian ancestors in a number of significant ways (Hood 2008). For one, they were generalists and seem to have moved around more than their neighbors. Living in smaller groups, Paleoeskimos were able to exploit resources that were cost ineffective for groups who were more stationary and larger in number. Their technology was different too. Paleoeskimos brought bow and arrow technology to the Eastern Subarctic, while the Maritime Archaic used harpoons and thrusting weaponry, including the toggling harpoon. Neither technology crossed ethnic boundaries, despite advantages to both. Paleoeskimos also preferred different raw material for stone tools, chert from Cape Mugford, not Ramah. They struck microblades from cores to tip their arrows with stone points. Taken together, the distinctions in economy, settlement, and technology suggest more than simply divergent traditions. Instead we can imagine an active process of "othering," of asserting difference, presumably on the part of both groups. Maritime Archaic people not only avoided the newcomers, they quickly abandoned much of the northern reaches of the Eastern Subarctic (Holly 2013:53–55). Newfoundland was completely abandoned by 1500 BCE and scarcely visited by Amerindian people for the next 1,200 years (Holly 2013:61).

Groswater Complex

Worsening climate may have contributed to the end of northern Amerindian settlement (Hood 2008), but if so, it did not deter Paleoeskimo people. At about 3,000 years ago a new Paleoeskimo culture arose in a complex archaeologists refer to as Groswater (Fitzhugh 1972). These were coastal people who fished, and hunted seabirds and seals, much like the Maritime Archaic, but with different technology. They made side-notched endblades, along with other flaked stone tools, many with traces of surface grinding (Figure 7.10). At the Phillip's Garden West site on the west coast of Newfoundland, Groswater people deposited unusually large and well-crafted endblades in assemblages dominated by harp seal bones. Renouf (2005) surmises that Phillip's Garden West was a place where hunters could spot the first seals of the season, an event accompanied by great fanfare and ritual. Groswater people also took advantage of migrating caribou by making seasonal forays into the interior (Holly and Erwin 2009). Like their Paleoeskimo ancestors, Groswater people were organized into relatively small mobile groups and maintained a flexibility that served them well in dealing with the vicissitudes of nature.

Dorset Paleoeskimos

Another Paleoeskimo tradition appeared on the scene about 500 BCE, first on the northern coast of Labrador, and then farther south a few centuries later. The Dorset Paleoeskimos mark such a break from what came before that most regional specialists consider the change to be yet another population replacement, this time of Groswater by Dorset (Holly 2013:82–83). The technological inventory is certainly different and Dorset people preferred Ramah chert. Oddly, they seem to have dropped the bow and arrow and may have had little in the way of watercraft. Still, people of the Dorset tradition were heavily reliant

Fig 7.10 Groswater endblades from the Phillip's Garden West site at Port au Choix, Newfoundland. Photography by Priscilla Renouf, reproduced with kind permission from the Port au Choix Archaeology Project.

0   5 cm

on marine resources (seals especially, plus walruses and seabirds) and they stayed put at coastal sites longer than their forebears. Compared with other Paleoeskimo people, the Dorset were specialists.

The density of seal bones at many Dorset sites is staggering. At Port au Choix, for instance, harp seals migrating north in the spring were dispatched in large numbers as they basked on nearshore ice (Figure 7.11). Spring was the time of social aggregation, when Dorset settlements ballooned in size. The largest of the large sites is Phillip's Garden near Port au Choix, where as many as 88 Dorset dwellings have been identified (Holly 2013:86). These were semisubterranean houses with overhead frames of whale rib bones anchored in postholes and covered in seal skins (Renouf 2011). They varied from 7 to 9 m in diameter and had axial cooking features that divided interior spaces into two parts, presumably to house two families. Holly (2013:86) surmises that upwards of 200 people may have occupied Phillip's Garden at peak season.

One of the big differences between early and late Paleoeskimo people was in their respective relations with Amerindians. By the time much of the north was resettled by Amerindians (i.e., Recent Indians) after about 300 BCE, the Dorset were supplying Ramah chert to their new neighbors. With Dorset communities focused on coastal resources and Amerindian communities venturing into the interior,

Fig 7.11 Harp seal mother and her pup. Wikimedia.

Fig 7.12 Exhibit at The Rooms (museum) in St. John's, Newfoundland, depicting quarrying of soapstone bowl preforms from the Fleur de Lys site in northeastern Newfoundland, excavated by John Irwin (2005) in the late 1990s. Kenneth E. Sassaman photo, 2015.

relations between the two may have been symbiotic. They likely traded more than rock between them and even congregated occasionally for communal events. At the Gould site near Phillip's Garden, for example, a combination of Amerindian and Dorset material is seen as evidence of a joint feast (Renouf et al. 2000). Holly (2013:99–100) points to other evidence to suggest Dorset–Amerindian relations were not always so warm and friendly.

Amerindian reoccupation of places like Newfoundland, which was home to only Paleoeskimos for more than fifteen centuries, must have challenged existing social and economic organization. The shift from generalized economies of Groswater times to the specialized harp seal hunting of Dorset people may very well have been stimulated by the return of Amerindians (see Holly 2005). Economic intensification like this signals not merely greater production, but also the demands of an emerging political or ritual economy, some perhaps geared toward interethnic relations. Even seemingly mundane activities and products, like soapstone vessels, could have been integral to economies of regional, multicultural interaction (Figure 7.12).

Dorset occupation of Newfoundland ended about 800 CE, when global warming of the Medieval Climatic Period diminished pack ice and the harp seals that depended on it. The people migrated north, along the Labrador coast. Along the way they had to navigate lands that were at least occasionally visited by Amerindians who spent much of their time in the interior. They could have adjusted their subsistence, mobility, and group sizes to accommodate new social and ecological circumstances, but they did not. Rather, the Dorset held steadfast in many respects. What did change noticeably was their production of art. Late period Dorset art (ca. 1,200–700 years ago) intensified to involve figurines of animals, humans, and things in-between

Sidebar 7.4 Dorset soapstone quarries

A fascinating dimension of Dorset culture is seen in the quarrying of soapstone. The soft, talc-rich rock was used to make cooking vessels and oil lamps. At Fleur de Lys in northeastern Newfoundland, outcrops of soapstone cluster in six locations, the largest of which, Locality 1, consists of 300 m of quarry face with 654 scars from removing vessel preforms. Excavations by John Irwin (2005) in the late 1990s showed that Dorset miners excavated below the ground surface at the base of the quarry face to extract fresh soapstone. The trenches they dug became saturated, providing exceptional organic preservation, including branches used to infill the trench and keep the area workable.

Irwin found evidence for a full range of production stages, from roughening out faces, to extracting preforms, to finishing vessels. The stone tools of quarrying and finishing were recovered too. In addition to the usual lamp and cooking vessel forms, miniature vessel scars were concentrated in outcrops close to the ground. Interpreted as "child's play," the small vessels signal a greater social context for quarrying than the work itself (Irwin 2010).

Fleur de Lys is the only known soapstone quarry in Newfoundland, so presumably it was the source of raw material for vessels and lamps island-wide, if not also beyond. Tracing soapstone to its geological source is a tricky business, however, so the reach of Fleur de Lys soapstone remains uncertain (Irwin 2005). Radiocarbon dating places its use between 1,600 and 1,200 years ago. A couple of centuries later, on the Ungava peninsula of Quebec, a quarry site known as Qajartalik was a place of shamanistic practice, as well as vessel production (Arsenault 2013). Carved into the quarry face are scores of human faces, many resembling the wooden shamanistic masks of the late period Dorset. Arsenault sees in this array of images, and their placement in mosaics of expression, an opportunity to pass shamanistic practice to the next generation, not unlike the mimicry of Fleur de Lys miniature vessels, but with serious mojo. Later, Thule Eskimos – who show up around 900–800 years ago – would use the Qajartalik quarry for strictly practical purposes, perhaps unaware that it was a source of Dorset power, although the faces in stone may have made it hard to deny.

(see Chapter 8). Bear imagery was popular, some of it suggestive of shamanistic practices. Wooden human masks of various expressions and painted in red ochre are also considered to be the instruments of shaman, used perhaps in rituals of curing and conjuring. The resemblance between wooden masks and faces carved in soapstone is unmistakable.

If changing climate and Amerindian neighbors were not enough for the Dorset, by about 900 years ago people of the Thule Eskimo tradition arrived across the Arctic from the west. Ancestors of today's Inuit, the Thule arrived with an impressive inventory of technology: large skin boats, kayaks, dog sleds, toggling harpoons, bows and arrows, and more. They may never have encountered the Dorset, but they certainly took their place. Global warming likely factored into the eastward migration of the Thule, much as it did the northern retreat of the Dorset, leaving southern coastlines open for colonization by Amerindians from the south. We'll take up the Thule expansion further in Chapter 8.

Marginal Myth

Our review of Paleoeskimo and Amerindian migrations and interactions has covered a lot of ground, but there were actually even more events of displacement and relocation. Not long after early Paleoeskimos migrated into Labrador and points farther south, seemingly replacing Maritime Archaic people, another incursion emanated from the south. About 4,000 years ago, members of the Susquehanna tradition of southern New England reached Nova Scotia and New Brunswick. Like the pre-Dorset Paleoeskimo, Susquehanna immigrants were more generalized than their Maritime cousins, relying on terrestrial game (mostly deer) more than marine mammals. At this same time the interior of the Quebec-Labrador peninsula began to be populated. Hitherto covered in ice, this region blossomed into dense boreal forests that supported small, short-term settlements by people who used some Ramah chert but mostly local stone, particularly Mistassini quartzite (Denton 1998). The homeland and cultural affiliation of immigrants into the interior is unknown, but connections both east and south are evident in the use of nonlocal materials (McCaffrey 2006).

We can add another incursion of Amerindians from the south or west about 2,000 years ago, arguably the influx of Algonkian speakers (Holly 2013:68–76). Pottery made an appearance at this time too, as did the bow and arrow, independent of the much earlier Paleoeskimo technology.

It is beyond ironic that a region of North America considered so marginal in so many ways should be a hotbed of cultural diversity. Sure, those who were either pushed or pulled into the Eastern Subarctic over the past 5,000 years experienced warmer climate than those before or after (Friesen 2013). Of course, warmer climate does not explain migrations, but it did enable people to expand both northward, with receding ice, and eastward, with migrating whales. It also enabled the Norse to further their reach. Ultimately, a return to a colder climate in the fourteenth and fifteenth centuries sent the Norse packing. Hostilities with native people likely contributed to their failure, reminding us that no matter the direct impacts of climate change, negotiating relations among people of distinct heritage, language, and culture can be just as challenging. We are thus compelled to understand how social inequality among the aboriginal peoples of the Eastern Canadian Subarctic traces to intercultural encounters and interactions. All of the aboriginal people moving through this "marginal" land were living off that land, and thus can be rightfully described as "hunters and gatherers" even as we acknowledge the diversity this entailed. Rather than dwell on differences in subsistence pursuits (sealing, whaling, fishing, caribou hunting, etc.), it would seem appropriate to ask how the social formation and alignments of groups constrained or enabled certain practices, notably those we might describe as "intensification."

Conclusion

We have covered vast portions of North America in this chapter and the one before to showcase the range of variation among those who lived off wild plants and animals during the Holocene. In each case covered here we questioned the concept of equality by considering that social formations took shape not simply from the relationship people had to land and its resources, but from that to other people as well, people of distinct identity and heritage. The consummate Great Basin foragers that Steward regarded as "natural man" were not constrained by nature as much as they were by practices that involved routine movements, cached resources, and the infrastructure of hunting. Ethnic differences in the Eastern Woodlands help to explain the differential acceptance of innovations, persistent land-use, and the contours of violence. The coming and going of diverse people in the Eastern Subarctic seems to have been the engine of change and a source of economic intensification.

In the early decades of Americanist archaeology, Steward's concept of Culture Core and its emphasis on human–environment relationships became conflated with a cultural evolutionary model that assumed everyone was born equal, naturally. More recent thinking illustrates how egalitarian social relations indeed arise out of certain ecological and technological conditions, but this form of egalitarianism emerges from engagement with the world, not some hard-wired primordial existence. Rousseau showed how "equality" as a social concept arose in the context of French inequalities. We think that ancient North America has its share of social revolutions that made egalitarianism an institution, at least for a while. These too, we imagine, gained traction in the context of inequalities that arose from communities who settled into particular places, built infrastructure to offset the diminished returns of staying put, and intensified economies to meet the demands of ritual and social life, and to assert and defend boundaries of exclusion. In the next chapter we will consider that these sorts of social and cultural challenges extend into the supernatural realm of otherworldly beings and forces.

8 Animism, Shamanism, and Technology
Life in the Arctic

When men came home from seal hunting in the spring, and when the seals were brought into the house, they had ipuutet [wooden ladles]. The women took the ladles and got fresh and pure snow. Then they gave the dead seal a drink saying, "Because you are thirsty, we are giving you good pure water. If you are thirsty, come here so you can have excellent water." They sprinkle snow below their mouth [on the chin] and also on their flippers, all the time talking to them. That is the way our mother did it.

> Yup'ik Eskimo, Clara Agartak, 1987 (Fienup-Riordan 1994:96–97)

As we delve into the details of Arctic history, let us step back from our own western perspectives on cultural variation and change to consider another way of seeing and being in the world. The alternative is sometimes called a *relational ontology*, meaning a worldview that considers the relations between things or beings as more fundamental than the things or beings themselves. This contrasts with a *substantivist* or *essentialist ontology*, in which the entities themselves are primary and the relations among them secondary. Western ontology is essentialist and the periodic table of elements in chemistry, for example, is one measure of this way of thinking. Chemists, of course, know a lot about reactions between elements, but through essentialist ontology, elements can be understood in their own right; the atomic weight of an element alone is enough to distinguish it from any other element. We do not need to ask how carbon reacts with nitrogen to understand what carbon is.

Imagine, instead, a worldview in which nothing can be understood in isolation from those things to which it is related. We made this exercise in the previous chapter, where we considered that many of the societies that were once thought of as independent and autonomous actually owed their existence to relations with others. Here we expand the purview to include nonhuman and otherworldly agents. We can consider, for instance, that game animals are more than targets for feeding. Through the act of hunting, humans and their game are each made. Consider further that game in this case is not only an animate creature, but one with a spirit or soul and the power to affect human outcomes. In the quote of the Yup'ik Eskimo woman at the start of this chapter, seals are persons of the sea who seek land and freshwater, which women are happy to oblige. How seals are treated by people – from the preparation of the hunt to the disposal of bones – determines future success in hunting (Fienup-Riordan 1994). The Yup'ik would say that seals have their own protocols to follow in their interactions with humans. The futures of seals and people alike depended on carefully regulated interactions between them.

Now, imagine a world where not only animals and humans are interactive, but also plants, water, rocks, the sky, the earth, and more. In relational ontologies, anything can be an agent. It is a worldview that anthropologists classify as *animistic*. Consistent with relational ontology, animism does not distinguish between spiritual and physical realms of the world inasmuch as all things have souls or spirits (e.g., Descola 2013). Animism is participatory religion, in which individuals actively engage nonhuman agents in the course of everyday practice (Figure 8.1). However, certain interactions between humans and supernatural forces rise to a level of learned practice that anthropologists classify as *shamanism*. As a practitioner able to

Fig 8.1 Yup'ik Eskimo mask with seal or sea otter spirit, Yukon River area, Alaska, 1800s. Dallas Museum of Art/Wikimedia.

Fig 8.2 Chuonnasuan (1927–2000), the last shaman of
the Oroqen people, photographed in July 1994 in Manchuria near the
Amur River border between the People's Republic of China and Russia
(Siberia). Richard Noll photo, 1994/Wikimedia.

access supernatural realms and forces, a *shaman* draws on a variety of knowledge, substance, and action to intervene as circumstances demand. They are agents of the spirit world, transcendent of the time–space boundaries of physical bodies. They variously heal, conjure, divine, protect, forecast, and more. Altered states of consciousness are involved at times, and shamans may be shape-changers (Figure 8.2).

The practice and term, *shamanism*, ultimately traces to Siberia, and Alice Kehoe (2000) gives us good reason not to export the term outside its original context. But here we are interested not so much in any historical lineages between, say, a nascent Siberian tradition of shamanism and those it influenced, as in any practice informed by relational ontology and animism. As we will see at the end of this chapter, these ways of thinking and being were pervasive, perhaps a good measure of their sustainability in our modern sense of the term.

Thinking and being in the Arctic is, of course, tough today and it must have always been that way. It takes ingenious technology, intimate knowledge of the environment, and dependable social connections to make a living there. Native people did not have to await the introduction of snow mobiles, kerosene heaters, or cell phones to make a go of it. And they did not have to await the melting of Arctic ice to expand across the region (Figure 8.3).

The human presence in Arctic Siberia has recently been pushed back to 45,000 years ago, when a mammoth and wolf were dispatched by Paleolithic hunters in the thick of the Ice Age (Pitulko et al. 2016). Of course, colonization of the North American Arctic came much later, but it was not precluded by ice. Humans were in central Alaska by 13,000 years ago, and farther east not much later. The latitude of central Alaska is just below the Arctic Circle and thus currently part of the forested subarctic, where monthly temperatures are above 10 degrees Celsius (50 degrees Fahrenheit) for only one to three months of the year. And yet, the northern reaches of the subarctic today would have seen arctic conditions when people first arrived. Besides temperatures that

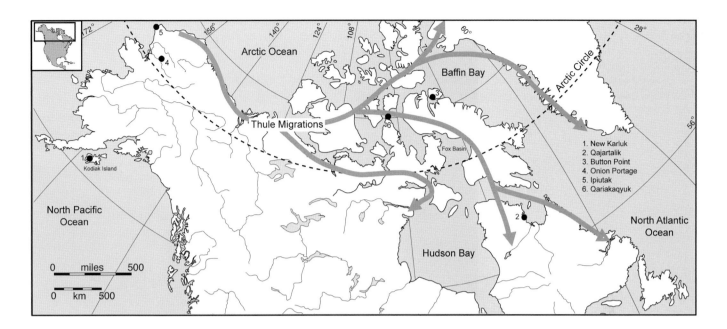

1. New Karluk
2. Qajartalik
3. Button Point
4. Onion Portage
5. Ipiutak
6. Qariakaqyuk

Fig 8.3 Map of the North American Arctic and Subarctic, showing sites mentioned in the text and the generalized route of Thule eastward migrations. Timothy R. Pauketat map, 2018.

rarely get above freezing, much of the Arctic gets little to no sunlight from October to March.

Technically, the Arctic is the region encompassed by the Arctic Circle, the invisible line of latitude at 66.5°N. From west to east this encompasses the northern third of Alaska, most of Nunavut and the northern extreme of the Northwest Territories, and the northern three-fourths of Greenland. The portions of northern Quebec, Labrador, and Newfoundland we covered in Chapter 7 are part of the Eastern Subarctic.

Given its limited sun and warmth, the Arctic supports little vegetation (Figure 8.4). The province lies north of the subarctic treeline, and consists mostly of tundra vegetation: dwarf shrubs, sedges, mosses, and lichens. In the northern parts of the Arctic, groundcover is bare. Across much of the province, the ground is frozen much of the year (permafrost), winds blow hard, and precipitation is minimal. When temperatures rise in the summer, parts of the tundra turn wet with melting permafrost and the marshes, lakes, and bogs of its scoured glacial plains.

Sea ice is a defining feature of the Arctic. This is basically frozen ocean water, not the ice sheets of glaciers that form on land. During the winter months, sea ice reaches land across much of the Arctic, essentially extending the range of terrestrial access to maritime biomes.

Fig 8.4 The alpine tundra landscape of the Gates of the Arctic National Park in the Brooks Range of northern Alaska. The park is situated entirely north of the Arctic Circle. Weiler Greg photo/Wikimedia.

The sea provided marine mammals (walruses, whales, seals) and fish for the various Arctic people we cover in this chapter. Changes in the distribution of sea ice over the course of Arctic human history have been instrumental in structuring the distribution of people and the game they came to depend on.

Arctic History

Arctic history is largely the history of Inuit people, those of Eskimo-Aleut language whose ancestors include people of the Thule culture who encountered the Norse in thirteenth-century Greenland and Newfoundland. Tracing this ancestry beyond the expression of Thule culture ca. 1,000 years ago is difficult. As we saw in Chapter 7, distinct, coeval traditions of Paleoeskimos converged in places like the eastern Arctic, attesting to multiple waves of eastward migration from Alaska, the apparent homeland of the Inuit, via the Thule (Table 8.1).

Some general observations on culture history will help to situate the histories we cover in this chapter. First, cultures of the Pacific coast of Alaska, including the Aleutian Islands, were long-lived, spanning a 7,000-year-long sequence that was punctuated at times by cultural changes leading ultimately to complex social and economic organization about 900 years ago (Fitzhugh 2003). Pacific Alaska is not technically part of the Arctic, as it is both at lower latitude and influenced by oceanic

Table 8.1 Chronology of culture history across the North American Arctic, from west to east (adapted from Neusius and Gross 2014:110).

Years BP	Pacific Alaska	North Alaska	High Arctic	Greenland
800–400			Thule	Thule
1,000–600				Norse
2,000–400		Thule		
2,500–800			Dorset	Dorset
3,000–1,500		Norton		
4,000–2,500			Pre-Dorset/ Independence	Sarqaq
4,500–400	Kodiak			
4,500–3,000		Arctic Small Tool		
5,500–400	Aleutian			
7,000–3,500	Ocean Bay			

fronts that bring greater warmth and moisture than the Arctic receives more generally. Much of the history of this maritime setting parallels developments on the Northwest Coast, which we cover in Chapter 13. Nonetheless, we review developments in the Aleutians and on Kodiak Island in this chapter as these inflected Arctic histories elsewhere.

Second, northern Alaska and the High Arctic (i.e., the northern Canadian archipelago) has a history that began at about 4,500 years ago with migrations eastward by communities of the Arctic Small Tool tradition, with roots in Siberia. They were the first to colonize the Arctic Ocean coast. They made it all the way to Greenland within a few centuries. The Independence and Pre-Dorset traditions of the eastern Arctic and the Pre-Dorset equivalent in Greenland, Sarqaq, are the presumed descendants of these early pioneers.

Third, as the name implies, Pre-Dorset "evolved" into the Dorset traditions of 2,500–800 years ago. Dorset was an eastern Arctic development, and it appears to have flourished through the time of Norse colonization of Greenland, and then dwindled with the arrival of Thule people about 800 years ago.

And that brings us to a major watershed of Arctic culture history: the eastward migration of Thule people, whose origins on islands on the Bering Strait 2,000 years ago were apparently rooted in Norton culture of the earlier millennium. We will take a close look in this chapter at the Thule migration, one of the most impactful events of Arctic history. As noted earlier, Thule traces directly to Inuit people of the modern era. Some of their Thule ancestors were in contact with the Norse, and they may have had a penchant for Norse iron (Chapter 3).

Pacific Alaska

An early and long-lived maritime tradition of the Pacific coast of Alaska is the Ocean Bay tradition of ca. 7,500–3,500 years ago. The oldest coastal occupations actually predate Ocean Bay by at least 1,500 years, and they occur on islands of the eastern Aleutian region. That region consists of volcanic islands that jut westward toward Asia. Assemblages of blades, microblades (Figure 8.5), transverse burins, stone bowls, and oil lamps are found associated with tent-like houses in shallow depressions at sites of the early Anangula phase (ca. 7000–5000 BCE). These rather ephemeral occupations likely represent the initial occupation of the Aleutians, and they reflect a full-blown maritime economy, although seasonal use of the interior of Alaska cannot be ruled out (Davis and Knecht 2010).

Ocean Bay is the better-known and well-established early maritime tradition of Pacific Alaska. Sites of this tradition are centered on Kodiak Island and extend into adjacent parts of Pacific Alaska, including the Aleutians. Like Anangula, from which it may be derived, Ocean Bay was a maritime tradition. Harpoon-like weapons, made from both stone and bone, were used to dispatch seals, sea lion, sea otter, porpoise, and whale. They also used bone hooks to catch fish. Ocean Bay sea-mammal hunters introduced ground-slate tools to an existing inventory of chipped-stone tools. Evidence for the kinds of boats they used for fishing and hunting remains elusive.

Changes ensued at about 2500 BCE on Kodiak Island. Oil lamps become more common as architecture became more elaborate. Small pithouses appear in the late Ocean Bay period. Walls were made from sod with floors partially sunk into the ground and often covered in red ochre. Filled with sea-mammal oil that was ignited at a wick, lamps provided not only illumination inside pithouses during long winter nights, but also a source of heat, even if modest (Figure 8.6).

Fig 8.5 Multiple views of three microblade cores from the Anangula site, which show distinctively Aleutian attributes, such as pressure flaking, within an overall Alaskan tradition of microblade and blade technologies (Gómez Coutouly 2015). Research continues on the historical and cultural relationship of Anangula technology to Siberian microblade industries and those of interior Alaska. Courtesy of Yan Axel Gómez Coutouly.

Fig 8.6 Kodiak oil lamp with animal effigy (Object A375349). Smithsonian National Museum of Natural History.

Developments on Kodiak Island took a strong pathway toward greater scale and complexity. During the Kachemak period of 3,500–1,000 years ago, a number of additional innovations were introduced, such as the toggling harpoon, which was a composite weapon with a detachable spearhead. The "toggle" of this design means that the head turned sideways after it entered prey and thus lessened the chance of it being dislodged (Figure 8.7). Cordage tied to the head enabled hunters to stay connected to the prey and eventually pull it in. With the toggling harpoon, the effectiveness of sea-mammal hunting sky-rocketed. Expanded use of net weights would suggest that fishing also intensified in the Kachemak period.

Another important innovation was the ground-slate *ulu*, which is a curved blade mounted parallel to a handle. Ulus are still used by modern Eskimos, and you can buy something like it at any well-stocked

Fig 8.7 Illustration of the components and function of a toggling harpoon from Barrow, Alaska (Dumas 1984).

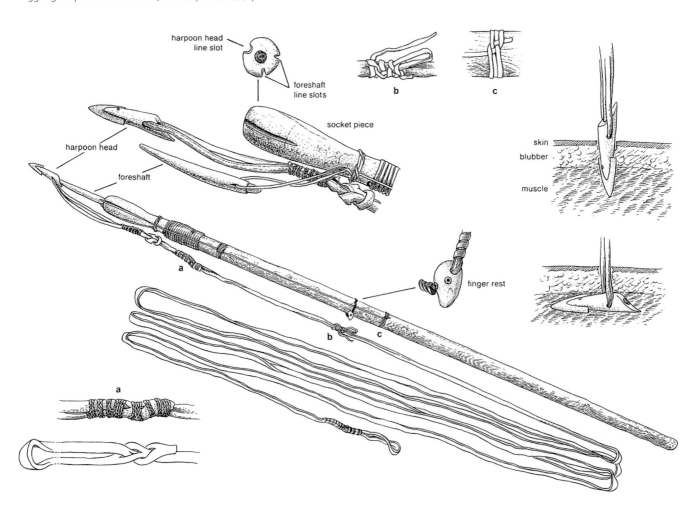

kitchen store. Great for butchering meat, ulus are today regarded as women's knives by the Inuit.

Social change was underway too. Pithouses began to be clustered in the Kachemak period in village-like fashion. Oil lamps were sometimes made larger than usual and decorated with relief carvings of animals or humans. Objects of personal adornment known as labrets appeared (see Chapter 13). Mortuary practices became more formal and geared toward ancestor veneration.

Big changes culminated on Kodiak Island after about 800 years ago in what is known as the Koniag period (1200 CE to European contact). Houses expanded from small, single-unit dwellings to multifamily units with a large central room and smaller side rooms. One such village of Koniag houses was occupied permanently for 600 years, through Russian occupation in the eighteenth century. Uncovered at the New Karluk site were various ceremonial objects, some evidently relevant to rituals of warfare and social competition, and others the instruments of shamans (Jordan and Knecht 1988). Evidence points to the emergence of institutions of power and leadership, evidently tied to the accumulation and distribution of symbolic wealth, but ultimately the ability to intensify food acquisition and storage. Archaeologist Ben Fitzhugh (2003) explains this process in ecological terms but with great attention to technological innovations, like toggling harpoons, nets, and ulus, that enabled people to offset the diminishing returns of more permanent and larger-scale settlement. These same technologies afforded opportunities to intensify production and amass surpluses for political ends, activities that fell to hereditary leaders much like those of the Northwest Coast (see Chapter 13).

The Aleutian Islands were home to other descendants of the Ocean Bay tradition, starting about 5,000 years ago. Some aspects of Aleutian material culture after this time, notably oil lamps and bone tools, match those of the Kodiak tradition, but missing in the Aleutians until very late are ground-slate tools. Middens of Aleutian sites contain the same sea mammals and fish of their Kodiak counterparts, but also sea urchin, birds, and foxes, plus occasional caribou and bear at sites in the eastern Aleutians. There is little to suggest that communities of the Aleutian tradition experienced the level of social and political complexity of the Kodiak islanders.

Trans-Arctic

Moving now to north Alaska, our attention shifts from long-term sequences of the North Pacific islands to a 5,000-year-long history of trans-Arctic migrations, literally people migrating across the Arctic Ocean coast, which was frozen most of the time. Transportation technology factors into this history in a huge way, as do all sorts of innovations for surviving in subfreezing weather most of the year.

Arctic Small Tool Tradition

This history begins with communities of the Arctic Small Tool tradition (ASTT). The first to colonize the Arctic Ocean coast of the High Arctic, communities of the ASTT established sites from northern Alaska to Greenland over a relatively short period of time. As the name implies, the ASTT consisted of small, finely made blades of flaked stone that were probably mounted into handles to make composite tools (Figure 8.8). Antler or wooden handles, hafts, or other organic components for mounting blades are rarely preserved in the ground. From sites with extraordinary preservation – generally in

Fig 8.8 Flaked-stone tools of the Arctic Small Tool tradition: (a) microblade; (b) burin; (c–e) projectile points; (f) side blade; (g) scraper; and (h) adze with polished bit (Dumond 1977: figure 48). Artifacts collected in the 1960s from National Park Service land in Alaska (now Katmai National Park) and curated by University of Oregon Museum of Natural and Cultural History, Eugene.

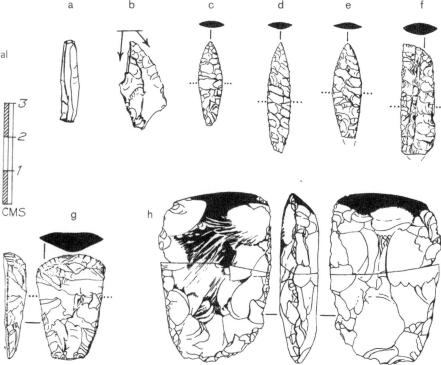

the eastern part of the ASTT range – we know that in addition to handles for composite tools, bone was used to make needles, harpoon heads, and foreshafts for projectiles. Small blades were often shaped into projectile points. Given their small size and the presence of bone foreshafts, these projectiles were likely the first true arrow points, used of course with a bow, which was an entirely new technology for North America. In addition, flaked stone was used to make burins for engraving, scrapers for hide processing, and adzes for working wood. Given the differences between ASTT technology and the older technologies of Pacific Alaska and the Aleutians, some specialists argue that the ASTT came with a second major wave of migration out of Siberia, where a similar small tool tradition flourished (Dumond 1984).

Houses have been documented at sites of the ASTT in northern Alaska (Figure 8.9). These are generally square structures about 4 m on a side and dug partially into the ground. An entry ramp on one side opened into an interior with a central fire hearth, and occasionally

Fig 8.9 Excavation of an Arctic Small Tool tradition semisubterranean house from the Brooks Range of southwest Alaska. Used with permission of Don E. Dumond.

four postholes that presumably supported a roof structure. Sod was most likely used to cover roofs made from wooden or whale-bone beams.

Independence and Pre-Dorset

The first indication of migration eastward across the High Arctic is found in the far north of Greenland and not that much later than the oldest ASTT sites in Alaska. Known as the Independence phase, sites dating from 4,000 to 3,700 years ago in the eastern High Arctic include tools nearly identical to those of the ASTT, if slightly larger on average. Houses were a good bit different, however. Independence houses tended to be elliptical in plan, with a ring of rocks around the perimeter and vertical rock slabs down the middle. A central hearth also lined with vertical rock slabs attests to substantial internal fires. Good evidence for the superstructure of houses is lacking, but they must have been sturdy enough to protect against months of extreme weather, but open enough to allow smoke to escape. Human passage in and out of houses may have been through the roofs.

Bear in mind that Independence settlement extended much farther north in the east than the ASTT did in Alaska, to within 700 km of the North Pole! With nearly three months of total darkness every winter, Independence communities must have practiced the human equivalent of hibernation. Cache pits in the floors of their houses attest to winter food storage.

Postdating Independence in northeast Canada and the southern part of Greenland are sites of the Pre-Dorset phase, called by some Sarqaq (or Saqqaq). The tool types of Pre-Dorest and Sarqaq are similar enough to those of Independence to show ancestry, but different enough to warrant separate nomenclature. In addition to the blades, burins, scrapers, and points made from stone, Pre-Dorset inventories include socketed bone harpoons. Soapstone lamps at some Sarqaq sites exemplify technology for indoor heat and light much like the oil lamps of Pacific Alaska. Despite the similarity, DNA from the hair of an individual dating to 2000 BCE shows no genetic affinity to Inuit people or modern Native Americans (Rasmussen et al. 2010). The individual is most closely related to indigenous people of northeast Asia, supporting the notion that the ASTT represents a separate migration of people into North America.

Dorset

We introduced the Dorset culture in the previous chapter and we discussed their history in the context of intercultural encounters. Here we continue where we left off by considering the beliefs of Dorset people in the context of Arctic living. Relationships to other people are still important in this respect, but let us instead consider the relationship Dorset people had with animals and other nonhuman entities, many of which were sources of food. You may recall from Chapter 7 that the Dorset people had a penchant for seals. They also hunted walruses and seabirds, but seals were primary targets. Ironically, Dorset people may not have used watercraft, at least not big boats, and thus depended on sea ice to gain access to seals. The going must have been tough, for we see in Dorset technology and art a sense of seriousness, arguably fear. But before we go any further with the Dorset worldview, let us review briefly some of the details of culture history and lifeways we covered in Chapter 7.

Dorset was a Paleoeskimo tradition and it clearly was centered on maritime resources. However, compared with other Paleoeskimo people, the Dorset had a more specialized subsistence economy. They also had a desire for Ramah chert from Labrador, which was tough to obtain, but they did not use bow technology, like their predecessors of the ASTT. You would be right to assume that Dorset culture has its origins in the Pre-Dorset, given the name alone. However, the appearance of Dorset in the eastern High Arctic and Greenland at about 2,500 years ago marks a turn away from a Paleoeskimo tradition of mobility and flexibility and, perhaps because of greater specialization, more vulnerability to the winds of change. Some of the Dorset sites mentioned in Chapter 7 attest to repeated, if not permanent, large-scale habitation. For instance, upwards of 200 people may have occupied the Phillip's Garden site in Newfoundland (Bell and Renouf 2003; Holly 2013:86). As we discussed earlier, Newfoundland sat at the interface between Paleoeskimo and Amerindian people, and Dorset specialization may have been stimulated by interactions between these distinct populations. Recall that encounters like this were triggered by southern migrations of Dorset people into the Eastern Subarctic. When the Medieval Warm Period began about 1,200 years ago, Dorset people migrated back north as sea ice diminished and curtailed the availability of harp seals. Although bone items believed to be sled parts are occasionally found at Dorset sites, the lack of dog remains or the hardware of harnesses suggests sleds must have been pulled by humans.

They could have adjusted their diet and settlement patterns in response to climate change, but instead the Dorset tried to maintain tradition by relocating northward. It is at this time, after about 750 CE, the late Dorset period, that we see an explosion in artwork, some of it involving animals, notably polar bears. Beyond the shamanistic practices evident in wooden masks and the carved soapstone faces, Dorset artwork may have had a practical effect, as in the use of polar bear effigies to teach young hunters how to dispatch seals (Figure 8.10).

What else does Dorset artwork tell us about their worldview? First of all, humans are the most common subject of the portable art and human faces figured prominently in the soapstone quarry at Qajartalik in Quebec (Arsenault 2013). Life-sized human masks carved from wood were found at Button Point, just north of Baffinland. Miniature human masks are more common. Small human figurines include examples of persons who appear to be killed. Additionally, carved bone was sometimes formed into human mouths with teeth, the canines exaggerated in size. Wear patterns on carved teeth, sometimes referred to as "shaman's teeth," suggest they were worn in the mouth much in the fashion of fake vampire teeth at Halloween.

Fig 8.10 Ivory carvings of polar bears either swimming or stalking prey. Courtesy of Matthew Betts.

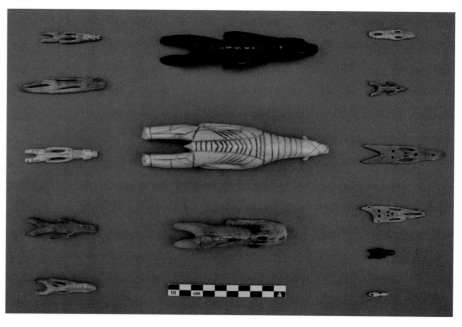

Sidebar 8.1 Relational ecology of polar bears

Dorset hunters took a variety of game but they were particularly keen on seals, both harp and ringed seals (e.g., Harp 1976; Hodgetts 2005; Renouf 2011). With such great emphasis on seals for subsistence, it stands to reason that these creatures would have factored into the ritual practices of the Dorset. It is thus curious that seals do not figure heavily in the prodigious Dorset art industry. Throughout their history but especially after about 1,300 years ago, Dorset artists carved a variety of miniature figurines of humans, bears, and other human–animal themes from bone, antler, ivory, soapstone, and wood. Polar bears were a particularly popular theme, second only to humans. As carved effigies, polar bears are rendered in all sorts of poses, some evidently flying.

Why so many polar bear effigies? And why so many postures and poses? Polar bears are certainly formidable creatures, arguably more dangerous to humans than grizzly bears. In an explanation that draws on relational ecology, Matthew Betts and colleagues (2015) suggest that Dorset people attempted to gain the perspective of polar bears as skilled hunters of seals. The range of postures and poses

of bear effigies suggests to them that Dorset carvers were capturing behaviors associated with seal hunting, such as stalking, leaping, and diving. These then served both as mnemonic devices for teaching hunting skills to fledgling Dorset hunters, and as a measure of the animistic belief that polar bears made the Dorset. Betts and colleagues (2015:108) see this connection as generative of Dorset culture and history: "the polar bear brought the Dorset into existence, both existentially, as a means to think about their place in the world, and practically, as a means to draw power, gain abilities and perspectives, and to teach/remind the Dorset of the correct actions on the sea ice." Notably, the production of polar bear effigies intensified in the centuries prior to the end of the Dorset, coincident with the warming trend known as the Medieval Warm Period and the influx of Thule people. Their long history of living on the edge of ice, like polar bears, was on the decline. Greater production and use of polar bear effigies may signal efforts on the part of the Dorset to apply their traditional beliefs and practices to mitigate the impact of devastating change.

Masks, figurines, and other depictions of humans and human body parts are usually attributed to shamanism by Dorset specialists (Figure 8.11). What exactly shamans were doing with human masks and other items is unknown, but if truly shamanistic, then the term "art" is misleading. As discussed in Sidebar 8.1 on polar bear effigies, so-called "art" consists of instruments of intervention, objects or substances that produce effects. They are, in their own right, agents of culture, not merely symbols or representations. To wear a human mask is to become another person, or another type of person. To depict an animal is to be that animal. The usual goals of shamanism may apply: that is, objects and masks may have been used to divine, protect, damage, or heal. But in a relational ontology, they are only a part of something bigger, more complex. Where, when, with what, and by whom an object was made and used may have been more important than the object itself.

The social context for all this object agency was one of rapid change. As noted above, the Medieval Warm Period undermined

Fig 8.11 Dorset wooden masks, 500–1200 CE, from the Button Point site on Bylot Island, Nunavut, Canada (Photos PfFm-1: 1773, S89-1827, PfFm-1: 1728a, S89-1828). Courtesy of Canadian Museum of History.

Dorset economies in its effects on sea ice and the seals that depended on it. Subsistence economies eventually diversified to include many other resources besides seals. Encounters with other people were on the rise, and not long after climate began to warm, Dorset people may have confronted the eastbound Thule, not to mention the Norse and various Amerindian people.

In the context of such change, Dorset people began to construct longhouses (Figure 8.12). This innovation actually occurred on the outskirts of what is sometimes called the "core area" of late Dorset settlement, the Foxe Basin (Maxwell 1976). People apparently moved rapidly out of the Foxe Basin in the eighth century CE to occupy sub-regions that were abandoned centuries earlier by people of Dorset ancestry. Their expanded settlements were enabled by a diversified economy, seasonal settlement adjustments, and food storage. Winters were times of dispersal and the use of semisubterranean houses or occasionally snow houses. But, in the summer, groups of up to a hundred people aggregated at sites of longhouses, where, according to archaeologist Max Friesen (2007), they reaffirmed their sense of group affiliation, evidently in opposition to a growing trend toward inequality and competition in the Foxe Basin, where longhouses are absent.

Friesen (2007) makes a good case for the egalitarianism of longhouses. These structures consisted of linear arrangements of boulders or gravel from 5 to 7 m in width and 8 to 45 m in length. How, or even

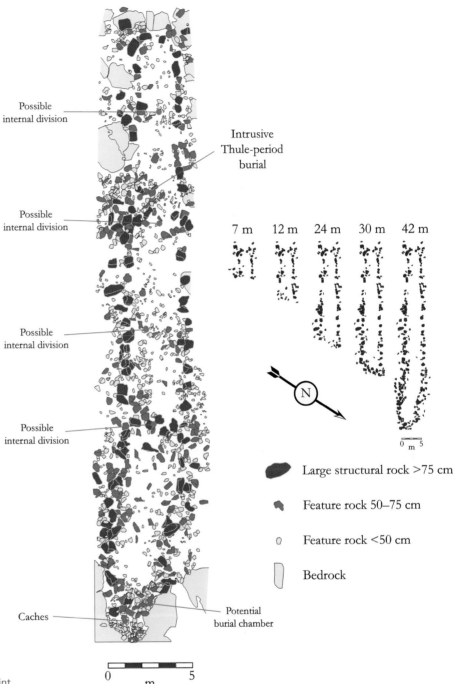

Fig 8.12 Planview of the 42 m long Reindeer Point longhouse in Greenland, showing possible internal divisions and various length configurations (Darwent et al. 2008). Courtesy of John Darwent.

if, longhouses were roofed is uncertain, but regional specialists have suggested that they enclosed multiple tents, probably one for each family. Associated with longhouses are hearth rows, which are concentrations of stones that are presumed to be related to food preparation but rarely have food remains associated with them. They vary in form and come in either single- or double-row arrangements. Although hearth rows vary in style and arrangement from site to site, they do not vary within a site. That is, each hearth, or pair of hearths in double rows, is identical, as if builders took great care to ensure no differences in size or form. What is more, artifact distributions within longhouses and hearth rows express no clear intrasite variations; it would appear that all classes of material culture, including animal carvings, were available to everyone.

The lack of spatial differentiation in late Dorset longhouses suggests to Friesen (2007) a lack of social differentiation. The striking aspect of longhouses is that most, if not all, members of a regional group could come together in one enclosure and live together as equals. This architecture, Friesen argues, was constructed as a conscious act of resistance to the tendency for inequality in late Dorset society, expressed most readily in the Foxe Basin, where population density was the greatest. The upshot here is that social change in late Dorset society has as much, if not more, to do with internally generated tension as it does the forces of environmental change. That late Dorset people opted out of growing tensions goes to show that they intervened in their relationship not only with animals and ice and water, through animistic practices, but also with each other.

Norton

The Thule tradition that would eventually supplant Dorset in the eastern Arctic is believed by some regional specialists to have roots in the Norton tradition of the western Arctic. Perhaps even deeper roots are found in the ASTT of Alaska, but added to the legacy of stone tools is the first pottery in the Arctic, evidently introduced from northeast Asia some 3,000 years ago (Figure 8.13). Pottery would not last, however, as it disappeared from Norton inventories roughly 1,000 years after it appeared.

Norton is divided into three successive phases or cultures: Choris, from 1000 to 500 BCE; Norton, from 500 to 50 BCE; and Ipiutak from about 50 BCE, when rudiments

Fig 8.13 Replica of a Choris pot and some sherds from a similar vessel (photo by Tim Rast, courtesy of Elfshot).

of later Thule culture began to appear. Choris sites are distributed across northern Alaska and include oval houses measuring up to 7 x 13 m in plan. At Onion Portage a series of smaller circular structures surrounded a central oval semisubterranean structure with a central hearth (Anderson 1988). Passageways from each of the round structures led to the central structure, which contained the by-products of manufacture of hunting implements and wood carvings. Artifacts from the round structures included pottery and other items related to food preparation, as well as hide scraping. Early Choris pottery consisted of small, cordmarked, round-bottomed vessels; later Choris vessels were fiber-tempered with exterior surfaces decorated with linear- or check-stamped designs. The organization of space at Onion Portage may suggest a division of labor with men's activities in the central, oval structure and the women's activities in the exterior, round structures. Occupied on and off for thousands of years, Onion Portage was an ideal location for intercepting migrating caribou.

The Norton phase or culture evolved from Choris culture at sites extending from Alaska to northwest Canada about 2,500 years ago. Check-stamped pottery is one of the more conspicuous elements of continuity between Choris and Norton. Houses of the Norton phase varied in size and shape, but were generally square and dug into the ground about 0.5 m deep. Larger, oval structures have been documented at some sites, and, like those of Choris culture, were likely men's houses. In addition to caribou hunting, Norton hunters took seals and whales, and they engaged in salmon fishing in the southern end of the range.

Ipiutak culture of post-50 BCE shows affinity to Choris and Norton and no doubt was derived from them even though it lacks pottery and stone lamps. Houses, subsistence pursuits, and stone tool technology do not deviate much from earlier practices, but Ipiutak art clearly stands out as a distinctive innovation. Found mostly in burials, objects of Ipiutak art include elaborate carvings of animals and humans, as well as masks and chain-like forms, mostly made from ivory. Everyday objects like harpoon parts and snow goggles often have elaborate carvings too, many with zoomorphic designs indicative of animistic beliefs. The distinctive linear, circle and dot aesthetic of Ipiutak carving resembles the Old Bering Sea tradition of the Thule culture (see below), as well as the Scthyo-Siberian of Ukraine.

Fig 8.14 Ipiutak ivory burial mask from Point Hope, Alaska. Image 3527, American Museum of Natural History Library.

The namesake site of this culture, Ipiutak, at Point Hope in northwest Alaska, consists of hundreds of house depressions along four beach ridges (Larsen and Rainey 1948). Three or four centuries of occupation are represented, and during any given generation perhaps 100–200 people occupied 20–30 of the houses. As discussed in Sidebar 8.2, successive occupations over periods of uplift and related geomorphological processes have stratified villages on landforms of successive age. In addition to a robust assemblage of square domestic structures, Ipiutak contained scores of human burials, one of which contained a walrus ivory mask that is believed to have been placed over the face of a shaman after death (Figure 8.14). With a distinctively human nose and mouth, this mask had 80 cavities that were apparently inlaid with jet (or lignite, a poorly compressed sort of coal) and perhaps feathers, hair, and other perishable materials. Based on more recent Inuit beliefs, this mask was likely placed over the face of a shaman to prevent evil spirits from reanimating the corpse.

Thule

The ancestors of Inuit (Eskimo) people today have a material past in the archaeological record of the Thule tradition of 900 CE contact. Before we get into questions about the origins of the Thule, or exactly when they first appeared as a people of distinct identity, let's consider what makes their experiences so remarkable:

(1) People of Thule culture were part of one of the most impressive diasporas of human history. In short order they and their descendants traversed the north Arctic from Siberia or Alaska to reach Greenland by 1200 CE. It may not be as expansive as other human diasporas, but it was across the northern Arctic, a world of fatal constraints.

(2) Their successful, rapid expanse across the northern Arctic was enabled by an ingenious repertoire of tools and technical knowledge. Thule people were experts at engineering transportation, weaponry, and architecture to challenge the limits of what is humanly possible.

Sidebar 8.2 Beach ridge archaeology in Alaska

Archaeology relies heavily on the concept of superposition that it borrowed from geology. The concept is pretty simple: in an undisturbed stratigraphic sequence (i.e., layered vertical deposits that have not been disturbed since they were laid down), the layer at the bottom is oldest, and the one at the top is the youngest. The same logic sometimes applies to horizontal sequences. Imagine, for instance, a store shelf stocked with cans of soup. The person stocking the shelf must emplace the back row of cans before the second row, which comes before the third row, and so on. If you have ever stocked store shelves you may have been told by your supervisor to "rotate the stock," which means remove the old ones from the back and replace them with fresher stock while bringing the older ones to the front. That is the sort of "disturbance" that would confound the interpretation of a stratigraphic sequence.

The Arctic of North America provides many good examples of "horizontal stratigraphy." This is often the case with beach ridges on capes that jut into the ocean, as well as any landform subject to postglacial rebound, which is when land rises after being relieved of the weight of glacial ice.

One great example of beach-ridge archaeology in Alaska can be found at Cape Espenberg on the Seward peninsula of coastal Alaska (Figure 8.15). John Darwent and colleagues (2013) documented 11 intervals of beach ridge development, mostly due to dune formation. Thule-Ipiutak occupation over more than a millennium tracked the evolution of this dune plain. The settlement pattern mimicked vertical stratigraphy and its law of superposition: a beach ridge closest to water formed only after the one landward of it formed, which formed after the one farther landward, and so on. Darwent and colleagues documented 117 house depressions across all 11 ridges and were able to use that sequence to analyze changes in house form and site activity over time. Comparing the distribution and form of houses across beach ridges, they were able to infer a shift from larger and more concentrated settlements to smaller and more dispersed settlements, evidently coincident with the onset of the Little Ice Age in the early fifteenth century.

(3) And they did it through the largess of whales, among other creatures. Others before them figured out how to dispatch whales and make use of their sizeable resource, but Thule people took the practice to a much higher level. Whales provided not only meat for getting through long winters, but also blubber to make oil for lamps, and bones that were large enough to substitute for architectural timbers in a world without wood. We should note that although whale hunting may have been critical in the eastward expansion of the Thule, seals were the more common quarry (Ramsden and Rankin 2013).

As mentioned earlier, the Thule tradition is believed to have arisen from the Norton tradition, perhaps as early as 2,000 years ago, when the Ipiutak phase commenced. However, a separate wave of migration from northeast Asia (Siberia) is implicated in the introduction of new technologies, like the sinew-backed bow, as well as new genetics data that show no connection between Paleoeskimos and Thule (Raghavan et al. 2014). If, as some argue, we place the beginning of Thule culture

Fig 8.15 Beach ridges at Cape Espenberg on the Seward peninsula of coastal Alaska contain house depressions of Thule-Ipiutak occupation over a millennium of shoreline progradation. Wikimedia.

at the time of its spread eastward, that is, after 900 CE, then its cultural roots lie in the late Birnik period of northern Alaska and Siberia. Some genetics research supports a direct connection between Birnik and Thule in the eastern Arctic, but perhaps not in the west (Hollinger et al. 2009). Genetics data in general are revealing the limits of inferring genealogies from material culture alone. Still, from an archaeological standpoint, what may be considered "classic" Thule culture stands out from other Arctic traditions in its inventory of technology for transportation, whaling, and housing. No matter the genetic histories of people introducing technological innovations, the result was rapid and successful colonization of the High Arctic and Greenland.

Setting aside the discrepancies between genetics and archaeological data for now, let us take a look at some of the innovations that made Thule migration so successful. Foremost perhaps is the large, open boat known as an *umiak*. Made by stretching seal or walrus skins over a frame of driftwood or whalebone, an umiak could be up to 18 m long and hold up to 30 passengers (Figure 8.16). They were light

Fig 8.16 Inuit moving an umiak (skin boat) on a sled to the water of Point Barrow, Alaska, 1935. Wikimedia.

enough to be carried over land when necessary, and sturdy enough to ply the open waters of the Arctic Ocean to hunt whales and haul lots of people and gear. Umiaks were usually paddled, although in the historic era they were known to occasionally be outfitted with sails made from seal intestine.

Umiaks may have originated in the Okvik and Old Bering Sea cultures of the Alaska and northeast Asian coasts, which date from about 2,200 to 1,250 years ago and are considered ancestral Thule by some specialists. Roughly coeval with the Birnik culture, the Okvik and Old Bering Sea cultures were hunters of sea mammals, including whales. Harpoons of this era were composite tools with toggle heads, the sort of technology known to be used for landing whales and other large game. They also used ice picks for hunting seals at breathing holes. In addition to umiaks, they made and used kayaks, which are smaller, enclosed one- or two-man boats, and sleds, but evidently not yet with dogs. An assortment of other tools and equipment includes cooking pots, lamps, groundstone projectiles and ulus, drills, needles, scrapers, and more. Decorating much of their material culture with geometric and zoomorphic engravings, Okvik and Old Bering Sea cultures are distinguished more by style than by technological attributes.

People of the Birnik culture of the northern Alaska coast are distinguishable from their eastern Arctic counterparts by technological as well as stylistic differences, notably a flat form of toggling harpoon. Sleds were improved over earlier designs, but were still pulled by people, not dogs. Umiaks and kayaks were used, and their houses tended to be small (3–4 m) and square, with driftwood or whalebone superstructures covered with sod, subterranean passageways, planked floors, and raised sleeping platforms.

Whether Thule culture grew out of Birnik or represented an entirely new influx of people from northeast Asia, by 1200 CE some of its people made it from Alaska to Greenland in as little as a few years. Umiaks enabled rapid migration with the transport of lots of people and gear. For decades, the motivation for migrating east, across the High Arctic, was believed to be pursuit of bowhead whales. Thule people were indeed excellent whale hunters. Umiaks equipped with the technology of whale hunting could venture far offshore (Figure 8.17).

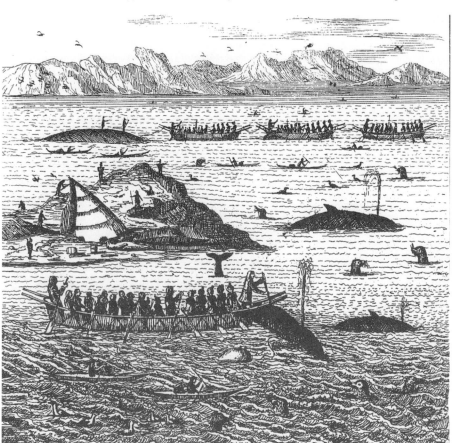

Fig 8.17 Whaling by umiak in Greenland, by Hans Egeda, 1741. Wikimedia.

We know from more recent times that hunters would harpoon whales and then attach to their prey a series of floats made from seal skins. Floats enabled hunters to track whales they had harpooned and the drag caused by floats helped to wear down these creatures so that they could be hauled to shore, where they were butchered.

Organizing a whale hunt by umiak required some leadership. We know historically that not all people had umiaks, or the ability to organize a whale hunt. Those vested with these capacities were known as *umialiks*, essentially whale boat captains. Not only was access and operation of umiaks a potential source of social differentiation, the distribution of whale parts likewise reinforced status distinctions. At the Thule winter village of Qariaraqyuk on Somerset Island, for example, archaeologist Peter Whitridge (1998, 2002) found that whale tongues, tails, and flippers were clustered at houses that also contained evidence of privileged status, as well as at a major ceremonial structure, known historically as a *karigi*. Associated with exotic commodities, an abundance of whaling gear and prized whale parts at certain households suggested that wealth and prestige accrued to umialiks and was the basis for nonegalitarian relationships in the community. Inequality likely extended to gender, as the use of the karigi appears to have been restricted to men. At the same time, cooperative efforts among households and between men and women may have subverted tendencies for inequality (Whitridge 1998). After all, Thule people did not live by whale alone. As critical as whales were to overwintering, during the rest of the year Thule people hunted other game and fished and generally made use of whatever resources they could collect. Dogsleds appeared at the time of Thule expansion, so travel over land with gear and resources was vastly improved (Figure 8.18).

If Thule people migrated east to pursue whales, changing climate likely played a big role in instigating this process. The Medieval Warm Period started at about 800 CE and would have caused Arctic ice to recede and open passage eastward for whales and humans alike. Seasonal blossoming of zooplankton and the fish that fed on it would have been a strong inducement for bowhead whales to migrate east.

Robert McGhee (2009) offers an alternative hypothesis for Thule expansion eastward. Having come to rely on sources of native iron for the manufacture of cutting and engraving tools, Thule people of northern Alaska sought out sources of meteorite iron and copper in the

Fig 8.18 Tandem hitched team of dogs pulling a sled in the western Arctic in the early twentieth century. Photo credit: Dogica.com.

eastern Arctic. Moreover, the presence of Norse people in Greenland may have been added incentive for Thule iron acquisition in the twelfth or thirteenth century. If indeed iron was the real motive for venturing east, Thule migration would not necessarily have been tied to climatic warming, and thus perhaps not as early as imagined. Improved radiocarbon chronology for Thule migration tends to support a later date (Friesen and Arnold 2008; Ramsden and Rankin 2013).

Thule people almost certainly came into contact with people of the Dorset tradition, as well as other native peoples, including the Norse. As mentioned earlier, new genetics data preclude biological admixture between the Thule and Paleoeskimos, but that does not mean they did not interact and influence one another. After about 1200 CE, some Thule moved south into the Hudson Bay area and down the coast of Labrador. As they moved south they likely encountered other people besides the Dorset and they had to make adjustments to their economy, as whales were not as abundant farther south. Caribou, bear, musk ox, birds, fish, and ring seals grew in importance to their diet. By about 1350 CE the climate grew colder with the Little Ice Age, a change that drove the Norse back to their homeland. Bowhead whaling all but ceased for the late period Thule, at least in the eastern Arctic. Their descendants across the Arctic would thrive in the many Inuit communities that continue to make a living in a world that even the Norse found hard to negotiate.

Animism and Shamanism Elsewhere in North America

As noted earlier in this chapter, the concepts of animism and shamanism have an Arctic pedigree, and some scholars warn that the concepts are not transferrable outside that context (e.g., Kehoe 2000). Others take a more liberal approach in seeking examples of relational ontologies involving human–animal relations, and for them animism and shamanism are pervasive in the nonwestern world, indigenous North America included. We therefore close this chapter with some brief examples from outside the Arctic.

Northwest Coast (see Chapter 13)

Salmon were intrinsic to successful life on the Northwest Coast and its native human inhabitants respected that. A variety of technologies were used to capture salmon as they entered bays and rivers to spawn. Notable for their capacity to capture salmon *en masse* were fish traps or weirs that were emplaced in intertidal flats or river channels. Salmon swimming to spawning locations were trapped by these enclosures and guided to an impoundment, where they could be harvested. The wooden stakes and occasional boulders of traps are visible at many sites today (Figure 8.19). In his survey of Willapa Bay in

Fig 8.19 Remains of a fish weir in Willapa Bay, Washington. Courtesy of Robert Losey.

Washington, Robert Losey (2010) observed many partial traps, ones that were missing portions of the fence-like components and thus no longer serviceable. On first blush, these incomplete traps would appear to have been victims of time, the ruins of once-complete and serviceable fishing technology.

Knowing how important salmon are to the cosmology and beliefs of Northwest Coast people, Losey proffered an alternative explanation for the incomplete traps: they were dismantled to avoid retaliation by salmon against people who treated them badly. This follows from the belief that salmon were sentient beings with lives much like humans. They lived in little houses in the sea, used canoes, and had kinship systems. They offered their lives to people in return for actions that would ensure their regeneration. For instance, the first catch of an annual harvest was ritually consumed and the remains burned or put back into the water to renew the population. Similarly, fish traps were dismantled, according to Losey (2010), to ensure future generations of salmon by allowing some to pass through after the harvest.

Not only were salmon sentient beings, fish traps had agency too, and this is true of many Northwest Coast technologies, much like those of the Arctic. Particularly noteworthy are the composite halibut hooks adorned with carvings of anthropomorphic and zoomorphic figures who negotiated with fish to offer their lives to people. Nets, boats, and other tools for fishing and travel were likewise animate. Meticulous care went into making and using such equipment, some of which, like nets, were regarded as humans.

Northeast Maritime Archaic (see Chapter 7)

In the last chapter we introduced the Maritime Archaic of the Northeast in the context of a multicultural Eastern Subarctic. The archaeological record of this ancient tradition offers a variety of evidence for animism and shamanism. Although not directly applicable, ethnohistoric accounts of subarctic groups like the Mistassini Cree provide insight into animistic practices involving the hunting, butchering, consumption, and disposal of animals (Tanner 1979). Here we will mention only a few of the mortuary practices of the Maritime Archaic where the remains of animals and people co-occur.

The Maritime Archaic cemetery at Port au Choix in Newfoundland is among the best examples (Tuck 1976). Locus II of this cemetery contained 52 graves and 95 burials, one grave with as many as 15 individuals. Distributed in three clusters, the burials are estimated to date to the third millennium BCE. Among members of Cluster C – the largest cluster, with 47 burials – was an elderly male buried with 200 great auk bills, 49 beaver incisors, and other items of stone and bone (Figure 8.20). It seems likely that the bills and incisors were attached to a bird-skin cape. Burial with parts of birds that forage in the sea might have symbolized great success as a fisherman, but in the case of this individual that seems unlikely. Stable isotopic analysis of his bones suggests that he lived off mostly terrestrial foods (Jelsma 2006:91). Alternatively, given the superior diving ability of the flightless great auk, Jelsma (2006:91) suggests that it may have "been perceived as a helping spirit in submarine descents into the underworld." If so, the individual buried with so much spiritual power was likely to have been a shaman.

The inventory of materials and substances in Maritime Archaic graves throughout the Northeast evokes imagination about a variety of animistic and shamanistic practices. Among the other prominent animal parts are the tusks of walruses, rostrums of swordfish, and the teeth of polar bears, sharks, and killer whales (Betts et al. 2012; Sanger 1973;

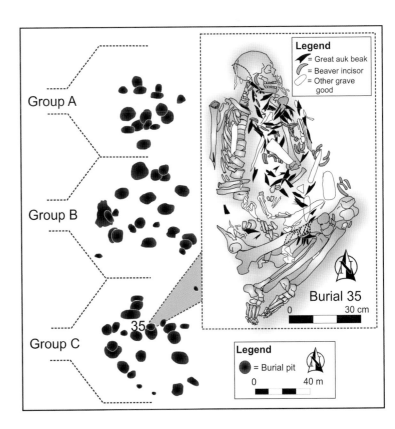

Fig 8.20 One of 47 burials in Group C at the Port au Choix cemetery was an elderly male with 200 great auk bills, 49 beaver incisors, and other items (Holly 2013:39).

Tuck 1976). These are all from formidable creatures, known to attack hunters and boats (Bourque 2012), and thus a likely source of inspiration for animistic practices to minimize risk. Those able to summon the spirits of the sea to succeed in walrus or swordfish hunting may have been the Maritime Archaic version of shamans (www.pc.gc.ca/en/lhn-nhs/nl/portauchoix for Parks Canada website on Port au Choix).

Great Lakes (see Chapter 10)

The Ojibwa people of the ethnohistoric Great Lakes region, along with other Algonkian people of the Northeast, participated in a religion known as *Midéwiwin*. The practices of Midéwiwin are called *Midé*, which translates roughly as "spiritual medicine." In its broadest terms, Midéwiwin is an institutionalized framework for teaching the worldview of the Ojibwa (Angel 2002). Consisting of both initiation and healing rites, Midé involved a variety of sacred objects, substances, places, and gestures used in formalized ceremonies that lasted several days. Origins narratives were a large part of Midéwiwin. One of two narratives centers on Bear as a savior of the Ojibwa. Having lost their way after being brought into existence, the ancestors of the Ojibwa needed help. Their Earth-Supernatural, Shell, called upon Bear to journey through the country with the Midé "pack of life" (i.e., sacred bundle) and deposit things along the way. In doing so, Bear gave the Ojibwa all that they would need to thrive; he gave them knowledge and wisdom about their world, he gave them Midéwiwin.

Archaeologists Meghan Howey and John O'Shea (2006) argue that a materialization of Bear's journey can be found in the pre-Columbian earthworks of Michigan. These are generally low-relief earthen enclosures, up to 120 m in diameter, and they date back at least 2,500 years. The connection between these built features and the ethnohistoric Ojibwa is tenuous (Mason 2009), but parallels between the layout of enclosures and details of Bear's journey are compelling. The enclosures Howey and O'Shea document, dating back some 800 years, were locations of ritual gathering by regionally dispersed communities, presumably places at which Midé occurred. They were the pre-Columbian versions of the bark scrolls of ethnohistory, on which Bear's journey was inscribed. In the post-contact era, when many nature communities became displaced and circumscribed, the ritual landscape of Midéwiwin could no longer be experienced through movement and gathering, but could be perpetuated as history through Midé ritual involving graphic representation (scrolls), narrative, and performance.

Zoomorphic effigy mounds were not part of the sacred landscape Howey and O'Shea analyzed, but they are common to the Late Woodland period of the upper Midwest, mostly in southern Wisconsin (Figure 8.21; see Chapter 10). Animals shaped from earth include birds, bison, deer, panthers, turtles, and, yes, bears. Many such mounds include human interments, but with or without burials, the ritual importance of animals in the worldview of those who constructed effigy mounds cannot be overstated. We delve more deeply into mound building in the next chapter, but first consider, in this final example, some of the portable objects in mounds and mound-related features that embodied animal spirits.

Portable Effigies of the Midwest and Southeast (see Chapter 9)

Mound building in the Southeast and Midwest goes back at least 7,000 years, but it was during the era known as Hopewell, about 2,000 years ago, that a tradition of portable animal effigies blossomed in media such as stone, copper, and clay. Notable among the Hopewell items of the Midwest were platform pipes with a menagerie of animals: birds, mammals, reptiles, and amphibians. Occasionally humans are depicted. Nearly all known pipes are from mortuary contexts, which is

Fig 8.21 Aerial view of Great Bear mound group, Effigy Mounds National Monument, Iowa. Wikimedia.

what Hopewell mounds are primarily about. These were not ordinary smoking devices. They are generally interpreted by archaeologists as totemic spirits that were important to native cosmology. In this regard it may be significant that few of the animals on platform pipes are species that were consumed (Rafferty 2016). Some have speculated that they were smoked by shamans to induce a trance state to assist in rituals of healing, although that cannot be substantiated on the basis of residues in pipes, many of which appear not to have been smoked at the time of their burial. It is nonetheless interesting that animals on pipes generally face toward the user, suggesting it was a personal, as opposed to public, experience.

Birds figure prominently in much Hopewell ritual paraphernalia. Copper sheets embossed with raptors are iconic items (Figure 8.22). Occasional headdresses with avian themes are found too. One from Hopewell Mound 25 on the Scioto River in Ohio is a double-headed raptor that Giles (2013) suggests may embody cosmic principles of the relationality between humans and bird spirits, perhaps complementary earth and sky forces.

Hopewell influences in the lower Southeast led to a thriving pottery industry in animal effigies, and again birds are very prominent. At the Weeden Island site of McKeithen, for instance, effigy vessels included roseate spoonbill, wood stork, great horned owl, turkey vulture, and an assortment of unidentified birds (Milanich et al. 1997[1984]:168). As we saw with the great auk of the Maritime Archaic, water birds in Hopewell-influenced religion may have held particular significance

Fig 8.22 This Hopewell copper cutout of a peregrine falcon from Mound City in Ohio is one of hundreds of images and effigies of birds in native metal, stone, mica, and pottery. Wikimedia.

for their ability to transcend the upper and lower worlds, but in these cases by actually flying in the air, as well as diving in the water.

The extent that birds and other animals depicted on pottery include species that were eaten is a matter of archaeological study involving food remains, and we have to be careful to distinguish meals in burials from ritual deposits that may have involved the use of plumage and other bird body parts that were not consumed. Mortuary feasting was among the ritual activities associated with Hopewell and related mounds, as well as later ones. Analysts seeking evidence for the protocols of ritual deposition may be able to infer narratives about native cosmology from the placement and association of certain animals and animal parts, as well as other substances and objects, in contexts such as feasting pits (e.g., Wallis and Blessing 2015). We may not be able to infer much about the meaning of animistic practices, or to find shamans wherever they existed, but it is clear that for many native people across the continent, animals, as well as plants, were far more than just food resources.

Conclusion

The examples of ritual practices and objects outside the Arctic with which we close this chapter are intended not to suggest that Siberian-derived animism and shamanism spread like wildfire across the continent, but only to note that relational ontologies were pervasive. The examples here barely scratch the surface. Consistent with the relational logic that nothing exists apart from other things, humans and their cultures are not separate from nature and its plants, animals, and other matter. Each is constituted in its relationships with others. And, also consistent with relational logic, things are not fixed in form, but are instead free to change as their relationships to other things change with time and space. It takes a good deal of effort to keep all this in balance, in harmony. Things did not always go as one would hope, of course, and so we can expect challenges to tradition in the interventions people undertake to deal with the unknown.

Above all perhaps, we see in animism a preoccupation with renewal and replenishment, a sense of long-term futures from not overdoing anything in the present or taking the present for granted. This applies to technology, as well as natural resources, and to landscapes and the built environment, which encode knowledge necessary to maintain balance. In this sense, animism is far more than a receptacle of ecological knowledge; it is a philosophy that does not privilege humans over other creatures and things. To animists, other things and creatures were not created by some supreme being to be exploited by people; there is no preordained hierarchy that puts people at the top, just under their god. Rather, as in the Yup'ik worldview expressed at the head of this chapter, the world into which they emerged was undifferentiated. It was the charge of people, with their nonhuman partners, to construct both boundaries and passages of mutual benefit (Fienup-Riordan 1994:48). The world was fluid, even when it was frozen solid.

9 Building Mounds, Communities, Histories

… The red man came –
The roaming hunter tribes, warlike and fierce,
And the mound-builders vanished from the earth.
The solitude of centuries untold
Has settled here they dwelt.
… All is gone;
All – save the piles of earth that hold their bones,
The platforms where they worshipped unknown gods,
The barriers which they built from the soil
To keep the foe at bay – till o'er the walls
The wild beleaguerers broke, and, one by one,
The strongholds of the plain were forced, and heaped
With corpses. The brown vultures of the wood
Flocked to those vast uncovered sepulchres,
And sat unscared and silent at their feast …

The Prairies, William Cullen Bryant, 1852

Back in Chapter 2 we encountered the Mound-builder Myth, a perplexing saga of nineteenth-century racism. The words of this 1852 poem by William Cullen Bryant narrate a mindset that granted no credit to ancestors of Native Americans for the construction of thousands of earthen mounds across the Eastern Woodlands. The myth was busted in the 1890s, through the intervention of the federal government and its Smithsonian Institution. More than a century of professional investigation since has led to a robust understanding of the history, diversity, and complexity of mound building. This chapter summarizes what we know about the so-called Mound-builders of the Eastern Woodlands. What we have learned since the days of Bryant is that there was no single Mound-builder culture. People who built mounds did so for many different reasons, in many different settings, in many different forms, out of many different substances, and across 7,000 years of time (Figure 9.1).

Fig 9.1 Portion of ca. 1850 painting by John Egan of mounds and mound communities of Caddo Parish, Louisiana, from the field notes of Montroville Dickeson. Although fanciful, the painting is one of few from the nineteenth century that associated native people with mounds. Wikimedia.

Fifty years ago a textbook on North American archaeology would start discussion of mound building with the Hopewell culture of the Midwest because it was thought to be the first. We have learned since that mounds go back much further. Dating to about 2,000 years ago, Hopewell was not the oldest mound-building tradition of the continent, even if it was perhaps the most prolific. The hundreds of Hopewell mounds and other earthworks erected along rivers of Ohio and Illinois figured prominently in the nineteenth-century myth that denied Native American authorship. But before Hopewell there was Adena, a closely related predecessor in the Ohio River valley. And before Adena there was Poverty Point in northeast Louisiana, a 3,500-year-old complex unlike any other. And before Poverty Point there were mound-builders in the Southeast dating back to 7,000 years ago.

As we will see both here and in Chapter 10, the geographic boundaries of mound-building traditions are sometimes hard to draw and that is because some of these traditions were time-transgressive, meaning they spread to other places over time. Whereas we do not suggest that processes of diffusion from core areas to outlying regions amount to an explanation for why people anywhere built mounds, most of the communities that did so were involved in large-scale networks of interaction. Objects and materials of long-distance exchange are one measure of cosmopolitan living, as are similarities in mortuary customs, settlement organization, and celestial alignment. We will see big breaks in history, too, as centuries elapsed between major episodes of mound building.

Above all, we emphasize in this chapter that the disparate traditions of mound building in the Eastern Woodlands – spanning many millennia and thousands of square kilometers – often involved efforts by native people to interpret their own past and project their vision into the future, all as a means of building communities. It follows that communities in this sense were never simply local and immediate, but instead cosmopolitan and historical; they had legacies going back many generations that involved people distributed across vast geographies. It also follows that mounds were never simply piles of dirt or heaps of shell. They were a medium of historical practice, much like archives and records, which were assembled from events and activities and then interpreted and reinterpreted as circumstances dictated. If William Cullen Bryant got anything right in his assessment of the mound-builders, it was that the mounds endured long after those who made them. It did not matter that mound building was not continuous; what matters is that mounds had to be reckoned with.

We start our review of mound building not at the beginning, but nearer the end, when the Hopewell tradition took shape (Table 9.1). Hopewell had an immediate predecessor in the Adena tradition, so we will take a look at these together before moving back in time, and across much space, to pick up threads of potential historical connection, with or without continuity in practice (Figure 9.2).

A couple of points of clarification are warranted before we launch into the archaeological details. First, we want to be clear what we mean by our use of the phrase "building communities." We all live in communities, so we have a good sense of what it means to bring people together. Suspend those thoughts for a moment. The mound-building communities we review in this chapter were held together not in the literal sense of living together, and not in the sense that they spoke the same language or dialect, had similar subsistence economies, or made the same sort of stone tools. In a word they were held together by religion, but not in the way you might think. Anthropologists tend to look at religion in the most abstract way possible, and that is belief in something bigger than yourself. For monotheists, that means a

Table 9.1 Chronological highlights of the Archaic and Woodland period mound-builders of the Eastern Woodlands.

Year BCE/ CE	Historic periods		Cultural patterns
	Midwest/ Midsouth/Lower Mississippi River valley	Southeast	
5000 BCE	Shell Mound Archaic (through ~1200 BCE)	Mount Taylor (FL)	shell mounds and ridges, some with mortuaries; domestic midden-mounds
3500 BCE	Middle Archaic mounds (LA)	Thornhill Mount Taylor (FL)	first earthen mounds, some mortuary; multi-mound complexes of probable ritual gathering
2500 BCE	Late Archaic mortuary mounds (IL)	Stallings (GA, SC) Orange (FL)	shell rings, first pottery in North America; increased regional diversity; initial native plant domestication
1500 BCE	Poverty Point (LA)	"Transitional"	coalescence of regional network; smaller-scale networks contract; widespread abandonment 1200 BCE
500 BCE	Adena	Early Deptford Tchula (LA)	earthen mortuary mounds; regional exchange
100 BCE	Hopewell	Late Deptford	elaborate earthworks in Midwest; spread of Hopewell into Southeast spawned local expressions of mortuary mounding and mound caching; early civic-ceremonial centers in Southeast
400 CE	Hopewell demise	Copena (AL) Marksville (LA) Swift Creek (GA/FL)	Continued civic-ceremonial centers in Southeast

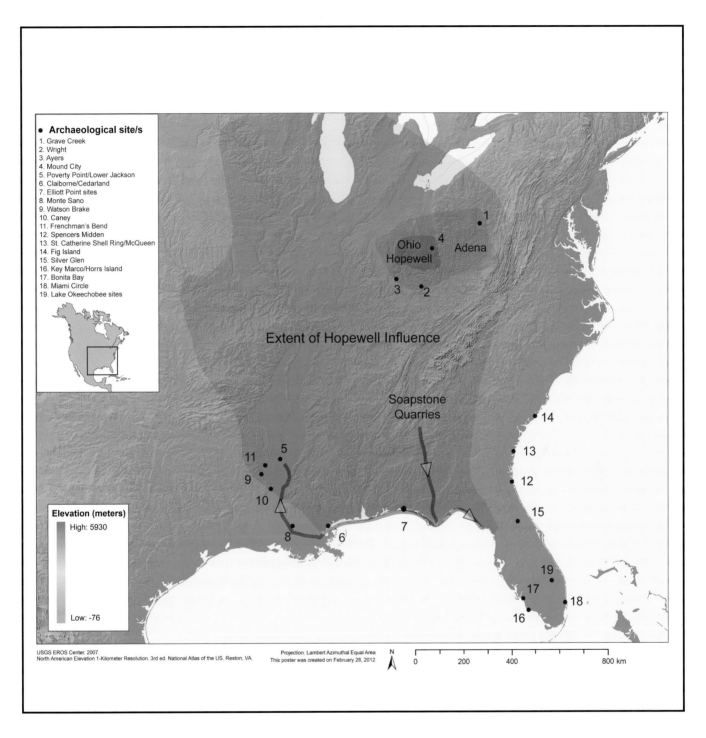

Fig 9.2 Map of the Eastern Woodlands showing sites mentioned in the text, the Adena and Ohio "heartlands" of the Midwest, the extent of Hopewell influence, and the likely route of soapstone vessel exchange during Poverty Point times.

supreme deity. Mound-builders of the Eastern Woodlands, as far as we know, were not monotheists, but instead animists (see Chapter 8). Communities to them included members who monotheists would not consider animate, and that includes the mounds themselves. And we need to add the sun and other stars, the moon, and planets to the mix, because the communities of earth had members in the sky too. As we will see, virtually all mounds and other earthworks were sited and aligned with reference to cycles of celestial bodies, although not in exactly the same way.

And this brings us to the second point of clarification: what we mean by "building histories." History in the western sense of the term is predicated on a linear sense of time, and on a recognition that linear time can be segmented into periods or eras. It also considers time to be objective and irreversible. History in the sense we use it in this book is not beholden to a linear narrative nor is it dependent on the actual events that fill time. It is, rather, what people make of the past, however that may be conceived. In nonlinear time structured by cycles like those of the sun or moon, history does in fact repeat itself because it never went away, which means it can be articulated with futures in ways that linear time disallows. We realize this may be a hard concept to wrap one's head around – if one's head is westernized – but try opening your mind to the alternatives that come from building histories with earth and other-than-earthly beings.

Early and Middle Woodland History-Builders of the Midwest

Two closely related cultural traditions of the Midwest involved the construction of mounds for mostly mortuary purposes. Disposal of the deceased in mounds was often elaborate, starting with a subterranean log-covered crypt in which bodies were accompanied by objects and substances of ritual import, many from far away. In addition to mortuary mounds, Adena and Hopewell communities built earthen enclosures and occasionally effigy mounds, as well as a variety of ritual structures such as charnel houses, where the dead were processed and stored. Mounds were sometimes constructed over charnel houses that were first burned.

Adena is the older tradition of the two, appearing around 500 BCE and lasting about three centuries, when it was superseded by Hopewell. If we judge its distribution based on mounds alone, Adena is confined to the central Ohio Valley and adjoining areas of Indiana, Kentucky, West Virginia, and Pennsylvania. Because Adena mounds were sited away from places of habitation, it is not easy to identify Adena settlements. Certainly there exist some diagnostic types of stone tools and pottery, but starting with Adena and continuing with Hopewell, we see a division between not only types of sites (villages vs. mounds) but the material culture associated with each. Bear in mind that Adena and Hopewell, as religious phenomena, likely cross-cut ethnic boundaries to encompass considerable diversity in everyday living. It is perhaps somewhat akin, albeit at much smaller scale, to the diversity of communities and families who practice a monotheistic religion like Catholicism: you might find the same sort of rosaries, crucifixes, and images of the Mother Mary in any Catholic home, but if you snooped around the garbage cans of those homes, you might find vastly different sorts of consumer patterns, different cuisines, and perhaps different levels of alcohol consumption.

This caveat goes to the point that there is not likely to be a modal Adena settlement-subsistence pattern. For the most part people who participated in Adena mound-related ritual were hunter-gatherers who supplemented their diet with garden products. Maize may have made an appearance in the greater region toward the end of the Adena period (e.g., Chapman and Shea 1981), but it is highly unlikely to have made an impact in local economies this early. Rather, most cultigens were local species of starchy- and oily-seeded annuals – *Chenopodium* (goosefoot), marsh elder, and sunflower – along with bottle gourd, plants that had been manipulated in the region since about 2000 BCE (Figure 9.3; see Smith and Yarnell 2009).

The ambiguous relationship between local practice and the pan-regional religion of Adena applies to Hopewell too. As a culture-historical benchmark, Hopewell began at ca. 200 BCE and lasted to about 400 CE in the lower Midwest. The two main centers of Hopewell mounding are in Ohio and Illinois, the latter mostly in the Illinois River valley. Objects of Hopewell ritual, plus the mounds, demarcate a much larger area and longer history than that of the heartland in the lower Midwest. Hopewell "spinoffs" occur as far afield as Florida, the lower Mississippi Valley, the mid-Atlantic, and

Fig 9.3 *Chenopodium berlandieri*, whose seeds and young greens were consumed by Native Americans for thousands of years. By 5,000 years ago, the seeds of *Chenopodium* from some archaeological sites in eastern North America show the telltale signs of domestication, notably larger seed mass, thinner hulls, and a truncated margin. Wikimedia.

Sidebar 9.1 Eastern agricultural complex

If the Mound-builder Myth had a lingering effect after it was debunked, it is found in the longstanding assumption that only agricultural people had the wherewithal to build mounds. We now know this to be untrue, as the many hunter-gatherers who built mounds attest. But even so, archaeologists tend to find substitutes for agriculture that could account for the energetic needs of public works projects of enormous scale. Exceptionally productive riverine and estuarine habitats are an example among people who did not grow their own food.

For the Adena and Hopewell people of the Midwest, gardening may have made a difference. This was not agriculture per se, like the corn agriculture of Mississippian times (see Chapter 10), but simply gardening, or what Bruce Smith (2001) calls "low-level food production." That doesn't sound like the sort of economy that could support large groups of people, but if Adena and Hopewell households were self-sufficient, as they seem to have been, then gardening may have been just the key to free up time for public works projects.

Domesticated varieties of corn from the Southwest may have made their way into the Eastern Woodlands about the time of Hopewell, but the evidence is debated. More importantly, indigenous species of oily and starchy seed-bearing plants and indigenous varieties of squashes had been collected in wild form throughout the Holocene. After about 5,000 years ago, morphological changes in several plant species signal trends toward cultivar status. Smith (1987, 1992) pointed out long ago that most of the species in question are fast-growing weeds, plants that would thrive in places disturbed by natural or human agents. He surmised that floodplains of major rivers in the region would be ideal habitat for colonizing weeds owing to floods that periodically disturbed old surfaces. Dispersed Hopewell settlements along rivers fit the bill.

Over the interval from ca. 5,000 to 3,800 years ago, at least four indigenous seed-bearing plants were domesticated: squash, sunflower, marsh elder, and chenopod. Three other native plants (erect knotweed, little barley, maygrass) do not show the morphological changes (i.e., increased seed size and reduced thickness of seed coat) of the domesticated species, but they were likely cultivated (Smith and Yarnell 2009).

At about the time of Hopewell we find a boost in the food utility of some of these species, owing largely to greater seed size, presumably a consequence of selection. At this point we might say we have an agricultural complex, but qualify it as the "eastern agricultural complex," to distinguish it from what was to come later with corn.

Archaeologists debate the role of farming in Hopewell communities, and beyond. For Hopewell cognates of the Southeast, farming appears to have been insignificant. For those subject to shorter growing seasons, stored seeds may have provided critical resources for overwintering. And yet, even in locations where gardening may have been beneficial as a seasonal resource, it was not thoroughly adopted. In a series of papers, paleoethnobotanist Kristen Gremillion (2002, 2004; Gremillion et al. 2008) applied models of behavioral and evolutionary ecology to explain the uneven distribution of early food production. Her approach is based on the principle that involvement with native seed crops depended on the costs and benefits of farming under particular environmental circumstances. The benefits of adopting seed crops, for example, are outweighed by the high processing costs involved when alternatives, such as hickory nuts, are widely available (Gremillion 2004). Like the aquatic resources of nonagricultural mound-builders, mast (nuts, acorns) indeed provided opportunities for surplus gathering and storage.

Alternative explanations for use of native cultigens turn on ritual practices. Some of the best evidence for the use of indigenous cultigens comes from deep inside caves in the Midsouth and Midwest, places in which no one could live. Human paleofeces in caves dating to the Early Woodland period contain chenopod, maygrass, knotweed, marsh elder, and sunflower (Yarnell and Black 1985). If such waste was not left by residents, then by whom? A variety of evidence points to ancient miners, people who ventured deep into caves to extract minerals and salts (Crothers et al. 2002; Tankersley 1996; Watson 1969, 1974). Other activities in caves involved rituals in which plants may have played a critical role, and mining itself was likely ritualized practice. Caves were, after all, portals into the underworld, not the kind of places one wanders into idly or without justifiable cause and authority.

the upper Midwest. Many of these distant occurrences date to the time when Hopewell was on the decline in the heartland, an example of the time-transgressive trends noted earlier. The term "Hopewell Interaction Sphere" was introduced in the 1960s to describe whatever process accounted for the widespread occurrence of things like copper earspools, panpipes, and gorgets, cut sheets of mica, platform pipes, pottery effigies, marine shell beads, and other objects of ritual import (Figure 9.4), almost all found in mounded mortuary contexts (Struever 1964). Researchers since then have documented considerable differences among those who shared in Hopewell religion (e.g., Carr and Case 2005; Charles and Buikstra 2006), even between the Illinois and Ohio communities which not only interacted, but evidently intermarried (Bolnick and Smith 2007).

Fig 9.4 Materials and objects of ritual import to Hopewell people came from places throughout the continent and were then circulated among Hopewell-related communities across much of eastern North America (Lepper 2005). Image courtesy of Voyageur Media Group, Inc. and Ohio History Connection. Jim Giles, graphic designer.

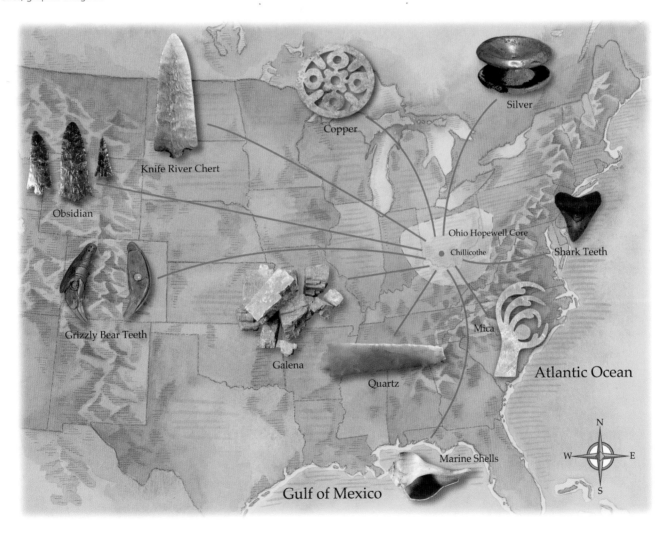

The Adena Moundscape

Adena mounds are generally conical, made of earth and/or stone, and vary in size from modest to enormous. The largest known Adena mound is Grave Creek in West Virginia (Figure 9.5). At 90 m in diameter and 21 m high, Grave Creek was constructed in successive stages over a period of at least 100 years (ca. 250–150 BCE). When it was first recorded in the early nineteenth century, the mound was encircled by a 12 m wide ditch. Illicit digging at that same time exposed numerous human burials, many alleged to have come from two chambers deep inside the mound. Unfortunately, records of this early digging are too scant to infer much about mound construction, but from work elsewhere we know that Adena burial mounds were *accretional*. That is, mounds grew in size as additional earth was deposited, each stage coinciding with the interment of additional human bodies. Thus, the size of mounds and the number of human interments within them is

Fig 9.5 Grave Creek Mound in Moundsville, West Virginia (https://www.nps.gov/places/grave-creek-mound.htm). Wikimedia.

a function of time or duration of use, not differential status or rank. Interments in Adena mounds include extended burials in log-covered crypts, cremations, and secondary (bundle) burials.

Excavations have often revealed postholes at the base of Adena mounds (Figure 9.6). These are apparently the remains of paired-post structures, circular in shape and up to 18 m in diameter. It is not at all clear if these structures were ever roofed, and they do not seem to have been used for domestic purposes. Given the mortuary uses of mounds, the structures were likely related to the storage and processing of human remains. Submound structures were sometimes burned, presumably just before the first load of earth was emplaced. Subsequent structures were then built on each successive stage of mounding, each presumably burned or razed in turn. It is worth noting that Adena domestic structures are also circular, paired-post structures, in this case scattered singularly or in small groups at sites removed considerable distances from mounds.

A third element of the Adena moundscape is the so-called "sacred circle." These are low-relief embankments of encircled earth, ranging from but a few meters to hundreds of meters in diameter, and generally with exterior ditches (Figure 9.7). The function of these circles, like the submound structures, is uncertain. They actually may not have had intrinsic meaning but rather were meaningful in relationship to

Fig 9.6 Paired-post structures, such as this one beneath Crigler Mound in Kentucky, were likely facilities for storing and processing the dead before they were decommissioned and covered in earth. The William S. Webb Museum WPA/TVA Photograph Archive.

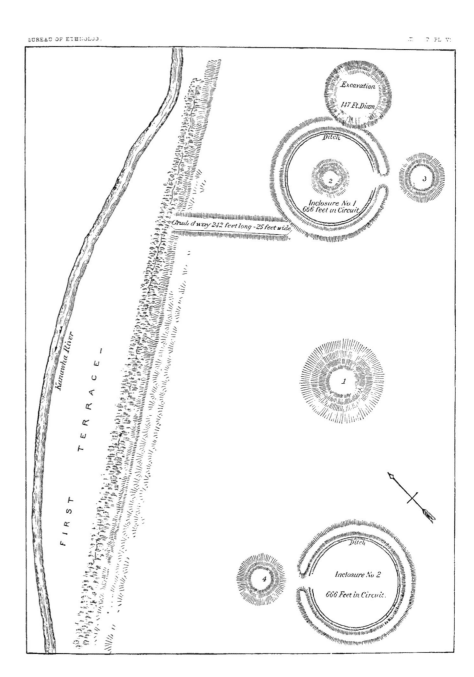

Fig 9.7 Two large earthen enclosures ("Sacred Circles") flanking the Criel Mound on the Kanawha River in West Virginia. Both enclosures have interior ditches and measure about 200 m in diameter. The enclosure at the top of the map surrounds a conical mound. It is open to the southeast, where a second conical mound was placed. The enclosure at the bottom lacks an interior mound but has one outside an opening to the northwest (https://library.si.edu/digital-library/book/annualreportofbu518831884smit).

other features in the landscape, including persons, human and otherwise. This is consistent with the thinking of archaeologist Berle Clay (1998), who sees Adena constructions as parts of integrated ritual landscapes. Because mounds and circles were emplaced in locations between areas of settlement, ritual activities likely involved members of different communities. Mounds and circles would thus have been instruments of regional integration, and not the corporate resources of territorially bounded communities.

Ritual involving the deceased was intrinsic to Adena religion, as it was for the later people of Hopewell religion, and of course for many other people. Ancestry must have factored heavily into the rites and beliefs of death. But connections across generations of people buried in mounds were perhaps not only those of blood relations, but also some sort of crosscutting social organization that connected people across vast geography, as well as time. Cross-culturally, sodalities and fraternities serve this purpose, enabling people who are otherwise distributed across different residential communities to unite for collective acts. A clan structure that links persons to totems or some other material symbol of membership comes to mind. At this level of abstraction we can appreciate the role of objects and material symbols as brokers of integration, themselves moving across the landscape, gathering up people and their history.

Persons and Objects

Objects interred with individuals of the Adena culture include groundstone celts and axes, carved stone tablets, hematite and other minerals, and copper beads, bracelets, rings, and gorgets. Pottery is noticeably absent in graves, although Adena people used pottery in their daily lives. The palm-sized carved stone tablets are notable for elaborate designs involving geometrics and animal and human-like imagery (Figure 9.8). Some of the earliest motifs continued to be important in Hopewell and later iconography. It is not unreasonable to suggest that zoomorphic motifs were totemic symbols for clans, for animals are pervasive in the folk taxonomies of Native American societies. However, and consistent with a relational ontology, artwork may have actually constituted persons, and not merely symbolized them. Some of the art invokes the idea of transformation from animal to human, or vice versa. Birds, wolves, deer, and bear occur commonly. In addition to tablet motifs, modified animal parts factored into all sorts of paraphernalia, most of which archaeologists classify as "ritual." Deer antlers, the jaw bones of large mammals, bear teeth, beaver incisors, and no doubt all sorts of soft tissue that did not survive (i.e., skin, hair, feathers, etc.) were used for ritual regalia. Modified wolf palates were found with human remains at the Wright and Ayers mounds (Webb and Baby 1957). The incisors and canines were intact, but the palates were cut to fit inside a human mouth. One individual

Fig 9.8 One of the Berlin stone tablets of the Adena culture. Some of these engraved tablets have residues of paint, suggesting they may have been used to stamp cloth or other media, or perhaps as templates for tattoos. Bird imagery, like the raptor depicted here, grows more common in the ensuing Hopewell tradition. Courtesy of Ohio History Connection. Image A340/000001.

at the Wright Mound had his front teeth removed to enable the modified palate to be inserted.

Associations between zoomorphic objects and particular individuals, such as the one at Wright Mound, may signal the presence of a shaman or equivalent practitioner. Shape-changing is not unexpected of those able to move between natural and supernatural realms. This must have been a powerful skill and a potential source of authority. On the other hand, to the extent that objects, art, and even shamanistic performance were effective at reminding people of the connections of persons across time and space, then networking must have defined Adena ritual power more than discrete persons, or even places (e.g., Giles 2010; Wallis 2011). It bears mentioning that nothing in the Adena mounded landscape would suggest that ritual practices were exclusive or private; the construction of such large earthworks alone speaks to considerable communal effort. The nature of social networking that fostered more-or-less communal relations among Adena people – what Edward Henry and Casey Barrier (2016) call the "organization of dissonance" – would be amplified in the ensuing Hopewell era.

The Hopewell Era

Grounded in the legacy of Adena, Hopewell appeared as a distinctive set of religious practices about 200 BCE. It grew over the next few centuries to become one of the more widespread ritual traditions of native North America. Recent research in the Midwest, where Hopewell arose, has shifted attention away from mounds to the analyses of community organization and settlement, particularly the relationship between earthworks and domestic life (Byers and Wymer 2010; Carr and Case 2005; Case and Carr 2008; Charles and Buikstra 2006; Dancey and Pacheco 1997). The latest work also builds on a conceptual shift away from Hopewell as a cluster of religious symbols and practices that operated socially at the *interregional* scale (e.g., Caldwell 1964) and toward the *local* experiences of constituent communities, what Christopher Carr (2005:67) calls "personalized reconstructions of local societies and cultures." How participation in Hopewell religion was motivated by local needs and rationalized by local logics is of growing concern. It follows that "being" Hopewell meant different things to different people. Although the symbols of Hopewell religion may have served as a sort of "lingua franca" for people of diverse language and culture (Seeman 1995), the interactions they facilitated no doubt varied across social contexts.

Like Adena, Hopewell people attended to their dead through infrastructure that included earthen mounds, crypts, and charnel houses. But they also constructed a panoply of geometric earthworks of enormous scale, forms that take us well past the infrastructure of interment. In the 1840s Ephraim Squier and Edwin Davis clambered over dozens of earthworks in Ohio to map a large portion of the Hopewell monumental landscape (Figure 9.9). Their work was impeccable, an enduring, accurate record of mounds and geometric enclosures distributed over hundreds of square kilometers. Their maps and descriptions became the Smithsonian Institution's first publication, *Ancient Monuments of the Mississippi Valley* (Squier and Davis 1848). As seen in the examples shown here, their renderings of sites with geometric enclosures and associated mounds stir the imagination. Like many of their contemporaries, Squier and Davis assumed the enclosures were defensive. No one thinks that now, but is there little consensus among modern analysts on the purpose and uses of enclosures (Figure 9.10).

In Ohio, enclosures were built in different ways, sometimes made from earth that was extracted from adjoining ditches, sometimes assembled from earth that was scraped up from the surface, and in other cases carried in from a borrow pit (Dancey 2005). They were constructed on both the level ground of river terraces and on dissected upland landforms, along the edges of cliffs. Especially large and

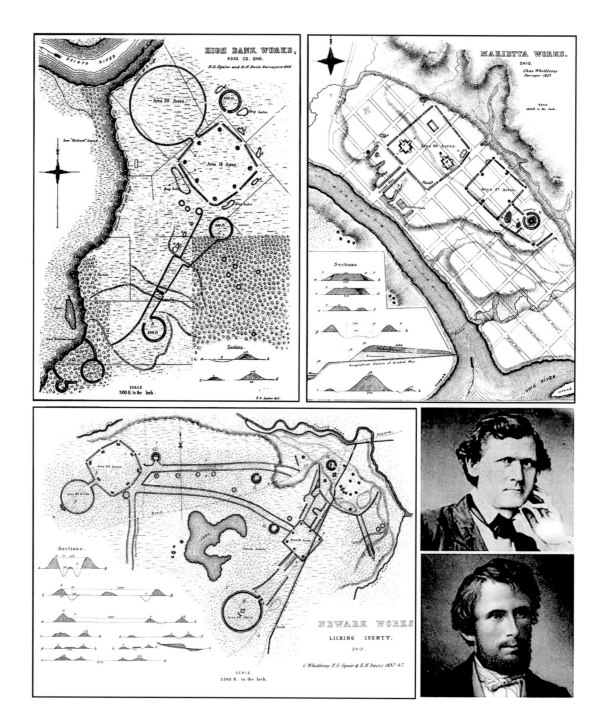

Fig 9.9 Three of the many detailed maps of Hopewell earthworks that Ephraim Squier (bottom right) and Edwin Davis (above Squier) drafted in the 1840s.

complex enclosures evidently came into being in stages, added late in some cases. Almost all are associated with mortuary mounds.

If enclosures were not intended to keep people out, were they designed to keep something in? Maybe, but not likely the dead, because burial mounds at some sites lie outside enclosures. If instead enclosures were dedicated spaces for the ritual activities of living humans,

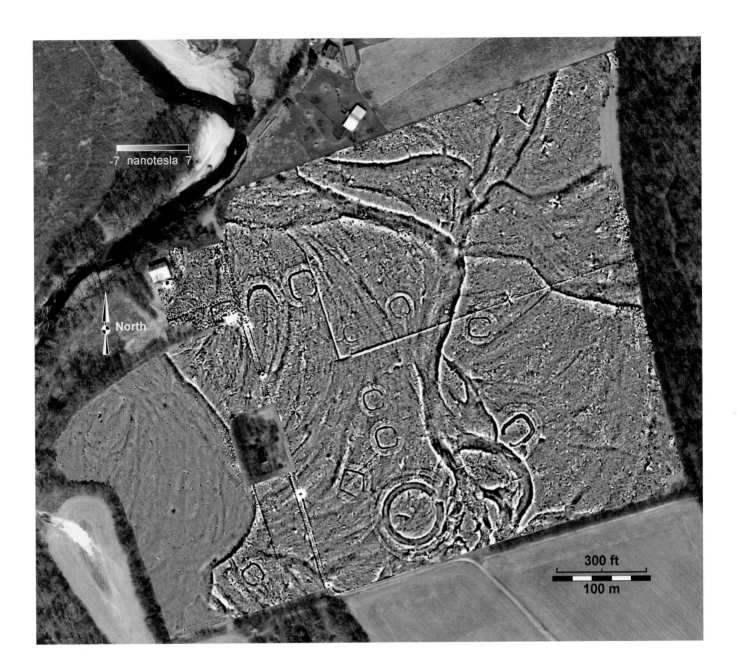

Fig 9.10 The output of a magnetometer survey of Steel
Earthworks in south-central Ohio by Jarrod Burks is
superimposed over aerial photography of the modern
landscape. The large circle to the south (one of two mapped
by Squier and Davis) was the only feature of this complex
that was clearly visible on the plowed ground surface. Note
the partially in-filled relict channels of the North Fork of
Paint Creek, a tributary of the Scioto River. Courtesy of Jarrod
Burks.

the scale of gatherings must have been enormous. Theoretically,
thousands of people could have congregated inside the largest enclosures. Yet, despite the potential for accommodating lots of people,
enclosures were not the homes of large resident populations. As with
Adena, Hopewell domestic life was distributed across small hamlets
and villages, usually away from mounds.

Enclosures of conjoined circles and squares common in the Scioto
Valley of Ohio have been interpreted as village surrogates (Dancey and

Sidebar 9.2 The remote sensing revolution

To map Hopewell earthworks, Squier and Davis had to pull chains of known length across vegetated mounds and ridges. They recorded their directions with a compass situated at the top of a pole with a sight. They transcribed these measurements of azimuth and distance to paper and then stylized contours with shading. It is a remarkable testimony to their skill that maps of Hopewell earthworks are so accurate and detailed.

Today's archaeologists are armed with an array of remote sensing technology that allows them to collect and display spatial data more quickly and more accurately than ever before. In one study using magnetometry, Jarrod Burks and Robert Cook (2012) showed that earthworks mapped by Squier and Davis were more complex than their nineteenth-century rendering shows. They also found earthworks that were hitherto unmapped, in some cases owing to degradation by agricultural plowing. Remote sensing is likewise useful for investigating the internal structure of mounds and other constructions, including submound features. The advantage here should be obvious: large tracts of land can be investigated for subsurface patterning without destructive excavations.

Remote sensing has gained widespread utility in mound studies across the East (Henry 2011; Henry et al. 2014; Thompson et al. 2014; Wright and Henry 2013), including work on shell deposits (e.g., Mahar 2013; Thompson et al. 2004). Besides magnetometry, specialists deploy ground-penetrating radar, gradiometry, and resistivity to detect subsurface anomalies. Data collected from the sky are widely used as well. For example, work in archaeoastronomy that we mention elsewhere in this chapter benefits from the availability of LiDAR data for vast portions of the Eastern Woodlands. Detailed topographic maps can be rendered from LiDAR data collected by aircraft. Not only are archaeologists free from the drudgery that Squier and Davis suffered, they can find spatial data on sites through various sources and construct maps without setting foot in the field. Remote sensing technologies have truly revolutionized the field.

Pacheco 1997) or "big houses" (DeBoer 1997), places of ritual gathering for communities otherwise dispersed across the landscape. Other researchers have emphasized astronomical alignments (Lepper 1998; Marshall 1996; Romain 2000), structured depositional sequences (Charles et al. 2004; Greber 2006; Van Nest et al. 2001), or the regional integration of dispersed sites (Dancey and Pacheco 1997). New theoretical perspectives emphasize experiential approaches to examine the relationship between symbol and action (Bernandini 2004). In one such interpretation, Bretton Giles (2010, 2011) argues that Hopewell enclosures were liminal places where rituals of world renewal took place (see also Byers 1996). Enclosures in this regard were instruments of social action whose engagement may have been routinized in ritual practice, but whose material effects were seen in the mobilization of large numbers of people. It is noteworthy that roads or pathways connect some of the sites of enclosures and mounds, a sign perhaps of routinized movements of people and other beings, such as the moon, between them (Figure 9.11).

Fig 9.11 3D model of moonrise over Newark earthworks. Lunar, solar, and other astronomical alignments have been inferred from the siting and configuration of many Hopewell mound centers, as well as spatial relationships among them. Image courtesy of John E. Hancock and Ancient Ohio Trail, whose interactive website (www.ancientohiotrail.org) offers a wealth of information on and imagery of Ohio's vast landscape of Hopewell earthworks.

Hopewell burials include flexed and extended primary interments, secondary "bundle" burials, and primary and secondary cremations. Individuals were placed on the ground or the surface of an existing mound and covered with earth, or, more commonly, placed in a crypt or charnel house, which was later covered with earth. Subterranean crypts were lined with stone or bark and fitted with a log lid. Such facilities were used repeatedly to deflesh corpses that were then interred in mounds as bundle burials. After some period of use crypts would be capped with earth and another started on top, much like the paired-post structures of Adena. The Ohio Hopewell above-ground equivalent was the charnel house, which often contained a crematorium. Even cremation in these cases followed a period of defleshing, often on clay platforms in spaces separated by partitions. After a charnel house was filled, it was burned and then covered with earth. Most were relatively small, but one at the Edwin Harness site was 35 m long and housed more than 175 persons (Greber 1983).

The connection between enclosures and mortuary mounds is a matter of spatial proximity, but possibly more salient was the spatial arrangement of mounds and enclosures in reference to cosmology or myth, and in this regard astronomical alignments bear relevance. Archaeoastronomer William Romain (2000, 2009) has documented scores of solar and lunar alignments at Hopewell sites across the region. Lately he has argued that constellations of sites and other landscape features materialized celestial movements related to mythological journeys of the dead. The Milky Way Path of Souls, as detailed by George Lankford (2007:205) from numerous ethnohistoric accounts, describes a series of built and "natural" landscape features along a path to the Land of the Spirits. Romain (2016) makes a compelling case that for many Hopewell people this journey began at the Newark earthworks in Ohio. The Great Hopewell Road heading to the southwest from Newark is, according to Romain, the earthen equivalent of the Milky Way, which aligns with this azimuth at the summer solstice. The pathway marked by this alignment heads directly to Sugarloaf Mountain, 80 km (50 mi) to the southwest, then crosses the Scioto River, and ends at Mound City, a place of 23 burial mounds enclosed by a low embankment. Romain's proposal accounts for interconnections among sites through all sorts of movement: bodily, astronomical, and other-worldly.

Hopewell Things

Like stars and moons and souls, things in the Hopewell network of interaction traveled far and often. Deposited in mounds were objects made of obsidian from Yellowstone, mica from the Appalachians, copper from the Great Lakes, and marine shell from the Gulf coast. Chert for making edged stone tools came from multiple sources stretching from Ohio to North Dakota. Among the variety of other minerals and rocks drafted into Hopewell uses were meteoric iron, galena, soapstone, silver, gold, hematite, quartz crystal, hornstone, gypsum, cannel coal, pipestone, sandstone, and more. The bone, antler, and teeth of a variety of animals were involved too, as were untold organic materials that do not typically survive in archaeological contexts. Of course, not all objects of Hopewell religion were made from nonlocal materials, but many were, and determining the sources of nonlocal materials is an enduring goal of modern archaeology (e.g., Fie 2006; Hughes et al. 1998; Seeman 1979).

The inventory of Hopewell things is vast (Figure 9.12). Pottery vessels diversified into an array of forms, including effigies and incised zoomorphic images, notably raptors. Platform pipes – not the long stem of a smoking pipe, only the distinctive bowl – were made from stone and sometimes adorned with an effigy of a bird, bear, frog, or other creature. Human figurines were made from clay. Marine gastropods were fashioned into dippers or cups. Mirrors were made from mica, as were cutouts of animal and human parts, such as wings or hands. Cooper was fashioned into earspools, beads, rings, bracelets, breastplates, gorgets, pendants, and panpipes. Copper was also used to make cutouts and embossed figures, like the famous peregrine falcon from Mound City (see Chapter 8). Antler, claws, horns, and other animal parts were also shaped from copper, and were presumably parts

Fig 9.12 An assortment of Hopewell ritual objects. Clockwise from upper left: mica claw, copper cutout, head effigy, bird effigy pipe, swan effigy cutout, gray fox effigy pipe. Items not to scale. Courtesy of Ohio History Connection (Images A283/000292.002, A283/000366, A0957/000123, A0957/000027, A0957/000015, A125/000038).

of ritual regalia, as they were with Adena. The list goes on. Suffice it to say, as William Dancey (2005:114) once did, that the inventory "includes nearly everything in the natural world, animal (including human), vegetal, and mineral alike, with special emphasis on things that glitter."

It goes without saying that fancy objects in Hopewell graves held special significance, but exactly how? Many such objects were no doubt linked to shamanism (Brown 1997), like the shape-changer imagery we mentioned earlier. Much of it is masterful art, to be sure, but is it also emblematic of worldview or cosmology? Because we know most of the iconic Hopewell material culture from graves, it would seem reasonable to assume that it relates to beliefs about death and the afterlife. And yet, not all of it is mortuary. If we think of the objects like we do the mounds and enclosures, relational qualities of sets of things take precedence over the intrinsic value or meaning of individual objects. So, for instance, Warren DeBoer (1997) sees a tripartite division among animal effigy pipes that is indicative of relationships among sky, earth, and water. Others have proposed dualisms based on paired substances or materials in mounds, as well as the contrast of yellow and red fill in mounds, and the enchaining of circles and squares at enclosures (Greber and Ruhl 2000).

The Scale of Daily and Ritual Life

Away from the mounds and enclosures, Hopewell settlement in the Midwest was dispersed, small-scale, and at least semi-mobile. Very few nuclear settlements are known for the region, which contrasts with the civic-ceremonial centers of Hopewell cognates to the south (see Chapter 10). Dispersed settlement in the heartland appears to have been relatively stable for most of the Hopewell period. At sites in the lower Illinois Valley, settlements were often located at the mouth of tributaries, while in Ohio they are known to stretch along many kilometers of river courses.

Houses were square or round bent-pole structures with associated hearths, pits, drying racks, and other "appliances." A nearby midden received food refuse, ash, and broken artifacts. In most cases only one house was in use at a time, suggesting each settlement consisted of a single household, although the composition of any given household was not necessarily limited to relations of blood and marriage.

Each household was likely capable of supplying their own food from a combination of foraging, hunting, fishing, and gardening. Nonetheless, connections among nearby settlements afforded insurance against short-term failure, such as a lost garden harvest or bad hunting season.

Mechanisms for leveling differences among households must have been in place, as they were in communal mound-related rituals. It is worth noting that objects of the Hopewell religion turn up occasionally at sites lacking ritual infrastructure, and go to show that they were not simply the material accoutrements of human interment (Dancey 2005:126). They also speak to the social scale of gatherings at ritual centers. In this respect, the difference between Adena and Hopewell reveals an expanded social sphere. Whereas Adena mounds and related earthworks were widely dispersed in Ohio and served local communities, Hopewell centers were fewer and more spatially clustered. Beyond the implication that Hopewell centers gathered people from a wider area than did those of Adena times, Hopewell centers arguably gathered more history. Mark Seeman and James Branch (2006:121) see this as "a shift away from a mounded landscape composed of many places where history took place (cyclical ritual activity) and toward a few places that carried the 'weight of history.'" Perhaps Hopewell gatherings were less frequent than those of Adena, but no doubt of greater scale. Judging from the labor involved in the construction of some of the largest Hopewell enclosures, the geographic (and social) scale of participating communities was well beyond the local (Bernardini 2004).

Demise or Reprise?

Hopewell as it is known to archaeologists fell into decline in the Midwest after about 400 CE. Some analysts have pointed to changes in daily life that dampened participation in large-scale social gatherings. Improvements in pottery for direct-heat cooking, the introduction of the bow and arrow, and perhaps better farming practices could have rendered households more self-sufficient. However, this reasoning presupposes that households were not already self-sufficient, and that gatherings were among the means by which groups pooled the risk of going alone. This is consistent with the argument made long ago by David Braun and Stephen Plog (1982), as well as David Brose

(1994), namely that social networks were a form of insurance against failure. That may well have been, but was that their sole purpose? Did Hopewell people need to invest so much in the rituality of ancestry and the cosmos to make that happen?

No, there was likely more to this history than buffering risk. Is it not curious that as Hopewell started to decline in the heartland it rose to prominence elsewhere? Inferred connections between heartland Hopewell and places in the Southeast, for instance, hinge on the presence of iconic objects, like earspools, mica cutouts, and quartz crystals. Such items appear in the Southeast during Hopewell times, but were deposited at ceremonial centers that persisted or were founded well after Hopewell declined in the heartland (see Chapter 10). That this was simply a removal of Midwest folks to the south seems unlikely; indeed, the Southeast had its own traditions of mounding, the one arguably with the greatest historical impacts, having preceded the Hopewell era by a thousand years.

Poverty Point and Shell Rings

In the quiet rural corner of northeast Louisiana is a place of remarkable history. It is called Poverty Point, named after a nearby, early twentieth-century plantation (https://www.nps.gov/popo/index.htm). It is a place where, between 1600 and 1200 BCE, people built a massive complex of earthworks like no other before or since. It is a place where, over this same period of time, objects and substances arrived from across a network as big as Hopewell. It is a place where visionaries materialized histories spanning at least two millennia and nearly half a continent. And it is a place of enduring mystery, perhaps as it should be. In 2014, Poverty Point was named a UNESCO World Heritage Site, only the twenty-second in the United States. Fittingly, it has joined the ranks of Stonehenge, the pyramids of Giza, the Acropolis of Athens, and Cahokia (Figure 9.13; see also Chapter 10).

To ask what Poverty Point was at the time of its construction and occupation is to invite rigorous debate among archaeologists. But no matter one's perspective, the scale and complexity of Poverty Point are undeniable. And no matter one's pet theory, all agree that this place was not simply a large village. Poverty Point was a place of big ideas, to be sure. We will do our best here to first describe the

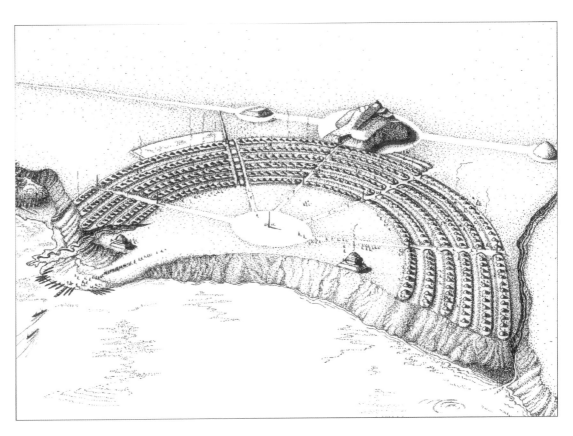

Fig 9.13 Jon Gibson's rendering of Poverty Point at the peak of its occupation, ca. 3,300 years ago.

archaeological substance of Poverty Point, and then consider in some detail its broader context in the fourth millennium Southeast, a journey that will take us to the Gulf coast and peninsular Florida, where sites known as "shell rings" factor into Poverty Point's history.

The Ridges and Mounds of Poverty Point

The moundscape that is Poverty Point is distributed over a 3 km^2 area of Maçon Ridge, high above a bayou in which channels of the Mississippi and Arkansas rivers once flowed (Ford and Webb 1956; Gibson 2000). Its defining features are six concentric earthen ridges that form a half circle 1.1 km in diameter and demarcate an open, plaza-like area about 600 m wide (Figure 9.14). The ridges are closed to the west and open to the east, where they front Bayou Maçon. Historic-era plowing and other disturbances have subdued the relief of ridges that were originally a few meters tall. Four aisles emanating from the plaza divide the ridges transversely, and 20–30 m wide swales between the ridges must have accentuated the relief. Presumably the swales are where soil was taken to form the ridges. Postholes, hearths, and middens under and on ridges attest to habitation or related activities.

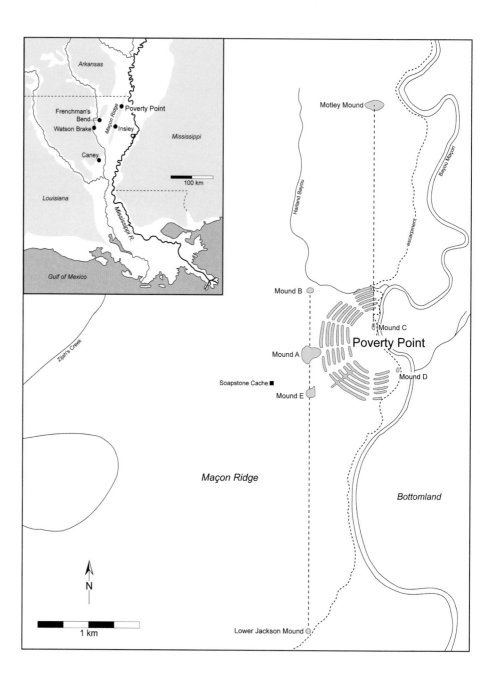

Fig 9.14 Plan map of Poverty Point, showing concentric ridges, associated mounds, and the two meridians that connect mounds. Kenneth E. Sassaman map.

On a north–south axis immediately west of the ridges are three mounds. The largest, Mound A, measures 195 x 216 m at its base and stands 21 m tall. When viewed from above, Mound A resembles a bird flying to the west. About 600 m north of Mound A is Mound B, a dome-shaped mound 6 m high and 55 m in diameter. To the south of Mound A at a distance of 183 m is the flat-topped Mound E, also known as Ballcourt Mound, which is 30 m on a side and 2.5 m tall.

Together, these three mounds frame the north–south extent of the concentric ridges.

East of the north–south axis of the three mounds, at 600 m distance, is a second north–south axis defined by Mound C in the plaza and Motley Mound 2 km to the north. Like Mound A, Motley Mound has been likened to a bird in flight, in this case flying north. Not far to the east of this second axis is the small, unassuming Mound F, located just north of the ridges. One additional mound, Mound D, lies to the east of the innermost ridge at its southern end, directly south of Mound F, arguably on a third axis. However, Mound D was built nearly 2,000 years after Poverty Point was abandoned, perhaps by persons who claimed affinity to the original inhabitants.

The building sequence of ridges and mounds at Poverty Point is well documented by recent field investigations (Gibson 2000; Ortmann 2010). Middens beneath each portion of the concentric ridges suggest that people were living in a semicircular fashion around a central plaza before any earth was mounded. According to Jon Gibson (2000), the inner ridge came first, followed by each of the five other ridges in sequence from inside out. As for the mounds, Anthony Ortmann (2010) has shown that Mound B came first, followed by mounds E and C, and Mound A and Motley Mound. Ortmann and Kidder (2013) provide a compelling case that the platform of Mound A, the second largest mound north of Mexico, was constructed in less than three months and would have taken some 2,000 laborers and a support staff of another 1,000 people (see also Kidder 2011). The newly dated Mound F came last (ca. 1200 BCE), along with a series of large posts emplaced in circles in the area (plaza) enclosed by the concentric ridges.

The People of Poverty Point

Estimates of the labor needed to mound earth at Poverty Point should not be confused with the size of its residential population, although some analysts imagine that figure to be equally large. For Gibson (2004), Poverty Point was a large town occupied by local people he has dubbed the *Tamaroha*, a Tunica word meaning "Mound Cave People" (see also Clark et al. 2010). If people occupied houses in semicircular fashion around a plaza and then expanded outward as ridges were added, the total potential population of residents would indeed be quite large. Definitive evidence for houses, however, has remained elusive. The site certainly has a large volume of midden debris and discarded material culture, notably an enormous number of baked-earth objects that are believed to be associated with earth-oven cooking (Gibson 2000:112–116). But so much of the material culture at Poverty Point was delivered from far away, as we detail later. In considering the vast amount of imported material, Ed Jackson (1991) suggested it was a trading center that attracted people from all over the Southeast. Whether for trade, mound building, or any other activities we can imagine, Poverty Point must have had regular visitors, so its residential population occasionally swelled in number.

From where did visitors to Poverty Point come? Judging from the diversity of nonlocal materials at the site, people came from many different places. However, we do not know if nonlocal materials were delivered routinely by visitors from afar or if residents of Poverty Point traveled to acquire things. Probably both. Before we consider these alternatives, let us first look at the immediate surroundings of the site.

Gibson (2000) has developed a typology of Poverty Point settlements that helps to put into perspective the social and geographic scope of this culture. Without question, Poverty Point was the center place; there is no other place of its age like it. However, in an area about 4 km in radius around this center are more than a dozen settlements with material culture much like that found at Poverty Point, what Gibson calls "core" settlements. A radius of about 20 km from Poverty Point encompasses another score of sites he calls "periphery," and we can go out another 100 km to find what he classifies as "distant" settlements.

With increasing distance from northeast Louisiana, affinity to Poverty Point culture fades judging from material culture alone. Affinity is especially tenuous at places hundreds of kilometers away from Poverty Point. Claiborne at the mouth of the Pearl River in Mississippi (Bruseth 1991) and sites of the Elliott Point culture of Choctawhatchee Bay, Florida (Thomas and Campbell 1991) have produced objects that link them to Poverty Point, but how and when these items got there is not altogether clear. Soapstone vessels, for instance, have been found at these and other Gulf coast sites and could signal the route by which such items traveled to Poverty Point from source areas in the southern Appalachians. We simply do not know how this happened, but we can be certain that little, if any, material from Poverty Point found its way to soapstone outcrops in Georgia and Alabama. The lack of more direct connections across hundreds of kilometers of the Southeast persuades some analysts to downplay the integration and complexity of social networks at this time (e.g., Milner 2004). That may have been the case, but considering the enormous amount of nonlocal material at Poverty Point, it is hard to imagine that the movement of things and people was incidental or random. The greatest contradiction about Poverty Point is that it is both a unique place in the landscape, seemingly parochial in form, and the locus of objects and materials from across half a continent, a sign of cosmopolitan living.

The Objects of Poverty Point

Among the most common artifacts at Poverty Point are spheroid objects that were shaped from local silt (loess) and then fired to harden them, like pottery (Figure 9.15). As noted above, these are thought to have been used as cooking stones in earth ovens. At Late Archaic sites across the Eastern Woodlands, stone was used for cooking purposes, resulting in the ubiquitous "fire-cracked rock" of sites near geological sources of stone. But northeast Louisiana is bereft of rock. Poverty Point chefs found a workaround with "artificial" cooking stones. They got creative too, making forms described by archaeologists as biconical, cylindrical grooved, cross-grooved, and melon-shaped. Most of these so-called "Poverty Point objects" would fit in the palm of your hand.

Fig 9.15 Baked clay objects, also known as "Poverty Point objects," are believed to have been used in earth-oven cooking. Courtesy of Jenny Ellerbe.

There were no good workaround solutions to the lack of local rock when it came to making projectiles, cutting edge tools, and other items of practical value. For many products made at Poverty Point the raw materials had to be imported or otherwise acquired, most likely by boat. Up the Mississippi River they had access to Mill Creek chert in southern Illinois, and farther up into the Ohio River valley outcrops of northern gray flint. Tributaries of the Mississippi connected them to sources of novaculite in Arkansas and closer sources of Citronelle gravel in Louisiana. Less direct sources of toolstone include the Pickwick cherts of the middle Tennessee River valley and Tallahata quartzite of Alabama. All of these materials were used to fashion flaked stone dart points, knives, scrapers, and the like. The smaller gravels, which were generally local, were not suited to most tool production but were used as a source of microblades and flakes for a variety of tasks, notably engraving and perforating other materials.

Heavy minerals and rocks were imported to Poverty Point for the manufacture of ground and polished tools. Among the more common are plummets, which are teardrop-shaped objects thought to have been used as weights for fishing nets (Figure 9.16). Many were made from magnetite from central Arkansas, also the source of hematite and quartz crystal. From farther north, in the Ozarks of Missouri, came galena, a lead ore. Sources of galena from Iowa were likewise transported to northeast Louisiana. The largest volume of nonlocal rock at Poverty Point is soapstone from southern Appalachian sources in Georgia and Alabama. Unlike all other lithic materials that arrived at Poverty Point, soapstone came in as finished products, namely cooking vessels.

Soapstone bowls remind us that much of the imported material to Poverty Point was drawn into ordinary uses, like collecting and cooking food. Bone preservation at Poverty Point is not good so we have little direct evidence for subsistence. Having noted this bias, fish bones are the most common bony remains found, lending credibility to the idea that plummets were used with nets for mass capture. The many bayous of the area would have been teeming with fish that could be harvested with drag nets or cast nets. Turtle, small mammals, and deer were also taken regularly, as were pecans, walnuts, persimmons, wild grapes, and other edible plants. Recall that Poverty Point people were not agriculturalists; there has been no evidence to date that they

Fig 9.16 Stone plummets (top photo) were likely used as weights for nets, as in the cast nets being thrown in this artist's impression of Poverty Point fishing. Plummet photo courtesy of Jenny Ellerbe; painting by Martin Pate, Newnan, Georgia, courtesy of Southeastern Archaeological Center National Park Service, and Louisiana Office of State Parks.

engaged in any form of food production, even though cultivation of native crops was underway at this time in the lower Midwest.

The not-so-ordinary items of Poverty Point culture include a variety of ornaments such as pendants, gorgets, and beads. Besides the nonlocal rocks already mentioned, some beads were made from copper that came from as far away as the Great Lakes. Most beads are simple tubular forms, occasionally with engravings but mostly plain. More elaborate are the owl pendants of Poverty Point, made most often from red jasper, a fine-grained quartz (Figure 9.17). These are actually quite rare at the site but have been found as far afield as Florida. Other figurines at Poverty Point include human forms made from fired earth. Many resemble women, often with the heads and arms removed. Decorated fired-clay objects of various geometric forms are like Poverty Point objects but are rarely found in the vicinity of cooking hearths and are thus not considered merely practical items.

On balance, the inventory of material culture points to a combination of everyday items and ritual objects. Because so much of the imported material was used in ordinary ways, efforts to supply the residents with tools appear to have been out of necessity. However, some activities, like cooking in heat-resistant vessels, could have been accomplished without having to import heavy soapstone bowls over hundreds of kilometers. In fact, Poverty Point residents knew how to make pottery and they did so occasionally (Gibson and Melancon 2004). There must have been something more to their logic of extralocal acquisition than meeting mundane needs.

Fig 9.17 Jasper owl beads of Poverty Point culture. Courtesy of Jenny Ellerbe.

The Logic of Poverty Point

Why were ridges shaped in half-circles, and nested? What were the reasons for orienting mounds along meridians, or leaving the nested ridges open to the east? Answers to these and related questions beg information we may never have. However, we can perhaps begin to recognize the rudiments of Poverty Point logic in the siting and orientation of mounds and other features of the built environment.

We again look to the sky for inspiration. As Brecher and Haag (1983) suspected long ago, Poverty Point is laid out in reference to celestial bodies and their movement, notably the sun. Archaeoastronomers Bill Romain and Norm Davis (2013) have substantiated solstitial alignments of mounds with various points of reference in and outside the plaza. Exactly how the plaza figured into alignments is uncertain, but beneath its surface are large pit features that likely supported large wooden poles, possibly for astronomical alignments. Some postholes assume circular arrangements up to 60 m in diameter (Louisiana Division of Archaeology 2014).

The usual arguments about solstitial alignments (e.g., calendrical calculations) may bear relevance at Poverty Point, but beyond the usual is one alignment that brings us back to the cosmopolitan nature of its culture. A line emanating from Mound C in the plaza towards the setting winter solstice sun runs along the southern base of Mound A and arrives in an open field to the west where more than 200 broken soapstone vessels were deposited in a pit (Webb 1944). Some of the vessels had embossed zoomorphic figures, including a raptor and a panther. By a long shot, this assemblage of soapstone vessels is the largest ever documented in North America and it is the farthest removed from geological sources of soapstone. Why were they broken and emplaced to the west of the mounds? We may never know, but given that the enclosure is closed to the west, the cache was located outside whatever the ridges enclosed.

Jon Gibson (2000) suggests that the enclosure was protection against the dark or unpredictable forces of Poverty Point cosmology, which resided in the west. It also could have been the direction associated with death. Remarkably, human interments have never been encountered at Poverty Point; if there was a formal cemetery to the west, in association with the soapstone, it may not have survived the ravages of time, especially modern tillage. Burials aside, west is the direction of the setting sun, traveling each night to the underworld, only to appear again in the east, to start anew. Journeying west may thus have been not so much a movement into the unknown or afterlife as much as a portal for getting back to the known world.

Considering that the concept of rejuvenation or renewal had a western orientation at Poverty Point, the placement of Mound A on the western margin of the mound complex makes sense. This massive mound was, as mentioned earlier, erected in a very short period of time by a large group of people. Its construction was an audacious act, bold and confident. T. R. Kidder (2011) sees it as the materialization of a cosmogonic myth, a story of earth origins (Figure 9.18). One

Fig 9.18 T. R. Kidder of Washington University examining the soils used to construct Mound A at Poverty Point. Photo courtesy of T. R. Kidder.

such myth, known widely as the Earth Diver myth, describes a watery world into which a bird or turtle dives to the bottom to retrieve some mud and bring it to the surface to beget land.

Whether the bird-like Mound A was literally a myth sculpted from earth, it came not at the beginning of Poverty Point's history, but near the end, when the site and an entire way of life were abandoned. Kidder (2006) has documented the onset of turbulent climate at this time, ca. 3,200 years ago, when flooding of rivers like the Mississippi and Arkansas increased in severity and frequency. Indeed, the river along the eastern margin of Poverty Point jumped its channel at this time, stranding the site from an artery of water transport. Moreover, the ever-rising seas of prior centuries took a turn downward, with cooler global climate known widely as the Neoglacial. Not only did climate change catalyze higher-energy river systems for more flooding, but it perhaps touched off an existential crisis in belief systems. Mound A, in this context, may have been an intervention against change, a way to get things back to normal.

The Hidden History of Poverty Point

The construction of Mound A materialized native history in earth. But what exactly was historical about this effigy mound, or any other parts of the mound complex, for that matter? As indicated earlier, Poverty Point appears unique in the larger scheme of North American archaeology, arguably the "culture that did not fit." That's how James Ford and Clarence Webb described it in 1956. Since that time we have come to realize that Poverty Point indeed has a deep history, one that goes beyond the site itself to encompass older mound traditions in Louisiana and surrounding areas, as well as the Gulf coast, where shell rings abound. This history is "hidden" in the sense that parts of it are integrated in the very moundscape that is Poverty Point – making them appear coeval with the later mounds – and because of significant gaps in regional chronology, when mounds were not constructed.

A gap of well over 1,000 years separates the oldest mound at Poverty Point from later constructions. And this oldest mound, known as Lower Jackson Mound, is actually about 3 km to the south of the main complex, so one could rightfully question whether it factored into the moundscape of Poverty Point at all (Saunders et al. 2001). However, Lower Jackson sits on the same meridian as Mound

A and its companions. Plus, the distance between Lower Jackson and these other mounds is a multiple of a standard unit of measurement that was used to lay out Poverty Point. That's the inference of archaeologist John Clark (2004b), who compared the geometry and layout of many mound complexes in the region to detect commonalities that recurred over nearly 3,000 years of terraforming, starting in the Middle Archaic period.

Middle Archaic Mounds

At least 13 sites with earthen mounds in Louisiana and 2 in Mississippi were erected between about 5,700 and 4,700 years ago, at least a millennium before Poverty Point (Saunders 2010). No doubt others in in the region date to the Middle Archaic too, some of which are now partially or fully encased in the silt and clay of later floods (e.g., Arco et al. 2006). All known mounds of this age were made from earth, and those that have been profiled or cored show they were built in stages. A few of the mounds have evidence for in-ground post structures at the base, below the mound fill, but none has produced evidence for mound-top buildings. Only one, Monte Sano (Kuttruff 1997; R. Saunders 1994), is known to include human burials.

Isolated mounds like Lower Jackson are not uncommon and these are generally conical or dome-shaped constructions, ranging from 1 to 7.5 m in height. Multiple mounds are also common, but they vary in number, form, and arrangement of mounds. The largest known complex is Watson Brake, an oval array of 11 mounds (Saunders et al. 1997). Connecting the mounds at Watson Brake are low earthen ridges, portending perhaps the nested ridges at Poverty Point (Figure 9.19).

Much of what we know about the Middle Archaic mounds of Louisiana is owed to the work of Joe Saunders and colleagues. Their excavations have produced enough domestic refuse and food remains to suggest that complexes were places of residence. Subsistence data from Watson Brake indicate that habitat was perennial (Saunders 2010:71–72). Fish bone dominates the vertebrate faunal remains (Jackson and Scott 2001). Fire-cracked rock and baked clay objects abound. Workshops for making stone beads and edged tools have been documented. This too seems to portend Poverty Point, but very

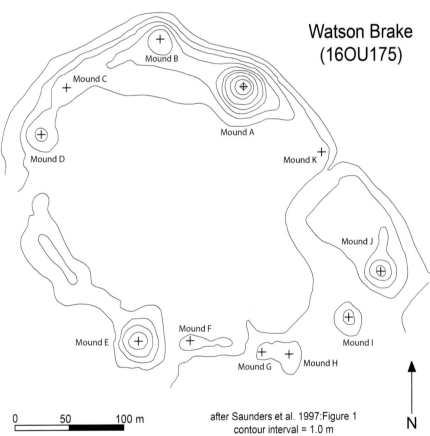

Watson Brake
(16OU175)

Mound B

Mound C

Mound A

Mound D

Mound K

Mound J

Mound I

Mound E

Mound F

Mound G   Mound H

0   50   100 m

after Saunders et al. 1997:Figure 1
contour interval = 1.0 m

N

Fig 9.19 Plan map (bottom) and artist's impression (top) of Watson Brake mounds in Louisiana. Painting courtesy of Steve Patricia.

little of the Middle Archaic assemblages of stone and other material culture is nonlocal. Joe Saunders (2004) sees nothing in the record to suggest that mound centers were economic centers, or places of extraregional gathering.

Middle Archaic mounds in Louisiana are located on terraces overlooking wetlands. Beyond that regularity, little in the size and configuration of mounds indicates an integrated or unified cultural tradition. That's the view of Saunders (2010:73–74) and others who rightly point to the local autonomy enabled by highly productive aquatic habitat. Food economies aside, connections among the various mound sites may instead be seen in shared practices of measurement and design.

Three multi-mound sites – Watson Brake, Caney, Frenchman's Bend – were arranged using similar geometric principles and units of measure (Clark 2004b; Sassaman and Heckenberger 2004). They vary in orientation relative to cardinal directions, so they do not seem to recapitulate astronomical alignments, at least not as autonomous complexes. They instead may have been components of a regional-scale moundscape. If so, alignments may point to pathways or circuits of movement among complexes, something akin perhaps to the inter-site alignments of Hopewell. It follows that each place was enchained with others in webs of reference, which were activated by movement of people. That such movement did not leave material traces in the form of nonlocal goods or materials stands in contrast to what was to become Poverty Point.

No matter the pedigree of Middle Archaic objects, what was to become Poverty Point as a moundscape had strong precedent in ancient ways, especially those involving circular enclosures and the spaces they enclosed. Watson Brake is the best example. Its oval plaza – encircled by mounds and connecting ridges – presages Poverty Point, despite the long gap between them. Why? How? Because Watson Brake and its contemporary mound sites persisted on the land long after those who built them. Continuity of use is not required for any people to confront the material residues of the past and try to make sense of them. It's what archaeologists do.

Looking back nearly 6,000 years, we find that life in the round had precedent in Middle Archaic mound complexes of Louisiana – if not also at much earlier, albeit faraway places, like Bull Brook in Massachusetts (see Chapter 4). Another pervasive set of related traditions involving circles resulted in deposits on the Gulf and lower Atlantic coasts known as "shell rings."

Shell Rings

At the mouth of the Pearl River in Mississippi, on the Gulf coast, are two arcuate ridges of shell, one on each side of the outlet channel. Cedarland and Claiborne are merely two places in a large inventory of coastal sites with above-ground shell in the shape of a ring or arc, but they are perhaps the most directly implicated in the genesis of Poverty Point (Figure 9.20; see Bruseth 1991). Claiborne is the later of the two, dating to the time when nonlocal materials and goods began to appear in the greater region, on the eve of Poverty Point. Copper, galena, and a cache of 11 soapstone vessels were recovered from Claiborne. The vessels were cached at the apex of the arc, on a bisecting line that intercepts a conical mound to the east, outside the enclosure. In some respects, the layout of Claiborne is a reciprocal of Poverty Point, at one-sixth the scale (Sassaman 2005). Other sites along the Gulf coast, notably those of the Elliott's Point complex centered on Choctawhatchee Bay in Florida (Thomas and Campbell 1991), contain objects of Poverty Point affinity. Archaeologists

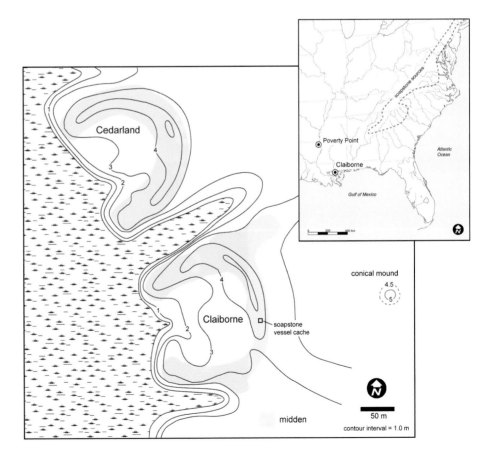

Fig 9.20 Topographic map of Cedarland and Claiborne sites at the mouth of the Pearl River in Mississippi. Kenneth E. Sassaman maps.

disagree about the level of integration necessary to explain the similarities, but whatever the cause, its history runs deeper than the time when objects started to move about the region across great distances.

That history traces to the greater shell ring traditions of the coastal Southeast (Figure 9.21). With some exceptions along rivers, shell rings are coastal sites, ranging widely in shape and size (Russo and Heide 2001), and dating mostly to the Late Archaic period. At 6,200 years in age, Spencers Midden in northeast Florida is the oldest (Russo 1996), the only one known to have a Middle Archaic pedigree. Most

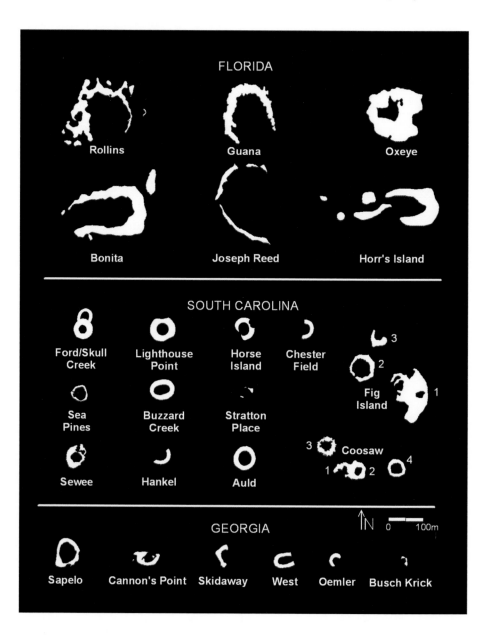

Fig 9.21 The plan outline of shell rings of the greater Southeast USA. Image courtesy of Michael Russo.

others date from 4,600 to 3,200 years ago and coincide with the onset of pottery making in the region. Other than Spencers Midden, older shell rings occupied at times of lower sea level either are now under water and marsh sediment, or did not survive the energy of transgressive sea. The ~4,600-year-old benchmark for terrestrial visibility of shell rings coincides with a drop in the rate of sea-level rise, and has been widely regarded as the point after which estuarine environments became productive and stable enough to support intensive coastal living. We know that is not entirely the case as regards food potential, but it certainly explains why an older coastal record is truncated.

Many rings are modest deposits with little relief, while others assume monumental proportions. Florida rings in general are about three times larger on average than those to the north along the Atlantic coast (Russo and Heide 2001). Examples on both the Atlantic and Gulf coasts, as well as freshwater sites on the St. Johns River, reach up to 300 m in length in U-shaped configurations. South Carolina and Georgia rings are usually less than 100 m wide, often enclosed, and occasionally grouped with others.

Shell rings consist of shell, of course, along with associated matrices of sand, bone, and artifacts. The shells of oyster are the most common constituent at most coastal rings, with some localities including coquina, other clam species, and gastropods such as the lightning and knobbed whelks. Rings and other shell formations on the St. Johns River in Florida are dominated by small freshwater snails, larger apple snails, and lesser numbers of freshwater clam. Stratigraphic sections of rings vary wildly, although many include layers of crushed shell and other indications of living surfaces. Massive layers of nearly pure shell are likewise common, regarded by some analysts as evidence for large-scale feasting (R. Saunders 2004). Solid traces of architecture are lacking, but pits for cooking food are common along the edges of rings. At the St. Catherines shell ring of coastal Georgia, large pits were likewise found in the center of the ring (Sanger and Thomas 2010), an exception to the pattern of clean plaza-like interiors. Likewise, a second shell ring on St. Catherine Island, McQueen Ring, contained cremations in the center of the ring, accompanied by copper (Sanger 2015). Like Claiborne, McQueen defies the general trend for limited material culture and virtually no nonlocal goods at rings across the region. McQueen is also unusual for its mortuary feature.

Debate continues among regional specialists over the function or purpose of shell rings. Most would agree that rings were places of habitation, but they disagree about the scale, seasonality, and permanence of occupations. Greater contention centers on inferences about social complexity and ceremonial life, and the extent to which rings can be considered monumental. Michael Russo (2004) sees in the asymmetry of rings a measure of social differentiation. The asymmetry of places like Fig Island on the South Carolina coast is owed in his argument to feasting events that were sponsored by households at locations of privilege, in this case the apex of the ring, where the most shell accumulated. Critics downplay the social or ceremonial uses of shell in explaining accumulations in practical terms, with much of the variation attributed to taphonomic processes beyond human agency (e.g., Marquardt 2010). That may well be the case, but no matter the initial conditions under which shell accumulated in a ring, those who came later had to reckon with it, and some of that reckoning likely involved the historical significance of rings to communities. As Victor Thompson (2007) sees it, shell rings that started off as places of everyday living became, through persistent use, historically significant, and occasionally the locus of feasting and other ritual activities that resulted in large accumulations of shell. It follows that shell rings were not all that much different than the monuments seen elsewhere insofar as they gained significance from histories of prior use.

Places of Gathering

To the extent that shell rings attracted large numbers of people from across the region, like a gravitational field pulling in bodies from across space, they were places of gathering not unlike Poverty Point, albeit at smaller scale. A good example is Silver Glen Run on the St. Johns River in northeast Florida (Figure 9.22). Because Silver Glen is a freshwater environment, its massive U-shaped shell ridge is not usually counted in the ranks of shell rings. Still, it is a construction not unlike those of coastal Florida, and it provides some of the best evidence for large-scale social gatherings that included guests from far away. In the 1870s, Jeffries Wyman of Harvard described the U-shaped ridge at the mouth of the run as the largest shell deposit in all of northeast Florida. In 1923 it was mined away, as were other shell deposits up the run and, eventually, the "amphitheater" of shell that surrounded the spring pool of Silver Glen.

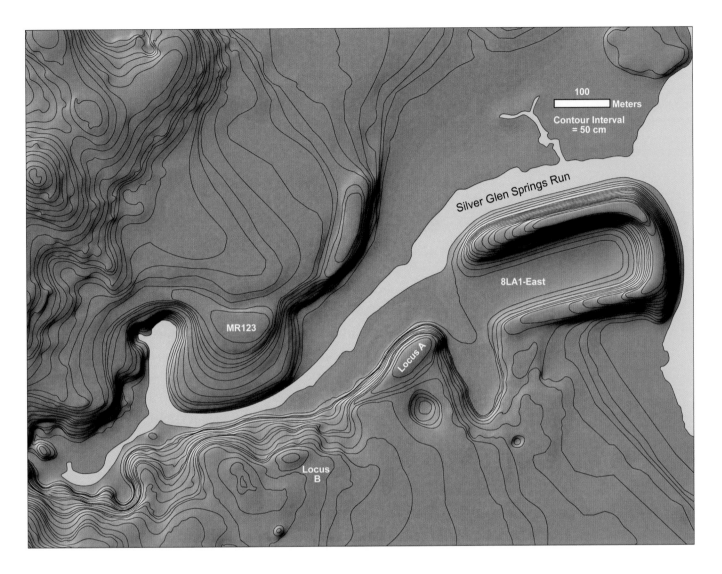

Fig 9.22 Reconstruction of Silver Glen Run on the St. Johns River of northeast Florida before it was mined for shell in the 1920s. Courtesy of Asa R. Randall.

Since 2007, University of Florida students have worked to document the monumental landscape of Silver Glen that survived mining operations. Collections from mining spoil include a large assemblage of Orange Incised pottery, dating from 4,500 to 3,700 years ago. The style and technology of Orange pottery is distinctive, like Stallings pottery that we discussed in Chapter 7, to which Orange is related. But the Orange tradition was widespread in Florida, and it is not easy to distinguish locally made pottery from imports, at least not with the naked eye. Zackary Gilmore (2016) applied the methods of neuron activation analysis (NAA) and petrography to identify microscopic and chemical signals for nonlocal wares. He found that about half of the pottery that was used and discarded at the U-shaped ridge came from places as far away as southwest Florida. Moreover,

Gilmore documented a location to the west of the ridge where massive pits were dug to process large quantities of shellfish, in this case freshwater clam and pond snails. Gilmore views these activities as a form of social reproduction, during which networks spanning half the state were reinforced and perhaps transformed through periodic gatherings.

Silver Glen and other shell mounds of Late Archaic age were preceded in the middle St. Johns River valley by shell ridges and mounds dating from the eighth millennium before present (Randall 2015). Water levels in early Holocene Florida were rising fast, along with the sea, supporting emergent wetland habitat within a low-gradient river with impoundments in lakes, lagoons, and backwater sloughs, many of them fed by large springs, like Silver Glen (O'Donoughue 2017). These newfound aquatic adaptations in northeast Florida have been presumed sustainable for thousands of years, judging from an apparent continuity of land-use and lack of dietary change (Milanich 1994).

Ongoing field research shows a much less stable and much more eventful history to early shell mounds. Environmental adjustments attending rising water may have been the ultimate reason for instability in land-use, but realignments of communities affected by environmental change had immediate consequences. Places of intensive habitation that had to be abandoned were perhaps no longer capable of sustaining a resident population, but they sometimes served as hubs of networking, again through ritual practices involving the mounding of shell, and at times human interments. Many of the oldest accumulations of shell and associated materials (artifacts, vertebrate fauna, plant remains) started off as locations of dwellings, with strata of stacked living surfaces and middens, often interspersed with mantles of clean shell or sand. At Silver Glen Run, a shell ridge dating to ca. 6,000 years ago is underlain by an assemblage of pits dating to nearly 9,000 years ago (Randall 2015). Histories of land-use spanned millennia and the resulting stratigraphic records are robust. However, histories materialized in pits and strata show considerable gaps in time, more than a millennium in some cases. Like the gap separating the Middle Archaic mounds of Louisiana from those of Poverty Point, time gaps in the middle St. Johns are no deterrent to historical significance. That is, continuity in practice did not matter as much as the enduring materiality of place.

Disruptions in practice over three millennia took a variety of forms. The oldest mounds in the middle St. Johns, dating from 7,200 years ago (5200 BCE) and part of the Mount Taylor tradition (Randall 2013), show that former locations of dwellings were capped with shell and then received multiple layers of structured deposition intermittently over the next century or two (Randall 2015; Sassaman and Randall 2012). A few centuries later the first mortuary mounds were established in the region, which, in addition to shell, involved the emplacement of white sand and black swamp muck over burial clusters (Aten 1999). These followed on the heels of a pond burial tradition going back to the early Holocene (see Chapter 5 on Windover). Another few centuries later, at about 3600 BCE, the mounding of earth over shell ridges ushered in a twist on tradition (the Thornhill Lake phase), coincident with an influx of nonlocal goods (Endonino 2010; Randall 2013). A fourth major change ensued after 4,500 years ago (2500 BCE), when a handful of mounds, notably the one at the mouth of Silver Glen, were reconfigured into massive U-shaped or multi-ridge structures, forms highly reminiscent of some of the larger shell rings of the Florida coast.

The twists and turns of middle St. Johns history most certainly have environmental triggers. In the case of the oldest mounds, abandonment seems to have followed a climate event that caused the adjacent river channel to jump its course. The shift from pond burials to shell mounds tracks generally the rise of surface water and inundation of terrestrial spaces from the early Holocene on (Sassaman 2012). The gathering at Silver Glen arguably rose out of human experiences with sea-level rise and coastal flooding, a way to perhaps reallocate people across the land in the context of major environmental change.

All that is true from an environmental standpoint. It does not begin to address the cultural value assigned to places and to the historical consciousness people had about the experiences of those who came before. It is not yet possible to draw all the connections that enabled people spread out over such a vast area to coalesce into large collectives, even if for only a short while. Shared principles, like those we reviewed for the Louisiana mounds, are hard to pinpoint, although some aspects of mound stratigraphy may hold clues. Florida Archaic mounds routinely juxtapose light matrix (unburned shell, white sand) with dark matrix (burned shell, muck, brown sand), and they often involve large caps of whole, clean shell, and less frequently sand.

Among Hopewell mound-builders, soil color and texture indexed a variety of relationships, such as direction, earth and sky, or birth and death (Buikstra et al. 1998; DeBoer 2005), while in the Mississippian tradition, the capping of mounds was an expression of rebirth (Knight 1986). In this earlier context, perhaps water was among the core symbolic referents, a consequence of living through times of rapidly rising water (Sassaman 2012). If shared experience can motivate large groups of people to connect and act collectively, then the scale of collective action must be commensurate with the scale of change. Is it possible that Poverty Point was a collective intervention against environmental change? If so, it must have been epic.

Mounding on the Edge of the Tropics

Left out of many summaries of North American archaeology is much discussion of developments in subtropical south Florida. Some casual observers have quipped that south Florida, in cultural terms, is more Caribbean than it is continental, and there is something to that indeed. But south Florida was hardly an island unto itself, and much of its history and character is owed to extralocal connections with other parts of the region. Any review of it can only scratch the surface of the complexity of south Florida's history or the nuance of its investigation by archaeologists, which begins with the historically known Calusa of the Caloosahatchee region of southwest Florida.

When the Spanish arrived in Florida, the Calusa occupied territory centered on Charlotte Harbor, one of the region's richest estuaries. The history of Caloosahatchee culture goes back to at least 500 CE and arguably much earlier. The Calusa are known to us through a combination of ethnohistory and archaeology. From the former we know that in the sixteenth century they were a complex society organized by rank or hierarchy (Figure 9.23); that they occupied massive site complexes of mounds, causeways, water courts, and canals; that they lived primarily off marine resources; that they resisted being brought under Spanish control for nearly two centuries; and that they interacted amicably with people to the south (Glade) and east (Belle Glade).

Through the lens of archaeology we see that the ancestors of the Calusa led different lives than their descendants, except perhaps for

Fig 9.23 Museum exhibit of the inside of the domicile of a Calusa chief, where he and his entourage greet a visitor. Southwest Florida Hall, Florida Museum of Natural History, University of Florida. Wikimedia.

their marine economies, which were longstanding. Based on 25 years of research, Marquardt (2014:14) argues that the Calusa "kingdom," as known to us through ethnohistory, "was in large part an attempt to imitate and compete with the Spanish invaders and survive within the new world order." It was thus a contact phenomenon, unique to the sixteenth century. Sociopolitical organization before contact was, in Marquardt's view, less hierarchical and more flexible. This seems to have served well the need to respond to rapid, short-term changes in environment, one of the key challenges to coastal dwellers. Moreover, periods of diminished estuarine productivity put constraints on the size and permanence of coastal settlements, countering trends toward hierarchical political organization.

Inarguably, the Calusa at contact were at the apogee of sociopolitical complexity, verging on statehood. But was their newfound identity at the time of Spanish contact without history? Of course not. Going back many centuries, even millennia, were communities that terraformed the landscape with mounds, ridges, and other emplacements of shell. We can stretch this back to at least the time of Late Archaic shell rings, such as Horrs Island and Bonita Bay, both located south of Charlotte Harbor, in what would later become Calusa territory. Whether or not we can trace a genealogy of culture back to 4,500 years ago, ancient shell works of the region likely factored in Calusa senses of the past, and of themselves.

The deep history of Caloosahatchee culture, according to Widmer (1988), can be characterized as a long, gradual climb to complexity. He places the beginning of this process at about 700 BCE, the time after which sea levels became relatively stable and promoted the development of productive seagrass, mangrove, and mudflat habitat for fish and shellfish. Widmer sees communities taking advantage of secure resources with stationary settlements that grew in number. Growth reached its limits at about 800 CE, when competition and warfare became endemic. Widmer posits that hierarchy arose at this time to manage the redistribution of scarce resources. This outcome, he argues, appeared long before European contact and endured until then virtually unchanged.

Recent work at the sixteenth-century capital of the Calusa – Mound Key near present-day Fort Myers Beach – adds historical nuance to the emergence of state-like political organization (Thompson et al. 2018). This midden-mound complex includes large mounds separated by a central canal, along with smaller mounds, ridges, and water courts that were likely used as fish traps. Remote sensing on the summit of Mound 1 revealed the remains of an oval-shaped building estimated at 24 m in length and 20 m wide. Spanish accounts confirm the presence of a large building on the mound summit, but radiocarbon age estimates show that earlier incarnations of a large building date to the ninth century CE when the Calusa returned to Mound Key after a hiatus in occupation, evidently under the favorable conditions of the Medieval Warm Period. Calusa political organization thereafter appears to have vacillated between competitive and cooperative relationships among regional communities until Spanish contact pushed them toward state-like institutions of power and control. Arguably, long-lived lineages housed figuratively in big houses like the one atop Mound 1 rose to power through their ability to mobilize labor to take advantage of favorable estuarine conditions with the engineering of canals, causeways, water courts, and more.

Ten Thousand Islands and Glades Culture

The built environment of Ten Thousand Islands in the Everglades, to the south of the Caloosahatchee, was expansive and complex, even mind boggling. This is an archipelago of mangrove islands with little inhabitable land over the past 7,000 years, when the Everglades came into existence. Margo Schwadron (2010) of the National Park Service has documented many of the shell works in the area, which range from small ring-shaped middens to entire island complexes of elaborate design (Figure 9.24). The term *terraforming* is especially apt in this case because these ancient people literally constructed inhabitable land out of mangrove swamps. They then went beyond the necessities of life to create a landscape of intricate form, structuring the perpetual motion of water, fish, and people with complex geometry. This was the work of people of the Glades culture, whose beginnings trace to ca. 500 BCE, when plain sand- and grit-tempered pottery became prevalent. Glades culture extended beyond the Ten Thousand Island region to encompass virtually all of the Everglades, as well as the south Atlantic coast and the Florida Keys.

Thirteen major shell works range from 10 to 50 ha in extent, all the location of major settlements, arguably shell cities. Recurring spatial arrangements among built components of these places suggest some shared principles of landscaping and architecture starting at about 600 CE. Among them is Key Marco, a site made famous by Frank Hamilton Cushing, who, in the 1890s, uncovered remarkable wooden artifacts in a muck pond. Like several other mega-sites, Key Marco shows bilateral symmetry in plan with a crescent at one end, a central ridge and mound district, and a series of radiating finger ridges at

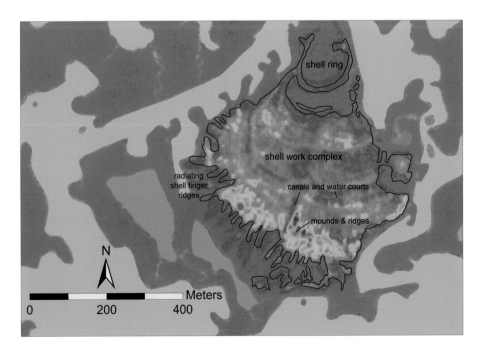

Fig 9.24 Topographic map of the Russell Key complex in the Ten Thousand Island area of southwest Florida. Ridges, rings, mounds, and platforms are interspersed with canals and water courts across a shell works of bilateral symmetry. The complex formed through centuries of terraforming. Older features, such as shell rings, were modified and repurposed for both practical and ritual needs. Courtesy of Margo Schwadron, NPS/SEAC.

the opposite end of the crescent. Ridges are interspersed with water courts and canals, not unlike the marinas of modern coastal Florida communities. These public works projects reached their apogee at ca. 900–1300 CE, after which the region was largely abandoned, perhaps owing to southward territorial expansion of the Calusa.

Some of the rings and crescents of shell in the Ten Thousand Island region clearly date to the Late Archaic period. Schwadron (2010) suggests that some of the oldest rings were incorporated into shell works of the Glades era, dating at least 1,000 years later. It is reasonable to presume that an ancient terraformed landscape preconfigured Glades settlement in practical ways, but did it also structure the way Glades people viewed themselves and the world despite the discontinuity of practice? We may never know, but the Ten Thousand Island region offers archaeological potential that has only begun to be explored. The same can be said about the terraformed landscape of the Okeechobee region to the north.

Belle Glade Culture of Okeechobee

A distinct cultural tradition on the northern edge of the Glades world involved elaborate sites of mounds, ridges, water courts, and canals. Centered on Lake Okeechobee in south-central Florida, the Belle Glade culture of ca. 1000 BCE through 1700 CE is best known for sites of complex terraforming that feature circular ditches up to one-half mile in diameter. William Sears (1982), who excavated at Fort Center in the late 1960s, thought that the ditches were for draining land for corn agriculture, but that idea finds no support today (Thompson et al. 2013). Soils in this wetland region are not terribly conducive to corn agriculture, with or without draining, and indeed corn was never part of the subsistence economy in south Florida until Europeans arrived. Because the Okeechobee Basin is subject to frequent flooding, it seems reasonable to posit that ditching was aimed to control the flow of surface water. A third hypothesis proposed by archaeologist Robert Carr (1985) is that the ditches were used as fish traps, another reasonable hypothesis given an emphasis on aquatic resources in the Belle Glade diet.

Circular ditches go back to the beginning of Glades culture, and they were often surrounded by small platform mounds, presumably the locations of dwellings. At Fort Center, for instance, two overlapping ditches 8 m wide and 2 m deep formed circles about 90 m in diameter; a third one about four times that size encloses the smaller circles. Glades circular ditches bear some resemblance to Adena and Hopewell enclosures, a parallel that did not escape notice by Sears (1982). But the oldest Glades examples are as old if not older than those of northern provenance, so we do not have to look north for inspiration. Indeed, Sears and others tended to look south instead, toward the Caribbean and South America, where ditches were part of agricultural infrastructure.

With no evidence for farming among Glades communities, ditches may have instead operated as material expressions of belief, much like those of Hopewell. However, Glades settlements with circular ditches, from early on, were apparently residential centers, unlike Hopewell. Over time locations of circular ditches expanded to include mortuary mounds, artificial ponds, and linear embankments. Fort Center after about 200 CE became a prominent civic-ceremonial center. A pond adjacent to a mound that included many secondary burials was likewise constructed for mortuary purposes. Sears (1982) called this a "charnel" pond, meaning a place where the dead were stored. The term is usually associated with buildings, as with the charnel houses of Hopewell noted earlier. The remains of a wooden platform found in the pond may very well have served in this capacity. Judging from an array of wooden carvings from the pond, the platform was adorned with a menagerie of animals, notably birds. The bony remains of about 300 people were recovered from the pond and the adjacent mound combined. Sears conjectured that the platform burned at about 500 CE and many of the skeletal remains that fell into the pond were recovered and emplaced in the mound in bundles. Whether or not any of the individuals in the pond were actually interred underwater – as with the Early Archaic tradition of pond burials noted in Chapter 5 – a meaningful association between death and water is likely.

Fort Center is but one of several Belle Glade centers of terraforming and ritual practice. Looking past any practical value that obtains from ditching and mounding wet earth, many sites have linear alignments that strongly suggest a Hopewell-like attention to the cosmos. Archaeologist Nathan Lawres (2017) has been reconstructing alignments, the most complex of which postdate 1200 CE, when the geopolitical reach of the Calusa peaked. In his analysis, Lawres sees two

Fig 9.25 View of the Miami Circle as it was being excavated in 1999. Courtesy of Florida Division of Historical Resources (http://info.flheritage .com/miami-circle).

levels of alignment: one dealing with cyclical events such as the solstices and equinoxes, and others projected across the landscape to connect with other places of monument construction. Like stars in a constellation, Belle Glade mound complexes most likely took their significance from their relative positions in the landscape.

The Miami Circle

Florida archaeology has enjoyed its share of surprising discoveries in recent decades. In 1998 a developer in Miami began construction of luxury condos at a place called Brickell Point, prime real estate at the mouth of the Miami River. Revealed in the underlying limestone after an existing apartment building was demolished was a circle of 24 subrectangular holes (Figure 9.25). Archaeological middens associated with the holes indicated that the 11.5 m diameter circle was likely to be the remains of an ancient building, but the contractor and other skeptics tried to argue that the holes were recent, ostensibly related to a septic system of the now-destroyed apartments. In 1999 the state of Florida purchased the land for 26.7 million dollars to save what came to be known as the Miami Circle. The purchase and the site drew considerable press attention and more than its share of controversy.

The Miami Circle is just that, a circle, in this case of a circle of holes that were sculpted out of limestone (Carr 2012). Most regional specialists agree that the holes likely supported posts of a building, in this case one large enough to be a public building. Radiometric dating of organic matter associated with the holes places them in the range of 2,000–1,800 years ago. Because buildings of this scale and elaboration had not before been documented in south Florida, some speculated that the structure was built by people of the Maya or Olmec tradition, having evidently paddled across the Gulf of Mexico to colonize south Florida. We now know that the Miami Circle is in fact not unique; other circles have been documented in the downtown Miami area over the past few years. The details of these buildings may never be known to us, but given some of the material culture associated with them (e.g., pottery, shell tools, shark teeth), they were constructed by ancestors of the historic-era Tequesta, an indigenous native tribe. Two basalt axe heads from Georgia attest to distant connections, but nothing from the Yucatan peninsula supports a Maya or Olmec pedigree for the buildings.

The function or purpose of buildings like those that stood at Brickell Point 2,000 years ago is unknown, although given their size and the labor involved in pecking out postholes, they were not likely to be merely domestic structures. Buildings of this scale and elaboration must have housed important public activities, although not necessarily open to all. In and amongst the architectural features of the Miami Circle were some unusual deposits, namely the remains of a shark, a sea turtle, and a dolphin. These were emplaced in the circle much later, during the early colonial era. Evidently, members of the Tequesta tribe, in the context of European disruptions, returned to Brickell Point to enjoin the forces of their ancestors in a place of enduring significance. Like so many of the mounds and other monuments we reviewed in this chapter, the Miami Circle may have drawn its greatest significance as a historical resource of intervention against change, in this case, irreparable change.

Conclusion

If you can pardon the pun, the Miami Circle brings us full circle in our coverage of Indian mounds. The Miami Circle, of course, was not a mound, but it was monumental in its elaboration and scale, and it was historical in the sense that it was called upon to assert community identity at a time of crisis. More to the point, we see in this recent discovery the same sort of bias that discounted any Indian authorship of mounds encountered by Europeans in their expansion west across America. How could mobile hunter-gatherers of the Everglades ever have constructed such a great building? Just as earlier observers of mounds looked to the Lost Tribes of Israel or the Welsh for the builders, skeptics and fanciful thinkers looked to Mexico, to the complex societies of the Maya and Toltec.

In the early twenty-first century, only the most fanciful thinkers would attribute mounds or public buildings in this continent to anyone other than the ancestors of Native Americans. But having learned in recent years that many mounds were not simply the constructions of local communities but rather the result of large gatherings, how far did people travel to participate in mound-related activities? As we have seen, in many cases, they traveled very far. Water would not seem to have been a huge impediment for people familiar with boat travel. Indeed, the historic-era Calusa traveled to and from Cuba regularly. We may not have smoking gun evidence for contact with the Caribbean or Mexico or South America in pre-Columbian North America, but not for the implausibility of ocean travel. In the middle part of the last century, famed archaeologist James Ford (1969) looked to the Caribbean and South America for the origins of pottery, village life, and mounds in the Southeast. Knowing now how old some of those features are in the region, Ford might have looked in the opposite direction were he to research the question today.

10 The Momentous Late Woodland–Mississippian Millennium

The Turk declared that in a country called Quivira, near his homeland, "there was a river flowing in the Plains, with fish as big as horses, and a vast number of very large canoes with sails, and carrying more than twenty oarsmen on each side." The nobles, he said, "rode in the stern, seated under canopies, and at the prow there was a great golden eagle." The lord of that land, the powerful Tatarrax, took his siesta under a tree from which hung numerous golden bells that amused him as they played in the breeze.

(Bolton 1990:198)

It seems entirely likely, given his proclivities, that a young John Muir would have gone out of his way to see the dozens of mysterious "effigy mounds" that dotted the University of Wisconsin campus while a student there in the late 1850s and early 1860s. These had been built in the shapes of thunderbirds and water spirits by generations of Native Americans from the 700s to the 1100s CE, or the second half of the Late Woodland period in the upper Midwest (400–1200 CE). Muir, even as a student, was frequently outdoors studying botany and geology. The mounds, one would suspect, affected him. Perhaps they encouraged some reflection and soul-searching, and stimulated his still-nascent eco-spiritualism.

Certainly, for indigenous Americans, the effigy mounds remain a physical "narrative of our own country," according to Aaron Bird Bear, native Mandan of the Three Affiliated Tribes of the Fort Berthold reservation and formerly staff of the American Indian Studies program on the Madison campus (Richter 2008). These unique burial mounds are part and parcel of Indian identities as the latter emerge from fundamental, lived relationships: past with present, living with dead, and people with other-than-human beings (Hallowell 1960). Such soul-searching, identity-laden entanglements alter one's sense of time, space, causality, and meaning. (Who am I in relation to the earth, sky, spirits, etc.?) They change the very sensibilities, emotions, and feelings that motivate you (Figure 10.1).

(a)

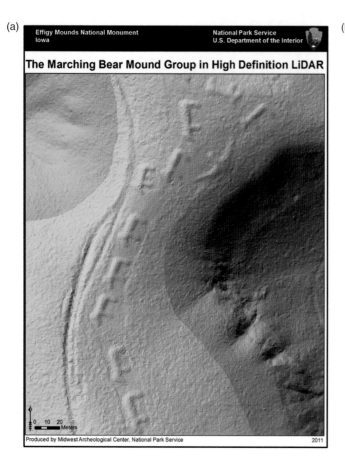

(b)

Fig 10.1 Animal-spirit mounds at Effigy Mounds National Historical Park, Iowa: (a) LiDAR view of Marching Bear group. National Park Service, Wikimedia; (b) grand-level view of the same group. Timothy R. Pauketat photo, 2009.

Considered at a mass scale, where entire populations of people are affected in some way, it seems plausible that the particulars of such entanglements need to be considered when attempting to understand the history of pre-Columbian North America. Periods of profound change might not happen the same way on this continent as on others: Africa, Asia, Europe, South America, or Australia. Such periods, the focus of this chapter, subsume the rise of a city, the birth of a civilization, the foundation of a formal religion, the coalescence of new provinces and ethnicities, agricultural intensification, wars, and the beginnings of what might have become – had not Europeans arrived – closer relations with Mesoamerica.

This chapter is about the people who comprised that history: founding fathers and mothers, godly impersonators, migrants, and anonymous farmers – men, women, and children who built impressive earthen pyramids, produced bumper crops, and underwrote societal movements that, in some ways, still affect all of us today. But the chapter is also about the relationship of history to humanity. How were human qualities in the heartland shaped by history? Taken together, history and humanity, the chapter is also about the places, things, and elemental powers that defined people. Just as the effigy mounds of Wisconsin continue to move anyone who sees them, walks alongside them, smells their deep-woods earthiness, or hears the chirps of songbirds that flit along their edges, so the great places of the Midwest and Southeast changed the people who lived relatively brief lives, generation after generation, in the centuries following the great Hopewellian "history-building" episode (see Chapter 9). All of this took place over the course of a thousand years and before the invasion by Spaniards, Frenchmen, and Englishmen, along with their exhaled billions of microbes, their measled bodies, and their smallpox-infected clothes (Figure 10.2).

Fig 10.2 Map of Late Woodland and Mississippian cultural complexes and sites in the Eastern Woodlands.

Anglos in a Late Woodland World

In the 1500s, indigenous North Americans living Late Woodland lifestyles met English colonists along the mid-Atlantic seaboard. In North Carolina in the 1580s, the artist John White painted native life as he saw it, or at least as his benefactors, Sir Walter Raleigh and Sir Richard Grenville, wanted it seen by potential colonists back in England (Figure 10.3). White would die in Ireland as ex-governor of the lost colony of Roanoke, south of Chesapeake Bay, hoping against

Fig 10.3 Native life at the village of Secotan, North Carolina. John White painting, British Museum. Wikimedia.

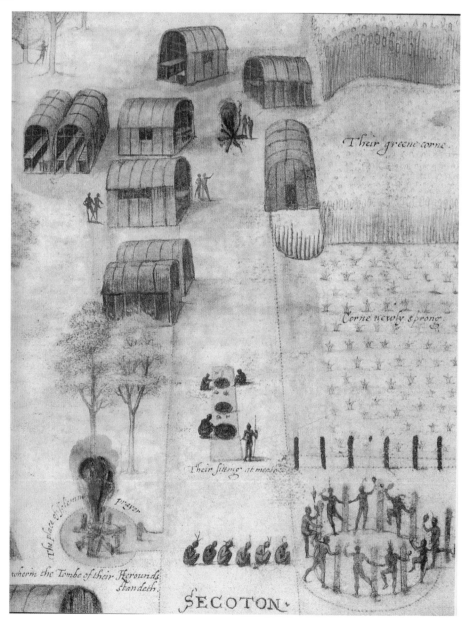

hope that his daughter and granddaughter had survived his failed attempts to resupply them and the other starving colonials he had left behind in early September 1587.

The colony had been failing in part owing to "the most extreme growing season drought in 800 years" (Stahle et al. 1998). After White's departure, at least some of Roanoke's 115 residents – minimally the women and children – were likely taken captive and then, perhaps, "adopted" by locals. In time, they may have become full-fledged community members and, eventually, progenitors of blue-eyed, blond-haired Native American descendants rumored for generations thereafter (Miller 2000). If so, then they lived in one of the many villages of bent-pole wigwam-style houses that White himself had illustrated years earlier, sometimes with defensive vertical-post palisade walls surrounding them, sometimes not, depending on localized threats of attack. In White's painting of the village of Secotan, boys sit atop wooden-pole platforms out in fields to drive off animals seeking to snack on the corn, beans, and squash growing there. Nearby are village houses and, beyond that, people placing foodstuffs into subterranean pits and, then, a ceremonial dance around an anthropomorphized post-circle monument. In another watercolor, White illustrated a burial mound atop which a large marine shell had been placed.

As it turns out, the enlightened Thomas Jefferson excavated just such a burial mound, 4 m (12 ft) high, on his estate in the 1770s (see Chapter 2). He had specific research questions in mind, in part after seeing a group of natives visiting a mound on his estate in the 1750s. They "went through the woods directly to it," he wrote, "without any instructions or enquiry, and having staid [sic] about it some time, with expressions which were construed to be those of sorrow, they returned to the high road, which they had left about half a dozen miles to pay this visit, and pursued their journey" (Jefferson 1999:106).

By the time of Jefferson's investigations, most such Monacan Indians, Siouan-speaking people who had lived near his estate, were gone. Some of them were probably descendants of a once-great Late Woodland era Chesapeake Bay area political confederation, complete with a central government lorded over by prominent ruling families in the early 1600s. With English trade via Jamestown into the region in the early 1600s, one Algonkian-speaking ruler – named Wahunsenacawh, a.k.a. Powhatan – had consolidated his power by violently deposing rivals and manipulating the English colonists. He resided in four or five long, wigwam-style houses, one of which (about 7 x 24 m) was excavated by Martin Gallivan and colleagues at the capital settlement of Werowocomoco (Gallivan 2012; Gallivan et al. 2013). The councils held in and around those buildings seem to have helped bring together a diverse series of Algonkian-speaking communities, and possibly some of the Monacans and others, Iroquoian-speaking Nottoways and Meherrins who otherwise lived outside of Wahunsenacawh's domain, which he called "Tsenacomacoh" (Gallivan 2012). It was an incipient kingdom and it might have lasted for some time had it not been for the European onslaught, both physical and biological, which brought the Late Woodland era in the mid-Atlantic region to a close.

The American Dark Ages (400–900 CE)

It turns out that the Late Woodland period had begun in a similar fashion with the closure of the great Hopewell sites and dissolution of long-distance relations (see Chapter 9). In parts of Illinois, Iowa, and Wisconsin, this may have happened as early as 250 CE (Benn and Green 2000). In Ohio, the Hopewellian phenomenon probably lasted until almost 400 CE (see Chapter 9). After that time, people whose ancestors had traveled far and wide now seem to have turned inward, becoming parochial in outlook, insular in character, and prone to intercommunity feuds if not small-scale wars. However the Hopewell people had integrated the great river valleys of the Eastern Woodlands, it was clearly over by the early years of the fifth century (Table 10.1).

In and around the Driftless Area of Wisconsin, the preceding Middle Woodland mode of relating to the dead through specific mortuary practices continued in attenuated form, increasingly with fewer people involved in mound building and lacking the exotic things and references of the earlier era. Across the Midwest, the scattered domestic occupations of the first half of the Late Woodland period are barely visible on the archaeological landscape. Meager evidence exists of low-density settlements with widely spaced semisubterranean huts, increased numbers of storage and cooking pits, and denser concentrations of plant cultivars and local faunal remains among burned and discarded refuse, all indicating self-reliant and relatively small-scale communities (Figure 10.4).

Table 10.1 Chronological highlights of the pre-Mississippian, Late Woodland era (adapted from Anderson and Mainfort 2002; Emerson et al. 2000).

Year CE	Historic periods		Cultural patterns
	Midwest/ Midsouth	Southeast	
250–400	Hopewellian demise	Deptford	Continued ceremonial centers in Southeast
		Swift Creek	Crystal River site with stelae
400–600	early Late Woodland	Weeden Island	Kolomoki, McKeithen sites; earliest appearance of bow and arrow
600–700		Troyville	Troyville site; rapid adoption of bow and arrow in parts of Midwest and Midsouth
700–900	late Late Woodland	Baytown, late Weeden Island Coles Creek	Effigy Mound culture in north; small mound-and-plaza complexes in south; maize intensification and early chunkey game in central Mississippi Valley
900–1000s	terminal Late Woodland		earliest Caddo culture in trans-Mississippi west; growth of pre-Mississippian village of Cahokia; Late Woodland occupation at Aztalan

Typically, the Late Woodland families of the Midwest used minimally decorated and unslipped semi-conoidal (or half-coconut-shaped) cooking pots made using simple paddle-and-anvil techniques (Figure 10.5). Holding a shaping tool or anvil on the inside of the would-be pot while slapping the outside with a paddle would weld the coils of clay into a solid vessel wall. In the Late Woodland Midwest, those paddles were usually wrapped with cordage, which then left impressions or "cordmarks" on the soft clay (Rice 1987). Walk over practically any Late Woodland site in the midcontinent and you will find three things: a few broken chipped-stone tools, fire-cracked rock, and a low-density scatter of cordmarked potsherds; such was the grist of what archaeologists once called the "Good Gray cultures." Plenty of others thought of the period as the American Dark Ages.

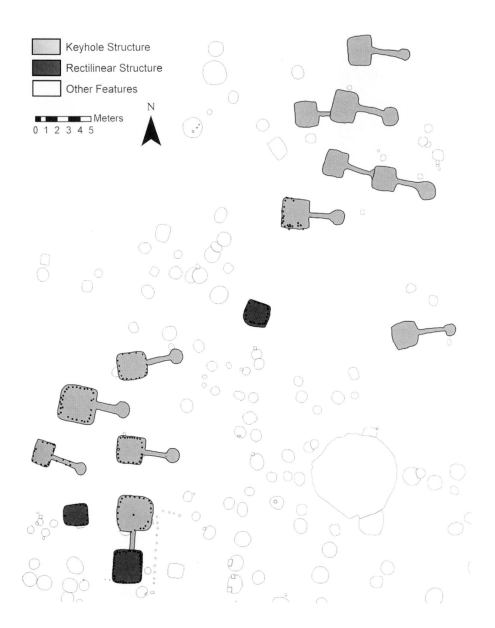

Fig 10.4 Portion of the Fish Lake site, southwestern Illinois (from Fortier 2014: figure 4.48). Courtesy of the Illinois State Archeological Survey, University of Illinois, Champaign-Urbana.

From Arkansas south into northern Louisiana, the rift separating the preceding Middle from the subsequent Late Woodland worlds was not as great. Certain storied places, such as the Helena to Marksville complexes, had become homes to ghosts, with subsequent scaled-back habitations of the early Late Woodland people at the northern end of the lower Mississippi Valley dubbed the "Baytown" culture by archaeologists (Phillips et al. 1951). But into central Louisiana, the parochial era yet saw the construction of another great, mounded complex: Troyville (Figure 10.6). Likely taking place over a period of generations, Troyville was doubtless a coordinated labor effort, seeing women, men, and children playing a part. Perhaps a storm cell

Fig 10.5 Late Woodland cooking pots: left, Deptford stamped cooking jar from Georgia, ca. 25 cm wide and tall (Ocmulgee National Monument); right, cordmarked and lip-notched bowl from Fish Lake, 26 cm diameter (from Zelen 2014: figure 5.10). Courtesy of the Illinois State Archaeological Survey, University of Illinois, Champaign-Urbana.

interrupted their labors now and then. Certainly they were punctuated by the appropriate ritual processions of finely dressed supplicants and visiting helpers, songs and prayers, orations, and great celebratory dances and feasts. Initially, visitors or pilgrims helping to build the complex may have stayed in a tent city located off to one side. Later, they probably stayed in one of the site's many circular lodges, 7–12 m in diameter with four cardinally aligned roof-support posts in their interiors (Lee 2010). They would remember the experience for the rest of their lives.

First recorded during the Dunbar Expedition, commissioned by President Jefferson, Troyville's central Great Mound (a.k.a. Mound 5) was impressive: 24 m (80 ft) in height with a stepped quasi-Mesoamerican profile. Neither this nor any of the other 8 to 13 mounds was a burial facility. Rather, they were four-sided platforms, the Great Mound having been built using alternating layers of clay and river cane (layers up to 1 m thick!) topped with wooden boards. "Ramps had been constructed at the four corners … and a series of posts formed a palisade-like screen on the south side of the mound. A causeway connected Mound 5 to Mound 4" (Lee 2010:146). True to its Marksville heritage, a massive D-shaped earthen embankment surrounded its 160 ha (400 acres). Unfortunately, little of this once-impressive complex survived the 1800s and 1900s. Confederate soldiers dug rifle pits into the top of the big mound in the 1860s, and later residents of the sleepy burg of Jonesville finished the job of leveling most of the remaining Troyville mounds. (Find Jonesville via

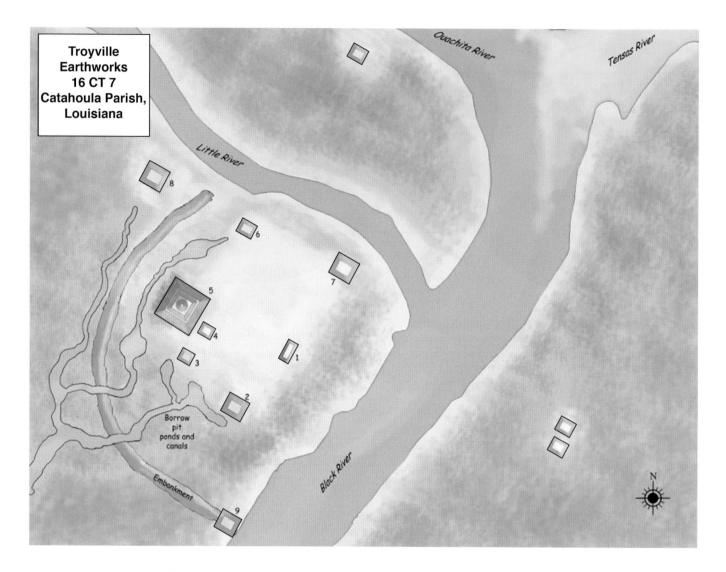

Fig 10.6 Troyville (adapted from a painting by Herb Roe). Wikimedia.

Google Earth and check out in Street view the intact Mound #4, now the property of the Archaeological Conservancy.)

East of Troyville

With Mound 5 being the third or fourth tallest earthen pyramid ever built in North America, and the site covering an area that rivals the largest of the earlier Hopewell and later Mississippian mounded centers, the historical impacts of Troyville were likely profound (if underappreciated today). To the east across the South's Coastal Plain toward Florida and up into the Carolinas, the divide between Middle and Late Woodland had been less obvious than in the Midwest. Indeed, the Hopewell phenomenon had never taken hold in the Southeast as it had in the main valleys of the Ohio and Mississippi rivers. Across much of Georgia, the Carolinas, and adjacent regions, archaeologists recognize the so-called late Deptford and Swift Creek cultural complexes. Potters of those cultures used wooden paddles, carved to depict spiritual beings and handed down from generation to generation, to finish their coiled, conoidal-shaped cooking vessels (see Figure 10.5; Wallis 2011). And they built a series of modest ceremonial complexes coeval with and postdating Hopewell, as at the Mandeville site along the Chattahoochee River in Georgia. Built as late as 700 CE, there was no apparent dissolution of Swift Creek ceremonial complexes in the South (Williams and Elliot 1998). Instead, other regional-cultural variants, including Weeden Island, first became recognizable after 200 CE and, in some cases, lasted until after 700 CE, when archaeologists recognize a "Weeden Island II" period in southern Georgia and northern Florida (ca. 700–1200 CE).

An example of a civic-ceremonial complex dating to the Deptford and Swift Creek periods is the six-mound Crystal River site, in west-central Florida (Figure 10.7). Covering an area of 8 ha including habitation debris, the site dates to the centuries between 100 BCE and the 600s CE (Pluckhahn et al. 2010). It is oddly organized with "two flat-topped ramped mounds bracketing its northern and southern ends, two burial mounds … an extensive comma-shaped shell middle with two smaller shell mounds, and three limestone boulders interpreted as stelae" (Pluckhahn et al. 2010:164). Two of the three limestone boulders stood in the plaza on either side of the burial mound, each visible from the summit of one of two opposing flat-topped mounds. One stele was carved to depict a human face, reminiscent of Taíno or Maya upright stones (cf. Bullen 1966). It rose almost 2 m out of the ground. The others were unadorned and extended about a meter above the surface.

Were these apparent stelae emplaced by expatriate Caribs or migrant Maya? The most recent archaeologists to work at the site, Thomas Pluckhahn, Victor Thompson, and Brent Weisman (2010), doubt it. And most Crystal River residents were surely local Floridians. Of course, that does not mean that the history of this unusual place can be explained in purely local terms any more than modern-day local cultures in Africa or Indonesia can be explained without also understanding global social history (Appadurai 1996; Wolf 1982). Perhaps it would help to look at another great Swift Creek-to-early-Weeden-Island period site dating slightly later than Crystal River.

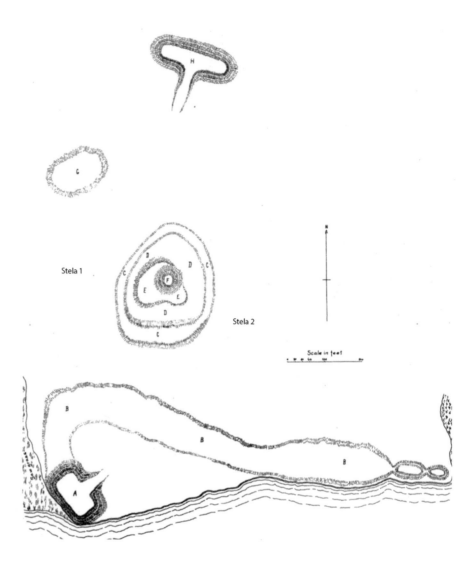

Stela 1

Stela 2

Fig 10.7 Schematic plan of the Crystal River site with stelae locations noted (adapted from Moore 1903: figure 16).

The Kolomoki site sits along the Chattahoochee River in south-eastern Georgia. Proclaimed by archaeologist Thomas Pluckhahn (2003:198) to have been, between 350 and 550 CE, "the largest and most densely settled community north of Mexico," the entire complex covers about 49 hectares and had a resident population of perhaps 500 individuals at its peak. Hundreds to thousands more people presumably lived in lands nearby and would have identified with Kolomoki. Identity here might have been a partial result of the work they dedicated to the construction of Kolomoki's central monumental core, which incidentally shares certain features with other ceremonial centers in the Coastal Plain all the way back to the Hopewellian-related Marksville site in Louisiana.

Fig 10.8 Weeden Island ceramic vessel, 30 cm tall (C. B. Moore 1901: figure 23).

With one large 17 m high rectangular pyramid, Kolomoki and its seven other mounds appear to have been aligned to either the summer solstice sunrise or the rising sun at the vernal and autumnal equinoxes. All were surrounded by a discontinuous, low curvilinear embankment of earth and, on either side of that, small, semisubterranean keyhole-shaped pithouses, the floor of one covering about 6 m², including an entrance ramp (Pluckhahn 2003). Within Mound D, excavated in 1950–1951, wooden mortuary scaffolds, cremations, and log-tomb burials are evidence of great mortuary spectacles. The pots made for such rituals feature humanoid and animal creatures or spirits, and have distinctive wall cutouts (Figure 10.8). A great site-wide closure event may have accompanied the death of a prominent leader.

A similar if slightly smaller configuration of mounds was found at the Weeden Island complex at McKeithen, coeval with but south of Kolomoki along the Chattahoochee in the modern-day Florida panhandle. There, three mounds form an isosceles triangle inside another circular earthen berm, a line bisecting the triangle from an earthen platform, Mound B also being aligned to the summer solstice sunrise (Milanich et al. 1997[1984]). Apparently, these were at the center of a highly organized ritual-administrative complex overseen by an apparent priestess. This leader might have been responsible for processing the bodies of dead community members atop Mound C for burial in Mound A. Her home or temple seems to have been a rectangular building on the summit of Mound B at the apex of the isosceles triangle (Figure 10.9). A healed-over arrow wound in her hip and red dye in her hair at death, she must have been a sight to see. Excavated by archaeologists Jerald Milanich and colleagues in the 1970s, she had died around the year 475, when her body was laid out in state on the floor of her mound-top building, presumably to be viewed or, perhaps, to continue leading the community even in death (Milanich et al. 1997[1984]). Judging from rodent-gnawing marks on her bones, her body lay there for a long time, perhaps many weeks. Finally, the townspeople dismantled her former home, and heaped earth over her in an act of ritual closure. Then, many, if not all, left the McKeithen site for points unknown.

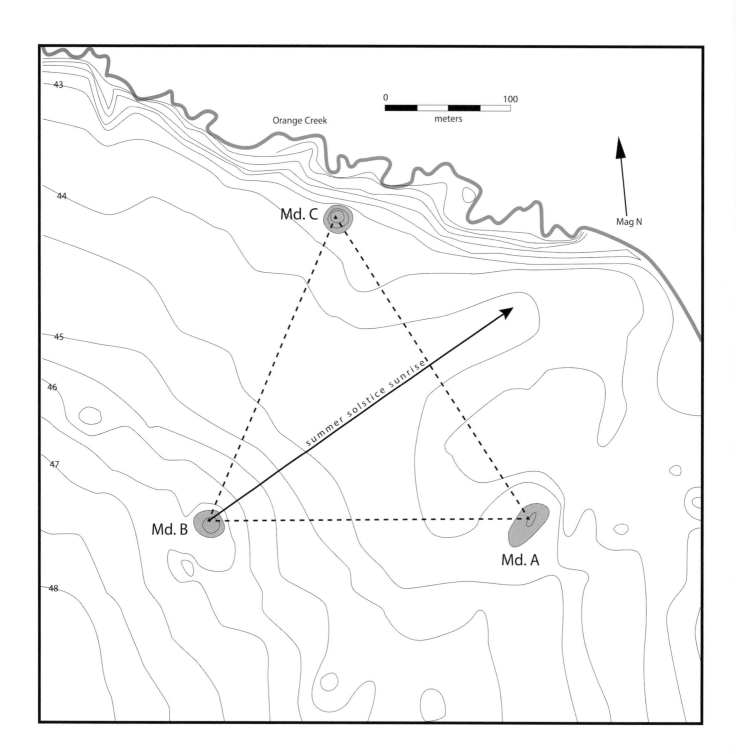

Fig 10.9 Plan map of the McKeithen site, Weeden Island culture, Georgia, showing site symmetry and summer solstice sunrise alignment to the northeast (adapted from Milanich et al. 1997[1984]: figure 5.1).

Bows and Arrows, Pots and Bears

As the arrow in the priestess's hip reveals, the American Dark Ages witnessed important social and cultural-technological changes. Up to that time, and as late as the year 800 CE in some parts of eastern North America, most people used atlatls to shoot stone-tipped missiles at their animal prey or at each other. Many in the East had not yet adopted the bow and arrow, and the reasons remain a mystery. After all, the bow had long been known in the far north, having been introduced into the Arctic from Siberia as early as 2000 BCE. Yet the bow seems to have only slowly spread south across eastern North America, initially into the northern Plains and down along the eastern seaboard into the Carolinas by about 200 CE. Interestingly, it did not penetrate some portions of the Midwest and South until the year 600, when the bow surged in popularity, replacing the atlatl in most places by 700 CE. Possibly, communities in America's heartland resisted bows until then. This seems to be the case even into Mesoamerica, where bows and arrows seem not to have been widely adopted until around 1100 CE (Ross Hassig, personal communication). As witnessed by the Spaniards, the Aztecs continued to use the atlatl in warfare alongside bows and arrows into the 1520s (see Chapter 3).

In the Midwest and Southeast, the transition to the bow seems to correspond to the increasingly complicated social relationships and landscapes of the Late Woodland era. Archaeologists debate whether or not the bow was a superior weapon in terms of the hunt, depending on what one was hunting. Simple bows and arrows may have had less killing power than the larger atlatl-thrown dart, making them less desirable when hunting large animals (Tomka 2013). Chipped stone arrowheads, after all, are much smaller than an average dart or spearpoint, which is the primary reason archaeologists are able to identify the introduction of the new weapon (Figure 10.10).

Fig 10.10 Late Woodland projectile points from the midcontinent before (left) and after (right) the introduction of the bow. Timothy R. Pauketat photo.

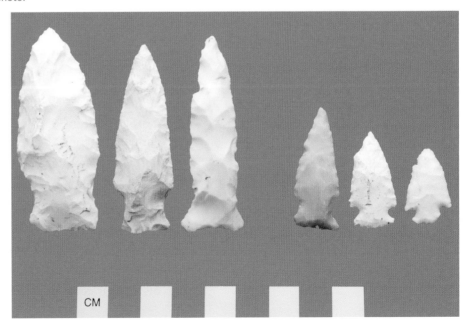

Then again, what the bow lacked in penetration power it made up for in stealth. Imagine a landscape in which you, a hunter or a warrior, tracked your prey or repelled your enemy's attack using darts propelled by atlatls. Before firing, you would have to stand upright, fully exposed, in order to let fly that missile. This would limit how and how effectively one might hunt or fight. The spear-thrower with dart is not an exceedingly stealthy weapon. On the other hand, a bow enables one to hide behind trees, bushes, and rocks to fire from a crouching position, protecting oneself from being seen. If you lived in a landscape where your enemy could attack you from behind rocks while you had to stand in the open to fire a return volley, you too might have adopted the bow and arrow in short order. The consequences of not switching to the bow could be dire.

Whatever the local reasons for switching to the bow, we must remember that technology is an extension of one's body to which one becomes habituated (Dobres 2000). Bows and arrows were not simply things that people might utilize without effect on their very being. Using them would have changed one's sense of self and, by extension, would have changed how people related to and identified or *communed* with other people and animals. As extensions of self and identity, the very basis of what constituted community and personhood would have become increasingly circumscribed – lived from behind a rock rather than revealed boldly in the open. In subtle ways, that is, face-to-face engagements with others might have been diminished, if only for fear of being seen or injured. In that kind of world, community itself might have taken on a different character, with communities of others increasingly considered as potential threats. The physical narratives of Indian country – the social landscape itself – would have been reordered in much the same way as Aaron Bird Bear had noted regarding effigy mounds in Wisconsin.

The effects were visible across the Great Lakes region of present-day Ontario, Michigan, and Wisconsin, and into Minnesota, northern Illinois, and Iowa. The cooking pots of the many Late Woodland cultures of that region reveal a heightened concern with projecting community identities and narratives. Wares made by people after the adoption of the bow and arrow were effusively decorated in locally standardized ways. Blackduck culture potters in Ontario added punctates or impressions of various kinds on the exteriors of their cookware (Mason 1981). Spring Creek, Saginaw Valley,

Juntunen, and Mackinac (pronounced Mak'-ĭ-naw) ceramics, among many other types, from Michigan, were incised, cordmarked, and punctated, with some rims "castellated" to square the appearance of the orifice when viewed from above (Brashler et al. 2000). Port Sauble and Aztalan Collared pottery from around Lake Michigan possessed distinctively cordmarked and impressed, thickened or collared rims, while Madison, Hartley, and a series of other cord-impressed wares made by Effigy Mound culture people and their relatives and neighbors west into Iowa exhibit arrangements of cords and net-like fabrics pushed into the soft prefired clay during manufacture. The effect was one where horizontal lines, tick marks, or even icons gave the vessel exterior the look of woven fabric. In such ways, perhaps, the pots were the narratives and identities of people woven and impressed on to the powerful medium of a communal pot made from earthly substances.

On a more superficial level, projecting one's identity on a pot might have come to the fore in part because potters were on the move at this time. We know this because the natal styles of some potters from, say, one end of Lake Superior sometimes appear in a foreign context at the other end of this or another of the Great Lakes. Potting was a habitual practice, of course, done repeatedly and without a lot of analytical thought in the doing. Potters made pots the way they were trained in their youth and, if relocating from one community to another, most probably continued to make pots in the same way unless there were compelling reasons to stop. The thing is, local people in the new

Sidebar 10.1 Who cooked what in Late Woodland pots?

In many parts of the Eastern Woodlands, Late Woodland pots were minimally decorated, thin-walled, cooking vessels. As in other parts of North America, the pots were commonly made in one sitting by coiling and then paddling the clay walls into shape (often tempered with crushed rock called "grit" or crushed potsherds called "grog"). In the Great Lakes region, which was a maize-free zone until the 1100s or later, wild rice (*Zizania* spp.) and a mix of native grasses could be boiled into porridges or parched ("popped") quickly over an open fire using such ceramic utensils. Wild rice could be threshed with beaters directly into canoes, and was a favorite of peoples from Saskatchewan and Manitoba to Michigan and Minnesota. Other starchy- and oily-seeded grasses were collected on foot by tapping the seed heads over baskets (not fragile pots). Once boiled or parched, the starchy seeds – goosefoot or lambsquarters (*Chenopodium berlandieri*), erect knotweed (*Polygonum erectum*), pigweed (*Amaranthus* spp.), maygrass (*Phalaris caroliniana*), and little barley (*Hordeum pusillum*) – could be ground into meal and stored or used to make bread. Along with oily-seeded sunflower (*Helianthus annuus*) and marsh elder (*Iva annua*), the seeds might be used to make porridges or stews in pots, the latter by adding meat and other greens, tubers, or squash. Many of the pots were large and could be used to cook generous portions, perhaps enough to feed entire extended families (see also Sidebar 9.1).

community would probably have noticed the immigrant potter's subtle variations in pot shape, finish, or functional characteristics and would have readily identified that potter or potting community as different (Longacre and Skibo 1994).

No doubt, the motivations for the relocation of one or more potters from here or there might often have been peaceful, as in a recently married spouse accompanying her husband back to his homeland. Harkening back to the long-forgotten Hopewellian era of their ancestors, marriage alliances forged between families and communities might have allowed future cooperation between distant peoples. To this end it is worth noting that archaeologists David Benn and William Green (2000) see in some cord impressions on Iowa pots a widespread "network of women potters" that "must have swept across the prairies within 50–100 years" (Benn and Green 2000:466). Then again, other relocations were not peaceful. Wife capture was a well-known tribal practice in the historic-era Midwest and Plains. War parties sometimes raided enemy villages and captured young women who might then be "adopted" by the captors, eventually to become full-fledged members of the captors' community. Well-known examples of this practice from New York to Texas in the historic era resulted in native men kidnapping Euro-American women; Mary Jemison and Cynthia Ann Parker are famous cases. Foreign wives who were forcibly relocated might have clung to their old natal identities in defiance of their captors, despite living far from home. Whether peacefully or defiantly done, pottery-making practices under these conditions can produce confusing, overlapping regional distributions of pottery styles. Moreover, played out over centuries, the effect of such practices in the Late Woodland era was the creation of hybrid communities composed of people from diverse cultural backgrounds, from the Canadian shores of the Great Lakes south into Illinois, Iowa, and Indiana.

Elsewhere, changing landscapes of peace and violence led to a new game and the intensification of crop production. By about 600 CE, a truly ancient kids' game called "hoop-and-pole" appears to have morphed into an early version of a sport later known as "chunkey" (Culin 1992; Pauketat 2009). Originally involving a rolling hoop and darts, a stone disk or discoidal stone replaced the hoop in a stretch of the Mississippi River valley in what is today eastern Missouri, western Illinois, and southwestern Wisconsin (Figure 10.11). Presumably, as later recorded by colonial French historian and naturalist Antoine-Simone le Page du Pratz, a Euro-American

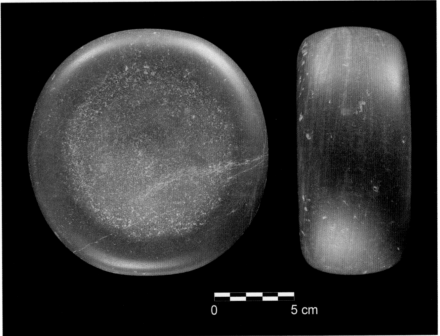

Fig 10.11 Late Woodland chunkey stone from the Janey B. Goode site, Illinois: top, *in situ*; bottom, face and side views. Courtesy of the Illinois State Archaeological Survey, University of Illinois, Champaign-Urbana.

naturalist William Bartram, and the wayfaring artist George Catlin, among others, two or more players took turns rolling the puck-like stone across flat ground, each attempting to throw their chunkey sticks either at the rolling stone or at the location at which it might stop. Among the Choctaw of Mississippi, the game was played in the plaza around an upright post, but there was no formal court similar to those used in the Southwestern or Mesoamerican ballgame. Whatever the rules of and grounds used for chunkey, archaeologists find that the distinctively shaped stones were increasingly associated at sites in southwestern Illinois with adult, ceremonial, or public buildings or courtyards by the year 800 or 900, suggesting something more than a kids' game. Possibly the chunkey game was becoming a way for people within or between communities to share in common narratives or to resolve disputes without resorting to violence, much like sports events between rival teams today. This was certainly the case during the historic era, when the American Indian team sporting events – chunkey and then stick ball (later known as *la crosse*) – were understood to be alternatives to war (see Chapter 12).

After Troyville, No Turning Back

That territorial relationships were increasingly becoming a concern among the otherwise-insular Late Woodland peoples of the Midwest might help to explain not only the chunkey game but also the intensification of crop production. Besides the actual remains of more seeds, the intensification of cultivation is evident in the appearance of large hoe blades in southern Illinois. Although small versions of these garden tools were evident at Middle Woodland villages in the Midwest, Late Woodland hoe blades dating to ca. 700 CE now included foot-long blades of polished limestone that, not counting the wooden handle, weighed up to 1.5 kg (or more than 3 lb) (Figure 10.12). Today,

Fig 10.12 Midwestern garden hoe blades from southwestern Illinois: left, Middle Woodland chipped stone blade; center, Late Woodland ground limestone blade; right, Mississippian chipped stone blade. Scale to right is in centimeters. Timothy R. Pauketat photo, 2012.

as in the past, such heavy tools are used in sod busting, breaking up and turning over the soil in fields to get them ready for planting in the springtime.

At the same time, two other obvious changes to everyday life in the Mississippi Valley were introduced. First and foremost, the maize plant appeared as a dietary staple in the refuse of families in a restricted portion of the valley, from central Illinois south into central Arkansas. Maize as a staple is evident by perhaps 700 CE at the Toltec site, a large ceremonial center with great earthen platform mounds near modern-day Little Rock, Arkansas. Gayle Fritz and other paleoethnobotanists believe that this influx of maize may have been a result of borrowing from the Southwest – where corn had been a staple for centuries (see Chapter 14). After all, at contact the well-worn Santa Fe Trail led from the Mississippi Valley west to Pecos Pueblo and, from there, into the Puebloan Southwest. Maize possibly introduced into the East at that time from the Southwest might have been significantly more productive than that purported to have been used by earlier Hopewell peoples, an association currently under debate (see Chapter 9).

Of course, similar to the arrival of the bow or pottery centuries earlier (see Chapter 7), the new corn plants were not uniformly greeted as a panacea. In fact, as far as we now know, maize was ignored by all of the people south of the Toltec site, near present-day Little Rock, Arkansas, until after 1100 CE. The lower Mississippi Valley, as it is known, was a land of "Coles Creek" ceremonial centers that, from about 700 to 1200 CE, developed out of the Troyville–Baytown phenomenon and were contemporaries with the later Swift Creek and Weeden Island II cultures of the Southeast. Coles Creek people met for their major ceremonials at prominent mound-and-plaza complexes. Some of the many dozens of such places, for instance Greenhouse, Raffman, or Feltus, were quite large, covering up to 10 ha (Figure 10.13). Their platform mounds reached impressive heights of 15–20 m, and their open plazas covered as much as 1,000 m². Importantly, archaeologist Tristram R. Kidder (2004) proved at the Raffman site that these plazas were great constructed features. People had hauled in thousands of cubic meters of earth and packed it into a rectangular area at the very inception of each center in order to create their huge community square. At Feltus, archaeologist Vincas Steponaitis and colleagues (2015) discovered that large marker posts were set into place in such plazas.

(a)

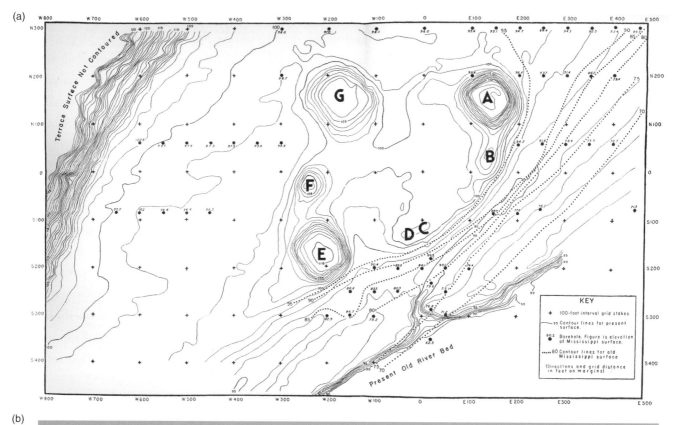

(b)

Fig 10.13 Coles Creek and Plum Bayou complexes: top, map of the Greenhouse site in central Louisiana (Ford 1951: figure 1); bottom, one of 18 mounds at the Toltec site, central Arkansas. Timothy R. Pauketat photo, 2006.

Yet, unlike Toltec to the north, with its novel intensification of field agriculture, the Coles Creek peoples still seemed insulated from the outside world. The bow and arrow didn't penetrate the region until the seventh century. Few exotic artifacts are known. And, as already noted, maize was unknown until 1100 CE. In short, the Coles Creek-like Toltec mound center was unique at the time. It was larger than any Coles Creek complex to the south, and was situated at the center of a clear cultural region – the so-called "Plum Bayou culture" – that included at least two lesser mound complexes and was populated by at least 1,000 farmers (Nassaney 2001).

At Toltec, a prominent earthen embankment up to 3 m (10 ft) high surrounded 18 earthen mounds and two likely plazas. The enclosure was probably not a defensive feature, but a spiritual barrier that prevented outside pollutants from entering and the resident spirits from roaming the earth (see Chapter 9). Among the monuments inside, three or four platforms reach 12–15 m in height (Rolingson 1998). Of these, Mound A has a surprisingly narrow base, yet was built tall, perhaps to impress the gathered throngs in ways not unlike billboards or the false fronts of frontier-town stores in the old American West. As seen from the east, the skyline of Mound B and the other great mounds of Toltec was impressive against the backdrop of a watery bayou and the setting sun. Of course, the sun was not the only impressive reference point. A recent archaeoastronomical study by William Romain (2015) makes it clear that, like earlier Hopewell and Marksville sites, Toltec's plan was laid out with reference to a once-in-a-generation moonrise, a function of the fact that the moon revolves around the earth at a different angle than the earth does around the sun (a.k.a. the "ecliptic"). Given its lunar configuration, it seems likely that the Toltec site was laid out from the start as a great cosmic center. Its effects would have presumably been at least as momentous as those of its predecessors back through the centuries: Troyville, Kolomoki, Marksville, Newark, Poverty Point, Watson Brake, and more.

Was the introduction of maize to the Midwest one of its effects? We are unsure, but by the 800s, Late Woodland villages to the north also began to plant fields of maize as well. Indeed, within a stretch of the Mississippi River floodplain called the "American Bottom" at the end of the so-called "Patrick phase" in that region, corn growing was becoming entangled in a cascade of social changes sufficient for archaeologists to give the era a new name: the Terminal Late Woodland period (900–1050 CE). This period has also been called the "Red Filmed Horizon" owing to the use of red slips on the outside of pots used in ritual gatherings (Pauketat 2004). Pots that are red slipped, which is to say coated with fine clay slurry to which an iron-based pigment has been added, have clear-cut visual qualities about them. They can be readily seen from afar, which may have been the point. Or the idea might have been to associate the contents or the contexts of usage with the color red and the emotions or feelings that this color inspired. If so, then the effects of a red-slipped pot in public would be like that produced when people wore elaborate or colorful clothing in public. The Terminal Late Woodland or Red Filmed Horizon seems to have been a time of increasingly public rituals and elaborate ceremonies. The old parochial ways of the Late Woodland era were coming to an end.

It was also the period during which the use of spindle whorls spread across the central Mississippi Valley (Figure 10.14). Spindle whorls are miniature spinning wheels, and were used in conjunction with a stick or spindle to mass produce twine and thread with which to weave fabric (Alt 1999). Sometime after 700 CE at Toltec and by 900 CE in outlying lands, that is, people appear to have scaled-up their production of cloth. And in other places around the world, cloth is often needed in order to make the fancy clothes worn by high-status

Fig 10.14 Potsherd spindle whorls from Cahokia, Illinois. Timothy R. Pauketat photo, 2002.

people in public rituals. If true, then social changes were very definitely afoot.

Whatever those changes were, they extended to the south of Toltec and to the west of old Troyville, into an area that would become the Caddo homeland. You may recall that Hernando de Soto had plunged into Caddo country in 1542, though he did not stay long (Chapter 3). Coronado too had skirted the territory, passing by the Caddo-speaking Wichita in Kansas in 1541. The Pawnee people of the eastern Plains, of whom Coronado's guide (The Turk) was a member, also spoke a Caddo language. It will be recalled that he had told Coronado of a native lord in the kingdom of Quivira who sat under a tree festooned with metal ornaments and who worshipped a goddess. Coronado had believed him up to a point before deciding that The Turk's stories were lies. But were they? Or was there a place, in some ways linked to Caddoan history, that had lived on in the collective memory of people (Kehoe 1998)?

Certainly, there seem to have been historical linkages between the formation of Caddo complexes in western Arkansas, eastern Oklahoma, northwestern Louisiana, and north-central Texas and those of Cahokia, an American Indian city to the northeast (Girard et al. 2014). After 800 CE, the Fourche Maline way of life in that region was becoming increasingly homogeneous, perhaps indicating an ethnic or linguistic coalescence. In that era, an early ceremonial center on the Red River, known today as Crenshaw, may have driven historical change. There, and at other early Caddo sites, mass burials of people, skulls, and deer antlers are known (Figure 10.15). The pottery appears similar to, if not derivative of, the Coles Creek and Plum Bayou peoples to the east and northeast, respectively. By the late 1000s CE, a suite of Cahokia's finest objects – long-nosed god earpieces, copper ornaments, chunkey stones, and carved redstone figure smoking pipes (see below) – ended up with the dead of a number of Caddo centers. Likewise, some, if fewer, Caddo and Caddo-like pots are also found at Cahokia (Figure 10.16). Possibly, the circular architecture of the early Caddo villages of the region – eastern Oklahoma, north-central Texas, and adjacent portions of Arkansas and Louisiana – inspired the circular ritual architecture introduced around greater Cahokia after 1050 CE (Figure 10.17).

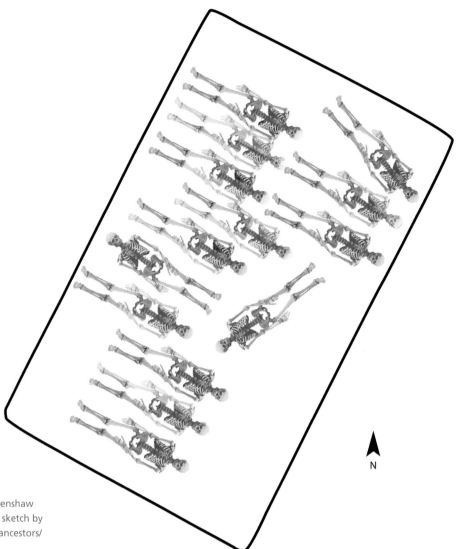

Fig 10.15 Schematic map of mass grave at the Crenshaw site. Timothy R. Pauketat image, adapted from a sketch by Glen Martin (www.texasbeyondhistory.net/tejas/ancestors/images/crenshaw-e25.html).

The Medieval Warming and Post-Classic Revitalizations (900–1200s CE)

A day's horse-and-buggy ride west of Madison, Wisconsin, sit the Baraboo Hills of Sauk and Richland counties, Wisconsin. Here lie four great earthen men, humanoid-spirit tumuli, or "man mounds" (Figure 10.18). They share some characteristics of other anthropomorphic bird mounds known from the Effigy Mound culture of 700–1200 CE, but the man mounds suggest something more: a restricted locality where a mythical human being or demi-god was thought to reside. Had an actual historical figure appeared who embodied such

Fig 10.16 Haley Engraved bottle of the early Caddo culture, 23 cm tall (C. B. Moore 1913: figure 20).

a mythical person? Do these mounds commemorate such an actor on the stage of ancient Wisconsin history?

A bigger social, political, and military history does seem evident to all who visit the Aztalan site, east of Madison, once thought to be an ancient "citadel" by John Muir's antiquarian contemporaries, Nathanial Hyer and Increase Lapham. Tucked away on the side of a slope that leads down to a particularly shallow stretch of the Rock River is a wooden fortification wall with its regularly spaced bastions and four-sided pyramidal mounds (search for "Aztalan State Park" in Google Earth). Nearby were rows of other conical and effigy mounds (Lapham 2001). The rectilinear angles of Aztalan contrast with the quiet curvilinear shapes of southern Wisconsin's effigy mounds and this cries out for an explanation. What happened here? In Muir's day, it was commonly assumed that the Aztalan citadel was the original homeland of the Aztecs of central Mexico. Hence, it came to be known as that legendary place: Aztlán. Today, we know that Wisconsin's Aztalan was a place where Late Woodland and Mississippian cultural realms converged in a great moment of historical change that came to the American Midwest and Southeast near the middle of the eleventh century CE. That historical change was initiated, it seems, by both the introduction of maize into the daily lives of some Terminal Late Woodland people and the beginning of what paleoclimatologists term the "Medieval Warm Period" around 800 CE (Table 10.2).

Beginning in that century and lasting three to four more, the average temperature on the continent increased by perhaps 2 degrees Fahrenheit (or about 1 degree Celsius). The temperatures were still cooler than our own twenty-first century's warming climate, but in the American midcontinent, the tenth century's warmer weather was also accompanied in some regions by additional rainfall per annum (Benson et al. 2009a). By themselves, such slightly altered conditions might not directly cause anything in particular to happen to people, depending on what they were doing or ready to do at the time. And, of course, in most parts of the continent, nothing historically dramatic did happen. In Iowa, no

Fig 10.17 Caddo house floors at the George C. Davis site, Texas. Courtesy of the Texas Archeological Research Laboratory, University of Texas at Austin (Image 41CE19-2818).

Fig 10.18 The Man Mound near Baraboo, Wisconsin in 1910. Courtesy of Sauk County Historical Society.

Table 10.2 Chronological highlights of the Terminal Late Woodland and Mississippian era (adapted from Cobb and Butler 2002; Emerson 2002; Fortier et al. 2006; Girard et al. 2014; Hally 1994; King 2003; Pauketat 2004).

Year CE	Historic periods		Cultural patterns
	Midwest/ Midsouth	Southeast	
900–1000s	Terminal Late Woodland	Terminal Late Woodland	Earliest Caddo culture in trans-Mississippi west; growth of pre-Mississippian village of Cahokia; Late Woodland occupation at Aztalan; earliest shell-tempered pottery
1050 ± 25	Cahokia's Big Bang	Terminal Late Woodland	Reconstruction of old village into proto-urban city
1050–1150	Early Mississippian	Terminal Late Woodland Early Mississippian	Cahokianism transported to Angel, Kincaid, northern outposts, Gahagan; centers of Shiloh, Ocmulgee, Etowah founded
1150–1350	Late Mississippian	Mississippian	Cahokia palisaded in its decline; Illinois Valley towns and Common Field site rise and fall; Moundville, Lake George, Winterville, Hiwassee Island, etc. founded or expanded
1350–1520s	Vacant Quarter	Mississippian	Etowah expanded; Spiro Great Mortuary event
	Oneota expansion		

great late ninth- or early tenth-century transformation occurred. In Mississippi, the Coles Creek people went on being Coles Creek people. In Florida, Weeden Island folks probably didn't notice any change in the weather.

However, in the center of the Midwest, especially around what would soon become the Cahokia region – the lands centered on the "American Bottom" (a river bottom is a flat floodplain) opposite modern-day St. Louis – the Medieval Warm Period saw change quite possibly linked to the wetter, warmer years of the early 1000s. Across the central Mississippi Valley, from the American Bottom south into the Bootheel of Missouri, clusters of corn-growing villages appear to have grown in prominence and visibility. Some of them, in southeast Missouri and northeast Arkansas, switched to making their pottery by adding crushed, burned mussel shell obtained from the rivers as temper to the clays used to produce the pots. The clays too were often dug from riverbanks or other exposures. One such village, known as the Zebree site, appears to have been surrounded by a ditch, later destroyed by a modern channel built by the United States Army Corps of Engineers. Archaeologists Dan and Phyllis Morse and volunteers excavated what they could of the site, finding a distinctive Terminal Late Woodland red-slipped pottery, Varney Red Filmed, in association with houses and storage pits (Morse and Morse 1983). That pottery was among the first shell-tempered pottery in the valley; some of the potters who made it migrated to Cahokia and elsewhere (Figure 10.19).

On the American Bottom, villages were booming, with human populations at each surging into the hundreds. Excavations at a site destined to be destroyed by a new interstate highway (I-255) during the 1970s (named the Range site after its owner) revealed the typical village pattern of the day: small pole-and-thatch huts built

Fig 10.19 Varney Red Filmed pottery-making tool kit (from Morse and Morse 1983: figure 10.5). Courtesy of Dan and Phyllis Morse.

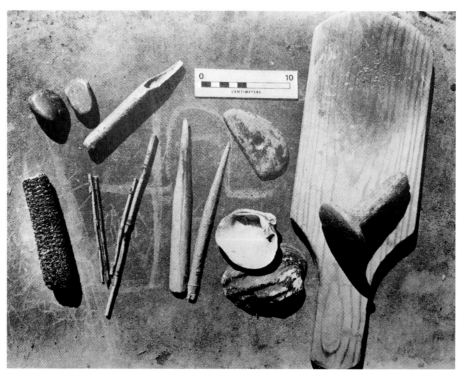

Sidebar 10.2 Why shell temper and red slips?

Experiments by Zebree project personnel confirmed materials-science studies of the technological aspects of shell-tempered pottery. Crushed and burned mussel shells add desirable chemical and structural properties to "montmorillinitic" clays from river bottoms. In addition, the shell weighs less than the crushed grit or grog previously added as temper to Woodland pots. Thus, potters could now make round-bottomed, portable dishware. Adding slips to the interior, common to Varney Red Filmed ceramics, reduced the permeability of the vessel walls.

Then again, red slips on the exterior walls, more common to later, early Mississippian wares, would seem to signal the importance of the color itself to people using the pot (see Red Filmed Horizon, above). Though few archaeologists have considered it, the addition of mussel shell to the pot might also have been less for purely technological reasons and more a means of the potter relating to the powers of the water and the creatures or spirits living under the water – always apparent in the iconography of Woodland and later Mississippian peoples. That is, a pot that built into its fabric both earth and water – to be used by people over fire – was a container that embodied all of the fundamental forces of the cosmos. The fact that it was also a superior technological container would not have been lost on people, but was probably understood in their own culturally meaningful terms.

around courtyards no bigger than a tennis court today, with a "council house" or "temple" off to one side (Figure 10.20). Chunkey stones and carved stone smoking pipe bowls were found buried near the central marker post of some courtyards (Kelly 1990b). One such village – the pre-Mississippian site of old Cahokia – exceeded 1,000 people by the mid-eleventh century, all strung out along a sandy floodplain ridge covering several square kilometers.

Founders

Perhaps it was the warmer and wetter weather. Perhaps it was the relatively peaceful lives led by the farmers in and around the American Bottom. Perhaps it was the arrival of strangers from the south – maybe people from Toltec in Arkansas – or the return of local dignitaries from a far-off land. Or possibly strange happenings in the sky – comets, meteor showers, and supernovae in 1006 and 1054 – induced people to seek the guidance of some visionary who, then, persuaded followers to build an unprecedented new cityscape that stretched for miles across the region. Something happened. And it beckoned people by the thousands to leave their old villages and distant homelands and join in what must have been a religious movement to build a new order of human experience. Today we know it as Cahokia, but its original name is not known for certain.

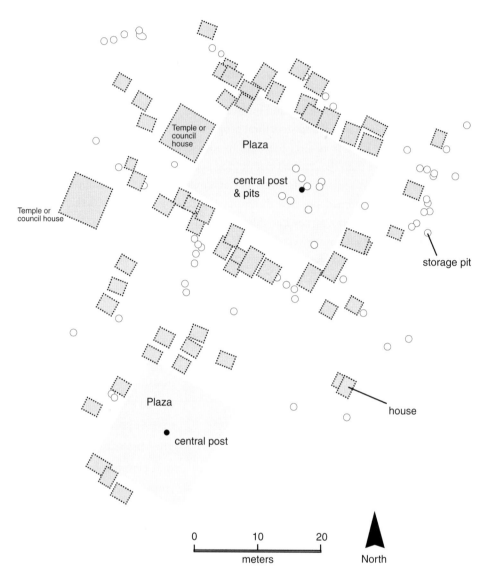

Fig 10.20 Plan view of one of the Terminal Late Woodland courtyard groups at the Range site (adapted from Kelly 1990b: figure 40).

Sometime around the year 1050 CE, portions of the old village of Cahokia were demolished. Superimposed over the top was a well-designed city plan, presumably the big idea of someone or some small group of people. That plan seems to have been large indeed, extending into the hills to the east, if not west, of the American Bottom. Over a period of time covering as little as a few years to as much as a few decades, the new city of Cahokia was constructed (Figure 10.21). Low-lying areas were filled, ridges were re-contoured, and entire plazas were leveled in the first hundred years of Cahokia's existence in an effort to remake a landscape such that it aligned with the fundamental powers of the cosmos.

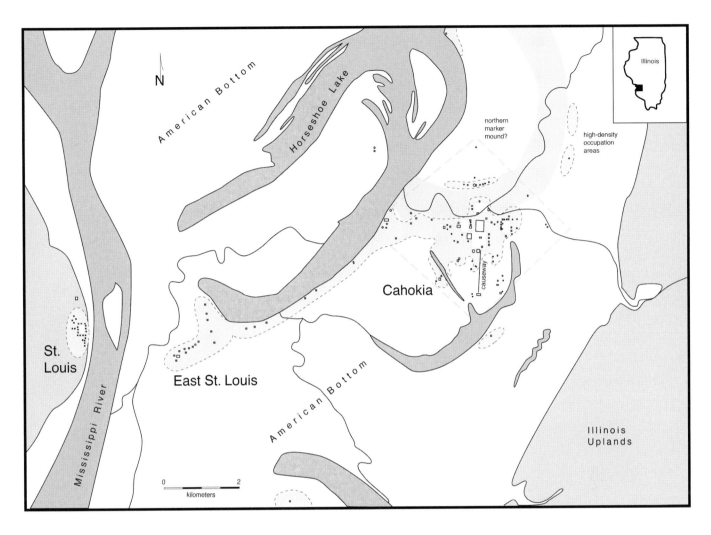

Fig 10.21 The precincts of Cahokia at about 1100 CE. Timothy R. Pauketat map.

We presume that the laborers were the local farmers and newly relocated people from outside the region. But whoever they were, the labor that they contributed to build this extraordinary capital must have equaled many tens, if not hundreds, of thousands of person-hours. That needed just to bring one-quarter to one-third of a new "Grand Plaza" into existence is 10,000 person-days – which is to say, 10,000 people working for one day, or 1,000 people working for 10 days (Alt et al. 2010). Other construction projects were underway at the same time, or shortly before or after. These included the relatively short-term construction of the third-largest pyramid in the Americas, locally called Monks Mound (Figure 10.22). It is composed of about 624,000 cubic meters of earth.

Thanks to recent excavations and new LiDAR imaging of the earth's surface, we can now recognize the design of the Cahokia precinct and infer the meaning it may have held. A central raised causeway, the

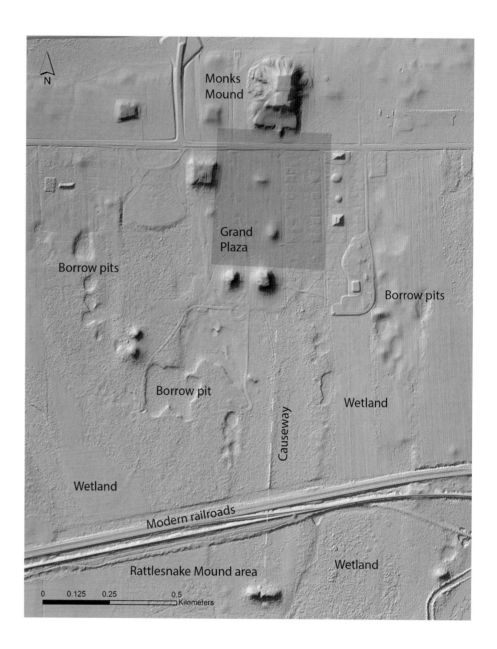

Fig 10.22 LiDAR image of Monks Mound, Grand Plaza, and Rattlesnake Causeway. Timothy R. Pauketat image, made using public domain data, 2018.

width of a paved highway today, was laid out from the "Grand Plaza" south for a kilometer (0.6 mile) at an azimuth of 5 (or 185) degrees, where 0 degrees is true north (Figure 10.23). Most of the central rectangular pyramids, along with the ridge-top mound at the south end of the causeway, are also angled at 5 degrees of azimuth. Someone designed this complex, but who?

One of the earliest interments in a small ridge-top burial mound, number 72 of Cahokia's total, dates to the decades around 1050 and contains the burials of a couple, a man and a woman. Alongside them were the bundled bones of another male and female, and a child, whose deaths had preceded those of the first couple, who in turn

Sidebar 10.3 Why call Cahokia a city?

A legacy of Euro-American ethnocentrism may account for archaeological debates in the 1980s through the early 2000s over what to call Cahokia and how to evaluate its historical significance (Kehoe 1998). Even today certain archaeologists shy away from labeling Cahokia a "city," some because they believe that American Indians would never build a city (ignoring indigenous Mesoamerican cities, of course) and others because of Cahokia's dissimilarities with other ancient cities in, say, Mesopotamia. However, Cahokia's population, its elaborate monumentality, and its rigidly ordered design compare well with early cities in the Americas, such as Tiwanaku in Bolivia and La Venta or Monte Alban in Mexico. Its pyramids were not, of course, built of stone. Stone would have been inconsistent with the legacy or tradition of earthen mound construction for the indigenous people of the Eastern Woodlands. But Cahokia covered as much area as, or more than, other early cities – some 20 km² if we include all three

monumental and ritual-residential complexes (Cahokia proper, East St. Louis, and St. Louis). Minimum population estimates for the overall city fall under 10,000. Maximum population estimates reach upwards to 20,000, not counting greater Cahokia's outlying farming population, which boosts the overall population of people from 20,000 to as many as 50,000. More farmers, who may have identified less closely with the city, would have lived beyond 80 km (50 mi) of Cahokia.

Each of Cahokia's three central precincts possessed great plazas, large platform mounds, and at least one oversized ridge-top mound, the primary place of rest for Cahokia's most important dead. The largest, Cahokia precinct, comprised 120 earthen pyramids, including Monks Mound. It and the other 200 or so platforms in the region were topped by great pole-and-thatch buildings, some probably temples and council chambers, others homes, and yet others storage rooms for sacred bundles or personal possessions.

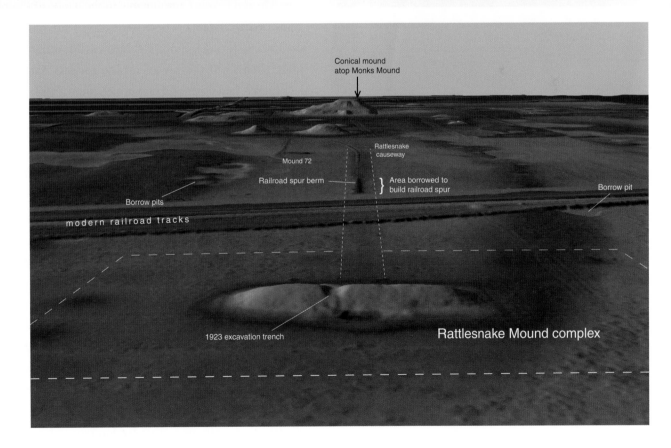

Fig 10.23 Oblique LiDAR view of the central Cahokia precinct from the south, with the ridge-top burial mound at the end of a kilometer-long causeway. Base map by Michael Farkas. Courtesy of the Illinois State Archaeological Survey, University of Illinois, Champaign-Urbana.

Fig 10.24 Cahokian goddess pouring liquid from a marine shell cup: carved from red flintclay stone quarried from sinkholes west of the city. Courtesy of the Illinois State Archaeological Survey, University of Illinois, Champaign-Urbana.

had been laid on or under 10,000 marine shell beads made locally from imported conch shell from the Gulf of Mexico (Emerson et al. 2016). Were these the founders of Cahokia? Were these, or their kinsfolk, the people who had envisioned the glorious new convergence of earth and sky and living and dead that became the city of Cahokia? Archaeologists do not know, but we can surmise that the layout of the greater complex – long known to archaeologists as the "Cahokia grid" – was the implementation of someone's plan. Some person or small group of people, that is, conceived and organized the place in the beginning (possibly not unlike Romulus and Rome, Akhenaten and his Egyptian capital of Amarna, or Yax-Kuk-Mo and the Maya capital of Copan).

The cosmic principles that underwrote the whole Cahokia experiment are on display in two dramatic ways: stone idols and human sacrifices. With regard to the first, a set of some two dozen stone idols have been discovered at and around Cahokia and beyond, presumably in the hands of Cahokian allies or descendants. These were carved for only a hundred years, during Cahokia's golden twelfth century. Of the idols, almost half portray a feminine goddess. She sits with legs tucked under her and is routinely shown with open lips while holding or emerging out of the baskets of ancestral bones. Sometimes she digs a garden hoe into the back of an earth monster. In other poses, crops sprout from her hands while a great serpent wraps around her body. In still another representation, she pours a liquid from a marine shell cup (Figure 10.24). In all cases, the image seems to be of a deity who harnesses the power of the earth to bring human beings crops and who is closely connected to ancestral spirits living in the land of the dead (the goddess's open lips suggest a dead body after the skin has undergone shrinkage).

Perhaps this goddess required human sacrifices to be sustained, because in several different contexts, the bodies of young people – mostly women – have been discovered either singly or in groups of 4, 19, 22, 24, and 53 (Figure 10.25). At least five burial pits that stemmed from individual sacrificial events exist in and under Mound 72 (Fowler et al. 1999). Others are known from several of the 15 or so other

Sidebar 10.4 Cahokian statuettes

With the growl of FAI-270-project belly-scrapers in the background, Thomas E. Emerson – 34-year-old native of Chippewa Falls, Wisconsin – bent over to pick up a red stone, perhaps a brick fragment. Rolling it over in his hand, he thought otherwise. It was an open-lipped fragmentary humanoid face, a piece of the now well-known Birger-figure statuette from the BBB Motor site, a modest pair of temples or shrine buildings at the edge of central Cahokia. In the weeks that followed the discovery of the Birger-figure fragment, Emerson and his crew would uncover the rest of its feminine body and the broken pieces of a second redstone statuette, the Keller figure, *in situ* in or near the two small buildings. Many others have been found or recognized since, though most of the feminine figures, probably Earth Mother, Corn, or even Moon goddesses, were kept in temples around Cahokia (Emerson 1997). There are also masculine or ambiguously sexed humanoid images, some of which depict shamans or priests, along with various animal or animal-spirit carvings. Many of the masculine and animal images are found far away from Cahokia, up and down the Mississippi River, in Caddo country, and into the Deep South at places such as Shiloh, Tennessee or Mobile, Alabama. One, from the Great Mortuary at the Spiro site, shows a masculine culture hero wearing a shell-bead necklace and human-head earpieces.

Since finding his first in 1979, Thomas Emerson has conducted mineralogical studies of the redstone used to carve all of them and found that all were made from a soft "flintclay" stone found only in natural sinkholes in Missouri due east of Cahokia (Emerson et al. 2003). That Cahokians kept and buried most of the feminine carvings but not the masculine or animal-spirit specimens, which often doubled as smoking pipe bowls, suggests that the central deity of the ancient city was a goddess. In a possible coincidence, The Turk reported to Coronado in 1542 that Tatarrax, ruler of the legendary Quivira, also worshipped a woman, "queen of heaven" (Bolton 1990:232). In the historic era, many American Indians in the Eastern Woodlands recognized "Our Grandmother" or her daughter as deities.

ridge-top mounds around greater Cahokia, most of which have been destroyed. Newspaper accounts written when the largest ridge-tops in St. Louis, East St. Louis, and elsewhere were destroyed in the 1860s and 1870s describe group burials of many skeletons in trenches in association with shell beads and more. One thing seems clear: the sacrifice of young females was a periodic ritual practice at Cahokia. Such human sacrifice is rare to unheard-of in earlier times: one pit at the Middle Woodland site of Pinson in Tennessee seems a testament to a one-off sacrificial event. A few burials at the Coles Creek site of Lake George in Mississippi also confirm the intermittent sacrifice of women and children. Yet the practice at Cahokia was different in that it was sustained and repeated, a routine, ritual aspect of this experiment in Native American urbanism. Was human sacrifice at Cahokia an import from Mesoamerica, where the Post-Classic "Toltec horizon" had reached its climax in the eleventh century as well? Perhaps.

Some archaeologists have long speculated about Mesoamerican contacts. Certainly maize, a Mesoamerican crop adopted in the region 150 years earlier, probably came with ritual knowledge that would have

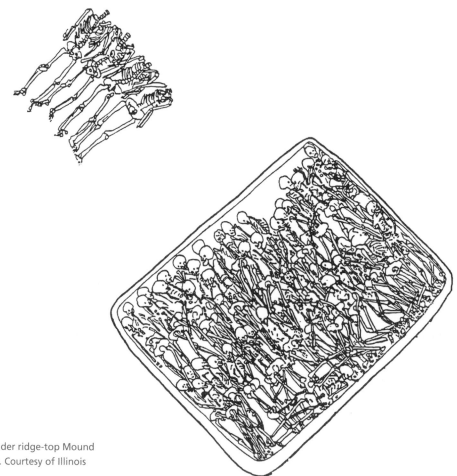

Fig 10.25 Map of 53 sacrificed human beings under ridge-top Mound 72, Cahokia (from Fowler et al. 1999: figure 6.6). Courtesy of Illinois State Museum.

Sidebar 10.5 Cahokians contact the world

We know that northern Mesoamerican artifacts – jadeite beads, a few bits of obsidian, and Huastecan pottery – have been found in the lower Rio Grande Valley of southern Texas, likely acquired by the hunter-gatherers of the "Brownsville complex" from southern sources (Hester 2004). And we know that Cahokians traveled, minimally from Wisconsin to Louisiana and beyond to the east and west. Perhaps a Cahokian traveler – a priest or would-be leader seeking knowledge of the exotic – returned from Mesoamerica with stories of strange gods and practices. And while we have found no traces yet of Mesoamerican chocolate, unlike in the Southwest (see Chapters 14 and 15), we have found evidence that they obtained the leaves of the yaupon holly plant from Arkansas, Mississippi, or Louisiana, with which they made a caffeine-rich ritual drink known historically as the "Black Drink" (Crown et al. 2012). Perhaps Cahokians or their contemporaries may also have returned home with a new strain of tobacco, the more potent *Nicotiana rustica*, widely known in Mesoamerica but found in the Mississippi Valley only after about 1100 CE (Wagner 2000). Since the Middle Woodland era, only the milder *Nicotiana quadrivalis* had been available in the Midwest.

referenced new corn spirits. Archaeologist Robert Hall and others long wondered if the "long-nosed god" earpieces and the chipped stone daggers that appeared without precedent at Cahokia after 1050 might indicate such a long-distance inspiration for the emergent Cahokian polity, sometimes called the "Ramey state" (Hall 2000; Kehoe 2005; O'Brien 1989). But there is no evidence of "trade" between Cahokia or any other Mississippian center and Mesoamerica – nor should we necessarily expect trade in common necessaries. Cahokia did not need economic goods from the south, and those exotic materials that they did acquire were not a result of trade. Cahokians traveled to acquire knowledge, spiritual power, and exotic materials and substances (such as tobacco or yaupon holly). They may have traveled to Mexico, but it did not result in trade – and no Mesoamerican artifacts are known north of south Texas from the Mississippi Valley, except for one blade-let of Mexican obsidian from the site of Spiro on the Arkansas River (Barker et al. 2002).

Mississippianization

The esoteric and spiritual powers of Cahokia were felt across the mid-continent and into the South in the decades after Cahokia's urban rebirth. Those powers were doubtless translated into political power every time a human being channeled them on earth. At least as early as 1050, some Cahokians traveled great distances, seemingly to worship the spirits of unusual or ancestral places. A mounded shrine 900 river-km (560 river-mi) north of the city at Trempealeau, Wisconsin appears to have been one such place. Dated to the years at or just before Cahokia's "big bang," this quasi-colony may have been maintained by one or more relocated Cahokian support communities who occupied the empty "no-man's land" at the edges of Effigy Mound territory (Pauketat et al. 2015). Other such colonies likely existed to the south as well, possibly indicated by Cahokian microlithic tool kits – used for the ritual production of shell beads – in present-day Arkansas and Mississippi. By 1150, Cahokians likely occupied some portion of the Plaquemine period Lake Providence site, in Louisiana (Wells and Weinstein 2007).

The Angel site, on the Ohio River in southwest Indiana, may have begun as just such a place. Founded sometime after 1050 CE, the site originally consisted of two or three platform mounds surrounded by a palisade wall, all of which were aligned to the same moonrise or moonset once every 18.6 years (Figure 10.26). Possibly this lunar knowledge came from Cahokia. Susan Alt notes that the distinctive "Yankeetown culture" pottery of Late Woodland farmers who lived in the vicinity of the future Angel site is relatively common around Cahokia, suggesting that they were visitors or immigrants from southwestern Indiana (Alt 2002). Possibly some of them, now newly Cahokianized, set up the new center of Angel. Later, the Angel outpost grew into a town of hundreds or more, known for its fine "negative-painted" plates and

Fig 10.26 Angel site Mound F, lower stage showing large temple (from Black 1967: figure 261). Courtesy of the Glenn A. Black Laboratory of Archaeology and the Trustees of Indiana University.

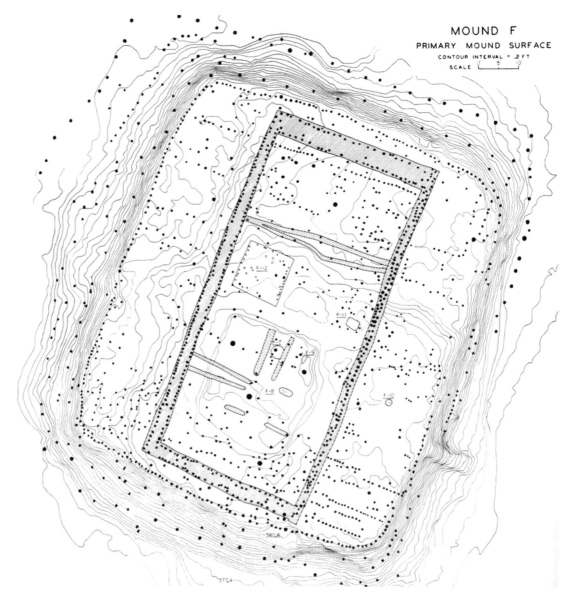

MOUND F
PRIMARY MOUND SURFACE
CONTOUR INTERVAL = .2 FT
SCALE

serving wares (Hilgeman 2000). The palisade wall there and at Angel, complete with bastions spaced to enable archers to fire arrows down upon would-be attackers, strongly suggests that these Mississippians feared attack or reprisal. But by whom?

Farther up the Ohio River, in the modern-day states of Kentucky, West Virginia, and Ohio, lived Late Woodland people who, after 1000 CE, are called the Fort Ancient culture (www.fortancient.org). They did not build large platform mounds or align their settlements on a rectangular grid (see also Chapter 12). Most did not build wall trench houses, though discoveries by archaeologist Robert Cook show that, at some sites, they did. Some of them, in fact, may have been relocated Mississippians from the lower portions of the Ohio Valley. Other Fort Ancient people may have resented the Mississippians at places such as Angel.

The Mississippian Southeast (1200–1600 CE)

At the same time, downriver was the even larger Mississippian town of Kincaid, with two or more plazas and a sturdy palisade wall enclosing more than 25 ha (62 acres). Founded in the twelfth century, Kincaid's earthen pyramids were surmounted by great circular and rectangular buildings. Its pyramids and houses were aligned to both an adjacent bayou and the moon. Excavations there since the 1930s have produced surprising numbers of artifacts made to look like owls or owlmen (Cole et al. 1951). Possibly the identity of the people of Kincaid was tethered to the owl, water, the night, and the moon. Whoever they were, we may presume that their identity, if not their claim to the Ohio, was also contested, as indicated by the palisade wall.

A series of substantial Mississippian towns, each with its own outlying farming hinterland or political territory, stretched up the Tennessee and Cumberland rivers through modern-day Kentucky and into the state of Tennessee. In the central portion of Tennessee geologically known as the Nashville Basin are several prominent "Middle Mississippian" towns, each presumably the political-administrative and religious center of a polity, which is to say a regional-scale territory governed from a capital center. Among the largest of these was Mound Bottom, which covered an area of some 40 ha (www.harpethriver.org/watershed-info/about/mound-bottom). Farther upriver was another great town, this one located on an island in the Tennessee River. Called Hiwassee Island, the complex featured an unusual dual-pyramid (Lewis and Kneberg 1946). Atop both sides of this structure and on the summits of other such great tumuli would have stood one or more town temples, a place where the bones of key ancestors or founders would have been kept for consultation by priests if not the leaders themselves (Figure 10.27). Also in it or an adjacent medicine lodge would have been held other bundles of religious materials, bones, and sacred things wrapped in fabric or animal hides that acted as a sacred barrier between the contents and the outside world.

Described by later French and Euro-American travelers, bundles in Mississippian temple complexes were held on altars or wracks and probably treated much like those better known among Plains peoples. That is, these were the all-important material texts on which all ceremonies were based. They were also oracles. No councilor, priest, or lord might make a significant decision for the entire community without consulting the appropriate bundle in some way. Indeed, Prairie-Plains people treated them as persons or gods to whom prayers might be offered, food given, and on whom attention might

Fig 10.27 Excavated building remains atop the twin pyramid at the Hiwassee Island site (Lewis and Kneberg 1946). Courtesy of the University of Tennessee Press.

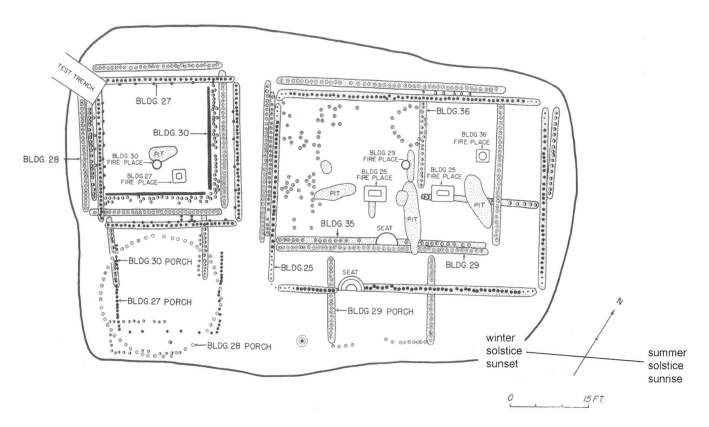

be showered. Based on the burials of sacred things found by archaeologists in mounds, it appears that such things as smoking pipes, chunkey stones, other heirlooms, certain ceremonial hats or items of dress, shell beads and bead-making kits, some arrows, and various other pieces of ritual regalia or materials were all bundled. Individually, such things probably were imbued with sacred life-giving power or occupied by spirits. As a package, the bundles were themselves beings able to influence the history and well-being of an entire people. James Murie, himself of Pawnee descent, was one of many anthropologists who described bundles as including the most fundamental animate powers: pieces of meteorites (stars), parts of animals, human remains, rocks, and more, all wrapped in a hide or textile that was the skin of what they considered to be a living bundle being (Murie 1981).

Far too little is known of the histories of these great sites or their inhabitants, though nearby were cemeteries of the dead where corpses were buried in the flesh ("inhumations"). In the upper reaches of the Tennessee, bodies were placed in individual graves, sometimes in the floors of houses (Sullivan and Rodning 2001). Around Nashville, the dead were often placed in "stone box" graves lined with slabs of limestone or sandstone, a practice that extended up into the American Bottom region during late Mississippian times (was there a historical connection?). Studies of the remains of these and nearby Middle Mississippian peoples reveal high rates of child mortality, and average lifespans, if you made it into your early twenties, of only another 20 years or so (Powell 1988). Few people lived beyond the age of 40 and, at that age, many women had lost one or more children and many men and some women had suffered broken limbs, dental caries, or systemic infections. Not an insignificant number, mostly men, also had died of arrow wounds or trauma suffered in hand-to-hand combat. Small infections mattered: an infected wound might fester and lead to death. So could an abscessed tooth if left untreated. Healers, the physicians and nurses of their day, were all-important to the community.

Was Middle Mississippian life in native North America as grim as all that? Perhaps not. More important may be how differently people of the Mississippian world related to each other and to the wider world and the forces therein. For instance, children were not sheltered from the realities of domestic or political life. You help your family grow crops or capture game and you learn the basics of life, death, fertility, and anatomy. You live in a one-room house with your parents

Sidebar 10.6 Middle Mississippians and chiefdoms

Sometimes used by archaeologists to refer to a time period, the designation "Middle" is also understood to refer to a type of Mississippian culture common to the "Middle" of the Mississippi Valley, from Cahokia south to Memphis and up the Tennessee and Cumberland rivers (Griffin 1967). Up through the 1970s, archaeologists identified Middle Mississippians based on their cultural-material attributes, especially shell-tempered pottery, earthen substructure mounds, and wall-trench architecture. By the 1970s, many archaeologists believed that such Middle Mississippian polities were best thought of in societal terms as "chiefdoms," centralized territories ruled by hereditary leaders or chiefs. While such societal classifications had the advantage of avoiding the trap of assuming that cultural materials (such as how one made a pot) correlated perfectly with political allegiances, community identities, and even ethnicities, they homogenized both the forms of governance and the social histories of the nominally Mississippian peoples (Pauketat 2007). After all, maybe some Mississippians were ruled not by hereditary chiefs but by councils of governors or priests. Perhaps some were more or less communal versus hierarchical. Some late Mississippian leaders may have been petty tyrants or warlords. Others, as at Cahokia, may have been great priestly administrators. Rather than assume society-wide institutions or evolutionary trajectories of entire societies, archaeologists need to document and explain cultural and social histories of peoples – dominant and subordinate, male and female, local and foreign – and their wider relationships to other peoples, places, materials, and powers through time.

and you might, for instance, routinely witness the sexual activity of your mother and father. In addition, compared with today, there may have been considerably more gender equity, with women holding significant political power within the community, especially when it came to the disposition of property (Sullivan and Rodning 2001).

Archaeologist Lynne Sullivan, who has devoted a significant portion of her career to the study of gender in the past, is fairly certain that most Mississippians were largely matrilineal (Figure 10.28). Inheritance and participation in community affairs, she and others argue, were probably based on the identity of your mother and maternal relatives. Men might have political power, but only through their mothers, grandmothers, or aunts. Likewise, the Mississippians – along with other Plains and Eastern Woodland peoples – almost certainly recognized multiple genders and transgendered individuals as integral to the community's social fabric. Difference and diversity, we presume, was valued. Other genders and transgendered people were special and powerful, blessed by cosmic forces. No archaeological or historic evidence exists to suggest that LGBTQ experience was anything but empowering. Shamans or priests, for instance, might be able to shape-shift between genders and between human and nonhuman beings (Emerson 2003). They might be able to move between dimensions of the seen and unseen worlds.

Fig 10.28 Archaeologist Lynne Sullivan, left, at the Hiwassee Island site, Tennessee. Courtesy of Tennessee Valley Authority and Lynne Sullivan.

Indeed, certain Mississippian capital towns may have been built to facilitate such movement. At Moundville, in central Alabama, a two-mound complex was established around 1120 CE, followed by a great expansion near the end of that century, when multiple "mounds were built around the perimeter of a large central plaza, a log palisade with tower bastions was erected, and new residential areas" were laid out (Blitz 2012:539). The site became home to perhaps 1,000–2,000 people, yes, but it was also the likely location where the priests might commune with a mythical winged serpent of the underworld (Figure 10.29). That being empowered one or more feminine goddesses who, in turn, lived in the land of darkness and the dead. Since Moundville's symbolism is dominated by the winged serpent and related imagery, this great Mississippian complex appears to have been the place where "the deceased" left "to embark on the 'Path of Souls'" (Knight and Steponaitis 2011:237).

Indeed, in later years, families would bring their departed kin here to inter their bodies in the grounds where family houses used to stand. The power of the place was such that an immense wooden palisade wall, similar to Cahokia's, was constructed to protect the sacred temples, ancestral bones, and religious articles from attack by those who disagreed with Moundville's claim as an *axis mundi*, or convergence of heaven and earth in this part of central Alabama. And while the

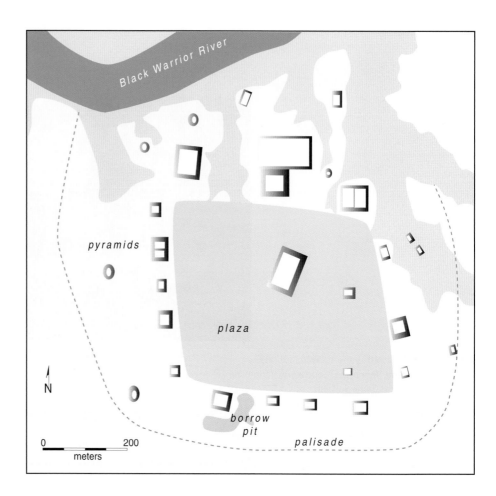

Fig 10.29 Moundville site plan.
Timothy R. Pauketat image, 2007.

great site was depopulated by the 1500s, some believe that descendants of its people include those proto-Choctaws or other Muskogean-speakers who battled Hernando de Soto's army in 1542 at Mabila, led by the hereditary lord Tuscaloosa (see Figure 3.7).

So too had the people formerly attached to the great site of Etowah in northern Georgia struggled with the Spaniards. Etowah was at the center of another proto-Muskogee province that may have begun in the early 1100s when Mississippian people, perhaps from the Tennessee-Cumberland regions, moved southward into the Etowah River basin (King 2003). Certainly, such population intrusions, ranging from a few prominent individuals to whole communities, seem evident in the Ocmulgee and Chattahoochee river drainages to the south of Etowah (Hally 1994). Unlike Moundville's inhabitants, Etowah's and Ocmulgee's elites drew inspiration from the story of a falcon-man hero, one of the twins, as seen in the elaborate burials of presumed leaders in Mound C at Etowah and in a great modeled clay sculpture on the floor of an "earthlodge" at Ocmulgee (Figure 10.30).

(a)

(b)

Fig 10.30 Ocmulgee earthlodge: (a) reconstructed exterior; (b) modeled falcon-shaped platform on the floor of the earthlodge. Wikimedia.

The political culture of Etowah had especially profound effects, copied at places as far away as Lake Jackson, Florida, 400 km (250 mi) to the south (King 2003:123). Similarly, Moundville's pottery and symbolism seem to have been copied by people at similar distances down to Mobile Bay, presumably acts that reveal their multifaceted cultural, political, economic, and military influence. Doubtless, Moundville could have projected a sizable fighting force, hundreds of warriors in organized units, at least that far (Figure 10.31).

The Mississippian era could be violent, and some believe that warfare of a sort is a defining feature of it (Dye 2009). Then again, archaeological evidence of site location, fortifications, and trauma from northern Georgia and Alabama indicate that the preceding Terminal Late Woodland era had been more violent, with the early Mississippian era ushering in a time of "peace" (Cobb and Garrow

Fig 10.31 Chief Outina and a Timucuan military unit, aided by Spaniards, confront an Indian enemy. Engraving by Theodore de Bry, based on painting by Jacques Le Moyne. Wikimedia.

1996; Little 1999). Keep in mind, of course, that geopolitical peace does not necessarily mean an absence of violence – it just means that violence is managed by politicians who may yet project their own sanctioned use of military force. This is what we seem to see, in other words, with the public energy diverted into the building of impressive bastioned palisade walls. Mississippians who moved into areas occupied by locals could establish great fortified settlements in ways that allowed them to dominate the region and organize violence (presumably directing organized violence outwardly). Such big fortified sites probably would have been understood by those less-organized locals as offensive threats (not "defensive" structures)!

In any event, two social-historical outcomes of these aggressive Mississippianizing developments are readily apparent to us today. First, Mississippian iconography and weaponry celebrated warriors, elevating the practice as a means of gaining prestige in this life if not advantage in the next. Second, boundaries or no man's lands formed rapidly around the territories claimed by the leading families of each Mississippian capital. Within those territories, the inhabitants of lesser towns, villages, or isolated farmsteads probably owed some portion of their farm produce to the capital town. The effect, over the long term, was to create social classes consisting of an upper tier of powerful patron kin groups from whom leaders would be selected to lead a lower stratum of common farmers.

In this way, through the centuries, at least from 1200 to the arrival of the Spanish conquistadors, many tens of thousands of people farmed for themselves and for Mississippian surplus-taking elites. They fished using hooks and line, nets, or elaborate fish weirs, and they hunted small game and deer, always first consulting their spirit guides via their personal religious bundles and probably turning over a share to local high-status leaders. They were spread across many dozens of political territories from the Coastal Plain of the Carolinas into the Midsouth of Tennessee and Kentucky and westward into Arkansas until one arrived in Caddo country. Conservative estimates of the overall population of the Mississippian world – which is to say the American Southeast and portions of the Midwest – in 1492 begin at about half a million. More generous estimates suggest several million people. Clearly many millions of Mississippians had lived and died in eastern North America over the course of the three centuries before the arrival of Columbus in the Caribbean (see Chapter 3).

The Legacy of the Mississippians

Whoever they were, warring in the central Mississippi Valley worsened after Cahokia was downsized from a city into a town and, finally, a ghost town by 1350 CE. In the Illinois River valley 150–300 km north of Cahokia, former Cahokian allies or expatriates may have become some of Cahokia's enemies. Certainly they fought amongst themselves. Whole fortified villages show evidence of either ritual incineration – burning because of the death of a prominent local citizen or some other planned closure – or enemy attack.

Farmers were seldom themselves the target of warriors nor were they warriors themselves, the practice of warring being an elite prerogative that aimed to undercut the powers resident in some town – especially by despoiling the ancestral temples of that place. There are exceptions, one being the Common Field site in southeast Missouri around the year 1300 CE. The attackers, thinks archaeologist Meghan Buchanan (2015), may have been Cahokians desperately seeking to remain in control of the central Mississippi Valley. The same phenomenon may explain entire burned towns south of Common Field in Missouri into Arkansas (Figure 10.32). In the later 1300s, northern Oneota people (also formerly called "Upper Mississippians" because they used shell-tempered pottery) had moved in alongside the Illinois Valley Mississippians. Local alliances and family relations were transformed, and small-scale disagreements turned into grim no-holds-barred wars between villages or small regions that lasted years.

Fig 10.32 Burned Powers-phase villages: Turner and Snodgrass sites. Timothy R. Pauketat map, 2007.

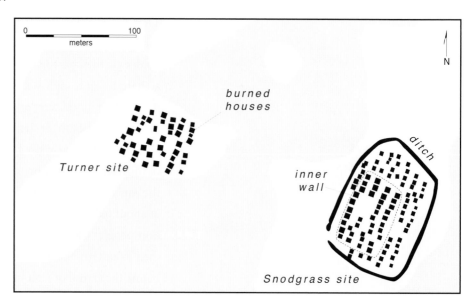

Cemeteries from the period contain buried men and women, up to 40 percent, who met violent deaths. They were scalped, bludgeoned, or arrowshot (Milner et al. 2013). The intent in that late Mississippian case seems to have been to kill people (rather than damage a temple or wreak other infrastructural damage). And as a result, the entire Illinois Valley region south through the former greater Cahokia region, and continuing, after about 1350, down to present-day Memphis and east into southern Indiana, was depopulated. Stephen Williams called this the "Vacant Quarter," and it marks the beginning of the end of the Mississippian civilization (Cobb and Butler 2002; Williams 1990).

Some people took refuge in the interior of Illinois; one population in Indiana stayed the course; others moved west on to the Plains or southeast into the Deep South, perhaps to form a new confederacy of Mississippians that Hernando de Soto described as the Coosa nation. Still others may have regrouped to lay the foundations of the historically known Choctaw, Muskogee, and Chickasaw Nations. But the ceremonial grandeur and monumentality of the previous Middle Mississippian peoples did not survive 1350, and another climatic shift less conducive to agricultural surpluses – the Little Ice Age – began that century: more droughts, more cold snaps, less tribute for elites.

With the opening of the Vacant Quarter to the north and a movement of peoples from those regions southward, the social fabric of the lower Mississippi Valley was probably stressed. If Cahokia had been a convergence of religious pilgrims and immigrants, then each late Mississippian lower valley town was probably its own little melting pot, exacerbated by captives who might be married into or "adopted" by locals, a late Mississippian version of the ages-old Woodland tribal practice. That composite character of the late Mississippians was only exacerbated when diseases from, first, the Spanish and then the French eliminated thousands in pockets across the Coastal Plain. The first Spanish explorers who entered the Deep South met the Mississippians. They were organized into a series of nations, confederacies, or provinces, and, often, ruled by hereditary leaders. Europeans called the rulers lords, queens, kings, caciques, chiefs, etc. depending on their own experiences back in Europe.

11 Two Worlds on the Great Plains

Indians lived in two worlds at the same time. There was the practical world where they hunted, traveled, loved, fought and died. And there was the equally real world of the spirits. Trees, animals, springs, caves, streams and mountains might each contain a life force, spirit or soul and must be treated with caution and respect … Especially revered were the locations where their creators, or spirit beings, had formed the cosmos: the planets, the earth's topography and plants and fellow creatures.

(Nabokov 2006:xi)

Skirting the Caddo regions northeastward into the Great Plains of present-day Kansas, Coronado failed to see what was right before his eyes. His Caddo-language-speaking guide, the captive Pawnee man nicknamed "The Turk," was not, strictly speaking, lying. Many Pawnee recognized a creator god and goddess connected with the sun and moon, named Tirawa and Atira. And earlier in time, ancestors of at least one tribal segment of the Pawnee may have lived in the vicinity of Kansas City, comprising what archaeologists call the Steed-Kisker culture (900–1400 CE). Their pottery was decorated with Cahokia-inspired symbolism. They, or a contingent of them – perhaps a clan, priesthood, or series of diplomats – may have resided alongside Siouan- and Algonkian-speaking peoples at that ancient city for a time (O'Brien 1993). The city, after all, was then just a canoe trip down the Missouri River.

Cahokia had by Coronado's time disappeared from the geopolitical landscape of the Mississippi Valley and the eastern Plains. The Cahokian things buried around 1400 in the Great Mortuary at Spiro, Oklahoma, just beyond the southern edge of the Plains, may have been a ceremonial closure of the earlier Mississippian world that had ended (see Chapter 10). Afterwards, at Spiro, shell engravings depict scenes that are reminiscent of Mesoamerican inspirations: Quetzalcoatl-like snake-men emerging out of a crack in the earth or a sacrificial victim of the dreaded arrow sacrifice. The latter is known both from Mesoamerican codices and from the historic Skidi branch of the Pawnee people (Hall 1997). Other possible icons and practices that may have originated from the American Southwest and Mesoamerica are known from Plains and Caddo territories after the 1300s as well (Lankford 2004). But no Mesoamerican trading network had yet extended into the Caddo area, at least not until the Spaniards brought portions of this area into their orbit in the 1600s. The impacts on native people were, of course, dramatic.

Dramatic events characterize the past as well, all the way back to the peopling of the continent and the travels of Plano and Plains Archaic hunter-gatherers (see Chapter 5). In this chapter, we pick up that history in the Middle Pre-Contact (a.k.a. Middle Prehistoric) era, beginning about 500 BCE on the Plains (Table 11.1). At that time, we can see the roots of the intensification of bison hunting in the northern Plains, which ultimately led to a kind of complex hunter-gatherer society and big historical change from Alberta south into the Dakotas. A few hundred years later, we can also see the influence of the Woodland-era Midwest exerted out into the Plains, probably via indigenous travelers from the east moving up the Missouri River to Yellowstone to obtain obsidian, Knife River flint, grizzly bear teeth, and wild sheep horns. These things from Wyoming and the Dakotas were seemingly critical to ritual life in Ohio and Illinois (see Chapter 10). In the end, the Hopewell connections into the Plains were but a harbinger of the even more complicated transcontinental historical relations and migration waves to follow during the Plains Village era. Of course, those relations came to a close soon after the passage of the Lewis and Clark expedition up the Missouri.

Journey up the Missouri

On May 14, 1804, Meriwether Lewis, William Clark, and their men departed their winter camp at the north end of the American Bottom, near St. Louis, to travel up the Missouri River in a keelboat en route to the Pacific Ocean. Along with 38 other men, they were about to enter the Great Plains, that immense and largely unbroken subtropical to semi-arid grassland that stretches from southeastern Alberta and south-central Saskatchewan to central Texas. With northern portions leveled by Pleistocene glaciers, the Plains consists of flat to rolling hills

Table 11.1 Chronological highlights of the Plains Woodland and Village periods (adapted from Henning 2005; Johnson and Johnson 1998; Mitchell 2012).

Year BCE/CE	Historic periods	Cultural patterns
500 BCE	Middle Pre-Contact	Besant points, bison kill sites with ritual features
CE		
100–500	Middle Pre-Contact	Bow and arrow at 200 CE
	Plains Woodland	Hopewell-inspired developments; earliest horticulture in Kansas City region
500–1000	Late Prehistoric/ Late Plains Woodland	Specialized bison drive systems in northern Plains
		Continued mound burials south; geometric mounds north; bow and arrow everywhere; horticulture in south and central Plains
1000–1250	Old Women's Phase	Labor organized around drive systems and jump sites
	Plains Village (early)	Migrations of Late Woodland peoples westward; horticultural intensification; Cahokian influence; appearance of dense villages of the Great Oasis culture and later Initial Middle Missouri tradition and Central Plains tradition sites
1250–1450	Plains Village (late)	Cahokian influence ends; initial Coalescent period; increased violence; Crow Creek massacre; drought allows grasslands and bison to extend range eastward
1450–1600	Plains Village (Proto-Historic)	Extended Coalescent period; nucleation of villages; spread of Oneota culture westward; initial waves of European pandemics
1700s	Historic	French exploration and fur trade into the Plains
1803	–	Louisiana Purchase
1804–1806	–	Lewis and Clark expedition

punctuated by eroded badlands and rocky escarpments, such as the Black Hills of South Dakota and the Alibates Hills in Texas. Thought a vast desert by European-American citizens of the United States in 1803, native people knew another world. The Plains was a landscape distinguished by great herds of bison, along with elk, antelope, bear, and many smaller mammals. Great flocks of migratory birds, including cranes, swans, geese, and ducks, passed through the Plains' Central Flyway – second in avian numbers only to the Mississippi Flyway – as they winged their way each year from Canada south to Mexico and beyond. Winters could be extreme, but so could summers with their high temperatures, grass fires, and mid-latitude cyclones complete with tornadoes.

Plains Indians stood at the center of this world (Figure 11.1). When purchased by the United States from France, the High Plains of the west – from Montana and eastern Colorado south into west Texas – were inhabited by horse-mounted foragers. They were known to others as the Blackfeet, Assiniboines, and Cheyennes in the north, and Apaches, Arapahos, Kiowas, Comanches, and more Cheyennes in the south – all of whom might trade with or raid both the Pueblos to the southwest and "Plains Villages" to the east. The latter people occupied the major waterways that flowed into the Mississippi River, namely the Missouri, Arkansas, and Red rivers that divide the Great Plains into northern, central, and southern divisions (see below).

Thomas Jefferson had urged the US Congress to commission the Lewis and Clark expedition in order to explore this territory, which was part of the newly acquired Louisiana Purchase. They were to continue all the way to the Pacific Ocean, passing into territory claimed by the United States, Spain, and Great Britain. Along the way, their expedition, dubbed the "Corps of Discovery," was to document the native peoples, biota, landforms, and archaeological sites encountered. Before ever leaving on the journey, William Clark had already almost died that winter doing as Jefferson had requested. He fell through lake ice while investigating an ancient Cahokian town (today called the Mitchell site) just 12 km (7 mi) north of the ancient city itself. Of course, he did not know it was a former Cahokian settlement, and even Cahokia had yet to be officially rediscovered by the new citizens of the expanding United States, though a French monastery chapel had been built atop the great pyramid in the late 1700s and the entire site sat just 6 km east of St. Louis, where the men gathered supplies

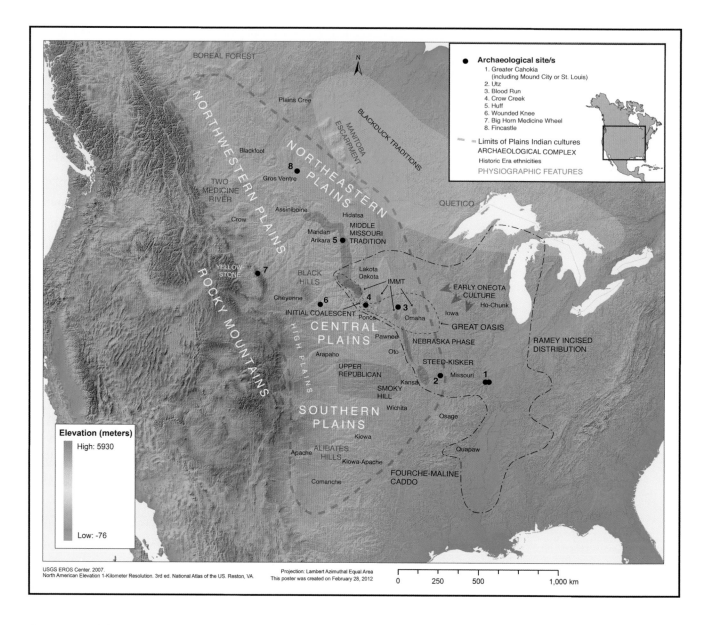

Fig 11.1 Map of Plains Indian identities, complexes, and sites.

and spent their time off during that long winter. Cahokia's tall central pyramid would have been visible from St. Louis, though shrouded by trees and brush.

William Clark had also described the mounds of St. Louis, also known by its nickname "Mound City." Unknown at the time, the 26 earthen pyramids there had been one of greater Cahokia's major precincts, an ancient gateway to the Great Plains just like its modern-day counterpart at the mouth of the Missouri River. Plains Village pottery has been found in recent years by archaeological excavations around Cahokia (see also O'Brien 1969). It was this precinct over which, in

1810, the young frontier lawyer Henry Marie Brackenridge had hiked, having recently decided to leave Ste. Genevieve, Missouri. In so doing, he was impressed by the giant earthen monuments and continued walking several miles from the East St. Louis precinct and its 45 pyramids into the ruins of the central Cahokia precinct, with its 120-plus pyramid-shaped tumuli. Following a row of mounds that connected the precincts, he ended up at the foot of Monks Mound, amazed at its enormity (Brackenridge 1962). The group of French Trappist monks who had founded the monastery there the previous year gave the wayfaring lawyer an icy reception.

Writing to Jefferson about his supposed discovery, Brackenridge would accompany the Manuel Lisa fur-trading expedition into the Plains just seven years after Lewis and Clark. As part of the Lisa expedition, he proceeded up to the Mandan villages in present-day North Dakota, as had Lewis and Clark before him. Both sets of explorers wrote extensively about the lands and peoples that they encountered: first the territories of Siouan-speaking Osage, Kansa, and Iowa peoples and into Pawnee territory in Nebraska. Continuing north, Lewis and Clark barely managed to avoid an encounter with a Spanish military force sent out from Santa Fe to intercept them, the Spanish having received word from an American spy that the Corps of Discovery would be traveling into the disputed Northwest to the Pacific Ocean. Recall that, almost a century earlier, Mexico City had sent the Villasur expedition out from Santa Fe to kill or capture a French, Pawnee, and Oto force (see Chapter 3). Three more Spanish forces were later sent to intercept Lewis and Clark, but all failed, often owing to their encounters with the Pawnee.

North of Pawnee territory in 1804, Lewis and Clark met with representatives of the Missouri, Oto, Omaha, and Iowa. The Corps of Discovery gave them "peace medals," among other things, before encountering the Dakota and Lakota (Teton, Yankton, Yanktonai, and Oglala Sioux) and then entering the lands of the Arikara and Mandan. Here they spent their first winter, building a fort across from a large, snowed-in village of Mandans, who helped them survive the extreme cold of that season (Coues 1979[1893]). The following spring they passed the Yellowstone River and, on their return trip in 1806, a member of the Corps would discover what was called "Coulter's Hell" – the geysers and boiling sulphuric springs later enshrined as Yellowstone National Park. Just as the Yellowstone River was followed westward by Lewis and Clark, so too was the Yellowstone region a cross-roads for pre-contact Americans moving between the Plains and the Rocky Mountains to the west.

Bison Hunter Complexity on the Northern Plains (500 BCE to Today)

Beginning around 500 BCE, in the so-called late Middle Pre-Contact or Prehistoric period, notable change in the relationships of people to bison and to the landscape is recognizable in this cross-roads area, and adjacent regions. Here, communal autumn bison hunts would be organized to obtain stores of meat for winter. This may have long been an annual affair, though the timing and frequency of bison kills must have been affected by yearly and longer-term fluctuations in the availability of forage, namely grass, which depends on sufficient moisture and sunlight to thrive (see Chapters 5 and 6). Eventually, however, the relationships included the construction of a complex monumental infrastructure on the northern Plains and, with it, growth in human and bison populations. The development of that infrastructure – elaborate constructions of piled stone cairns in rows along with stone effigies, tipi rings, and special ritual sites known as Medicine Wheels – can best be understood by traveling back in time 2,500 years, when the climate was a little warmer and drier than today, and stopping off at a single kill site in southern Alberta.

Sitting on an unassumingly flat, old glacial lake bottom covered with sand dunes was the site of a one-off bison kill that archaeologists would later dub Fincastle. There, just before 500 BCE, "a group of sufficient size made a substantial kill by ambushing a herd of bison watering in a marshy, interdune area in southern Alberta in the late summer or early fall" (Bubel 2014:237). The hunters butchered the animals, leaving behind primary concentrations of articulated feet, legs, vertebral columns, and rib cages. Off to the side, they continued the butchering process, smashing and splintering the long bones and other remains with hammers in order to extract the bone marrow and grease, producing secondary concentrations of fragmented bison bone. Then, they did something that continues to baffle archaeologists. The bison hunters took select long bones and mandibles and drove their ends deep into the sand and clay beneath their feet to produce a series of "bone uprights" (Bubel 2014). Eight such uprights were known, none with any identifiable practical purpose. Indeed, they were arranged for effect, with sets of three or so bison mandibles stuck in the ground such that the teeth still in the jaws "fanned outward" (Bubel 2014:221). The hunters then moved on, leaving the site to the carnivores and the flies. Not long thereafter, it was covered over by dunes and forgotten.

The projectile points and bifacial cutting tools that the Fincastle hunters had used were primarily of a type called the Besant side-notched point, with some showing careful resharpening and reuse before being left behind at the site (Figure 11.2). At a ratio of almost 6:1, the dart points were made from the high-quality Knife River flint from North and South Dakota, some 800 km to the southeast. Indeed, the hunters may have had cultural affiliations in that direction, though Besant points are found alongside other styles possibly indicative of multiple ethnic groups across the northern Plains. To be sure, Besant people were bison hunters, although some may have moved into the Rocky Mountains and into the Great Basin, as noted earlier (see also Greaves 2012). To the south, in North and South Dakota, Besant dart points are found at sites with distinctive cordmarked, conoidal pottery cooking jars, bone uprights, and even small burial mounds, part of what archaeologists there identify as the Sonota complex. To the north in Alberta and Saskatchewan, pottery is rare.

Bison was never the sole animal hunted on the northern Plains, but it was relied upon increasingly through time. To some extent, the reliance was facilitated by the bow and arrow, which swept through Alberta, Saskatchewan, Montana, the Dakotas, and points southward around 200 CE. By 600 CE, a clear bison hunting preference, more elaborate "game-driving systems," and new (Avonlea) projectile point styles and tool types indicate the beginning of the Late Prehistoric period. Whereas Middle Prehistoric bison "kills most commonly involved luring a few animals into pounds or traps rather than cliff jumps … the classic jump with its extensive cairn-lined driving systems predominated in the Late Prehistoric period" (Zedeño et al. 2014:24). Also during the Late Prehistoric period, labor pools grew, and pemmican and storable dry meat allowed Plains communities to more fully realize the benefits of larger kills.

Specialized intensive bison hunting reached a climax during the Old Women's phase, dating from 900 to 1750 CE, which began with the Medieval Climatic Anomaly (Zedeño et al. 2014). At that time,

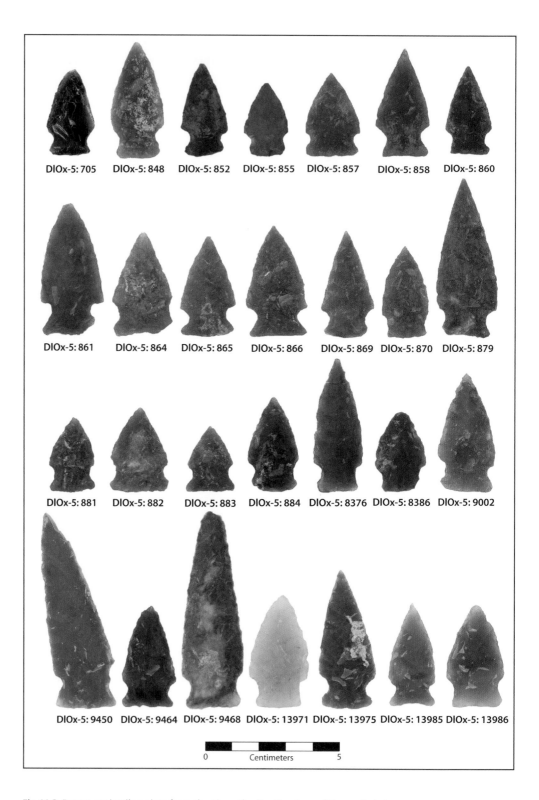

Fig 11.2 Besant projectile points from the Fincastle site. Courtesy of Shawn Bubel.

amalgamations of local and nonlocal people comprised the groups who built and used complicated "driveline" and jump systems. These were carefully designed piles of rock set in rows with respect to landscape topography to facilitate movement of bison herds toward their death over the edge of a steep drop-off. In the Two Medicine River landscape of Montana, there are multiple locales featuring multiple drivelines (i.e., rock cairns in set rows) that channeled herds to jump sites (Figure 11.3). Nearby were stone rings, the foundations for tipis, rock art and vision quest sites, and even Medicine Wheels (Zedeño et al. 2014) that comprised parts of an even more elaborate "kill site complex" that included grazing areas, drive lanes, cliffs, bone beds, camps, and processing areas (Oetelaar 2014).

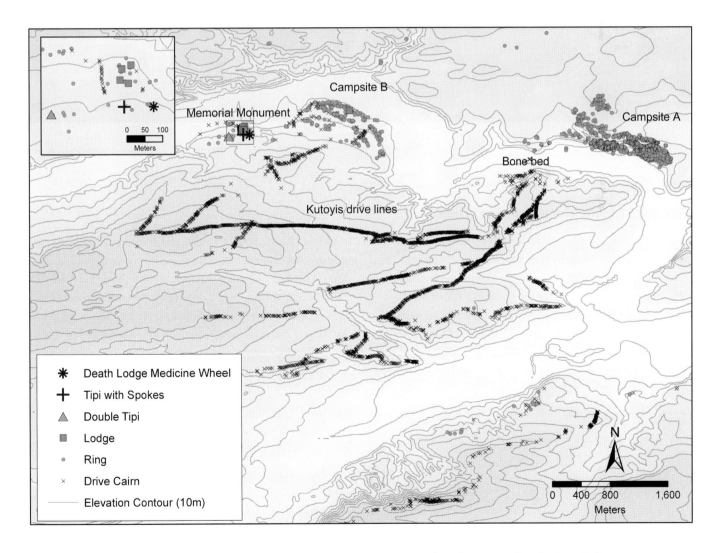

Fig 11.3 Sites and features of a northern Plains drive system landscape (from Feathers et al.2015). Courtesy of Maria Nieves Zedeño.

Fig 11.4 Big Horn Medicine Wheel, Wyoming. I. Merriot photo/Wikimedia.

Sidebar 11.1 Big Horn Medicine Wheel

Find "Medicine Wheel, Big Horn, WY" on Google Earth. Advance the date to the Winter Solstice, or December 21, and move in close to the image at an oblique angle. Rotate the image so that you can see the sunrise or sunset on the southeastern and southwestern horizon. By looking across the middle of the wheel and moving the time forward and backward, you can see that both the rising and setting of the sun on the day of the solstice are marked by special perimeter rock piles. Moreover, the sunrise position also aligns with the narrow cliff edge that, in turn, points to the peak of Medicine Mountain in the distance. Archaeologist Robert Hall, born into the Stockbridge Mohican tribe of Wisconsin, concluded that such "astronomical alignments served also to magically gather and direct powers from nature for the benefit of the people" and enable "communication between cosmic levels, including those of the sky and the Underworld" (Hall 1985).

The most famous vision quest site is the "Big Horn Medicine Wheel" in Wyoming, well known for its astronomical alignments and dramatic landscape position (Figure 11.4). Such Medicine Wheels (or World Center Shrines) were often arrangements of boulders in remote locations to which people might make pilgrimages and where they might leave offerings to the spirits. The Big Horn Medicine Wheel was aligned to key sun and star rises or sets (Eddy 1974; Williamson 1984).

The period that witnessed this complex bit of landscape engineering was probably related in some way to social and agricultural developments in the Middle Missouri River region (see below). Northern people, that is, engaged the southerners both peacefully and through raids, folding captives from those raids into their local northern kin-based organizations (Zedeño et al. 2014:27). The result was an amalgamation of kin and nonkin and, by the colonial era, elaborate physical and social cultural landscapes tethered to monumental stone surface architecture. Another way of saying this is to note that the northern people were very much active agents in the management of a social and physical landscape tethered to engineered features that directly intervened in herd movements.

With regard to this human intervention in the herd, Gerald Oetelaar (2014) has illustrated how people, namely the ancestors of the Blackfeet or Pikaani people, were guided by a different ontological relationship with the spirit world and the land. Kill sites were part of an "alliance" with spiritual beings that defined Pikaani life and identity. The people were, as noted in the epigram at the outset of this chapter, of two worlds. The homeland of the Blackfeet today consists of a vast stretch of the Plains up against the Rocky Mountains of southern Alberta, southwestern Saskatchewan, and northern Montana (Figure 11.5). Blackfoot movements across this landscape always had an economic dimension for sure (all human experience always does). However, that dimension was and is just an aspect of Blackfoot identity and life journey, which first and foremost involves a way of living simultaneously in this world and in a spiritual world. Historically, an annual

journey and ritual pilgrimage involved travel along well-established trails extending from the wintering grounds in the Foothills [of the peripheral mountains] to the sun dance ground on the open prairie. The named places visited along the way served as navigational aids and repositories of traditional knowledge. These landmarks were created in the long ago by ancestral beings who left behind songs, sacred objects (Napi figures), and practices to commemorate their creative acts on earth.

(Oetelaar 2012:344)

Spirits and ancestors resided in mountain peaks or other landforms. Moving through the landscape, seeing them or visiting them, was to commune with those spirits and ancestors. So was hunting a spiritual engagement in addition to an economic pursuit. The spirit guides of

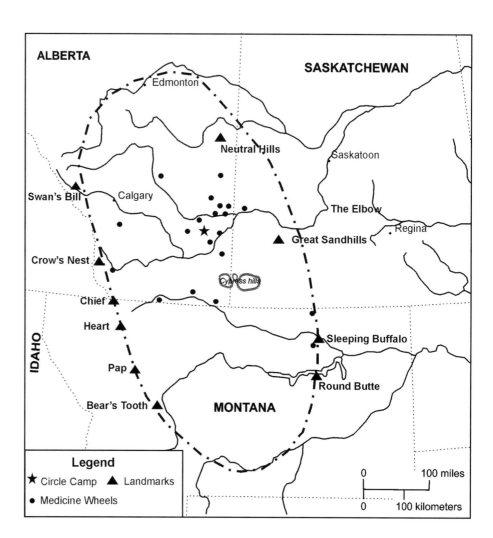

Fig 11.5 The northern Plains cultural landscape of the Blackfeet. Courtesy of Gerald A. Oetelaar.

Blackfeet hunters would be consulted through the sacred objects in one's personal medicine bundle before each hunt. It was about living completely, in terms of obtaining both sustenance and spiritual balance. Making such a regular journey was the very essence of being Pikaani. To move in general was to live in the now, to be a part of the narration of sacred Blackfeet stories and to take part in the larger cosmology. Their experiences and beliefs were indistinguishable.

The Eastern and Central Plains (100–1000 CE)

From the Dakotas southward into northern Texas, Plains religiosity was likely affected in some way by the Hopewell phenomenon that swept the American midcontinent beginning about 2,000 years ago (Chapter 9). At the northeastern edge of the northern Plains, this includes the burial mound complexes south of the Laurel culture in the Canadian Boreal forest zone (see also Chapter 12). On to the northern Plains itself, the low mounds of the Besant culture – the pottery-using, foraging, and bison-hunting people who lived in tipis – have also been linked to the general Hopewell phenomenon. The distribution of Besant burial sites is irregular across North and South Dakota, and interpreted to indicate that Hopewellian practices were "transmitted along different routes by different stimuli from the Midwest and Central Plains" (Johnson and Johnson 1998:218).

Besant foragers probably did not include actual immigrants from the east. Rather, the Besant hunter-foragers had adopted and adapted nonlocal mortuary practices such that they fit local realities. Of these, the previously mentioned Sonota complex people made some use of Hopewell-style subfloor tombs containing processed bodies and body parts. "Gulf coast conch shell, [and] *Olivella, Marginella*, and *Dentalium*" shells are found in association, as are "pottery and artifacts with Hopewellian overtones such as carved human palates and worked bear maxillae" (Johnson and Johnson 1998:221).

To the south in the vicinity of present-day Kansas City is the better-known Kansas City Hopewell culture area, another localization of the otherwise exotic Hopewellian phenomenon. As in eastern variants, the Kansas City Hopewell culture was preceded by Early Woodland practices that are also comparable to their eastern cognates, suggesting that whatever Hopewell was, it began centuries before the 100–500 CE florescence on the Plains as well (Johnson and Johnson 1998). To the south into northeastern Oklahoma, the "Cooper phase" people appear even more localized if not peripheral, with distinctive pottery and omnipresent "Gary contracting stem" dart points making up typical domestic artifact assemblages. These were nonsedentary foraging people for the most part, though horticulture is known, especially from the latter half of the Kansas City Hopewell phenomenon.

By that time, these Middle Woodland-era people cultivated marsh elder and squash. Possibly, they also grew an early strain of maize, perhaps secured and later moved eastward from Basketmaker III people living in present-day New Mexico (see Chapter 14). Comparable to their Basketmaker contemporaries, the central Plains Hopewellians lived in a series of villages, each covering as much as 6 ha (15 acres). Village size shrank as one traveled west, doubtless because fewer forager-horticulturalists could be supported in any one location in the heart of the central Plains. Biomass on the Plains was patchy; winters were harsh. It is no surprise that the average mound size of a western "Schultz phase" Plains Woodland occupation also was much reduced, indicating smaller communities of people. It is difficult to imagine more than a few dozen people living at most such sites throughout most times of the year; however, warm season aggregations of hundreds were possible. These would have been the times when people would have hosted important ceremonials, perhaps including early forerunners of contemporary Powwows (www.britannica.com/EBchecked/topic/1367720/powwow).

More localized Hopewellian characteristics, from elaborate pottery forms and broad chipped-stone projectile points to submound tombs, illustrate that some limited suite of Hopewell cult knowledge had been imported into the region (Figure 11.6). Other attributes of the eastern Hopewell are absent, perhaps because they made no local sense. For instance, rather than the log construction common to Eastern Woodlands Hopewell crypts, the submound burial chambers in the nine well-known Kansas City area burial mounds consisted of "dry-laid masonry tombs covered with rock or earth mounds" (Johnson and Johnson 1998:203). As a result, archaeologists used to note that Plains Woodland people were not actively involved in a "Hopewellian Interaction Sphere" or "Exchange System," which was presumed to be an actively maintained trading network in the Mississippi and Ohio river valleys.

However, today it seems clearer that even the eastern Hopewell phenomenon was not driven by economic exchange (see Chapter 9). Regardless of how much face-to-face engagement various Middle Woodland people had with one another, the thrust of the larger Hopewell phenomenon into the Plains was religious fervor and pilgrimage. Over several generations there were probably a series of localized social and religious movements. Likely each had its own shrines, sacred bundles, leaders, and followers that were based to some degree in the newly adopted and then adapted religious practices from back east. These were carried great distances and transplanted in new lands almost certainly via the transfer of sacred medicine bundles – the consequences of which need to be considered in terms of culture "contact" (see Chapter 3).

Historically, and still today, major Plains Indian rituals or ceremonials were all based around a bundle. Indigenous ethnographer Francis La Flesche (1921:71ff.) recognized such bundles to be portable

Fig 11.6 Kansas City Hopewell ceramic jar. Courtesy of Kansas Historical Society.

shrines. Later archaeologist Preston Holder (1970:213) did too, calling them "portable ceremonial centers." Bundles were carefully enshrined on special altars inside special lodges, and were opened only on special occasions by special people (priests and bundle keepers) in order for a certain ceremony to take place. Some village or tribal bundles contained the history and identity of a people, which could be read by some priests. For instance, a Hidatsa bundle contained the skulls of the two ancestral "first men" of Hidatsa culture, who were said to have come to earth as thunderbirds (Bowers 1965).

Historically, the powers of certain bundles were such that, once they were introduced into a new land, they enabled the new practice to (literally and figuratively) take place. And, since duplicate copies of various bundles could be made, the new religious practice might spread rapidly as a religious movement from one village to the next and one people to other peoples, even crossing language barriers (Pauketat 2013). Thus, Hopewellian practices may have emanated out of the Midwest via bundle transfers or copies. That said, the bundled practices were always localized, and whether in Ohio or in the northern and central Plains, they would have been a dynamic source of Middle Woodland change. Once in place and ceremonially opened on special occasions, new practices would overlay or be syncretized with extant local traditions (not unlike globalized culture today).

So, bundles were the source of ritual, identity, belief, and heritage on the Plains from early times. They were even understood to be prominent living beings, deserving of respect, homage, and offerings (which were accepted on behalf of the bundle by a bundle keeper). But bundles could also be decommissioned or grow powerless, sometimes because no suitable bundle keeper or curator could be found. It took years for one apprentice bundle keeper to learn how to care for and maintain the power of the bundle. The end of the Hopewell world may have been a crisis of increasingly weak bundles (see also Spielmann 2013).

Being more distant from the Hopewellian heartland, it comes as no surprise that, to the south and north in the Plains, distinctly Plains Woodland ways of being human did not end sharply at 500 CE. Bundle power may have lived on there. Rock mound or cairn construction continued, from the central Plains into the Ozarks of southern Missouri. Oklahoma and Texas panhandle sites dating as late as the 900s comprise small temporary or seasonally occupied settlements of foragers and gardeners. Merging into the Fourche Maline (pronounced "foosh mayleen") culture of Arkansas and Oklahoma, such people yet used Gary dart points, after 500 CE alongside small arrow points, and made a multi-purpose flowerpot-shaped type of ceramic cookware known as Williams Plain. The large vessels, with small flat bases, are found into the Caddo area farther to the southeast (Brown 1996). In the Dakotas north into Manitoba, pottery-using Late Plains Woodland people are known up until 1000 CE. Moreover, between 600 and 900 CE, some of them built linear and geometric mounds, possibly related in some way to the Effigy Mound culture phenomenon known farther east in Iowa and Wisconsin (see Chapter 10).

Early Plains Villages (1000–1250 CE)

There are disagreements about precisely when or where, but at least by the eleventh century CE, dramatic changes came to the Plains sufficient for archaeologists to recognize a new "Plains Village period" from about 1000 to 1600 CE (Mitchell 2012). During their maximum point of population nucleation in the Proto-Historic era, great villages of up to 2,000 people living in dozens of impressive thatched (grass-roofed) or earth-covered lodges dotted the major river ways of the Plains. The homes of the Caddo-speaking Wichita in Kansas were circular and thatched. Those of other Caddo-language speakers, such as the Pawnee, and various Siouan-speaking Mandan and Hidatsa to the north were circular or rectangular and covered with earth (Figures 11.7–11.8).

Fig 11.7 Plains Indian houses: left, Wichita grass-covered circular house near Anadarko, Oklahoma, Thomas Croft photo/Wikimedia; right, Mandan earthlodge, Edward S. Curtis photo/Library of Congress, Washington, DC.

Fig 11.8 Mandan village as seen by George Catlin. Smithsonian Institution/ Wikimedia.

Brackenridge had visited these crowded, roiling centers of social life on the Plains in the spring and summer after his rediscovery of Cahokia. His eastern Euro-American sensibilities were beset by the winter's accumulation of refuse and human waste in the backyards of one Arikara village. I "[r]ambled through the village," he says, "which I found excessively filthy, the 'villainous smells,' which every where assailed me, compelled me at length, to seek refuge in the open plain. The lovers of Indian manners, and mode of living, should contemplate them at a distance" (Brackenridge 1962:247). Of course, he also noted that wherever he went, "the children ran away, screaming, and frightened at my outré and savage appearance."

Such great smelly accumulations probably were uncommon in the early Plains Village period, when fewer people lived in more widely spaced lodges inside smaller, unfortified villages. Between 1000 and 1250, some people in the central and northeastern Plains also lived in scattered rural farmsteads, indicating a time of general security. All existed by mixing farming and hunting, including periodic forays to cull bison herds (on foot, of course). They grew fields of maize, squash, and wild grasses. They processed animal materials in each

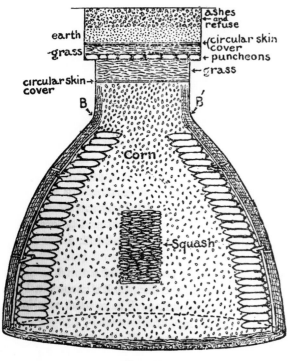

Figure 25
Redrawn from sketch by Goodbird.

Fig 11.9 The corn storage pit of the Hidatsa farmer Maxi'diwiac (Buffalo Bird Woman) (from Wilson 1917: figure 25).

village: meat and certain organs for food; brains and bone grease for hide processing and insect repellent; hides for robes, bedding, and door coverings; and the bones themselves for hoe blades, needles, awls (or punches), shuttles (for weaving cloth), and more. Annually, they put away sizeable stores of dried cultigens in bell-shaped storage pits able to hold thousands of liters of foodstuffs (Figure 11.9). The Missouri River trench and its major tributaries – the Nebraska, Platte, Republican, and Kansas rivers – were dotted by these dense population clusters, as Lewis and Clark had witnessed even after European diseases and historic reshuffling had occurred. So too were the Arkansas, Canadian, and Red rivers to the south.

Initial Middle Missouri Tradition

In the northern Plains, the first such villages included the "Initial Middle Missouri tradition" (IMMT) settlements (Henning 2005; Mitchell 2012). "The origins of the Middle Missouri tradition (MMT) lie in a transformation among regional terminal Late Woodland groups in the Missouri basin and western Prairies from dispersed, unfortified farming hamlets into nucleated, fortified farming villages" (Tiffany 2007:3). The Late Woodland farming hamlets were made up of a few oval homes featuring horseshoe-shaped entrances (Ahler 2007; Benn and Green 2000). After 900 CE, the predominant terminal Late Woodland occupation of western Iowa and portions of eastern Nebraska and South Dakota is called the "Great Oasis" culture (Mitchell 2012). By 900 CE, such Late Woodland village horticulturalists were tending gardens of maize, wild grasses, sunflower, and squash planted near their homes, especially in floodplains.

Great Oasis farmers, alongside the "Glenwood" people of eastern Nebraska, the "Mill Creek" farmers of northwest Iowa, and "Cambria" peoples of southern Minnesota, were in direct or indirect contact with outsiders, acquiring, for instance, exotic shells from the Pacific Ocean via down-the-line (or hand-to-hand) gifting or trading relationships with foragers to the west and east. This network existed across the northern Plains for centuries. They also sought what the city dwellers of Cahokia, a boat ride down the Missouri River, had to offer. Cahokians produced marine shell beads, axe heads, projectile points, and fancy pots. In small numbers, such things show up among the later Late Woodland hamlets of the eastern Plains.

By the 1100s, there were IMMT villages to the east, in the Great Oasis homeland, and to the west (and north) up the Missouri. The eastern villages (IMMTe) were consolidations of Great Oasis hamlets, while those to the west (IMMTw) included Great Oasis people who relocated into a new land (Ahler 2007; Krause 2016; Tiffany 2007). Both sets of populations were amalgamations and transformations of earlier kin groups, resulting in significant historical change (in the sense of Murray and Swenson 2016). Some Initial Middle Missouri pottery attributes, such as S-shaped jar rims, were copied by Cahokians (or some Middle Missouri potters were living at Cahokia; Figure 11.10).

The earliest IMMT villagers, east and west, framed large, semisubterranean, rectangular homes using timbers retrieved from wooded floodplains; roofs were probably covered with earth in part, though others suspect that thatch from prairie grasses may also have been used (Figure 11.11). These homes were capable of housing newly *extended* families and were sometimes situated in isolated locations, with the residents being part of a larger village-based community nearby. The fact that such families could reside away from the main village is strongly suggestive of a peaceful existence, at least more

Fig 11.10 Initial Middle Missouri "Foreman Cord Impressed" pottery with S-shaped rim, orifice diameter 20.5 cm (Lehmer 1954: plate 15).

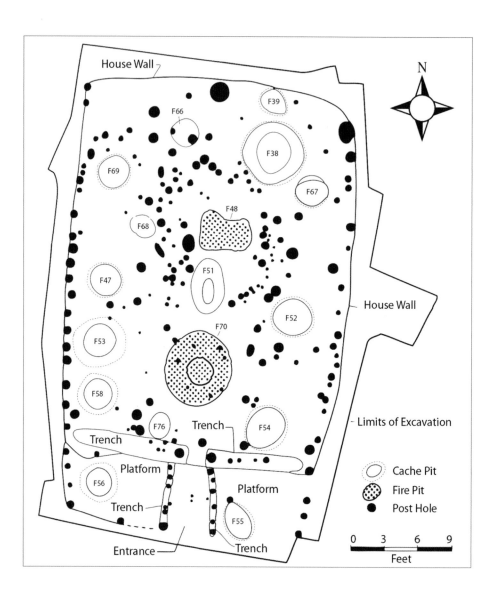

Fig 11.11 Middle Missouri tradition pithouse or earthlodge. Courtesy of Mark Mitchell.

peaceful than in years to come. Accordingly, both the IMMT farmsteads and the larger villages were not initially fortified, indicating that fear of attack was minimal. No doubt, this time of relative peace probably means that the new IMMT community territories did not significantly infringe upon those of others. Up to that point, the land was relatively open and underpopulated.

Central Plains Tradition

The same seems true of Plains Village life as it was emerging in the central Plains, south of the IMMT villages. There, so-called Central Plains tradition people built small rectangular earthlodges, similar to the southern Plains, that comprised smaller "autonomous farmsteads"

(Figure 11.11; see Mitchell 2012:360). Their pots were made in a grit-tempered, collared-ware style reminiscent of the Woodland era, though some incised globular vessels could have been inspired by Cahokia's "Ramey Incised" style. In eastern Nebraska and adjacent states, archaeologists have identified a series of phases based on pottery style variants and settlement details. Even at this early date, these may correspond to ethnic groups or tribal identities: the Nebraska, Smoky Hill, Solomon River, Lower Loup, and Upper Republican phases. A variant of the Central Plains vessel mode has been identified in eastern Kansas and western Missouri as well. Dated to about 1000–1250 CE, the Steed-Kisker peoples produced this decorated style using shell-tempered pastes, seemingly replicating Cahokian pottery technology to a degree. They also made local versions of classic "Cahokia Notched" arrow points, built rectangular semisubterranean lodges (probably at least partially covered over with earth), and buried some of their dead in low mounds (O'Brien 1993). The easternmost such site seems to be the Cloverdale site near St. Joseph, Missouri (http://users.stlcc.edu/mfuller/Cloverdale/index.html).

The historical implications of the central Plains villager relationships with Cahokia have been debated for years. Some suggest that Cahokians sought and depended on Plains Village products (Tiffany 1991; Tiffany and Alex 2001). As evidence, we might consider the close correspondence between the Plains Village period and Cahokia's own mid-eleventh- through twelfth-century heyday, as well as the presence of certain Cahokian objects or close copies. But others suspect less direct causal relationships (Henning 2005). Plains Village culture, after all, was under construction before 1050, or so it seems now. Thus, Cahokia's impacts on Plains people may have been more in terms of how they or their things were used by Plains folks or – in the case of medicine bundles – what was transferred and how from one place to the other.

Thus, archaeologist Mark Mitchell (2012:364) notes that, while "not every community interacted exclusively with Cahokia," prominent Plains men may have been adopted members of, or simply allied with, Cahokian peoples downriver, acquiring "objects and materials signifying their connection to distant sources of power, which they in turn used to bolster their claims to local prestige and leadership." Among the IMMTe people of the Mill Creek culture (1100–1200), Cahokian imports included Ramey Incised and Powell Plain polished pots, chunkey stones, earspools, marine shell beads and pendants, Cahokia-style points, and long-nosed god earpieces (see Chapter 10). As argued by an earlier generation of archaeologists familiar with both Cahokia and Plains-Prairie peoples, the latter earpieces were probably especially prized, and indicate likely direct contact by at least one Plains leader with Cahokian politicos (Gibbon 1974; Hall 1997) – not unlike the peace medals handed out by Lewis and Clark and others (see Chapter 3). At such times, families may have exchanged marriage partners, cementing long-lasting affinal ties and creating heritage connections along the Missouri River.

There is another potential dimension of Cahokia–Plains Village relationships that should also be recognized, in part owing to recent work at and around greater Cahokia. The great complex grew in the eleventh century far too fast to have been a function of birth-rate increases, and both ceramic and isotopic evidence suggests that immigration was key to Cahokia's rapid rise (see Chapter 10). The result would have been a composite, diverse kind of cityscape, with different social, ethnic, and even linguistic groups possibly present. The presence of Plains contingents – factions, visitors, or emissaries to Cahokia – is an entirely plausible scenario. Plains representatives might well have traveled to the city to learn a sacred practice or ceremony, later to return home with a medicine bundle (an updated version of the earlier Hopewell dynamic). Whole groups of priests or leaders seeking understanding and knowledge may have visited, or even stayed for years, not unlike the practice of visiting Washington, DC in later history. Certainly, there is no good reason to assume, as some archaeologists have, that Cahokian descendants include only one off-shoot Siouan-speaking ethnicity. Likewise the demise of Cahokia may have also had both direct and indirect cultural impacts on the Plains, direct because of expatriate subpopulations that eventually migrated on to the Plains, and indirect owing to its absence after a century or more of being a cultural reference point or source of cultural power.

Coalescence on the Plains

Of more immediate concerns to IMMT and Central Plains peoples, of course, were the "region's two most important resources … maize and bison" (Mitchell 2012:364). The effects of communities coalescing around maize and bison played out in local political terms as time went on, but could well have been complicated by Cahokia's dissolution and the appearance of expatriate subpopulations, or the reshuffling of expatriates, ex-allies, or ex-enemies on the Plains. After 1200 CE, whatever position Cahokia itself had played in Plains life was rapidly coming to a close. And, around that time, changes in Plains Village life are manifest, including a greater reliance on horticultural products and wild foods: besides corn, squash, and goosefoot (*Chenopodium*), beans now made an appearance, presumably imported from the Southwest. Other starchy grasses were also cultivated, including knotweed, maygrass, little barley, and marsh elder. In addition, "fruits such as grapes and plums … nuts, and probably tubers such as prairie turnips were gathered by most villagers" (Drass 2012:376). More plant foods, in short, were being used to feed families.

Of animal products on the central and southern Plains, archaeologist Richard Drass says this:

The larger streams in the east could supply significant amounts of fish and other aquatic resources, but western groups had access to few aquatic animals and relied more on game. Deer were hunted by all groups; rabbits, rodents,

Sidebar 11.2 Plains Village horticulture

In 1913, 1914, and 1915, Maxi'diwiac (Buffalo Bird Woman) relayed her knowledge of how she and her Hidatsa family (father, two wives/mothers, and grandmothers) cleared fields and planted, harvested, processed, and stored crops to Presbyterian pastor-turned-anthropologist Gilbert Livingstone Wilson (Wilson 1917). The following are Maxi'diwiac's words:

In old times we Hidatsas never made our gardens on the untimbered, prairie land, because the soil there is too hard and dry. In the bottom lands by the Missouri, the soil is soft and easy to work … With their hoes, my mothers [and grandmothers] … dug and softened the soil in places for the corn hills, which were laid off in rows. These hills they planted. Then all summer they worked with their hoes, clearing and breaking the ground between the hills … The first seed that we planted in the spring was sunflower … around the edges of a field … Corn planting began the second month after sunflower-seed was planted, that is in May; and it lasted about a month … We Hidatsa women

were early risers in the planting season; it was my habit to be up before sunrise, while the air was cool … The season for watching the field began early in August when green corn began to come in; for this was the time when the ripening ears were apt to be stolen by horses, or birds, or boys … Two girls usually watched and sang together … [and] often worked at porcupine embroidery as they watched.

(Wilson 1917:9–31)

Squash seed was planted early in June … [and the] squash harvest began a little before green corn came in … We picked a good many squashes in a season. One year my mother fetched in seventy baskets from our field. We stored our corn, beans, sunflower seed and dried squash in cache pits for the winter, much as white people keep vegetables in their cellars. A cache pit was shaped somewhat like a jug, with a narrow neck at the top, the width of the mouth, or entrance, was commonly about two feet … Descent into one of these big cache pits was made with a ladder.

(Wilson 1917:87–88)

birds, and other small animals supplemented the larger game. Turtles, especially box turtles, seem to have been regularly collected … Bison, however, was by far the … primary meat source … Few bison may have been present at eastern Plains sites before about AD 1250, but bison remains increase significantly at later sites in this area.

(Drass 2012:376)

Importantly, Plains Villages were increasingly large and more numerous during the thirteenth century. To the south, certain rivers were lined with villages, each separated from the next by sometimes less than an hour's walk (ca. 2.5 km). To the north, "Extended variant" Middle Missouri villages remained populous, about the same size as earlier IMM peoples. They averaged some 300 people per settlement, though lodges doubled in size, suggesting that, increasingly, extended family households were acting as the primary units of communal labor (Mitchell 2012).

After 1300 and the end of the Medieval Warm Period, a drying trend set in, and additional changes occurred. Most Plains villagers began growing corn more intensively and, in the southern Plains, obtaining more foodstuffs from the Southwest and Southeast. With regard to the latter, Caddo–Mississippian contacts are evident, with the ancestors of the Wichita, Pawnee, and Arikara – all Caddo-speaking horticulturalists – likely visiting sites such as Spiro from time to time. Certainly, the lodges of the southern Caddos on the Plains are virtually identical to those of the Central Plains tradition.

Initial Coalescent People

At this time, some of the central Plains peoples, such as the Arikara, began migrating northward, up the Missouri River, where archaeologists label them the "Initial Coalescent" people (Krause 2016). Although a consensus over the precise demographic dynamics of the Plains is lacking, the presence of fortifications at later Middle Missouri sites in the northern Plains and at the so-called Initial Coalescent period sites suggests that social tensions were high between communities of dissimilar people. Gone were the outlying extended household sites that once indicated peace. From about 1300 to 1450, Initial Coalescent villages were established in the Middle Missouri trench, sometimes directly superimposing earlier Middle Missouri sites, and likely displacing contemporary people in the process (Johnson 1998). Many of the Initial Coalescent villages and their material remains do indeed look very similar to those of the Central Plains tradition, all being the likely ancestors of the Pawnee, Arikara, Hidatsa, and Mandan. Initial villages range in size from about 10 to 50 earthlodges, covering, on average, 10 ha (25 acres), with one massive village of more than 100 ha (250 acres) (Johnson 1998:313). Depending on ethnicity and tradition, communities might bury their dead in the flesh in cemeteries or place them on scaffolds in a special location. Typically, both were often located high on a river bluff (www.nps.gov/knri/index.htm).

The earthlodges in these Initial Coalescent villages were spaced widely. Each building was of similar shape – usually circular to slightly rectangular in outline, having floor areas averaging almost 60 m^2, and with an interior post framework and an upper wall consisting of in-slanted timbers extending from the ground surface to the ceiling, all heaped over in earth (Roper and Pauls 2005). Some lodges were larger and more centrally located than others, likely an indication of the higher status or greater community importance attached to them and their residents. But "[p]erhaps the most distinguishing feature of the Initial Coalescent villages is a fortification system composed of a ditch, an interior palisade, and protruding bastions set at 120- to 180-foot intervals" (Johnson 1998:313). Considering that these settlements are situated in the midst of Plains grasslands, the cutting and hauling of wood from bottomland locations to build a palisade that encloses 10 ha would suggest a serious commitment to defense and the need for a generous supply of wood, never mind the labor to build it (Figure 11.12). Presumably, such defenses were thrown up at

Sidebar 11.3 Inside the earthlodge

Earthlodges embodied the two worlds of Plains Village life. Inside were the household's tools and possessions, sleeping mats and robes, and work areas, all around a central hearth. Also inside was a microcosm of the wider world, or "a universe within the universe" (Chamberlain 1982:155). The hearth was the focal point of that world which was often divided into four sacred quarters using large roof-support posts. These posts might be painted with the color associated with the north, south, east, or west. In the rear of some,

especially the "medicine lodges" of bundle keepers and priests, were altars – elevated areas or wooden frameworks atop which might lie a bison skull and on or from which medicine bundles, sacred corn ears, and more were laid or hung. The entire lodge, especially of avid skywatchers such as the Skiri Pawnee, was often aligned to astronomical phenomena, including the equinoxes or solstices, such that light from the sun at various times of the year would strike the interior of the lodge through the doorway.

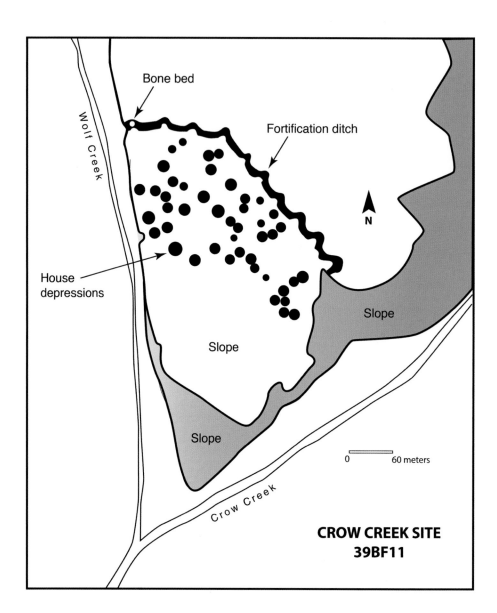

Fig 11.12 Map of the Initial Coalescent village of Crow Creek, North Dakota, showing large defensive ditch (adapted from Willey and Emerson 1993: figure 2).

the very foundation of each village, meaning that the selection of the village location was contingent on the existence of a heavily wooded river bottom nearby.

We have little understanding of these founding moments. Who decided where? How was labor appropriated and order established at the outset? Were people guided to a site based on some convergence of spiritual associations and physical properties? After their initial layout, we presume that the "labor which maintained the village was communal … [and] shared by all" (Holder 1970:56). Regardless of the answers to questions of their foundations, there were doubtless social effects: foundational constructions establish senses of identity and community relations. Communities, personalities, and modes of governance based on collective constructions and experiences of barriers surely varied from those that were formed around open plans. So it may not be enough to say that each Plains Village was self-governing.

Certainly, the absence of clusters of sites along with the diversity in house shapes and sizes between villages indicates that the residents, or leaders, of each site decided on their own construction standards and made their own decisions. Brackenridge (1962:254) had called the later Plains villagers "oligarchical." Some archaeologists today might call them heterarchical – or laterally ordered. No doubt households, lineages, and clans integrated each village and provided the possibility for between-village alliances and political confederations. But each village also must have had its own unique history that affected the larger trajectory of the Plains. A settlement such as the Huff site, near Bismark, North Dakota, suggests a strong within-village authority. This Middle Missouri tradition settlement consists of many dozens of lodges arranged in rows and surrounded by a symmetrical ditch and palisade fortification that encloses 3.4 ha (Figure 11.13; see Wood 1961).

Some Plains peoples, especially the Caddo-speaking Pawnee, Wichita, and Arikara, were ranked into incipient classes, perhaps helping to explain the Initial Coalescent reshuffling of the Plains (Krause 2016).

In any village there was a fundamental interest in stable hierarchical ranking which appears most strikingly in the lives of the men. Essentially there were two groups of men: those with high rank, the leader group; and those without significant rank, the commoners. However, since each man was maintained by the labor of a stable household, and was in effect the representative of the household, it is more accurate to say that any village was divided into leader households and commoner households … [T]here was a small core of leading families whose rank was assured by religious sanctions and reinforced by economic position, and within that small core there were a few families whose high status was clearly hereditary.

(Holder 1970:37)

High-status lodges (lineages) had more influence and rights to inherit certain tribal bundles that, in turn, afforded them more power, while "commoner" lodges did not. There were other regulatory bodies involved with the maintenance of civic order within and between villages. Besides kin groups – lineages or clans – whose duties

Fig 11.13 Huff site, North Dakota: top, aerial view of site showing locations of houses and palisade wall and ditch; bottom, excavated house (Wood 1961: plates 1 and 4).

it might be to ritually manage information or resources, there were also sodalities (a.k.a. "societies"). There were men's groups, warrior societies, tobacco societies, and more, each basing its membership on age cohorts, gender, or life experiences, not kinship. Such sodalities or societies controlled the timing and performance of various ceremonies or the management of all-important medicine bundles that were, in turn, absolutely essential for the performance of the songs, prayers, or ritual components of the ceremonies. Even the making of pottery for such ceremonial occasions was bundled and produced exclusively by some clans and not others (Bowers 1965).

One might presume that resource availability within and around villages was managed by such kin groups or sodalities and led by a high-ranking household well back into the Plains Village period (particularly wood for use in construction and cooking fires). This was critical because, for example, after some period of time, people might run out of firewood. Likewise, a palisade wall might need to be rebuilt, such that any village would have to consider carefully its wood supply. If you could not build a wall, your safety would have likely been in jeopardy.

A case in point? The villagers of the Crow Creek site had to rebuild their palisade wall and dig a new ditch at one point around 1350. Unfortunately, they were unable to complete the reconstruction before an unknown enemy attacked the settlement. The community was decimated (Willey and Emerson 1993).

Sidebar 11.4 The Crow Creek massacre

Likely settled by Arikara villagers, the 50 earthlodges at Crow Creek village were occupied by an estimated 800 people in the fourteenth century CE. They and their parents and grandparents had lived there for enough time that the first wooden palisade wall and outer ditch around the settlement had been allowed to deteriorate and be filled in. Around the year 1350, a new ditch was begun, a project that would have taken days if not weeks. Perhaps they were aware of a threat. This ditch was particularly wide (2 m) and deep (1.5 m). Unfortunately, they had not completed the defensive feature or begun the palisade wall when an enemy attacked and overwhelmed them. Earlier excavations at the site had documented that at least some of the earthlodges had been burned, and the remains of victims of the attack were found yet inside. Then, in 1978, archaeologists working for the state of South Dakota received word that human remains were falling out of the sides of the cut bank atop which sits the Crow Creek site. Some local looters had commenced their own diggings there and the archaeologists arrived to stop it and to determine the source of the remains.

Excavating into what was determined to be the new but unfinished defensive ditch, the archaeologists found the remains of at least 486 individuals in a mass grave: men,

women, and children. Most had suffered severe perimortem trauma (near or at the time of death) that included blows to the head and decapitations with clubs and axes, some made while they were attempting to escape (as skull fractures were located on the back of the cranium). Others had been arrowshot. At least 90 percent of them had been scalped. Others had suffered additional perimortem or postmortem mutilation, ranging from having their limbs, hands, or feet cut off, tongues cut out, noses sliced away, teeth pulled out or bashed in, and genitalia removed (Willey and Emerson 1993).

Given the unusual ratio of adults to juveniles and men to women, it is likely that many young women were taken captive. Some unknown number of residents may have escaped, presumably hiding for their lives. The bodies of the slain were then allowed to lie exposed in the village and, over the next period of days to weeks, were scavenged by wolves, coyotes, and dogs, leaving behind carnivore gnawing marks on the bones. At some point, however, a party of people, probably the surviving relatives of the slain, returned to collect all of the scattered body parts for burial in the yet-open and incomplete defensive ditch (Willey and Emerson 1993; Zimmerman 1985; see also http://en.wikipedia.org/wiki/Crow_Creek_massacre).

Tensions on the northern Plains may have lessened after the 1300s, but not in the south. Instead, site densities on the central and southern Plains "decline dramatically" around 1450, marking a relocation of populations possibly owing to a surge in violence there (Drass 2012:380). By about 1500 CE, villages disappeared from western, more arid zones, and fortifications became more widespread in the southern Plains. Possibly a drier "Little Ice Age" climate – the cooler, drier conditions across the northern hemisphere until 1800 or so – is to blame. Then again, geopolitical conditions across the Southwest and Plains and into the Mississippi Valley may also have been a cause (cf. the Pueblos and Mississippians, Chapters 10, 14, and 15). Southwestern pueblos were nucleating at the time, the Vacant Quarter had opened up in the central Mississippi Valley, and Illinois River valley Mississippians were engaged in conflicts with "Oneota" people from the north.

Oneota Expansion

Oneota peoples are identified primarily by their settlements and material culture, and seem to have descended from Woodland groups in the upper Midwest, especially Wisconsin. Adopting some of the Ramey symbolism and shell-tempered pottery technology of Cahokia, they were initially a series of village-horticultural groups similar to Plains villagers. Archaeologists identify their precursors as early as 1000 CE, and a developed Oneota culture by 1200 CE (Henning 2007). Their everyday cooking pottery is distinctive for its use of "thunderbird" tail and wing motifs; children in Oneota longhouses would have grown up associating such spirits and their aggressive, war-like characteristics with everyday life. Their "bone and stone tool complexes are in great measure Plains-derived, with bison scapula digging tools, shaft straighteners, unifacial flake end scrapers, manos, and grinding slabs commonly found" in western Wisconsin and, eventually, out on to the northeastern Plains (Henning 2005:170).

By the 1300s, the Oneota peoples expanded their domain well out into the Plains regions as far as western Iowa and southeastern Nebraska. This expansion reached a climax during the 1500s and 1600s, when Oneota communities seem to have established great village sites. The Utz site in modern-day central Missouri was the principal village of the Chiwere-Siouian-speaking Missouri Indians, a late Oneota group. Utz residents were in intermittent contact with or managed to obtain access to objects from both Late Mississippians in the Bootheel of Missouri and Puebloan farmers in the far-off Southwest. Another community was Blood Run, known from the late seventeenth century as the great village of the Omaha, a Dhegiha-Siouan-speaking people in far northwestern Iowa. This latter site covers an impressive 240 ha (593 acres) on either side of the Big Sioux River. It featured "275 large conical [burial] mounds, from 150 to 800 stone circulars and ovals that are probably house outlines, a possible effigy mound, an earthen enclosure covering ca. 6 ha, an earthen serpent effigy over 90 m long, and at least seven large pitted Sioux Quartzite boulders" (Henning 2005:175). These last have hundreds of pecked depressions and were powerful medicine to the proto-Omaha (www.watchablewildlifenwia.org/sites-BloodRun.htm).

Proto-Historic Plains Villagers

By the beginning of the Proto-Historic era around 1500, the widespread historical and geopolitical effects of Central Plains movements north and Oneota migrations west had transformed the Plains. But more was to come in the form of European pandemics and the horse. The former exacerbated intertribal warfare of land and labor; the latter enabled territories to be extended, pemmican and dried meat movements to be expanded, and fighting forces to be projected over vast distances (Holder 1970). In the wake of such great change, rituals that might ameliorate enmities and create alliances between villages and nations became widespread, again now carried even farther afield by people on horseback. Among these were the Grass Dance, the Dream Dance, Midéwiwin, and the Sun Dance (Young 2001). The last was known in some form among many of the Plains peoples, though most of them also told stories of how they had acquired the bundles to conduct the ritual from elsewhere. The Sun Dance involved a circle of upright posts and a large forked center post to which supplicants would be tethered by means of leather straps or ropes fastened into their pectoral flesh (Figure 11.14). Possibly this was a

Fig 11.14 Cheyenne Sun Dance, ca. 1909. Henry Chaufty photo/Library of Congress, Washington, DC.

Sidebar 11.5 Plains sweat baths

"The sweat bath has become one of the most persistent elements of American Indian religion" (Hall 1997:124). Sweats took place in modest circular buildings usually constructed as simple bent-pole or wigwam huts. Exteriors were covered with mats, skins, or earth. A hearth in the middle would have held red-hot rocks on which water would be poured to produce steam and obtain the desired result: to cause individuals to perspire heavily and thereby purify the body. Doing so was often necessary before engaging in other ritual activities. A Lakota priest recounted the reasons: "This sweat removes from your body all evil, all touch of woman, and makes you wakáⁿ [cosmic power], that the spirit of the Great Mystery may come close to you and strengthens you" (Bucko 1998:43). The roots of sweat baths may be ancient and connected to uterine metaphors (Hall 1997), though specific forms or associations of sweat lodge practices were altered through time, likely as parts of (re)bundled religious movements. Such was the case with the arrival of sweat lodges at Cahokia at about 1050 CE, and such was also the case with circular shrine buildings in Mesoamerica (McAnany 2012).

version of Mesoamerican pole ceremonialism (similar to contemporary Mesoamerican pole acrobats called *voladores*). On the Plains, it was connected to warfare, the veneration of culture heroes, and the adoption of souls of enemies that might accompany the community's own dead (Hall 1997). Robert Hall thought that it, if not also the well-known Plains sweat lodge (which was a necessary component of the Sun Dance and other ceremonies), may have been historically related to Cahokian developments.

Perhaps the most important of the Plains rituals was the Calumet ceremony, which originated a couple of centuries earlier on the Plains and eventually spread into the Southeast (Brown 1989; Rodning 2014). The Calumet (or "peace pipe") was a revered object smoked at the culmination of a long ceremony wherein one party "adopted" a non-relative into his kin group. Rooted in Middle Woodland ritual smoking of tobacco, it was similar to the earlier noted Cahokian adoption practices via long-nosed god earpieces (Hall 1997). Misunderstood by early Euro-American travelers as a temporary sign of a truce, such ritual adoption via the Calumet pipe established lasting relations between Plains groups. Anyone carrying the Calumet would not be harmed but allowed to pass (Figure 11.15). Among the Pawnee, for instance, ritual envoys would process across the Plains carrying the Calumet, which they called the Hako, in front so as not to be molested by enemy war parties (Fletcher 1996).

An early Jesuit missionary traveling on the Mississippi, Father Jacques Gravier, described it this way in 1701:

Fig 11.15 Calumet.

There is nothing among these Indians that is more mysterious or more reverenced. No such honors are paid to the crowns and scepters of Kings as those that they pay to it. It seems to be the God of Peace and of war, the arbiter of life and of death. It suffices for one to carry and to show it, to walk in safety in the midst of Enemies, who in the hottest of the Fight lay down their weapons when it is displayed … There is one Calumet for Peace and one for war, and they are distinguished solely by the Color of the feathers that adorn them. Red is the sign of war. They use it also to terminate their quarrels, to strengthen their alliances and to speak to Strangers. It is a sort of Pipe for smoking Tobacco, made from a red stone polished like marble, and bored out in such manner that one end serves for holding the tobacco, while the other fits upon the stem. The latter consists of a hollow stick two feet long, as large as an ordinary cane. Hence the French have called it "calumet," from a corruption of the word Chalumeau, because it resembles that instrument – or, rather, a long flute. It is ornamented with the heads or Necks of various birds, whose plumage is very handsome. They also add long feathers of red, green, or other colors with which it is entirely covered. They esteem it chiefly because they look upon it as the Calumet or Pipe of the sun; and, in fact, they offer it to the sun to smoke when they wish to obtain a calm, or rain, or fine weather.

Another means of communicating across linguistic boundaries was Plains Indian sign language. Although the precursors to this nonverbal lingua franca may extend as far back as the Plains Woodland era or to Plains–Cahokia relationships, it seems likely that the Proto-Historic era was the maximum point of its use. That is, despite ethnic boundaries and the dangers of moving across the Plains, information clearly spread far and wide – everyone knew everything. Even an African crop – the watermelon – took only decades to move from the sixteenth-century Spanish borderland colonies into the interior Great Plains, in some cases "contacting" native people before European people themselves (Blake 1981)! People on the Plains knew what was happening across their great expanse of grassland. Plains sign language enabled Siouan-, Caddo-, and Algonkian-language speakers on the Plains to convey messages across ethnic and language boundaries, even at a distance. Eventually, French and later American fur traders themselves also learned to communicate via signs, first described during Cabeza de Vaca's travels through Texas and, later, by Coronado's account through the southern Plains.

Doubtless, signs were a means whereby the Proto-Historic villagers of the Plains established communications with neighbors. However, we should not underestimate the long-distance travel by would-be leaders, priests, and other ritual specialists. Historically, clan priests did not distinguish such long-distance travel from one's spiritual journey through life and into other dimensions of human existence. The well-known ritual and warrior leader – they weren't always separable – Sitting Bull reached out later in his life as part of Buffalo Bill's Wild West Show, for instance, because it was a part of his being. The equally well-known Lakota priest Black Elk traveled in both his dreams and his waking hours to commune with sacred forces and otherworldly beings (Neihardt 2008). Many Plains peoples believed that they were descended from the stars and would return there, following the Milky Way's Path of Souls after death. Among the Crow in the northern Plains, time and social life were utterly inseparable from the movements of planets and stars (McCleary 1997).

The same seems to have been true of the various Caddo-speaking peoples of the central Plains. As the Caddo world shifted its attention southward after the demise of Cahokia, so Plains people also seem to have acquired ceremonial trappings and practices strikingly similar to those of the Southwest, northern Mexico, and Mesoamerica. During the Proto-Historic era, this included the adoption of Peyote ritualism among southern Plains groups (Stewart 1987), and earlier, the appearance of a four-pointed depiction of the Morningstar (usually Venus). They had also included the adoption of a kind of ritualized warring known among the Aztec, warriors who would tether themselves to the ground and fight an enemy hand-to-hand to the death. And they include the infamous Arrow or Morningstar sacrifice of a young captive female, suspected to have been practiced by the Wichita, Pawnee, and perhaps the Arikara (Chamberlain 1982; Holder 1970). Certainly it was performed by the sedentary Caddo-Mississippians to the south (see Chapter 10).

By the early 1540s, the social landscape of the southern Plains had been thoroughly transformed, with great areas once filled with Plains Villages now devoid of settlement. Into that void in modern-day west Texas came the Apaches and Comanches, who had been living in the High Plains of Colorado and New Mexico. Their effects were keenly felt there, especially after horses arrived on the Plains, having escaped the Spaniards during various entradas. They raided southwestern Pueblos and eastern Plains Villages. In the 1600s and 1700s, this new horse culture enabled the once-marginal foragers of the West to dominate the Plains. Some, such as the Algonkian-speaking Cheyenne, had migrated to the central Plains from Minnesota in the fifteenth or sixteenth century, and took to horses quickly. So did the Pawnee and Wichita. Others, mostly Plains villagers, were slower to adopt the horse or were tethered to their fields, placing them at a significant disadvantage in relationships with the new nomadic western Plains horse peoples and the soon-to-arrive Euro-Americans (Holder 1970). As a result, some of the first Indian peoples to be moved on to reservations were the horticultural villagers.

Even in this period, of course, Plains Indians continued to live in two worlds. Peace pipes were smoked, peace medals were received, treaties were forged, and spirit journeys continued. After 1807, the journeys occasionally involved Indian emissaries traveling to St. Louis. There, they would meet with William Clark, a sympathetic ear, who had been assigned by Jefferson as the US Agent for Indian Affairs after his return from the Pacific Northwest. Later in the century, native prophets and visionaries would emerge who could envision alternative futures – spiritual and real. Among the most widespread and historically impactful of these was the Ghost Dance, promulgated by the Piute visionary Wovoka, who carried his vision on to the Plains (Kehoe 2006).

That ended, during the US presidency of Benjamin Harrison, in the 1890 massacre of Lakota people at Wounded Knee on the Pine Ridge Reservation in South Dakota (see also http://en.wikipedia.org/wiki/Wounded_Knee_Massacre). Peace medal production was discontinued shortly thereafter (see Chapter 3), while both US and Canadian governments were carving up the central and northern Plains into provinces and states, a process largely complete by the time of the massacre. For all intents and purposes, the pre-colonial Plains Indian world was over just 86 years after Lewis and Clark had begun their trip up the Missouri.

12 The Final Centuries of the Northeast

There were different things in the olden days, strange happenings, strange animals and birds, and strange people.

Aurelia Jones Miller, Seneca (in Parker 1989:394)

Monumental complexes, population centers, and cosmic centerplaces lent a definite shape to the American Southwest, Southeast, and Midwest before the arrival of the Spanish, French, and English. Were it not for the historical contrasts between those subcontinental areas, in their final centuries, and the American Northeast, one might conclude that such centralization was the natural culmination of societal evolution. But the Northeast puts the lie to that conclusion.

Anthropologists and historians there speak not of complex polities, ceremonial centers, or regional cultures. Indeed, over the course of the continent's final indigenous millennium, roughly 500 to 1600 CE, government in the Northeast emerged without great planned central sites, a significant contrast to, say, the Southwest or Southeast. What's more, there were no expansive Puebloan- or Mississippian-style horizons in the Northeast. And, unlike what we will see in the far west (Chapter 13), there were no great trade networks or class stratification in the Northeast. The minimally centralized confederacies that did form there were built from "sachemdoms" and "tribes" (Salwen 1978; Simmons 1978).

What are we to make of these divergences? And what were the larger historical consequences? Answers to these questions, based on northeastern indigenous history, tell us something unique about the causes and effects of human history generally. Big historical contingencies matter much more than any supposed societal-developmental generalities. To see how, we begin at the end.

Historic Introductions

In 1621, the great sachem (a.k.a. Massasoit) of the Wapanoag Confederacy, Ousamequin, was justifiably wary of the Europeans who had been coming and going along the New England coastline. His position as leader, while hereditary, was always tenuous (Figure 12.1). For starters, the powerful Narragansett Confederacy was located just to the west, across Narragansett Bay. Moreover, he – like other Algonkian sachems – had to look out for the best interests of all the inhabitants of his dominion. Massasoit's authority, that is, rested on how well he personified the relationships between the various forces and beings of and on the earth.

Massasoit's people and their neighbors spoke Algonkian dialects and cultivated maize, beans, sunflowers, and squash like many others in the Northeast at the time. They hunted wild game and fished the rivers and the coasts. They stored up foodstuffs in subterranean pits against the prospects of harsh New England winters. They lived in scattered hamlets and small villages composed of clusters of oval, single-set-post wigwams. Several such settlements might comprise a community, though one's identity was always tethered in some way to one's natal settlement. Community wellbeing depended on successful hunting seasons, productive gardens, and peaceful relations with neighbors.

Fig 12.1 Massasoit visits the pilgrims (www.flickr.com). Library of Congress, Washington, DC.

But now, foreign intruders who arrived in large wooden ships offshore had plundered the food stores of coastal villages and were occupying Wapanoag land (Washburn 1978). Massasoit first greeted them in March of 1621, wearing shell beads and face paint, at the head of a mass of several dozen warriors, all standing atop a hill overlooking the colony of Plymouth (Adams 1933). In league with an allied Abenaki sachem from modern-day Maine (named Samoset), Massasoit directed Squanto to intercede. Peace and order seem to have been Massasoit's goal, and Squanto was the perfect operative. After all, Squanto had been captured by the English and taken abroad years earlier. He was eventually able to return to native New England and, now, spoke both English and his Algonkian dialect. Squanto also intimately identified with the location being occupied by the foreigners, which happened to be his original homeland. At the behest of Massasoit, we presume, Squanto stayed behind after the great sachem and nearly 100 of his people left the harvest festival in October of that year, hosted with prayerful solemnity by the 50-plus English survivors of the colony's first year (Philbrick 2006). Roasted wild turkey, venison, corn bread, and pumpkin soup, among other local victuals, had probably all been on the menu of that first Thanksgiving. These had either been procured from the interior New England-Acadian oak, spruce, and pine forests, lakes, marshlands, and coastal areas of New England, or grown in the shallow rocky soils of the many garden plots around Wapanoag settlements.

There was a limit to how much the thin soils could produce. In New England, rocks are everywhere. Many are cobbles translocated from the Canadian interior or the nearby Appalachian Mountain ranges tens of thousands of years earlier by Pleistocene-era glaciers. Bedrock is also exposed on the surface in places and in the nearby mountain ranges locally known as the Taconics, Berkshires/Green Mountains, and White Mountains. These ranges parallel each other in a north–south direction through modern-day eastern New York, Connecticut–Massachusetts–Vermont, and New Hampshire–Maine–New Brunswick, respectively. The Hudson Valley is a large north–south trough to the west of the Taconic and Green mountains, with the immense Lake Champlain at its northern end. It separates New England from the interior of New York and the Iroquoian homeland (Figure 12.2).

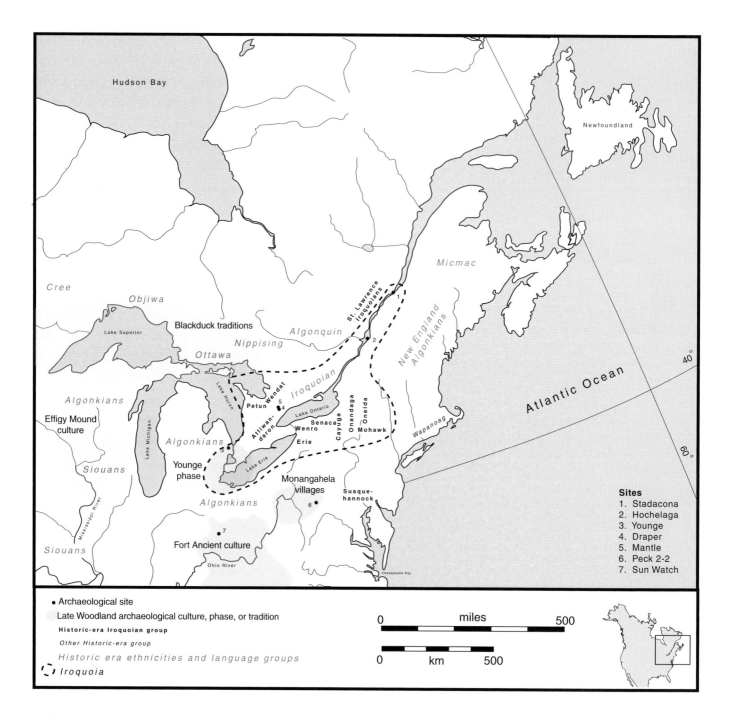

Fig 12.2 Map of the Northeast showing major Late Woodland and early historic era cultural complexes. Timothy R. Pauketat map.

West of Lake Champlain are the dome-shaped Adirondack Mountains, heavily glaciated and used by the Mohawk historically as a hunting territory. South of the Adirondacks, the Hudson's main tributary from the west, the Mohawk River, provides access into the Great Lakes drainage and the great interior lands to the west. Here were "the communication routes of the Iroquois and of their neighbors. They were the Indians' corridors of trade, war, and peace … The Iroquois were strategically located to exploit the geopolitics of the region" (Fenton 1978:297). South of the Mohawk River in New York State and northern Pennsylvania are the heavily forested Catskills, Poconoes, and the "southern tier," the last being the northern fringe of Pennsylvania's Appalachian Plateau. The Finger Lakes between these highlands and Lake Ontario were the homeland of Iroquoian-speaking peoples. These included the Attiwandaron (a.k.a. Neutral), Erie, Petun, Susquehannock, Wendat (a.k.a. Huron), Wenro, and other St. Lawrence Iroquoians, and also (from west to east) the Seneca, Cayuga, Onondaga, Oneida, and Mohawk who would unify in the 1600s as the Five Nations of the Haudenosaunee (adding the Tuscarora from eastern Carolina later as a sixth nation).

Owing to the communicative potential of this corridor, Iroquoian- and even Cree-speaking peoples of New York, Quebec, and Ontario to the north and west were fully aware of the English by 1621. Indeed,

Sidebar 12.1 Lakes

Across New England and into Ontario, Quebec, and New Brunswick, the horizons are dominated by trees and hills interspersed with marshes and lakes. The Laurentide ice sheet had scoured the Northeast during the Pleistocene, leaving flat plains in areas around the St. Lawrence River and allowing large pre-Columbian settlements occupied by St. Lawrence Iroquoians to flourish there (and, later, the cities of Montreal, Toronto, and Quebec City). Beyond the great dome of rock known as the Adirondack Mountains, the ice had gouged out the Lake Ontario basin and rode over the Niagara Escarpment, a great ledge of sedimentary rock that cuts across New York State into Ontario, where the water pouring over it led to one of earth's natural wonders: Niagara Falls. In Google Earth, search for "Niagara Falls" and enter street view for closeups. Past the escarpment, glacial ice radiated southward into the rocky highlands to the south (New York State's "southern tier"). In so doing, the ice was channeled into linear glaciers, gouging great U-shaped valleys that later filled with water: the famous "Finger Lakes" of New York. In Google Earth, search for them. Compare their shape with that of other glacial scars filled with water to the north: the great "Lake Champlain," and the thousands of random-shaped lakes in Maine, Nova Scotia, and Quebec. Then search for "Lac Manicouagan." Though it had been covered in glacial ice, it was not originally a glacial lake but a late Triassic-era asteroid impact crater some 214 million years ago (see https://en.wikipedia.org/wiki/Manicouagan_crater)!

the native Quebecois and Ontarians had already allied themselves with the French against them. Jacques Cartier had navigated his ships up the St. Lawrence River in 1535, and he was followed by others including Samuel Champlain in 1603. With the aid of the missionaries of an all-male Catholic order known as the Jesuits (Thwaites 1898), founded in 1540, Champlain established lasting alliances with the Montagnais, who were unconsolidated semisedentary foragers occupying the northern lands of the Northeast's Acadian oak, spruce, and pine forest. He did the same with the St. Lawrence Iroquoians, who were sedentary horticultural peoples to the south, even founding Quebec City on the site of the proto-Wendat (or Huron) village of Stadacona.

Since before the arrival of Cartier, the Montagnais, Wendat, and other St. Lawrence Iroquoians were the mortal enemies of the Five Nations of the Haudenosaunee Confederacy of southern Ontario and New York State, sometimes generically known as the Iroquois. Champlain exploited this rift, and waged war against the Haudenosaunee, especially the Mohawk to the east. One of the largest settlements seen by Cartier was a St. Lawrence Iroquoian longhouse town called Hochelaga, the future site of Montreal. It boasted a human population of at least 1,000 and possibly more, aggregated in part for safety and protected by a circumferential palisade wall. The Five Nations of the Haudenosaunee – the Cayuga, Mohawk, Oneida, Onondaga, and Seneca – targeted Hochelaga, among other northern villages, into the 1600s. Inevitably, this led to village abandonments and population relocations. The *coup de grâce* of such attacks came in 1649, when 1,000 Haudenosaunee warriors attacked Wendat and related settlements, forcing their inhabitants to scatter as refugees. Through such military campaigns, the Haudenosaunee became a powerful nation that, oddly, lacked a permanent political capital.

The Haudenosaunee made similar attacks elsewhere, with the dynamics of intra-village, inter-ethnic, and Indian–European contacts of the time portrayed effectively in the 1991 film *Black Robe*, filmed in part around one of Quebec's natural wonders: Lac Manicouagan (https://en.wikipedia.org/wiki/Black_Robe_(film)). One famous Haudenosaunee campaign was witnessed and recorded by French operative Henri de Tonti to the west in Illinois country in 1680. To get to central Illinois, the raiders had to paddle some 400 km across Lake Erie and then walk the same distance or more to their destination. Their raid led to the killing or capturing of some 800 members of the Illini Confederacy. Some captive women and children were marched and canoed back to New York, tethered together with leather straps and captive collars. Others were burned at the stake or killed outright on site, their unburied skeletonized remains evident on the ground for years thereafter.

How had it come to this? What were the motivations for such attacks? Was it their worldview or ontology (a way of relating to life and death), their "tribal" organization, or their geopolitical position (a way of relating to the French and English)? Should our explanations of this unusual history consider the history-altering qualities of the maize plant, intensified 600 years before Champlain, or perhaps the formation of the "village" itself? What about the historically known cult-like fascination with a team sport later dubbed "lacrosse"? Answers are to be found only by gaining a better historical perspective. That perspective comes in part by looking deeper into the social history of the Northeast's earlier centuries.

Late Woodland Transformations in the Northeast

Like so many people across the Eastern Woodlands and into the Plains 2,000 years ago, the hunting-foraging-gardening people of the St. Lawrence River valley from New York and Ontario up through northern Vermont, New Hampshire, New Brunswick, Maine, and Quebec had also been pulled into the mysterious Middle Woodland-era Hopewellian phenomenon that was flourishing in the Ohio River valley up until the 400s CE (see Chapter 9). Along the St. Lawrence, a watered-down Hopewellian phenomenon nevertheless involved more than just burial mounds or beliefs about the dead. It somehow extended into the realm of the everyday, with cooking pots zoned and decorated using familiar rows of punctates, rocker and dentate stamping, and cord-wrapped stick impressions (Chapdelaine 2012). Such stylistic and technological pottery changes had infiltrated New England as well, where archaeologist Elizabeth Chilton (2012:266) interprets them as signaling an "expanding … subsistence base." Along with pottery, she observes a greater visibility of sites during this time as evidence of increased human settlement sizes.

Of course, such enlarged subsistence bases and increased settlement sizes would have played out as an altered if not enlarged field of relations between people, plants, earth, and the various beings or spirits seen and unseen entangled along the paths trod by people moving between fields, rivers, and home. As with all pre-Columbian North Americans, northeastern people had animistic sensibilities. Hopewellian animism was different, of course, and possibly involved a greater religiosity in everyday life, enhanced peaceful engagements with neighbors, and influential shamans, priests, or prophets (see Chapter 9). Whatever the case, the Hopewellian legacy lasted longer along the St. Lawrence and in New England – until around 1000 CE – than it did in the Midwest. Possibly, this was because it was less politicized than its Ohio Valley neighbors, which is to say less attached to enormous central sites where would-be prophets and leaders might perform their visions for would-be followers in ways that, contingent on the followers following, produced great historical effects. On the other hand, possibly, the resilient Middle Woodland era in the Northeast indicates that there were unique qualities to these local cultures yet to be appreciated.

In the St. Lawrence drainage, especially southern Ontario and New York, archaeologists identify the usually small habitation areas and modest burial mounds dating to this period as the "Point Peninsula culture" (Fitting 1978). This vague category grades into or overlaps with the Laurel tradition or the Lake Forest Middle Woodland cultures of the northern spruce forests of the Canadian Shield (see also Chapter 11). There, Late Woodland-era Black Duck culture lived at the very edge of the Plains in southern Manitoba. These likely Algonkian-speaking peoples, who included the proto-Ojibwa, were the heirs to the Laurel tradition of the Middle Woodland era, the latter mostly living in the boreal forest zone of Manitoba, Saskatchewan, Minnesota, and northern Michigan. The descendant Black Duck people would engage in Plains bison hunts during the summer and fish in lakes during the spring and fall. Late summer would see the wild rice harvest, still conducted by Ojibwa people today (www.youtube.com/watch?v=X8R1p9mMq_I).

The autumn would then see aggregations of people and a move into the sheltered valleys of the upland forests to the north (Graham 2005). During the Proto-Historic era, Midéwiwin ceremonialism swept the Cree, Menominee, Ojibwa, Ottawa, and Pottawatomie of the region (see Chapter 8); red painted pictographs still seen in the Boundary Waters Canoe Area and Quetico Provincial Park in

Minnesota and Ontario, respectively, show scenes of Midéwiwin lodges and healing rites along with bears and other spirit beings (Weeks 2012). The landscape of the region is characterized by a myriad of irregularly shaped lakes that drain into one another via rapids and waterfalls. Scraped down to the granite basement rocks by Ice Age glaciers, the thin soils are covered in coniferous forests, brush, and blueberry bushes, providing food, cover, and lodging materials for moose, elk, bear, and beaver. Zoom into the wilderness on Google Earth by entering "Quetico Provincial Park."

The so-called Point Peninsula culture also grades into the "Western Basin" tradition sites in southeastern lower Michigan, which archaeologist David Stothers (1975; Stothers and Graves 1983) understood to have been a precursor to the early "Younge phase" Iroquoian villagers who, in later centuries, occupied that portion of the state around the modern-day cities of Flint and Detroit. A principal attribute of all such Middle Woodland sites – and an oft-unstated characteristic of the era generally (which would change soon) – was the lack of large, sedentary domestic settlements. The difficulty of archaeologists to even identify prominent residential sites in Canada ends when we enter the Late Woodland period. The Late Woodland villages of dozens to hundreds of people, that is, were in no way natural or inconsequential societal developments. They formed for reasons not present in the Middle Woodland era, and had implications, as we shall see (Table 12.1).

In the Northeast, the end of the Middle Woodland era and the beginning of the Late Woodland period correspond rather closely to the intensification of maize horticulture, beginning around the year 1000 CE. Of course, this may not have been the earliest maize in the region, since archaeologist John Hart and associates (2003, 2007) have argued, based on the presence of maize phytoliths in the kitchen middens of Middle Woodland settlements in New York State, that the plant had been cultivated in some places off and on since 200 BCE. Then again, this is controversial, and the "macro-botanical" remains of maize kernels and cobs themselves, recovered from domestic deposits, are known only after 1000 CE. This means that, for all intents and purposes, American Indian people in the Northeast came to rely on the plant as a foodstuff only during the time period we know as the Late Woodland era (500/1000–1600 CE).

Table 12.1 Chronological highlights of the Late Woodland era in the St. Lawrence, upper Ohio, and New England regions (adapted from Birch and Williamson 2013; Chapdelaine 2012; Chilton 2012; Fitting 1978; Means 2012; Snow 1978; Stothers 1975; Williamson 2012).

Year CE	Historic period	Cultural patterns
500s	Middle/Late Woodland	Point Peninsula complex in St. Lawrence River valley; Lake Forest/Laurel traditions in Quebec and Ontario; Riviere aux Vases Late Woodland in southeastern Michigan.
700		Bow and arrow adopted.
1000s	Late Woodland	Villages consolidate. Adoption or intensification of "Northern Flint" maize horticulture; proto-Iroquoian Owasco and Princess Point cultures in New York and Ontario; Younge phase in southeastern Michigan; Monongahela and Fort Ancient traditions in the upper Ohio Valley.
1200		Younge tradition Springwells phase in southeastern Michigan and northwestern Ohio.
1300s		St. Lawrence Iroquoian population expansion, peaks in the 1400s. Enlargement of longhouses. Increased sexual division of labor. Appearance of sweat lodges and ossuary burials.
1500s	Proto-Historic	First appearance of European metals and objects.
1550s–1600		Village amalgamations and abandonment of lower St. Lawrence. Increased access to European materials.
1600–1650	Historic	Regional confederations; reduction and displacement of other groups.

Given insufficient samples, the details of the transregional history of maize intensification – who grew it first and how it was distributed, stored, and prepared – are unknown. Thus, the question also remains as to whether the intensification of maize at 1000 CE was more of a cause or a consequence of social change (Tuck 1978:325). Presumably, either something led people to produce more food or, as argued in the case of Alabama Mississippian history (Chapter 14), the sweet taste of maize had lulled people into its sticky web. In the latter case, if maize itself significantly altered the ways – culinary habits, daily routine, annual scheduling of activities, spiritual associations of the plant and its needs – in which people experienced the world, then why would it have led to political and ethnic confederations in the Northeast unlike those of other continental areas in which it was grown: the Southeast, Midwest, Southwest, and Mexico (see Chapters 10, 14–15)?

The answer, for some archaeologists and paleoethnobotanists – usually from an economic or subsistence-based perspective – is that maize did *not* have revolutionary historical effects. In New England, this conclusion is based on empirical grounds. Archaeological evidence suggests that "mobile farmers" in the interior merely "tacked on" maize as one of several cultigens. Moreover, that same evidence argues that maize "did not become a staple food until after European colonization" (Chilton 2012:269). Generally speaking, the Late Woodland people of New England relied much more heavily on foraged wild plants and animals, including shellfish from coastal waters. In addition, judging from historical-linguistic and archaeological evidence, upstream and downstream communities depended upon one another in ways that formed the basis of multi-settlement, tribal alliances. Their settlements were small, consisting of oval wigwam-style bark-covered huts in the north (modern-day New Brunswick and Newfoundland), intended for small families, and those in the south (New England) "large enough to accommodate extended family groups" but not as large as Iroquoian longhouses to the west (Snow 1978:58). Their pottery was distinctive, similar to Iroquoian wares in its conoidal shape, collared rims, prominent castellations, and effigy appliques. The pots' vertical dualism (upper geometrically incised collar clearly separated from a lower body) and the quadri-partitioned collar itself, sometimes featuring inset maize and anthropomorphic characters, are suggestive of the pot's role as mediator between heavenly and earthly realms (Figure 12.3).

The relationship between maize and social change in the St. Lawrence River valley is clearer, though alternative readings of the history of maize and the origins of Iroquoian populations are possible. Many have suggested some sort of cultural intrusion, in part because the transition to maize-gardening village life was relatively abrupt. Moreover, Iroquoian languages are, in fact, related to Cherokee and

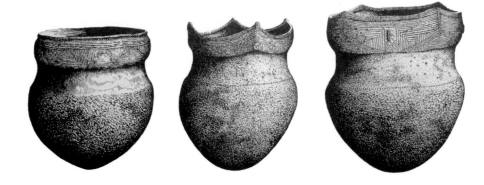

Fig 12.3 New England Late Woodland pots (Fowler 1966: figure 18). Used with the permission of the Massachusetts Archaeological Society.

Sidebar 12.2 Green corn and Mesoamericanoid trappings in New York?

Since at least the 1800s, Iroquoian-speaking peoples practiced a more than week-long Green Corn ceremony similar to those of other native North Americans from the Southeast to Mexico (Witthoft 1949). They also possessed a Corn Mother story, as did the Narragansett, Rhode Island's Algonkian-speaking neighbors to the Wapanoags. Iroquoian groups even possessed accounts of Hero Twins remarkably similar to those known from Mesoamerica into the Plains and Midwest.

According to the usual Iroquois version, maize grew from the body of the woman who gave birth to the Creator and his evil-minded twin. This Corn Mother, in turn, was the daughter of a pregnant woman who was let down from heaven, and for whom the earth was formed by the animals (the earth-diver story). The Corn Mother was impregnated by a man from the heavens, who … laid a sharp arrow and a blunt arrow on her body, these forming the good and bad brothers. When the twins were ready to be born, the evil-minded one went in the direction of a beam of light, so killing his mother, but the Creator was born naturally. The maize sprang from her body. Flint, the evil-minded brother,

and the Creator grew up together, always engaged in struggle. The Creator made man and many useful animals and plants; Flint made carnivorous animals and enemies to man. Finally, the Creator overcame his brother (in the bowl game, according to some variants), and thus ensured the continuance of man and his world.

(Witthoft 1949:80–81)

The age and origins of the Green Corn ceremony – which involved various gendered dances, recitations, and the celebration of the first ripe maize – and the Corn Mother and Hero-Twin narratives are unclear. Did they accompany the first maize into the Northeast, or were they tacked on later? If later, perhaps Iroquoian prophetic leaders, from Hiawatha to Handsome Lake, borrowed the practices and narratives from the Tuscarora, Cherokee, or other southern Mississippians as they reinvented Haudenosaunee culture and confederated the Iroquois into a larger league. Either way, the tight associations would seem to constitute evidence of the ways in which maize was bundled with other cultural associations that would affect historical development locally.

Tuscarora in south Appalachia, the latter confederating with the Haudenosaunee after the early 1700s Tuscarora War (Lounsbury 1978). Thus, historical linguistics would seem to suggest some kind of infiltration of outside people or proto-Iroquoian language into New York and Ontario before 1000 CE, as do genetic studies (Williamson 2012). However, Dean Snow's (1995) argument for a first-millennium CE mass migration of Iroquoian speakers into the Northeast is doubted by many. Instead, most argue for a less-simplistic scenario in which Algonkian and Iroquoian populations become amalgamated in the centuries leading up to 1000 CE (Engelbrecht 2003).

Villagizing the Past

Clearly, not only is leadership an insufficient explanation of northeastern historical development, so are maize and migration by themselves. History is more complex. After all, the impetus for change around the year 1000 CE did not affect only Iroquoia or New England. It radiated in all directions (see Chapters 10–11). For such reasons, archaeologists have also looked to other globalizing explanations. These have included big-historical models, where the intensification of maize and the development of Mississippian civilization are asserted to have had domino effects on non-Mississippians up into New York State (Dincauze and Hasenstab 1989). And they have also included climatic models, where the Medieval Warm Period is assumed to have forced social change upon all peoples across North America.

As a matter of principle, our understanding of the relationships between all of the variables (maize, migration, climate, contacts, etc.), even if climate is a culprit, must remain historical – which is to say appreciative of the contingencies: the material and experiential bases of social history and the wide-ranging engagement by people with other people across great distances (à la Chapter 3). The most powerful if often overlooked elements of the causes of northeastern history involve villages themselves. We see such village-related changes around 1000 CE to the south of New York's southern tier into western Pennsylvania, where archaeologists identify the Monongahela culture (Means 2007, 2012). Here, in the Ohio River drainage where the Allegheny and Monongahela rivers meet, around modern-day Pittsburgh, Pennsylvania, lie a series of circular or arc-shaped villages. Some have open plazas and circumferential palisade walls. The site known as the Peck 2–2 village featured large circular dwellings and intervening arcs of other smaller circular dwellings (Figure 12.4). In explaining them, archaeologist Bernard Means (2012) recognizes that the villages themselves caused specific forms of community and kin-group organization, in turn entangled with the history of maize if not also the history of interregional violence and fear. Building a wall, for instance, imparts exclusivity to a community that was, in turn, destined to affect people's identities and actions.

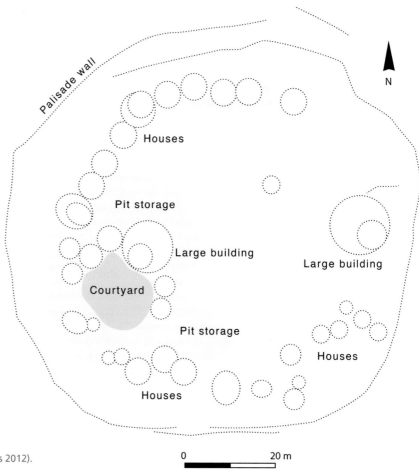

Fig 12.4 Monongahela village site (adapted from Means 2012).

With regard to the latter, it is important to note that downriver from the Monongahela people were the "Fort Ancient" culture farmers, a Mississippian-influenced Algonkian people. The "Fort Ancient" villages had also developed, it seems, as part of the maize-related social changes of the times, especially as these emanated from sources along the Mississippi River (Chapter 10). The Fort Ancient villages consisted of one or two dozen rectangular houses around an open courtyard, increasingly palisaded through time (Figure 12.5). The well-known Sun Watch site near Dayton, Ohio, today the scene of contemporary community and Native American engagement (as any Google search demonstrates), was just one of scores of large Fort Ancient culture settlements. As shown by archaeologist Robert Cook, these are now known to have incorporated nonlocal Mississippians into their otherwise Late Woodland and likely Algonkian-type social fabric (Cook 2008).

Fig 12.5 Sun Watch village, partial reconstruction, 2006. Wikimedia.

Upriver from the Monongahela people, of course, were Iroquoian-speaking populations, simultaneously undergoing their own village consolidations. The earliest peoples identifiable as Iroquoian forager-farmers date as early as 900 CE, plus or minus a century (Tuck 1978), and may be presumed to have had some kind of causal effects on those who would become Monongahela people, among others. "In both Ontario and New York, villages of this period seem to have consisted of unwalled clusters of round and/or oblong houses, implying some permanence of settlement" (Tuck 1978:326). Shortly thereafter, new village sites were founded on higher, defendable ground and were also enclosed by palisade walls (Wright 1966). Single-set-post homes were also expanded, becoming increasingly lengthy, with multiple partitions indicating the presence of multiple families comprising single extended families. Archaeologist Ronald Williamson (2012:278) summarizes the cascade of changes that followed:

Toward the end of the 13th century, small communities amalgamated to form larger villages of approximately 1.5 hectares (three acres) in extent, with twice the population of the earlier base settlements. With this development came widespread similarities in pottery and smoking pipe styles that point to an increasing level of intercommunity communication and integration ... The hamlets and camps of the previous centuries were to a large degree replaced by agricultural cabin sites, which were situated within the vast agricultural fields that surrounded the major villages. These changes in settlement-subsistence patterns probably related to the need to produce more maize for more people in one place.

This was also when maize consumption peaked, at least in some localities. Detailed isotope analysis of human remains from the ca. AD 1300 ancestral Wendat Moatfield ossuary, located approximately five kilometers north of Lake Ontario in the city of Toronto, indicates that for at least one generation maize comprised 70 percent of the diet. Such intensified cultivation may have been a necessary, temporary response to increased population concentration within a newly amalgamated settlement …

At the height of St. Lawrence Iroquoian development, in the 1400s, great villages of hundreds of people occupied key defensive locations along the north shore of Lake Ontario. These villages were often allied with each other, the mollusk-shell beaded "wampum" belts gifted from one group to another signifying such an alliance. (European attempts to treat wampum as a kind of money ultimately led to the collapse of wampum exchange.) Inter-village alliances became tribal and national alliances as one scaled them up, and scaling up the alliance structure enabled populations of regions to grow. The population density of southern Ontario alone was some 24,000 people (Birch and Williamson 2013). More Iroquoian speakers lived down the St. Lawrence and on the New York side of Lake Ontario. Even more lived in southeastern Michigan, south of Lake Huron, and at the far western end of Lake Erie (Stothers 1975). Like those in Ontario, the Michigan branch of Iroquoians were, by the 1300s CE, building longhouses, smoking tobacco from Iroquoian pipes, cultivating maize, engaging in Iroquoian-style reburial and modification of skulls, and making Iroquoian-style pots. At the type site of the "Younge phase," two longhouses sat isolated, each one on a hill, as if each building was its own distinct settlement (Figure 12.6). One was about 10 m wide and 83 m long. Another was 192 m long (Greenman 1967); 100 people could have lived inside (Figure 12.7).

Canadian archaeologists have devoted significant energy to excavating the longhouses of larger villages north of Lake Ontario in their entirety, providing unique glimpses into detailed domestic, communal, and regional histories in the region sometimes called Huronia. One of these sites, Draper, consisted of a walled area (rebuilt repeatedly) covering 3.4 ha and enclosing several longhouses at any one time (Figure 12.8). The arrangement of the longhouses, along with the varieties of pottery around them, suggested to archaeologists that the

Fig 12.6 Reconstructed Huron longhouse (for the film *Black Robe*), Saint-Félix-d'Otis, Quebec, Canada. Wikimedia.

occupants had coalesced at Draper from multiple natal settlements, which is to say the places where people were born. Such coalescent moves produced hybrid communities, comprising people from multiple different backgrounds. This hybridity is evident in the broken pots lying about in this and other village middens, where one finds broken cooking wares "reminiscent of St. Lawrence Iroquoian, New York Iroquois, or Attiwandaron [a.k.a. Neutral Confederacy] types" (Williamson 2012:281).

Fig 12.7 Draper site house 6 plan: note that the building walls and interior posts and pits were rebuilt and replaced through time (adapted from Finlayson 1985: figure 34).

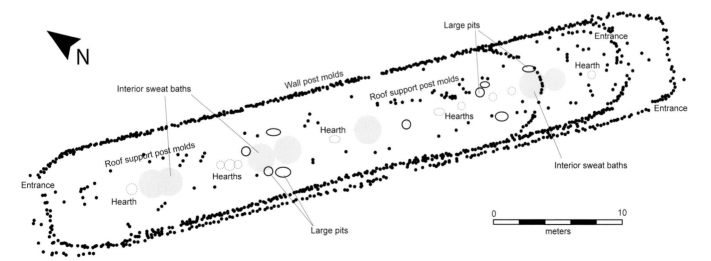

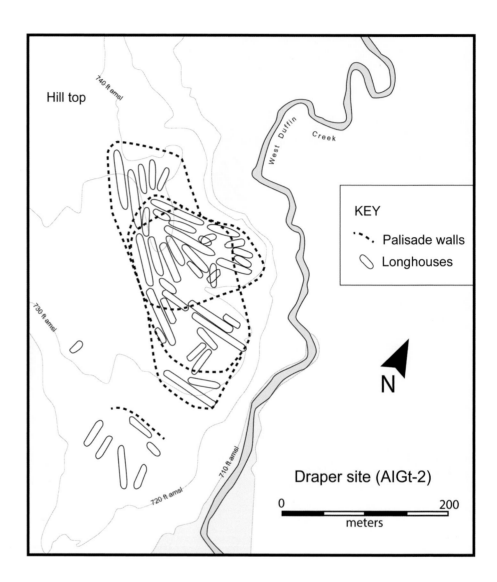

Fig 12.8 Draper site village plan: note that the village palisade was rebuilt multiple times (adapted from Finlayson 1985: figure 3).

That hybridity is also evident in the rise of great "Feast of the Dead" ceremonies, evident early on among the proto-Wendat in ossuary burials. Such ossuaries contained the remains of many mourned dead, the bodies of whom would be curated until the year and day that the great ceremony was held (Figure 12.9). Also in the midden around the buildings of Iroquoian villages here and at other such fifteenth- and sixteenth-century sites were scattered unarticulated bits of human bone (Birch and Williamson 2013; Finlayson 1985). Most are from human crania, and attest to the historically known practices of warfare, enemy capture, and sacrifice. In contemporary sites in other regions of the continent, archaeologists find no pieces of human bone, indicating the great differences between them and the Ontario Iroquoians.

Fig 12.9 Huron Feast of the Dead as witnessed by Father Jean de Brébeuf in 1636. Wikimedia.

The early sixteenth-century successor village to Draper, the Mantle site, was located only 5 km upstream, the implication being that Draper's residents regrouped at Mantle immediately after leaving their former home. Here, a palisade wall enclosed an area of 4.2 ha. Within the settlement's bounds were up to 40 longhouses at any one time, many oriented toward a town plaza, and all rebuilt at one time or another as new people moved in, older ones passed away or moved out, and the settlement reinforced. Like Draper, the Mantle site was

Sidebar 12.3 Spirit capture, adoption, and reincarnation

As in other North American cultures, Iroquoian peoples understood there to be two souls in any human being. One was the "animating soul" and was contained in a person's bones. Another was an intellectual soul and was contained in the head (Hewitt 1894). The first soul would stay with the bones. The second could be released and sent on its way to the spirit world. Perforating skulls or cutting out cranial sections, as seen at the Younge site in Michigan or at Draper and Mantle in Ontario, was a way of "releasing" the soul. This accounts for Iroquoian motivations in executing captives and their treatment of the dead as part of great Feast of the Dead celebrations.

In warfare, the "death of an important person" in the Iroquoian world demanded

a community response in proportion to the degree to which the person's death … disrupted the community … Another kind of response to death was to take to the warpath … Taking the life of an enemy never served purely to indulge a warrior in the self-ish satisfaction of blood revenge. It was widely believed necessary to obtain the spirit of an enemy as a servant for the mourned

kinsman while on the spirit trail [i.e., the journey into the after-life]. It was also widely believed that a spirit freed by death could not rest until someone had been adopted to replace its loss, often taking the name of the deceased … The person adopted did not have to be a member of the tribe of the deceased, so warfare for the purpose of taking captives was sometimes a part of the mourning process.

(Hall 1997:32)

Captives not adopted into the community were executed. "These were often subjected to prolonged and agonizing forms of torture. Examples on record typically involved burning coals, red-hot iron, and such other cruelties as fancy and opportunity suggested, ending with the victim's death and not infrequently with a feast in which the captive was eaten" (Hall 1997:32). By the same token, the spirit of a person might reinhabit another human being, much the way the second soul of a dead Attiwandaron sachem was witnessed by a Jesuit priest in the early 1700s to enter the body of his successor (Hall 1997:35).

inhabited for only 25 to 30 years, or about one-and-a-half human generations. Yet, archaeologically, the site is a palimpsest of rebuilt longhouses with hundreds of postmolds in rows (Figure 12.10). This was a planned settlement, as the longhouse orientation and midden areas reveal. Large middens appear to have been located with respect to the placement of buildings and palisade wall, the largest being a communal dump beyond the wall. There is also evidence of some pottery-making specialization, presumably a function of the organizations that came about because of the complexities of social life inside this specific Iroquoian settlement (Birch and Williamson 2013).

Interfaces of History

If villages were causal in pre-Columbian northeastern history, then longhouses were causal in a more intimate way, educating, clothing, disciplining, and enculturating the human bodies who resided therein with the lessons of what it meant to be Attiwandaron,

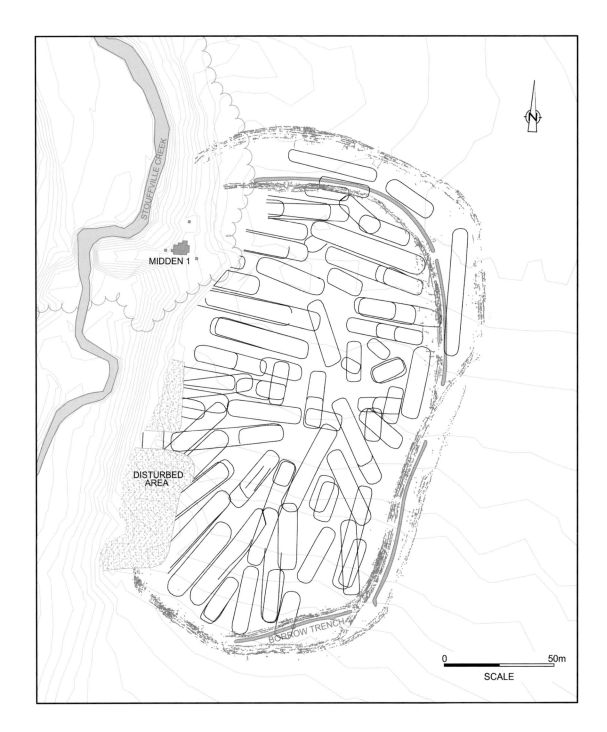

Fig 12.10 Mantle site village plan: ovals are longhouse constructions surrounded by both palisade walls and ditches (from Williamson 2012: figure 23.3). Courtesy of Archaeological Services, Inc.

Cayuga, Erie, Mohawk, Onondaga, Oneida, Petun, Seneca, Wendat, and Wenro. A longhouse was a great arbor-roofed structure entered from the ends or sides and divided into multiple rooms, each with its own hearth, beds, and storage. Though partitioned, one could and in some cases must have entered or exited one's immediate family room via the rooms of other families. Even if you were not related by

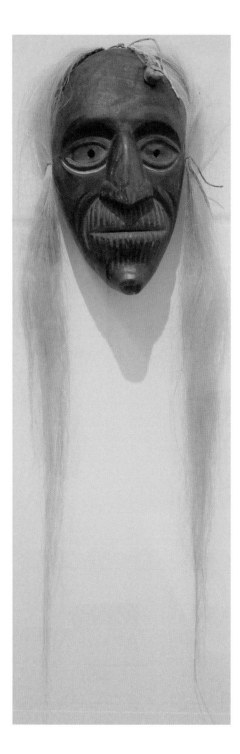

Fig 12.11 False Face Society mask, Seneca, late nineteenth to early twentieth century, Honolulu Museum of Art, Accession 5057.4. Wikimedia.

blood in the first place, such a daily trek through the intimate areas of other nuclear families would have engendered a sense of relating to everyone as one big family. Such extended families, lineages, or clans would have eaten together, communed as a group, worked together, and warred together. The longhouse truly was simultaneously a household, an extended kin group, and a community. In fact, the longhouse itself was a metaphor that defined in the historic era the unified Haudenosaunee. Any Iroquoian sense of self or personhood, whether local or national, was tethered to the longhouse (Creese 2012).

The materiality of the building and its nonhuman contents was also an integral part of the longhouse way-of-being, or ontology. Wood and trees, for instance, held a special place in Iroquoian life, a great mythical tree being central to the Iroquoian cosmos (Hewitt 1903; Parker 1989). Members of various "Medicine Mask Societies," sodalities within communities that included the "False Face Society," wore wooden masks and used turtle rattles to perform healing rituals for the community (Figure 12.11). The mask itself possessed an animate spirit owing in part to its relationship to the lifeforce of the world tree, red and black paint, and the sun. The same is true today, and the Haudenosaunee maintain a strict policy regarding the manufacture, circulation, and display of these items (www.indiantime .net/story/2009/06/18/cultural-corner/haudenosaunee-confederacy-policy-on-false-face-masks/2564.html).

Faces and disembodied heads were powerful images that animated other aspects of Iroquoian life. On pots, they appear in modeled clay under or as part of the vessel's collar or thickened upper rim (Figure 12.12). Like the masks, these are not human depictions but anthropomorphic spirits and gods that infuse the pot and its contents with vitality. Such nonhuman beings comprised a kind of polytheistic pantheon (not quite the equivalent of "totemism" because individual Iroquoian clans are not rigidly connected to specific spirits). Along with a transformative life force that Iroquoian speakers call Orenda, the spirits "pervade all nature and affect man for good or evil." Indeed, like people, "good spirits are constantly making war upon evil spirits" (Parker 1989:3). Human beings, such as the members of the False Face Society, might channel Orenda and thereby embody spiritual powers, enabling them to engage in healing rites and other ritual intercessions on behalf of the community.

Fig 12.12 Mythical faces on potsherds, each 2–3 cm in width. Annual Report of the Bureau of American Ethnology, 1895. US Government Printing Office, Washington, DC.

Such life forces and deities infused Iroquoian gaming as well. Popular games, with supernatural underpinnings, included the bowl (or platter) game, which consisted of tossing zoomorphic, painted, or abstract dice-like game pieces into the air from a wooden bowl into which they would be caught. One scored points depending on the position of the gaming pieces. The game was played to help cure illness. It also led to gambling.

Team sports were played for reasons that exceeded the physical exhilaration of the game. Of these games, lacrosse may have had profound history-making effects owing in part to its spiritual foundations. After his arrival in Quebec among the Wendat in 1625, French Jesuit missionary Father Jean de Brébeuf "complained that the Huron [Wendat] resorted to sorcerers [shamans] for divination when someone was ill. Among their cures were feasts, dances, and games … Of these, lacrosse seemed the most powerful …" (Vennum 1994:13). Even today, lacrosse or *dehuntshigwa'es* among the Onondaga, which they consider to be "the Creator's game," is played to strengthen body and mind and "to heal the sick" (Vennum 1994:7). Originally, opposing teams included dozens to hundreds of players, each of whom held one or two wooden lacrosse sticks to catch and toss the rawhide or wooden balls (Figure 12.13). These balls, in turn, were metaphors for the flying heads of deities, which included a wind or storm god with long flowing hair.

Given the integral relationship of players, balls, disembodied heads, and healing, Iroquoian villagers were highly motivated to play lacrosse, bowl, and other games. Their community wellbeing depended on it. Moreover, team play – happening in a specially designated and prepared field and involving most able-bodied, male community members – was related to warring. Lacrosse, for instance, was also called the "Little Brother of War" by some (Vennum 1994). Playing it might avert or lead to war and, hence, directly influence a community's physiological and emotional wellbeing, if not also its social or political history. In terms of its history-making effects, consider too that children, inculcated from their youth in the game, were thereby also educated in the ways of warfare as a basis of social life. And, as warfare and enemy capture, adoption, and killing were sacred acts, so the lacrosse game itself must be credited to some degree with having a religious power.

We presume that one or more members of some unknown Iroquoian village invented or reinvented the game as early as the 1000s or, more likely, as part of the crescendo of population aggregation, hybridity, and intercommunity violence in the 1300s–1500s. Of course, from there, lacrosse or stickball, as it is also known, swept the Eastern Woodlands, supplanting the Cahokia-Mississippian game

Fig 12.13 Native stickball or lacrosse players. George Catlin painting, Smithsonian Institution Wikimedia.

of chunkey (see Chapter 10). It was even adopted in the Plains, where George Catlin would paint scenes of its play in the 1830s and where it may have contributed to the consolidation of Plains Indian nations, who were in turn about to challenge the cavalry of the United States government. The game, though known among a few groups in British Columbia, California, and Washington State, was seldom played in the far West (see Chapter 13).

Conclusion and Epilogue

It would be a mistake to conclude that any of the peoples of the Northeast were variations of tribal societies that evolved in similar ways owing to "human nature" or noncultural factors (population growth and organizational necessity). While some present-day words, such as tribes and confederacies, encourage contemporary comparisons, the comparisons lead us to an awareness of the differences within and between New England and Iroquoia versus other sedentary village societies in North America. Those differences, as they are caught up in a web of houses, villages, wooden masks, corn, and gaming in the Northeast, suggest that societies do not "evolve" in any sense of that word because societies themselves are but a suite of contingent relationships spread out across space and through time. Margaret Mead's famous comment, "a small group of thoughtful committed citizens can change the world," is pertinent here (see also Chapter 15). The evidence is in the historical contrasts embodied by native North America.

Perhaps no greater contrasts exist among North American contemporaries than they do between the villagized, nation-building, lacrosse-playing Haudenosaunee and those of the far West: the non-pottery-using, non-agricultural, and densely inhabited settlements of native Californians and their aristocratic fisher-forager Haida, Tligit, Kwakiutl, Salish, and other Northwest Coast neighbors (Chapter 13). Those contrasts will make the northeasterners even more historically singular, as their ways of life seem to have been historically contingent on the physical media through which people related to others and to water, mountains, trees, plants, fish, weather events, climate, and more. Maize, lacrosse, and village formation defined the Northeast, a land already shaped by the Hopewellian phenomenon of 1,500–2,000 years ago. Perhaps such developments are directly related to the ability of later Iroquoian people to nation-build.

Such contingencies carry right on into the historic era, after 1600 CE, to define native relations within increasingly Euro-American-dominated contexts. There were consequences of the prolonged contacts for all sides, though certainly more devastating for native peoples. Thus, unallied Iroquoian nations would be driven to near-extinction by Euro-American and Haudenosaunee campaigns to control the northeastern fur trade. Smallpox and measles would finish the job, particularly on peoples closely connected to the Jesuit missions. Individually, the missionaries fared little better. Father Jean de Brébeuf would be captured along with Wendat warriors by the Iroquois and tortured to death in 1649.

In New England, attacked by Captain Miles Standish and subject to other English excesses, the Narragansett and other Algonkian peoples were much reduced owing to the same combination of warfare and disease. For instance, Wapanoag self-determination came to an end in 1675 following a failed campaign to oust the English led by Metacomet (a.k.a. King Philip), son of the great sachem Massasoit. The English slaughtered the Wapanoag and chopped Metacomet's body into pieces. His head was mounted on a pike in Plymouth for two decades (Kroeber 1907).

13 Divergence in the Far West

Up and down the West Coast of North America – from British Columbia and Alaska south to Baja California before and after the 1600s – lived sedentary and semisedentary fishers and foragers (Figure 13.1). Aspects of their California, Oregon, Washington, British Columbia, and southeast Alaska cultures paralleled those known from other such sedentary village people, including in New York and the Northeast as discussed in the previous chapter. However, unlike the Northeast, where, for instance, the Haudenosaunee – a "League of the Iroquois" – constituted a "most conspicuous" and singular historical development of "civil organization" (Morgan 1962[1851]:3), there is little evidence in the far West that locally dense population concentrations – some of which at European contact were led by hereditary elites who engaged in long-distance trade and craft specialization – were parts of large-scale political confederacies or regional polities (Ames and Maschner 1999; Perry 2012). Moreover, Northwest Coast, Interior Plateau, and California peoples of the pre-Columbian era never built great ceremonial centers as happened in other portions of the continent. Yet portions of the Interior Plateau were unmatched in the longevity of the human occupations, some lasting in a near-continuous manner for centuries.

Certainly, stable, multi-community native provinces existed in California, led by hereditary leaders. Spanish explorer Juan Rodríguez Cabrillo, for instance, mentioned an elderly female cacique living in present-day Santa Barbara County in 1542 who lorded over one province composed of a series of coastal towns and adjacent to a second province: "The chief of these towns," the expedition log recorded, "is an old Indian woman who came on board the ships and slept two nights in the *Capitana* [i.e., the Spanish ship], many others doing the same" (see also Chapter 3). Speaking to the question of political organization, Cabrillo infers that the "town of Ciucut seemed to be the head of the other towns because they came there from them when called by the chief" (Wagner 1941:51).

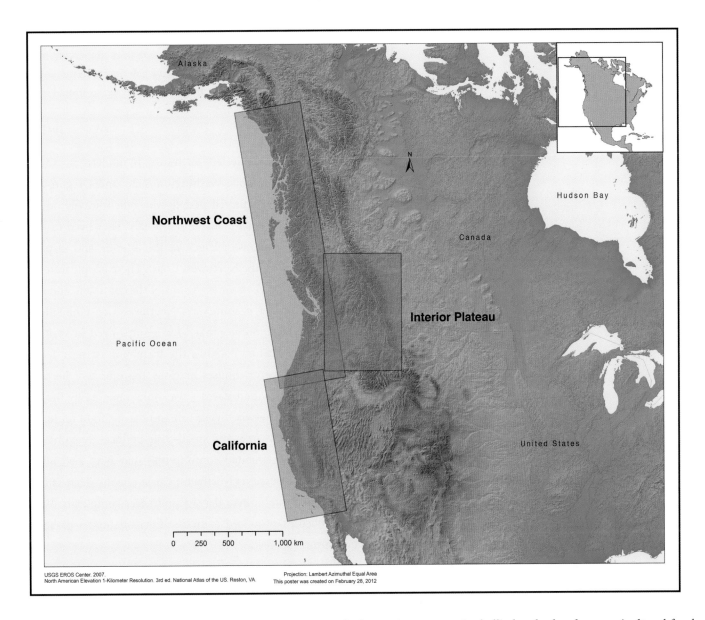

Fig 13.1 Map of the far West.

Such provinces comprised allied and related nonagricultural food collectors living in permanent "rancherias" and "pueblos," at least as described by the Spaniards. These native Californians harvested the sea in the spring and summer, managed stands of oaks and wild grasses in the fall, and foraged and hunted the interior in the winter. Cabrillo described the coastal towns in some detail:

They have round houses, well covered down to the ground. They wear skins of many different kinds of animals, eat acorns and a white seed the size of maize, which is used to make tamales. They live well ... Indians who came on board with water and fish ... displayed much friendship. In their towns they have large plazas and circular enclosures around which imbedded in the ground are many stone posts which stand about three palm-lengths above it. In the middle of these enclosures there are many very thick timbers like masts sunk in the ground. These are covered with many paintings, and we thought they must worship them because when they danced they did so around inside of the enclosure.

(Wagner 1941:52)

Things changed as one traveled northward. In modern-day southeast Alaska, British Columbia, Washington State, and Oregon were villages of up to several hundred people who relied heavily on riverine, coastal, and terrestrial plants and animals. They lived in scattered pithouses and pithouse villages, in the interior, and in plank house settlements, along the Northwest Coast. These people were not highly centralized, relative to other regions of the continent, and only weakly territorialized. Yet, in some ways, Northwest Coast inhabitants were more hierarchical. Some ranked kin groups lived in veritable proto-feudal arrangements. Possibly, the formation of fully feudal relationships – where great houses or clans appropriated the labor of community members and slaves – was only hindered by the uneven distribution of otherwise dense fish and marine food resources. Extensive exchange networks and small-scale political domains that crosscut rather than cemented communities may have also inhibited confederation of various Northwest Coast regions. That said, in at least one region, the human density and sheer complexity of the ranked relationships produced a unique form of hunter-gatherer-fisher "urbanism" (see below).

Meriwether Lewis and William Clark passed through the southern portions of the Northwest Coast and Interior Plateau in 1805 and described what they saw. At the juncture of the Snake and Columbia rivers, near present-day Kennewick, Washington, they recorded the appearance and housing of people who Lewis and Clark described as linguistically and culturally differentiated into a series of "nations":

In their dress and general appearance ... the men wear ... a robe of deer- or antelope-skin, under which a few of them have a short leathern shirt ... [F]emales have no other covering but a truss or piece of leather tied round the hips and then drawn tight between the legs. The ornaments usually worn by both sexes are large blue or white beads, either pendant from their ears, or around the neck, wrists, and arms; they have, likewise, bracelets of brass, copper, and horn, and some trinkets of shells, fish-bones, and curious feathers. The houses ... are made of large mats of rushes, and are generally of square or oblong form, varying in length from 15 to 60 feet, and supported in the inside by poles or forks about six feet high; the top is covered with mats, leaving a space of 12 or 15 inches the whole length of the house, for the purpose of admitting the light and suffering the smoke to pass through; the roof is nearly flat, which seems to indicate that rains are not common in this open country; the house is not divided into apartments, the fire being in the middle of the large room, immediately under the hole in the roof; the rooms are ornamented with their nets, gigs, and other fishing-tackle, as well as the bow for each inhabitant, and a large quiver of arrows, which are headed with flints ... The men ... are said to content themselves with a single wife, with whom we observe the husband shares the labors of procuring subsistence ...

(Coues 1979[1893]:637–638)

Arriving on the coast in 1805, the pair of American explorers described the Clatsop people who lived in plank houses. The buildings, they said, were

sunk about four feet deep into the ground; the walls, roof, and gable-ends were formed of split pine boards; the descent was through a small door down a ladder. There were two fires in the middle of the room, and the beds disposed round the walls two or three feet from the [floor], so as to leave room under them for their bags, baskets, and household articles. The floor itself was covered with mats.

(Coues 1979[1893]:730)

Lewis and Clark also saw overlapping or hybrid styles of dress, bodily comportment, everyday practice, and housing as they traveled west. No doubt this was due in some part to the fact that, along the major rivers and coastline, everybody knew what everyone else was doing. That wide-ranging knowledge, in turn, was a function to some degree of the physical movements of people up and down the rivers. Many people relocated themselves in order to improve their chances of catching fish or collecting other riverine resources. Some had to move in order to accompany a new spouse to a distant homeland. Others were relocated as captives or slaves, transported in one or another direction along the major rivers against their wills.

It was a remarkably varied physical, linguistic, political, familial, and even spiritual landscape. In some areas of the coast, population densities were high, and feudal dealings invariably crosscut complicated community landscapes. There were raids, intra- and inter-community politics, and captive taking. There was also long-distance travel, perhaps not surprising given the possibilities of moving materials in watercraft. The exchange of craft items during such trading expeditions doubtless mitigated some of the misunderstandings between peoples, and were ritually formalized, known historically as Potlatches (e.g., www.youtube.com/watch?v=QqzvOumX2fs). These exchanges reached historical highs late in the history of the native Northwest Coast with a rituality that far exceeded most other parts of North America.

The extremes and contrasts of the far West's native history with that of other portions of the continent call out for explanations. Surely, we believe, such explanations cannot be boiled down to the simple presence or absence of hereditary leadership or the one-way causality of climate change. After all, there were always leaders everywhere, including hereditary community heads and war chiefs along the West Coast (similar in some ways to Massasoit and his peers in New England or the Iroquoian sachems in the interior, as we saw in Chapter 12). And certain climatic shifts, as we have seen elsewhere in this volume, seem to have had little social-historical impact.

Possibly we need to think more broadly about the configurations and kinds of relationships between peoples, between people and things, and between humans and nonhuman beings. Were these historically constituted relationships somehow different within the far West or between it and other subcontinental areas? What differences specifically might have produced the divergent histories of the far West? Let us turn to each of the three major physiographic areas – the Interior Plateau, Northwest Coast, and California – to find out.

Interior Plateau

North of the Great Basin, south of the subarctic, west of the Rockies, and east of the Pacific coast lies the plateau of the interior Northwest (Figure 13.2). This physiographic province is usually divided into the Canadian Plateau of British Columbia to the north, and the Columbia Plateau of Washington, Oregon, and Idaho to the south. Like much of the Great Basin and the western Plains, the Interior Plateau is semi-arid, sitting in the lee of tall mountains to the west. Unlike the Great Basin, great rivers – the Columbia and the Fraser – connect the Interior Plateau to the Pacific Ocean. In fact, the Columbia and its tributaries comprise the fourth largest river system in North America, channeling a tremendous volume of water to the sea. Together, the

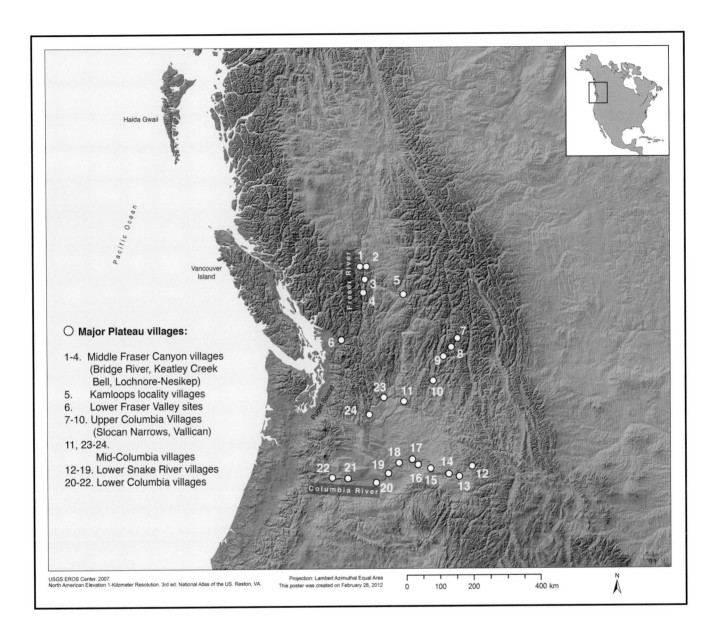

Fig 13.2 Map of the Interior Plateau and portions of the adjacent Northwest Coast.

great rivers enabled considerable human movement throughout the interior Northwest, much as it afforded Lewis and Clark's journey to the coast in 1805.

The terrain between river valleys ranges from flat to rolling hills and, in the central portion of the province (i.e., the Thompson Plateau), low ridges with valleys in-filled with glacial till. Most parts of this diverse landscape were utilized by people at one time or another, but we will focus discussion below on settlement along rivers, where villages of upwards of 1,000 persons were established over the past two millennia. The history of these people is one of change.

Fig 13.3 Tlakliut man standing on a fishing platform holding a fishing net containing fish caught in a natural rock weir below. Edward S. Curtis, 1923/Library of Congress, Washington, DC.

Climate change figures prominently in this history, with changing sea-surface temperatures along the northern Pacific coast affecting the timing and magnitude of anadromous fish migrations up the rivers. In fact, the biggest trends in culture change are tied to the waxing and waning of salmon runs deep into the interior to spawn in the fresh waters of the Fraser and Columbia rivers and their tributaries (Figure 13.3).

Not surprisingly, the biggest social change in the Interior Plateau was the appearance of large and permanent villages at upriver locations of salmon harvesting. Notably, this was neither a gradual nor irreversible trend (Prentiss and Chatters 2003). Diverse foraging practices existed across the greater region, at times simultaneous and perhaps even interdependent of one another. How and why some of these tactics for making a living trended toward social inequality is a matter of considerable research in the region. Recent work in the middle Fraser Canyon, deep in the Interior Plateau, shows that complexity in the region was not only marked, but also causally connected to communities of the Northwest Coast proper. It also hints strongly at the existence of multiple streams of history in the Interior Plateau.

Sidebar 13.1 Forager diversity on the plateau

During the fifth millennium BP, communities of the greater Pacific Northwest engaged in at least four different ways of living off the land (Prentiss and Kuijt 2012:45–52). *Mobile* or *generalized foraging* was employed by small coresident groups who moved frequently from place to place to access diverse resources as they became available. It worked best in environments with a relatively even distribution of resources (Binford 1980), as in parts of the Canadian Plateau, where people of the Nesikep tradition dwelled. *Serial foraging* involved seasonal movements across a series of specific locations to access specific resources, such as summer and early fall salmon runs. It was practiced by communities of the Gulf of Georgia, Vancouver Island, and Puget Sound, members of the Charles culture, part of the Old Cordilleran tradition. *Sedentary foraging* took place in the Columbia Plateau during Pithouse I times and possibly in the Fraser Valley during the Eayam phase. As the name implies, sedentary foragers stayed put for much if not all of the year, but they did not practice storage, at least not at a large scale. To guard against failure, sedentary foragers positioned sites at ecotones in the environment: places at the boundaries between two or more distinct habitats. *Collecting* first appeared on the island of Haida Gwaii and a few centuries later on the coastal mainland of British Columbia. Collectors lived in permanent settlements and employed logistical mobility (Binford 1980) to acquire large amounts of food that could be stored for later use, notably during the winter.

Because these various strategies coexisted during the fifth millennium BP, they cannot be attributed purely to change over time, as if mobile foraging gradually evolved into collecting in a pervasive, irreversible way. Environmental diversity clearly was at play, but that alone does not account for all this variation. The pithouses of sedentary foragers in the Columbia Plateau, for instance, have a precedent in the Great Basin, implicating northern migrations of people with traditions foreign to the region. For our purposes, we are interested in how these various strategies affected social history, notably the rise of social equality and its antithesis in asserted egalitarianism. Population movements, social action, habitat diversity, climate change, and environmental disasters all factor into these processes.

Sidebar 13.2 Diversity from the start

Who occupied the Interior Plateau first? The best answer is now the people of the Western Stemmed tradition, known from work at Paisley Caves in the northern Great Basin and almost certainly of Pacific coastal derivation (see Chapter 4). Added to this mix after about 12,000 years ago were people of the Old Cordilleran tradition. Known best by willow-leaf-shaped projectile points, Old Cordilleran sites are distributed from the central Northwest Coast through the southern Interior Plateau, where they are usually attributed to the Cascade phase.

The greater diversity of peoples of the Interior Plateau and Northwest Coast factored into later developments in the middle Fraser. On the coast, people of the Old Cordilleran tradition established the first shell middens along the lower Fraser and Columbia rivers, as early as 8,000 years ago. These were seasonal sites, but apparently reoccupied repeatedly by the same people and thus indicative of serial foraging. Some of these shell middens contain abundant salmon bone, along with the bones of smaller fish and, of course, the shells of mollusks. Some of the larger sites (e.g., Namu, Milliken, and The Dalles) may have supported seasonal aggregations by multiple groups for fishing, but there is little to suggest that any such sites were permanently occupied. Sea-level instability to this point made both marine resources and anadromous fish runs unpredictable, and evidence for housing and storage is lacking.

Early Pithouse Villages

After 5,000 years ago, sea level stabilized, shellfish beds expanded, and fish and marine mammal populations burgeoned. Salmon runs became bigger and more predictable. The stage was set for big change. In the Columbia Plateau, mobile foragers of the Cascade phase settled into more or less permanent villages to become sedentary foragers by about 5,000 BP, living in pithouses during what is aptly called the Pithouse I phase. The residential buildings of these Pithouse I people were relatively modest, circular in outline, and several meters in diameter, similar to those described by Lewis and Clark. Long straight poles would be leaned together in a conical fashion up from the edges of the semisubterranean basin to form the roof. One entered from the side. Interiors were divided into activity zones (sleeping, tool making, cooking).

Archaeologically, the remains of such buildings are often found clustered into small village settlements, such as those from the Mack Canyon site along the Deschutes River, a tributary of the Columbia (Figure 13.4). Similar pithouse villages, early and late, extended south into the California interior and north into British Columbia (Figure 13.5). Typical domestic possessions often left behind when a home was abandoned include stone, wood, and other perishable processing tools used for processing food and animal and plant byproducts (Figure 13.6). Such things tell us that foods were not cooked in pots, but were usually roasted over fires, baked in pits, or boiled in baskets and skin bags with the aid of red-hot stones.

Lacking below-ground storage, villagers of the Pithouse I phase took advantage of diverse seasonal resources by positioning villages at the interface of two or more biological communities, what ecologists call an *ecotone* (Chatters 1995). The interface between riparian zones and adjacent mountainsides is a good example, where summer fishing in rivers and winter hunting in the adjacent uplands could be accomplished from a single home base. It follows that the diet of Pithouse I people was diverse, when measured over seasons, and that no single food resource was dominant over others.

This early start to permanent villages was short-circuited after about 4,100 years ago as the region entered into a period of colder and wetter climate known as the Neoglacial (Prentiss and Kuijt 2012:52–53). Although salmon migrations into the interior benefited from this change, winter forays into upland forests for game and other resources

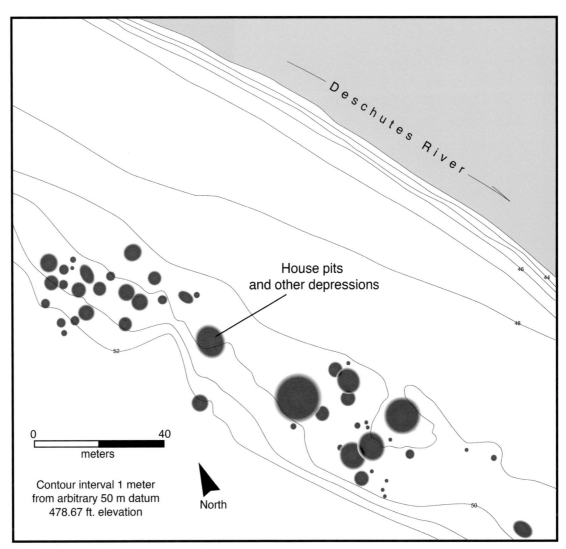

Fig 13.4 Pithouse village along Deschutes River, Oregon (adapted from Aikens et al. 2011: figure 3.26).

were increasingly challenged by heavy snowfall. The Pithouse I villages of the Columbia Plateau were abandoned. Communities may have reverted to mobile foraging, but evidently foraging in the Canadian Plateau was likewise impacted by Neoglacial conditions as traces of the so-called Lochnore culture there disappeared around 4,000 years ago. Whether mobile or sedentary, interior communities did not fare well under changing climate and for the next 500 years the region was ignored, save for occasional passers-through (Table 13.1).

After 3,500 years ago in the Columbia Plateau, villages were once again settled and occupied, leading archaeologists to identify a Pithouse II phase (Chatters 1995). It would be fair to wonder at this point about lines of ancestry. Who, for instance, were the immediate ancestors of these new Pithouse II people in the Columbia Basin? They apparently could not

Fig 13.5 Archaeologists inspect a house basin in the Stein River valley, British Columbia. Courtesy of Ian Kuijt.

Fig 13.6 Food processing mauls and pestles from pithouse midden in The Dalles. Courtesy of the University of Oregon Museum of Natural and Cultural History.

Table 13.1 Chronological highlights of the Northwest Coast and Interior Plateau (adapted from Aikens et al. 2011; Ames 2005; Ames and Maschner 1999; Kirk and Daugherty 2007; Maschner 2012b; Prentiss 2012).

Year CE	Historic period	Cultural patterns
0	Late Middle Pacific period	Coast: large coastal plank house villages; offshore fishing; large cemeteries.
	Pithouse II	Interior Plateau: large pithouse villages in the interior.
500	Late Pacific period	Coast: increased Pacific fishery productivity; increased interpersonal violence; fortified villages.
	Lillooet horizon	Interior Plateau: bow and arrow.
800–1300	Medieval Warm Period	
	Late Pacific climax	Peak village aggregation and fortification; end of the Lillooet phenomenon interior; subsistence specialization on salmon and deer.
1150–1350	Late Pacific disruption	Coastal abandonments; demographic reshuffling.
1400s	Late Pacific reoccupation	Large sedentary plank house villages; intensive warfare; craft specialization; ranked social hierarchies.

have been people of the Pithouse I phase, who are thought to have abandoned the area 500 years earlier (Prentiss and Kuijt 2012:56). But where did those earlier people go? Did they die off, or relocate elsewhere? Did some communities wind up on the coast, only to return generations later to life on the river? The evidence of absence hints at a complex history. In any event, the next 1,000-year-long Pithouse II period also ushered in a greater reliance on salmon coeval with the growth of pithouse villages across the Interior Plateau. To the north in the Canadian Plateau, this growth is also correlated with the occasional construction of pithouses as large as 15 m in diameter (Prentiss and Kuijt 2012:60).

The Dalles

The most densely populated Columbia Plateau occupation (characterized by continuous village areas and deep refuse middens) was "The Dalles" (rhymes with pals). This region "flourished increasingly as a fishing and trading center after about 3,000 years ago, reaching its peak during the nineteenth-century contact-historic period" (Aikens et al. 2011:178). Melvin Aikens and colleagues (2011:188–189) infer a migration of Chinookan-speaking people into The Dalles, on the falls of the Columbia River between modern-day Washington State and Oregon. And this migration, they surmise, was a cause of major historic change in the region, particularly as they would have displaced if not subordinated locals.

Certainly, The Dalles was one of the best, if not the best, salmon fisheries in the world. For all intents and purposes, this made The Dalles a great "rendezvous" site, or a meeting place for many different peoples on an annual basis (Figure 13.7). "When Lewis and Clark came down the Columbia in 1805, The Dalles area was home to a multi-ethnic community dominated by the Wishram and Wasco tribes, who respectively controlled the Washington and Oregon sides of the Long Narrows [a set of rapids]" (Aikens et al. 2011:179).

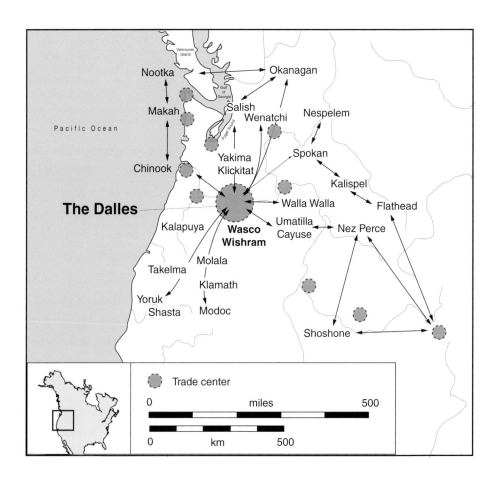

Fig 13.7 The Dalles' network (adapted from Aikens et al. 2011: figure 3.23).

As descendants of "a Chinookan-speaking nation on the lower Columbia and Pacific coast that was famous for long-distance trade throughout the Northwest," one can presume that a "Chinook Jargon" or trade language facilitated commerce between distant, unrelated groups from the beginning (Aikens et al. 2011:188). That goods might have been transferred in a more controlled way at this and other rendezvous locations or at annual gatherings means that trade became connected to place and, therein, laden with fixed social relationships, such that wearing various beads and pendants – common in village middens from The Dalles – identified one's community, ethnic identity, and natal affiliation. Moreover, these places were the locations where people connected to nonhuman forces that defined their own identities and histories. Portions of The Dalles, for instance, are covered with petroglyphs and pictographs showing the faces of animals, animal spirits, or monstrous beings or deities (Figure 13.8).

Fig 13.8 She-Who-Watches (Tsagiglalal) petroglyph on a rock along the Columbia River near The Dalles, attributed to the Wishram/Tlakluit Indians of the Chinook Nation. Edward S. Curtis, 1910/Library of Congress, Washington, DC.

Pithouse Villages of the Mid-Fraser Canyon

The course of Interior Plateau history was convoluted and necessarily involved developments in adjacent regions, especially on the coast. The big twist in this history was the emergence of an economy of salmon storage. Irrespective of lines of ancestry, blood, and marriage, the salmon storage economy had historical ramifications, taking on a life of its own and structuring settlement, labor, property rights, power, prestige, and ultimately institutions of social inequality.

Another place that witnessed the emergence and growth of pithouse villages at strategic places of salmon harvesting after 2,500 years ago was the mid-Fraser Canyon. Here, pithouses ranged from 5 to 20 m in diameter, sunk into the ground about 0.5 m. Interior posts in the center supported roof beams stretching from a circumferential rim of earth. Entrances could be to the side or through the roof, and interiors with benches, hearths, and various activity areas included numerous storage pits, which were also common around the outside of pithouses. Larger houses must have accommodated either multiple families or some sort of larger corporate unit. House size variability may also indicate social or economic differences between families.

Pithouse villages of the mid-Fraser have occupation histories spanning many centuries, the longest-lived starting at about 2,500 years ago (rooted in earlier villages elsewhere identified as the Shuswap horizon of ca. 1500–500 BCE). At that time, or about 500 BCE, the expanding pithouse villages seem related in some ways to the so-called "Locarno Beach" phase of the Middle Pacific period around Northwest Coast's Gulf of Georgia (see below). In fact, Prentiss and Kuijt (2012:63) read the similarities between the coastal and plateau peoples at this time as the expansion of Locarno Beach lifeways from the coast into the interior. They suggest further that multiple efforts to establish villages up the Fraser River during the early Shuswap horizon may have been thwarted by periodic climatic events of the Neoglacial, notably severe winters.

In any event, by 2,000 years ago, descendant communities worked out the solution to tough winters with a full-blown salmon storage economy, the result coming to be known as the Lillooet horizon (ca. 0 CE to 1200 CE). During this period, villages grew in sometimes "dramatic" fashion, with populations reaching as large as 1,000 residents

(Prentiss 2012:176–177). The drama in the dramatic expansion of these villages may have resulted in part from the arrival of people from lower stretches of the Fraser River into the high-altitude interior, possibly because ideal conditions out in the Pacific Ocean made a rugged stretch of British Columbia's Fraser River – a.k.a. Fraser Canyon – a more desirable place to live than it had been (Figures 13.9–13.10). Archaeological excavations at two sites with protracted histories – Keatley Creek led by Brian Hayden (1997) and Bridge River led by Anna Prentiss and colleagues (2008) – have richly informed our perspectives on social changes attending the rise and fall of big villages.

The residents of these mid-Fraser Canyon pithouse villages did not live by salmon alone. Roots, berries, and deer were important resources too. However, villages evidently grew as salmon became more plentiful in the area. Villages were sited in proximity to some

Fig 13.9 Mid-Fraser River terrain, near Big Bar, British Columbia. Murray Foubister/Wikimedia.

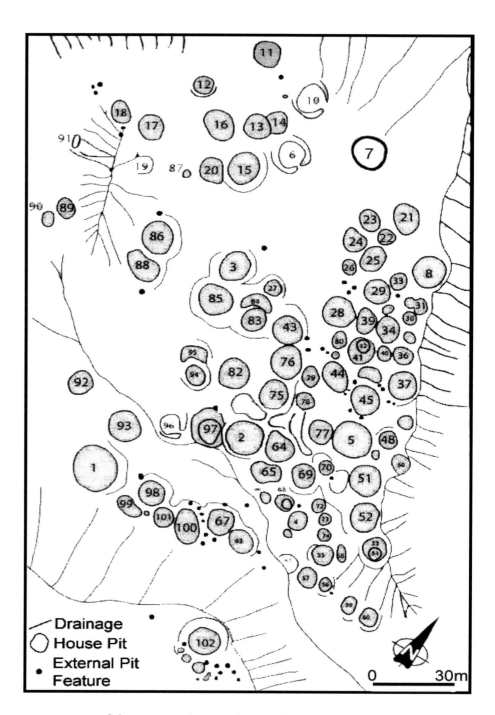

Fig 13.10 Keatley Creek site plan. Courtesy of Anna Prentiss.

of the most productive places to harvest spawning fish. In the mid-Fraser area that meant locations where salmon congregate before continuing their journey up tributaries like Bridge River or Keatley Creek. At these locations salmon could be taken by the thousands, provided you had adequate labor and the right technology.

Adequate labor was a matter of people power, and the more people you had the more fish you could harvest, process, and store. Of course,

Fig 13.11 Cross-section view of a mid-Fraser River house and house members. Courtesy of Eric Carlson.

the more people you had the more mouths you had to feed. The right technology meant not only the nets used to harvest salmon – generally dip nets, but also float nets and set nets (see Prentiss and Kuijt 2012:135 for illustrations of each) – but also fishing platforms and drying racks. The combination of strategic places to fish, infrastructure to harvest and process, and the labor needed to make it all happen put considerable demand on people to aggregate and stay put. We might add that mass harvesting of salmon was intended to get people through tough winters, and big pithouses were good places for large households to hole up (Figure 13.11).

Social Inequality

To understand how life in large villages led to social inequality, we might consider that something other than getting through the winter drew people into larger, more permanent communities. The growth of villages came in fits and starts, not gradually, and the biggest jumps in population came late in the history of mid-Fraser villages. This was also a time of diminishing salmon supplies. Surely salmon were reliable over many generations, but as they grew less reliable – arguably thanks to a period of global warming (Chatters 1995) – some households enacted strategies to ensure their survival, presumably at the expense of others. Competition for prime resource

Sidebar 13.3 Prepping salmon

Mid-Fraser people ate a variety of plant and animal foods, but salmon was a critical resource for those living in large villages. The bony remains of salmon turn up routinely in village excavations, mostly in the form of postcranial elements: vertebrae, ribs, and spines. Missing are the head bones, whose absence suggests heads were cut off and discarded elsewhere. The separation of heads from bodies offers insight into the significance of salmon for winter food. As we have already seen, salmon migrate up the rivers of the Interior Plateau in summer and early fall and can be harvested by the thousands. A good portion of the annual catch was no doubt consumed upon arrival, but in order for it to be prepped for latter consumption it had to be dried, and that took place at fishing stations apart from villages. Although whole fish also could be preserved by smoking or salting, if drying is the preferred method, increasing surface area by splitting the fish in half made good sense. This was the preferred method of First Nations people of the mid-Fraser region at the time of European contact (Prentiss and Kuijt 2012:117–125, 136). At locations of mass capture along the river, work parties began processing salmon by cutting off their heads. The bodies were then split along the underside, up to the tail, and the roe sacks and guts separated for other uses. With backbones left intact, bodies were splayed open and the meat scored to the skin at close intervals perpendicular to the length. The resulting packages were then strung over drying racks that were constructed in locations where dry, warm air blew strong. In the historic era, fish-drying racks consisted of horizontal poles suspended on vertical posts. Ramada-like roofs shaded the racks from direct sunlight. The combination of fish capture and fish processing infrastructure at locations ideally suited to both tasks meant that fishing camps were typically proprietary.

From an archaeological standpoint, the lack of head parts back at villages is good evidence that salmon were processed for storage. There certainly were plenty of salmon vertebrae and other body parts deposited at village sites, as well as the cache pits in which stores were presumably kept. It follows that salmon was a critical resource for getting through tough winters. Processing salmon at fish camps maximized their food potential for later use while reducing the costs of transport and storage.

So what became of the heads, roe, and guts? Heads and guts in the historic era were boiled to render fish oil, which also could be stored for winter. Roe was sometimes buried in baskets underground for use in late winter or spring (Prentiss and Kuijt 2012:124). One pit at Keatley Creek contained nothing but salmon skeletons, which has been interpreted as a reserve for making fish broth in times of need. Through these ingenious ways of processing and storing salmon, nothing was wasted. However, the upshot here is that archaeologists can infer differences between immediate and delayed use of salmon through subtle clues like the absence of head parts at locations of consumption.

patches and the labor to exploit them ensued. From this arose institutions of territorial control, property, and inheritance. These novel arrangements led to inequities not only between villages, but also within villages, as larger households may have been able to cope with changes better than smaller ones by diversifying as well as intensifying their efforts.

In this respect, we have to wonder if the sudden growth in a village like Bridge River – notably the emergence of two distinct pithouse clusters – resulted when certain corporate groups, from failing settlements, relocated to this more successful village. If so, the realignment of groups on the landscape produced instant inequality:

those with heritage claims to villages and the infrastructure to prove it, and those who had to carve out a new niche among their fully ensconced neighbors. Ironically, the regional networks of reciprocity and sharing that structured the mid-Fraser cultural landscape of the previous centuries may well have been the mechanism for an enterprising individual to take advantage of an otherwise bad situation in the interest of his or her own people, as Hayden (1994) has surmised.

Ultimately, the big Lillooet horizon villages disappeared sometime around 1050–1250 CE. On the lower Fraser River, the construction of burial mounds also ceased about this time, perhaps for climatic reasons (mediated by social relations, as always). The Medieval Warm Period likely adversely impacted the movements of anadromous fish and, from there, the social life of human beings (Prentiss 2012:177). That climatic episode did pass, and Interior Plateau regions were again reoccupied after about 1450 CE by people re-entering from the coast, to which we turn next.

Northwest Coast

The Northwest Coast encompasses portions of present-day northern California, Oregon, Idaho, Washington, British Columbia, and southeast Alaska. This rugged subcontinental area covers mountains, arid intermontane plateaus, river gorges, lush coastal slopes, rocky shorelines, and islands teeming with marine life (Figure 13.12). The Pacific weather patterns in the past thousand years led to an incredible range of environmental conditions and ecozones, from temperate rainforests along the coast to high deserts and snow-packed mountains in the interior, all moderated by periodic Pacific environmental cycles, such as El Niño, and subject to longer-term climatic shifts (Maschner 2012a; Moss 2011).

By about 5000 BCE, archaeologists recognize a "Pacific" period, a more than six millennia span of time that followed the earlier Archaic era (Ames and Maschner 1999). Generally, the early Pacific or middle Holocene period (ca. 5000–1500 BCE) witnessed the beginnings of pithouse settlements and their associated shell midden formation (Maschner 2012b; Moss 2011). There, bone harpoon tips and lance heads for killing large sea mammals seem to go along with the increasingly sedentary coastal lifestyle, particularly

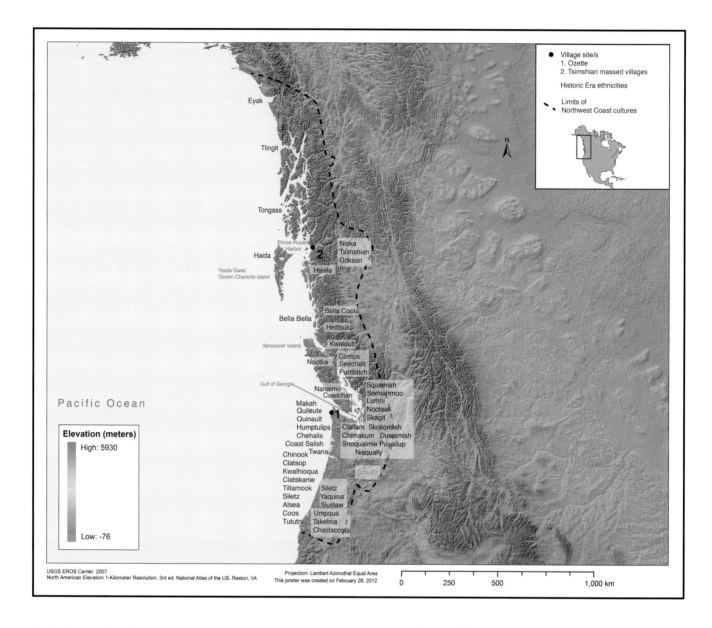

Fig 13.12 Map of the Northwest Coast.

climate-related phases of expansion after 2000 BCE. Groundstone woodworking tools correspond with the cutting and splitting of boards for housing and other articles, as well as the spread of the rainforest that, today, we think synonymous with these regions (Maschner 2012b:90–93).

By 1500 BCE, the coastal mainland of British Columbia was home to relatively large, sedentary (if not permanent) settlements of people who harvested salmon and, now, began storing dried salmon for use later in the year. By this time, known as the beginning of the late Holocene era or the middle Pacific period, people also harvested offshore fish such as herring and cod more intensively. Recognizable from southeast Alaska south to Prince Rupert Harbor and the southern coast (around Vancouver Island), the initial phases of this period, such as the Locarno Beach phase in Georgia Bay (see Interior Plateau, above), suggest that populations had grown and the more numerous inhabitants had begun living in surface plank houses. The subsequent Marpole phase of the southern coast, beginning around 500 BCE, betrays "extensive evidence of status differences, especially in regard to cranial deformation and the wealth of grave goods" in burials (Maschner 2012b:166). Specialization of craft production and food harvesting followed shortly thereafter (Ames 2005:64).

Archaeologist Herb Maschner (2012b) considers this southern coast Marpole phase and the cognate phases of other regions to have been something of a social "experiment" that did not last. Indeed, many of the large middle Pacific villages disappeared about 2,000 years ago. The reasons may not be climatic, since the cooler climate of the Neoglacial episode continued throughout much of this period, though ostensibly with far less impact here, on the Northwest Coast, than in the Interior Plateau.

Late Pacific Period

The later pre-Columbian history of the rugged waterways and salmon fisheries of North America's Northwest is known to archaeologists as the late Pacific period (of the late Holocene era), the final period prior to the arrival of Europeans (ca. 500–1750 CE). In the Northwest, late Pacific communities were not only multi-ethnic but also stratified, with high-ranking families controlling prime riverine locations and owning slaves, who were captives taken from other communities. Lesser or "middle class" community members included the relations of those who had achieved some degree of prominence in life (Aikens and colleagues [2011] include the families of shamans and war chiefs in this grouping). At the bottom were slaves (see below).

Late Pacific period "trade" here too is significant for what it reveals about indigenous Northwest Coast social relationships and historical contexts. Extensive "interaction spheres" or exchange networks existed across the Northwest, divisible into the northern, central, and southern segments (Ames and Maschner 1999). By the late Pacific period, the central and southern networks were most prominent. Obsidian, copper, dentalium shells, and nephrite (an igneous rock used for making axe and adze heads) moved between communities within these spheres (Figure 13.13). So did slaves.

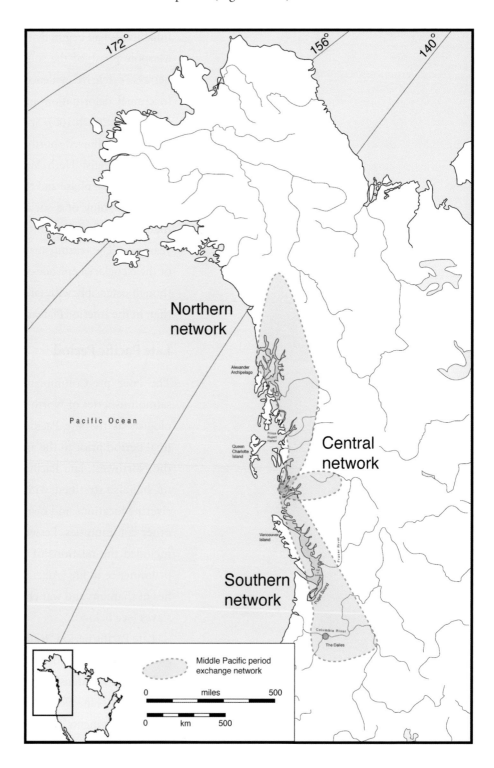

Fig 13.13 Northwest Coast trade networks during the middle Pacific period (adapted from Ames and Maschner 1999: map 59).

Sidebar 13.4 Trade, trade fairs, and the Potlatch

There are multiple kinds of relationships between people that we might conflate if we uncritically use the deceptively simple word "trade." That is, there is gift-giving and social exchange that happens between people with the effect (though possibly not the intent) of cementing familial ties, establishing bonds of friendship, and setting up political alliances. Gifting and social exchanges of this kind – which may involve transfers of portable things, marriage partners, titles, or invisible powers – are often parts of trade fairs, loosely organized annual gatherings at central sites. They are also parts of more tightly organized ceremonials, such as the Northwest Coast "Potlatch," where food is also consumed in great feasts. Such exchanges come with expectations of returns and indebtedness (Mauss 1990).

The Potlatch in the Northwest was conducted in the winter months and involved transferring ceremonial objects, marriage partners, and titles to others and succeeding generations as well as distributing food and "wealth" to the dozens if not hundreds gathered at the event. High-status households hosted these events, and additional prestige was gained by doing so. Dances and feasting occurred over a period of days, the latter involving large wooden containers and spoons used to dispense the foods. In the historic era, so much wealth was accumulated for distribution, as elites attempted to maintain their positions in the face of commoner potlatches, that goods were simply burned and destroyed.

Much of what was exchanged – even some of that categorized as "wealth" – was "inalienable" – unable to be divested of the social relationships within which the trade occurs (Mills 2004; Weiner 1992). A variant of this, common in other locations in North America, is direct acquisition of materials or powers through long-distance travel (Helms 1993). Here, the exchange may not be person-to-person but person-to-place or thing, as in the transfer of bundle power (see Chapter 10). All of these sorts of exchanges contrast with the "commodity" exchanges of "alienable goods," which accompany the formation of markets (as happens in ancient Mexico) and is especially well known from modern-day capitalist relationships, where the trade goods are often dissociated from social relations (Kopytoff 1986). None of these forms of trade are necessarily exclusive, and one can grade into another.

All of this was happening in the absence, by and large, of sizeable centralized towns or great ceremonial centers on the coast. Also absent, or at least highly localized, were territorially bounded polities (Ames and Maschner 1999:171). For all intents and purposes, the seat of political authority and ceremony was the house. And there were great "houses" (literally and figuratively speaking) or lineages of people who identified with specific animal-spirit totems as their ancestors. Historically, the linguistic and ethnic diversity of the Northwest Coast was remarkable, with some valleys having their own language (much like California to the south). Here, the emergence of the ranked, corporate-kin houses became the basis of community and, by extension, the regional cultural landscape.

The high and low ranked lineages were distinct and maintained through warring and the ceremonial dispensation of wealth to such an extent as to comprise actual social classes. In the early modern era, Tlingit war leaders organized raiding parties of hundreds of warriors wearing slate body armor and traveling in large canoes to attack enemies for the purpose of capturing slaves and taking booty (Ames and Maschner 1999:195). At home, especially in the north, high-ranking families displayed their status by wearing "lip labrets" – plugs of stone, wood, or bone set in perforations in the lip (Figure 13.14). In some areas and times, "all free women … wore labrets" – and size mattered: "high-status women wore large labrets" (Ames and Maschner 1999:182). Historically, some high-status people in central and southern coastal areas practiced cranial deformation, binding the skulls of children such that the face appeared broader as adults. Certainly, all high-status families lived in bigger, better homes, owned more slaves, were descended from more powerful ancestral totems, and possessed more rights of access to sea-mammal hunting. The hereditary chiefs of lineage heads of such families wore special garments and hats that both embodied spiritual energies in ritual and denoted their status. Such was especially the case in the northern Northwest Coast (Figure 13.15).

Individual plank houses and the villages in which they stood were larger to the north, in British Columbia and southeast Alaska, and smaller to the south, in Oregon and northern California. At contact, the coastal villages of southeastern Alaska and British Columbia were great complexes of plank houses and carved wooden monuments:

Fig 13.14 Labret worn in the lower lip of a Haida woman. Richard Maynard, 1880s/Public domain.

Fig 13.15 Haida chief "Highest Peak in Mountain Range" in ceremonial garb and in front of "House Where People Always Want to Go." Wikimedia.

totem poles. The world of the Haida people living on the Haida Gwaii (a.k.a. Queen Charlotte) island archipelago

> was like the edge of a knife cutting between the depths of the sea, which to them symbolized the underworld, and the forested mountainsides, which marked the transition to the upper world … [T]hey embellished the narrow human zone of their villages with a profusion of boldly carved monuments and brightly painted emblems signifying their identity. Throughout their villages these … creatures of the upper and lower worlds presented a balanced statement of the forces of their universe.
>
> (MacDonald 1983:3)

Northwest Coast Indian cultural identities were thoroughly entangled with places at the interface of forested land and open water, and the nonhuman inhabitants or resident powers thereof. As a result, hunting, fishing, gathering materials for the production of tools, craft objects, and ornaments, and moving about generally were all acts of identity formation and history making (Thornton 2008). Among the Tlingit, who live north of the Haida in southeastern Alaska, "almost all production took place in the context of lands and sites that were owned, defended, and inherited through … clans and house groups" (Thornton 2008:134), meaning that kinship – in this case matrilineal (inherited through the mother's bloodline) – was also inseparable from the experience of place and all of the resident forces, things, and beings therein. This strong sense of belonging and inheritance helps to explain the development of inequality between those with the right to inherit and those deemed unworthy of inheritance.

For many, "[w]ealth consisted of the right of access to both natural and supernatural resources" which

belonged to the lineage and were exercised by the lineage chief. Prerogatives assigned to a particular lineage might include the rights to hunting lands and fishing streams, rocky islets where sea mammals could be clubbed, berry-picking areas, stands of fine timber [for the building of plank houses], or stretches of beach where whales might be stranded. Each lineage had a founding ancestor and an accumulated history which was the basis for claiming these rights and privileges. Linking the lineage with the ancestral and supernatural sources of power were the songs, dances, crests for use in carving, and names belonging to the lineage.

(MacDonald 1983:5)

On the Northwest Coast, the house itself was the seat of such power, status, belonging, and identity. The great structural anthropologist Claude Levi-Strauss even considered Northwest Coast people exemplars of "house societies" (Moss 2011:122). In such societies, houses – both the buildings and the groups of people – were microcosms of the greater universe (not unlike central sites elsewhere). The roof of a house might be likened to the starry sky above, with the sun entering and exiting by front and back doors, and the house positioned between the watery underworld down on the beach and the high upperworld accessed through the trees behind the settlement (Figure 13.16). The spirits of the dead moved between these worlds, and were subject to being reincarnated as children (MacDonald 1983:7). The totem poles that crowded the house fronts in some settlements were "portals" that enabled relationships between the living and the dead (like trees themselves) and also physical commemorations of the histories of the community, detailed through their elaborately carved figures.

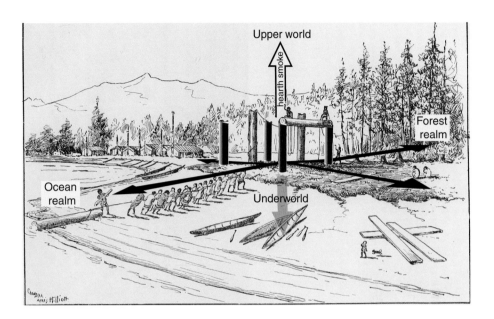

Labels within image: Upper world · hearth smoke · Forest realm · Ocean realm · Underworld

Fig 13.16 The Haida construct the cosmos by building a plank house at the Tsimshian village of Port Simpson, British Columbia, 1866 (adapted from Niblack 1890: plate 70).

The rich materiality of such village life is amply documented in the buried remains of a relatively recent, pre-European-contact Makah settlement, named Ozette, on Washington State's Olympic peninsula. At the beginning of the eighteenth century, an earthquake shook the West Coast from northern California to southeast Alaska, causing a mudslide at Ozette. Recorded as a tsunami by scribes in Japan, the earthquake is projected to have been centered in the American Northwest and to have taken place "on January 26, 1700, at 9 p.m. (Northwest time)" (Kirk 2015:79). The mudslide took out at least eight plank houses occupying the slope along the ocean, and buried under wet, oxygen-poor mud the walls and roofs of the flattened buildings (Figure 13.17). One of the buildings, House 1, was a high-status residence. It was cleaner and larger, and contained evidence that its residents ate more salmon and halibut and, possibly, more whale meat (Ames and Maschner 1999:165).

In the collaborative recovery project that began in 1966, archaeologists working with the Makah found beneath the debris all of the bone, stone, textile, leather, and wooden articles, tools, and possessions where they were left before the mudslide. The walls had been covered with elaborately carved panels of mythical beings: spirit-being bears, wolves, whales, and thunderbirds. Inside there were more wooden carvings, one of a whale fin inlaid with sea otter teeth (Figure 13.18). There were also pieces of fishing tackle, projectile

Fig 13.17 Ozette, a Makah Indian village, as it probably looked before the arrival of white explorers. Getty Image.

Fig 13.18 Ozette wooden bowl. Photograph by Ruth Kirk, in Kirk and Daugherty 2007. Reprinted with permission of the University of Washington Press.

points, carved wooden bowls showing anthropomorphic characters, wooden boxes of all sizes, cradles, bone hair combs carved with bird designs, baskets of all kinds, bone awls for leather work, spindle whorls and battens for making thread and weaving, wooden clubs and canoe paddles, a child's whale-blubber pacifier, and the beaver-tooth dice from some household's bowl game (Kirk 2015; Kirk and Daugherty 2007). There were no ceramic containers; wooden boxes were used in conjunction with hot rocks to bring liquid foods to a boil.

Late Pacific Period Complexities

Of course the late Pacific period people were heirs to middle Pacific traditions that had already seen the establishment of intercommunity inequalities, inherited status differentiation, and frequent violence-related bodily trauma. However, with the late Pacific changes of 500 CE, Northwest Coast social relations became a thick tangle of contingencies that played out in different ways depending on location. For instance, late Pacific villages not only grew larger and, likely, more internally diverse, they also were palisaded and positioned in more defensible locations, at least up to about 1100 CE. Archaeologist Herb Maschner (2012b) tracks the changes over the next two centuries. First, he notes, some people focused their previously unfocused diet, eating more salmon and deer, a pattern that lasted for a couple hundred years. Then, he observes, some regions were abandoned and others show a marked decrease in human population, only to be reoccupied in the last 200–300 years before European exploration. "This disruption in settlement and demography between 800 and 600 years ago is visible in the archaeological record from southeast Alaska southward to the Gulf of Georgia, where the Coast Salish Pattern develops after this time" (Maschner 2012b:167). The Coast Salish comprise a series of related ethnic and linguistic groups who, unlike other coastal people, emphasize patrilineal rather than matrilineal descent.

Late Pacific complexities can also be seen in the "institutionalization" of slavery. A key item of Northwest Coast trade was human slaves. These human beings had been captured by war parties and then forcibly held for the rest of their lives as the lowest of the low. Historically, the numbers of slaves per household in parts of the Northwest is estimated to have been about one in four household members (Ames 2008: table 6.3). During their lifetimes, they could expect to be traded, sometimes moved across northern California, Oregon, Washington, and British Columbia. At death, they were denied burial in village cemeteries, some bodies simply being dumped out at sea.

Not all Late Pacific complexities occurred uniformly along the Northwest Coast. As with earlier eras, certain regions were more or less intensively inhabited into the Late Pacific period, doubtless related in complicated ways to the all-important Pacific-mediated climate. In fact, one of the more significant localized changes – the appearance of a form of Northwest Coast urbanism – began with an occupational hiatus. Around Prince Rupert Harbor, the beginning of the Late Pacific period was marked by the disappearance of villages, with the causes still talked about today (Ames et al. 2016). According to their contemporary oral histories, the Northern Tsimshian fought and lost a war against intruders who they called Tlingit. The defeated Northern Tsimshian withdrew and, for a time, moved away.

Centuries later, the Tsimshians returned and retook the harbor, forming a new alliance of nine tribes and settling "in such a way that they can withstand attack" (Ames et al. 2016:1). Their return appears to date to about 1000 CE, and at that time Tsimshians reoccupied some of the old village areas. However, of these, the old sites most exposed to attack were never reoccupied, while those villages that were reoccupied witnessed the construction of some of the densest stands of housing ever seen in the Northwest. The unprecedented density led archaeologist Kenneth Ames and his colleagues (2016) to identify the result as "massed villages," and to consider Prince Rupert Harbor an unusual experiment in urbanism, unlike anything seen before, here or elsewhere (Ames et al. 2016).

Given the basis of Northwest Coast community in hierarchically ranked houses (and not monolithic ethnicities or unified tribal entities as elsewhere in North America), such widespread synchronous changes can only be understood by untangling the local village-based landscapes of identity and inheritance that were tethered to trade and warring. In the case of Prince Rupert Harbor, there were no climatic shifts that correlated with the Late Pacific hiatus and reoccupation (Ames et al. 2016). Interestingly, this episode of social transformation also did not correlate with any sort of great social or religious movement, as one might expect from other North American cases. Loose relational webs, not overarching religious or social movements or ideologies, characterized the Northwest Coast. Interregional interaction there was unlike that in other parts of the continent. And it was rooted in a very different kind of community experience and, ultimately, a unique form of "complexity," involving class hierarchy, warfare, slave-taking, and trade.

California

In some ways, the native history of central and southern California paralleled that of the Northwest Coast and Interior Plateau, and the mediating effects of the oceans in combination with climatic factors cannot be dismissed (Table 13.2). In other ways, the histories of these areas diverged markedly and for cultural, not environmental, reasons (Wengrow and Graeber 2018). Certainly the cultural and linguistic diversity of California is notable, most of which was based in populations of intensive or "complex" food collectors and foragers, not farmers. These sedentary and semisedentary groups were loosely networked across great stretches of space via the circulation

Table 13.2 Chronological highlights of the central and southern California Middle and Late periods (adapted from Arnold 2004; Lightfoot and Luby 2012; Perry 2012; Schwitalla and Jones 2012).

Year CE	Historic period	Cultural patterns
400 ± 100	Middle Period (a.k.a. Upper Archaic)	San Francisco Bay shell mound building; Penutian migration into Central Valley. Southern California droughts, coastal reorientation of settlements, deep-sea fishing, plank canoes and barbed harpoons, bow and arrow, intensification of exchange.
800–1300	Medieval Warm Period/Transitional period	Increased violence and biological stresses. San Francisco Bay shell mound building.
1300	Late Period	Intensive foraging-fishing, hierarchical organization, craft specialization, central towns along coasts and major rivers, money.
1542	First contact	Juan Rodríguez Cabrillo explores California coast.
1769	Historic era	Franciscan mission system established.
1848	American	California gold rush, end of Mexican–American war; extermination of native groups by miners and ranchers.

of obsidian, marine shell, and other articles. Reminiscent of Archaic period developments in eastern North America, some California groups consciously distinguished themselves from others, and from nearby Northwest Coast peoples, through the adoption or rejection of certain cultural practices (e.g., Wengrow and Graeber 2018).

Cultural Landscape Diversity

When first encountered by Juan Rodríguez Cabrillo, California was occupied by more than 300,000 native people speaking a tangle of 50 major languages, many comprising multiple dialects (Cook 1978; Shipley 1978). Others would estimate the population at even higher levels. The great diversity (especially in central and northern regions, compared with Iroquoia, for instance) is often attributed to the country's rugged topography and its patchy distribution of food resources. To the east, the pine-fir forest-covered Sierra Nevada range and, south of that, the barren Mojave Desert cut off California from the Interior Plateau, Great Basin, and Southwest. The Central Valley, an area of grassland throughout the Late Period, was fringed by an oak savannah where it met coastal mountain ranges to the west. Around San Francisco north to the Klamath Valley, stunning redwood forests grew in the moist coastal zone. There, in the north, coastal Yoruk peoples built plank houses from redwood and cedar in a Northwest Coast style, but they did not engage in slave-taking (Pilling 1978; Wengrow and Graeber 2018). In a similar but drier zone around modern-day Los Angeles, on the Channel Islands, and south into Baja California, drought-resistant annuals interspersed with oak trees comprised a coastal chaparral environment (Figure 13.19).

Walking even for just a day or two across almost any portion of California except the Central Valley would have involved crossing several small valleys and ecological zones that are, in turn, structured by altitude, slope, orientation, and geology. Local populations, one argument goes, would have been bounded by natural features and, over centuries, isolated socially, culturally, and linguistically. The last California native man to live in such isolation, up to 1911 in fact, was Ishi (Kroeber 1961). Then again, scenarios that hold people to have been mere adaptations to local environments greatly oversimplify the complex historical landscape of California. After all, California was populated by people as early as any place in North America, and

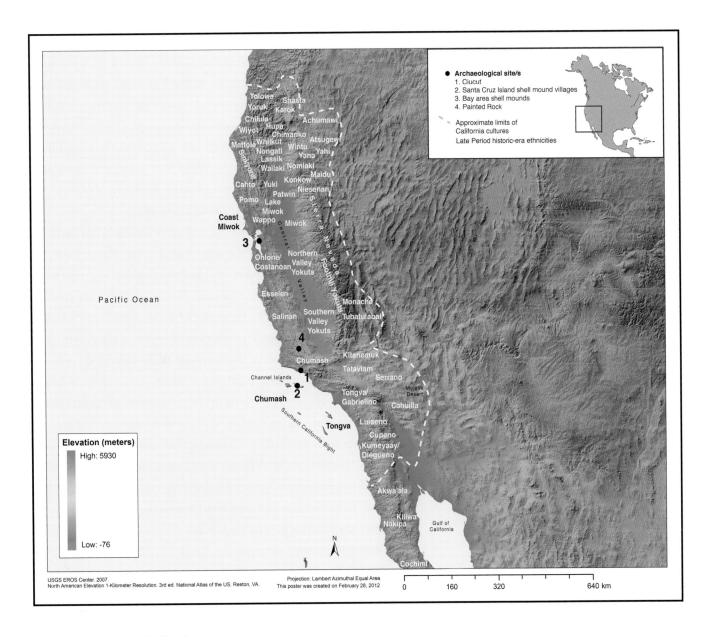

Fig 13.19 Map of Late Period California.

its linguistic diversity is partly a function of the 12,000-plus years of historical change (see Chapters 4–5). DNA and historical linguistic evidence supports arguments for migrations within and between California regions throughout the past.

Middle Holocene Developments

California's middle Holocene period (5000–2000 BCE) overlaps with its "Archaic" period, which is also called the "Early" (ca. 5500–600 BCE) and "Middle" horizons (ca. 600 BCE–1000 CE), generally speaking. During this long stretch of time, small groups of foragers appear to have carved up the interior into territories tethered to groves of oaks, among other things (see Chapter 6). In the wetlands of the Central Valley – known as the Delta, where the Sacramento and San Joaquin rivers meet – and around the San Francisco Bay area to the west, domestic sites dot the landscape. These sites, here and in southern California, are generally small, with few exceptions, and produce evidence of fishing, shellfish harvesting, and acorn processing, the last in the form of groundstone mortars and pestles (Arnold and Walsh 2010; Erlandson and Glassow 1997).

Mostly, we presume that many if not most Early horizon foragers lived in pithouses. In one coastal instance, the Nursery site on San Clemente Island, pithouses were built with whalebone roof supports (Raab 1997). Here and elsewhere, human burials were found with shaped shell ornaments, indicative of the importance or relationship of mollusks to people. That relationship became even more apparent later, during the Middle horizon (600 BCE–1000/1150 CE), or early late Holocene era, as populations of hunter-gatherers grew larger and became less mobile, tethered to semipermanent home settlements.

After that, during California's Late horizon or period (of the late Holocene, ca. 1000/1050 CE to contact), things became even more complex (Gamble 2015c). Villages dotted the Central Valley's Sacramento and San Joaquin valleys while, along the coast around San Francisco Bay, semisedentary and sedentary foragers lived atop and around mollusk-shell and earthen mounds that were growing large through accretion and planned enlargements (Figure 13.20). Archaeologists Kent Lightfoot and Edward Luby (2012) suspect some of the Bay area shell mounds to have been monuments that marked group territories (compare the shell mounds in Chapter 9). Many of these are characterized by some combination of shell or earth middens and construction fills from 1 m to (around the Bay) 10 m high "extending across the equivalent of a couple of football fields" (Lightfoot and Luby 2012:214). Interred in many of these were dozens to hundreds of human burials, possibly suggesting a long-term continuous occupation over thousands of years. Animal burials or offerings are also known.

During the Middle Period's "golden era" (ca. 600 BCE–1000/1150 CE), a series of these large shell mounds were built around the San Francisco Bay area, each about 3 km from the next and topped with bent-pole buildings. The politicized character of these mounds may be indicated by the increased evidence of interpersonal violence on

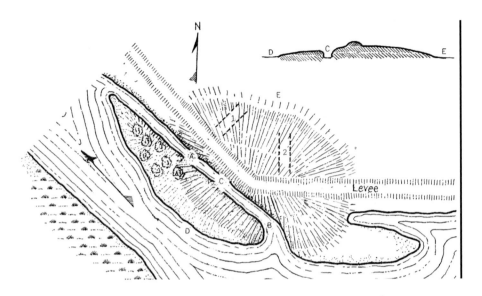

Fig 13.20 Plan of a California shell mound near Stockton, California (Jones 1922:117).

the bodies buried within some. This is called the "Berkeley Pattern" around the Bay (Arnold and Walsh 2010:72). Forearm fractures are found in numbers that suggest hand-to-hand fighting. Isolated hands or heads are found, indicating trophy taking. Puncture and arrow wounds are known, as is scalping.

Far to the south, an even larger Early and Middle Period shell mound, El Montón on Santa Cruz Island, is also believed by Lynn Gamble (2017) to have been a monumental construction, a platform mound that would have served as site of memory construction and the seat of macrocommunity governance. Such coastal integration of sites also makes sense in practical and theatrical terms. Owing to the reliance of the island people on boat transportation (see Late Period, below), shoreline settlements could scarcely have been isolated as distinct communities. Moreover, the people, buildings, or performances associated with a shell mound summit would have been visible from the landward side as well as during a water approach, making El Montón an ideal community-theatrical feature. Its early date may mean that El Montón's construction set the stage, so to speak, for Chumash history-to-come (Figure 13.21).

Back in central California after 400 CE, Penutian speakers, possibly from the east, are thought to have replaced Hokan-speaking people around the Bay and along the interior Sacramento and San Joaquin rivers and their tributaries (Elsasser 1978; Hull 2012; J. R. Johnson et al. 2012). Around San Francisco Bay, the population replacement

Fig 13.21 Archaeologist Lynn Gamble standing in her excavation trench on El Montón, Santa Cruz Island, California. Timothy R. Pauketat photo, 2012.

is called the "Meganos intrusion" and may have been short-lived (Arnold and Walsh 2010:72). The intrusion lasted longer in the Central Valley, and had happened about the same time as the bow and arrow appeared which, in California, is generally correlated with a rise in human-on-human violence (Perry 2012).

Presumably, the Penutian speakers filtering into the Central Valley at this time included several distinct tribal groups of sedentary or semisedentary hunter-gatherers who relied on deer, other small terrestrial animals and waterfowl, acorns, grasses, and other wild berries, nuts, roots, and seeds. Near many settlements were exposures of bedrock covered with "milling stations," the concavities worn into the rock from the processing of acorns using rock hammers and pestles, some today preserved on public lands (www.parks.ca.gov/?page_id=553). You will recall from Chapter 6 that acorns were the region's principal staple food (Figure 13.22).

In general, such Central Valley people lived in pithouses that were most often grass-, tule-, bark-, or fern-covered cone-shaped frameworks of poles built over shallow semisubterranean basins. Several such buildings comprised the typical small settlement, with some featuring earthen middens or, again, mounds a meter or so high, in which the dead were interred (Lightfoot and Luby 2012:217–218). A couple of large Patwin towns (Penutian speakers) were known along the Sacramento River historically, each administered by a prominent hereditary chief and each featuring small sweat lodges, ordinary living quarters, and an earth-covered "dance house" (Kroeber 1922). Inside such buildings, community groups and secret societies met to perform sacred rites.

Historically, one such society was the *Kuksu* sodality or cult into which young men were initiated (Kroeber 1976). When they danced, they wore heavy paint makeup, feathers, and garments. Sometimes,

Fig 13.22 Circular milling and processing depressions in bedrock, Sequoia National Forest, California. Timothy R. Pauketat photos, 2017.

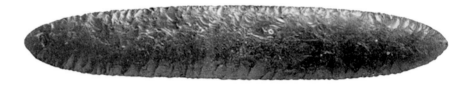

Fig 13.23 Obsidian dance blades, 25 and 33 cm (10 and 13 in) long (Rust 1905: plate XLI).

inalienable community objects, such as large obsidian knives most common in northern California, accompanied the dances (Figure 13.23). Initiates in the society, the children of wealthy families, endured two or three months of being sequestered after a ritualized bloodletting, induced in turn by being shot by small arrows (Thakar and Gamble 2015).

As on the Northwest Coast, pottery was rarely made and used by Middle Period Californians (cf. the historic-era Yokuts of the San Joaquin Valley; Kroeber 1976:537). Instead, Middle Period peoples made a diverse array of baskets with which to store, cook, and serve food and drinks, some lined with water-resistant pitch and others featuring extremely tight weaves. Games of chance and skill played by people were largely interpersonal, not communal (in contrast to the Eastern Woodlands and Plains; see Chapters 10–12). At contact, for example, only the Yokut, Pomo, and Miwok played a scaled-down version of lacrosse (Kroeber 1976:847).

Central Valley towns in the Middle Period, and subsequent Late horizon times, were sustained by an intensive harvesting of salmon and other anadromous fish in the river with the help of community fish weirs, traps, and dams (Gamble 2012:181). They and the other residents of the Central Valley managed the landscape, burning off grasslands to promote those grass species with edible seeds and culling undesirable trees from wooded groves to maximize the growth of oak trees that yielded the most acorns

Fig 13.24 Ada Lopez Richards, a Tolowa woman: note the woven hat, shell bead necklaces, and dentalium shell embroidered skirt. Edward S. Curtis, ca.1923/Library of Congress, Washington, DC.

annually (typically called "arboriculture"). Everything was scheduled to the season, with little left to chance (see Sidebar 6.2).

Of course, it was hard work, and the hardest work – collecting wood, seeds, and tubers using collection baskets and digging sticks, hauling the same back to the village in burden baskets on one's back with a tumpline strapped to the head, then processing the many seeds and nuts using stone grinding tools – was left to women and, especially, lower-status women. Carrying and grinding over many years strains the lower back, hips, and knees, and Middle and Late Period skeletal remains show such wear, along with spinal degeneration and osteoarthritis, particularly in older females (Hollimon 1996; Hollimon and Murley 2012).

The food, tool, and utensil remains of such sedentary foragers include many bone, stone, and mollusk-shell artifacts, the remains of cooked foods, food-processing tools (especially groundstone mortars and pestles), projectile points, fishing gear, net weights or sinkers, awls, sewing needles, and much more. Included among the village remains are many beads made from gastropod and bivalve shells. Besides minimally modified *Olivella* species shells, these included disk, globular, tubular, and cylindrical forms as well as pendants. The bead shape, of course, varied owing to raw material type, the group of producers who made them, the production technology involved, and the relative value of the shells. Historically, California native people wore many beaded garments, sashes, belts, and necklaces, and villagers in restricted coastal areas manufactured and then circulated these across and between regions (Figure 13.24). Those loci of manufacture included the Napa Valley to the north of San Francisco Bay, today famous as wine country but in the past the scene of both obsidian extraction and shell bead production. The locality was "a waypoint in the marine mollusk trade from the coast to the Sacramento Valley … [and] a source of obsidian for San Francisco Bay, Marin County, and the Sacramento–San Joaquin Delta regions" (Elsasser 1978:46).

Late Period Patterns

Subsequently, as part of the Bay area's "Augustine Pattern" of the Late Period, construction of shell mounds ceased, though people – now probably refocused on the acorn-producing regions of the interior – yet placed their dead in them. Doubtless, these changes are related to the effects of the Medieval Climatic Anomaly, which covered the period of about 800–1300 CE. Certainly the effects were felt in the San Joaquin and Sacramento valleys, where "drought conditions" would have "increased the lure" of the major rivers and lakes (Arnold and Walsh 2010:97). "Foothill regions, for the most part, held their primary attraction in the fall alone, when acorns ripened and game animals returned from their summer migrations to the high Sierra" (Arnold and Walsh 2010:97). Where substantial foothill settlements did occur, they were "along permanent streams that feed the valley floor from sources high in the Sierra." Two known sites in such a situation "yielded a substantial corpus of burial data possibly indicating heritable status differentiation" (Arnold and Walsh 2010:97). But that status differentiation, as judged by numbers of shell ornaments, was itself variable across the region.

Though it varied across Late Period California after the eleventh century CE, access to many types of beads, beaded necklaces, or beaded garments signified high rank, much as it did on the Northwest Coast. Some types of *Olivella* or clamshell beads were used as money (cf. historic-era wampum in the Northeast; see Chapter 12). As opposed to other beads, that is, native Californians' "money beads" were "used by anyone regardless of the status position they were born into" (King 1978:61). Throughout the Late horizon and into the historic era, new bead types and increased quantities of beads seem to attest to the monetized value of such items. Not surprisingly, this value would have encouraged increased shell-craft production and, from there, a kind of inflationary spiral that led increasingly to craft specialization (i.e., the production by a few members of a community for the consumption by many others, locally and beyond).

At the same time, evidence from southern California points to a more clear-cut case of "occupational specialization, ascribed status, and formalized leadership, as well as associated technologies such as ocean-going watercraft and shell bead currencies" (Perry 2012:224).

The effect seems to have been the production of a new kind or level of "complexity on the southern California coast" (Coupland 2004:180). Such developments are clearest among the Chumash of the southern California Bight (see below).

Besides the effects of money and craft production, Late Period historical development was also contingent on the warmer and drier effects of the Medieval Climatic Anomaly (Schwitalla and Jones 2012:94). On the one hand, droughts during the eleventh and twelfth centuries – the "Transitional period" between the Middle and Late periods – appear to have had dilatory impacts on diet and health. Increased levels of dietary deficiencies – evidenced by cribra orbitalia (eye socket lesions), enamel hypoplasia (tooth enamel defects), and periostitis (bone infections) along with a reduced average stature – correlate with the Medieval Warm Period and are particularly acute in some regions in the late 1200s and 1300s. On the other hand, such physical stresses played out socially as intercommunity violence, seen osteologically as higher incidences of cranial fractures (from being hit over the head), broken forearms (from attempting to deflect an enemy's blows), and embedded projectile points. Historically, community raids and feuds were linked to disputes over resources, and we presume the same applied to this early Late Period transition.

Certainly, the history of relations between people and the plants and animals upon which they subsisted produced a hierarchical society in certain regions at least by 1150 CE. Ascribed or inherited status was common as was a nascent political hierarchy of leaders, called "wots" by the Chumash and "sektus" by the Penutian speakers in the Central Valley (Gamble 2012). The "Chumash chief enjoyed influence and honor to a rather unusual degree ... [and] received food and shell money from the people – no doubt for a return of some kind ... Ordinarily, he alone had more than one wife" (Kroeber 1976:556). In appearance, the wots were distinctive: "Draped in otter skin capes, they wore their hair up, secured with delicately carved bone pins and large, inlaid chert knives" (Gamble 2015a:67). Among the Penutian speakers, the chief was less influential, though among the southern Maidu, the "chief was hereditary, received part of all larger game, and sometimes had young men hunt for him outright. He lived in the village dance house, or this dwelling served as assembly chamber for the group" (Kroeber 1976:399).

The Late Period Chumash

Late Period craft production was becoming specialized, such that higher status people controlled the production and exchange of valuable materials and shell money (Gamble 2015b). The effects of the shell-article production and exchange cycles are particularly pronounced among the Chumash on the Channel Islands off the coast of modern-day Santa Barbara, where many beads were manufactured. Here and on the mainland of the southern California Bight are special quarry sites and habitations involved in shell bead-making. Chert quarries were the sites from which raw material was obtained to produce small microdrill bits, each to be fitted on to a wooden drill turned with the help of a bow. These were made by striking small "microblades" off a core or prepared chunk of raw material. Those flakes and bits of debitage that proved useless for drill bits were simply left behind. The drills themselves, broken or dulled from use, are found in the middens of settlements all around the Channel Islands, and particularly on the large Santa Cruz Island (Gamble 2015b).

Nearby, small shell mound middens 3–4 m deep dot the coastline, each surmounted by at least several – and some with 20 or more – visible depressions, many a meter or so deep. These were the locations of former Late Period buildings (Figure 13.25). Some buildings were large, being the dwellings of families of higher status and others being dance houses for ceremonials.

Fig 13.25 Large house depression on a shell mound, Santa Cruz Island, California. Timothy R. Pauketat photo, 2012.

According to all accounts, the Chumash house was large – up to 50 feet or more in diameter – and harbored a community of … as many as 50 individuals by one report, 40 by another, three or four families according to a third. The structure was hemispherical, made by planting willows or other poles in a circle and bending and tying them together at the top. Other sticks extended across these, and to them was fastened a layer of tule mats, or sometimes, perhaps, thatch. There was no earth covering except for a few feet from the ground, the frame being too light to support a burden of soil.

(Kroeber 1976:557)

Their floors were either dug into or surrounded through time by the heaped-up mollusk shell and marine mammal, fish, and bird bone scrap that resulted from the many meals consumed there. Intermixed with the debris are exhausted and broken igneous rock mortars, pestles, hammerstones, chert flakes and pieces of projectile points, microdrills, and, always, whole and broken shell beads (Figure 13.26).

The population estimates for each site, from a family to 100 people residing in up to 40 contemporary houses, belie the likely close ties between adjacent settlements, many of which along the Channel Island shorelines were visible one from another (Figure 13.27). In all probability, a cluster of settlements comprised a community. Indeed, recall that the Early– Middle Period shell mound, El Montón on Santa Cruz Island, is believed by Lynn Gamble to have been a monumental construction – a platform mound – that would have also served as the seat of macrocommunity governance, tying multiple settlements together. Such coastal integration of sites also makes sense in practical and theatrical terms. Owing to the reliance of the island people on boat transportation, shoreline settlements could scarcely be isolated

Fig 13.26 Chumash shell mound artifacts: left, igneous rock mortar fragment; top right, chert biface; lower right, mollusk shell and shell bead. Timothy R. Pauketat photos, 2008.

Fig 13.27 Intervisible sites along the coastline of Santa Cruz Island, California. Timothy R. Pauketat photo, 2008.

as distinct communities. Moreover, the people, buildings, or performances associated with a shell mound summit would have been visible from the landward side as well as during a water approach, making it an ideal community-building theatrical feature. Given the importance of long-distance and cross-channel trade, such shell mounds would seem to have been well placed. Given the multiple experiential linkages of both land and water in a shoreline shell mound site, one should suspect that any community was about more beings than just people.

For the Channel Island dwellers as well as the mainland Chumash, much of the movement of materials and goods took place with the aid of substantial plank canoes, also known as tomols (Figure 13.28). These had been built since around 500 CE using boards glued together with asphaltum (also found in archaeological contexts). In them, the island Chumash exported beads (including bead money), dried fish, and groundstone, and imported acorns, deer bone, obsidian, and baskets (Kroeber 1976:557). Although such exchange relations never unified all of the Chumash, who occupied the lands from modern-day Malibu north to San Luis Obispo, it is clear that some capital towns governed provinces and, presumably, imposed some degree of unity among the people.

Fig 13.28 Chumash plank canoe or tomol.
W. Langdon Kihn, 1946/Wikimedia.

Possibly more important than political unification, pan-Chumash identity and societal integrity was further imparted by the presence of a religious society known as the 'antap (Hollimon 2001; Perry 2012; Thakar and Gamble 2015). This society (or sodality) comprised shamans, canoe owners, and political leaders who paid shell-bead money to join and were responsible for organizing and performing annual rituals correctly. Although the genealogy of this sodality is unclear, most towns at contact had multiple 'antap practitioners and so they might have more than one shaman, who typically specialized in curing and matters surrounding death (Corbett 2004). Such people, historically more common in southern California than in the Central Valley, also sought spirit guides that might include the sun, performed rites timed to the solstices, and predicted weather, which might vary drastically with the El Niño cycle.

Shamans and Shamanic Sites

Archaeologically, rattles and bone whistles, the latter used in shamanic rituals and ceremonial dances, are found in association with shamans or ritual sites (Figure 13.29). The magic of the whistle, possibly owing to its association with breath and the human soul, was also used in courtship. Medicinal and hallucinogenic plants, especially jimsonweed (*Datura* sp.), are known from shamanic contexts, including those surrounding the puberty rites of boys and girls, which might

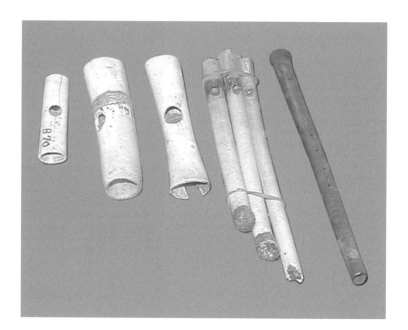

Fig 13.29 Bone whistles used in California Indian rituals, San Luis Obispo Mission museum. Timothy R. Pauketat photo, 2002.

Fig 13.30 Chumash Painted Cave State Historic Park, Santa Barbara, California: left, rockshelter opening; right, panel of polychrome pictographs. Timothy R. Pauketat photos, 2016.

include vision questing, where shamans or young people sought spirit guides to help them in life.

Shamanic and vision-quest sites are known from across California, with Chumash locations featuring polychrome paintings of supposed world-center or sun symbols along with "entoptic" imagery (often associated with drug-induced trance states). In one instance above modern-day Santa Barbara, the vision-quest site is remote, located in the mountains above the Chumash coastal villages (Figure 13.30). It would have taken a shaman or vision seeker a day or more to climb to it. The most famous sacred site, still used by modern-day Chumash, is Painted Rock, in the Carrizo Plain near San Luis Obispo. Today, Painted

Sidebar 13.5 Tree carving in California: cultural survival

By Matt Kettmann, February 9, 2010, *Time* magazine:

An "arborglyph" or tree carving was discovered in 2006 on an old gnarled oak in a grove atop the San Luis Mountains near San Luis Obispo. A "Chumash family that lived on a nearby hillside until they all died in the 1918 flu epidemic may have tended to the arborglyph …" It consisted of the meter-high image of a six-legged lizard, thought to be a mythical nightsky being. There are "similar designs on rock formations from San Luis Obispo south through Santa Barbara and into Malibu." The being's "carved crown" appears to show "the constellation Ursa Major – which includes the Big Dipper – related to the position of Polaris, the North Star … [T]he ancient images were deliberate studies of the stars and served as integral components of the Chumash people's annual calendar" that, amazingly, survives to this day.

Rock is part of the Carrizo Plain National Monument and managed by the Bureau of Land Management. To protect it from vandalism, you visit it with a park escort (www.blm.gov/programs/national-conserva tion-lands/california/carrizo-plain-national-monument). In Google Earth, search for "Painted Rock, Carrizo Plain National Monument" or just "Painted Rock, CA." Zoom into its interior, which is shaped like a giant vulva with walk-in access from the north. Adjust the time of day using the "time slider" and see how the sun would have passed above the feature, casting shadows along the walls in different areas depending on the season. Enter street view, still facing north, and advance the time of day hour by hour through the night. See how all of the stars revolved around one brighter star. This is the north star.

Historic Epilogue

So much changed with the arrival of the Spanish and, in the Northwest, the Russians and English. The Northwest Coast peoples were spared some of the early European and Euro-American incursions, though native Californians, "universally characterized … as shy and friendly people" by early nonnative explorers, suffered greatly, unable to mount large-scale resistance (Washburn 1978). The Spanish missions employed a strategy known as *reducción*, whereby dispersed village peoples were forcibly moved into single mission sites. The mission's orderly layout and its temporality marked by church bells – along with whippings, solitary confinement, "and even execution" of non-compliant native individuals – instantiated a new, authoritarian cultural hegemony that altered the ways in which human beings came to know their place in the world (Castillo 1978).

There was organized Indian resistance, but the dispersed and unallied forager-fisher peoples in California, particularly after the 1848 gold rush and absorption of the territory by the United States, could not anticipate or stave off the horrific massacres of native people by the intruding Euro-Americans, as recounted by ethnohistorian Edward Castillo (1978:107–108): "Indian life, which was more valuable to the Mexicans because they institutionalized Indian labor for wealth, was seen as worthless to the Americans." Attacks on Indians by the "Anglos commenced almost at once. Anglo invaders began to seize land in the interior valley and along the northern coast." In one episode, Indian families had grouped together into a winter settlement, and the

whites thought it was a favorable opportunity to get rid of them altogether. So they went in a body to the Indian camp, during the night … shot all the men, women, and children at the first onslaught, and cut the throats of the remainder. Very few escaped. Next morning 60 bodies lay weltering in their blood …

(Castillo 1978:108)

The US military assisted in other episodes, leading to instances such as the Clear Lake Massacre, which reportedly began when some Pomo Indians killed two white traders who had enslaved them. In response, the US government sent a military force under the command of Captain Nathanial Lyon, later the first Union general killed in the Civil War. Lyon's men landed on an island and slaughtered 135 of 400 resident men, women, and children (Castillo 1978:108).

14 Order and Chaos in the Southwest
The Hohokam and Puebloan Worlds

Fig 14.1 Zuni girl with pottery jar on head. Edward S. Curtis, ca. 1903/Library of Congress, Washington, DC.

A Zuni girl, living just north of the Mogollon Rim, witnessed Coronado's parade of Spanish horsemen and Tlaxcaltec warriors marching north in 1540. She saw them return south two years later. The times, it must have seemed to her, were changing. Then again, being Zuni already meant embodying a borderland blend of cultures and languages with roots in the Keresan-speaking Pueblos to the east, the Uto-Aztecan-speaking Hopi and Tohono O'odham communities to the northwest and southwest, and the Mogollons to the southeast. The girl was the result of centuries of order and chaos in the Southwest dating from the very beginnings of village life (Figure 14.1).

This chapter outlines the happenings, places, and variable fortunes of people who lived through the beginnings of pithouse village life, around the Grand Canyon and Four Corners, south across the Mogollon Rim, and into the Sonoran Desert and west Mexico (Figure 14.2). It examines the explanations of how and why later adobe compounds and astronomically aligned masonry centers arose at places such as Snaketown, Casa Grande, Pueblo Bonito, and Wupatki. Along the way, we seek to answer some important questions about human history. Among the questions is: how were community, monumentality, agriculture, religion, and migration connected to the Zuni girl's lived reality and to the unique human experience of the greater Southwest and northwest Mexico?

Agricultural Background

At contact in northwestern Mexico and the American Southwest, in the present-day states of Sonora, Chihuahua, Arizona, and New Mexico, most indigenous people lived sedentary, agricultural lifestyles. They farmed domesticated crops used for food, including maize (*Zea mays*), squash (*Cucurbita pepo*), beans

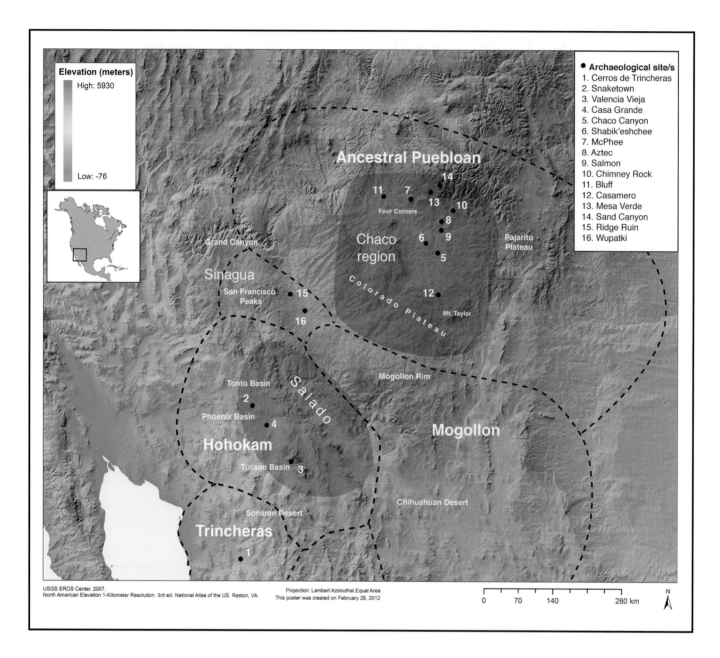

Fig 14.2 Map of the greater Southwest/northwestern Mexico.

(*Phaseolus vulgaris*), and native starchy seeds (including amaranth, goosefoot, lambsquarters, ricegrass, and sunflower, varying by location). They also cultivated the bottle gourd or calabash (*Lagenaria* spp.) for use as containers, grew cotton for textile production, and kept domestic turkeys in pens. These crops and practices have sometimes been lumped together and called the "Sonoran Agricultural Complex" (Ford 1985). As a set, the food products possessed nutritional qualities that complemented each other. They grew well together on the plateau to the north and in the desert to the south.

Sidebar 14.1 Agricultural landscapes in the Southwest

The Colorado Plateau is a heavily dissected 34 million ha (85 million acre) geological uplift covered by desert scrublands and scattered mountain forests in the northern Southwest (i.e., northern Arizona, northwestern New Mexico, southeastern Utah, and far western Colorado), the ancestral homeland of the Puebloan Indians and their Basketmaker period forerunners. The southwestern edge of this plateau – sometimes called "The Big Empty" – is defined by the Mogollon Rim, a sharp vertical and forested escarpment that rises up to 2,400 m (8,000 ft) above sea level. To its south one descends into the Salt River and, eventually, into the Sonoran Desert. The desert stretches from central Arizona south to the tip of California and into Sonora, Mexico, and includes the treeless river basins and mountains that ring them. Farmers on the Colorado Plateau did not irrigate their fields, their "dry farming" techniques including various water conservation and water-capture or rainfall-retention features. Farmers in the Sonoran Desert, on the other hand, turned to irrigation farming techniques to make the desert bloom.

But this northwestern Mexican and greater southwestern pattern developed over a period of centuries, beginning during the "Late Archaic" and "Early Ceramic period" as early as 3,500 years ago in the Sonoran Desert, from present-day Phoenix, Arizona south into Sonora, Mexico. The reliance on domestic crops came later to people on the Colorado Plateau, with maize and squash becoming staples during the thousand-year-long "Basketmaker II" period (500 BCE–500 CE). In both areas, early agricultural life revolved around the pithouse village, a seemingly stable residential lifestyle. Pithouses were comfortable homes, framed with wooden poles and covered with earth but with floors dug down below the ground surface. They were large enough for an entire family and would be cool in the summers yet warm in the winters (Figure 14.3). A pithouse village was the locus of community, and community, in turn, was the heart of civic and ceremonial life. But communities frequently have fuzzy boundaries. In the ancient Southwest, they might be dispersed across some wider locality to include people living at other villages or at smaller farmsteads and field houses.

In the Southwest, the landscape set the outer limits to community. The reason is not difficult to see. Unlike other parts of the continent, where forests, mountains, or featureless plains limit visibility or provide few distant visual cues, the Southwest's combination of treeless horizons and great basins studded with distant mesas or mountains locates the human observer at the center of a vast, rich relational field. Clearly, for southwestern people, says anthropologist Keith Basso (1996), cultural knowledge and social memory "sits in places."

Fig 14.3 The remains of superimposed Hohokam pithouses at Mescal Wash, Arizona (from Vanderpot 2017: figure 28). Courtesy of the Arizona Department of Transportation and Statistical Research, Inc.

Historically, various native groups associated great mythic events, deities, and historical accounts with distant landmarks or directions. Their very identities – who they were, where they came from, and where they or their souls were going – were entangled with the experience of such places near and far. A person was tied to the land from the moment her or his young eyes glimpsed the distant horizon.

Sidebar 14.2 Southwestern community

As we noted earlier in this book, community was more than a place, an identity, or a group of people. It was a dynamic set of social relationships realized through experience. Communities would form and reform contingent on the people, places, and things involved in the acts of communion. One quite literally communes with people and with other aspects of the world, if not also with the forces of the cosmos. Such acts are not merely imagined in one's head. They have a materiality – a shape or form that enables communion with others. Southwestern pots, for example, embodied community – this active communing and relating to others. How? First, ancient people knew that the pot was made from earthen materials (clay and temper), and that it was made to contain the produce of the earth. Right away that knowledge established a bond between the potter

and the earth. Second, large "communal" pots were made to contain food for dispersal to some larger group of people, such that the user would end up intimately related to them. Third, the pot might be decorated with meaningful patterns, colors, and icons that evoked emotions, memories, or opinions that were, in turn, subject to discussion and negotiation by a larger group. Thus, merely positioning such a pot, with all of its potential implications, in the middle of a plaza to feed people attending a feast, for instance, would have had clear communal effects. It would have drawn people into a set of social relationships – community – whether they liked it or not by communing through the pot. To put it another way, the pot would have embodied community. Wherever it was, there would be community also.

Multiply that sort of experience by community and agriculture and you have the basic ingredients of native southwestern/northwestern civilization. Civilization's agricultural and communal recipe, as it turns out, was also deeply affected by an important social change around 500 CE: the bow and arrow was introduced, replacing the standard hunting equipment across the Southwest up to that time, the atlatl-thrown spear or dart. The reasons for the adoption of the bow at 500 CE have been debated by archaeologists. Was it simply a superior hunting weapon? Perhaps, although people accustomed to the atlatl might have shied away from the bow because of what the technology entailed. For one thing, it forced people to shift their hunting tactics and techniques; the bow provided greater stealth and, conceivably, allowed small game to be shot rather than simply snared. For another thing, this new stealthy weapon gave bow users a distinct advantage over spear-throwing Luddites. Perhaps these two reasons were sufficient for most people across the landscape to switch, more or less simultaneously, to the bow. In the long run, the bow almost certainly changed the calculus of when and how one village might raid another, making the world a more dangerous place for these early agriculturalists (see also Chapter 10).

The second and most important alteration to the social and physical landscape resulted from extensive labor investment in land. Labor investments on the Colorado Plateau involved clearing and maintaining diverse field locations, constructing run-off detention ponds and water collection pools, and establishing shrines to ensure the community's balanced relationship to cosmic forces. Landscape modifications in the desertlands of Chihuahua and Sonora north into the Tucson, Phoenix, and Tonto basins of central Arizona included even more labor-intensive and permanent alterations.

In the far south, these improvements involved contouring hills and building settlements atop what locals call *cerros de trincheras* (or "trenched hills"). These terraced-hill settlements, primarily in Chihuahua, Mexico (and possibly southern Arizona and Sonora), date to as early as 1500 BCE, though they were discontinued before seeing a later resurgence. The vast majority dated to a later period, after 1200 CE. The largest of these settlements, bearing the name Cerros de Trincheras, is 150 m high and covers a square kilometer (McGuire et al. 1999; Zavala 2006, 2012). Of course, such hilltop settlements may also have afforded a certain sort of visibility that would have, literally, changed people's outlooks. Some may also have provided places of refuge or defense under threat of attacks from outsiders, perhaps even the Hohokam with whom they seem to be unrelated. In the future Hohokam homeland north of the Trincheras region, beginning along the Santa Cruz River and present-day Tucson, the principal agricultural investment was the construction of irrigation canals (Table 14.1).

The Early Hohokam

Obviously, irrigation canals would offset the severe water availability restrictions in the Sonoran Desert, which otherwise would have made agriculture impossible. But, much like the Sonoran's saguaro cactus, which collects and retains water for its plant cells and produces luscious edible fruits, people had recognized how to move water to where they needed it. The earliest Early Agricultural period canals in

Table 14.1 Chronological highlights of the Hohokam area (adapted from Fish and Fish 2007b).

Year CE	Historic period	Cultural patterns
200–450	Early Ceramic	Widespread adoption of plain-surfaced pottery and anthropomorphic figurines; population levels low or populations localized.
450–700	Pioneer	Pithouse villages with courtyards and plazas; large-scale irrigation; ritual use of palettes and censers; bow and arrow adopted.
700–900	Colonial	Ballcourts in villages; red-on-buff pottery appears; widespread exchange relationships.
900–1150	Sedentary	Expanded irrigation in Phoenix Basin; platform mounds appear, used to elevate dance performances; possible emigration into the Sierra Sin Agua to the north; Wupatki and other Great Houses founded; ballcourts de-emphasized in the Sonora, while they continue to the north.
1150–1300	Early Classic	Regional reorganization; platform mounds elevate public buildings; Salado "culture" emanates from Tonto Basin.
1300–1450	Late Classic	Great platform mounds and adobe buildings within compound walls; population concentration and migrants enter region.
1450–1500	–	Regional depopulation.

the Tucson Basin were just short ditches 20–30 m long, and are known to predate the beginnings of Sonoran agriculture, or about 1500 BCE. They also predate the coalescence of a Hohokam cultural tradition, as recognized by archaeologists. The people of the time seem to have lived in small bent-pole brush huts with circular ground plans. Their dried food stores were held from one season to the next in subfloor pits (Wallace 2007). Their agricultural lives depended on the grade of and waterflow in local streams, with some hints that localities might be abandoned if the rivers became entrenched and downcut too deeply for the canal builders to tap their waters.

Soon, the irrigation system and food production outputs would be expanded across the Tucson Basin and to the north in the Phoenix and Tonto basins along the Gila and Salt rivers, respectively. This marked the beginning of the Hohokam culture and the Pioneer period, at about 450 CE (Fish and Fish 2007a, 2007b, 2012). Why did this expansion happen? The standard archaeological argument is that the Hohokam peoples were the consequence of irrigation farming. In such harsh conditions, irrigation would allow more people to live off the land. Certainly, the opposite was also true. Depopulations of certain localities, the Tucson Basin in the early Pioneer period or the entire Hohokam heartland after 1450 CE, seem to have been the result of changes in the local grades of rivers, inhibiting irrigation and making dense populations untenable.

But are such simple cause-and-effect explanations sufficient? Would they be enough to explain the histories of the United States, Canada, and Mexico? After all, those nations are the result of an agricultural system based on both Old and New World crops, such as wheat and barley, on the one hand, and maize, beans, and squash, on the other. Yet the USA, Canada, and Mexico have separate and, in some ways, radically divergent historical trajectories. So, clearly, the histories of who-did-what-where-when-how-and-why matter, and there is doubtless as much social, political, economic, and religious history behind the Hohokam as there is for modern North America.

At present, a good deal of Hohokam history is conjectural, based on logical extrapolations of general knowns: "What were the effects of irrigation on, say, social organization or inequality? Was it heavy-handed elite rulers or cooperative community organizers who organized the labor to build the canals or said when, why, and how water should flow and where or to whom it should be directed?" We do not yet have definitive answers to these questions, but not because archaeologists are unable to provide such answers. We are. But Hohokam archaeology was stunted in the early twentieth century, lagging behind other portions of the Southwest until the 1930s and beyond.

Part of the reason for lag in the development of Hohokam archaeology is itself historical and, partly, climatic. Hohokam sites, apart from Classic Period Great Houses (see below), have only modest surface expressions and relatively poor preservation, especially compared with Puebloan sites in the Four Corners region (Randall McGuire, personal communication, 2013). Unreconstructed Hohokam houses, at least on Pioneer period sites, can be difficult to find. The lack of standing architecture (in the early Hohokam era and across most of North America) makes excavation efforts challenging. In such situations, archaeologists have to distinguish subtle soil color and texture changes even to recognize architectural remains. And then, once found, Hohokam pithouses lack the visual presence and sex appeal of Puebloan masonry.

In the meantime, the temperate Four Corners area of the Colorado Plateau had seen important and extensive late nineteenth- and early twentieth-century ethnological and archaeological investigations that established a continuous Puebloan chronology. Possibly, this was also due to milder weather conditions on the plateau. After all, the extreme summertime heat and dry conditions in the Sonoran Desert, where the Hohokam sites were located, can be a challenge to archaeology students and professors on an academic schedule, with only the summers at their disposal to do research. Given the intense heat and infrared rays in these pre-airconditioning and pre-sunscreen times, some academic archaeologists went elsewhere (such as the Colorado Plateau).

Thus, the early Hohokam region work of Frank Hamilton Cushing, in the 1880s, and the spotty excavations by the Smithsonian, in the early 1900s, did not result in the recognition of a Hohokam culture or a regional chronological sequence (the latter being a prerequisite for historical studies). That came mostly after the Gladwins' 1927–1932 investigations of Casa Grande (a.k.a. the Grewe site), assisted by a young Emil Haury. Later in the 1930s, the team carried out a two-year excavation project at the great Pioneer period site of Snaketown. At both places, the team would establish the facts of the Hohokam cultural-historical sequence and obtain the first glimpse of possible relationships of the Hohokam to Mesoamerica. But not until Haury's

(1976) later excavations and analysis of Snaketown, followed by the emergence of cultural resource management (CRM) archaeology in the 1970s, was there an infusion of archaeological information of the sort that might begin to clarify the hows and whys of Hohokam history. CRM was, in turn, a development that responded to the need to mitigate the adverse effects of federally funded construction on ancient sites determined to be historically significant, as mandated by federal legislation (see Chapter 2).

Pioneer Hohokam (450–700 CE)

To solve these more-encompassing social-historical questions, archaeologists begin with the diachronic evidence of settlements, subsistence practices, ritual activities, and exchange patterns. There are several important big-picture patterns that can be delineated for the Pioneer Hohokam (Doyel 1991). First and foremost, the beginning of this era witnessed a significant increase in the population density in central and southern Arizona. Settlements grew large and more frequent, with major habitations stretched out like beads on a necklace along river ways and their associated irrigation canal systems. Presumably this gave people both improved subsistence security and safety from physical violence or raids.

This earliest period is exemplified well by the late 1990s CRM excavations of Valencia Vieja by Desert Archaeology, Inc. on the outskirts of Tucson, Arizona (Wallace 2007). Valencia Vieja was one of a couple dozen such early Pioneer period Hohokam villages scattered in the Tucson Basin. Initially a small settlement of a few houses, Valencia Vieja grew in a matter of three or four generations to a village of some 10–20 households, a household being a co-residential group or family; they varied in size and kind then as they do now – as small and "nontraditional" as a parent and child or as large as an extended family. After 500 CE, these houses were arranged in clusters or "courtyard groups," which were, in turn, grouped around a 2,000–3,000 m^2 plaza, with the largest and best-constructed buildings being council houses and the domiciles of leaders or high-ranking families.

Whether of high or low status, individual families lived in the multiple houses of any one courtyard group cluster during these early Pioneer period days, according to David Wilcox and colleagues (1981) (Figure 14.4). The largest public or high-status homes of any

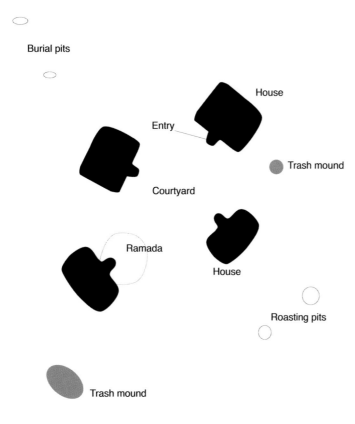

Burial pits

House

Entry

Trash mound

Courtyard

Ramada

House

Roasting pits

Trash mound

Fig 14.4 Idealized early Hohokam courtyard group (adapted from Craig and Henderson 2007: figure 4.2).

such courtyard cluster fronted the plaza, and excavators have found evidence that, in any sizeable early Hohokam village, there was not one leading family. Rather, there were several prominent families, perhaps members of a number of clans that comprised the village. Presumably, each kin-group or clan leader might have had a seat on the village council that governed settlements, ranging from 100 inhabitants, such as Valencia Vieja, to more than 1,000.

The ordinary refuse associated with Pioneer Hohokam family life included broken groundstone manos, metates, mortars and pestles (corn- and seed-grinding implements), exhausted groundstone axe heads (grooved to facilitate attachment of a simple handle), and the broken sherds of a variety of distinctive Hohokam pots (Figure 14.5). Stephanie Whittlesey (2007:68) concludes that "Hohokam cuisine was based on meal made from ground seeds and maize kernels, and we think that large pieces of broken vessels, even painted ones, were used to parch seeds …" Added to the ordinary mix beginning before 700 were things one might consider extraordinary, including small stone palettes, censers, and fired-clay anthropomorphic figurines. The palettes and censers were basic equipment needed to pulverize pigments and incense, and then burn the latter (a characteristically Mesoamerican practice). They are found with the cremation of human remains and were often burned themselves. That is, the burning of incense was somehow connected to

Fig 14.5 Hohokam red-on-buff jar and cauldron, each ca. 20 cm wide. Dallas Museum of Art/Public domain.

the treatment of the dead, who were typically cremated, their ashes buried in the yard of the respective household clusters. The many clay figurines may be the depictions of ancestors whose physical remains had already been reduced to bits of bone and ash buried in pots or pits. As such, the figurines might "presence" a deceased ancestor or her or his soul in the midst of the living (note that this is more than merely "representing" an ancestor, as it means the spirit is there, in the room with you).

Snaketown and the Colonial and Sedentary Periods (700–1150 CE)

Such ritual items became more numerous and varied during the Colonial (700–900) and Sedentary (900–1150) periods. These included more elaborate versions of articles known from the Pioneer period – stone censers now with anthropomorphic and zoomorphic imagery and elaborate stone palettes adorned with carved bird, human, and frog imagery and appendages – and more anthropomorphic pottery vessels (Figure 14.6). The last included the special red-on-buff painted pots that first appeared at the end of the Pioneer period; they had tripod legs and were modeled to look like human or animal forms, presumably used as serving dishes and for seed storage. There were also carved bone hairpins and stone and bone needles, some perhaps for ritual bloodletting, another Mesoamerican practice. And there were high-quality chipped-stone arrow points and marine-shell items, including trumpets, cut-and-shaped pendants, rings, and bracelet parts (Figure 14.7). The most common of these was the bracelet (Randall

Fig 14.6 Hohokam incense-grinding palette, ca. 20 cm in length. Timothy R. Pauketat photo/Heard Museum, Phoenix.

Fig 14.7 Bracelet pieces, made from *Glycymeris* clam shells from the Gulf of California, each about 5 cm in diameter. Courtesy of the Huhugam Heritage Center.

McGuire, personal communication, 2013). Most of these craft items are concentrated in the debris of likely high-status residences at the larger, principal villages (Bayman 2007). At such places, the trumpets probably heralded announcements or important moments in great ceremonies.

The heightened rituality of Hohokam social life during the Colonial and Sedentary periods was perhaps due in no small measure to an all-important sport introduced into the Hohokam world after 700. This was the Mesoamerican ball-game. In Mesoamerica, according to Randall McGuire (personal communication, 2013), there were elite and nonelite forms of the game. In the elite or nobles' game, a rubber ball would have been bounced between players and through a hoop or into a goal using only one's body (no hands), the point being to score points. The ballgame was a public spectacle played in a sunken court to be viewed from above by scores of people, who probably gambled on the play below. The play probably had religious if not political implications and overtones. "The commoners' form of the game," on the other hand, involved "a rubber ball about the size of a red gym ball that was played off the hip" or

a ball about the size of a tennis ball played off of the wrist. In both of these games there was no hoop or goal and the point was to pass the ball back and forth between teams with a score occurring if a team failed to return the ball. This game is still played in Sinaloa today. From Hohokam sites we have no hoops and the walls of Hohokam ballcourts are generally too low and too sloped to play the noble game. They would be quite adequate to play the commoner game.

(Randall McGuire, personal communication, 2013)

Ovoid-shaped ballcourts dating to the Colonial and Sedentary periods remain among the most conspicuous features of this sport (Figure 14.8). Opposing teams from different Hohokam families and villages would have met for a game or tournament, a ritual battle of sorts, with the winning team taking home material goods or winning political concessions if not water rights. The most and biggest ballcourts are known from the largest and most powerful Hohokam towns, each spaced some 5 km from the next in major river and irrigation systems.

Fig 14.8 Hohokam ballcourt at Casa Grande, Arizona.
Timothy R. Pauketat photo, 2003.

Such settlements are conspicuous also for their fixity. Many Colonial and Sedentary period villages and towns were founded during the preceding Pioneer era, with the later household clusters – each averaging two to three dozen residents – repeatedly rebuilding their pithouses atop those of earlier generations. The results are complex superimposed palimpsests of domestic remains. These domestic feature clusters, commonly including outdoor cooking pits ("hornos") and courtyard cemeteries, were arrayed in concentric patterns around courtyards. Town-sized settlements in the Tucson, Phoenix, and Tonto basins routinely comprised one or two ballcourts and 10–20 corporate household or courtyard groups, each made up of perhaps 16–20 people, all arrayed around a central town plaza. The average population of such towns reached several hundred individuals.

At 900 CE, there were between 100 and 200 such sporting facilities in the Hohokam regions, 40 percent of them in the Phoenix Basin, where the center of Hohokam cultural and economic power had by then shifted. Soon there would also be dozens of another sort of monument: earthen platform mounds. These pyramidal constructions were introduced after 900 CE, perhaps as part of a new politico-religious movement from Mexico, where pyramids have an ancient history. In any event, they seem to have replaced the ballcourt, which gradually ceased being constructed in the Hohokam heartland.

Archaeologists have pointed out that both ballcourts and platform mounds were at one time or another integral to Hohokam community – now complex, hierarchical relationships crosscut with multiple familial interests, religious organizations, councils, and other nonkin factions or assemblies – sometimes called "sodalities" – based on age, gender, life experience, etc. In terms of their experience, the ballcourt would seem to have been a less elite-centric facility and, as such, may have fallen out of favor later. Ballcourts at Snaketown (see below) were, after all, built by digging down into the earth, that great life-giving and democratizing realm to which the ashes of people would return. Moreover, during the ballgame or any other ceremony in that ballcourt space, spectators *looked down* upon players (or dancers or orators). Platforms on the other hand *elevated* the orators and performers atop a four-sided construction. They were built skyward, the direction to which spectators would need to look. Taking a page from a Mesoamerican handbook, ballgames probably involved mythic struggles in the underworld, but pyramids linked stories of people with the sky gods. The divergent practical and performative implications of each might have had real communal and political consequences.

Among the consequences was the emergence of a regional powerhouse at a place called Snaketown, excavated by Gladwin and Haury in the 1930s and 1960s. This Hohokam settlement, founded back in Pioneer days, grew to be considerably larger than the rest during the Colonial and Sedentary periods, ultimately home to 500–1,000 people living in courtyard groups arrayed in a concentric configuration around a great plaza, all covering an area of about 100 ha (250 acres). It appears that, at Snaketown and a lesser settlement known as Valencia Viejo, the residential remains of families who flanked the plaza included larger and better-built homes that faced the town plaza (Wallace 2007). These, in turn, produced debris from the production of ritual objects and ornaments from the exotic materials key to Hohokam economy and religion. The people who resided in these superior homes seem to have controlled materials that originated from the Mimbres and Mogollon regions to the east, the Puebloan world to the north, the Trincheras area to the south, and California to the west.

Doubtless the scale of this powerhouse is a reflection of the amount of irrigated land, now connected via larger canals, at the disposal of would-be Snaketown elites. Here and elsewhere, the largest canals were more than 20 m wide at the surface and up to 6 m deep (Figure 14.9). They ran for miles, with the Snaketown system providing water for some 30,000 ha (70,000 acres) of tillable land. Each canal would have consumed tens of thousands of person-days to complete, indicating an astronomical effort on the part of Hohokam laborers who would have identified with the water, the network, and the crops. But if successful, as they seem to have been, these canals would have led to the production of tens of thousands of bushels of maize, beans, and squash every year. This was the food of an emergent civilization that relied on greater cooperative relationships of communities upstream and downstream. Social life, cultural meanings, and communities were inseparable from the water, the canals, and the crops that grew in the fields. To make it all work, some reserves were surely

Fig 14.9 Archaeologist Emil Haury and Hohokam irrigation ditch in cross-section at Snaketown, Arizona. Courtesy of the Huhugam Heritage Center.

kept aside to host the work crews and to sponsor the great ballgames and ritual events of the Hohokam calendar. But there are very few bell-shaped storage pits (a long-term storage facility). Perhaps this means that foodstuffs were stored, at least in the short term, within buildings. If not, then we might question the long-term viability of such a place.

Geopolitical Implications and a Colorado Plateau Alternative

The historical impacts of a series of large towns in the Sonoran Desert – each governed perhaps by a council or group of clan leaders – are worth considering, given the potential geopolitical implications of periodic, inter-annual rainfall and food shortages. What did the Snaketown people do between 700 and 900 CE to ensure their own subsistence and, by extension, political security in hard times? Did they raid their neighbors? Moreover, what might the distant neighbors of Snaketown – communally organized farming groups with occasional food-production shortages of their own – do in times of desperation? Might distant people, or their movements, have impinged on, say, Snaketown's interests or security? Or, perhaps from the point of view of the outsiders, would Snaketown have been perceived as a threat to other Hohokam towns or to ancestral Puebloans and Mogollon people living a couple hundred kilometers (a hundred or more miles) away?

Archaeologists interested in the historical relationships of southwestern and northern Mexican people, including Randall McGuire and Maria Elisa Villalpando C. (2007) and Ben Nelson (2006), have given considerable thought to these geopolitical questions. Stephen Lekson (2008) has also pondered the possibility that developments in the ancestral Puebloan homeland were stimulated, directly or indirectly, by the growing Hohokam phenomenon in central and southern Arizona. Distance and the Mogollon Rim, a physical barrier, may not have stopped cultural exchanges through the greater Southwest. Certainly it did not centuries later, after 1140 CE, when expatriate Puebloans moved from the Colorado Plateau south across the Mogollon highlands and into Hohokam territories. Certainly distance alone – the hundreds of kilometers involved in moving from one end of the greater Southwest to the other – was probably not much of a deterrent. Remember how far historic-era Native Americans raided, how the awareness or knowledge of others stretched across the continent (Chapter 3), and how far Late Archaic folks traveled in eastern North America to get to Poverty Point, among other ceremonial sites (Chapter 9).

Oddly, the Mogollon Rim was at least as much a barrier to twentieth-century archaeologists, who perfected the Puebloan chronology and cultural history first, with significant studies by A. V. Kidder at Pecos Pueblo, Earl Morris at Aztec, and Edgar Lee Hewett at Chaco (Cordell 1984; Lekson 2008; Plog 1997). These digs were facilitated by a pleasant climate and an ease of recognizing and excavating Puebloan masonry structures. Indeed, their visibility was problematic to the extent that looters and early archaeologists mined the rooms of pueblos with abandon. In the bad old days of antiquarian treasure hunting (see Chapter 2), for instance, Richard Wetherill had conducted large-scale excavations of Mesa Verde in 1888 before turning his sights and his "non-Native ... hunger for adventure, things, and knowledge" to Chaco Canyon in 1896 (Swentzell 2004:52). Many archaeologists followed, refining the regional chronology as they went (Table 14.2).

Late Basketmaker to Early Puebloan Transition

Up on Mesa Verde, a prominent forested tableland visible for miles rising above the uplifted Colorado Plateau, the Basketmaker III (BM-III) people experienced what archaeologist Richard Wilshusen (2006) describes as rapid and dramatic change. There had been few Basketmaker inhabitants in the area before 575 CE. These scattered residents lived in small, isolated farmsteads of one to a few families, farming the mesa tops and hunting the canyons much like Basketmaker III people dispersed across the plateau. They used unadorned cooking and storage pots, including the jar, olla (bottle), and seed jar (or "tecomate" – a globe-shaped vessel), and decorated (black paint on white) bowls for serving food, now including maize, squash, *and* beans. The bow and arrow was a relatively new weapon, and Mesa Verde was isolated and relatively safe yet productive, with few people. Of course, perhaps owing to its safety, the population of the region surged at the end of the sixth century, says Wilshusen. Immigrants moved in from Basketmaker lands to the east and west, creating villages of up to 20

Table 14.2 Chronological highlights of the Puebloan area (adapted from Glowacki and Van Keuren 2011; Lekson 2006; Noble 2004, 2006).

Year CE	Historic period	Cultural patterns
500–700/750	Basketmaker III	Pithouse villages widespread; pottery adopted; the bow and arrow appears across the landscape.
750–900	Pueblo I	Masonry pueblos, now with pithouses/kivas in yards and above-ground slab houses, become common; localized conflicts evident.
900–1040	Pueblo II	Migration into Chaco Canyon; Great House construction happens in pulses; timbers, pots, corn imported into canyon.
1040–1100	PII, Classic Bonito phase	Major constructions and Great Kivas at Chaco; Chacoan outliers built across ≥52,000 km² (20,000 square mile) area.
1100–1140	Early Pueblo III	Major new construction at Aztec as Chaco Canyon declines.
1140–1300	PIII McElmo and Mesa Verde phases	Totah region population surges, references Chacoan past; violence.
1300–1540	Pueblo IV	Totah region depopulated; Rio Grande Pueblos established; continued violence; Katsina religion develops.

families, cutting trees for timber and cooking fires, and planting fields in the new openings.

Tensions seem to have arisen among these later BM-III groups, potentially giving rise to conflicts over lands, resources, or social exchanges, thinks warfare expert Stephen LeBlanc (1999). The BM-III evidence for such violence includes arrowshot victims and apparent fortifications. Some settlements built defensive walls, such as a hamlet near Mesa Verde called "Knobby Knee Stockade" (Figure 14.10). At this site, which dates to the first half of the seventh century, one or two pithouses were surrounded by a wall. We do not know if the reason for building such a wall was a serious, continuous threat or just a periodic one, but the fact that the site was burned around 650 might indicate that someone attacked the occupants inside the wall. Then again, the residents had already removed most

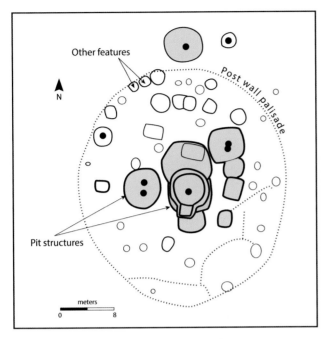

Fig 14.10 Basketmaker homes and defensive wall at the Knobby Knee site (adapted from LeBlanc 1999).

of their possessions and buried a dog on the floor of a pithouse just before the site burned, leading Wilshusen to surmise that this particular burning might have (also) been a ceremonial act to commemorate the decommissioning of the settlement, a practice known at other BM-III and later Pueblo I and II settlements.

Ceremonialism was certainly on the rise as well, as evidenced by BM-III developments south of Mesa Verde. Here, atop the Chacra Mesa overlooking Chaco Canyon, were two exceptionally large BM-III settlements dating to the early 500s. Chaco guru-archaeologist Thomas Windes (2004, 2007) is uncertain whether or not these were year-round villages or summertime residences, but the sites, called Shabik'eshchee and 29SJ423, sprawled across the mesatops, each with some 100 pithouses and uncounted ramadas and outdoor work areas. Their size made them unique and, perhaps, uniquely safe locations to live or visit. Why then did they fall into disuse by 600 CE? The reasons are unclear, but Windes makes the argument that these large sites were early precursors to the later "Great Houses" that would come to define Chaco Canyon.

Formalizations of Pithouses and Storage Bins

But these Great Houses were still a century-plus in the future. At the beginning of the eighth century, coincidentally (?), the Hohokam world was entering its more elaborate Colonial period and the Basketmaker agriculturalists were expanding their outdoor village facilities. In the latter case, this entailed the construction of adobe or masonry room blocks in backyards and around the work areas of pithouses. This development, for archaeologists, signals the beginning of the Pueblo I period, though it did not happen everywhere uniformly. Through the Pueblo I and II periods (see below), "80–90 percent of the population during the Pueblo period from AD 900 to 1200 in the area between Kayenta and Red Lake Trading Post were living in pithouses rather than masonry pueblos" (Ward 1976:17).

In any event, where it did happen, the move to masonry room blocks indicates an architectural formalization of two kinds of spaces. The first formalization was that of the pithouse. During P-I times, some of these seem to have been reserved for higher-status families or for ceremonial gatherings and, hence, archaeologists call them "kivas" – semisubterranean Puebloan temples of a sort. However, the timing of such a formalization is debated, with the first real kivas perhaps being the oversized Basketmaker III examples and the later "Great Kivas" of Chaco Canyon (Van Dyke 2007b). In any case, pithouses had taken on new purposes or meanings by early Pueblo times, making use of anachronistic (old-time) characteristics to tie people's beliefs to ancient principles; this is what temples do worldwide (Renfrew 1985). Before 1500, most pithouses and kivas were circular in plan shape, with fire pits and other features on the floors and ventilation shafts (to provide oxygen to the fire) exiting one side, giving them keyhole shapes in plan view. On their floors still today is the all-important *sipapu*, a small hole that connects the people in the kiva to the previous world from which their ancestors had emerged. The sipapu, in other words, is a "portal" between dimensions and supernatural realms (Figure 14.11).

The second formalization was of the outdoor storage bin or workspace facility. Whereas BM-III settlements made use of scattered outdoor areas, sometimes roofed, for outdoor activities or shelters, the P-I period saw the construction of adobe and masonry rooms strung together in a single row in the backyards of the pithouse/kiva. This

Fig 14.11 Small kiva at Cliff Palace, Mesa Verde, Colorado, showing ventilation shaft opening, stone deflector screen, fire pit, and sipapu. Timothy R. Pauketat photo, 2006.

was a plateau-wide development that demands just a little creative logic to explain:

(1) Since the BM-III period, folks stored food over the long-term, say a season or more, in subterranean pits or stone-lined underground "cists" (similar to root cellars). This is something that agrarian peoples did (in fact *had* to do) around the world – including the ancestors of everyone reading this book – before the advent of twentieth-century refrigeration technology. Pits allow dried meats and durable grains to be sealed off in a near-anaerobic state and out of the reach of varmints. Storage of foods in pithouse rafters and above-ground bins or rooms is a short-term sort of storage, intended to allow periodic access and replacement of what was warehoused therein. This is what one does if one is hosting visitors or anticipating that some portion of one's stores will be shipped out.

(2) The same logic applies to putting up visitors. Visitors are a short-term storage problem; you have to let them sleep someplace. Since additional rooms were being added to residential areas between 700 and 900 CE, maybe there were more visitors – more movement on the landscape having to do with the hosting of ceremonies and feasts or the development of ceremonial places visited by people, as Windes had argued for Shabik'eshchee and 29SJ423.

Whatever the Pueblo I formalizations actually entailed, it was not long before some of the new pueblos – kivas/pithouses and masonry room blocks – grew large. Among the largest were P-I settlements in the Dolores region of southwestern Colorado. One of these was the McPhee Pueblo, the earliest version of which dates to 780 CE. In the year 861 (an accuracy only possible via the dendrochronological dates of the Southwest), the people of McPhee rebuilt and expanded their pueblo into what Windes recognizes as among the first so-called "Great House." In McPhee's case, the Great House comprised two large crescent-shaped blocks of some 100 rooms with interior plazas containing pithouses. Like their smaller counterparts, the residents of these larger buildings discarded trash off to one side, the result being an ever accumulating "trash mound" (Figure 14.12).

Standing back from these settlement alterations, we may see that this was a period of significant social change, at least in parts of the Four Corners region. P-I groups may have staked out territories or

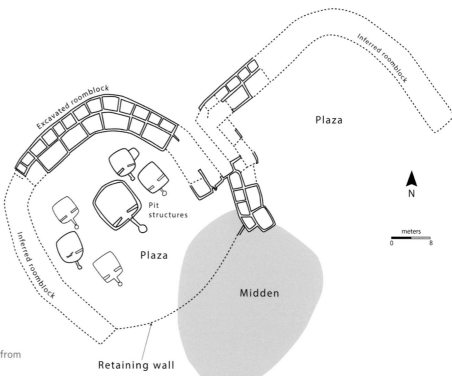

Fig 14.12 McPhee Pueblo/Great House (adapted from Windes 2004: figure 3.2).

formed alliances. In one location along the Animas River, situated between two recognizable P-I cultural groups, this jostling for position on the landscape had tragic consequences. Sometime shortly after 809 CE, there was a "massacre of no fewer than thirty-five men and women of all ages" capped off by "the extensive processing/desecration of their remains" (Potter and Yoder 2008:37). The bones of those killed were crushed. The problem in this case was not subsistence stress, according to the analysis by James Potter and Thomas Yoder, but identity politics played out over land. The site was burned in a final act following the massacre.

Compounding identity politics was the fact that the northern portions of the Four Corners region had dangerously short growing seasons. Perhaps because of this, by the late 870s, the Dolores Basin was largely drained of its people. They had moved on to a warmer, bigger, and brighter future. Most Chacoan archaeologists now believe that many of the Dolores people migrated south toward and into Chaco Canyon. In the year 861, and in one of the Southwest's bleakest canyons, they began to build two of three early McPhee-style Great Houses, Una Vida and Pueblo Bonito. A few decades later, the third was built, named Peñasco Blanco. All were impressive buildings even in their initial two-story form. But, unlike McPhee Pueblo and other P-I settlements, there was a considerably smaller residential occupation associated with these early Chacoan Great Houses than one would expect if these were big villages. In addition, all three were built in a row along the long axis of Chaco Canyon that happens to coincide with a rare astronomical event. Coincidence? Thus begins the mystery of what Cynthia Irwin-Williams, the excavator of one oversized northern Chacoan "outlier" (see below), dubbed "the Chaco Phenomenon."

The Place beyond the Horizon (861–1140 CE)

Shortly after the Mexican–American War in 1849, a US cavalry detachment was sent to gather information on the new lands the United States had just taken from Mexico. The group happened into Chaco Canyon and wrote the first description of its Great Houses, naming each one. The scale of the ruins impressed them, as it does any visitor to Chaco Culture National Historic Park today (www.nps.gov/chcu/index.htm).

So impressive is this place that memories of it seem to linger in the stories of its descendants. The Hopi speak of "The Place beyond the Horizon" where clans "from all directions" gathered and "became astute observers of the cosmos" (Kuwanwisiwma 2004:43). Those cosmic powers, they explain, produced a complicated history where people may have "embraced a social-political-religious hierarchy and envisioned control and power over place, resources, and people" (Swentzell 2004:50). Echoes of such Puebloan accounts are heard among the Navajo, later arrivals to the region. They speak of a Gambler who manipulated people into becoming his "pawns" (Begay 2004). Archaeological findings increasingly seem consistent with these narratives.

Great Pulses of Labor

Between 861 and 1140 and in several great pulses of activity, a series of nine monumental masonry Great Houses, several other lesser great buildings, and many dozens of single-family "unit pueblos" were constructed on the canyon floor and mesa top (Figure 14.13). Formal roads were built, with stone staircases chiseled into the canyon walls, to connect or pass by the canyon's Great Houses and dozens of "outlier" Great Houses, some running just a few hundred meters and others many miles. People traveling into and out of the canyon may have used some such roads, invariably built in arrow-straight segments. Others appear to have been built to run past long-abandoned archaeological sites or landmarks. Still others seem to have seen little to no human foot traffic, instead pointing in possibly culturally significant directions. Archaeologist Barbara Mills, among others, suggests that these roads could have been links to the past or avenues along which spirits might pass. The longest road heads due north out of the canyon, passing alongside Huerfano Mesa and heading north to the San Juan River. Later Great Houses would be built on this Great North Road.

Additional Great Houses were built outside the canyon and in distant outlying locations (i.e., the outliers), many on or along Chacoan roads. All of these houses, within the canyon or beyond, are distinctive in form and masonry style. Most had associated "trash mounds." The largest is Pueblo Bonito, built in at least seven major construction

Fig 14.13 The layout of Chaco Canyon, showing proposed organizational axes and (inset) locations of some roads and unit pueblos. Timothy R. Pauketat map.

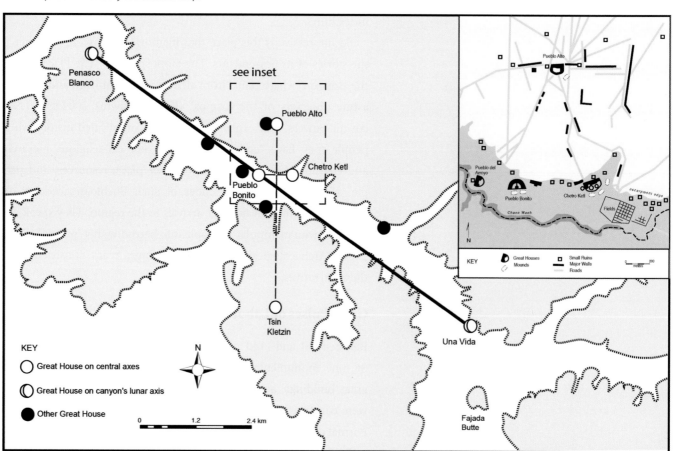

Fig 14.14 Pueblo Bonito, Chaco Canyon, New Mexico, view from canyon rim. Timothy R. Pauketat photo, 2008.

stages (Figure 14.14). At the end, it possessed 650 rooms stacked five stories high. Like the other eight Great Houses (and like those of outlier buildings), the lower load-bearing walls are thick, with flat slab exteriors produced by breaking sandstone slabs in half and using the broken long edge as the exterior. Wall interiors were filled with rubble. As one ascended to the upper rooms, the masonry walls would thin. Each upper-story floor was built using beams (vigas) or girders atop which secondary vigas or joists would be laid, finally covered with latillas (sticks) and paving material.

Chaco archaeologists estimate that major Great House construction projects, expansions or entirely new buildings, were carefully pre-planned by (part-time?) engineers and masons and carried out over a period of one to several years.

How many laborers were needed for construction of the Great Houses? We know (from wall abutments and masonry styles) that major sections of the houses were constructed as single projects … Based on calculations of the amount of stone, clay, water and wood beams needed to build a single room, we estimated that over a 10-year period the equivalent of about 30 men working between two and four months a year could have successfully completed a major construction project at Chaco.

(Lekson et al. 1988:104)

If that time span covered only a year, then 300 laborers would be needed for the construction season. This does not, of course, count the hours cutting and hauling the trees from distant mountains (50 miles away). "We estimate that in order to construct the floors and roofs of these multistory houses, 215,000 trees, some of them 25 centimeters (10 inches) in diameter, were cut from forests as many as 80 kilometers away ..." (Lekson et al. 1988:104). These timbers – logs of ponderosa pine from the Chuska Mountains 80 km (50 mi) to the northwest and Mount Taylor, 88 km (55 mi) to the south-southeast – were carried into Chaco along some of these roads.

Such labor estimates, even including the logging of distant forests, still do not account for the construction of roadways or the provisions and supplies needed by the workers to accomplish the construction projects or by the hosts to feed the people attending their great ceremonies. Most analysts recognize that the agricultural potential of the canyon is, to say the least, limited. An apparent gridded field covering some 6 ha (15 acres) is known next to Chetro Ketl, sitting almost undetected today beneath the desert scrub. Presumably, crops might have been reliably grown in such a special field. However, by measuring the amount of trace elements (particularly strontium) in the corn cobs, it is now known that most maize was imported from outside the canyon (Benson 2010; Benson et al. 2009b; Cordell et al. 2008). Also imported from the Chuska Mountains, to the east, and Red Mesa Valley, 70 km (45 mi) to the south, were thousands of "grayware" ceramic cooking pots, painted Gallup black-on-white and Chaco black-on-white pottery containers, and pieces of chert for making tools.

Those were the more mundane items. Also carried in was exotic raw turquoise, from the Cerillos hills between modern-day Santa Fe and Albuquerque, New Mexico. Moreover, chocolate was carried in from Mexico and consumed using special cylinder jars, most of which have been found in Pueblo Bonito (Figure 14.15). Along with that chocolate, the Chacoans imported live macaws, whose home range is tropical Mesoamerica, their colorful feathers being prized for ritual uses.

The Order of Downtown Chaco

Some archaeologists interpret Chaco Canyon, with all of this evidence of labor investment and ritual elaboration, as the remains of a series of quasi-independent pueblos, not unlike today's descendant

Fig 14.15 Chaco black-on-white cylinder jars found in Pueblo Bonito, each 25 cm tall. Courtesy of Patricia Crown and the Smithsonian National Museum of Natural History.

Sidebar 14.3 Google Earth views of Chaco's great houses and gridded field

Enter "Chaco Culture, Pueblo Bonito" into the search bar of Google Earth, and it will take you straight to the heart of the Chaco Canyon. Below you will see the largest and oldest of the Great Houses, a D-shaped construction with circular kivas in its plazas and rectangular rooms along its arching back wall (Latitude 36.0606 N, Longitude 107.9616 W). Go west about 300 m to Longitude 107.9657 W and hover over Pueblo del Arroyo with its circular "tri-wall" structure projected toward the arroyo. Now, go back to the east almost a kilometer, following along the canyon wall to Longitude 107.9542 W. You will be above Chetro Ketl, a Great House almost as large as Pueblo Bonito. Note that

a Great Kiva can be seen in its southeastern corner. Just a few meters across the small arroyo along Chetro Ketl's southeastern edge, and on the north side of the larger stream bed of the "Chaco River" or "wash," is a discolored geometric area four times the size of the Great Houses you were just viewing. This discolored area is bifurcated by the modern park road. Gwinn Vivian (2004) believes that this discolored anomaly is an ancient gridded field. Zoom out to see both Chetro Ketl and Pueblo Bonito; note that another Great House may be seen to the north atop the mesa, occupying the apex of an isosceles triangle that connects all three. This is Pueblo Alto.

pueblos. Others see in it political hierarchy, centralized governance, and farmers subordinated to become commoners. The former group might infer that the canyon was home to a "heterarchical" (i.e., horizontally organized) society where nonranked autonomous clans met to conduct rituals in their own independent houses of worship. The latter might call Chaco a kind of oddly sprawling "cityscape" that governed a wider region. Still others, including descendants, see elements of both in the ruins of Chaco Canyon, a historically singular development produced by the unique place and its events and people. A few more facts might help us infer what Chaco was and was not.

The resident population of the canyon probably never exceeded around 2,000 people, in large part owing to the extreme environmental conditions. Chaco Canyon, most agree, simply couldn't support any more people. In fact it had few to no trees for much of the Pueblo II period and was not the best place to grow corn. So, who lived in the Great Houses? Analyses of the archaeological remains of living debris point to a remarkable fact. Only about 15 percent of the room suites in any Great House were used for living! Moreover, the trash mounds of many of the Great Houses are too small, with too few broken pots and discarded bones, to have been the accumulations of large populations. Thus, Lekson and colleagues (1988) estimate that no more than about 100 people probably occupied any one Great House. Many of the rooms were simply uninhabitable: poorly lit and even more poorly ventilated. These were probably for storage. Some might have remained empty by intent, perhaps built just to permit the exterior form of the Great House to take shape (Lekson 2007). Conversely, some may have been built for use by invisible spirits and ghosts.

Consider this: one room deep in the oldest part of Pueblo Bonito contained the honored remains of two men who died in the late 800s. At least one of these men was buried with an assortment of ritual objects that may identify him as a leader or priest of a particular sacred society – sometimes called a "sodality" (Ware 2014). The powers associated with these men and their things may not have ended with their interment, but may instead have made Pueblo Bonito a powerful place (Mills 2008). A few later residents appear to have re-entered this burial room to leave offerings and the bones of a few later people. But doing so was doubtless not a casual act.

It is worthy of note that entrance into Pueblo Bonito and the other Chacoan Great Houses was by means of a special exterior doorway. These doorways, as seen in all Great Houses (and in fact in later Puebloan constructions), had T shapes (Figure 14.16). T-shaped doorways have been argued by some, seeking a functional answer to the strange form, to have facilitated people entering with their arms full – perhaps carrying in a pot or sack of corn. However, why then not make all doorways on the inside of such buildings T-shaped? Interior doorways are almost all built in a simple rectangular form. The Ts were special.

Moreover, the T-shaped opening shows up elsewhere, most importantly on ceramic vessels, where it is sometimes the opening of the pot and sometimes the point of contact between a human thumb and

Fig 14.16 T-shaped doorway on an old exterior wall of Pueblo Bonito. Timothy R. Pauketat photo, 2012.

the handle of a Puebloan mug. The T opening in these cases and, we would argue, in the exteriors of buildings constitute "portals" – the points of contact between different dimensions of existence (exterior living and sunlit world vs. interior ancestral and earthly darkness) or substances (the foods inside a pot with the person outside, or the skin of a person with the fired earth of a ceramic mug). In some respects, the T shape may be a vertical depiction of the ancient pithouse, which had a T shape in plan view.

Whatever the derivation of the T form, it would seem to be a symbolically charged portal that denoted the movement from one realm to another. Thus, Chaco evinces a remarkable large-scale yet highly intimate experiential pattern: great quantities of basic construction supplies, food, and cooking pots were imported into the canyon on the backs of people – many thousands of whom probably arrived periodically for great political, religious, and civic events organized by a few elites – all to build awe-inspiring monuments entered through portals. Such a seemingly noneconomical pattern, where resources used to build and support it could not be generated locally and where both ordinary and extraordinary movements through constructed spaces consist of passage through portals, screams of being motivated by religious devotion. So, too, does the tremendous amount of human energy that was diverted into the building of Great Houses – some taking several years to complete – smack of people who believed in what they were doing or, at least, in what the Chacoan leaders and priests were doing. What the T-shaped doorways meant specifically to people has yet to be resolved. However, quite possibly, gathering, construction, and basic bodily movements into and out of great architectural spaces in Chaco Canyon were, for all intents and purposes, religious acts.

Like medieval cathedrals in Europe or Old Kingdom pyramids in Egypt, Great Houses were religious and political monumental constructions. All such monuments were more than just public commemorations of some idealized shared heritage, political actor, or event (such as the Washington Monument or Lincoln Memorial in Washington, DC). Great Houses and other great monuments inspired awe. They enabled people to connect or relate to cosmic forces, if not the essence of "being" itself. They may have built a sense of a greater macrocommunity – via an *esprits de corps* – as people built them (again, just like European cathedrals and Egyptian pyramids). But then the canyon itself and its various landmarks, such as Fajada Butte, were monumental and, as many visitors today know, remain monumental. And monuments have effects on people that may be, through time, compounded by people.

In the 1970s, archaeologist John Fritz (1978) noticed that there was a greater order to the arrangement of the canyon's Great Houses. He identified intra-canyon cardinal axes, one running from Pueblo Bonito to Chetro Ketl and the other bifurcating this east–west line and connecting Pueblo Alto to the north with Tsin Kletzin to the south. In the 1980s, archaeoastronomer Anna Sofaer began her well-known "Solstice Project" – which sought to establish the underlying celestial referents of Fritz's observed symmetries (https://solsticeproject.org). As highlighted in her film *The Mystery of Chaco Canyon* (1999), Sofaer and her colleagues identified a technically elegant calendrical device known as the "Sun Dagger" (Sofaer 2008). High atop Fajada Butte, three sandstone slabs were positioned upright on edge intentionally or accidentally against a vertical cliff wall. A spiral petroglyph, consisting of 19 rings, had been pecked into the cliff face behind the slabs. When the light of the sun shone through the slab openings on the annual solstices and equinoxes, or when the moon's rays did likewise on the extreme moonrise positions every 18.6 years, daggers of light would cross the spirals at key positions. That such astronomical happenings were important to the Chacoans can be confirmed by other spiral petroglyphs in the canyon, positioned such that shadows bisect them during the year, or by the well-known pictograph below Peñasco Blanco, interpreted by some to commemorate the supernova of 1054.

Sofaer also argues that the major walls of most buildings were aligned with solar (solstitial or equinoctial) or lunar-standstill (maxima or minima) rise or set positions on the horizon (as also known among the Ohio Hopewell; see Chapter 9). As importantly, the buildings also align with each other and with the canyon overall, which happens to be naturally configured to channel the eye toward certain maximum lunar and solar positions (Sofaer 2008). The overall effects of this canyon-wide configuration may have been profound. Ancient people, many of whom would have been more aware of celestial movements than city-dwellers today, would sense that their bodies could be positioned at the intersection of the moving heavens here on earth. Such an effect is known as a "hierophany" (Ashmore 2007). People may well have identified this location as a cosmic center – a place where space and time coincide with human life. As such, Chaco Canyon in some sense may have possessed agency of a sort, the power to affect human history. It gathered people unto itself, a microcosm of the greater southwestern landscape.

In fact, during the three human generations between 1040 and 1100, also called the Classic Bonito phase, the Chacoan phenomenon was transforming and expanding. At this time, numerous "Great Kivas" were added to the canyon. These were exceptionally large kivas with other monumental features, including great fireplaces, four giant roof support posts (sitting atop foundation stone slabs), chambers under or at the floor (possible foot drums where sounds would resonate beneath a plank floor), and possible hidden subfloor entrances. Great Kivas, in short, were the ultimate ritual space. Puebloan priests may have been able to cast their voice from beneath the floor or appear magically from under the floor, perhaps veiled by smoke or fabric. The flurry of Great Kiva construction may indicate that some new religious practice or organization, or some powerful leader or governing body, had taken hold in the canyon during the Classic Bonito phase (Van Dyke 2004, 2007a).

Classic Bonito Phase (1040–1100 CE)

Whatever it was, the Classic Bonito phase also witnessed the construction of Chacoan outliers across the San Juan Basin and beyond, the farthest being 210 km (130 mi) from Downtown Chaco (Cameron 2009). Well-known examples include Canyon de Chelly's White House (Arizona), Bluff (Utah), Lowry (Colorado), and Chimney Rock (Colorado). Certain outlier sites appear to have been selected by Chacoans or would-be Chacoans for effect. They were built and positioned in ways that took full advantage of topography, visibility, and distant landmarks (Figure 14.17). Many were aligned to distant features, making the Great House a place where lines of sight or landmarks converge or intersect in powerful ways. In some locations, these outliers look remarkably similar to their Chacoan Great House archetypes. Others vary in construction technique, internal configuration, or some other attribute. More than likely, local people – most of whom would have seen Chaco Canyon at some point in their lives – were the builders of most outlier Great Houses. But exactly who resided in some of them remains a mystery. Some could have been Chacoan leaders or priests, perhaps residing there for variable periods of time.

Some such Great Houses were small, especially in outlying locations. For instance, a modest Chacoan Great House sits atop a hill behind the Anasazi Heritage Center at the opening of the Dolores Basin in southern Colorado (www.blm.gov/visit/anasazi-heritage-center). This location was the ancestral (P-I) homeland of at least some P-II Chacoans, and it looks to the south past Mesa Verde to the Chuskas, 80 km (50 mi) away, where many P-II Chacoans resided. Thus, the site visually linked the past and present worlds of Chaco. Moreover, the small Great House was aligned with the cardinal directions – as established by watching the sun move across the sky daily – such that history and the movements of the sun might be brought together (see if you can find this site on Google Earth, recognizable as a circular kiva at the center of a small room block @ Latitude 37.4777 N, Longitude 108.5456 W).

Some outlier Great Houses rivaled the scale of those in the canyon proper, for example the Salmon Ruins built along the Great

Casamero Great House ruins

Fig 14.17 Ruins of the Chaco outlier at Casamero, near Thoreau, New Mexico. Note the unusual eye-like natural features on the cliff. Timothy R. Pauketat photo, 2015.

North Road between 1090 and 1094 CE. Excavated by Cynthia Irwin-Williams in the 1970s, the 300 rooms in two stories aligned with a lunar standstill. More dramatic than this is the even more distant Great House at Chimney Rock, Colorado. Here, atop a nearly inaccessible and narrow butte, a classic Chacoan Great House was constructed. From its rooftop, one could have viewed the maximum northern moonrise between two great spires of rock, an event that took place once in every 18.6 years. Cutting dates of the wood used to build the roofs of the Chimney Rock Great House match each of the standstill years between the 1070s and the 1090s (Malville 2004), verifying that the building was expanded or repaired during each lunar event. Downslope sits a string of dozens of unit pueblos, the homes of local residents or pilgrims who, like the Chacoans in the Great House, positioned themselves at this seemingly powerful location (Figure 14.18).

As Chimney Rock attests, Chacoan Great Houses were typically "overengineered" or, in the words of John Stein (in *The Mystery of*

Chaco Canyon), "overbuilt and underused" (Lekson et al. 1988). Throughout the course of Chacoan history, the masonry styles common to the canyon morphed for reasons that are only partly because of ancient engineering concerns. The earliest style is Type I, made using small locally procured rock slabs. Later Types II through IV featured alternating rows of thick and thin blocks. The later styles could support the weight of walls up to five stories high.

In addition, the alternating masonry bands may have mimicked the layered sandstone of Chaco Canyon itself, if not also the balanced opposition of earth to sky or life to death. Archaeologist Stephen Plog (2003) has also suggested that the Ancestral Pueblo sometimes used texture to denote color, meaning that the thick and thin masonry layers might connote light and dark colors, respectively. Even more interesting, it seems likely that the masonry walls, once constructed in the elaborate Type II through IV modes, were covered over (Figure 14.19). There are hints of plaster being smeared over the masonry such that visitors might not be able to see it. Only the builders would remember the meaning and power of the walls themselves, and there might, in turn, be a kind of power in knowing about the walls.

Today, visitors to the canyon encounter a great empty sandstone landscape covered with brush, the stratified cliff

Fig 14.18 Chimney Rock, Colorado. Timothy R. Pauketat photo, 2009.

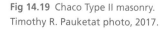

Fig 14.19 Chaco Type II masonry. Timothy R. Pauketat photo, 2017.

Fig 14.20 Archaeologist Ruth Van Dyke at Pueblo Bonito, Chaco Canyon, New Mexico in 2013. Courtesy of Jim Wetherill Shaffner, grandson of Richard Wetherill.

walls on either side of Chaco Wash rising 20–50 m above the canyon floor. A thousand years ago, on the occasion of a great ceremony, the canyon rim and floor might have been lined with thousands of people watching the festivities from above and below, viewing a rising full moon, or performing sacred dances atop the multistoried Great Houses or in a natural amphitheater between Pueblo Bonito and Chetro Ketl. It seems undeniable that Chaco Canyon, its Great Houses, and kivas were theatrical spaces ready made for political, communal, and religious spectacles. Merely moving through Chaco Canyon is a richly sensuous experience (even via Google Earth!).

Archaeologist Ruth Van Dyke (2007a) has been at the forefront of arguments that recognize the critical role played by pilgrimage in the development of Chaco (Figure 14.20). A thousand years ago, she has argued – based on her own retracing of such pilgrimage routes – one's senses would have all been stimulated by the changing vistas, scents, and sounds experienced when moving in and out of the canyon. Clear night skies were and yet are filled with stars. In the backcountry, total silence reigns on windless days. Thus, Chaco Canyon would seem to have possessed all of the characteristics of a powerful place that might enable great religious movements. And perhaps it did, with each pulse of construction being a renewal or revitalization of religion.

Of course, such movements are invariably political as well, or at least have political implications, as was noted in Chapter 3. It is possible that, in emphasizing the religiosity of Chaco Canyon, we may overlook the region's political underbelly during the P-II period. All of that unbridled experiential power, one might suspect, could have been harnessed by politically minded leaders. Such leaders or would-be leaders may have competed with others in seeking to maintain or expand their own powers. Indeed, Pueblo and Navajo stories exist today that tell of the cosmic powers of the canyon having been co-opted and abused by human beings.

Moreover, archaeologists have found evidence of violence that may have resulted from the political machinations of leaders and would-be leaders. Archaeologists point to skeletal evidence that suggests Chacoans may have carried out violence against enemies and outsiders during Chaco's heyday (Bustard 2008; Kohler and Turner 2006; Lekson 2002). Unlike the skeletal evidence from before and after the P-II period, little human skeletal trauma of the sort that would result from small-scale raids and feuding was suffered by Chacoans in the greater San Juan Basin during the Chacoan era. Sometimes archaeologists refer to the regional pattern as Chaco's "Halo" effect, produced when diverse people belonging to a unified or centrally governed macrocommunity seem to have lived relatively peacefully together. But such a peace may have been actively – even aggressively – maintained too. Chacoan leaders, that is, may have kept a lid on internal fighting, presumably by settling disputes and punishing violators. This is what political governments do worldwide; philosopher Michel Foucault (1979) noted that state-sponsored violence against nonconformists – those that might be declared enemies of the state, terrorists, or, simply, criminals who need imprisonment – is a way to keep the peace. Some have interpreted a series of human skeletal parts in ceremonially sealed kivas as executions of witches (Walker 2008). If so, then perhaps ridding one's community of evil might double as a political act. Recall that this was something the Shawnee Prophet did in Indiana in the early 1800s (see Chapter 3).

Whatever the actual governmental structure of Chaco – whether a council of clan leaders, a ruling Gambler, or even a temporary ritual association of kin groups – big aggregations of people have big historical effects. They provide order for people, at least for a time. And around Chaco the effects were a diminution of random acts of violence. Chacoan leaders may have gained the power to punish violators of rules on behalf of the community by virtue of declaring them witches (again conflating politics and religion). Certainly, the uptick in endemic violence after the depopulation of the canyon by 1140 would seem to confirm that a region-wide peace – what Lekson (1999) calls *pax Chaco* – had once existed, maintained voluntarily or by force, such that it could dissolve by 1150.

The End is a New Beginning (1100–1150 CE)

Two significant multi-year droughts hit the Southwest between about 1120 and 1150 CE, facts that may have hastened the Chacoans' exodus from Chaco Canyon. But those climatological facts may have only been part of the background to the reasons for the final depopulation of Chaco and the migrations to the northern San Juan and, it turns out, to the south into and beyond the Mogollon highlands. Indeed, the beginning of the end for Chaco may have resulted from a Classic Bonito phase expansion that planted the seeds of depopulation.

Early on, some outliers were probably established through missionizing movements, with Chacoan leaders and priests converting or gathering outlying locals into the fold back at Chaco. These would have been *centripetal* movements that centralized human effort and cosmic order back in Chaco Canyon. But other outlier foundings, such as at Salmon, likely had *centrifugal* effects. In essence, by carrying Chacoan religion with them to new places, they had begun to decentralize Chaco's economy and polity. These would have been out-migrations in effect, with expatriates setting up new "colonies."

Notable large-scale movements to the north are known into the Totah or Mesa Verde region, which includes the northern San Juan Basin, Mesa Verde, and contiguous portions of the Dolores River. Besides Salmon and Chimney Rock, such later Bonito phase Great Houses were built at places such as Bluff, Utah, Lowry, Colorado, and Aztec, New Mexico (Cameron 2009). Of these outward-bound movements, Aztec was the greatest. It was built in stages, beginning at 1110 CE, 80 km (50 mi) north of Chaco and just 13 km (8 mi) north of Salmon on the Great North Road (which itself may have been extended or rebuilt by the founders of Aztec in the early twelfth century). Indeed, the earliest of three Great Houses at Aztec, the West House, is very nearly a duplicate of Salmon. Possibly, the builders of Salmon also built this first Aztec Great House.

Moreover, in their final configuration, Aztec's three Great Houses appear to be an off-cardinal replica of the three central buildings of Downtown Chaco: Pueblo Bonito, Chetro Ketl, and Pueblo Alto (Van Dyke 2008). Near the western Aztec structure, similar to that of Chaco, a tri-walled circular building was raised. Within the West building, Chaco-style kivas can be seen in the eastern bank of rooms while Mesa Verde-style kivas – those with a prominent keyhole shape – were built in the western wing. Apparently, these kivas were built, if not used, by two distinctive Puebloan clans or ethnic groups whose identities were joined at Aztec.

In the middle of Aztec West, a Great Kiva occupied the plaza space (Lister and Lister 1987). This impressive structure, excavated by Earl Morris and the American Museum of Natural History in 1921, was the successor of Chaco's Great Kivas, the largest of which are examples in Pueblo Bonito and Chetro Ketl and immediately south of

(a)

(b)

Fig 14.21 Great Kivas: (a) excavated example at Chetro Ketl, Chaco Canyon, New Mexico; (b) reconstructed interior at Aztec, Colorado. Timothy R. Pauketat photos, 2006.

Sidebar 14.4 Temporalities of experience

Psychological studies have been done that examine the "temporalities" of various different sorts of experiences in large and small spaces with variable external stimuli. One of the results of these studies is that miniaturizing experience, as in kids playing with dolls or adults using miniature ancestral figures (e.g., the Hohokam), speeds up one's experience of time. It seems to people engaging in such practices that more

time has elapsed than actually has (according to one's clock). On the other hand, grand spaces – such as Great Houses or Great Kivas – and dark cavernous spaces slow down the rate at which one's brain receives sensory stimuli and increase one's sense of "awe." That is, grand spaces slow down one's experience of time, leading people to assume that less time has elapsed than actually has.

Bonito – the isolated hilltop Great Kiva known as Casa Rinconda (Figure 14.21). Aztec's Great Kiva floor covers 122 m², not counting its exterior rooms, and may have been up to 4.5 m in height from its semisubterranean floor to its ceiling. This gives the kiva an interior volume of 556 cubic meters, a voluminous interior with cavernous, sonic qualities. The kiva was reconstructed in 1931, and the visitor today experiences a relatively dark interior, lit by natural daylight that enters indirectly through doorways and a number of T-shaped windows into the adjoining ground-level exterior rooms.

Back in Chaco Canyon, there is evidence for two closing developments. The first takes the form of a final addition to Chetro Ketl, one of the central D-shaped Great Houses (aligned to a lunar standstill). This was the addition, sometime after 1105 CE, of a Mexican-style colonnade to the façade of the central living suite facing the site's elevated plaza. Possibly, one might reason, the Chacoans had adopted some new Mexican-derived reference if not ceremony.

The second closing development followed shortly thereafter as another construction boom (or so it seems). A series of small Great Houses or Great House additions were made between 1115 and 1140 CE in the distinctive "McElmo" style of Aztec and, as we will see shortly, Mesa Verde (Van Dyke 2004). The McElmo constructions are small and compact with strongly rectilinear plans and few kivas. Their wall style consists of more massive sandstone blocks, rather than thin-faced slabs. In the canyon proper, Pueblo del Arroyo had a new wing added in the McElmo style. New McElmo buildings include Kin Kletso, New Alto, Casa Chaquita, and Tsin Kletzin. Wijiji probably also dates to the McElmo phase, although it was built using thinner tabular sandstone.

Given that there was some shift of activity from Chaco Canyon to Aztec by this time, it remains unclear what exactly the McElmo constructions at Chaco mean or where the builders were coming from. Was the McElmo form simply the latest in a series of construction modes laid out and executed by people living in and around Chaco Canyon? Or were these small buildings some sort of commemorative link that was being made by people from northern San Juan? That is, the religious underpinnings if not the political legitimacy of the people of Aztec may yet have been heavily tied to an increasingly empty Chaco Canyon. Quite likely, priests and farmers made pilgrimages to Chaco in these later years. While there, they built new but smaller Great Houses as a form of worship or to connect themselves to the great cultural heritage of the canyon, increasingly a distant memory for many of those who came (Lipe 2006a, 2006b).

Western Pueblos, Salado, and the Classic Hohokam (1150–1450 CE)

It may come as no surprise: as the Colonial and Sedentary period Hohokam may have engendered historical change in the Pueblo country to the north, so the Chacoan phenomenon probably affected the Hohokam. Clearly, Chaco's extensive regional web of religious fervor combined with a political-military halo is evident in Chacoan outliers. Into the 1100s, these were established far and wide, including to the south beyond Red Mesa Valley (where so many Chacoan supplies originated), past the Zuni Mountains, and just over the Little Colorado River almost to the Mogollon Rim.

At about the same time, during the Sedentary period (900–1150 CE), Hohokam society may have experienced serious social if not political and economic "disruption." The all-important ballgame, for instance, appears to have been on its way out, a pattern that Jeffery Clark (2007) believes was part and parcel of significant Hohokam social change. Whether or not Chaco can be implicated in this change is uncertain, but later changes in the Chacoan world – namely its twelfth-century depopulation – did have effects. During the twelfth century, there were apparent Hohokam migrations from the south to the north into Puebloan territory, and there were Puebloan migrations from north to south in the Hohokam regions.

With regards to the south-to-north movement, it is unclear precisely which or how many Hohokam people may have moved into the northwestern edge of the Colorado Plateau around the San Francisco Mountains. But that area, known as the Sierra Sin Agua (the mountains without water), saw the appearance of Hohokam ballcourts, Sonoran-style pithouse villages, and Hohokam craft industries beginning near the end of the 1000s. The people living there, at one time simply labeled the "Sinagua" culture, were primarily of Puebloan derivation, likely ancestors of some Hopi, and can be tied back to Chaco (Gruner 2018). In fact, the late twelfth-century burial of the "Magician," a leader interred with all of his ritual accouterments (including prayer sticks) at the site of Ridge Ruin only a couple of decades after the final depopulation of Chaco, is probably a descendant of Chaco (McGregor 1943). Erina Gruner (2015, 2018) argues persuasively that he was a member of the same Chaco religious sodality as one of the two men buried at Pueblo Bonito in the late 800s, and that he "may have brought Chacoan cult to Ridge Ruin" (Gruner 2018:35). Then again, upon his death, the cult objects – an amazing assortment of inlaid wands, prayer sticks, and fancy pots – were buried with him, so perhaps the living were unable to, or perhaps decided not to, pass along his ritual objects to an apprentice or heir (Gruner 2015).

So, aspects of Chaco were alternately being carried away from or left behind quite intentionally. Within a few decades, impressive multi-storied Great Houses, copies of Chacoan archetypes, were under construction in the Sierra Sin Agua at Tuzigoot, Elden, and Wupatki. At Wupatki, the masonry veneers of the initial Great House are Chacoan (Gruner 2018), though a Hohokam-style ballcourt and an unusual

Fig 14.22 Ballcourt at Wupatki, Arizona. Timothy R. Pauketat photo, 2013.

roofless "Great Kiva-like" building are also present (Figure 14.22). Later, when the P-III people of Mesa Verde began building cliff dwellings, so too did the Puebloan residents of the Sierra Sin Agua, moving to places today called Walnut Canyon and Montezuma's Castle (see P-III and IV below).

The north-to-south movement of Puebloans into the Hohokam country is even more obvious. Many Ancestral Puebloan people traveled in this direction in the early 1200s, possibly owing to rainfall shortages in places such as the Mogollon highlands. The Puebloan migrations involved people both moving down from the north into the Verde and Tonto basins, and swinging across the eastern Mogollon highlands and into the San Pedro and Tucson basins. By about 1250, and out of this intermediate, hybrid world of immigrants and locals speaking very different Puebloan and Hohokam languages, there developed another "phenomenon" that was neither simply a culture or an identity: the Salado (Crown 1994; Dean 2000).

The Salado phenomenon (1250–1450 CE) appears to have begun in and around the Tonto Basin, just south of the Mogollon highlands, where it may be associated with immigrant potters from the north seeking "to compete with others who made decorated pottery" for a series of communities in the area (Lyons 2003). Some of the potters were probably ancestral Hopi. But, whoever the initial Salado groups were, polychrome pottery production "spread beyond these groups

Fig 14.23 Salado polychrome pot (20 cm wide orifice). Courtesy of the Amerind Foundation, Inc., Dragoon, Arizona. Timothy R. Pauketat photos, 2012.

within the context of the diffusion of a regional cult associated with weather control and fertility" (Lyons 2003:81). Aspects of the Salado phenomenon spread across the Mogollon and Hohokam regions and as far south as the great pueblo of Paquimé (a.k.a. Casas Grandes) in Chihuahua, Mexico, where the wares were imported (see Chapter 15). It has precursor and cognate polychrome styles to the north in the Sierra Sin Agua region where the mix of Hohokam and Puebloan traditions had been intermingled already for a century.

Patricia Crown (1994) also calls Salado a religious ideology. Wherever it took hold, Salado seems to have involved ceremonies employing elaborate variations of Salado polychrome pots with names such as Pinto, Gila, Tonto, and Roosevelt Red Ware (Figure 14.23). These pots betray a concern with color, symmetry, and balance, featuring icons depicting Venus, the sun, clouds, rain, wind, and flowers. If such pots have the ability to embody or evoke "community" by their very presence in social spaces, then Salado pots in and of themselves may well have afforded a religious movement. The Salado movement may have rebalanced the cosmos, or at least people's relationships to the cosmos relative to the dynamic, unsettled cultural landscapes in which they lived.

In the Tonto Basin, such unsettled landscapes had existed for a century. In about the year 1150, significant organizational changes were already underway in the Hohokam desertlands of the Sonora during the "Classic" period (1150–1450 CE). Populations along the Salt, Gila, and San Pedro rivers appear to have been consolidated into more compact, monumental sites centered on impressive adobe compounds, each of which enclosed the social space of several households (each being an elaborate version of the courtyard households described for the Colonial and Sedentary period era). Some compounds were elaborate, self-contained, rectangular, multi-roomed facilities covering up to 9,000 m^2 (more than 2 acres) and, no doubt, housing an elite kin group. Some of these were clustered into localities.

At the center of the compounds of the most important families are earthen platforms, now larger than before and with above-ground adobe buildings on their summits. Some of these, such as the buildings at Mesa Grande, Pueblo Grande, Los Muertos, and Casa Grande are great buildings (Figure 14.24). They call to mind the equally large-scale Great Houses of Chaco, the pyramids of Mesoamerica, or the earthen pyramids of the far-off Mississippians in eastern North

Fig 14.24 Adobe Great House at Casa Grande, Arizona. Timothy R. Pauketat photo, 2010.

America (Chapter 10). In any event, the earthen mounds and surmounting buildings are outgrowths of a long Hohokam history. And unlike the more corporate, group-oriented, all-inclusive theatrical performances and monumental constructions of the Ancestral Puebloans, the greatest Classic Hohokam buildings were the exclusive domains of a few elite households. Hence the compound walls that shielded those inside from the ordinary world outside.

Perhaps such walls were important for defense, since the Classic Hohokam economy was in some ways less extensive and weaker than in Sedentary and Colonial period times. Many of the elaborate crafted ritual articles of the earlier era ceased to exist in these later times. Notable was the disappearance of censers and palettes and the fall-off in the once-prevalent shell bracelet. Other shell-work continued and turquoise-and-shell mosaic makes an appearance.

So too did the management of irrigation systems continue, reaching their maximum extent during the Classic era. David Doyel (2007:83) summarizes: "In the lower Salt River valley … where the city of Phoenix now stands, 14 irrigation networks with an estimated aggregate length of 300 miles watered 400 square miles of agricultural land and settlements." More specifically, he describes the Classic period systems associated with each community of several "platform mound villages" along primary "trunk-line" canals 20 miles (32 km) in length and each watering up to 15,000 acres (6,000 ha) (Doyel 2007:89). Each village and each trunk line was probably part of an irrigation community, all of which were also political entities that controlled about 15 square miles (40 km²) of irrigated land.

The peak population of the Phoenix Basin, the largest of the Classic period occupations, is currently estimated to have been about 15,000–20,000 individuals (Doelle 2000). The entire Hohokam region had at least double that number in the Classic period. That is lower than earlier estimates, but a respectable concentration of farmers nonetheless, especially given the desert environment. A reconstruction of a Classic period segment of the Salt River basin shows the relationship of central places and community territories to irrigated lands (Figure 14.25). Remarkably, such archaeological maps resemble

Fig 14.25 Hohokam territories and canals along the Salt River, Arizona (adapted from Fish and Fish 2007: figure 5.8).

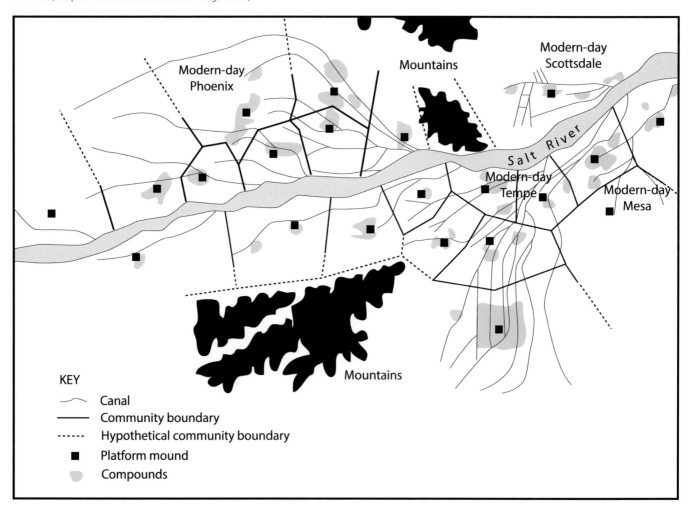

known Hohokam petroglyph maps (Doolittle 1988), with the ancient map-makers using dots to signify a population locus or community, short lines to depict territories, and long lines to show irrigation canals. The Hohokam, it would seem, understood their social landscape in much the same ways as archaeologists do.

Doyel would use the word "chiefdom" to describe each of the political entities in any irrigation system. Glen Rice (1998, 2000) would label each a community "segment." Whatever the political units are called, the salient attribute of Classic Hohokam life was the interdependence of the various political-social-economic units, each headed by likely hereditary elites. Possibly, as the maps support, Hohokam life was approaching proto-urban conditions. The capital-intensive land investments, dense populations, and compounded social barriers were unique in the Southwest and west Mexico. In contrast to Chaco, where a singular macrocommunity and a cosmic center sat at the middle of a vast network, the Classic Hohokam were more socially localized and economically autonomous, if more hierarchical and stratified, with greater incipient wealth and power disparities.

Pueblo III and IV (1140–1540 CE)

In various ways, the later pre-Hispanic history of the Ancestral Puebloans on the Colorado Plateau converged with, paralleled, and diverged from the Classic Hohokam. The convergence involved various Ancestral Puebloan clans and communities during the twelfth century migrating south into the Mogollon and Hohokam areas and west into the Sierra Sin Agua, as previously noted. For the parallels and divergences, we stay on the Colorado Plateau, where there was a twelfth-century rekindling of the Pueblo world.

Into the Cliffs

The best representative of this rekindling is found in the Totah region, beginning with the earlier-noted colonizing movements of Chacoans to Salmon and Aztec (Gruner 2018). Given the depopulation of Chaco Canyon and some significant social and material changes that followed, archaeologists designate the new period as Pueblo III (1150–1300 CE). At first, Aztec remained the center of P-III life, at least for a brief period, until its people relocated, many northward on to Mesa Verde. In the early 1100s, Mesa Verde was simultaneously experiencing a longer growing season with more precipitation and a population surge. Included among these early P-III settlements – note that most were built *on the mesa top* – were McElmo-style buildings, including that known as Far View House (Figure 14.26). Chaco, the place or the idea, may have yet loomed large in the heritage of these P-III people. Quite possibly, priests from Aztec, Lowry, or Far View made pilgrimages back to the great ancient canyon, much as Montezuma did to ancient Teotihuacan, as Charlemagne did to Rome, or as the devout still do to Jerusalem and Mecca. In fact, bits of P-III materials are known from some Great Houses at Chaco, quite possibly those entered by later Puebloan visitors.

The cosmologies of such later Puebloan priests or astronomers seem to have been very similar to those of their Chacoan forebears,

Fig 14.26 Mesa Verde landscape, with the D-shaped Sun Temple atop the mesa (left) and Cliff Palace built into the cliffside (right). Timothy R. Pauketat photo, 2009.

Sun Temple

Cliff Palace

as attested by four attributes of P-III sites. First, cosmic relationships were built into the settlements and localities, with masonry walls and shrines aligned to, say, solstices and equinoxes. Second, the rock art of Mesa Verde is similar to that of Chaco Canyon. Thus, common to the petroglyphs on various cliff faces in both places is the familiar spiral motif, some seemingly positioned such that the play of sunlight and shadow would appear to bifurcate them, similar to the Sun Dagger atop Fajada Butte. Third, T-shaped doorways and windows to the outside on the later Puebloan buildings would seem to indicate the same notion of a transcendental portal. Finally, inside some of the high "observatory" towers in the P-III ruins of Mesa Verde are red, white, and black painted murals that look like depictions of the horizon out of a window.

J. McKim Malville (2008) has interpreted Mural 30 inside a tower at Cliff Palace, painted around 1270 CE, as a horizon clock, where positions of the sun and annual time were ticked off by a sun priest. Scott Ortman (2000) sees this and similar paintings as physically and perceptually relating space, time, and cosmic order. Finally, Elizabeth Newsome and Kelley Hays-Gilpin (2011:174) note that such P-III art "placed the viewer in a center place that evoked the surrounding landscape, earth, and sky, within an orderly progression of time." Other depictions of landscape, time, and order are known from kivas in the Totah region. The P-III people, it seems, viewed the world much like their Chacoan ancestors.

Such active, historical relationships would help to explain Mesa Verdean mimicry of Chaco Canyon. For example, one early P-III construction, the Sun Temple, seems to be a miniaturized D-shaped replica of Pueblo Bonito. Like its Chacoan antecedents, this building and its exterior features, built in the late 1100s, were aligned to both the winter solstice sunrise and the southern maximum moonrise (Malville 2004). The later P-III site of Cliff Palace faces the old Sun Temple as if to acknowledge its place in the people's history (Figure 14.27). Similar references to or "appropriations" of earlier Chacoan ruins by later Pueblo III people are known from across the Colorado Plateau.

The P-III people of the plateau made such physical heritage claims and sought the temporal and spatial order of the cosmos in a time of increasing turmoil based on the volatile environmental conditions of the Totah region. Let's face it, the weather and long-term climatic conditions on the Colorado Plateau, especially these northern portions,

Fig 14.27 Cliff Palace ruins, Mesa Verde, Colorado. Timothy R. Pauketat photo, 2014.

were unpredictable. A particularly cold year, with frost arriving early, or a dry period might devastate that year's crop for some people. So too were social arrangements in some locales slightly chaotic. The cultural landscape around the Mesa Verde region had seldom been stable, but was home to migrants from different locations and with varying claims to the legacy of Chaco, among other more immediate resource claims. And without a superordinate macrocommunity that might resolve disputes and create an *esprit de corps*, small-scale disagreements between neighbors or in-laws might boil over into physical violence.

Besides the Chacoan-esque worldview of some, violence defined the P-III period, ultimately causing the depopulation of Mesa Verde, among other places, around 1300. The increased thirteenth-century security concerns of Ancestral Puebloans are one likely reason that communities relocated their masonry homes from the tops to the sides of mesas. At Mesa Verde, the largest P-III villages were constructed in locations easy to defend and difficult to attack: Cliff Palace, Long House, Square Tower House, and many others. Ladders were the only point of egress into and out of most, and food stores in some were even more inaccessible, placed in small masonry rooms on ledges high above their heads. Mortality rates from traumatic injuries, including arrow wounds, soared as one valley's community may have raided others to settle disputes over marriage debts, insults, or other infringements.

There was no centralized government and, left unsettled, minor disputes might, over the years, lead to uncontrolled small-scale wars, ethnic hatreds, and massacres. The worst violence currently known of happened in the McElmo Creek valley northeast of Mesa Verde shortly after 1277 CE. At that time, an overwhelming enemy of unknown origin swooped down upon Sand Canyon Pueblo, a dying settlement with a large defensive masonry wall around it. The circumstances and sequence of events, as reconstructed by archaeologists of the Crow Canyon Research Center, are telling of the reasons for and long-term effects of P-III life. Kristin Kuckelman (2008:111–118) outlines the circumstances and events, which we distill here into nine points:

(1) The village "housed an estimated four hundred to six hundred people …"

(2) "[P]opulation levels in this locality reached an all-time high between … 1260 and 1280" but the "residents of Sand Canyon Pueblo appear to have been healthy …"

(3) "Among the residents of Sand Canyon Pueblo was the primary agent of this case study, a man … [to be known as] Block 100 man … He was robust and had been well nourished during his lifetime," although he had seen a fight before, judging from the healed fracture on his skull.

(4) Block 100 man was related to others living at the pueblo, yet "was born with six toes on his right foot … [identical to a high status] individual whose remains were interred [a century or two earlier] in a room at Pueblo Bonito in Chaco Canyon …"

(5) "The remains of Block 100 man exhibit skeletal alterations known as musculoskeletal stress markers … [that] could have resulted from a lifetime of engaging in the activities of a craftsman."

(6) In the years prior to the attack, "natural resources of the region had probably been dramatically reduced by centuries of occupation … and one-fourth to three-fourths [or 100–450] of the residents of the village [had already] emigrated before final village depopulation …"

(7) "Block 100 man and other villagers, including … his blood relatives, chose to stay."

(8) One day after 1277 CE, the pueblo "was attacked, and Block 100 man, other members of his family, and numerous additional

residents who were in the village at that time were killed … [A] large depression fracture [to Block 100 man's cranium] … indicates that the fatal blow was probably delivered in a face-to-face confrontation by a right-handed assailant. The position, location, and context of his remains suggest that Block 100 man was killed while on the roof of Room 105, along the massive village-enclosing wall, possibly in a defensive or lookout position … [A]fter he was struck, his body was dropped, probably feet first, through a roof hatchway and came to rest in a sprawled position on the floor …"

(9) Subsequently, Sand Canyon Pueblo was burned. No one returned.

This may have been one of any number of such events that ultimately encouraged the near-total abandonment of Mesa Verde and the Totah region. By 1300 CE, few Ancestral Puebloans were left. Most had moved south and west.

Pueblo IV Migrations

Reasons for the depopulation come to mind as well – a combination of unbearable social conditions and an inability to see communities through lean years. But there may yet be more to the story (see "Katsina Religion" below). Archaeologist James Snead (2008) argues, using a similar case study dating to about the same time in the Galisteo Basin south of Santa Fe, that Puebloan people and their descendants would not return to a place where such violence had occurred. This was because of their beliefs that such places would be inhabited by the dark spirits of those who had died there. Better to avoid them. Even enemies of the former inhabitants would not visit such localities for many years owing to the perceived risks involved.

As people moved southward, the population densities of locales surged, including the Pajarito Plateau, home of Bandelier National Monument, north of Santa Fe. Here, the residents built multistory room blocks up against and carved into the soft volcanic tuff cliffs of valleys (Powers 2005). Standing atop their roofs, people would carve stories of their peoples into the walls. Some stayed; others moved on down the valley of the Rio Grande.

A series of new pueblos were established along the Rio Grande that, together, define the Pueblo IV period (1300–1540/1600 CE). These pueblos, some large and spacious and home to many hundreds of people, were built by the descendants of their northern P-III ancestors and, before them, the Chacoans. However, the relocation of the

Sidebar 14.5 The power of movement

Migrations are themselves social and cultural processes, where old ties and relationships to people, places, and things are severed and new ones established. Along the way, the narrative accounts that explain for people who they are, what they believe, and from whence they came are established in ways with long-lasting value. Migration accounts, for instance, are at the heart of contemporary Hopi, Zuni, and other Puebloan clan identities, homelands, religious practices, and art styles (e.g., Bernardini 2011).

Fig 14.28 Restored polychrome kiva mural at Kuaua, Coronado State Park, Bernalillo, New Mexico. Wikimedia.

Ancestral Puebloans southward entailed some marked changes in community life, worldviews, and religious practices. Severin Fowles (2012) has termed this a Puebloan "Age of Reformation." It lasted until the arrival of Coronado and the beginning of the mission period in the Southwest.

With regard to community life, the most notable alteration was the plaza-centric emphasis in villages, which were increasingly rectangular and less accessible to entrance from the outside (Figure 14.28). All sides of the pueblo were lined with masonry or adobe room blocks, meaning that plaza dances or gatherings could be viewed by residents sitting atop the roofs, but not by people outside (as in the case of Chaco by standing atop the canyon walls). The theatrical qualities of the interior space remained from earlier P-II and P-III times, but these were now theaters-in-the-round, meaning that movements through them would have been significantly different. Kivas were yet built in

Fig 14.29 Petroglyph showing Katsina figure, Petroglyph National Monument, Albuquerque, New Mexico. Timothy R. Pauketat photo, 2009.

the plazas, and still are today, but there are far fewer than in earlier years and, clearly, they are reserved for ceremonial purposes.

Katsina Religion

On the walls of these kivas were elaborate, painted (and frequently repainted) murals showing anthropomorphic supernaturals, ancestor spirits, and powerful cosmic forces in multicolored splendor. Beginning in later P-III times and efflorescing with the P-IV migrations was a new movement known as the Katsina (sometimes spelled Kachina) religion (Adams 1991). Believed to have been inspired by happenings at places such as Paquimé in Chihuahua and, ultimately, Mesoamerica, the Katsina religion built on Puebloan beliefs concerning the sky, rain, clouds, and ancestors.

The result was village ceremonials where Katsinas – sky gods, rain deities, clouds, and powerful ancestors – bring blessings, rain, and fertility or, better, are themselves believed to *be* the blessings, rain, and fertility. During celebratory dances, the Katsinas are presenced by costumed and masked Puebloan dancers and by sacred carved dolls. These same gods were prayed to and visited through kiva mural paintings and through rock art outside the village (Munson 2011). Connections to the gods were made through the act of painting and pecking glyphs into rock. Today, along the Rio Grande, thousands of Katsina petroglyphs cover the volcanic rock escarpments that border what would have been the cultivated valley of the river (www .nps.gov/petr/index.htm) (Figure 14.29).

This new emphasis on embodied gods over external cosmic forces was part and parcel of the inward-turned rituals of the P-IV people. Indeed, such a "revitalization movement" or movements may have caused the pervasive shifts of the era (Glowacki 2011; McGuire 2011). The effect of these repeated P-IV spatial and material religious practices on Puebloan worldviews was profound, as analyzed by Elizabeth Newsome and Kelley Hays-Gilpin. Newsome and Hays-Gilpin had earlier noted that P-III sensibilities involved occupying a node at the center of a vast *external* field of moving space–time relationships. For the Pueblo IV period, Newsome and Hays-Gilpin (2011:166) observe that "the confluence and merging of populations in the 1300s and 1400s led to more heterogeneous, densely populated centers" and "the viewership expressed in these murals and their settings shifted inward to accommodate a new emphasis on social interconnections."

None of this is to say that this revitalized, reformed Puebloan world was not subject to the same chaotic forces as before. Warfare is well known from the period, with entire pueblos occasionally attacked and incinerated. The inward-turned P-IV worldviews surely were partly a result of the concerns of external threats – one pueblo or group of allied pueblos might have been another's worst enemy. In addition, by 1300, the ultimate source of some of the violence experienced along the Rio Grande may have lain outside the region, perhaps in the Plains to the east, in the Sierra Sin Agua to the west, or across the Mogollon highlands to the southeast. In that direction, some 650 km to the south, sat the unusual city of Paquimé, which may have had its own claims to the Puebloan lands (see Chapter 15).

Postscript

The Classic Hohokam centers dissolved by about 1450, coincidentally at about the same time as Paquimé, discussed in the next chapter. Hohokam descendants dispersed into smaller O'odham family settlements and, perhaps, joined Yuman-speaking groups in the lower Colorado River valley (Randall McGuire, personal communication, 2013). In the meantime, the Pueblos – about to be invaded by the Spaniards – were not necessarily peaceful, orderly, and homogeneous places. At some scales and at some times in their past, order had been very much the norm. At other times, the worlds of southwestern and northwestern Mexican peoples had been chaotic, hybridized, and fluid fields of ever-changing relationships. The results were communities of locals and migrants speaking various dialects crosscut, in turn, by clan affiliations and divergent interests.

In 1540, the Zuni girl who witnessed the arrival of Coronado may have understood this intuitively. Her Zuni tradition – a unique Hopi–Pueblo–O'odham–Mogollon mix – was not a set of unchanging practices. Nor were any Puebloan or Hohokam traditions. Ultimately, the Spanish colonists and missionaries would not, and could not, control the minds of the indigenous southwesterners, the Zuni girl included. The events of 1680 put the lie to that flawed theory (see Chapter 3).

15 Pots, Peripheries, and Paquimé
The Southwest Inside Out

Never doubt that a small group of thoughtful committed citizens can change the world. Indeed, it is the only thing that ever has.

Margaret Mead (source unknown)

People can – you can, as Margaret Mead once said – change the world, even supposedly powerless, marginalized, or peripheral people. You do this *at and through* places *with and through* things. Demonstrating the historical impact of such people, places, and things is one of the most significant contributions of archaeology today. We find evidence of it all the time and from some surprising quarters. How did it and does it happen?

People in the past mobilized basic, everyday routines and ordinary things, such as the making and using of pots for cooking, in their history-making movements. The power of pots in making this happen resides in the ways that the ceramic containers relate people to the fundamentals of human experience. Pottery making and use are manifestations of one's rudimentary bodily motions, perceptions, and needs: hands shape clay; smells of cooking food whet taste buds; hunger pangs motivate actions. One cannot avoid the daily experience of eating and that usually means using food containers. Yet owing to this simplicity of association, pots (and the food therein) embody one's identity and relationship to everything outside the body. This is not an elaborate theoretical proposition; it is an essential metaphorical process. If "you are what you eat," to borrow a phrase, then you are also what you eat it from.

Now, not everybody made pots and not all potters made pots the same way across the pre-Hispanic Southwest or in northwest Mexico (e.g., see "Salado," Chapter 14). Most Puebloan and Hohokam potters constructed their pots by making coils of damp clay to build up a wall with their hands. No pottery wheels were used. The feel of the clay between one's fingers made the associations intimate. The coils on many Puebloan cooking pots were pinched together without paddling the outside, producing a "corrugated" exterior. Other pots, like those made by the Hohokam, were thinned by potters wielding a paddle in one hand, slapping it against the outside while holding an anvil on the inside. Some of the red-on-buff Hohokam ollas, those with sharply angled walls, were more complicated constructions – made in two or more pieces which were partially dried and then bonded together – by specialists at places such as Snaketown. So too were some Puebloan and Mogollon vessels made by expert potters. Archaeologists have identified some Mimbres black-on-white bowl sets as having been painted and possibly shaped by single individuals (see below). In other cases, some entire settlements in these regions specialized in making pots for use by other non-pottery-making consumers (remember the case of Chaco Canyon). Various chemical, geological, and archaeometric studies by archaeologists have pinpointed valleys from which the village specialists mined the clays (Mills and Crown 1995). In such cases, one's identity might also be connected to one's lived reality as a pottery consumer rather than maker. The same applies to the historic era.

Beginning in the late 1800s, indigenous potters in the greater Southwest and in northwest Mexico significantly altered their world (Figure 15.1). A Hopi potter, Nampeyo, of the Hano Pueblo in Arizona – originally refugees from the Pueblo Revolt of 1680 – single-handedly revived and transformed Hopi pottery art. So too did María Martínez (née Poveka) and her husband, Julian, of the San Ildefonso Pueblo in New Mexico during the first half of the twentieth century. Like Nampeyo, María and her husband – who added the designs to María's pots – traveled widely to venues such as the World's Fairs

Fig 15.1 Pottery of the US Southwest and northwestern Mexico: (a) Puebloan corrugated jar, ca. 25 cm tall, Salinas Pueblo Missions National Monument, New Mexico, Timothy R. Pauketat photo, 2009; (b) Zuni potters at work beneath drying platform, 1915. Wikimedia.

(a)

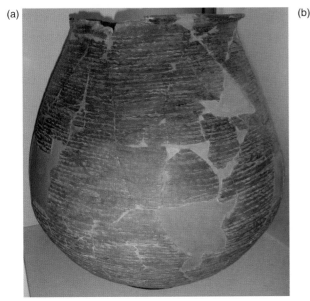

(b)

of early twentieth-century America, even being invited to chat with Franklin and Eleanor Roosevelt in the White House. Her ceramic art, subsidized by Edgar Lee Hewett in the early 1900s, helped bring about a renaissance of Puebloan pottery making, which is very much alive today.

More recently, a young Hispanic man, Juan Quezada (and his family), reinvented the lost pottery technology associated with the long-abandoned center of Paquimé, also known as "Casas Grandes" (great houses), in Chihuahua. Unfortunately, in the town of Mata Ortiz near the ruins of Paquimé, people dug up pots, selling them on the antiquities market. As a teenage boy in the early 1970s, Juan did likewise, though he and others also began to replicate the pots to sell on the market. He ended up training his family and they, in turn, trained scores of others in Mata Ortiz (Lowell et al. 1999).

In Chihuahua, or elsewhere, such re-productions of traditional technological practices have transformed gendered social and economic relationships at small and large scales. Among the Pueblos of New Mexico and Arizona, a tradition formerly passed along from mother or aunt to daughter or niece now also includes men who make and decorate pots. Meanwhile, the Rarámuri (a.k.a. Tarahumara), residents of the Mexican state of Chihuahua, now produce their rustic reddish-brown ollas (or jars), often covered with stretched cowhide, for use as décor in United States homes, hotels, and restaurants. And the ceramic vessels of Juan Quezada and the potters of Mata Ortiz are collected by art aficionados worldwide, boosting the economy of the formerly impoverished Mexican community.

In ancient North America, handmade pots often defined and embodied community. But they were also metaphors for the world as lived by these people. According to archaeologist Scott Ortman (2006), Puebloan kivas were even thought of as "containers," similar to (and even painted like) pottery bowls, with their wooden-framework roofs understood to be oversized and upside-down woven baskets. In light of that, perhaps it is easy to see that people's sense of who-they-were would be synonymous with the clay of and designs on the pot. These linked the elements of life to the everyday rhythms of life: the clay under one's feet, the polishing striations applied to give the ceramic vessel a sheen, the heat of fire which hardened the clay-container walls, and the smoke that ascended into the sky when one fired the pots. Before María Martínez dug clay or collected the grit with which to "temper" her pots, she said prayers and made offerings to cosmic forces (Marriott 1948).

So, pottery in the indigenous world of the greater Southwest and northern Mexico was and is the stuff of life, and as a result each ceramic container possessed a kind of power, spirit, or life force. That life force bound people to the elements of which the pot was made – clay, water, fire, pigments, fuel, ashes, and smoke. When broken or buried, pots may also have been the stuff of death. You will recall from Chapter 14 that, at both Chaco and Chacoan descendant sites in the Sierra Sin Agua, powerful Chacoans were buried with things that were a part of their very identity. In Pueblo Bonito at Chaco, a great cache of black-on-white cylinder vessels (used to drink liquid chocolate) was buried inside an old backroom. Nearby were the bodies of two important men and rooms containing turquoise, bracelets, and macaws, among other ritual items. Perhaps the pots themselves were deserving of burial. We shall also see that, in the Mimbres region of the Southwest's Mogollon area, black-on-white bowls were buried with the dead, most having been "killed" before burial. Small holes were punched into their walls, presumably to release the pot's spirit.

Clearly, pottery is also the stuff of archaeology, which seeks to examine if not revivify the historical relationships between, among other things, pots, people, and places. In this chapter, we examine such relationships by working from the outside in, moving from previously unexamined Southwest/northwestern Mexico cultures into the landscapes of Casas Grandes in Chihuahua, Mexico. We begin southwest of the Hohokam, with the Patayan, and then move to the extreme north to examine the peripheral Fremont culture, before heading south across the Mogollon regions to the indigenous city of Paquimé (Figure 15.2). History may have turned at Paquimé (Table 15.1).

Did Pots Make the Patayan Patayan?

From about 700 CE on, around the western edges of the Hohokam and Puebloan regions and following the Colorado River from the Grand Canyon south to the Gulf of California, lived the desert-dwelling Patayan (Cordell 1984; Stone 1987). Their world was harsh and comprised extreme desert conditions and rocky treeless mountains. Not

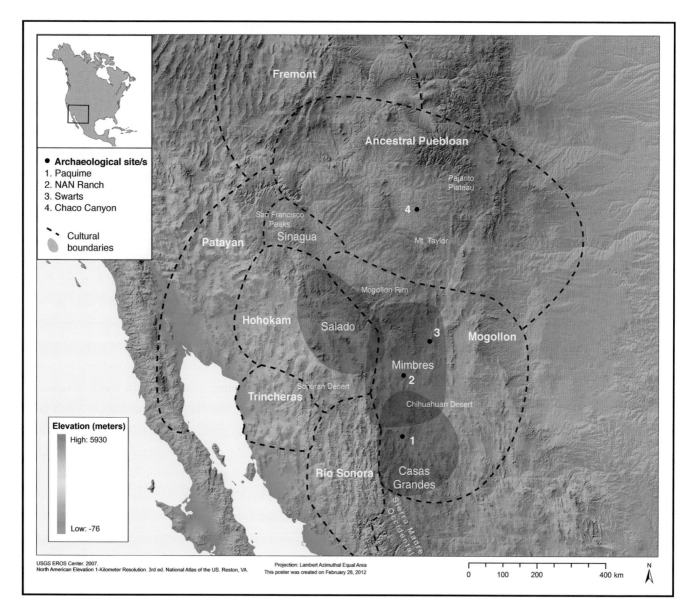

Fig 15.2 The peripheral Southwest and northern Mexico.

surprisingly, their lives and histories are poorly understood, although it is possible to say that most were foragers and part-time agriculturalists who probably engaged their more populous Puebloan and Hohokam neighbors to the east on a routine basis. Yet they probably did not speak the languages of the Pueblo and Hohokam. In the north, from eastern Nevada to southern California, the people calling themselves the Hualapai, Havasupai, Quechan, Mohave, and Yavapai at contact spoke Yuman dialects. So too did the historically known Cocopah in the south at the mouth of the Colorado River. Then again, so did other non-Patayan people in southern California and the Baja peninsula.

Table 15.1 Chronological highlights of the Mogollon and Casas Grandes regions (adapted from Minnis and Whalen 2015; Nelson and Hegmon 2010; Whalen and Minnis 2001, 2009).

Year CE	Historic period	Cultural patterns
200–550	Early Pithouse	Mogollon regions surge in population; sites located on high mesas and hilltops.
550–1000	Late Pithouse	Pithouse and courtyard settlements grow on low terraces nearer waterways; rectangular great kivas built; Mogollon interactions with Hohokam; red-on-brown pottery after 700 CE.
1000–1130	Classic Mimbres	Above-ground pueblos begin, reach maximum size, growing in unplanned fashion; classic black-on-white bowls produced by specialists; limited irrigation systems; likely close relations with Chacoans seeking Mexican materials.
1130–1200	Animas/Black Mountain	Mimbres region relocations; Mimbres black-on-white disappears.
	Late Viejo	Casas Grandes region population is modest; earliest jacal (mud-and-stick) roomblock construction in Chihuahua; red-on-brown pottery.
1200–1450	Medio (Casas Grandes)	Chihuahuan polychromes; planned constructions of Paquimé.
	Late Jornada Mogollon	Increased population density; Katsina cult; large western Mogollon pueblos (e.g., Grasshopper, Chavez Pass).
1500	–	Paquimé abandoned; northern Mogollon pueblos fragment and coalesce, the most successful being Zuni.

So what made the Patayan Patayan? The answer seems not to be the array of manos, metates, hide-processing tools, and arrowheads common to many of the Southwest's peoples. It is not also simply agriculture, in part since various Patayan groups practiced agriculture only to a limited extent. This was true mostly for the semisedentary Patayan people in low-lying areas along the Colorado River, who also subsisted by fishing and capturing waterfowl. Upland Patayans foraged for wild plants, such as agave and piñon, and hunted deer and antelope. Farther south, in Baja California, the native Yuman-speaking peoples did not rely on agriculture at all, which would seem to place them outside the Patayan culture if not the greater Southwest culture area. Of course, while the historically known Kumeyaay, Paipai, Kiliwa, and Cochimí of the north-central Baja California peninsula were foragers only, some lived in villages of thatched-roof houses along the coast, with territorial populations of a few thousand each at contact.

Perhaps Patayan culture stemmed from the lived experience of settlements or special-use sites. Like their Hohokam neighbors, the Patayan peoples built rectangular earthlodges along with a few small, rectangular masonry structures above ground (Cordell 1984). Large sites could yet lie buried under the alluvium of the Colorado River, but most settlements were small and dispersed, similar to the "rancherias" of historic-era O'odham people to the east. The Patayan also created distinctive rock art panels in the desertlands of northern Arizona, eastern Nevada, and southern California. These rock art sites typically include unusual geometric forms that some analysts identify as shamanic figures and "entoptic" imagery – figures envisioned during altered states of consciousness (Whitley 2000). Finally, the region around present-day Blythe, California contains scores of *geoglyphs* – landscape-sized drawings in the earth. Most of these are intaglios, depressions created by removing earth and rocks from the glyph area. They include humanoid and zoomorphic forms, the latter including quadrupeds and snakes (Figure 15.3). All of these may have been graphic components of lived narratives that related places and human experience to supernatural realms and beings, realized or told by traveling across the landscape over the course of a year or a lifetime. Certain people – specifically shamans or young men seeking visions – may also have trekked to such locations on special occasions.

Of course, pots were the "communal" artifact of Patayan and other southwestern settlements *par excellence*. Pots connected people to others, to landscapes, and to the cosmos on a daily basis. Certainly for archaeologists, the most diagnostic Patayan artifact is pottery. Patayan pottery includes plain gray wares early on, used for cooking food. But more diagnostic of Patayan culture were their red-slipped buffware, similar to Hohokam varieties. This was more common after 1050 CE, correlating roughly with both Chaco's Bonito phase and Snaketown's Sedentary period climax. Some of these have distinctive red, fine-line, geometric patterns that, if anything like any of the other pottery in the Southwest, were key to the living-out of relationships in this foreboding part of the world. Of course, to say that such pots may have been the essence of Patayan identity is to overstate things. Then again, doing

Fig 15.3 Humanoid geoglyph near Blythe, Arizona. Wikimedia.

so at least has the merit of encouraging us to consider the *materiality* of identity formation in other seemingly peripheral cultural regions. To explain better, let us look to the Fremont.

Were the Fremont Peripheral?

Calling anybody "peripheral" is a notion that needs to be proven. In many ways, for instance, the people living at Patayan rancherias were no more peripheral than the inhabitants of Hohokam compounds or Puebloan Great Houses. However, low-density, relatively powerless, or underprivileged populations are known in other parts of the world to gravitate economically, demographically, or culturally toward higher-density, powerful, and privileged people, given the perceived benefits of so doing. For such reasons, immigrants have arrived in the United States for centuries and would-be elites continue to clothe themselves in the garments and trappings of Paris, New York, or Hollywood. The people of some homeland, having accepted an inferior cultural status, become peripheral in this way. Their histories and cultural identities, that is, become contingent on other people.

Just such an inference has been mobilized to explain the Fremont culture (700–1300 CE). This culture corresponds closely to the northern Colorado Plateau and beyond into central Utah, extending a little into eastern Nevada, western Colorado, and southern Idaho and Wyoming (Janetski 2008; Madsen 1989; Simms 2008). Beginning about 700 CE, corresponding to the end of the Basketmaker III period, and continuing until about 1300 CE, the end of the Pueblo III period, the people of the plateau north of the Ancestral Pueblo had an identifiable cultural integrity. They lived in small villages or rancherias of between two and a hundred pithouses, much like the BM-III people had (Figure 15.4). They seem to have played a game involving a palm-sized spherical stone ball, in this case without a formal court. These were foragers and gardeners, collecting pine nuts and berries, hunting large game (mountain sheep, antelope, and deer), snaring small game (such as birds and jackrabbits), and growing corn, beans, and squash where possible. They processed the collected plant foods with manos and metates, and kept their seasonal food stores inside pots, upright-slab storage cists, and distinctive masonry or adobe granaries – something like small circular rooms with log and adobe roofs – often out of sight high up on rock ledges. Clearly, they worried about others stealing their foodstores, perhaps while they were away.

Fremont pottery and basketry were made on an as-needed basis by family members, characterized by simple coiled and

Fig 15.4 Fremont slab-lined house at the Dos Casas site, Museum of Peoples and Cultures, Brigham Young University. Courtesy of Richard Talbot and Scott Ure.

one-rod-and-bundle technologies, respectively (Janetski 2008; Madsen 1989; Simms 2008). The basic storage and cooking pot was a thin-walled plain and gray-paste olla or jar, some with pinched or corrugated exteriors like Puebloan cookpots to the south. Some jars and bowls were painted, usually with black geometric patterns similar to their Puebloan counterparts. Some were appliqued (Figure 15.5). Not surprisingly, this pottery is perhaps the most central element of Fremont material culture. As noted earlier, it is that which articulates

Fig 15.5 Fremont appliqued pitcher, CEUM 8490. Courtesy of the Utah State University, Eastern Prehistoric Museum.

people, places, and things with the wider world. But it is not the only distinctive cultural trait.

Fremont clothing and personal adornment was also unique. We know this in part because Fremont leather items, such as footwear, are often preserved owing to the high-altitude dry conditions at many sites. Unlike Puebloan yucca sandals, Fremont people wore high-top moccasins, sewn from two or three parts and sometimes insulated, with the small, upper dewclaws of a deer or sheep serving as heels. Other articles of clothing and personal ornamentation are evident on clay figurines that show anthropomorphic characters (Figure 15.6). These figurines have distinctive hairdos and face paint or tattoos, and wear elaborate necklaces, sashes, and skirts or breechcloths. The figurines themselves may have been intended to show deceased female and male ancestors or other superhuman beings from the land of the dead, as the eyes are almost always shown closed. They are also characteristically shown with large trapezoidal torsos lacking clay arms and legs and appear nearly identical in outline to certain Fremont rock art anthropomorphs (e.g., Janetski 1998; Schaafsma 2008).

Such characters in Fremont rock art are occasionally shown with limbs and horns, the latter possibly indicating that some were underworld beings similar to those described by Great Basin and Puebloan descendants today (Figure 15.7). Complicated panels of petroglyphs and a few pictographs are known from places such as Nine Mile Creek, Sego Canyon, Range Creek Canyon, and the San Rafael Swell in Utah (Metcalf 2008). These show the horned, triangular beings flanked by large game animals, long-necked birds, men or gods with bows and shields, and geometric motifs, including lightning, serpentine lines, and spirals. No doubt, such panels were the graphic elements of narratives that might be verbalized on site.

Fig 15.6 Unfired clay figurines found in a side canyon of Range Creek Canyon in Utah. Clarence Pilling/Wikimedia.

Fig 15.7 Early Fremont period petroglyphs in Sego Canyon, Utah. P. D. Tullman/Wikimedia.

Besides pottery, such great rock art panels may be among the most telling features of Fremont landscapes, which otherwise comprise modest settlements and campsites hidden away in canyons (e.g., Talbot and Richens 2004). Similar to some early Puebloan rock art, these were inscriptions that afforded human contact with the dead and deities of other worlds. But they were also clearly palimpsests, layers of superimposed glyphs and motifs that resulted from repeated episodes of telling stories and prognosticating futures as these involved superhuman figures. Such inscriptions fixed or emplaced the relatively small-scale settlements of the semi-mobile Fremont in space and time so closely that cultural knowledge and history actually *resided* in these places (following Basso 1996). Such places also imparted identity to the diverse assortment of Fremont peoples who, historically, probably became the Shoshone, Ute, Piute, and Navajo, among others.

The transfer of ownership of 1,700 ha of an unstudied and off-limits canyon near Price, Utah, from private to public hands, provided significant new discoveries pertaining to the relationship of Fremont people to the land (http://video.pbs.org/video/1192787828). From the 1940s on, rancher Waldo Wilcox had not allowed any archaeologists or artifact collectors on to his cattle ranch; he turned it over to the state in 2004 to ensure that it would be protected. In the process, multiple native, rancher, and scientific points of view about site preservation find a place, literally. In Range Creek Canyon, Fremont-era villages and campsites attest to the close, fragile connections between the past, the land, and the present (http://nhmu.utah.edu/range-creek). So fragile was this relationship in the past that it was pushed over the edge around the year 1300 (Janetski 2008).

Conflict seems evident in the placement of granaries and the depictions of anthropomorphic figures with shields and weapons. Droughts in the 1100s and 1200s surely added stress to Fremont lives. Then, beginning around 1300, the climate of this northernmost southwestern area turned colder. This was the beginning of the "Little Ice Age" which would last until European colonization. Fremont agricultural production could not be sustained in those years, and people dispersed or moved away, some perhaps into the Plains (to become the Dismal River culture), some perhaps into the Ancestral Puebloan homeland, where they may be ancestral to various Hopi clans (Powell and Smiley 2002). Across much of their one-time territory, there was a "clear break" marking the end of the Fremont way of life (Simms 2008:231).

It is worth recalling the Navajo stories of relationships with a Gambler at Chaco Canyon (or Salmon, Aztec, Mesa Verde). Perhaps some Fremont relationships with the Pueblo world were as peripheral clients to central patrons. In any number of ways, Fremont groups could have been pulled into that complicated Puebloan web to the south (see Chapter 14). Maybe some Fremont folks were actively Puebloanized and peripheralized. Or maybe the trappings of southwestern civilization amid the Fremont were inert adoptions with little historical significance. Knowing which was the case, when and where, at places such as Range Creek Canyon will go a long way toward understanding southwestern geopolitics generally and regional-cultural change farther to the south specifically.

Mogollon (200–1000 CE) and Mimbres (1000–1130 CE)

South and east of the Ancestral Puebloan and Hohokam cultural regions lies the so-called Mogollon area, a series of regions south of the Colorado Plateau extending from the Mogollon Rim into New

Mexico and, ultimately, Chihuahua. In some ways like the Patayan and Fremont cultures, this great stretch of territory might be thought of as peripheral – occupied by people on the receiving end of history who lacked the Great Houses and compounds of core southwestern developments. That would change after 1130 CE in the farthest southern reaches of the Mogollon area in Chihuahua, Mexico.

Certainly, throughout their history, the Mogollon people dealt with the various movements that emanated from the San Juan, Salt, and Gila river basins, among others, sometimes migrating or seeing migrations from one to the other. Equally clear, there were fewer standout historical phenomena to be noted in the Mogollon territory. Mogollon pottery, on the whole, includes versions of corrugated or plain cooking wares in the north or south, respectively, and painted serving or ceremonial red wares and white wares all over. With the appearance of the Salado phenomenon (Chapter 14), polychrome vessels became distributed throughout the Mogollon world too, with some pots made in Arizona ending up at the southern Mogollon center of Paquimé (see below).

Mimbres Settlements

The core of the Mogollon area comprises the Mimbres region, in turn centered on the Mimbres Valley in southwestern New Mexico. Based largely on research since the 1970s, it seems that the history of the people of the Mimbres region followed a unique trajectory while also being contingent on that of the Hohokam and the Ancestral Puebloans to the west and north, respectively. During the Pithouse period (200–1000 CE), Mogollon settlements were small and often impermanent (Gilman 2010). The subsurface homes were initially circular in outline. Later they were rectangular in shape.

By the final centuries of the late Pithouse period (800–1000 CE), the people of southwestern New Mexico seem to have been increasingly connected with the north. At Mimbres village sites, a few larger public buildings or Great Kivas were built, each covering 400–1,800 square feet (37–167 m²). One entered the building by walking down a sloping entryway on to its floor (Creel and Anyon 2010). That entryway often faced toward the winter solstice sunrise, indicating a connection between the annual return of the sun (from its southerly wintertime slide up to that point) and the rituals within these buildings (Figure 15.8). Inside each of these Great Kivas, like their

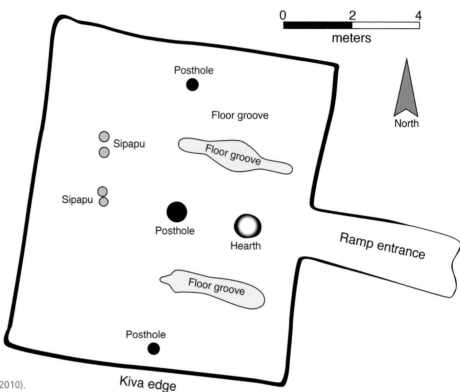

Fig 15.8 Mimbres kiva (after Creel and Anyon 2010).

Puebloan counterparts, were a hearth, opposing floor-groove foot drums, and a sipapu (the portal connecting the living to the previous world; see Chapter 14).

Puebloan inspirations or connections may have been the reason for a short-term transition in the Mogollon region from pithouse settlements to above-ground roomblock pueblos. This took place over just one or two human generations immediately prior to 1000 CE. The result was Mimbres villages and farmsteads, not as elaborate as the Pueblo I and Pueblo II Great Houses to the north for sure, but Puebloan in style nonetheless. These were single-story buildings constructed using river cobbles rather than masonry slabs, and they were more heavily populated than the other monumental architectural constructions.

Also unlike the oversized Puebloan buildings to the north, these post-1000 Mogollon constructions seem not to have been designed or built by large work crews during great social gatherings. Rather, the Mimbres pattern is one where a settlement grew or shrank depending on the fortunes and family sizes of the people who lived there. New rooms were added as needed, and old ones, after the deaths of their residents, were converted into the final resting places for the dead (Figure 15.9). In this way, some Classic Mimbres period (1000–1130 CE) pueblos, such as Swarts Ruin, Galaz Ruin, or NAN Ranch Ruin, grew large, reaching sizes of 150 or more rooms (Shafer 2003). In so developing, some ended up with a slightly haphazard appearance in plan view, lacking strict adherence to a single design or organizational axis. According to Stephen LeBlanc (2004:11), by the early 1100s, "some seventeen villages roughly the size of Swarts Ruin lay along the Mimbres River and its major tributaries, each about three miles from the next … A handful of other large sites" sat "along the Gila River and near the Rio Grande. In addition, dozens of smaller villages and farmsteads [i.e., unit pueblos] were situated in upland areas and along minor drainages."

There are yet indications of later connections with the Pacific Ocean, and perhaps the Hohokam, in the form of cut-shell ornaments,

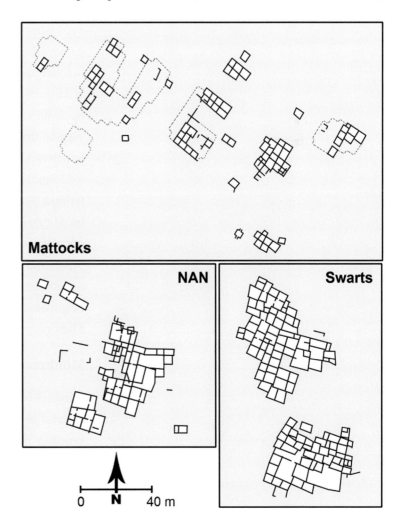

Fig 15.9 Plan schematics of three Mimbres settlements. Courtesy of Will C. Russell.

Sidebar 15.1 Actual pueblos!

The pueblos of the Mimbres Valley during the Classic period seem to have been actual pueblos or populated towns akin to those known from the historic era into the present day. Doubtless there was an established social hierarchy within a Mimbres town, with leaders, councils, and priests articulating and promoting community interests. However, the well-populated yet haphazard developmental tendencies of Mimbres sites, with simple cobblestone construction of rooms in fits and starts, and the use of old rooms for burials of family members, all suggest a corporate-familial organization and considerable familial autonomy within the community. This would have been very different from the Great Houses and compounds of the classic Chacoan and Hohokam worlds, characterized by exclusive and monumental architectural spaces and regional-scale practical and ideological order. Your life in such a place would have revolved around plaza events hosted by community leaders who were also your kin or affines (i.e., in-laws). In your likely matrilineal community, your kin would have included mostly your mother's relatives with whom you would have coordinated all major activities, from farming along the river to cooking dinner or expanding your home. Occasionally you may have had the opportunity to accompany, say, a maternal uncle on a great trip far to the south to acquire the colorful birds, bells, and chocolate powder that you might later carry in your family's baskets to "The Place beyond the Horizon" in the north.

a few paint palettes, the cremation of some deceased individuals, and, perhaps, irrigation technology. The first include the *Glycimeris* species bracelet parts, so diagnostic of Hohokam dress, buried with the dead at Mogollon sites and painted on the inside of the famous Mimbres black-on-white bowls (see Chapter 14). The palettes and cremations suggest that some people were familiar with Hohokam religious practices. On the other hand, irrigation may have been merely copied from their distant neighbors to the west, who had perfected canal technology well before the 1000s. Moreover, the images of ocean fish on Mimbres pots seem to indicate that Mimbres people visited the ocean in western Mexico, perhaps south of the Trincheras region (see below, and McGuire 2011). In any event, the people of the Mimbres region, after 1000, also became closely associated with their Chacoan neighbors to the north. This is evident through, among other things, Mimbres pottery.

Mimbres Pottery

Mimbres black-on-white bowls are the best-known Classic Mimbres cultural objects. These are simple, hemispherical white-slipped pots, generally made about the size of today's large mixing bowl, able to hold two or three liters of solid food. Each is painted in a somewhat minimalist design that begins with several black lines around the inside of the upper bowl interior. Below that may be some geometric embellishments that accentuate the pot's usual artistic subject matter: a scene showing anthropomorphic, zoomorphic, or ornamental figures from side or front views, often engaged in some activity (Figure 15.10). The figures range from geometric patterns to naturalistic and surreal depictions of *Glycimeris* bracelets, scorpions, grasshoppers, fish, rabbits, tortoises, turkeys, swallows, hummingbirds, ocean fish, macaws, bats, antelope, mountain goats, deer, and human or superhuman figures, the last possibly including local versions of Mesoamerican gods: a horned and feathered serpent and a goggle-eyed anthropomorph. All such beings are commonly shown engaging each other or using special ritual sword-like sticks, masks, burden baskets, pots, blankets, smoking tubes or cane cigarettes, and flowers.

Stephen LeBlanc (2004) has demonstrated that, of the hundreds of pots known, there are sets of two or more pots that were painted by single artisans. Such specialists, who may or may not have been the potters themselves, sometimes favored particular motifs or design patterns. One painter's rabbits or tortoises, for instance, are readily identified as hers or his. In rare instances, LeBlanc was even able to discern pots made over the course of a single artisan's life.

Some of the Mimbres bowls had been used and later buried in the ground, and their rim edges showed evidence of use wear. Other bowls were specially made for burial. One way or another, most of the whole pots known today were probably buried with the dead in Mimbres villages. Many of these vessels had themselves been killed, or intentionally damaged by punching a hole into the base. Almost all of them betray a simple naturalistic or surreal aesthetic that, unfortunately, appeals to modern-day art collectors. This has led to an

Fig 15.10 Mimbres black-on-white bowl interiors (each ca. 30 cm in diameter): left, bear; center, pronghorn antelope; right, rabbit. Dallas Museum of Art/Wikimedia.

Sidebar 15.2 Newsbrief: Mimbres Court Evidence, by Carolyn Swan, for *Archaeology* magazine, volume 54 (2001)

Three men have been arrested for digging up potsherds at the East Fork site, a Mimbres settlement in New Mexico's Gila National Forest. The looters, Aaron Sera and brothers James and Michael Quarrell, were convicted and may face up to two years' imprisonment and fines of $20,000 or more; sentences are pending.

Officers of the Forest Service Law Enforcement Agency had earlier found evidence of digging and had placed a seismic sensor in the area to monitor human activity. One month later, the sensor was activated and officers caught the men looting the site. Upon questioning, Michael Quarrell admitted their intention to sell the pottery they found. The

Mimbres, who lived in southwestern New Mexico and a small section of northern Mexico from AD 900 to 1200, produced pottery famous for its black-and-white geometric patterns and depictions of animals and humans. The vessels, often associated with burials, were likely placed on the head of the deceased, whose soul escaped through a hole punched in the bottom.

The 1979 Archaeological Resources Protection Act prohibits excavation without a permit and removal or damaging of archaeological materials and human remains located on public land. The act also prohibits the trafficking of artifacts wrongfully removed from sites.

(www.archaeology.org/0101/newsbriefs/mimbres.html)

illicit art market fed by unscrupulous looters, who have mined Classic Mimbres sites – sometimes with highly destructive machinery – simply to recover and then sell the ancient treasures for profit (e.g., www.savingantiquities.org/category/article). Most of the beautiful bowls one might view online were, in fact, stolen from their resting places by such looters.

Such looting forever destroys our ability to fit the Mimbres pieces into the larger puzzle of pre-Hispanic southwestern history. Of the most intriguing problems yet to be resolved is the Mimbres' relationship to Chaco, Paquimé (see below), and Mesoamerica. It is highly significant that no Chacoan Great Houses were built in the Mimbres region. However, Chacoans likely obtained Mesoamerican articles – macaws, chocolate, copper bells – via the Mimbres region, not the Hohokam. From a Mimbres point of view, relations with Chaco were doubtless important.

Then again, the paramount concern of these Mogollons may have been northern or western Mexico. Given their proximity, Mimbres people may have traded various materials from the south to the north. Hence, Chacoans may have tapped the Mimbres Mogollons for valuable Mesoamerican materials. During the Classic Mimbres period, both places had similar sorts of Mesoamerican objects. Never mind that the ritual sticks held in the hands of some Mimbres pots' characters, and the dancers depicted on other pots, appear to Zuni and

Hopi descendants today as the same sort of ritual objects and garb that their own leaders and sodalities use or used (remember the buried men in Pueblo Bonito and the Magician at Ridges Ruin). Both peoples believe themselves descended from the Mimbres Mogollons.

As the ocean fish and macaws would seem to attest, the Mimbres potters may have possessed wide-ranging knowledge of exotic animals that lived hundreds of miles away from their remote desert homeland. Thus it seems that these were no simple backwater Mogollons. They were well-informed and connected folks. The people at Mimbres villages, it seems, had somehow emerged as players in the complicated geopolitical world that was the eleventh- and twelfth-century Southwest. It is difficult not to see the imagery of Mimbres black-on-white bowls as historically linked to the orthodox religious practices emanating out of Chaco (making the Mimbres peripheral). However, it is equally difficult not to see Mimbres as an autochthonous regional development, benefiting from its proximity to (and contingent on) developments in) the Hohokam and Ancestral Puebloan realms, while also being far enough away to hold off incorporation into a Chacoan "cultural hegemony" (an umbrella-like regional order or orthodoxy made up of syncretized political ideologies and second-nature ways of being in the world that privileges some over others). While appearing peripheral in some ways, they may actually have been central in other ways. They certainly figure centrally in a subsequent major historical development in the greater Southwest: the Casas Grandes phenomenon.

Mysterious Gaps (1130–1200 CE)

Around 1130, "thousands of people left dozens of villages in the Mimbres region within the span of some 20 to 30 years – a dramatic event" (Nelson 2010:100). What was happening? There were significant droughts in the mid-1100s, some fields may have become exhausted (from generations of corn–beans–squash agriculture), or people may simply have felt an inexplicable urge to move. All are possible explanations offered by archaeologist Margaret Nelson (2010), reminiscent of scenarios previously discussed for other portions of the Southwest (Chapter 14). Of course, none of these necessarily explains the simultaneous termination of Mimbres black-on-white pottery production. That is, either before or during the emigrations of Mogollon peoples out of the Mimbres region, the well-known, eye-catching Mimbres black-on-white pottery ceased to be produced. Why?

Definitive answers to this question have yet to be given by archaeologists, and actually may depend on whether production stopped before or during the relocation of villagers to their new homelands. Some of their new pueblos were probably to the north or west; others were likely south, called by archaeologists the Animas and Black Mountain phases in southern New Mexico, where there is no Mimbres black-on-white to be seen after 1130 (Creel 1999; Nelson and Hegmon 2010; Shafer 1999). Still others seem to have migrated directly south into the Rio Casas Grandes Valley of northwest Chihuahua, where there is some Mimbres pottery, perhaps predating the 1130 cut-off (or perhaps not; see below). In any event, it is important to recognize that Mimbres pottery was not on its way out, a passing fad that had outlived its utility, before 1130. Instead, production was going strong up to the end. So if the manufacture of Mimbres black-on-white ceased simply as a function of moving away, then we might blame the rigors of the move – people wandering in the wilderness coming to associate the imagery with negative memories to be forgotten in their new homeland. Migrations are always opportunities for social reinvention. Leave the old furniture behind; change your name; restart anew; forget the past!

However, if production ceased before the valley's general depopulation, especially if cessation was abrupt, then one might suspect a major (almost catastrophic) event or a pervasive societal transformation or religious movement that involved or led to an intentional decision by people to cease a powerful, if perhaps dangerous, practice. Something similar may have happened with regard to the ancient Hopewell demise in the American Midwest (Chapters 9 and 10). But lacking evidence for an environmental catastrophe, and consistent with the introduction to this chapter, such a decision would seem to have been necessarily related to the meanings connected to or the implications of making or using the painted Mimbres pots. If ceramic vessels embody community as argued earlier, then elimination of them may have been an intentional rejection of that community, perhaps in favor of another. The pots, in such a scenario, would bear a great history-changing power.

It is worth remembering the correspondence between the end of the Mimbres art style, at ca. 1130, and the depopulation of Chaco

Canyon, which most place at 1140 CE. Were both related to a third cause (the climate?) but not each other? Or was there something about the greater Mimbres–Chaco connection – perhaps novel religious practices or sodalities shared by people in both places – that dissolved in the Mimbres Valley because of Chaco's demise, or vice versa (if the dendrochronology is taken at face value, then vice versa is the most likely scenario)? There are local southwestern precedents for this sort of planned, ceremonial termination to ritual practices. In the Ancestral Puebloan region to the north and the Mimbres Valley to the south, kivas were formally decommissioned by dismantling and burning them, an act of both remembrance and forgetting (Creel and Anyon 2010; Mills 2008). Perhaps the end of Mimbres bowl production was a similar sort of act, the potters and artisans in each valley pueblo, perhaps in a valley-wide coordinated ritual closure event, marking some historical turning point.

Casas Grandes and the Water City (ca. 1200–1450 CE)

Let's consider just such a possible historical turning point. After 1200, based on a series of dendrochronological dates, a new great town – some would call it a city – was emerging about 290 km (180 mi) due south of the Mimbres Valley (Dean and Ravesloot 1993). To a large extent, the description that we apply to this place – town or city – is irrelevant. Towns and cities come in different shapes and sizes throughout human history. What matters were its historical effects. Today we call this place Paquimé, a.k.a. Casas Grandes (Figure 15.11). Its actual founding date, if there was such a thing, is unclear, and may have happened at or decades after the cessation of Mimbres black-on-white pottery production. In fact, certain archaeological facts suggest that major construction at Paquimé didn't happen until after the year 1200 (Whalen and Minnis 2009, 2012). Did major construction break the historical continuity of the region, or were the builders of Paquimé merely the descendants of earlier Viejo period people?

The lack of clarity on something so basic as founding dates and cultural continuity can be attributed in part to a lack of appropriate biological, chronometric, and social data necessary to answer big questions. Archaeology is hard work, and working in Chihuahua (at the time of this writing during a drug war) isn't simple. But it is

Fig 15.11 Excavated residential area of Paquimé, showing roomblocks. Wikimedia.

possible with archaeological data and at some risk to one's personal safety to answer big questions. To borrow Margaret Mead's phraseology, archaeology is the only way to answer such questions!

The big questions include the following. Did people migrate to the Casas Grandes region and, if so, who, how many, when, and why? Was there a founding moment at all, and if so, when? Were there specific engagements with Mesoamericans (why and with whom specifically)? Did the people of Casas Grandes make major trading or warring expeditions northward? If so, did such things shape the Southwest's geopolitics? Unfortunately, in the past, researchers have become stuck in restrictive schools of thought. In the 1970s, too much emphasis was placed on the Mesoamerican origins of Paquimé's people. However, an opposite extreme has taken hold in recent years: Mesoamerica has been written out of the history of Casas Grandes, as if the phenomenon was simply the end result of a process of *in situ* human adaptation to the local Chihuahuan environment (Mathiowetz 2011). Such a scenario seems to ignore the possible gaps in the archaeological record and to downplay the possible influx of immigrants into Chihuahua. Indeed, the adaptationist line of thought also overlooks the power of places. Places, especially cosmopolitan cities, are never simply the products of history. Rather, *places cause history*. Today, we need to avoid the extremes and begin by investigating that history!

Let's begin with the origins of the Casas Grandes population. With regard to the mysterious disappearance of the Mimbres, few can doubt that sherds of Mimbres black-on-white bowls are known from sites in the Casas Grandes region, revealing some sort of Chihuahuan connection to these northern people. Possibly, migrants from the Mimbres Valley resettled the Chihuahuan desert lands to the south. They weren't that far away (290 km [180 mi] or several days' walk). In the Casas Grandes region, the Mimbres sherds presumably date to the end of what is called the Viejo period, a loosely defined era when a sparse population living in modest pithouse villages inhabited the Rio Casas Grandes Valley. Before 1000 CE, Viejo pithouses and small settlements look similar to Mogollon Late Pithouse period sites. After that date, also like the Mimbres Mogollon pattern, and for the next two centuries, the Viejo period people built modest above-ground roomblock pueblos. Very little about this period is currently known except that, for all intents and purposes, the Viejo people were the southernmost Mogollon population.

So, the preconditions for Paquimé were in place before 1150. In fact, a few scattered Viejo period village areas are known to underlie the subsequent Medio period occupation of Paquimé, which dates from about 1200 to 1450 CE. However, Viejo period sites are relatively small and few in number, and can hardly account for the significantly larger population of Paquimé after ca. 1200 CE, never mind the rest of the Casas Grandes people living at hundreds of Medio period sites in the valley (Figure 15.12). That is, the Viejo period may have been a necessary precondition to the founding of Paquimé, but it is unlikely

Sidebar 15.3 Southern terminus of the Chaco meridian?

In a provocative book, *The Chaco Meridian*, published in 1999, archaeologist Stephen Lekson proposed that Ancestral Puebloan people on the Colorado Plateau recognized a great north–south axis or meridian and built their most important sacred centers (and the Great North Road out of Chaco) along it. He posited that they did this to maintain a fundamental balance with the cosmos. Chaco Canyon was the first great center, contemporary with the Classic Mimbres (also generally on the meridian), followed by Aztec, and, finally, Paquimé (Lekson 1999). These places all fall within a fraction of a degree of longitude 107.9 degrees W. Find them on Google Earth for yourself. Perhaps, Lekson suggests in print, groups of Ancestral Puebloan migrants – likely small processions led by priests – used simple plumb lines and sighting sticks to maintain the same north–south line as they migrated south across hundreds of miles to a new homeland along Rio Casas Grandes. To do this, they would have needed to reference landmarks ahead of them and, once passing them, use them as backsights to check their position. They might also have used crude sundials (vertical sticks or "gnomons" in the ground against which the sun's shadow over the course of a day might be used to mark a north–south axis). Many southwestern archaeologists dismiss the idea. Others, presumably believing it too outlandish, refuse to even acknowledge it. Yet there are reasons to suspect that Ancestral Puebloan people were among the builders of Paquimé, regardless of the meridian scenario.

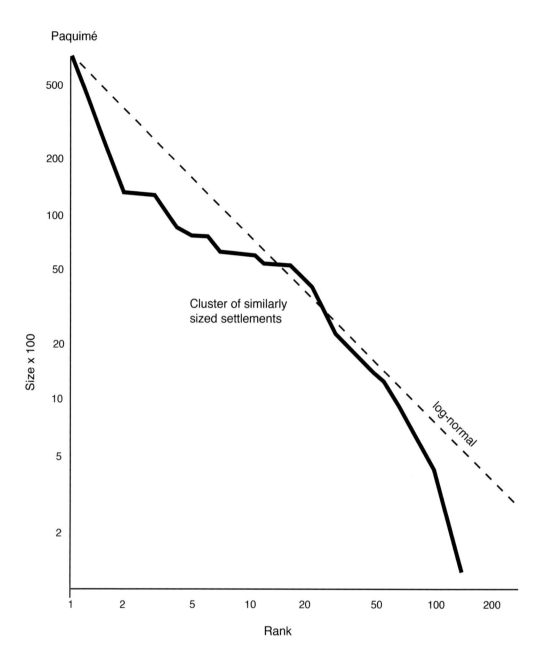

Fig 15.12 Regional site rank-size distribution graph, Medio period (adapted from Whalen and Minnis 2001).

that local people birthed enough offspring to then "evolve" into the Medio period phenomenon, with its unprecedented features and elaborate cosmology. Let's look at downtown Paquimé more closely.

Downtown Paquimé

For most of the twentieth century, little was known of a site first visited by the Spanish in the 1560s. A description of it in 1584, perhaps made just a century after Paquimé's abandonment, notes many houses of great size, strength, and height. These houses are six or seven stories high … [and] contain large and magnificent patios paved with enormous, beautiful stones. There are hand carved stones that supported the magnificent pillars made of heavy trunks brought from far away. The walls of the houses are stuccoed and painted in many shades and colors.

(Quoted in VanPool and VanPool 2007:3)

Three centuries later, the highest adobe walls – highly erodible when exposed to desert rains – had crumbled. Some were "still standing 30 feet above the 20-foot-high mound" of ruins (Wilcox 1999:98).

In 1959, archaeologist Charles Di Peso, the young director of the Amerind Foundation in Dragoon, Arizona, began major excavations of the anomalous historical phenomenon in conjunction with Mexico's Instituto Nacional de Antropología e Historia (www .amerind.org). The Amerind Foundation eventually published a masterful eight-volume set of the work (Di Peso 1974; Di Peso et al. 1974). In it, Di Peso interpreted what he found as a northern outlier of Mesoamerican civilization, a trading outpost set up, perhaps, by Toltecs who had migrated north from central Mexico. These new inhabitants, he thought, were Mesoamerican lords who had brought with them their elaborate religious practices.

Few agree with him today. But few who have worked in the Casas Grandes phenomenon, especially within the limits of downtown Paquimé, fail to identify this place as large, orderly, and cosmopolitan, much the way that Di Peso saw it. That cosmopolitan quality should be emphasized. While founded on some local northwestern Mexican

Sidebar 15.4 Paquimé from above

In Google Earth's search bar, type in "Casas Grandes, Chihuahua" (or "Museo de las Culturas del Norte"). Just meters to the southeast of the museum you can see many rectilinear rooms, small pyramids, effigy mounds, I-shaped ballcourts, and plazas of the excavated portions of Paquimé. Note that much of the site is aligned to the cardinal directions, including a cross-and-circle platform at the site's north end. Other walls and the ballcourt are off cardinal by a few degrees. Why? Was this planned or the result of a lack of central planning? Enter "Street View Mode" and take a tour of the pathways that lead you through the ancient site.

Imagine that the buildings were several stories high. You enter through a T-shaped doorway. Water might gurgle in the covered conduits beneath your feet. Echoes of macaws and turkeys squawking or gobbling would reverberate off the walls. You pass through hallways covered with murals and enter a great sunny patio with high painted walls. Greens and reds might predominate, the same as on the feather headdresses and costumes worn by priests and political elites here in the patio, outside in the plazas, or atop the platforms. The greatest platforms may have been the long-collapsed flat roofs of the adobe houses themselves.

principles, Paquimé's diverse parts and unique features seem to have transcended the older kinship organizations of villages and pueblos. Its very cosmopolitan quality is, in effect, the definition of a city.

Paquimé's rectilinear roomblock "houses" and walled-in courtyards are reminiscent of Hohokam towns to the north and Chalchuites settlements to the south. But the Casas Grandes city was bigger, and its walls higher, than most of them. The entire city covered about 20 ha, the core of which was composed of two large roomblock areas surrounded by a series of lesser houses (Figure 15.13). In total, there may have been 2,000 rooms in the excavated and unexcavated portions of the city. The maximum population was never great by urban Mesoamerican standards, but it was locally significant, comprising at least 2,000 people, not counting other pueblos and farming settlements in the region. One early twentieth-century guesstimate placed the population of Paquimé at 3,000–4,000 people.

Unlike the Great Houses of Chaco Canyon, few of the interior rooms inside the adobe houses at Paquimé appear to have been inaccessible and unlivable. Instead, they were functional, even posh, facilities for private living, corporate work activity, and public socializing and performance. An analysis of access potential using graph theory by David Wilcox (1999) suggests that many interior spaces were easily accessed via hallways and off patios and plazas. Some access ways were probably public. Others were private. There were a number of types of entrances into and out of the roomblock houses, including the idiosyncratic Ancestral Puebloan T-shaped "portal" doorways (see Chapter 14). These are known from outlier Casas Grandes settlements as well, and south all the way into Zacatecas (Randall McGuire, personal communication, 2013).

Each of Paquimé's house complexes included living rooms, storerooms, workshop rooms, and aviaries arrayed around patios, similar to Mesoamerican and north and west Mexican patterns (Randall McGuire, personal communication, 2013). In one complex was a Mogollon-style square kiva, one wall of which was decorated with a carved serpentine image (similar to those in kiva murals to the north). The walls of the residential houses were painted as well, as the Spanish had noted in the 1500s. And if Paquimé's painted room murals were anything like those of Pueblo IV kivas (or Teotihuacan's apartment complexes), then we might expect that a stroll through the spacious rooms and patios of Paquimé's houses would have been a sensually

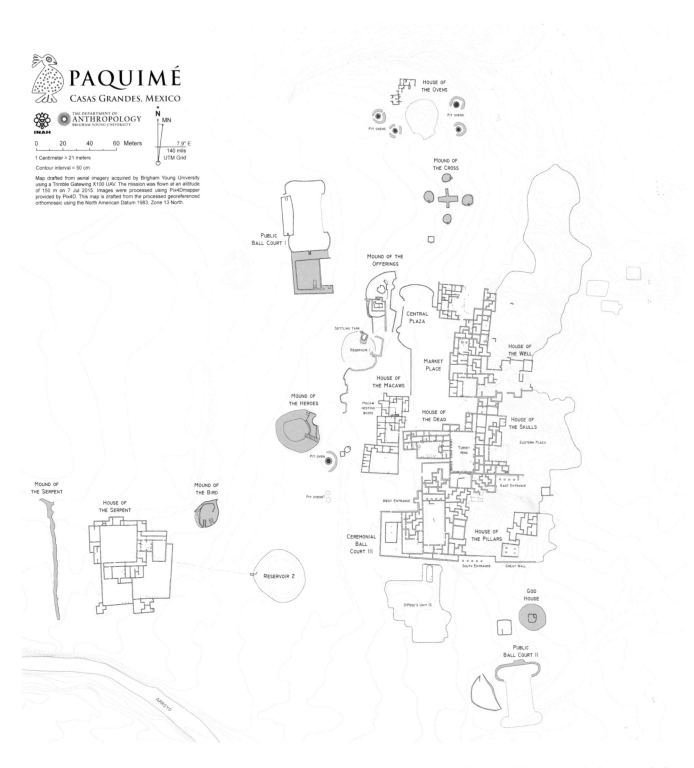

Fig 15.13 Map of Paquimé. Courtesy of Scott Ure and Michael Searcy, Brigham Young University.

rich experience (perhaps akin to walking through the stained-glass-lit naves of medieval European cathedrals). The interiors would have been cool and dimly lit compared with the sunny and warm desert outside. But blue sky would brighten the open-air patios at the heart of most roomblocks, linking the earthly adobe interiors to the rain and skylight from above. The painted imagery on the walls probably included oversized versions of the serpent, macaw, and anthropomorphized beings seen on polychrome pots in rich hues of green, red, brown, and white.

Some of the workshop areas of the residential houses were filled with the refuse of craft production activities, including tens of thousands of marine shell artifacts in one room alone. Some house compounds seem dedicated to specific purposes. The so-called House of the Wells had a large cistern inside. The House of the Serpent and House of the Macaw were composed of rooms of adobe and stone pens for raising and keeping macaws and turkeys (Figure 15.14). In one of them, more than a hundred macaws were found buried beneath room floors. Another hundred-plus more were found sacrificed elsewhere, some by beheading. Certainly they were not eaten for food, nor were many of the site's turkeys. The House of the Pit Ovens at the city's northern end seems to have been a large communal or elite kitchen, with great cooking pits associated in which to bake agave, a fleshy succulent. Di Peso's crew found a large pile of burned rock rubble just outside the building, the residual from pit-cooking events. On the other hand, the House of the Dead contained hundreds of turkey burials and many human interments as well, including possible elites in crypts, some buried with artifacts suggesting their connection to water.

Fig 15.14 Macaw pens at Paquimé. Courtesy of Stephen Lekson.

Besides the adobe roomblocks, several stories high, there are other monuments and public-works features. These include a sunken plaza, several other likely plazas, seven stone platforms, three large cisterns, a walk-in well, one exclusive and two public ballcourts, and a subsurface water-supply system that linked each of the major roomblocks. Of these, the platforms and cisterns occupy the western side of the site, opposite the sunken central plaza. These platforms are small pyramids in a variety of shapes that may mimic Casas Grandes deities. They include a circular pyramid, a rectangular one, a stone-faced horned-serpent mound, and a beheaded bird-effigy pyramid. They also include an anomalous cross-and-circle pyramid, with a circular stone-faced earth-filled mound at each end of the four-pointed cross. One or more of these pyramids, or the deities in association, may have been directly tied to the adjacent cisterns. One pyramid was a multi-terraced structure with adobe architecture on its summit and a ramp down to one of the cisterns. Another mound seems associated with one of the two open-air ballcourts. A third ballcourt was walled and presumably reserved for exclusive engagements. At Paquimé, and at a series of Casas Grandes outliers, these ballcourts take the shape of a capital letter I, similar to their elite-variety counterparts in Mesoamerica (and unlike the ovoid Hohokam courts).

Paquimé's Cosmology

It is easy to see why Di Peso and colleagues assumed that Paquimé was a northern trade center of Mesoamerican civilization. It is equally clear to see why VanPool and VanPool (2007:27) consider it metaphorically to have been a "water city." Besides the water-management features of the city, there was an astounding number – 3.9 million – of marine shell artifacts and discarded pieces associated with the rooms of the site. Clearly, these had to arrive at the site via transport from ocean sources, some in Mesoamerica and others in California. In some of these same and other rooms, many whole pots were also found. In fact, VanPool and VanPool (2007) note that pothunters dating back to the 1850s may have removed up to 15,000 pots from the rooms of Paquimé and its outliers. Many of these were readily identified nonutilitarian polychrome vessels (later emulated and reinvented by Juan Quezada and the Mata Ortiz potters). Many of these feature an elaborate polychrome iconography of cosmic symbols, serpents, macaws, and human beings or demi-gods. The serpents include naturalistic depictions of rattlesnakes, kingsnakes, and coral-snakes, among others, along with abstract horned or plumed serpents or serpent–human hybrids, all reminiscent of Mesoamerican gods such as Quetzalcoatl, the god of wind and earthly water associated with mountains (Figure 15.15). So too do the birds include a variety of forms, both macaws and turkeys, and also anthropomorphized macaw people. Michael Mathiowetz (2011) interprets certain anthropomorphized characters to be depictions of the rulers of Casas Grandes.

The form and iconography of the noncooking wares, which include the well-known Ramos style of the Chihuahuan polychromes, have been analyzed by VanPool and VanPool (2007) who seek to understand the religious practices and cosmology of Casas Grandes people. Especially important, they conclude, is water and mountain symbolism. The former, of course, might be amply evidenced by the great quantities of marine shell on site. Puebloan and Mesoamerican peoples typically associated wind and rain with mountains, and Di Peso and others believed that a temple atop the high hill Cerro de Moctezuma, a few miles east of Paquimé, may have been Paquimé's shrine to a wind god similar to Quetzalcoatl (VanPool and VanPool

Fig 15.15 Ramos polychrome vessel showing abstract serpent head. Courtesy of the Amerind Foundation, Inc., Dragoon, Arizona. Timothy R. Pauketat photo, 2012.

Fig 15.16 Ramos polychrome masculine human effigy bottle, smoking a cigar. Courtesy of the Amerind Foundation, Inc., Dragoon, Arizona. Timothy R. Pauketat photo, 2012.

2007:32). Such preoccupations with wind and rain were likely depicted by Casas Grandes imagery of horned or plumed serpents thought to "live in water" (VanPool and VanPool 2007:30). So too was macaw symbolism probably tied to water, since the macaw colors of red and green are connected to water among Puebloan and Mesoamerican people (Di Peso et al. 1974, vol. VIII; Mathiowetz 2011; VanPool and VanPool 2007).

Besides such cosmic symbolism on pots, there are also human or humanoid effigy vessels, pots where the being's crown doubles as the vessel orifice. Of these, there are feminine and masculine effigies, and some that seem to possess attributes of both sexes. Feminine figures typically show individuals holding vessels or children, with vulvas exposed, and sometimes pregnant or nursing. VanPool and VanPool (2007) identified this as a non-Mesoamerican focus on a fertility goddess. The masculine figures, on the other hand, are shown smoking cane cigars (or tubular pipes) or masturbating, typically with exposed penises in either case (Figure 15.16). The pipes may be a connection between smoke, clouds, and rain-making. VanPool and VanPool see this too as an indication of a non-Mesoamerican shamanic practice. Then again, it may also and alternatively be another indication of a Mesoamerican-style Quetzalcoatl cult, where the god "conveyed leaders from the underworld to positions of power in this world" (McGuire 2011:43). The use of hallucinogenic tobacco may have facilitated the process, involving an individual seeking a vision. Certainly, there have been discoveries of cane cigarettes (tobacco stuffed inside a hollow piece of cane) at Paquimé (see also Hodge 1910:768). Whether leaders or shamanic priests, they appear to have mediated the powers of the cosmos, prayed for rain, and ensured success in war and peace.

Paquimé's History-Making Power

Some of the iconographic elements and polychrome colors of Casas Grandes' organized religion were connected to the pan-regional politico-religious movements of the time, what Patricia Crown (1994) has called the "Southwestern cult"

Sidebar 15.5 The production of gender at Paquimé

Modern-day gender theory holds that biological sex and gender are not necessarily isomorphic. In fact, VanPool and VanPool (2007) argue that indigenous shamans sometimes had the sexual and behavioral attributes of both men and women, and the Casas Grandes human effigy pots may depict third and fourth genders (in addition to men and women). But these pots do more than just "represent" some reality. They create reality by defining the cultural

associations and sexual qualities that epitomize someone's ideal masculine and feminine genders. Associations with fertility or virility, for instance, may not have been common to southwestern cultures before they were linked via pottery imagery and then distributed to consumers who may only then come to assume that these associations or other sexual qualities were a natural part of being a man or a woman.

(Chapter 14) and what Michael Mathiowetz (2011) refers to as the religion of the Flower World. There were Salado and Salado-like wares and imagery at Paquimé, indicating some sort of connection between the people there and the happenings across the greater Southwest. Ultimately, there are also likely connections between Casas Grandes and the Katsina (or Kachina) religion in the north, which was historically derived from Mesoamerican religions. If we extrapolate from Whalen and Minnis' (2012) belief that Ramos polychrome – the finest of the Casas Grandes polychromes – dates mostly to the 1300s, then such pan-southwestern connections all seem coeval and related.

A principal mistake of many archaeological scenarios, especially adaptationist ones, has been to overlook the power of places in forging such historical connections. As noted earlier, towns and cities are not just the benign products of history, religious movements, or subsistence strategies. Similar to pots and other cultural things, places have effects on human history. To explain these effects, we need to consider Paquimé's history-making power in two ways. What was it about the place that attracted people to become part of it? And what were its bigger geopolitical impacts?

Understanding the attraction of Paquimé is critical. Did people move there simply for subsistence security? ("Gotta love that baked agave; let's move there!") Why the elaborate monumentality, rich sensuous surroundings, and great ballgames if not because such things were a part of the greater meaning and powerful experience of the place? More than likely, it is precisely because Paquimé was bigger and better than anything people had imagined in northern Mexico or the Southwest up to that point that it attracted people. Upon arriving, perhaps migrants converted or adopted the religion of the water city.

The place itself was proof that something was right – the cosmos was balanced – at Paquimé.

But not everyone moved to Paquimé. Some people to the north or south may have consciously resisted the attractions of the city. They may even have resented the controls that Casas Grandes people likely possessed over the acquisition or distribution of powerful substances and exotic raw materials. In the meantime, expatriate Mogollons or Puebloans living at Paquimé may have maintained kin ties with people or other claims to resources in their former homelands (New Mexico's turquoise for instance). Certainly the people of great places may well have come to believe that they were situated at the center of the cosmos and were, as a result, favored by the gods. They could do no wrong. If they needed something or desired to balance some perceived imbalance, they may have been impelled – simply on the basis of their own sense of self – to go and get it or to right the wrong. The people of such places as Paquimé and other early cities, in such ways, may become aggressors and threats to outsiders. As a result, the mere existence of a great place can set in motion a chain of events.

The Violence of Religion and the End of Paquimé

Thus, it may come as no surprise that the 1300s and 1400s in Chihuahua and north along the Rio Grande in New Mexico was an era of great religious fervor – all those movements – and significant violence. Great religious dedication comes with a commitment to defend one's beliefs. Certainly, religion and violence are conflated in human history: Medieval Europe was awash with warrior saints, religious-military politicians, and crusades. Various Christian and Islamic sects beat themselves and violently punish others. Wars are fought by soldiers seeking heavenly legitimacy. Fundamentalist jihadists and radical imams continue in this vein today.

Stephen LeBlanc contends that the Katsina (or Kachina) religion was the result of the changing social conditions of the time, of which warfare was a prime component. "While warfare may not have caused the Kachina cult," he concludes, "it is probable that warfare set off a series of cascading causes and effects that resulted in its adoption" (LeBlanc 1999:302). Such a cascading relationship is often illustrated in the rock art of the later Puebloan and Mogollon Rio Grande Valley as a mix of religious and military symbolism. In some Mogollon regions to the west, people's hold on landscapes was clearly tenuous. Some large pueblos, including the well-studied Grasshopper Pueblo, were built with enclosed plazas that afforded efficient defense in case of attack (LeBlanc 1999). The histories of some such places included abrupt and large-scale construction phases followed by attacks and depopulations (see Chapter 14). Grasshopper Pueblo, for instance, lasted no more than a century, and was possibly attacked and abandoned after only a couple of generations.

How much of this Mogollon instability and Rio Grande violence might be blamed on Paquimé? It is difficult to know, although it is important to note that the closest P-IV pueblos along the Rio Grande are less than 500 km (300 mi) north of Paquimé. Archaeologists John Ravesloot and Patricia Spoerl (1989:135) conclude that there exists "considerable direct and indirect evidence for warfare as an integral aspect of Casas Grandes society throughout the Medio period. The presence of trophy skulls and the association of objects made from human bone with a number of Casas Grandes burials suggests that warfare may have played a critical role" in the history of Paquimé. Conceivably, a war party from Paquimé packing jerky and covering 50 km (30 mi) per day (a common rate for a marching army) could have made a one-way overland trip north in 10 days. (In Google Earth, find Casas Grandes again, then cut northeast to Juarez City and follow the Rio Grande and I-25 north to Albuquerque.) It is only 210 km (130 mi) overland to the Rio Grande, meaning that returning warriors could have floated downriver before traveling just four days overland back to Paquimé. The trip was possible, but it's also possible that warriors from the south never ventured too far north. Local infighting may account for much of the evidence of violence.

Immediately north of Paquimé lived people possessing identifiable Casas Grandes culture. To the east and north between them and the Rio Grande pueblos lived the Jornada Mogollons (see Figure 15.2). Stephen LeBlanc (1999) notes that there were frequently gaps or "no man's lands" between these various clusters of Casas Grandes, Mogollon, and finally Puebloan settlements. He also has studied site layouts and histories, believing them to be related to the geopolitics of the time. North of Paquimé, the settlement patterns of Puebloan and Mogollon peoples include occasional settlement incinerations and periodic abandonments and resettlements. Consider one example just north of Paquimé:

Some 80 miles (130 km) north of the site of Casas Grandes was a group of sites in Hidalgo County, New Mexico, that may have formed one or more clusters. That they interacted with Casas Grandes is clear; whether they were a competing polity is not clear. Some sites had plazas enclosed by rooms, others had freestanding walls to complete the enclosures. Several burned.

(LeBlanc 1999:343)

Farther east and north, before reaching the Pueblo IV settlements along the Rio Grande, one passes through the territories of Jornada Mogollon peoples. There, evidence of warfare was less pervasive but, when present, had serious consequences.

One small 15-room pueblo in far southeastern New Mexico was found to have buried within it 30 human crania, among other skeletal remains, all burned. Possibly, nearly the entire community of three or four dozen people may have been killed during an attack somewhere around 1350 CE (LeBlanc 1999:344).

Paquimé itself may have come to a fiery end around 1450 CE. That is, Di Peso (1974), known to exaggerate his evidence, believed that invaders had brought down the site. LeBlanc agrees, reasoning that, of the

576 individuals [sets of human remains] from the Medio Period ... recovered at the site, 127 were not formally buried and seemed to represent individuals killed at the very end of the occupation. While this statistic is well known, the implications have been generally ignored. Because both the buried and the unburied bodies represent only a sample of the total population of the site, it can reasonably be estimated that the entire population of the settlement – some 1,000 to 2,000 people – were killed. Casas Grandes may represent the greatest massacre – with the possible exception of Awatovi – that ever took place in the prehistoric Southwest.

(LeBlanc 1999:252)

Ravesloot (1988) rejects such arguments. Certainly, he concedes, there were two unburied bodies lying on the floor of one sanctuary who may have died defending this inner sanctum. However, whether or not these

two burials, as well as the other 124 burials identified by Di Peso and others as unburied bodies, actually represent individuals killed during an attack is impossible to evaluate. Many of these "unburied bodies" were found in the fill of rooms mixed in roof-fall and scattered on room floors. However, numerous others were fully articulated and were recovered from contexts such as room fill or plaza drains.

(Ravesloot and Spoerl 1989:134)

In the end, we can only be sure that the population of the Casas Grandes region ultimately dispersed (Whalen and Minnis 2012:420). Some archaeologists think that the Casas Grandes people migrated west into Sonora. Others – some Hopi among them – suspect that they are among the descendants of Casas Grandes (Mathiowetz 2011). Most are unwilling to guess. Wherever they went, the abandonment of the Casas Grandes region was total. No one was left behind. Perhaps, like other southwestern locations, the descendants of Paquimé had wanted to forget the place. But we can't. Its great walls, plazas, and pots remain, pulling later Spanish explorers, Hispanic artisans, and archaeologists alike into the mysteries of the peripheral Southwest and, in some sense, turning its indigenous history inside out.

16 1984 BCE

Open up Google Earth one last time, and wait for North America to come into focus. The continent sits in a glowing blue ocean. In 19,840 BCE, to randomly pick a year, much of the Arctic, Subarctic, and North American interior would have been locked up in massive ice sheets that sat as far south as New England, the Ohio Valley, and the central Great Plains. As far as we can tell, no human beings yet inhabited North America. Tundra and spruce forests covered large swaths of the interior. Mammoths plodded through present-day California, Arizona, and New Mexico. Mastodons roamed the east. The earth would have glowed a bit less.

Check your "eye altitude" above earth on the screen. Even from a distance of more than 5,000 miles up, you can see the differently colored physiographic features of the continent. Run your eye from north to south, starting from Alaska and northwestern Canada. You should see the white caps of the snow-covered Rockies from Alaska south to British Columbia, today slowly melting into the sea. Zoom into one such mountain top – enter street view – and imagine yourself here in 19,840 BCE. Exit ground-level view and zoom back out. Four or five thousand years later, the first Americans may have been just off shore, hunting the "kelp highway" in the Pacific Ocean, making their initial forays inland but not crossing the frozen mountains (see Chapter 4).

Follow the Rocky Mountain spine of the continent south until it becomes the Sierra Madres of Mexico. Mexico City – originally Tenochtitlan – sits near the end of the mountain chain, where the continent wants to curve eastward around the Yucatan. Divert your gaze into the Gulf of Mexico and the Caribbean. Here, many centuries later, people in boats from South and Central America migrated to the great islands: Cuba, Hispaniola, Puerto Rico, and Jamaica. They may have also found Florida's flat green peninsula. Certainly, from thousands of miles above, Florida pulls the eye northward into the mainland of the eastern United States. There is less physiographic variability in eastern North America than there is in the West. In the distant past, more people more frequently moved across or laid claim to more area than was possible in portions of the heterogeneous, rugged West. These physiographic and locomotive realities would have definite historical ramifications.

Look across the St. Lawrence and the Great Lakes up into Hudson Bay. See the dark boreal green of the Subarctic's forests give way to the barren light green of the tundra. On the Subarctic's surface below, pick out a lake – any lake. Now, zoom down to its shoreline and enter street view. Those massive Pleistocene ice sheets had definitely flattened the landscape here, with whatever rocks you see having been scraped bare and exposed to human eyes only after the Holocene warmed the earth. Much later, say at 1984 BCE, to pick another arbitrary date, the diverse cultural landscapes of such regions were well established. Maritime Archaic people, living in longhouses, and Paleoeskimo people, residing in smaller pithouses, occupied interior and coastal zones and occasionally encountered one another. Tensions broke out from time to time, and Paleoeskimos – who had brought bow and arrow technology with them to the Eastern Subarctic around this time – "replaced" some Maritime Archaic people (see Chapter 7). The Maritime Archaic communities who remained continued to use harpoons and thrusting weaponry, seemingly as a mark of their ethnic identities.

Standing here, on the shoreline of some digital subarctic lake, imagine yourself in the moccasins of a Maritime or Paleoeskimo person on a bright cold day in April, 1984 BCE. How would you deal when encountering the "other," and what would be the immediate and long-term effects of your actions?

Contacts are powerful processes and are ongoing all of the time at various scales of human experience (see Chapter 3). They are historical inflection points, where the totality of all that you are and the ways in which you relate to everything around you – with or without your conscious understanding of it – might be brought to bear on the here and now. History turns on such moments, in one sense, although, in another sense, these moments are not truly discrete and isolatable but constant, happening at many scales simultaneously and continuously, such that only now – long after the fact – can we (the analysts) somewhat artificially separate and study them.

Such study is made all the more challenging because people, here in the Subarctic and all across North America at 1984 BCE, were not motivated in the same way that many of us are today. We live in a modern world with modern sensibilities. We view people, places, and things as having a primary reality, while relegating relations (seen and unseen) that bind them to each other to a derivative status in our explanations. Clearly, we elevate ourselves as the central arbiters of human (if not also earth) history. That sounds a lot like the capitalism and consumerism espoused by Henry Ford, as opposed to John Muir (see Chapter 1). And it certainly characterizes twenty-first-century America. Most people in the pre-Columbian past (and to some extent John Muir) instead moved through life as if vital, animate qualities – spirits, forces, powers – imbued people, places, and things and, in many ways, made history happen the ways that it did. Shamans were so highly regarded in the Subarctic and across much of the continent in different historical epochs because they, owing to their special characteristics or life experiences, were more centrally placed to mediate powerful nonhuman spirits and forces on behalf of their communities.

Of course, delineating one or more ontologies or worldviews in the past and contrasting them to modernist ontologies in the present is, as some archaeologists have pointed out, simply to reify modernism by essentializing ontologies as things (e.g., Harris and Cippola 2017; see especially Chapters 6–9). To better understand how to avoid this problem, and to realize some lessons from this book, let us leave our lakeside location and travel into the Archaic Southeast (see Chapter 9). In Google Earth, leave ground-level view and zoom back out to a position several thousand miles above the continent. Then, type in "Poverty Point."

When you arrive, looking down from a few thousand feet above on to the symmetrical earthworks below, you should be wondering about the historical genesis of this great Late Archaic complex and its connections to other mounded sites or mound-building people across the South's Coastal Plain. In 1984 BCE, impressive mollusk-shell ring mounds dotted the coast and the rivers that fed into the Atlantic Ocean. Some such places seem, to some analysts today, to have begun their histories as the periodic habitations of ordinary people doing ordinary things. Only later did some become prominent centers of religious activity.

Of course, such observations again belie our own modernist proclivities to distinguish the ordinary from the extraordinary, as if these were two recognized realms in the past as they are for us in the present (e.g., habitual everyday life versus intentional political or religious practice). However, across most of the North American past, such distinctions did not exist (and even today we delude ourselves into thinking that we always separate the two).

In 1984 BCE, there were no ongoing large-scale communal constructions taking place at the spot soon to become Poverty Point. However, in years to come, people would gather here in a semicircular fashion around an open plaza before any earth was mounded. Not long thereafter, the mounding itself would happen in a historically orchestrated sequence of events starting at 1600 BCE. The site plan suggests that the builders pulled the order of the heavens down to earth, such that to walk across the site was to align one's body with cosmic rhythms. Impressive oversized circles of upright posts lined the plaza, some outlining roofed buildings. People traveled from many hundreds of kilometers away to participate, bringing with them exotic materials that were then crafted into elaborate net weights, bodily ornaments, divination stones, chipped-stone tools, and more. Even the seemingly mundane clay cooking objects were often decorated in extraordinary ways.

That is, the ordinary at Poverty Point (and all comparable places in North America) was also extraordinary and vice versa. More than likely, even the initial pre-mound occupation at Poverty Point, or those at other Archaic mounded complexes, also possessed extraordinary qualities. The differences between ordinary and extraordinary were not of kind, that is, but of degree, at least up to a point. Elsewhere in space and time, some of those points – let us call them historical hinge points for the sake of argument – were constituted by places themselves: Poverty Point, Chaco Canyon, Snaketown, Cahokia, Prince Rupert Harbor, Emoryville, Silver Glen, etc. Some of those points were realized through things: Stallings pottery, Ramos polychrome, shell-bead necklaces, peace medals, La Conquistadora, etc. Some of the points were, obviously, embodied by specific persons: Pocahontas, Metacomet, an aged female Chumash leader, a mythical Wisconsin character enshrined by a "Man Mound," etc.

After these points in history were reached, which our review of pre-colonial North American history indicates happened a little differently everywhere, archaeologists can begin asking about the development of, say, formalized religions, inequalities, social classes, organized trade, economic infrastructure, political power, and even urbanism. But the process in every case, in North America, must take into consideration the ontological dimensions of humanity and history. Any archaeological explanations that fail to do so – instead drawing on uniformitarian, colonialist, and utterly modern notions of "human nature" – are themselves doomed to failure (see Chapters 1–2 and 6).

In recognizing those ontological bases, we now also recognize that nonhuman forces played a role in the human history of the continent. Doing so is an intellectual move consistent with indigenous, First Nations, and American Indian scholarship today, which was itself rebooted in a moment of protest (e.g., Deloria 1970; see Chapter 2). Doing so is also part of a larger theoretical movement to recognize that humanity and human history span nonhuman agencies of change as well as human ones. Today, that movement is called post-humanism and "new materialism" (Harris and Cippolla 2017). Unlike an old materialism and a contemporary modernism (which essentializes things, glorifies a few great men, and fetishizes technology; see Chapter 1), the newer forms of materialism treat people and nonhuman beings, as well as other entities, substances, and states of matter and energy, as co-mediators of history.

The key word here is history. An older materialism dismissed it; new materialism and related approaches incorporate it. For instance, sea-level rise itself possesses a history that helps to explain the human history of shell-ring sites across the Coastal Plain; the sea, in some ways, co-mediated human life. As another example, bison herds have histories that were partially responsible for the development of jump sites and, later, the specialized spiritual/economic driveline infrastructure in the northern Plains (see Chapter 11); bison pulled people into their web and, in the end, benefited from the relationship! Similarly, the making, wearing, and circulation of mollusk-shell jewelry in California, among other places, did not simply reflect human–human relationships and identities, nor did they merely "function" to create social solidarity; instead, the history of mollusks was entangled with people who understood the former to embody spiritual powers of water on land. To wear a shell was to merge one's own being with the shell's spirit. In the same way, to incorporate the crushed and burned particles of freshwater mussel shells as the temper of one's cooking pots, as in the post-900 CE Mississippi Valley, was to propitiously position oneself vis-à-vis the forces of water and the watery realm of the ancestors to which one owed one's very life. This was especially true following the adoption of maize, a water-sensitive plant that became a dietary staple across much of native America.

Thinking about the widespread historical impacts of maize brings us – yet hovering above Poverty Point – to another point. What, we must now ask, was the role of truly global processes in the history of history-making people? Besides sea-level rise and maize adoption, climate change itself comes back into scrutiny, though not as climate but as weather. That is, people even today deny climate change as long as it remains an abstract notion outside their own experience – outside their ontology. But the more numerous and more powerful hurricanes that blow through the Caribbean and up into the mainland, or the droughts, forest fires, and mudslides that plague the Southwest and California – all linked to palpable weather events – are in no way abstract. They affect how people relate to the world. They alter ontologies.

This is the reason that climate change does tend to correlate with certain cultural changes in the past. This is not to say that climate determines cultural change. However, where atmospheric phenomena and weather events (thunderstorms, lightning, floods, droughts) were understood as spiritual powers that mediated human life, people's actions might closely correspond to climate change. Native people, climate, crops, and sea-level rise share a history that, today, we have artificially and unfortunately broken up into categories: human history, climate history, earth history.

John Muir also understood this, and as a final reminder of the importance of his approach for us today, let us depart Poverty Point and travel, via Google Earth, to one final location: Yosemite National Park. After typing in the name and hitting "search," notice that you are flown to a point 50 or so miles above the Sierra Nevada. We visited these earlier in Chapter 1, where Muir was discussed. Notice that the peaks of some mountains are (hopefully) snow covered. Certainly they were in 1984 BCE, smack in the middle of California's Early Period, when the western slopes of the Sierra Nevadas were densely occupied by a diversity of native people intensively collecting acorns and moving seasonally from the lower foothills in the winter to higher elevations in the summer – what archaeologists have called a "California pattern" (see Chapters 6 and 13). As with the other historical forces considered above, we must acknowledge the acorn's historical effects – affording people ample winter stores and, later in the Middle and Late periods, dramatically impacting the organization and distribution of labor that, in turn, led to more rigid gender and ethnic divisions.

And we must acknowledge, in turn, the related historical impacts of those native California women and men, as well, partly in parenting generations of descendants who would transform the forests and leave their milling stone depressions across the region's rocky outcrops. Ultimately, the descendants of the Early Period Californians living in the Yosemite Valley in 1984 BCE would resist Euro-American invaders to the best of their ability – first the Spanish, then the Mexicans, and then especially the Anglo-Americans. Ironically, John Muir's religious conversion at Yosemite in 1868 came at the expense of the region's native inhabitants, who had been and were still being removed from California. Large numbers were simply exterminated (see Chapter 13).

We must remember, and learn the lessons of, this ironic, calamitous history, along with all of the lessons of all of the native histories reviewed in this book. Will we? Look back at the Google Earth image of Yosemite from 50-plus miles up in the air. To the northeast is Mono Lake, a natural water-collection basin at the edge of the Great Basin. Notice that the lake is much smaller than the grayish brown basin that surrounds it, proof positive that the basin used to contain much more water than it does now. In 1941, Los Angeles began to siphon off the lake's water to meet the growing demands of urban California. Described on tourist websites as a hauntingly beautiful, shimmering body of water, ecologists elsewhere describe its ecosystem as having collapsed.

Now look to the southwest of Yosemite in the direction of modern-day Merced and Fresno, out in California's Central Valley. The brown colors of the foothills reveal the increasing aridity of this global breadbasket, with repeated droughts taking great tolls on today's human–environmental infrastructure. Up into the Sierra Nevada – into the heart of Yosemite and south into Sequoia National Park – the great ancient trees are dying. By the time you read this, many may have withered and fallen.

Now, zoom out again – thousands of miles away from earth as you see it on your screen – and look back at North America. A central lesson of North American archaeology, in our mind, is a clarification of our own historical relationships to the whole: the human–nonhuman whole, the continental whole, and the global whole. The histories that we have sought to understand are not merely histories of people, and certainly not written histories. North American histories were lived, material, momentous, contentious, ontological, and impactful. The people in these histories related to and through the forces, matter, and beings of their worlds. They proactively engaged each other and those wider worlds. Their histories resulted in altered configurations of people, places, things, substances, and phenomena that then impinged on (but did not determine) their own, and our own, futures.

We are living out those futures today. We need to be as proactive as were the people of the past, and as respectful of the many historical moving parts, as were they. North American archaeology in the twenty-first century is part of a struggle to improve the world. It starts with rethinking our relationship to the past in the service of the future.

References

Adams, E. Charles, 1991. *The Origins and Development of the Pueblo Katsina Cult*. Tucson: University of Arizona Press.

Adams, James Truslow, 1933. Massasoit. In *Dictionary of American Biography*, vol. IV (part 2), pp. 380–381. New York: Scribners.

Adovasio, James M., and C. Andrew Hemmings, 2011. Inundated Landscapes and the Colonization of the Northeastern Gulf of Mexico. Paper presented at the 76th Annual Meeting of the Society for American Archaeology, Sacramento, California.

Ahler, Stanley A., 2007. Origins of the Northern Expansion of the Middle Missouri Tradition. In *Plains Village Archaeology: Bison-Hunting Farmers in the Central and Northern Plains*, edited by S. A. Ahler and M. Kay, pp. 15–31. Salt Lake City: University of Utah Press.

Aikens, C. Melvin, Thomas J. Connolly, and Dennis L. Jenkins, 2011. *Oregon Archaeology*. Corvallis: Oregon State University Press.

Alarcón, Gerardo, and Guillermo Ahuja, 2015. The Materials of Tamtoc. In *The Huasteca: Culture, History, and Interregional Exchange*, edited by K. A. Faust and K. N. Richter, pp. 37–58. Norman: University of Oklahoma Press.

Alt, Susan M., 1999. Spindle Whorls and Fiber Production at Early Cahokian Settlements. *Southeastern Archaeology* 18:124–133.

Alt, Susan M., 2002. Identities, Traditions, and Diversity in Cahokia's Uplands. *Midcontinental Journal of Archaeology* 27:217–236.

Alt, Susan M., Jeffery D. Kruchten, and Timothy R. Pauketat, 2010. The Construction and Use of Cahokia's Grand Plaza. *Journal of Field Archaeology* 35(2):131–146.

Ames, Kenneth M., 2005. Tempo and Scale in the Evolution of Social Complexity in Western North America: Four Case Studies. In *North American Archaeology*, edited by T. R. Pauketat and D. D. Loren, pp. 56–78. London: Blackwell.

Ames, Kenneth M., 2008. Slavery, Household Production, and Demography on the Southern Northwest Coast: Cables, Tacking, and Ropewalks. In *Invisible Citizens: Captives and their Consequences*, edited by Catherine M. Cameron, pp. 138–158. Salt Lake City: University of Utah Press.

Ames, Kenneth M., and Herbert D. G. Maschner, 1999. *Peoples of the Northwest Coast*. London: Thames and Hudson.

Ames, Kenneth M., Kisha Supernant, Andrew Martindale, Susan Marsden, Bryn Letham, and Robert Gustus, 2016. A Hunter-Gatherer-Fisher Urban Landscape in Prince Rupert Harbor, British Columbia? Paper presented at the 81st Annual Meeting of the Society for American Archaeology, Orlando, Florida.

Anderson, David G., 1996. Models of Paleoindian and Early Archaic Settlement in the Lower Southeast. In *The Paleoindian and Early Archaic Southeast*, edited by David G. Anderson and Kenneth E. Sassaman, pp. 29–45. Tuscaloosa: University of Alabama Press.

Anderson, David G., 2010. Human Settlement in the New World: Multidisciplinary Approaches, the "Beringian" Standstill, and the

Shape of Things to Come. In *Human Variation in the Americas: The Integration of Archaeology and Biological Anthropology*, edited by Benjamin M. Auerbach, pp. 311–346. Occasional Paper 38. Carbondale, IL: Southern Illinois University, Center for Archaeological Investigations.

Anderson, David G., and Glen T. Hanson, 1988. Early Archaic Occupations in the Southeastern United States: A Case Study from the Savannah River Basin. *American Antiquity* 53:262–286.

Anderson, David G., and Robert C. Mainfort (eds.), 2002. *The Woodland Southeast*. Tuscaloosa: University of Alabama Press.

Anderson, David G., and Kenneth E. Sassaman, 2012. *Recent Developments in Southeastern Archaeology: From Colonization to Complexity*. Washington, DC: Society for American Archaeology Press.

Anderson, David G., D. Shane Miller, Stephen J. Yerka, J. Christopher Gillam, Erik N. Johanson, Derek T. Anderson, Albert C. Goodyear, and Ashley M. Smallwood, 2010. PIDBA (Paleoindian Database of the Americas) 2010: Current Status and Findings. *Archaeology of Eastern North America* 38:63–90.

Anderson, David G., Albert C. Goodyear, James Kennett, and Allen West, 2011. Multiple Lines of Evidence for Possible Human Population Decline/Settlement Reorganization during the Early Younger Dryas. *Quaternary International* 242:570–583.

Anderson, Douglas D., 1988. *Onion Portage: An Archaeological Site on the Kobuk River, Northwestern Alaska*. Fairbanks: University of Alaska Press.

Angel, Michael, 2002. *Preserving the Sacred: Historical Perspectives on the Ojibwa Midewinin*. Winnipeg: University of Manitoba Press.

Appadurai, Arjun, 1996. *Modernity at Large: Cultural Dimensions of Globalization*. Minneapolis: University of Minnesota Press.

Arco, Lee J., Katie A. Adelsberger, Ling-yu Hung, and Tristram R. Kidder, 2006. Alluvial Geoarchaeology of a Middle Archaic Mound Complex in the Lower Mississippi Valley, USA. *Geoarchaeology* 21:591–614.

Arnold, Jeanne E., 1987. *Craft Specialization in the Prehistoric Channel Islands, California*. Berkeley: University of California Press.

Arnold, Jeanne E. (ed.), 2004. *Foundations of Chumash Complexity*. Los Angeles: Cotsen Institute of Archaeology, University of California.

Arnold, Jeanne E., and Michael R. Walsh, 2010. *California's Ancient Past: From the Pacific to the Range of Light*. Washington, DC: Society for American Archaeology Press.

Arsenault, Daniel, 2013. The Aesthetic Power of Ancient Dorset Images at Qajartalik, a Unique Petroglyph Site in the Canadian Arctic. *Boletín del Museo Chileno de Arte Precolombino* 18:19–32.

Ashmore, Wendy, 2007. Building Social History at Pueblo Bonito: Footnotes to a Biography of Place. In *The Architecture of Chaco*

Canyon, New Mexico, edited by S. H. Lekson, pp. 179–198. Salt Lake City: University of Utah Press.

Aten, Lawrence E., 1999. Middle Archaic Ceremonialism at Tick Island, Florida: Ripley P. Bullen's 1961 Excavations at the Harris Creek Site. *Florida Anthropologist* 52:131–200.

Auerbach, Benjamin M. (ed.), 2010. *Human Variation in the Americas: The Integration of Archaeology and Biological Anthropology.* Carbondale, IL: Center for Archaeological Investigations.

Aveni, Anthony F., 2012. Mesoamerican Calendars and Archaeoastronomy. In *The Oxford Handbook of Mesoamerican Archaeology*, edited by D. L. Nichols and C. A. Pool, pp. 787–794. Oxford: Oxford University Press.

Bamforth, Douglas B., 1988. *Ecology and Human Organization on the Great Plains.* New York: Plenum.

Barker, Alex W., Craig E. Skinner, M. Steven Shackley, Michael D. Glascock, and J. Daniel Rogers, 2002. Mesoamerican Origin for an Obsidian Scraper from the Precolumbian Southeastern United States. *American Antiquity* 67(1):103–108.

Barnard, Alan, 2004. Hunter-Gatherers in History, Archaeology, and Anthropology: An Introductory Essay. In *Hunter-Gatherers in History, Archaeology, and Anthropology*, edited by Alan Barnard, pp. 1–13. Oxford: Berg.

Barth, Fredrik, 1969. *Ethnic Groups and Boundaries: The Social Organization of Culture Difference.* Oslo: Universitetsforlaget.

Basso, Keith H., 1996. *Wisdom Sits in Places: Landscape and Language among the Western Apache.* Albuquerque: University of New Mexico Press.

Bayman, James M., 2007. Artisans and their Crafts in Hohokam Society. In *The Hohokam Millennium*, edited by S. K. Fish and P. R. Fish, pp. 75–81. Santa Fe, NM: School for Advanced Research Press.

Beck, Charlotte, and George T. Jones, 1997. The Terminal Pleistocene/Early Holocene Archaeology of the Great Basin. *Journal of World Prehistory* 11:161–236.

Beck, Charlotte, and George T. Jones, 2007. Early Paleoarchaic Point Morphology and Chronology. In *Paleoindian or Paleoarchaic? Great Basin Human Ecology at the Pleistocene–Holocene Transition*, edited by Kelly Graff and David N. Schmidt, pp. 23–41. Salt Lake City: University of Utah Press.

Beck, Charlotte, and George T. Jones, 2010. Clovis and Western Stemmed: Population Migration and the Meeting of Two Technologies in the Intermountain West. *American Antiquity* 75:81–116.

Beekman, Christopher S., 2012. Current Views on Power, Economics, and Subsistence in Ancient Western Mexico. In *The Oxford Handbook of Mesoamerican Archaeology*, edited by D. L. Nichols and C. A. Pool, pp. 495–512. Oxford: Oxford University Press.

Begay, Richard M., 2004. Tsé Bíyah 'Anii'áhí: Chaco Canyon and its Place in Navajo History. In *In Search of Chaco: New Approaches to an Archaeological Enigma*, edited by D. G. Noble, pp. 54–60. Santa Fe, NM: School for Advanced Research Press.

Bell, Trevor, and M. A. P. Renouf, 2003. Prehistoric Cultures, Reconstructed Coasts: Maritime Archaic Indian Site Distribution in Newfoundland. *World Archaeology* 35:350–370.

Bement, Leland C., 1999. *Bison Hunting at Cooper Site: Where Lightning Bolts Drew Thundering Herds*. Norman: University of Oklahoma Press.

Benn, David W., and William Green, 2000. Late Woodland Cultures in Iowa. In *Late Woodland Societies: Transition and Transformation across the Midcontinent*, edited by T. E. Emerson, D. L. McElrath, and A. C. Fortier, pp. 429–496. Lincoln: University of Nebraska Press.

Bennett, Jane, 2010. *Vibrant Matter: A Political Ecology of Things*. Durham, NC: Duke University Press.

Benson, Larry V., 2010. Who Provided Maize to Chaco Canyon after the mid-12th-Century Drought? *Journal of Archaeological Science* 37:621–629.

Benson, Larry V., Timothy R. Pauketat, and Edward Cook, 2009a. Cahokia's Boom and Bust in the Context of Climate Change. *American Antiquity* 74:467–483.

Benson, Larry V., John R. Stein, and H. E. Taylor, 2009b. Possible Sources of Archaeological Maize Found in Chaco Canyon and Aztec Ruin, New Mexico. *Journal of Archaeological Science* 36:387–407.

Bernardini, Wesley, 2004. Hopewell Earthworks: A Case Study in the Referential and Experiential Meaning of Monuments. *Journal of Anthropological Archaeology* 23:331–356.

Bernardini, Wesley, 2011. North, South, and Center: An Outline of Hopi Ethnogenesis. In *Religious Transformation in the Late Pre-Hispanic Pueblo World*, edited by Donna M. Glowacki and Scott Van Keuren, pp. 196–220. Tucson: University of Arizona Press.

Bernbeck, Reinhard, and Randall H. McGuire (eds.), 2011. *Ideologies in Archaeology*. Tucson: University of Arizona Press.

Bettinger, Robert L., 1999. What Happened in the Medithermal. In *Models for the Millennium: Great Basin Archaeology Today*, edited by C. Beck, pp. 62–74. Salt Lake City: University of Utah Press.

Bettinger, Robert L., and M. A. Baumhoff, 1982. The Numic Spread: Great Basin Cultures in Competition. *American Antiquity* 47:485–503.

Bettinger, Robert L., and Jelmer W. Eerkens, 1999. Point Typologies, Cultural Transmission, and the Spread of Bow-and-Arrow Technology in the Prehistoric Great Basin. *American Antiquity* 64:231–242.

Betts, Matthew W., Susan E. Blair, and David W. Black, 2012. Perspectivism, Mortuary Symbolism, and Human–Shark Relationships on the Maritime Peninsula. *American Antiquity* 77:621–645.

Betts, Matthew W., Mari Hardenberg, and Ian Stirling, 2015. How Animals Create Human History: Relational Ecology and the Dorset–Polar Bear Connection. *American Antiquity* 80:89–112.

Bever, Michael R., 2006. Too Little, Too Late? The Radiocarbon Chronology of Alaska and the Peopling of the New World. *American Antiquity* 71:595–620.

Binford, Lewis R., 1962. Archaeology as Anthropology. *American Antiquity* 28:217–225.

Binford, Lewis R., 1980. Willow Smoke and Dogs' Tails: Hunter-Gatherer Settlement Systems and Archaeological Site Formation. *American Antiquity* 45:4–20.

Binford, Lewis R., 2001. *Constructing Frames of Reference: An Analytical Method for Archaeological Theory Building Using Ethnographic and Environmental Data Sets.* Berkeley: University of California Press.

Birch, Jennifer, and Ronald F. Williamson, 2013. *The Mantle Site: An Archaeological History of an Ancestral Wendat Community.* Lanham, MD: AltaMira Press.

Black, Glenn A., 1967. *Angel Site: An Archaeological, Historical, and Ethnological Study.* Indianapolis: Indiana Historical Society.

Blake, Leonard W., 1981. Early Acceptance of Watermelon by Indians of the United States. *Journal of Ethnobiology* 1(2):193–199.

Blitz, John H., 2012. Moundville in the Mississippian World. In *The Oxford Handbook of North American Archaeology*, edited by T. R. Pauketat, pp. 534–543. Oxford: Oxford University Press.

Bolnick, Deborah A., and David G. Smith, 2007. Migration and Social Structure among the Hopewell: Evidence from Ancient DNA. *American Antiquity* 72:627–644.

Bolton, Herbert E., 1990. *Coronado: Knight of Pueblo and Plains.* Albuquerque: University of New Mexico Press.

Bourgeon, Lauriane, Ariana Burke, and Thomas Higham, 2017. Earliest Human Presence in North America Dated to the Last Glacial Maximum: New Radiocarbon Dates from Bluefish Caves, Canada. *PLoS ONE* 12(1): e0169486. https://doi.org/10.1371/journal.pone.0169486.

Bourque, Bruce, 2012. *The Swordfish Hunters: The History and Ecology of an Ancient American Sea People.* Piermont, NH: Bunker Hill Publishing.

Bowers, Alfred W., 1965. *Hidatsa Social and Ceremonial Organization.* Bureau of American Ethnology Bulletin 194. Washington, DC: Smithsonian Institution.

Brackenridge, Henry Marie, 1962. *Views of Louisiana Together with a Journal of a Voyage up the Missouri River, in 1811* (originally published 1814). Chicago: Quadrangle.

Brashler, Janet G., Elizabeth B. Garland, Margaret B. Holman, William A. Lovis, and Susan R. Martin, 2000. Adaptive Strategies and Socioeconomic Systems in Northern Great Lakes Riverine

Environments: The Late Woodland of Michigan. In *Late Woodland Societies: Transition and Transformation across the Midcontinent*, edited by T. E. Emerson, D. L. McElrath, and A. C. Fortier, pp. 543–579. Lincoln: University of Nebraska Press.

Braun, David P., and Stephen Plog, 1982. Evolution of "Tribal" Social Networks: Theory and Prehistoric North American Evidence. *American Antiquity* 47:504–525.

Brecher, Kenneth, and William G. Haag, 1983. Astronomical Alignments at Poverty Point. *American Antiquity* 48:161–163.

Brink, Jack W., 2008. *Imagining Head-Smashed-In: Aboriginal Buffalo Hunting on the Northern Plains*. Edmonton: Athabaska University Press.

Brokaw, Chet, 2009. Lawsuit Would Let Sioux Take Money for Black Hills. *Native Times*, October 20.

Brooks, James F., 2016. *Mesa of Sorrows: A History of the Awat'ovi Massacre*. New York: W. W. Norton.

Brose, David S., 1994. Trade and Exchange in the Midwestern United States. In *Prehistoric Exchange Systems in North America*, edited by Timothy G. Baugh and Jonathon E. Ericson, pp. 215–240. New York: Plenum.

Brown, Dee, 1970. *Bury My Heart at Wounded Knee: An Indian History of the American West*. New York: Holt, Rinehart, and Winston.

Brown, Ian W., 1989. The Calumet Ceremony in the Southeast and its Archaeological Manifestations. *American Antiquity* 54:311–331.

Brown, James A., 1996. *The Spiro Ceremonial Center: The Archaeology of Arkansas Valley Caddoan Culture in Eastern Oklahoma*. Museum of Anthropology Memoirs 29. Ann Arbor: University of Michigan.

Brown, James A., 1997. The Archaeology of Ancient Religion in the Eastern Woodlands. *Annual Review of Anthropology* 26:465–485.

Brown, James A., and Robert Vierra, 1983. What Happened in the Middle Archaic? Introduction to an Ecological Approach to Koster Site Archaeology. In *Archaic Hunter-Gatherers in the American Midwest*, edited by J. L. Phillips and J. A. Brown, pp. 165–195. New York: Academic Press.

Bruseth, James E., 1991. Poverty Point Development as Seen from the Cedarland and Claiborne Sites, Southern Mississippi. In *The Poverty Point Culture: Local Manifestations, Subsistence Practices, and Trade Networks*, edited by Kathleen M. Byrd, pp. 7–26. Geoscience and Man 29. Baton Rouge: Louisiana State University.

Bubel, Shawn, 2014. The Fincastle Site: A Late Middle Prehistoric Bison Kill on the Northwestern Plains. *Plains Anthropologist* 59(231):207–240.

Buchanan, Meghan E., 2015. Warfare and the Materialization of Daily Life at the Mississippian Common Field Site. Unpublished Ph.D. dissertation, Department of Anthropology, Indiana University, Bloomington.

Buckmaster, Marla A., and James Paquette, 1988. The Gorto Site: Preliminary Report on a Late Paleoindian Site in Marquette County, Michigan. *Wisconsin Archaeologist* 69:101–124.

Bucko, Raymond, 1998. *The Lakota Ritual of the Sweat Lodge.* Lincoln: University of Nebraska Press.

Buikstra, Jane, Douglas Charles, and Gordon Rakita, 1998. *Staging Ritual: Hopewell Ceremonialism at the Mound House Site, Greene County, Illinois.* Kampsville Studies in Archaeology and History 1. Kampsville, IL: Center for American Archaeology.

Bullen, Ripley P., 1966. Stelae at the Crystal River Site, Florida. *American Antiquity* 31(6):861–865.

Burks, Jarrod, 2014. Geophysical Survey at Ohio Earthworks: Updating Nineteenth Century Maps and Filling the "Empty" Spaces. *Archaeological Prospection* 21:5–13.

Burks, Jarrod, and Robert A. Cook, 2012. Beyond Squier and Davis: Rediscovering Ohio's Earthworks Using Geophysical Remote Sensing. *American Antiquity* 76:667–689.

Bustard, Wendy, 2008. Chaco Horrificus? In *Social Violence in the Prehispanic American Southwest*, edited by D. L. Nichols and P. L. Crown, pp. 70–97. Tucson: University of Arizona Press.

Byers, A. Martin, 1996. Social Structure and the Pragmatic Meaning of Material Culture: Ohio Hopewell as Ecclesiastic-Communal Cult. In *A View from the Core: A Synthesis of Ohio Hopewell Archaeology*, edited by Paul J. Pacheco, pp. 174–192. Columbus: Ohio Archaeological Council.

Byers, A. Martin, and Dee Ann Wymer (eds.), 2010. *Hopewell Settlement Patterns, Subsistence, and Symbolic Landscapes.* Gainesville: University Press of Florida.

Caldwell, Joseph R., 1964. Interaction Spheres in Prehistory. In *Hopewellian Studies*, edited by Joseph R. Caldwell and Robert L. Hall, pp. 133–143. Scientific Paper 12(6). Springfield: Illinois State Museum.

Cameron, Catherine M. (ed.), 2009. *Chaco and After in the Northern San Juan: Excavations at the Bluff Great House.* Tucson: University of Arizona Press.

Carr, Christopher, 2005. Historical Insights into the Direction and Limitations of Recent Research on Hopewell. In *Gathering Hopewell: Society, Ritual, and Ritual Interaction*, edited by Christopher Carr and D. Troy Case, pp. 51–70. New York: Kluwer Academic/Plenum.

Carr, Christopher, and D. Troy Case (eds.), 2005. *Gathering Hopewell: Society, Ritual, and Ritual Interaction.* New York: Kluwer Academic/Plenum.

Carr, Robert S., 1985. Prehistoric Circular Earthworks in South Florida. *Florida Anthropologist* 38:288–301.

Carr, Robert S., 2012. *Digging Miami.* Gainesville: University Press of Florida.

Case, D. Troy, and Christopher Carr (eds.), 2008. *The Scioto Hopewell and their Neighbors: Bioarchaeological Documentation and Cultural Understanding.* New York: Springer.

Castille, George Pierre, 1996. The Commodification of Indian Identity. *American Anthropologist* 98:743–747.

Castillo, Bernal Diaz del, 2008. *The History of the Conquest of New Spain.* Translated by D. Carrasco. Albuquerque: University of New Mexico Press.

Castillo, Edward D., 1978. The Impact of Euro-American Exploration and Settlement. In *Handbook of North American Indians, California,* vol. VIII, edited by R. F. Heizer, pp. 99–127. Washington, DC: Smithsonian Institution.

Chamberlain, Von Del, 1982. *When Stars Came Down to Earth: Cosmology of the Skidi Pawnee Indians of North America.* Los Altos, CA: Ballena Press.

Chapdelaine, Claude, 2012. Overview of the St. Lawrence Archaic through Woodland. In *The Oxford Handbook of North American Archaeology*, edited by T. R. Pauketat, pp. 249–261. Oxford: Oxford University Press.

Chapman, Jefferson, and Andrea B. Shea, 1981. The Archaeobotanical Record: Early Archaic Period to Contact in the Lower Little Tennessee River Valley. *Tennessee Anthropologist* 6:61–84.

Charles, D., and J. Buikstra, 1983. Archaic Mortuary Sites in the Central Mississippi Drainage: Distribution, Structure, and Behavioral Implications. In *Archaic Hunter-Gatherers in the American Midwest*, edited by J. L. Phillips and J. A. Brown, pp. 117–145. New York: Academic Press.

Charles, Douglas K., and Jane E. Buikstra (eds.), 2006. *Recreating Hopewell.* Gainesville: University Press of Florida.

Charles, Douglas K., Julieann Van Nest, and Jane E. Buikstra, 2004. From the Earth: Minerals and Meaning in the Hopewellian World. In *Soils, Stones and Symbols*, edited by Nicole Boivan and Mary A. Owoc, pp. 43–70. London: University College London Press.

Chatters, James C., 1995. Population Growth, Climatic Cooling, and the Development of Collector Strategies on the Southern Plateau, Western North America. *Journal of World Prehistory* 9:341–400.

Chatters, James C., 2010. Peopling the Americas via Multiple Migrations from Beringia: Evidence from the Early Holocene of the Columbia Plateau. In *Human Variation in the Americas: The Integration of Archaeology and Biological Anthropology*, edited by Benjamin M. Auerbach, pp. 51–76. Center for Archaeological Investigations, Occasional Paper 38. Carbondale, IL: Southern Illinois University.

Chatters, James C., Steven Hackenberger, Brett Lenz, Anna M. Prentiss, and Jayne-Leigh Thomas, 2012. The Paleoindian to Archaic Transition in the Pacific Northwest: *In Situ* Development or Ethnic Replacement? In *On the Brink: Transformations in Human*

Organization and Adaptation at the Pleistocene–Holocene Boundary in North America, edited by C. Britt Bousman and Bradley J. Vierra, pp. 37–65. College Station: Texas A&M University Press.

Chavez, Thomas E., 1994. The Villasur Expedition and the Segesser Hide Paintings. In *Spain and the Plains: Myths and Realities of Spanish Exploration and Settlement on the Great Plains*, edited by R. H. Vigil, F. W. Kaye, and J. R. Wunder, pp. 90–113. Boulder: University Press of Colorado.

Chazin, Hannah, and Stephen E. Nash, 2013. Moments, Movements, and Metaphors: Paul Sydney Martin, Pedagogy, and Professionalism in Field Schools, 1926–1974. *American Antiquity* 78:322–343.

Chilton, Elizabeth S., 2012. New England Algonquians: "Backwaters" and Typological Boundaries. In *The Oxford Handbook of North American Archaeology*, edited by T. R. Pauketat, pp. 262–272. Oxford: Oxford University Press.

Chilton, Elizabeth S., Thomas Ulrich, and Niels Rinehart, 2005. A Reexamination of the DEDIC Paleo-Indian Site, Deerfield, Massachusetts. *Massachusetts Archaeological Society Bulletin* 66(2):58–66.

Claassen, Cheryl, 1993. Black and White Women at Irene Mound. *Southeastern Archaeology* 12:137–147.

Claassen, Cheryl, 1996. A Consideration of the Social Organization of the Shell Mound Archaic. In *Archaeology of the Mid-Holocene Southeast*, edited by Kenneth E. Sassaman and David G. Anderson, pp. 235–258. Gainesville: University Press of Florida.

Claassen, Cheryl, 2010. *Feasting with Shellfish in the Southern Ohio Valley: Archaic Sacred Sites and Rituals*. Knoxville: University of Tennessee Press.

Claassen, Cheryl, 2015. *Beliefs and Rituals in Archaic Eastern North America: An Interpretive Guide*. Tuscaloosa: University of Alabama Press.

Claflin, William H., Jr., 1931. *The Stalling's Island Mound, Columbia County, Georgia*. Peabody Museum of American Archaeology and Ethnology Papers 14(1). Cambridge, MA: Peabody Museum.

Clark, Jeffery J., 2007. A San Pedro Valley Perspective on Ancestral Pueblo Migration in the Hohokam World. In *The Hohokam Millennium*, edited by S. K. Fish and P. R. Fish, pp. 99–107. Santa Fe, NM: School for Advanced Research Press.

Clark, John E., 2004a. Mesoamerica Goes Public: Early Ceremonial Centers, Leaders, and Communities. In *Mesoamerican Archaeology: Theory and Practice*, edited by J. A. Hendon and R. A. Joyce, pp. 42–72. Oxford: Blackwell.

Clark, John E., 2004b. Surrounding the Sacred: Geometry and Design of Early Mound Groups as Meaning and Function. In *Signs of Power: The Rise of Cultural Complexity in the Southeast*, edited by Jon L. Gibson and Philip J. Carr, pp. 162–213. Tuscaloosa: University of Alabama Press.

Clark, John E., and Dennis Gosser, 1995. Reinventing Mesoamerica's First Pottery. In *The Emergence of Pottery: Technology and Innovation in Ancient Societies*, edited by W. Barnett and J. W. Hoopes, pp. 209–219. Washington, DC: Smithsonian Institution Press.

Clark, John E., and Michelle Knoll, 2005. The American Formative Revisited. In *Gulf Coast Archaeology: The Southeastern United States and Mexico*, edited by N. M. White, pp. 281–303. Gainesville: University Press of Florida.

Clark, John E., Jon L. Gibson, and James Ziedler, 2010. First Towns in the Americas: Searching for Agriculture, Population Growth, and Other Enabling Conditions. In *Becoming Villagers: Comparing Early Village Societies*, edited by Matthew S. Bandy and Jake R. Fox, pp. 205–245. Tucson: University of Arizona Press.

Clausen, Carl J., H. K. Brooks, and A. B. Wesolowsky, 1975. The Early Man Site at Warm Mineral Springs. *Journal of Field Archaeology* 2:191–213.

Clausen, Carl J., A. D. Cohen, Cesare Emiliani, J. A. Holman, and J. J. Stipp, 1979. Little Salt Springs, Florida: A Unique Underwater Site. *Science* 203:609–614.

Clay, R. Berle, 1998. The Essential Features of Adena Ritual and their Implications. *Southeastern Archaeology* 17:1–21.

Clayton, Lawrence A., Vernon J. Knight, Jr., and Edward C. Moore (eds.), 1993. *The De Soto Chronicles: The Expedition of Hernando de Soto to North America in 1539–1543*. Tuscaloosa: University of Alabama Press.

Cobb, Charles R., 2005. Archaeology and the "Savage Slot": Displacement and Emplacement in the Modern World. *American Anthropologist* 107:563–574.

Cobb, Charles R., and Brian M. Butler, 2002. The Vacant Quarter Revisited: Late Mississippian Abandonment of the Lower Ohio Valley. *American Antiquity* 67:625–641.

Cobb, Charles R., and Patrick H. Garrow, 1996. Woodstock Culture and the Question of Mississippian Emergence. *American Antiquity* 61:21–37.

Coe, Joffre L., 1964. *The Formative Cultures of the Carolina Piedmont*. Transactions of the American Philosophical Society 54(5). Philadelphia: American Philosophical Society.

Cole, Fay-Cooper, Robert Bell, John Bennett, Joseph Caldwell, Norman Emerson, Richard MacNeish, Kenneth Orr, and Roger Willis, 1951. *Kincaid: A Prehistoric Illinois Metropolis*. Chicago: University of Chicago Press.

Collins, Michael B., 1999. *Clovis Blade Technology*. Austin: University of Texas Press.

Colwell-Chanthaphonh, Chip, and T. J. Ferguson (eds.), 2008. *Collaboration in Archaeological Practice: Engaging Descendant Communities*. Plymouth, UK: AltaMira Press.

Cook, Robert A., 2008. *Sun Watch: Fort Ancient Development in the Mississippian World*. Tuscaloosa: University of Alabama Press.

Cook, Sherburne F., 1978. Historical Demography. In *Handbook of North American Indians, California*, vol. VIII, edited by R. F. Heizer, pp. 91–98. Washington, DC: Smithsonian Institution.

Cooper, Jago, 2013. The Climatic Context for Pre-Columbian Archaeology in the Caribbean. In *The Oxford Handbook of Caribbean Archaeology*, edited by William F. Keegan, Corinne L. Hofman, and Reniel Rodriguez Ramos, pp. 47–58. Oxford: Oxford University Press.

Corbett, Ray, 2004. Chumash Bone Whistles: The Development of Ceremonial Integration in Chumash Society. In *Foundations of Chumash Complexity*, edited by J. E. Arnold, pp. 65–73. Los Angeles: Cotsen Institute of Archaeology, University of California.

Cordell, Linda S., 1984. *Prehistory of the Southwest*. Orlando: Academic Press.

Cordell, Linda S., H. Wolcott Toll, Mollie S. Toll, and Thomas C. Windes, 2008. Archaeological Corn from Pueblo Bonito, Chaco Canyon, New Mexico: Dates, Contexts, Sources. *American Antiquity* 73(3):491–511.

Coues, Elliott (ed.), 1979[1893]. *The History of the Lewis and Clark Expedition*. 3 vols. New York: Dover.

Coupland, Gary, 2004. Complex Hunter-Gatherers of the Southern California Coast: A View from One Thousand Miles North. In *Foundations of Chumash Complexity*, edited by J. E. Arnold. Los Angeles: Cotsen Institute of Archaeology, University of California.

Cowgill, George L., 2012. Concepts of Collapse and Regeneration in Human History. In *The Oxford Handbook of Mesoamerican Archaeology*, edited by D. L. Nichols and C. A. Pool, pp. 301–308. Oxford: Oxford University Press.

Craig, Douglas B., and T. Kathleen Henderson, 2007. Houses, Households, and Household Organization. In *The Hohokam Millennium*, edited by S. Fish and P. Fish, pp. 30–37. Santa Fe, NM: School for Advanced Research Press.

Creel, Darrell G., 1999. The Black Mountain Phase in the Mimbres Area. In *The Casas Grandes World*, edited by C. F. Schaafsma and C. L. Riley, pp. 107–120. Salt Lake City: University of Utah Press.

Creel, Darrell G., and Roger Anyon, 2010. Burning Down the House: Ritual Architecture of the Mimbres Late Pithouse Period. In *Mimbres Lives and Landscapes*, edited by M. C. Nelson and M. Hegmon, pp. 29–37. Santa Fe, NM: School for Advanced Research Press.

Creese, John L., 2012. The Domestication of Personhood: A View from the Northern Iroquoian Longhouse. *Cambridge Archaeological Journal* 22(3):365–386.

Cross, John R., 1999. "By Any Other Name …": A Reconsideration of Middle Archaic Lithic Technology and Typology in the Northeast. In *The Archaeological Northeast*, edited by Mary Ann Levine, Kenneth E. Sassaman, and Michael S. Nassaney, pp. 57–73. Westport, CT: Bergin and Garvey.

Crothers, George M., 1999. Archaic Period Subsistence and Economy: The Green River Shell Midden Sites of Kentucky. Ph.D. dissertation, Department of Anthropology, Washington University, St. Louis.

Crothers, George M., Charles H. Faulkner, Jan F. Simek, Patty Jo Watson, and P. Willey, 2002. Woodland Cave Archaeology in Eastern North America. In *The Woodland Southeast*, edited by David G. Anderson and Robert C. Mainfort, Jr., pp. 502–524. Tuscaloosa: University of Alabama Press.

Crown, Patricia L., 1994. *Ceramics and Ideology: Salado Polychrome Pottery*. Albuquerque: University of New Mexico Press.

Crown, Patricia L., and W. Jeffrey Hurst, 2009. Evidence of Cacao Use in the Prehispanic American Southwest. *Proceedings of the National Academy of Sciences* 106(7):2110–2113.

Crown, Patricia L., Thomas E. Emerson, J. Gu, William J. Hurst, Timothy R. Pauketat, and Timothy Ward, 2012. Ritual Black Drink Consumption at Cahokia. *Proceedings of the National Academy of Sciences* 109(35):13944–13949.

Crown, Patricia L., Jiyan Gu, W. Jeffrey Hurst, Timothy J. Ward, Ardith D. Bravenec, Syed Ali, Laura Kerbert, Marlaina Berch, Erin Redman, Patrick D. Lyons, Jamie Merewether, David A. Phillips, Lori S. Reed, and Kyle Woodson, 2015. Ritual Drinks in the Pre-Hispanic US Southwest and Mexican Northwest. *Proceedings of the National Academy of Sciences* 112(37):11436–11442.

Culin, Stewart, 1992. *Games of the North American Indians*. Lincoln: University of Nebraska Press.

Curet, L. A., and J. R. Oliver, 1998. Mortuary Practices, Social Development, and Ideology in Precolumbian Puerto Rico. *Latin American Antiquity* 9(3):217–239.

Curran, Mary Lou, 1999. Exploration, Colonization, and Settling In: The Bull Brook Phase, Antecedents, and Descendants. In *The Archaeological Northeast*, edited by M. A. Levine, K. E. Sassaman, and M. S. Nassaney, pp. 3–24. Westport, CT: Bergin and Garvey.

Cybulski, J. S., 2010. Human Skeletal Variation and Environmental Diversity in Northwestern North America. In *Human Variation in the Americas: The Integration of Archaeology and Biological Anthropology*, edited by Benjamin M. Auerbach, pp. 77–112. Center for Archaeological Investigations, Occasional Paper 38. Carbondale, IL: Southern Illinois University.

Dancey, William S., 2005. The Enigmatic Hopewell of the Eastern Woodlands. In *North American Archaeology*, edited by Timothy R. Pauketat and Diana DiPaolo Loren, pp. 108–137. Malden, MA: Blackwell.

Dancey, William S., and Paul J. Pacheco (eds.), 1997. *Ohio Hopewell Community Organization*. Kent, OH: Kent State University Press.

Daniel, I. Randolph, 1998. *Hardaway Revisited: Early Archaic Settlement in the Southeast*. Tuscaloosa: University of Alabama Press.

Darwent, John, Hans Lange, Genevieve LeMoine, and Christyann Darwent, 2008. The Longest Longhouse in Greenland. *Antiquity* 82(315).

Darwent, John, Owen Mason, John Hoffecker, and Christyann Darwent, 2013. 1,000 Years of House Change at Cape Espenberg, Alaska: A Case Study in Horizontal Stratigraphy. *American Antiquity* 78:433–455.

Dávila Cabrera, Patricio, 2005. Mound Builders along the Coast of the Gulf of Mexico and the Eastern United States. In *Gulf Coast Archaeology: The Southeastern United States and Mexico*, edited by N. M. White, pp. 87–107. Gainesville: University Press of Florida.

Dávila Cabrera, Patricio, 2015. Trapezoidal Shell Pectorals from the Huasteca. In *The Huasteca: Culture, History, and Interregional Exchange*, edited by K. A. Faust and K. N. Richter, pp. 128–151. Norman: University of Oklahoma Press.

Davis, Richard S., and R. A. Knecht, 2010. Continuity and Change in the Eastern Aleutian Archaeological Sequence. *Human Biology* 82:507–524.

Dawe, Robert J., and Marcel Kornfeld, 2017. Nunataks and Valley Glaciers: Over the Mountains and through the Ice. *Quaternary International* 444:56–71.

Dean, Jeffrey S. (ed.), 2000. *Salado*. Albuquerque: University of New Mexico Press.

Dean, Jeffrey S., and John C. Ravesloot, 1993. The Chronology of Cultural Interaction in the Gran Chichimeca. In *Culture and Contact: Charles C. Di Peso's Gran Chichimeca*, edited by A. I. Woosley and J. C. Ravesloot, pp. 83–103. Albuquerque: University of New Mexico Press.

DeBoer, Warren R., 1997. Ceremonial Centers from Cayapas (Esmeraldas, Ecuador), to Chillicothe (Ohio, USA). *Cambridge Archaeological Journal* 7:225–253.

DeBoer, Warren R., 2005. Colors for a North American Past. *World Archaeology* 37:66–91.

Deller, D. Brian, and Christopher J. Ellis, 1984. Crowfield: A Preliminary Report on a Probable Paleo-Indian Cremation in Southwestern Ontario. *Archaeology of Eastern North America* 12:41–71.

Deller, D. Brian, Christopher J. Ellis, and James R. Keron, 2009. Understanding Cache Variability: A Deliberately Burned Early Paleoindian Tool Assemblage from the Crowfield Site, Southeastern Ontario. *American Antiquity* 74:371–397.

Deloria, Philip J., 1999. *Playing Indian*. New Haven: Yale University Press.

Deloria, Vine, Jr., 1970. *Custer Died for Your Sins: An Indian Manifesto*. Norman: University of Oklahoma Press.

Deloria, Vine, Jr., 1992. Indians, Archaeologists, and the Future. *American Antiquity* 57:595–598.

Dent, Richard J., Jr., 1995. *Chesapeake Prehistory: Old Traditions, New Directions*. New York: Plenum.

Denton, David, 1998. From the Source to the Margins and Back: Notes on Mistassini Quartzite and Archaeology in the Area of the Colline Blanche. *Paleo-Quebec* 27:17–32.

Descola, Phillippe, 2013. *Beyond Nature and Culture*. Chicago: University of Chicago Press.

Di Peso, Charles C., 1974. *Casas Grandes: A Fallen Trading Center of the Gran Chichimeca*, vols. I–III. Dragoon and Flagstaff, AZ: Amerind Foundation and Northland Press.

Di Peso, Charles C., J. B. Rinaldo, and G. J. Fenner, 1974. *Casas Grandes: A Fallen Trading Center of the Gran Chichimeca*, vols. IV–VIII. Dragoon and Flagstaff, AZ: Amerind Foundation and Northland Press.

Dickason, Olive, and David T. McNab, 2009. *Canada's First Nations: A History of Founding Peoples from Earliest Times*. Oxford: Oxford University Press.

Diehl, Richard A., 1983. *Tula: The Toltec Capital of Ancient Mexico*. London: Thames and Hudson.

Dillehay, Thomas D., 1997. *Monte Verde: A Late Pleistocene Settlement in Chile, vol. II: The Archaeological Context and Interpretation*. Washington, DC: Smithsonian Institution Press.

Dillehay, Thomas D., C. Ramirez, M. Pino, M.B. Collins, J Rossen, and J. D. Pino-Navarro, 2008. Monte Verde: Seaweed, Food, Medicine, and the Peopling of South America. *Science* 320:784–786.

Dincauze, Dena F., 1976. *The Neville Site: 8000 Years at Amoskeag*. Cambridge, MA: Peabody Museum of Archaeology and Ethnology.

Dincauze, Dena F., 1984. An Archaeo-Logical Evaluation of the Case for Pre-Clovis Occupations. In *Advances in World Archaeology*, III, edited by Fred Wendorf and A. E. Close, pp. 275–323. Orlando: Academic Press.

Dincauze, Dena F., and Robert J. Hasenstab, 1989. Explaining the Iroquois: Tribalization on a Prehistoric Periphery. In *Centre and Periphery: Comparative Studies in Archaeology*, edited by T. C. Champion, pp. 67–87. London: Unwin Hyman.

Dixon, David, 2005. *Never Come to Peace Again: Pontiac's Uprising and the Fate of the British Empire in North America*. Norman: University of Oklahoma Press.

Dobres, Marcia-Anne, 2000. *Technology and Social Agency*. Oxford: Blackwell.

Doelle, William H., 2000. Tonto Basin Demography in a Regional Perspective. In *Salado*, edited by J. S. Dean, pp. 81–106. Albuquerque: University of New Mexico Press.

Dongoske, Kurt E., Michael Yeatts, Roger Anyon, and T. J. Ferguson, 1997. Archaeological Cultures and Cultural Affiliation: Hopi and Zuni Perspectives in the American Southwest. *American Antiquity* 62:600–608.

Dongoske, Kurt E., Mark S. Aldenderfer, and Karen Doehner (eds.), 2000. *Working Together: Native Americans and Archaeologists*. Washington, DC: Society for American Archaeology.

Doolittle, William E., 1988. *Pre-Hispanic Occupance in the Valley of Sonora, Mexico: Archaeological Confirmation of Early Spanish Reports*.

Anthropological Papers of the University of Arizona 48. Tucson: University of Arizona Press.

Doran, Glen H. (ed.), 2002. *Windover: Multidisciplinary Investigations of an Early Archaic Florida Cemetery*. Gainesville: University Press of Florida.

Doyel, David E., 1991. Hohokam Cultural Evolution in the Phoenix Basin. In *Exploring the Hohokam: Prehistoric Desert Peoples of the American Southwest*, edited by G. J. Gumerman, pp. 231–278. Albuquerque: University of New Mexico Press.

Doyel, David E., 2007. Irrigation, Production, and Power in Phoenix Basin Hohokam Society. In *The Hohokam Millennium*, edited by S. K. Fish and P. R. Fish, pp. 82–89. Santa Fe, NM: School for Advanced Research Press.

Drass, Richard R., 2012. Planting the Plains: The Development and Extent of Plains Village Agriculturalists in the Southern and Central Plains. In *The Oxford Handbook of North American Archaeology*, edited by T. R. Pauketat, pp. 373–385. Oxford: Oxford University Press.

Dumas, David (ed.), 1984. *Handbook of North American Indians, vol. V: Arctic*. Washington, DC: Smithsonian Institution.

Dumond, Don E., 1977. *The Eskimos and Aleuts*. London: Thames and Hudson.

Dumond, Don E., 1984. Prehistory of the Bering Sea Region. In *Handbook of North American Indians, vol. V: Arctic*, edited by David Damas, pp. 94–105. Washington, DC: Smithsonian Institution.

Dunbar, James S., 1991. Resource Orientation of Clovis and Suwannee Age Paleoindian Sites in Florida. In *Clovis: Origins and Adaptations*, edited by Robson Bonnichsen and Karen L. Turnmire, pp. 185–213. Corvallis: Center for the Study of the First Americans and Oregon State University.

Dunbar, James S., 2006. Paleoindian Archaeology. In *First Floridians and Last Mastodons: The Page Ladson Site in the Aucilla River*, edited by S. David Webb, pp. 403–435. Dordrecht: Springer.

Dunbar, James S., and P. K. Vojnovski, 2007. Early Floridians and Late Megamammals: Some Technological and Dietary Evidence from Four North Florida Paleoindian Sites. In *Foragers of the Terminal Pleistocene*, edited by Renee B. Walker and Boyce N. Driskell, pp. 167–202. Tuscaloosa: University of Alabama Press.

Dye, David H., 1996. Initial Riverine Adaptation in the Midsouth: An Examination of Three Middle Holocene Shell Middens. In *Of Caves and Shell Mounds*, edited by Kenneth C. Carstens and Patty Jo Watson, pp. 140–158. Tuscaloosa: University of Alabama Press.

Dye, David H., 2009. *War Paths, Peace Paths: An Archaeology of Cooperation and Conflict in Native Eastern North America*. Lanham, MD: AltaMira Press.

Eakin, Daniel H., Julie E. Francis, and Mary Lou Larson, 1997. The Split Rock Ranch Site: Early Archaic Cultural Practices in Southcentral Wyoming. In *Changing Perspectives of the Archaic on the Northwestern*

Plains and Rocky Mountains, edited by Mary Lou Larson and Julie E. Francis, pp. 395–435. Vermillion: University of South Dakota Press.

Echo-Hawk, Roger, 2000. Ancient History in the New World: Integrating Oral Traditions and the Archaeological Record in Deep Time. *American Antiquity* 65:267–290.

Eddy, John A., 1974. Astronomical Alignment of the Big Horn Medicine Wheel. *Science* 184(4141):1035–1043.

Eerkens, Jelmer W., and Carl P. Lipo, 2014. A Tale of Two Technologies: Prehistoric Diffusion of Pottery Innovations among Hunter-Gatherers. *Journal of Anthropological Archaeology* 35:23–31.

Ekholm, Gordon F., 1944. *Excavations at Tampico and Panuco in the Huasteca, Mexico.* Anthropological Papers of the American Museum of Natural History 38 (part 5). New York: American Museum of Natural History.

Ellis, Christopher J., and D. Brian Deller, 1997. Variability in the Archaeological Record of Northeastern Early Paleoindians: A View from Southern Ontario. *Archaeology of Eastern North America* 25:1–30.

Ellis, Christopher J., and D. Brian Deller, 2000. *An Early Paleoindian Site near Parkhill, Ontario.* Mercury Series, Archaeological Survey of Canada Paper 159. Hull: Canadian Museum of Civilization.

Elsasser, Albert B., 1978. Development of Regional Prehistoric Cultures. In *Handbook of North American Indians, vol. VIII: California*, edited by R. F. Heizer, pp. 37–57. Washington, DC: Smithsonian Institution.

Emerson, Thomas E., 1997. Cahokian Elite Ideology and the Mississippian Cosmos. In *Cahokia: Domination and Ideology in the Mississippian World*, edited by T. R. Pauketat and T. E. Emerson, pp. 190–228. Lincoln: University of Nebraska Press.

Emerson, Thomas E., 2002. An Introduction to Cahokia 2002: Diversity, Complexity, and History. *Midcontinental Journal of Archaeology* 27(2):127–148.

Emerson, Thomas E., 2003. Materializing Cahokia Shamans. *Southeastern Archaeology* 22:135–154.

Emerson, Thomas E., 2016. Paradigms Lost: Reconfiguring Cahokia's Mound 72 Beaded Burial. *American Antiquity* 81:405–425.

Emerson, Thomas E., Dale L. McElrath, and Andrew C. Fortier (eds.), 2000. *Late Woodland Societies: Tradition and Transformation across the Midcontinent.* Lincoln: University of Nebraska Press.

Emerson, Thomas E., Randall E. Hughes, Mary R. Hynes, and Sarah U. Wisseman, 2003. The Sourcing and Interpretation of Cahokia-Style Figurines in the Trans-Mississippi South and Southeast. *American Antiquity* 68:287–313.

Emerson, Thomas E., Dale L. McElrath, and Andrew C. Fortier (eds.), 2009. *Archaic Societies: Diversity and Complexity across the Midcontinent.* Albany: State University of New York Press.

Emerson, Thomas E., Kristin M. Hedman, Eve A. Hargrave, Dawn E. Cobb, and Andrew R. Thompson, 2016. Paradigms Lost:

Reconfiguring Cahokia's Mound 72 Beaded Burial. *American Antiquity* 81(3):405–425.

Endonino, Jon C., 2010. Thornhill Lake: Hunter-Gatherers, Monuments, and Memory. Ph.D. dissertation, Department of Anthropology, University of Florida, Gainesville.

Engelbrecht, William, 2003. *Iroquoia: The Development of a Native World*. Syracuse, NY: Syracuse University Press.

Erlandson, J., T. Rick, T. Braje, M. Casperson, T. Garcia, D. Guthrie, N. Jew, M. Moss, L. Reeder, J. Watts, L. Willis, and B. Fullfrost, 2011. Paleoindian Seafaring, Shell Middens, and Maritime Technologies on California's Northern Channel Islands. *Science* 331:1181–1185.

Erlandson, Jon M., and Michael A. Glassow (eds.), 1997. *Archaeology of the California Coast during the Middle Holocene*. Los Angeles: Institute of Archaeology, University of California.

Erlandson, Jon M., and Todd J. Braje, 2012. Foundations for the Far West: Paleoindian Cultures on the Western Fringe of North America. In *The Oxford Handbook of North American Archaeology*, edited by Timothy R. Pauketat, pp. 149–159. Oxford: Oxford University Press.

Erlandson, Jon M., Michael H. Graham, Bruce J. Bourque, Debra Corbett, James E. Estes, and Robert S. Steneck, 2007. The Kelp Highway Hypothesis: Marine Ecology, the Coastal Migration Theory, and the Peopling of the Americas. *Journal of Island and Coastal Archaeology* 2:161–174.

Erlandson, Jon M., Madonna L. Moss, and Matthew Des Lauriers, 2008. Living on the Edge: Early Maritime Cultures of the Pacific Coast of North America. *Quaternary Science Reviews* 27:2232–2245.

Fagan, Brian M., 2001. *The Little Ice Age: How Climate Made History, 1300–1850*. New York: Basic Books.

Fagan, Brian M., 2005. *Ancient North America: The Archaeology of a Continent*. New York: Thames and Hudson.

Fagette, Paul, 1996. *Digging for Dollars: American Archeology and the New Deal*. Albuquerque: University of New Mexico Press.

Fairbanks, Charles H., 1946. The Macon Earth Lodge. *American Antiquity* 12:94–108.

Fash, William L., and Mary E. Lyons, 2005. *The Ancient American World*. Oxford: Oxford University Press.

Faught, Michael K., 2004a. Submerged Paleoindian and Archaic Sites of the Big Bend, Florida. *Journal of Field Archaeology* 29:273–289.

Faught, Michael K., 2004b. The Underwater Archaeology of Paleolandscapes, Apalachee Bay, Florida. *American Antiquity* 69:275–289.

Faught, Michael K., 2008. Archaeological Roots of Human Diversity in the New World: A Compilation of Accurate and Precise Radiocarbon Ages from Earliest Sites. *American Antiquity* 73:670–698.

Faught, Michael K., and James C. Waggoner, Jr., 2012. The Early Archaic to Middle Archaic Transition in Florida: An Argument for Discontinuity. *Florida Anthropologist* 65:153–175.

Faust, Katherine A., and Kim N. Richter, 2015. The Huasteca as Heartland in the Hinterlands. In *The Huasteca: Culture, History, and Interregional Exchange*, edited by K. A. Faust and K. N. Richter, pp. 2–18. Norman: University of Oklahoma Press.

Fawcett, William B., 1987. Communal Hunts, Human Aggregations, Social Variation, and Climatic Change: Bison Utilization by Prehistoric Inhabitants of the Great Plains. Ph.D. dissertation, Department of Anthropology, University of Massachusetts, Amherst.

Feathers, James, Maria N. Zedeño, Lawrence C. Todd, and Stephen Aaberg. 2015. Dating Stone Alignments by Luminescence. *Advances in Archaeological Practice* 3:378–396.

Feder, Kenneth L., 2014. *Frauds, Myths, and Mysteries: Science and Pseudoscience in Archaeology*. New York: McGraw-Hill.

Fenton, William N., 1978. Northern Iroquoian Culture Patterns. In *Handbook of North American Indians, vol. XV: Northeast*, edited by B. G. Trigger, pp. 296–321. Washington, DC: Smithsonian Institution.

Fie, Shannon M., 2006. Visiting in the Interaction Sphere: Ceramic Exchange and Interaction in the Lower Illinois Valley. In *Recreating Hopewell*, edited by D. K. Charles and J. E. Buikstra, pp. 427–445. Gainesville: University of Florida Press.

Fiedel, Stuart, 2017. The Anzick Genome Proves Clovis is First, after All. *Quaternary International* 444:4–9.

Fienup-Riordan, Ann, 1994. *Boundaries and Passages: Rule and Ritual in Yup'ik Eskimo Oral Tradition*. Norman: University of Oklahoma Press.

Finlayson, William D., 1985. *The 1975 and 1978 Rescue Excavations at the Draper Site: Introduction and Settlement Pattern*. Archaeological Survey of Canada Mercury Series Paper 130. Ottawa: Canadian Museum of Civilization.

Firestone, R. B., A. West, J. P. Kennett et al., 2007. Evidence for an Extraterrestrial Impact 12,900 Years Ago that Contributed to the Megafaunal Extinctions and the Younger Dryas Cooling. *Proceedings of the National Academy of Sciences* 104:16016–16021.

Fish, Suzanne K., and Paul R. Fish (eds.), 2007a. *The Hohokam Millennium*. Santa Fe, NM: School for Advanced Research Press.

Fish, Suzanne K., and Paul R. Fish, 2007b. The Hohokam Millennium. In *The Hohokam Millennium*, edited by S. Fish and P. Fish, pp. 1–11. Santa Fe, NM: School for Advanced Research Press.

Fish, Suzanne K., and Paul R. Fish, 2012. Hohokam Society and Water Management. In *The Oxford Handbook of North American Archaeology*, edited by T. R. Pauketat, pp. 571–584. Oxford: Oxford University Press.

Fitting, James E., 1978. Regional Cultural Development, 300 BC to AD 1000. In *Handbook of North American Indians, Northeast*, vol. XV, edited by B. G. Trigger, pp. 44–57. Washington, DC: Smithsonian Institution.

Fitzhugh, Ben, 2003. *The Evolution of Complex Hunter-Gatherers: Archaeological Evidence from the North Pacific.* New York: Kluwer Academic-Plenum.

Fitzhugh, William W., 1972. *Environmental Archaeology and Cultural Systems in Hamilton Inlet, Labrador: A Survey of the Central Labrador Coast from 3000 BC to the Present.* Smithsonian Contributions to Anthropology 16. Washington, DC: Smithsonian Institution Press.

Fitzhugh, William W., 1978. Maritime Archaic Cultures of the Central and Northern Labrador Coast. *Arctic Anthropology* 15:61–95.

Fitzhugh, William W., 1984. Residence Pattern Development in the Labrador Maritime Archaic: Longhouse Models and 1983 Surveys. In *Archaeology in Newfoundland and Labrador 1983*, edited by Jane S. Thomson and Callum Thomson, pp. 6–47. St. John's: Historic Resources Division, Department of Culture, Recreation and Youth, Government of Newfoundland and Labrador.

Fitzhugh, William W., 2006. Settlement, Social and Ceremonial Change in the Labrador Maritime Archaic. In *The Archaic of the Far Northeast*, edited by David Sanger and M. A. P. Renouf, pp. 47–82. Orono: University of Maine Press.

Fladmark, Knut R., 1979. Routes: Alternate Migration Corridors for Early Man in North America. *American Antiquity* 44:55–69.

Flannery, Kent, and Joyce Marcus, 2012. *The Creation of Inequality: How Our Prehistoric Ancestors Set the Stage for Monarchy, Slavery and Empire.* Cambridge, MA: Harvard University Press.

Fletcher, Alice C., 1996. *The Hako: Song, Pipe, and Unity in a Pawnee Calumet Ceremony* (originally published 1904). Lincoln: University of Nebraska Press.

Ford, James A., 1951. *Greenhouse: A Troyville-Coles Creek Period Site in Avoyelles Parish, Louisiana.* Anthropological Papers of the American Museum of Natural History 44, pt. 1. New York: American Museum of Natural History.

Ford, James A., 1962. *A Quantitative Method for Deriving Cultural Chronology.* Technical Bulletin 1. Washington, DC: Pan American Union.

Ford, James A., 1969. *A Comparison of Formative Cultures in the Americas: Diffusion or the Psychic Unity of Man.* Smithsonian Contributions to Anthropology 2. Washington, DC: Smithsonian Institution Press.

Ford, James A., and Clarence H. Webb, 1956. *Poverty Point, a Late Archaic Site in Louisiana.* Anthropological Papers 46, pt. 1. New York: American Museum of Natural History.

Ford, Richard I., 1985. Patterns of Prehistoric Food Production in North America. In *Prehistoric Food Production in North America*, edited by R. I. Ford, pp. 341–364. Anthropological Papers of the Museum of Anthropology 75. Ann Arbor: Museum of Anthropology, University of Michigan.

Fortier, Andrew C. (ed.), 2014. *Late Woodland Communities in the American Bottom: The Fish Lake Site*. Illinois State Archaeological Survey, Research Report 28. Urbana: University of Illinois.

Fortier, Andrew C., Thomas E. Emerson, and Dale L. McElrath, 2006. Calibrating and Reassessing American Bottom Culture History. *Southeastern Archaeology* 25(2):170–211.

Foucault, Michel, 1979. *Discipline and Punish: The Birth of the Prison*. New York: Vintage Books.

Fowler, Catherine S., and Don D. Fowler (eds.), 2008. *The Great Basin: People and Place in Ancient Times*. Santa Fe, NM School for Advanced Research Press.

Fowler, Melvin, Jerome C. Rose, Barbara Vander Leest, and Steven R. Ahler, 1999. *The Mound 72 Area: Dedicated and Sacred Space in Early Cahokia*. Reports of Investigations 54. Springfield: Illinois State Museum.

Fowler, William S., 1966. Ceremonial and Domestic Products of Aboriginal New England. *Bulletin of the Massachusetts Archaeological Society* 27(3–4):33–66.

Fowles, Severin, 2012. The Pueblo Village in an Age of Reformation (AD 1300–1600). In *The Oxford Handbook of North American Archaeology*, edited by T. R. Pauketat, pp. 631–644. Oxford: Oxford University Press.

Franco, Maria Teresa, and Gonzalez Salas (eds.), 1993. *The Huastec and Totonac World*. Mexico City: Grupo Financiero Inverlat.

Friesen, T. Max, 2007. Hearth Rows, Hierarchies and Arctic Hunter-Gatherers: The Construction of Equality in the Late Dorset Period. *World Archaeology* 39:194–214.

Friesen, T. Max, 2013. North America: Paleoeskimo and Inuit Archaeology. In *The Encyclopedia of Global Human Migration*, edited by Immanuel Ness, pp. 1–8. Hoboken: Wiley-Blackwell.

Friesen, T. Max, and Charles D. Arnold, 2008. The Timing of the Thule Migration: New Dates from the Western Canadian Arctic. *American Antiquity* 73:527–538.

Frison, George C., 1971. The Buffalo Pound in Northwestern Plains Prehistory: Site 48CA302, Wyoming. *American Antiquity* 36:77–91.

Frison, George C. (ed.), 1974. *The Casper Site: A Hell Gap Bison Kill on the High Plains*. New York: Academic Press.

Frison, George C., and Bruce A. Bradley, 1980. *Folsom Tools and Technology at the Hanson Site, Wyoming*. Albuquerque: University of New Mexico Press.

Frison, George C., and Dennis J. Stanford (eds.), 1982. *The Agate Basin Site*. New York: Academic Press.

Frison, George C., R. L. Andrews, J. M. Adovasio, R. C. Carlisle, and Robert Edgar, 1986. A Late Paleoindian Animal Trapping Net from Northern Wyoming. *American Antiquity* 51:352–361.

Fritz, John M., 1978. Paleopsychology Today: Ideational Systems and Human Adaptation in Prehistory. In *Social Archaeology: Beyond Subsistence and Dating*, edited by C. L. Redman, W. T. Langhorne,

Jr., M. J. Berman, N. M. Versaggi, E. V. Curtin, and J. C. Wanser, pp. 37–59. New York: Academic Press.

Fuson, Robert Henderson, 2000. *Juan Ponce de Leon and the Spanish Discovery of Puerto Rico and Florida*. Blacksburg, VA: McDonald and Woodward.

Gallivan, Martin D., 2012. Native History in the Chesapeake: The Powhatan Chiefdom and Beyond. In *The Oxford Handbook of North American Archaeology*, edited by T. R. Pauketat, pp. 310–322. Oxford: Oxford University Press.

Gallivan, Martin D., E. Randolph Turner, III, Justine Woodard McKnight, David A. Brown, Thane Harpole, and Danielle Moretti-Langholtz, 2013. *The Werowocomoco Research Project: 2004–2010 Field Seasons.* Archaeological Research Report Series 3. Williamsburg, VA: College of William and Mary, Department of Anthropology.

Gamble, Clive, 2007. *Origins and Revolutions: Human Identity in Earliest Prehistory*. Cambridge, UK: Cambridge University Press.

Gamble, Lynn H., 2012. A Land of Power: The Materiality of Wealth, Knowledge, Authority, and the Supernatural. In *Contemporary Issues in California Archaeology*, edited by T. L. Jones and J. E. Perry, pp. 175–196. Walnut Creek, CA: Left Coast Press.

Gamble, Lynn H., 2015a. California Indian Chiefs and Other Elites. In *First Coastal Californians*, edited by L. H. Gamble, pp. 66–73. Santa Fe, NM: School for Advanced Research Press.

Gamble, Lynn H., 2015b. Shell Beads as Adornment and Money. In *First Coastal Californians*, edited by L. H. Gamble, pp. 82–87. Santa Fe, NM: School of Advanced Research Press.

Gamble, Lynn H., 2015c. Thirteen Thousand Years on the Coast. In *First Coastal Californians*, edited by L. H. Gamble, pp. 1–7. Santa Fe, NM: School for Advanced Research Press.

Gamble, Lynn H., 2017. Feasting, Ritual Practices, Social Memory, and Persistent Places: New Interpretations of Shell Mounds in Southern California. *American Antiquity* 82:427–451.

Garfinkel, Alan P., 2006. Paradigm Shifts, Rock Art Studies, and the "Coco Sheep Cult" of Eastern California. *North American Archaeologist* 27:203–244.

Garfinkel, Alan P., and Donald R. Austin, 2011. Reproductive Symbolism in Great Basin Rock Art: Bighorn Sheep Hunting, Fertility and Forager Identity. *Cambridge Archaeological Journal* 21:454–471.

Garfinkel, Alan P., Donald R. Austin, D. Earle, and H. Williams, 2009. Myth, Ritual, and Rock Art: Coso Decorated Animal-Humans and the Animal Master. *Rock Art Research* 26:179–197.

Gayton, A. H., 1948. Yokuts and Western Mono Ethnography II: Northern Foothill Yokuts and Western Mono. *University of California Anthropological Records* 10(2):143–301.

Gell, Alfred, 1992. The Enchantment of Technology and the Technology of Enchantment. In *Anthropology, Art and Aesthetics*, edited by J. Coote and A. Shelton, pp. 40–63. Oxford: Oxford University Press.

Gemillion, Kristen J., 2004. Seed Processing and the Origins of Food Production in Eastern North America. *American Antiquity* 69:215–233.

Gibbon, Guy, 1974. A Model of Mississippian Development and its Implications for the Red Wing Area. In *Aspects of Upper Great Lakes Anthropology*, edited by E. Johnson, pp. 129–137. Minnesota Prehistoric Archaeology Series 11. St. Paul: Minnesota Historical Society.

Gibbon, Guy, 2012. Lifeways through Time in the Upper Mississippi River Valley and Northeastern Plains. In *The Oxford Handbook of North American Archaeology*, edited by T. Pauketat, pp. 325–335. Oxford: Oxford University Press.

Gibson, Jon L., 2000. *The Ancient Mounds of Poverty Point Place of Rings*. Gainesville: University Press of Florida.

Gibson, Jon L., 2004. The Power of Beneficent Obligation in First Mound-Building Societies. In *Signs of Power: The Rise of Cultural Complexity in the Southeast*, edited by Jon L. Gibson and Philip J. Carr, pp. 254–269. Tuscaloosa: University of Alabama Press.

Gibson, Jon L., and Mark A. Melancon, 2004. In the Beginning: Social Contexts of First Pottery in the Lower Mississippi Valley. In *Early Pottery: Technology, Function, Style, and Interaction in the Lower Southeast*, edited by Rebecca Saunders and Christopher T. Hays, pp. 169–192. Tuscaloosa: University of Alabama Press.

Giles, Bretton T., 2010. Sacrificing Complexity: Renewal through Ohio Hopewell Rituals. In *Ancient Complexities: New Perspectives in Precolumbian North America*, edited by Susan M. Alt, pp. 73–95. Salt Lake City: University of Utah Press.

Giles, Bretton T., 2011. The Ritual Mnemonics of Hopewell Symbols: An Analysis of Effigies and Ceremonial Regalia from Tremper, Mound City and Hopewell. Ph.D. dissertation, Department of Anthropology, State University of New York at Binghamton.

Giles, Bretton T., 2013. A Contextual and Iconographic Reassessment of the Headdress on Burial 11 from Hopewell Mound 25. *American Antiquity* 78:502–519.

Gilman, Patricia A., 2010. Settling In. In *Mimbres Lives and Landscapes*, edited by M. C. Nelson and M. Hegmon, pp. 17–28. Santa Fe, NM: School for Advanced Research Press.

Gilmore, Zackary I., 2016. *Gathering at Silver Glen: Community and History in Late Archaic Florida*. Gainesville: University Press of Florida.

Girard, Jeffrey S., Timothy K. Perttula, and Mary Beth Trubitt, 2014. *Caddo Connections: Cultural Interactions within and beyond the Caddo World*. Lanham, MD: Rowman and Littlefield.

Glowacki, Donna M., 2011. The Role of Religion in the Depopulation of the Central Mesa Verde Region. In *Religious Transformation in the Late Pre-Hispanic Pueblo World*, edited by D. M. Glowacki and S. Van Keuren, pp. 66–83. Tucson: University of Arizona Press.

Glowacki, Donna M., and Scott Van Keuren (eds.), 2011. *Religious Transformation in the Late Pre-Hispanic Pueblo World*. Tucson: University of Arizona Press.

Goebel, T., 2004. The Search for a Clovis Progenitor in Siberia. In *Entering America: Northeast Asia and Beringia before the Last Glacial Maximum*, edited by D. Madsen, pp. 311–358. Salt Lake City: University of Utah Press.

Goebel, T., R. Powers, and N. Bigelow, 1991. The Nenana Complex of Alaska and Clovis Origins. In *Clovis Origins and Adaptations*, edited by R. Bonnichsen and K. Turnmire, pp. 49–79. Corvallis: Center for the Study of the First Americans, Oregon State University.

Goebel, T., M. R. Waters, and M. Dikova, 2003. The Archaeology of Ushki Lake, Kamchatka, and the Pleistocene Peopling of the Americas. *Science* 301:501–505.

Goebel, T., M. R. Waters, and D. H. O'Rourke, 2008. The Late Pleistocene Dispersal of Modern Humans in the Americas. *Science* 319:1497–1502.

Gómez, Coutouly, and Yan Axel, 2015. Anangula – A Major Pressue-Microblade Site in the Aleutian Islands, Alaska: Reevaluating its Lithic Component. *Arctic Anthropology* 52:23–59.

Goodyear, Albert C., 1974. *The Brand Site: A Techno-functional Study of a Dalton Site in Northeast Arkansas*. Research Series 7. Fayetteville: Arkansas Archaeological Survey.

Goodyear, Albert C., 1982. The Chronological Position of the Dalton Horizon in the Southeastern United States. *American Antiquity* 47:382–395.

Gosden, Chris, 1994. *Social Being and Time*. Oxford: Blackwell.

Graham, James, 2005. Blackduck Settlement in South-Western Manitoba: Land Use and Site Selection. Unpublished Masters degree, Natural Resources Institute, University of Manitoba, Winnipeg.

Graham, Russell W., and E. L. Lundelius, 1994. *FAUNMAP: A Database Documenting Late Quaternary Distributions of Mammal Species in the United States*. Illinois State Museum Scientific Papers 25. Springfield: Illinois State Museum. Available online at www.museum.state.il.us/research/faunmap/aboutfaunmap.html.

Gramly, Richard M., 1982. *The Vail Site: A Palaeo-Indian Encampment in Maine*. Bulletin of the Buffalo Society of Natural Sciences 30. Buffalo: Buffalo Society of Natural Sciences.

Grant, C., J. W. Baird, and J. K. Pringle, 1968. *Rock Drawings of the Coso Range, Inyo County, California: An Ancient Sheep Hunting Cult Pictured in Desert Rock Carvings*. Maturango Museum Publication 4. Ridgecrest, CA: Maturango Museum.

Gravlee, Clarence C., H. Russell Bernard, and William R. Leonard, 2003. Heredity, Environment, and Cranial Form: A Re-analysis of Boas's Immigrant Data. *American Anthropologist* 105:125–138.

Grayson, D. K., 2011. *The Great Basin: A Natural Prehistory*. Berkeley: University of California Press.

Grayson, D. K., and D. J. Meltzer, 2002. Clovis Hunting and Large Mammal Extinction: A Critical Review of the Evidence. *Journal of World Prehistory* 16:313–359.

Greaves, Sheila, 2012. A New Look at the Besant Phase in the Eastern Slopes of the Canadian Rocky Mountains. *Plains Anthropologist* 57(224):367–392.

Greber, N'omi B., 1983. *Recent Excavations at the Edwin Harness Mound, Liberty Works, Ross County, Ohio.* Midcontinental Journal of Archaeology, Special Publication 5.

Greber, N'omi B., 2006. Enclosures and Communities of Ohio Hopewell: An Essay. In *Recreating Hopewell*, edited by Douglas K. Charles and Jane E. Buikstra, pp. 74–105. Gainesville: University Press of Florida.

Greber, N'omi B., and K. C. Ruhl, 2000. *The Hopewell Site: A Contemporary Analysis Based on the Work of Charles C. Willoughby.* Washington, PA: Eastern National.

Greenman, Emerson F., 1967. *The Younge Site: An Archaeological Record from Michigan* (reprinted). Occasional Contributions from the Museum of Anthropology of the University of Michigan 6. Ann Arbor: University of Michigan Museum of Anthropology.

Gremillion, Kristen J., 2002. The Development and Dispersal of Agricultural Systems in the Woodland Period Southeast. In *The Woodland Southeast*, edited by David G. Anderson and Robert C. Mainfort, Jr., pp. 483–501. Tuscaloosa: University of Alabama Press.

Gremillion, Kristen J., 2004. Seed Processing and the Origins of Food Production in Eastern North America. *American Antiquity* 69:215–234.

Gremillion, Kristen J., Jason Windingstad, and Sarah C. Sherwood, 2008. Forest Opening, Habitat Use, and Food Production on the Cumberland Plateau, Kentucky: Adaptive Flexibility in Marginal Settings. *American Antiquity* 73:387–411.

Griffin, James B., 1967. Eastern North American Archaeology: A Summary. *Science* 156(3772):175–191.

Griffin, John W., 1974. *Investigations in Russell Cave.* Publications in Archeology 13. Washington, DC: National Park Service.

Gruner, Erina, 2015. Replicating Things, Replicating Identity: The Movement of Chacoan Ritual Paraphernalia beyond the Chaco World. In *Practicing Materiality*, edited by Ruth Van Dyke, pp. 56–78. Tucson: University of Arizona Press.

Gruner, Erina, 2018. The Mobile House: Religious Leadership at Chacoan and Chacoan Revival Centers. In *Religion and Politics in the Ancient Americas*, edited by Sarah B. Barber and Arthur A. Joyce, pp. 27–50. London: Routledge.

Hall, Robert L., 1985. Medicine Wheels, Sun Circles, and the Magic of World Center Shrines. *Plains Anthropologist* 30(109):181–193.

Hall, Robert L., 1997. *An Archaeology of the Soul: Native American Indian Belief and Ritual.* Urbana: University of Illinois Press.

Hall, Robert L., 2000. Sacrificed Foursomes and Green Corn Ceremonialism. In *Mounds, Modoc, and Mesoamerica: Papers in Honor of Melvin L. Fowler*, edited by S. R. Ahler, pp. 245–253. Scientific Papers 28. Springfield: Illinois State Museum.

Hallowell, A. I., 1960. Ojibwa Ontology, Behavior, and World View. In *Culture in History: Essays in Honor of Paul Radin*, edited by S. Diamond, pp. 19–52. New York: Columbia University Press.

Hally, David J. (ed.), 1994. *Ocmulgee Archaeology: 1936–1986*. Athens: University of Georgia Press.

Halsey, John R. (ed.), 1999. *Retrieving Michigan's Buried Past: The Archaeology of the Great Lakes State*. Bulletin 64. Bloomfield Hills, MI: Cranbrook Institute of Science.

Harp, Elmer, 1976. Dorset Settlement Patterns in Newfoundland and Southeastern Hudson Bay. In *Eastern Arctic Prehistory: Paleoeskimo Problems*, edited by M. Maxwell, pp. 119–138. Memoirs of the Society for American Archaeology 31. Washington, DC: Society for American Archaeology.

Harris, Marvin, 1968. *The Rise of Anthropological Theory*. New York: Crowell.

Harris, Oliver J. T., and Craig Cippola, 2017. *Archaeological Theory in the New Millennium: Introducing Current Perspectives*. London: Routledge.

Hart, John, R. Thompson, and H. J. Brumbach, 2003. Phytolith Evidence for Early Maize (*Zea mays*) in the Northern Fingers Lake Region of New York. *American Antiquity* 68:619–640.

Hart, John, H. J. Brumbach, and R. Lusteck, 2007. Extending the Phytolith Evidence for Early Maize (*Zea mays* ssp. *mays*) and Squash (*Curcurbita* sp.) in Central New York. *American Antiquity* 72:563–583.

Haskins, Valerie A., and Nicholas P. Herrmann, 1996. Shell Mound Bioarchaeology. In *Of Caves and Shellmounds*, edited by Kenneth C. Carstens and Patty J. Watson, pp. 107–118. Tuscaloosa: University of Alabama Press.

Hassig, Ross, 1985. *Trade, Tribute, and Transportation: The Sixteenth-Century Political Economy of the Valley of Mexico*. Norman: University of Oklahoma Press.

Hassig, Ross, 1988. *Aztec Warfare: Imperial Expansion and Political Control*. Norman: University of Oklahoma Press.

Hassig, Ross, 2001. *Time, History, and Belief in Aztec and Colonial Mexico*. Austin: University of Texas Press.

Hassig, Ross, 2006. *Mexico and the Spanish Conquest*. Norman: University of Oklahoma Press.

Haury, Emil W., 1976. *The Hohokam, Desert Farmers and Craftsmen: Excavations at Snaketown, 1964–1965*. Tucson: University of Arizona Press.

Hayden, Brian, 1994. Competition, Labor, and Complex Hunter-Gatherers. In *Key Issues in Hunter-Gatherer Research*, edited by Ernest S. Burch and Linda J. Ellana, pp. 223–239. London: Berg.

Hayden, Brian, 1997. *The Pithouses of Keatley Creek: Complex Hunter-Gatherers of the Northwest Plateau*. Fort Worth, TX: Harcourt Brace.

Hayden, Brian, 2001. A Prolegomenon to the Importance of Feasting. In *Feasts: Archaeological and Ethnographic Perspectives on Food, Politics, and Power*, edited by Michael Dietler and Brian Hayden, pp. 23–64. Washington, DC: Smithsonian Institution Press.

Hayden, Brian, 2007. *The Pithouses of Keatley Creek*. Fort Worth, TX: Harcourt Brace.

Hayes, Jack Irby, Jr., 2001. *South Carolina and the New Deal*. Columbia: University of South Carolina Press.

Haynes, C. Vance, Jr., 1973. The Calico Site: Artifacts or Geofacts? *Science* 181:305–310.

Haynes, C. Vance, Jr., 2008. Younger Dryas "Black Mats" and the Rancholabrean Termination in North America. *Proceedings of the National Academy of Sciences* 105:6520–6525.

Haynes, C. Vance, Jr., and Bruce B. Huckell (eds.), 2007. *Murray Springs: A Clovis Site with Multiple Activity Areas in the San Pedro Valley, Arizona*. Tucson: University of Arizona Press.

Haynes, Gary, 2002. *The Early Settlement of North America: The Clovis Era*. Cambridge, UK: Cambridge University Press.

Hays-Gilpin, Kelley, and Jane H. Hill, 1999. The Flower World in Material Culture: An Iconographic Complex in the Southwest and Mesoamerica. *Journal of Anthropological Research* 55:1–37.

Hays-Gilpin, Kelley, and Jane H. Hill, 2000. The Flower World in Prehistoric Southwest Material Culture. In *The Archaeology of Regional Interaction: Religion, Warfare, and Exchange across the American Southwest and Beyond*, edited by M. Hegmon, pp. 411–428. Boulder: University of Colorado Press.

Healan, Dan M., and Robert H. Cobean, 2012. Tula and the Toltecs. In *The Oxford Handbook of Mesoamerican Archaeology*, edited by D. L. Nichols and C. A. Pool, pp. 372–384. Oxford: Oxford University Press.

Helms, Mary W., 1993. *Craft and the Kingly Ideal: Art, Trade, and Power*. Austin: University of Texas Press.

Hemmings, C. Andrew, 2004. The Organic Clovis: A Single Continent-Wide Cultural Adaptation. Ph.D. dissertation, Department of Anthropology, University of Florida, Gainesville.

Henning, Dale R., 2005. The Evolution of the Plains Village Tradition. In *North American Archaeology*, edited by T. R. Pauketat and D. D. Loren, pp. 161–186. Malden, MA: Blackwell Press.

Henning, Dale R., 2007. Continuity and Change in the Eastern Plains, AD 800–1700. In *Plains Village Archaeology: Bison-Hunting Farmers in the Central and Northern Plains*, edited by S. A. Ahler and M. Kay, pp. 67–82. Salt Lake City: University of Utah Press.

Henry, Edward R., 2011. A Multistage Geophysical Approach to Detecting and Interpreting Archaeological Features at the LeBus Circle, Bourbon County, Kentucky. *Archaeological Prospection* 18:231–244.

Henry, Edward R., and Casey R. Barrier, 2016. The Organization of Dissonance in Adena-Hopewell Societies of Eastern North America. *World Archaeology* 48(1):87–109.

Henry, Edward R., Nicolas R. Laracuente, Jared S. Case, and Jay K. Johnson, 2014. Incorporating Multistaged Geophysical Data into Regional-Scale Models: A Case Study from an Adena Burial Mound in Central Kentucky. *Archaeological Prospection* 21:15–26.

Hensley, Christine, 1994. The Archaic Settlement System of the Middle Green River Valley. Ph.D. dissertation, Department of Anthropology, Washington University, St. Louis.

Hester, Thomas R., 2004. The Prehistory of South Texas. In *The Prehistory of Texas*, edited by T. K. Perttula, pp. 127–151. College Station, TX: Texas A&M University Press.

Hewitt, J. N. B., 1894. The Iroquoian Concept of the Soul. *Journal of American Folklore* 8(29):107–116.

Hewitt, J. N. B., 1903. Iroquoian Cosmology. In *Twenty-First Annual Report of the Bureau of American Ethnology*, pp. 127–339. Washington, DC: Government Printing Office.

Hildebrandt, W. R., and K. R. McGuire, 2002. The Ascendance of Hunting during the California Middle Archaic: An Evolutionary Perspective. *American Antiquity* 67:231–256.

Hilgeman, Sherri L., 2000. *Pottery and Chronology at Angel*. Tuscaloosa: University of Alabama Press.

Hill, James N., 1970. *Broken K Pueblo: Prehistoric Social Organization in the American Southwest*. Anthropological Papers 18. Tucson: University of Arizona.

Hill, Matthew E., Jr., Matthew G. Hill, and Christopher C. Widga, 2008. Late Quaternary Bison Diminution on the Great Plains of North America: Evaluating the Role of Human Hunting versus Climate-Change. *Quaternary Science Reviews* 27:1752–1771.

Hockett, Brian, Cliff Creger, Beth Smith, Craig Young, James Carter, Eric Dillingham, Rachel Crews, and Evan Pellegrini, 2013. Large-Scale Trapping Features from the Great Basin, USA: The Significance of Leadership and Communal Gatherings in Ancient Foraging Societies. *Quaternary International* 697:64–78.

Hodder, Ian, 2011. *Entangled: An Archaeology of the Relationships between Humans and Things*. Chichester: Wiley-Blackwell.

Hodge, Frederick W., 1910. *Handbook of American Indians North of Mexico*. Bureau of American Ethnology Bulletin 30. Washington, DC: Bureau of American Ethnology.

Hodgetts, Lisa M., 2005. Using Bone Measurements to Determine Season of Harp Seal Hunting at the Dorset Palaeoeskimo Site of Phillip's Garden. *Newfoundland and Labrador Studies* 20:91–106.

Hofman, Jack, 1985. Middle Archaic Ritual and Shell Midden Archaeology: Considering the Significance of Cremations. In *Exploring Tennessee Prehistory: A Dedication to Alfred K. Guthe*, edited by Thomas R. Whyte, C. Clifford Boyd, and Brett H. Riggs, pp. 1–21.

Report of Investigations 42. Knoxville: Department of Anthropology, University of Tennessee.

Holder, Preston, 1970. *The Hoe and the Horse on the Plains: A Study of Cultural Development among North American Indians.* Lincoln: University of Nebraska Press.

Holen, Steven R., Thomas A. Deméré, Daniel C. Fisher, Richard Fullagar, James B. Paces, George T. Jefferson, Jared M. Beeton, Richard A. Cerutti, Adam N. Rountrey, Lawrence Vescera, and Kathleen A. Holen, 2017. A 130,000-Year-Old Archaeological Site in Southern California, USA. *Nature* 544:479–483.

Holliday, Vance T., 2000. The Evolution of Paleoindian Geoarchaeology and Typology on the Great Plains. *Geoarchaeology* 15:227–290.

Hollimon, Sandra E., 1996. Sex, Gender and Health among the Chumash: An Archaeological Examination of Prehistoric Gender Roles. *Proceedings of the Society for California Archaeology* 9:205–208.

Hollimon, Sandra E., 2001. Death, Gender, and the Chumash Peoples: Mourning Ceremonialism as an Integrative Mechanism. In *Social Memory, Identity, and Death: Anthropological Perspectives on Mortuary Rituals*, edited by M. S. Chesson, pp. 41–55. Archeological Papers of the American Anthropological Association 10. Washington, DC: American Anthropological Association.

Hollimon, Sandra E., and Daniel F. Murley, 2012. A Land of Many Genders. In *Contemporary Issues in California Archaeology*, edited by T. L. Jones and J. E. Perry, pp. 295–301. Walnut Creek, CA: Left Coast Press.

Hollinger, R. Eric, Stephen Ousley, and Charles Utermohle, 2009. The Thule Migration: A New Look at the Archaeology and Biology of the Point Barrow Region Populations. In *The Northern World, AD 900–1400*, edited by Herbert Maschner, Owen Mason, and Robert McGhee, pp. 131–154. Salt Lake City: University of Utah Press.

Holly, Donald H., Jr., 2005. The Place of "Others" in Hunter-Gatherer Intensification. *American Anthropologist* 107:207–220.

Holly, Donald H., Jr., 2013. *History in the Making: The Archaeology of the Eastern Subarctic.* Lanham, MD: AltaMira Press.

Holly, Donald H., Jr., and John C. Erwin, 2009. Terra Incognita, Still: Archaeological Investigations in the Interior of the Island of Newfoundland. *Archaeology of Eastern North America* 37:65–84.

Holmes, Charles, 2001. Tanana River Valley Archaeology circa 14,000 to 9000 BP. *Arctic Anthropology* 38:154–170.

Hood, Bryan C., 2008. *Towards an Archaeology of the Nain Region, Labrador.* Smithsonian Institution, Arctic Studies Center, Contributions to Circumpolar Anthropology 7. Washington, DC: National Museum of Natural History.

Hotz, Gottfried, 1970. *Indian Skin Paintings from the American Southwest: Two Representations of Border Conflicts between Mexico and the Missouri in the Early Eighteenth Century.* Norman: University of Oklahoma Press.

Howey, Meghan C. L., and John M. O'Shea, 2006. Bear's Journey and the Study of Ritual in Archaeology. *American Antiquity* 71:261–282.

Hudson, Corey M., 2008. Walter Taylor and the History of American Archaeology. *Journal of Anthropological Archaeology* 27:192–200.

Hughes, R. E., T. E. Berres, D. M. Moore, and K. B. Farnsworth, 1998. Revision of Hopewellian Trading Patterns in Midwestern North America Based on Mineralogical Sourcing. *Geoarchaeology* 13:709–729.

Hull, Kathleen L., 2007. The Sierra Nevada: Archaeology in the Range of Light. In *California Prehistory: Colonization, Culture, and Complexity*, edited by Terry L. Jones and Kathryn A. Klar, pp. 177–189. Lanham, MD: AltaMira Press.

Hull, Kathleen L., 2012. A Land of Many People: Population Dynamics as Context and Catalyst. In *Contemporary Issues in California Archaeology*, edited by T. L. Jones and J. E. Perry, pp. 73–92. Walnut Creek, CA: Left Coast Press.

Hunter, Doug, 2011. *The Race to the New World: Christopher Columbus, John Cabot, and a Lost History of Discovery*. New York: Palgrave Macmillan.

Huxley, Julian, 1942. *Evolution: The Modern Synthesis*. London: Allen and Unwin.

Ingold, Tim, 2000. *The Perception of the Environment: Essays in Livelihood, Dwelling and Skill*. London: Routledge.

Irwin, John C., 2005. Revisiting the Dorset Soapstone Quarry in Fleur de Lys, Newfoundland. In *Contributions to the Study of the Dorset Palaeo-Eskimos*, edited by Patricia D. Sutherland, pp. 121–132. Archaeology Paper 167. Quebec: Canadian Museum of Civilization.

Irwin, John C., 2010. Dorset Palaeoeskimo Quarrying Techniques and the Production of Little Pots at Fleur de Lys, Newfoundland. In *Ancient Mines and Quarries: A Trans-Atlantic Perspective*, edited by Margaret Brewer-LaPorta, Adrian Burke, and David Field, pp. 56–66. Oxford: Oxbow.

Jackson, H. Edwin, 1991. The Trade Fair in Hunter-Gatherer Interaction: The Role of Intersocietal Trade in the Evolution of Poverty Point Culture. In *Between Bands and States*, edited by Susan A. Gregg, pp. 265–286. Center for Archaeological Investigations, Occasional Paper 9. Carbondale: Southern Illinois University.

Jackson, H. Edwin, and Susan L. Scott, 2001. Archaic Faunal Utilization in the Louisiana Bottomlands. *Southeastern Archaeology* 20:187–196.

Jackson, T. L., 1991. Pounding Acorn: Women's Production as Social and Economic Focus. In *Engendering Archaeology: Women and Prehistory*, edited by J. M. Gero and M. W. Conkey, pp. 301–325. Oxford: Basil Blackwell.

Janetski, Joel C., 1998. *Archaeology of Clear Creek Canyon*. Provo, UT: Museum of Peoples and Cultures, Brigham Young University.

Janetski, Joel C., 2008. The Enigmatic Fremont. In *The Great Basin: People and Place in Ancient Times*, edited by C. S. Fowler and D. D. Fowler, pp. 104–115. Santa Fe, NM: School for Advanced Research Press.

Jantz, R. L., P. Marr, and C. A. Jantz, 2010. Body Proportions in Recent Native Americans: Colonization History versus Ecogeographical Patterns. In *Human Variation in the Americas: The Integration of Archaeology and Biological Anthropology*, edited by Benjamin M. Auerbach, pp. 292–310. Center for Archaeological Investigations, Occasional Paper 38. Carbondale: Southern Illinois University.

Jefferies, Richard W., 2004. Regional Scale Interaction Networks and the Emergence of Cultural Complexity along the Northern Margins of the Southeast. In *Signs of Power: The Rise of Cultural Complexity in the Southeast*, edited by Jon L. Gibson and Philip J. Carr, pp. 71–85. Tuscaloosa: University of Alabama Press.

Jefferson, Thomas, 1787. *Notes of the State of Virginia*. London: Stockdale.

Jefferson, Thomas, 1999. *Notes on the State of Virginia*, edited by F. C. Shuffelton. New York: Penguin.

Jelsma, Johan, 2006. Three Social Status Groups at Port au Choix: Maritime Archaic Mortuary Practices and Social Structure. In *The Archaic of the Far Northeast*, edited by David Sanger and M. A. P. Renouf, pp. 83–103. Orono: University of Maine Press.

Jenkins, D. L., L. G. Davis, T. W. Stafford, Jr., et al., 2012. Clovis Age Western Stemmed Projectile Points and Human Coprolites at the Paisley Caves. *Science* 337:223–228.

Jennings, Jesse D., 1957. *Danger Cave*. Anthropological Papers 27. Salt Lake City: University of Utah Press.

Johnson, Ann Mary, and Alfred E. Johnson, 1998. The Plains Woodland. In *Archaeology on the Great Plains*, edited by W. R. Wood, pp. 201–234. Lawrence: University Press of Kansas.

Johnson, Craig M., 1998. The Coalescent Tradition. In *Archaeology on the Great Plains*, edited by W. R. Wood, pp. 308–344. Lawrence: University Press of Kansas.

Johnson, Jay K., 1997. Stone Tools, Politics, and the Eighteenth-Century Chickasaw in Northeast Mississippi. *American Antiquity* 62:215–230.

Johnson, Jay K., and Samuel O. Brookes, 1989. Benton Points, Turkey Tails and Cache Blades: Middle Archaic Exchange in the Southeast. *Southeastern Archaeology* 8:134–145.

Johnson, John R., Brian M. Kemp, Cara Monroe, and Joseph G. Lorenz, 2012. A Land of Diversity: Genetic Insights into Ancestral Origins. In *Contemporary Issues in California Archaeology*, edited by T. L. Jones and J. E. Perry, pp. 49–72. Walnut Creek, CA: Left Coast Press.

Jones, Philip M., 1922. *Mound Excavations near Stockton*. University of California Publications in American Archaeology and Ethnology 20(7). Berkeley: University of California.

Jones, Ruthe Blalock, 2004. The Bread Dance: A Shawnee Ceremony of Thanks and Renewal. In *Hero, Hawk, and Open Hand: American Indian Art of the Ancient Midwest and South*, edited by R. F. Townsend and R. V. Sharp, pp. 252–259. Chicago: Art Institute of Chicago.

Jordan, Aaron, and Richard K. Talbot, 2002. The Escalante Drainage Project: Big Flat and Escalante Canyon Areas 2001. *Museum of Peoples and Cultures Technical Series 01–13*. Provo, UT: Brigham Young University.

Jordan, Richard H., and Richard A. Knecht, 1988. Archaeological Research on Western Kodiak Island, Alaska: The Development of Koniag Culture. In *Late Prehistoric Development of Alaska's Native People*, edited by R. D. Shaw, R. K. Harritt, and D. E. Dumond, pp. 185–214. New York: Plenum.

Keegan, William F., 2007. *Taino Indian Myth and Practice: The Arrival of the Stranger King*. Gainesville: University Press of Florida.

Keegan, William F., Corinne L. Hofman, and Reniel Rodriguez Ramos (eds.), 2013. *The Oxford Handbook of Caribbean Archaeology*. Oxford: Oxford University Press.

Kehoe, Alice B., 1998. *Land of Prehistory: A Critical History of American Archaeology*. London: Routledge.

Kehoe, Alice B., 2000. *Shamans and Religion: An Anthropological Exploration into Critical Thinking*. Third edition. Long Grove, IL: Waveland.

Kehoe, Alice B., 2005. Wind Jewels and Paddling Gods: The Mississippian Southeast in the Postclassic Mesoamerican World. In *Gulf Coast Archaeology: The Southeastern United States and Mexico*, edited by N. M. White, pp. 260–280. Gainesville: University Press of Florida.

Kehoe, Alice B., 2006. *The Ghost Dance: Ethnohistory and Revitalization*. Long Grove, IL: Waveland.

Kelley, J. Charles, 1971. Archaeology of the Northern Frontier: Zacatecas and Durango. In *Handbook of Middle American Indians, vol. XI: Archaeology of Northern Mesoamerica, Part II*, edited by G. F. Ekholm and I. Bernal, pp. 763–801. Austin: University of Texas Press.

Kelley, J. Charles, and Ellen A. Kelley, 2001. Alta Vista de Chalchihuites. In *Archaeology of Ancient Mexico and Central America: An Encyclopedia*, edited by S. T. Evans and D. L. Webster, pp. 16–17. New York: Garland.

Kelly, John E., 1990a. The Emergence of Mississippian Culture in the American Bottom Region. In *The Mississippian Emergence*, edited by B. D. Smith, pp. 113–152. Washington, DC: Smithsonian Institution Press.

Kelly, John E., 1990b. Range Site Community Patterns and the Mississippian Emergence. In *The Mississippian Emergence*, edited by B. D. Smith, pp. 67–112. Washington, DC: Smithsonian Institution Press.

Kelly, Robert L., 1995. *The Foraging Spectrum: Diversity in Hunter-Gatherer Lifeways*. Washington, DC: Smithsonian Institution Press.

Kelly, Robert L., and Lawrence C. Todd, 1988. Coming into the Country: Early Paleoindian Hunting and Mobility. *American Antiquity* 53:231–244.

Kelly, Robert L., Todd A. Surovell, Bryan N. Shuman, and Geoffey M. Smith, 2013. A Continuous Climatic Impact on Holocene Human Population in the Rocky Mountains. *Proceedings of the National Academy of Sciences* 110:443–447.

Kelso, William M., 2006. *Jamestown: The Buried Truth*. Charlottesville: University of Virginia Press.

Kemp, Brian M., and Theodore G. Schurr, 2010. Ancient and Modern Genetic Variation in the Americas. In *Human Variation in the Americas: The Integration of Archaeology and Biological Anthropology*, edited by Benjamin M. Auerbach, pp. 12–50. Center for Archaeological Investigations, Occasional Paper 38. Carbondale: Southern Illinois University.

Kennett, Douglas J., 2012. Archaic-Period Foragers and Farmers in Mesoamerica. In *The Oxford Handbook of Mesoamerican Archaeology*, edited by D. L. Nichols and C. A. Pool, pp. 141–150. Oxford: Oxford University Press.

Kerber, Jordan E. (ed.), 2006. *Cross-Cultural Collaboration: Native Peoples and Archaeology in the Northeastern United States*. Lincoln: University of Nebraska Press.

Kidder, Tristram R., 2004. Plazas as Architecture: An Example from the Raffman Site, Northeast Louisiana. *American Antiquity* 69(3):514–532.

Kidder, Tristram R., 2006. Climate Change and the Archaic to Woodland Transition (3000–2500 cal BP) in the Mississippi River Basin. *American Antiquity* 71:195–231.

Kidder, Tristram R., 2011. Transforming Hunter-Gatherer History at Poverty Point. In *Hunter-Gatherer Archaeology as Historical Process*, edited by Kenneth E. Sassaman and Donald H. Holley, Jr., pp. 95–119. Tucson: University of Arizona Press.

Kilby, David J., 2013. Clovis Caches: Current Perspectives and Future Directions. In *Paleoamerican Odyssey*, edited by Kelly Graf, Ted Goebel, and Michael Waters, pp. 257–272. College Station: Center for the Study of the First Americans, Texas A&M University.

King, Adam, 2003. *Etowah: The Political History of a Chiefdom Capital*. Tuscaloosa: University of Alabama Press.

King, Chester, 1978. Protohistoric and Historic Archaeology. In *Handbook of North American Indians, California*, vol. VIII, edited by R. F. Heizer, pp. 58–68. Washington, DC: Smithsonian Institution.

Kirk, Ruth, 2015. *Ozette: Excavating a Makah Whaling Village*. Seattle: University of Washington Press.

Kirk, Ruth, and Richard D. Daugherty, 2007. *Archaeology in Washington*. Seattle: University of Washington Press.

Knight, Vernon J., Jr., 1986. The Institutional Organization of Mississippian Religion. *American Antiquity* 51:675–687.

Knight, Vernon J., Jr., and Vincas P. Steponaitis, 2011. A Redefinition of the Hemphill Style in Mississippian Art. In *Visualizing the Sacred: Cosmic Visions, Regionalism, and the Art of the Mississippian World*, edited by G. E. Lankford, F. K. Reilly, III, and J. F. Garber, pp. 201–239. Austin: University of Texas Press.

Kohler, Timothy A., and Kathryn K. Turner, 2006. Raiding for Women in the Pre-Hispanic Northern Pueblo Southwest? *Current Anthropology* 47(6):1035–1045.

Koldehoff, Brad, and John A. Walthall, 2004. Settling In: Hunter-Gatherer Mobility during the Pleistocene–Holocene Transition in the Central Mississippi Valley. In *Aboriginal Ritual and Economy in the Eastern Woodlands: Essays in Honor of Howard Dalton Winters*, edited by A.-M. Cantwell, L. A. Conrad, and J. E. Reyman, pp. 49–72. Scientific Papers 30. Springfield: Illinois State Museum.

Kopytoff, Igor, 1986. The Cultural Biography of Things: Commoditization as Process. In *The Social Life of Things: Commodities in Cultural Perspective*, edited by A. Appadurai, pp. 64–91. Cambridge, UK: Cambridge University Press.

Kornfeld, Marcel, George C. Frison, and Mary Lou Larson, 2010. *Prehistoric Hunter-Gatherers of the High Plains and Rockies*. Third edition. London: Routledge.

Kozuch, Laura, 2002. Olivella Beads from Spiro and the Plains. *American Antiquity* 67:697–709.

Krause, Richard A., 2016. An Explication of Arikara Culture History. *Plains Anthropologist* 61(240):308–335.

Krech, Shepard, III, 2000. *The Ecological Indian: Myth and History*. New York: W. W. Norton.

Kroeber, Alfred L., 1907. *The Religion of the Indians of California*. University of California Publications in American Archaeology and Ethnology 4(6). Berkeley: University of California Press.

Kroeber, Alfred L., 1922. *Elements of Culture in Native California*. University of California Publications in American Archaeology and Ethnology 13. Berkeley: University of California Press.

Kroeber, Alfred L., 1939. *Cultural and Natural Areas of Native North America*. Berkeley: University of California Press.

Kroeber, Alfred L., 1976. *Handbook of the Indians of California*. New York: Dover Publications.

Kroeber, Theodora, 1961. *Ishi in Two Worlds: A Biography of the Last Wild Indian in North America*. Berkeley: University of California Press.

Kuckelman, Kristin A., 2008. An Agent-Centered Case Study of the Depopulation of Sand Canyon Pueblo. In *The Social Construction of Communities: Agency, Structure, and Identity in the Prehispanic Southwest*, edited by M. D. Varien and J. M. Potter, pp. 109–121. Walnut Creek, CA: AltaMira Press.

Kunz, Keneva, and Gisli Sigurosson, 2008. *The Vinland Sagas*. New York: Penguin.

Kuttruff, Carl, 1997. Louisiana's Lost Heritage: The Monte Sano Mounds. *Louisiana Archaeological Conservancy* 7(2):4–6.

Kuwanwisiwma, Leigh J., 2004. Yupköyvi: The Hopi Story of Chaco Canyon. In *In Search of Chaco: New Approaches to an Archaeological Enigma*, edited by D. G. Noble, pp. 41–47. Santa Fe, NM: School for Advanced Research Press.

La Flesche, Francis, 1921. *The Osage Tribe: Rite of the Chiefs; Sayings of the Ancient Men*. Thirty-Sixth Annual Report of the Bureau of American Ethnology. Washington, DC: Bureau of American Ethnology.

Lamb, S., 1958. Linguistic Prehistory in the Great Basin. *International Journal of American Linguistics* 24:95–100.

Lankford, George E., 2004. Some Southwestern Influences in the Southeastern Ceremonial Complex. *Arkansas Archeologist* 45:1–25.

Lankford, George E., 2007. *Reachable Stars Patterns in the Ethnoastronomy of Eastern North America*. Tuscaloosa: University of Alabama Press.

Lapham, Increase A., 2001. *The Antiquities of Wisconsin as Surveyed and Described*. Madison: University of Wisconsin Press.

Larsen, Clark S., and Robert L. Kelly, 1995. *Bioarchaeology of the Stillwater Marsh: Prehistoric Human Adaptation in the Western Great Basin*. Anthropological Papers of the American Museum of Natural History 77. New York: American Museum of Natural History.

Larsen, Helga, and Froelich Rainey, 1948. *Ipiutak and the Arctic Whale-Hunting Culture*. Anthropological Papers 42. New York: American Museum of Natural History.

Larson, Mary Lou, 1997. Housepits and Mobile Hunter-Gatherers: A Consideration of the Wyoming Evidence. *Plains Anthropologist* 42:353–369.

Larson, Mary Lou, Marcel Kornfeld, and George A. Frison, 2009. *Hell Gap: A Stratified Paleoindian Campsite at the Edge of the Rockies*. Salt Lake City: University of Utah Press.

Lawres, Nathan R., 2017. Materializing Ontology in Monumental Form: Engaging the Ontological in the Okeechobee Basin, Florida. *Journal of Anthropological Research* 73:647–694.

Leacock, Eleanor, 1954. *The Montagnais "Hunting Territory" and the Fur Trade*. Menasha, MD: American Anthropological Association.

LeBlanc, Steven A., 1999. *Prehistoric Warfare in the American Southwest*. Salt Lake City: University of Utah Press.

LeBlanc, Steven A., 2004. *Painted by a Distant Hand: Mimbres Pottery from the American Southwest*. Cambridge, MA: Peabody Museum Press, Harvard University.

Lee, Aubra L., 2010. Troyville and the Baytown Period. In *Archaeology of Louisiana*, edited by M. A. Rees, pp. 135–156. Baton Rouge: Louisiana State University Press.

Lehmer, Donald J., 1954. *Archeological Investigations in the Oahe Dam Area, South Dakota, 1950–51*. Bureau of American Ethnology Bulletin 158. Washington, DC: Smithsonian Institution.

Lekson, Stephen H., 1999. *The Chaco Meridian: Centers of Political Power in the Ancient Southwest*. Walnut Canyon, CA: AltaMira Press.

Lekson, Stephen H., 2002. War in the Southwest, War in the World. *American Antiquity* 67:607–624.

Lekson, Stephen H., 2005. Chaco and Paquimé: Complexity, History, Landscape. In *North American Archaeology*, edited by T. R. Pauketat and D. D. Loren, pp. 235–272. Malden, MA: Blackwell Press.

Lekson, Stephen H. (ed.), 2006. *The Archaeology of Chaco Canyon: An Eleventh-Century Pueblo Regional Center*. Santa Fe, NM: School for Advanced Research Press.

Lekson, Stephen H. (ed.), 2007. *The Architecture of Chaco Canyon, New Mexico*. Salt Lake City: University of Utah Press.

Lekson, Stephen H., 2008. *A History of the Ancient Southwest*. Santa Fe, NM: School for Advanced Research Press.

Lekson, Stephen H., Thomas C. Windes, John R. Stein, and W. James Judge, 1988. The Chaco Canyon Community. *Scientific American* 259:100–109.

Lepper, Bradley T., 1998. Ancient Astronomers of the Ohio Valley. *Timeline* 15:2–11.

Lepper, Bradley T., 2005. *Ohio Archaeology: An Illustrated Chronicle of Ohio's Ancient American Indian Cultures*. Wilmington, OH: Orange Frazer Press.

Lewis, Thomas M. N., and Madeline Kneberg, 1946. *Hiwassee Island: An Archaeological Account of Four Tennessee Indian Peoples*. Knoxville: University of Tennessee Press.

Lightfoot, Kent G., 1995. Culture Contact Studies: Refining the Relationship between Prehistoric and Historical Archaeology. *American Antiquity* 60:199–217.

Lightfoot, Kent G., and Edward M. Luby, 2012. Mound Building by California Hunter-Gatherers. In *The Oxford Handbook of North American Archaeology*, edited by T. R. Pauketat, pp. 212–223. Oxford: Oxford University Press.

Lightfoot, Kent G., Antoinette Martinez, and Ann M. Schiff, 1998. Daily Practice and Material Culture in Pluralistic Social Settings: An Archaeological Study of Culture Change and Persistence from Fort Ross, California. *American Antiquity* 63(2):199–222.

Lipe, William D., 2006a. The Mesa Verde Region: Chaco's Northern Neighbor. In *In Search of Chaco: New Approaches to an Archaeological Enigma*, edited by D. G. Noble, pp. 105–115. Santa Fe, NM: School of American Research Press.

Lipe, William D., 2006b. Notes from the North. In *The Archaeology of Chaco Canyon: An Eleventh-Century Pueblo Regional Center*, edited by S. H. Lekson, pp. 261–314. Santa Fe, NM: School of American Research Press.

Lipo, Carl P., Robert C. Dunnell, Michael J. O'Brien, Veronica Harper, and John Dudgeon, 2012. Beveled Projectile Points and Ballistics Technology. *American Antiquity* 77:774–778.

Lister, Robert H., and Florence C. Lister, 1987. *Aztec Ruins on the Animas: Excavated, Preserved, and Interpreted*. Tucson: Western National Parks Association.

Little, Keith J., 1999. The Role of Late Woodland Interactions in the Emergence of Etowah. *Southeastern Archaeology* 18(1):45–56.

Longacre, W. A., 1970. *Archaeology as Anthropology: A Case Study*. Anthropological Papers 17. Tucson: University of Arizona.

Longacre, William A., and James M. Skibo (eds.), 1994. *Kalinga Ethnoarchaeology: Expanding Archaeological Method and Theory*. Washington, DC: Smithsonian Institution Press.

Lorant, Stefan, 1946. *The New World: The First Pictures of America*. New York: Deull, Sloan, and Pierce.

Loren, Diana DiPaolo, 2000. The Intersections of Colonial Policy and Colonial Practice: Creolization on the Eighteenth-Century Louisiana/ Texas Frontier. *Historical Archaeology* 34(3):85–98.

Loren, Diana DiPaolo, 2007. *In Contact: Bodies and Spaces in the Sixteenth- and Seventeenth-Century Eastern Woodlands*. Lanham, MD: AltaMira Press.

Losey, Robert, 2010. Animism as a Means of Exploring Archaeological Fishing Structures on Willipa Bay, Washington, USA. *Cambridge Archaeological Journal* 20:17–32.

Louisiana Division of Archaeology, 2014. Poverty Point. In *Discover Archaeology*. Louisiana Department of Culture, Recreation and Tourism. www.crt.state.la.us/cultural-development/archaeology/ discover-archaeology/poverty-point.

Lounsbury, Floyd G., 1978. Iroquoian Languages. In *Handbook of North American Indians, Northeast*, vol. XV, edited by B. G. Trigger, pp. 334–343. Washington, DC: Smithsonian Institution.

Love, Michael, 2012. The Development of Complex Societies in Formative-Period Pacific Guatemala and Chiapas. In *The Oxford Handbook of Mesoamerican Archaeology*, edited by D. L. Nichols and C. A. Pool, pp. 200–214. Oxford: Oxford University Press.

Lowell, Susan, W. Ross Humphreys, and Robin Stancliff, 1999. *The Many Faces of Mata Ortiz*. Tucson: Treasure Chest Books.

Lowie, Robert H., 1917. *Culture and Ethnology*. New York: Douglas C. McMurtrie.

Lyman, R. Lee, and Michael J. O'Brien, 1999. Americanist Stratigraphic Excavation and the Measurement of Culture Change. *Journal of Archaeological Method and Theory* 6:55–108.

Lyon, Edwin A., 1996. *A New Deal for Southeastern Archaeology*. Tuscaloosa: University of Alabama Press.

Lyons, Patrick D., 2003. *Ancestral Hopi Migrations*. Anthropological Papers of the University of Arizona 68. Tucson: University of Arizona Press.

MacDonald, G. F., 1968. *Debert: A Palaeo-Indian Site in Central Nova Scotia*. Anthropology Papers of the National Museum of Canada 16. Ottawa: National Museum of Canada.

MacDonald, George F., 1983. *Haida Monumental Art: Villages of the Queen Charlotte Islands*. Vancouver and Seattle: UBC Press and University of Washington Press.

McAnany, Patricia A., 2012. Terminal Classic Maya Heterodoxy and Shrine Vernacularism in the Sibun Valley, Belize. *Cambridge Archaeological Journal* 22(1):115–134.

McCaffrey, Moira, 2006. Archaic Period Occupation in Subarctic Quebec: A Review of the Evidence. In *The Archaic of the Far Northeast*, edited by D. Sanger and M. A. P. Renouf, pp. 161–190. Orono: University of Maine Press.

McCleary, Timothy P., 1997. *The Stars We Know: Crow Indian Astronomy and Lifeways.* Prospect Heights: Waveland Press.

McGahey, Samuel O., 1996. Paleoindian and Early Archaic Data from Mississippi. In *The Paleoindian and Early Archaic Southeast*, edited by David G. Anderson and Kenneth E. Sassaman, pp. 354–384. Tuscaloosa: University of Alabama Press.

McGhee, Robert, 2008. Aboriginalism and the Problem of Indigenous Archaeology. *American Antiquity* 73:579–597.

McGhee, Robert, 2009. When and Why did the Inuit Move to the Eastern Arctic? In *The Northern World AD 900–1400*, edited by Herbert Maschner, Owen Mason, and Robert McGhee, pp. 155–163. Salt Lake City: University of Utah Press.

McGhee, Robert, and James A. Tuck, 1975. *An Archaic Sequence from the Strait of Belle Isle, Labrador.* Mercury Series, Archaeological Survey of Canada Paper 34. Ottawa: National Museum of Man.

McGovern, Thomas H., 1994. Management for Extinction in Norse Greenland. In *Historical Ecology: Cultural Knowledge and Changing Landscapes*, edited by C. A. Crumley, pp. 127–154. Santa Fe, NM: School of American Research.

McGovern, Thomas H., Orri Vésteinsson, Adolf Fridriksson, Mike Church, Ian Lawson, Ian A. Simpson, Arni Einarsson, Andy Dugmore, Gordon Cook, Sophia Perdikaris, Kevin J. Edwards, Amanda M. Thomson, W. Paul Adderley, Anthony Newton, Gavin Lucas, Ragnar Edvardsson, Oscar Aldred, and Elaine Dunbar, 2007. Landscapes of Settlement in Northern Iceland: Historical Ecology of Human Impact and Climate Fluctuation on the Millennial Scale. *American Anthropologist* 109:27–51. DOI:10.1525/AA.2007.109.1.27.

McGregor, John C., 1943. Burial of an Early American Magician. *Proceedings of the American Philosophical Society* 86(2):270–298.

McGuire, Kelly R., and William R. Hildebrandt, 2005. Re-Thinking Great Basin Foragers: Prestige Hunting and Costly Signaling during the Middle Archaic Period. *American Antiquity* 70:695–712.

McGuire, Randall H., 1992. *A Marxist Archaeology.* New York: Academic Press.

McGuire, Randall H., 2008. *Archaeology as Political Action.* Berkeley: University of California Press.

McGuire, Randall H., 2011. Pueblo Religion and the Mesoamerican Connection. In *Religious Transformation in the Late Pre-Hispanic Pueblo World*, edited by D. M. Glowacki and S. Van Keuren, pp. 23–49. Tucson: University of Arizona Press.

McGuire, Randall H., 2012. Mesoamerica and the Southwest/Northwest. In *The Oxford Handbook of Mesoamerican Archaeology*, edited by D. L. Nichols and C. A. Pool, pp. 513–524. Oxford: Oxford University Press.

McGuire, Randall H., and Maria Elisa Villalpando C., 2007. The Hohokam and Mesoamerica. In *The Hohokam Millennium*, edited by S. K. Fish and P. R. Fish, pp. 56–63. Santa Fe, NM: School for Advanced Research Press.

McGuire, Randall H., Maria Elisa Villalpando C., Victoria D. Vargas, and Emiliano Gallaga M., 1999. Cerro de Trincheras and the Casas Grandes World. In *The Casas Grandes World*, edited by C. F. Schaafsma and C. L. Riley, pp. 134–146. Salt Lake City: University of Utah Press.

Madsen, D. B., 1989. *Exploring the Fremont*. Salt Lake City: University of Utah Press.

Madsen, David B., 1999. The Nature of Great Basin Environmental Change during the Pleistocene/Holocene Transition and its Possible Impact on Human Populations. In *Models for the Millennium: Great Basin Archaeology Today*, edited by C. Beck, pp. 75–82. Salt Lake City: University of Utah Press.

Madsen, David B., and Steven R. Simms, 1988. The Fremont Complex: A Behavioral Perspective. *Journal of World Prehistory* 12:255–336.

Mahar, Ginessa J., 2013. Archaeological Geophysics on St. Catherines Island: Beyond Prospection. In *Life among the Tides: Recent Archaeology on the Georgia Bight*, edited by D. H. Thomas and V. D. Thompson. New York: American Museum of Natural History.

Malville, J. McKim (ed.), 2004. *Chimney Rock: The Ultimate Chacoan Outlier*. Lanham, MD: Lexington Books.

Malville, J. McKim, 2008. *A Guide to Prehistoric Astronomy in the Southwest* (revised and updated). Boulder: Johnson Books.

Mandryx, Carole A. S., Heiner Josenhans, Daryl W. Fedje, and Rolf W. Mathewes, 2001. Late Quaternary Paleoenvironments of Northwestern North America: Implications for Inland versus Coastal Migration Routes. *Quaternary Science Reviews* 20:301–314.

Marquardt, William H., 1985. Complexity and Scale in the Study of Fisher-Gatherer-Hunters: An Example from the Eastern United States. In *Prehistoric Hunter-Gatherers: The Emergence of Cultural Complexity*, edited by T. D. Price and J. A. Brown, pp. 59–98. Orlando: Academic Press.

Marquardt, William H., 2010. Shell Mounds in the Southeast: Middens, Monuments, Temple Mounds, Rings, or Works? *American Antiquity* 75:551–570.

Marquardt, William H., 2014. Tracking the Calusa: A Retrospective. *Southeastern Archaeology* 33:1–24.

Marriott, Alice, 1948. *María: The Potter of San Ildefonso*. Albuquerque: University of New Mexico Press.

Marshall, James A., 1996. Towards a Definition of the Ohio Hopewell Core and Periphery Utilizing the Geometric Earthworks. In *A View from the Core: A Synthesis of Ohio Hopewell Archaeology*, edited by Paul J. Pacheco, pp. 210–220. Columbus: Ohio Archaeological Council.

Martin, Paul S., 1973. The Discovery of America. *Science* 179:969–974.

Maschner, Herbert D. G., 2012a. Archaeology of the North Pacific. In *The Oxford Handbook of North American Archaeology*, edited by T. R. Pauketat, pp. 135–145. Oxford: Oxford University Press.

Maschner, Herbert D. G., 2012b. Archaeology of the Northwest Coast. In *The Oxford Handbook of North American Archaeology*, edited by T. R. Pauketat, pp. 160–172. Oxford: Oxford University Press.

Mason, Ronald J., 1981. *Great Lakes Archaeology*. New York: Academic Press.

Mason, Ronald J., 2009. Bear's Journey and the Study of Ritual in Archaeology: Some Comments on Howey and Shea's Midewiwin Paper. *American Antiquity* 74:189–192.

Mason, Ronald J., and Carol Irwin, 1960. An Eden-Scottsbluff Burial in Northeastern Wisconsin. *American Antiquity* 26:43–57.

Mathiowetz, Michael D., 2011. The Diurnal Path of the Sun: Ideology and Interregional Interaction in Ancient Northwest Mesoamerica and the American Southwest. Ph.D. dissertation, Department of Anthropology, University of California: Riverside.

Mauss, Marcel, 1990. *The Gift: The Form and Reason for Exchange in Archaic Societies*. Translated by W. D. Halls. New York: W. W. Norton.

Maxwell, M., 1976. Introduction. In *Eastern Arctic Prehistory: Paleoeskimo Problems*, edited by M. Maxwell, pp. 1–5. Memoirs of the Society for American Archaeology 31. Washington, DC: Society for American Archaeology.

Means, Bernard K., 2007. *Circular Villages of the Monongahela Tradition*. Tuscaloosa: University of Alabama Press.

Means, Bernard K., 2012. Villagers and Farmers of the Middle and Upper Ohio River Valley, 11th to 17th Centuries AD: The Fort Ancient and Monongahela Traditions. In *The Oxford Handbook of North American Archaeology*, edited by T. R. Pauketat, pp. 297–309. Oxford: Oxford University Press.

Means, Bernard K. (ed.), 2013. *Shovel Ready: Archaeology and Roosevelt's New Deal for America*. Tuscaloosa: University of Alabama Press.

Meeks, Scott C., and David G. Anderson, 2012. Evaluating the Effect of the Younger Dryas on Human Population Histories in the Southeastern United States. In *Hunter-Gatherer Behavior: Human Response during the Younger Dryas*, edited by Meten I. Erin, pp. 111–138. New York: Routledge.

Meinholz, Norman M., and Steven R. Kuehn, 1996. *The Deadman Slough Site: Late Paleoindian/Early Archaic and Woodland Occupations along the Flambeau River, Price County, Wisconsin*. Archaeological Research Series 4. Madison: Museum Archaeology Program, State Historical Society of Wisconsin.

Meltzer, David J., 1989a. Was Stone Exchanged among Eastern North America Paleoindians? In *Eastern Paleoindian Lithic Resource Use*, edited by C. Ellis and J. Lothrop, pp. 11–39. Boulder: Westview Press.

Meltzer, David J., 1989b. Why Don't We Know When the First People Came to North America? *American Antiquity* 54:471–490.

Meltzer, David J., 2006. *Folsom: New Archaeological Investigations of a Classic Paleoindian Bison Kill*. Berkeley: University of California Press.

Meltzer, David J., 2009. *First Peoples in a New World: Colonizing Ice Age America*. Berkeley: University of California Press.

Meltzer, David J., Donald K. Grayson, Gerardo Ardila, Alex W. Barker, Dena F. Dincauze, C. Vance Haynes, Francisco Mena, Lautaro Nunez, and Dennis J. Stanford, 1997. On the Pleistocene Antiquity of Monte Verde, Southern Chile. *American Antiquity* 62:659–663.

Mensforth, Robert P., 2001. Warfare and Trophy Taking in the Archaic. In *Archaic Transitions in Ohio and Kentucky Prehistory*, edited by Olaf H. Prufer, Sara E. Peddle, and Richard S. Meindl, pp. 110–138. Kent, OH: Kent State University Press.

Mensforth, Robert P., 2007. Human Trophy Taking in Eastern North America during the Archaic Period: The Relationship to Warfare and Social Complexity. In *The Taking and Displaying of Human Body Parts as Trophies by Amerindians*, edited by R. J. Chacon and D. H. Dye, pp. 222–277. New York: Springer.

Merrill, William L., Robert J. Hard, Jonathan B. Mabry, Gayle J. Fritz, Karen R. Adams, John R. Roney, and A. C. MacWilliams, 2009. The Diffusion of Maize to the Southwestern United States and its Impact. *PNAS* 106(50):21019–21026.

Metcalf, Duncan, 2008. Range Creek Canyon. In *The Great Basin: People and Place in Ancient Times*, edited by C. S. Fowler and D. D. Fowler, pp. 116–123. Santa Fe, NM: School for Advanced Research Press.

Milanich, Jerald T., 1994. *Archaeology of Precolumbian Florida*. Gainesville: University Press of Florida.

Milanich, Jerald T., Ann S. Cordell, Vernon J. Knight, Jr., Timothy A. Kohler, and Brenda J. Sigler-Lavelle, 1997[1984]. *Archaeology of Northern Florida, AD 200–900: The McKeithen Weeden Island Culture*. Gainesville: University Press of Florida.

Miller, Lee, 2000. *Roanoke: Solving the Mystery of the Lost Colony*. New York: Penguin.

Mills, Barbara J., 2004. The Establishment and Defeat of Hierarchy: Inalienable Possessions and the History of Collective Prestige Structures in the Pueblo Southwest. *American Anthropologist* 106(2):238–251.

Mills, Barbara J., 2008. Remembering while Forgetting: Depositional Practices and Social Memory at Chaco. In *Memory Work: Archaeologies of Material Practices*, edited by B. J. Mills and W. H. Walker, pp. 81–108. Santa Fe, NM: School for Advanced Research Press.

Mills, Barbara J., and Patricia L. Crown (eds.), 1995. *Ceramic Production in the American Southwest*. Tucson: University of Arizona Press.

Milner, George R., 2004. *The Mound Builders: Ancient Peoples of Eastern North America*. London: Thames and Hudson.

Milner, George R., and Richard W. Jefferies, 1998. The Read Archaic Shell Midden in Kentucky. *Southeastern Archaeology* 17:119–132.

Milner, George R., George Chaplin, and Emily Zavodny, 2013. Conflict and Societal Change in Late Prehistoric Eastern North America. *Evolutionary Anthropology* 22:96–102.

Minnis, Paul E., and Michael E. Whalen (eds.), 2015. *Ancient Paquimé and the Casas Grandes World*. Tucson: University of Arizona Press.

Mitchell, Mark D., 2012. The Origins and Development of Farming Villages in the Northern Great Plains. In *The Oxford Handbook of North American Archaeology*, edited by T. R. Pauketat, pp. 359–372. Oxford: Oxford University Press.

Moore, Christopher R., and Victor D. Thompson, 2012. Animism and Green River Persistent Places: A Dwelling Perspective of the Shell Mound Archaic. *Journal of Social Archaeology* 12:264–284.

Moore, Clarence B., 1901. Certain Aboriginal Remains of the Northwest Florida Coast. *Journal of the Academy of Natural Sciences of Philadelphia*, 2nd ser., 11. Reprinted as *The Northwest Florida Expeditions of Clarence Bloomfield Moore*, edited by David S. Brose and Nancy Marie White. Tuscaloosa: University of Alabama Press (1999).

Moore, Clarence B., 1903. Certain Aboriginal Mounds of the Florida Central West-Coast. *Journal of the Academy of Natural Sciences of Philadelphia*, 2nd ser., 12. Reprinted as *The West and Central Florida Expeditions of Clarence Bloomfield Moore*, edited by Jeffrey M. Mitchem. Tuscaloosa: University of Alabama Press (1999).

Moore, Clarence B., 1913. Some Aboriginal Sites in Louisiana and in Arkansas. *Journal of the Academy of Natural Sciences of Philadelphia*, 2nd ser., 16. Reprinted as *The Louisiana and Arkansas Expeditions of Clarence Bloomfield Moore*, edited by Richard A. Weinstein, David B. Kelley, and Joe W. Saunders. Tuscaloosa: University of Alabama Press (2003).

Morey, Darcy F., 2010. *Dogs: Domestication and Development of a Social Bond*. Cambridge, UK: Cambridge University Press.

Morgan, Christopher, 2010. Numic Expansion in the Southern Sierra Nevada. *Journal of California and Great Basin Anthropology* 30:157–174.

Morgan, Christopher, 2012. Modeling Modes of Hunter-Gatherer Food Storage. *American Antiquity* 77:714–736.

Morgan, Lewis Henry, 1962[1851]. *League of the Iroquois*. New York: Corinth Books and Citadel Press.

Morrow, Juliet E., 2017. After Anzick: Reconciling New Genomic Data and Models with the Archaeological Evidence for Peopling of the Americas. *Quaternary International* 444:1–3.

Morrow, Juliet E., and Toby A. Morrow, 1999. Geographic Variation in Fluted Projectile Points: A Hemispheric Perspective. *American Antiquity* 64:215–230.

Morse, Dan F., 1997. *Sloan: A Paleoindian Dalton Cemetery in Arkansas*. Washington, DC: Smithsonian Institution Press.

Morse, Dan F., and Phyllis A. Morse, 1983. *Archaeology of the Central Mississippi Valley*. New York: Academic Press.

Moss, Madonna L., 2011. *Northwest Coast: Archaeology as Deep History*. Washington, DC: Society for American Archaeology Press.

Muir, John, 1911. *My First Summer in the Sierra*. Boston: Houghton Mifflin.

Mulloy, William T., 1954. The McKean Site in Northeastern Wyoming. *Southwestern Journal of Anthropology* 10:432–460.

Munson, Marit K., 2011. Iconography, Space, and Practice: Rio Grande Rock Art, AD 1150–1600. In *Religious Transformation in the Late Pre-Hispanic Pueblo World*, edited by D. M. Glowacki and S. Van Keuren, pp. 109–129. Tucson: University of Arizona Press.

Murie, James R., 1981. *Ceremonies of the Pawnee, Part I: The Skiri*. Smithsonian Contributions to Anthropology 27. Washington, DC: Smithsonian Institution Press.

Murray, Wendi Field, and Fern E. Swenson, 2016. Situational Sedentism: Post-Contact Arikara Settlement as Social Process in the Middle Missouri, North Dakota. *Plains Anthropologist* 61(240):336–360.

Nabokov, Peter, 2006. *Where the Lightning Strikes: The Lives of American Indian Sacred Places*. New York: Penguin.

Nassaney, Michael S., 2001. The Historical-Processual Development of Late Woodland Societies. In *The Archaeology of Traditions: History and Agency before and after Columbus*, edited by T. R. Pauketat, pp. 157–173. Gainesville: University Press of Florida.

Neihardt, John G., 2008. *Black Elk Speaks: Being the Life Story of a Holy Man of the Oglala Sioux*. Albany: State University of New York Press.

Nelson, Ben A., 1997. Chronology and Stratigraphy at La Quemada, Zacatecas, Mexico. *Journal of Field Archaeology* 24:85–109.

Nelson, Ben A., 2006. Mesoamerican Objects and Symbols in Chaco Canyon Contexts. In *The Archaeology of Chaco Canyon: An 11th Century Pueblo Regional Center*, edited by S. H. Lekson, pp. 339–371. Santa Fe, NM: School for Advanced Research Press.

Nelson, Ben A., J. Andrew Darling, and David A. Kice, 1992. Mortuary Practices and the Social Order at La Quemada, Zacatecas, Mexico. *Latin American Antiquity* 3(4):298–315.

Nelson, Margaret C., 2010. Mimbres, the Mystery? In *Mimbres Lives and Landscapes*, edited by M. C. Nelson and M. Hegmon, pp. 99–103. Santa Fe, NM: School for Advanced Research Press.

Nelson, Margaret C., and Michelle Hegmon (eds.), 2010. *Mimbres Lives and Landscapes*. Santa Fe, NM: School for Advanced Research Press.

Neusius, Sarah W., and G. Timothy Gross, 2014. *Seeking our Past: An Introduction to North American Archaeology*. Oxford: Oxford University Press.

Newsome, Elizabeth A., and Kelley Hays-Gilpin, 2011. Spectatorship and Performance in Mural Painting, 1250–1500: Visuality and Social Integration. In *Religious Transformation in the Late Pre-Hispanic Pueblo World*, edited by D. M. Glowacki and S. Van Keuren. Tucson: University of Arizona Press.

Niblack, Albert P., 1890. The Coast Indians of Southern Alaska and Northern British Columbia. In *Annual Report of the Board of Regents of the Smithsonian Institution*, pp. 225–386. Washington, DC: Government Printing Office.

Nicholas, George P. (ed.), 2010. *Being and Becoming Indigenous Archaeologists*. Walnut Creek, CA: Left Coast Press.

Nicholls, R. J., R. S. Tol, and A. T. Vafeidis, 2005. *Global Estimates of the Impact of a Collapse of the West Antarctic Ice Sheet: An Application of FUND*. FNY-78, Research Unit Sustainability and Global Change. Hamburg: Hamburg University and Centre for Maritime and Atmospheric Science.

Nichols, Deborah L., and Christopher A. Pool (eds.), 2012. *The Oxford Handbook of Mesoamerican Archaeology*. Oxford: Oxford University Press.

Noble, David Grant (ed.), 2004. *In Search of Chaco: New Approaches to an Archaeological Enigma*. Santa Fe, NM: School for Advanced Research Press.

Noble, David Grant (ed.), 2006. *The Mesa Verde World: Explorations in Ancestral Pueblo Archaeology*. Santa Fe, NM: School for American Research Press.

O'Brien, Patricia J., 1969. The Chronological Position of the Cambered Jar at Cahokia and its Implications. *American Antiquity* 34(4):411–416.

O'Brien, Patricia J., 1989. Cahokia: Political Capital of the "Ramey" State? *North American Archaeologist* 10:275–292.

O'Brien, Patricia J., 1993. Steed-Kisker: The Western Periphery of the Mississippian Tradition. *Midcontinental Journal of Archaeology* 18(1):281–283.

O'Donoughue, Jason M., 2017. *Water from Stone: Archaeology and Conservation at Florida's Springs*. Gainesville: University Press of Florida.

O'Shea, John M., and Guy A. Meadows, 2009. Evidence for Early Hunters beneath the Great Lakes. *Proceedings of the National Academy of Sciences* 106:10120–10123.

O'Shea, John M., Ashley K. Lemke, Elizabeth P. Sonnenburg, Robert G. Reynolds, and Brian D. Abbott, 2014. A 9,000-year-old Caribou Hunting Structure beneath Lake Huron. *Proceedings of the National Academy of Sciences* 111:6911–6915.

Oetelaar, Gerald A., 2012. The Archaeological Imprint of Oral Traditions on the Landscape of Northern Plains Hunter-Gatherers. In *The Oxford Handbook of North American Archaeology*, edited by T. R. Pauketat, pp. 336–346. Oxford: Oxford University Press.

Oetelaar, Gerald A., 2014. Better Homes and Pastures: Human Agency and the Construction of Place in Communal Bison Hunting on the Northern Plains. *Plains Anthropologist* 59(229):9–37.

Olson, Keith W., 1973. The GI Bill and Higher Education: Success and Surprise. *American Quarterly* 25:596–610.

Ortman, Scott G., 2000. Conceptual Metaphor in the Archaeological Record: Methods and an Example from the American Southwest. *American Antiquity* 65(4):613–645.

Ortman, Scott G., 2006. Ancient Pottery of the Mesa Verde Country: How Ancestral Pueblo People Made it, Used it, and Thought about it.

In *The Mesa Verde World*, edited by D. G. Noble, pp. 101–110. Santa Fe, NM: School of American Research Press.

Ortmann, Anthony L., 2010. Placing Poverty Point Mounds in their Temporal Context. *American Antiquity* 75:657–678.

Ortmann, Anthony L., and Tristram R. Kidder, 2013. Building Mound A at Poverty Point: Monumental Public Architecture, Ritual Practice, and Implications for Hunter-Gatherer Complexity. *Geoarchaeology* 28:66–86.

Ortner, Sherry B., 1984. Theory in Anthropology since the Sixties. *Comparative Studies in Society and History* 26:126–166.

Osborn, Alan J., 1977. Strandloopers, Mermaids, and Other Fairy Tales: Ecological Determinants of Coastal Adaptations: The Peruvian Case. In *For Theory Building in Archaeology*, edited by Lewis Binford, pp. 157–205. New York: Academic Press.

Osborn, Alan J., 2014. Eye of the Needle: Cold Stress, Clothing, and Sewing Technology during the Younger Dryas Cold Event in North America. *American Antiquity* 79:45–68.

Parker, Arthur C., 1989. *Seneca Myths and Folk Tales*. Lincoln: University of Nebraska Press.

Pauketat, Timothy R., 2004. *Ancient Cahokia and the Mississippians*. Cambridge, UK: Cambridge University Press.

Pauketat, Timothy R., 2007. *Chiefdoms and Other Archaeological Delusions*. Walnut Creek, CA: AltaMira Press.

Pauketat, Timothy R., 2009. *Cahokia: Ancient America's Great City on the Mississippi*. New York: Viking-Penguin Press.

Pauketat, Timothy R., 2013. *An Archaeology of the Cosmos: Rethinking Agency and Religion in Ancient America*. London: Routledge.

Pauketat, Timothy R., and Susan M. Alt, 2018. Water and Shells in Bodies and Pots: Mississippian Rhizome, Cahokian Poiesis. In *Relational Identities and Other-than-Human Agency in Archaeology*, edited by E. Harrison-Buck and J. Hendon. Boulder: University of Colorado Press.

Pauketat, Timothy R., Robert F. Boszhardt, and Danielle M. Benden, 2015. Trempealeau Entanglements: An Ancient Colony's Causes and Effects. *American Antiquity* 80:260–289.

Perego, U. A., A. Achilli, N. Angerhofer et al., 2009. Distinctive Paleo-Indian Migration Routes from Beringia Marked by Two Rare mtDNA Haplogroups. *Current Biology* 19:1–8.

Perez, Ventura R., Ben A. Nelson, and Deborah L. Martin, 2008. Veneration or Violence? A Study of Variations in Human Bone Modification at La Quemada. In *Social Violence in the Prehispanic American Southwest*, edited by D. L. Nichols and P. L. Crown, pp. 123–142. Tucson: University of Arizona Press.

Perry, Jennifer E., 2012. Diversity, Exchange, and Complexity in the California Bight. In *The Oxford Handbook of North American Archaeology*, edited by T. R. Pauketat, pp. 224–234. Oxford: Oxford University Press.

Philbrick, Nathaniel, 2006. *Mayflower: A Story of Courage, Community, and War*. New York: Penguin.

Phillips, Philip, James A. Ford, and James B. Griffin, 1951. *Archaeological Survey in the Lower Mississippi Alluvial Valley, 1940–1947*. Papers of the Peabody Museum of Archaeology and Ethnology 25. Cambridge, MA: Peabody Museum of Archaeology and Ethnology, Harvard University.

Pilling, Arnold R., 1978. Yurok. In *Handbook of North American Indians, California*, vol. VIII, edited by R. F. Heizer, pp. 137–154. Washington, DC: Smithsonian Institution.

Pinson, A. O., 2011. The Clovis Occupation of the Dietz Site (35LK1529), Lake County, Oregon, and its Bearing on the Adaptive Diversity of Clovis Foragers. *American Antiquity* 76:285–313.

Piperno, Dolores R., and Bruce D. Smith, 2012. The Origins of Food Production in Mesoamerica. In *The Oxford Handbook of Mesoamerican Archaeology*, edited by D. L. Nichols and C. A. Pool, pp. 151–168. Oxford: Oxford University Press.

Pitulko, Vladimir, Alexei N. Tikhonov, Elena Y. Pavlova, Pavel A. Nikolskiy, Konstantin E. Kuper, and Roman N. Polozov, 2016. Early Human Presence in the Arctic: Evidence from 45,000-year-old Mammoth Remains. *Science* 351:260–263.

Plog, Stephen, 1997. *Ancient Peoples of the American Southwest*. London: Thames and Hudson.

Plog, Stephen, 2003. Exploring the Ubiquitous through the Unusual: Color Symbolism in Pueblo Black-on-White Pottery. *American Antiquity* 68(4):665–695.

Pluckhahn, Thomas J., 2003. *Kolomoki: Settlement, Ceremony, and Status in the Deep South, AD 350–750*. Tuscaloosa: University of Alabama Press.

Pluckhahn, Thomas J., Victor D. Thompson, and Brent R. Weisman, 2010. Toward a New View of History and Process at Crystal River (8CI1). *Southeastern Archaeology* 29(1):164–181.

Pollard, Helen Perlstein, 2012. The Tarascan Empire: Postclassic Social Complexity in Western Mexico. In *The Oxford Handbook of Mesoamerican Archaeology*, edited by D. L. Nichols and C. A. Pool, pp. 434–448. Oxford: Oxford University Press.

Pool, Christopher A., 2012. The Formation of Complex Societies in Mesoamerica. In *The Oxford Handbook of Mesoamerican Archaeology*, edited by D. L. Nichols and C. A. Pool, pp. 169–187. Oxford: Oxford University Press.

Potter, Ben A., Joshua D. Reuther, Vance T. Holliday, Charles E. Holmes, D. Shane Miller, and Nicholas Schmuck, 2017. Early Colonization of Beringia and Northern North America: Chronology, Routes, and Adaptive Strategies. *Quaternary International* 444:36–55.

Potter, James M., and Thomas D. Yoder, 2008. Space, Houses, and Bodies: Identity Construction and Destruction in an Early Pueblo

Community. In *The Social Construction of Communities: Agency, Structure, and Identity in the Prehispanic Southwest*, edited by M. D. Varien and J. M. Potter, pp. 21–40. Lanham, MD: AltaMira Press.

Powell, Mary Lucas, 1988. *Status and Health in Prehistory: A Case Study of the Moundville Chiefdom*. Tuscaloosa: University of Alabama Press.

Powell, Shirley, and Francis E. Smiley, 2002. *Prehistoric Culture Change on the Colorado Plateau: Ten Thousand Years on Black Mesa*. Tucson: University of Arizona Press.

Powers, Robert P., 2005. *The Peopling of Bandelier: New Insights from the Archaeology of the Pajarito Plateau*. Santa Fe, NM: School for American Research Press.

Prentiss, Anna Marie, 2012. The Winter Village Pattern on the Plateau of Northwestern North America. In *The Oxford Handbook of North American Archaeology*, edited by Timothy R. Pauketat, pp. 173–184. Oxford: Oxford University Press.

Prentiss, Anna Marie, and Ian Kuijt, 2012. *People of the Middle Fraser Canyon: An Archaeological History*. Vancouver: University of British Columbia Press.

Prentiss, Anna Marie, Guy Cross, Thomas A. Foor, Mathew Hogan, Dirk Markle, and David S. Clarke, 2008. Evolution of a Late Prehistoric Winter Village on the Interior Plateau of British Columbia: Geophysical Investigations, Radiocarbon Dating, and Spatial Analysis of the Bridge River Site. *American Antiquity* 73:59–82.

Prentiss, William C., and James C. Chatters, 2003. Cultural Diversification and Decimation in the Prehistoric Record. *Current Anthropology* 44:33–58.

Preucel, Robert W. (ed.), 2002. *Archaeologies of the Pueblo Revolt: Identity, Meaning and Renewal in the Pueblo World*. Albuquerque: University of New Mexico Press.

Quinn, R. L., B. D. Tucker, and J. Krigbaum, 2008. Diet and Mobility in Middle Archaic Florida: Stable Isotopic and Faunal Data from the Harris Creek Archaeological Site (8vo24), Tick Island. *Journal of Archaeological Science* 35(8):2346–2356.

Raab, L. Mark, 1997. The Southern Channel Islands during the Middle Holocene: Trends in Maritime Cultural Evolution. In *Archaeology of the California Coast during the Middle Holocene*, edited by J. M. Erlandson and M. A. Glassow, pp. 23–34. Los Angeles: Institute of Archaeology, University of California.

Rafferty, Sean M., 2016. Smoking Pipes of Eastern North America. In *Perspectives on the Archaeology of Pipes, Tobacco and Other Smoke Plants in the Ancient Americas*, edited by E. A. Bollwerk and S. Tushingham, pp. 13–26. New York: Springer.

Raghavan, Maanasa, Michael DeGiorgio, Anders Albrechtsen, et al., 2014. The Genetic Prehistory of the New World Arctic. *Science* 345. DOI:10.1126/science.1255832.

Ragir, Sonia, 1972. *The Early Horizon in Central California Prehistory*. Contributions to University of California Archaeological Research Facility 15. Berkeley: University of California.

Ramenofsky, Ann F., 1987. *Vectors of Death: The Archaeology of European Contact*. Albuquerque: University of New Mexico Press.

Ramsden, Peter, and Lisa K. Rankin, 2013. Thule Radiocarbon Chronology and its Implications for Early Inuit–European Interaction in Labrador. In *Exploring Atlantic Transitions: Archaeologies of Transience and Permanence in New Found Lands*, edited by Peter E. Pope and Shannon Lewis-Simpson, pp. 299–309. Woodbridge, UK: Boydell Press.

Randall, Asa R., 2013. The Chronology and History of Mount Taylor Period (ca. 7400–4600 cal BP) Shell Sites on the Middle St. Johns River, Florida. *Southeastern Archaeology* 32:193–217.

Randall, Asa R., 2015. *Constructing Histories: Archaic Freshwater Shell Mounds and Social Landscapes of the St. Johns River, Florida*. Gainesville: University Press of Florida.

Randall, Asa R., and Kenneth E. Sassaman, 2010. Emergent Complexities during the Archaic in Northeast Florida. In *Ancient Complexities: New Perspectives in Precolumbian North America*, edited by Susan Alt, pp. 8–31. Salt Lake City: University of Utah Press.

Rankin, Lisa K., 2008. Un-caching Hunter-Gatherer Culture in Labrador: From Daily Life to Long-Term History. *North Atlantic Archaeology* 1:117–156.

Rasmussen, Morten, Yingrui Li, Stinus Lingren et al., 2010. Ancient Human Genome Sequence of an Extinct Paleo-Eskimo. *Nature* 463:757–763.

Rasmussen, Morten, Martin Sikora, Anders Albrechtsen et al., 2015. The Ancestry and Affiliations of Kennewick Man. *Nature* 523:455–458.

Ravesloot, John C., 1988. *Mortuary Practices and Social Differentiation at Casas Grandes, Chihuahua, Mexico*. Anthropological Papers of the Univerisity of Arizona 49. Tucson: University of Arizona.

Ravesloot, John C., and Patricia M. Spoerl, 1989. The Role of Warfare in the Development of Status Hierarchies at Casas Grandes, Chihuahua, Mexico. In *Cultures in Conflict: Current Archaeological Approaches*, edited by D. C. Tkaczuk and B. C. Vivian, pp. 130–137. Calgary: University of Calgary Archaeological Association.

Redman, Charles L., 1999. *Human Impact on Ancient Environments*. Tucson: University of Arizona Press.

Reher, Charles A., and George C. Frison, 1980. *The Vore Site, 48CK302, A Stratified Buffalo Jump in the Wyoming Black Hills*. Memoir 16. Lincoln, NE: Plains Anthropologist.

Reilly, F. Kent, III, 2004. People of Earth, People of Sky: Visualizing the Sacred in Native American Art of the Mississippian Period. In *Hero, Hawk, and Open Hand: American Indian Art of the Ancient Midwest and South*, edited by R. F. Townsend and R. V. Sharp, pp. 125–137. New Haven, CT: Art Institute of Chicago and Yale University Press.

Reilly, F. Kent, III, 2012. Mesoamerican Religious Beliefs: The Practices and Practitioners. In *The Oxford Handbook of Mesoamerican Archaeology*, edited by D. L. Nichols and C. A. Pool, pp. 764–775. Oxford: Oxford University Press.

Renfrew, Colin, 1985. *The Archaeology of Cult: The Sanctuary at Phylakopi*. London: Thames and Hudson.

Renouf, M. A. P., 2005. Phillip's Garden West: A Newfoundland Groswater Variant. In *Contributions to the Study of the Dorset Palaeo-Eskimos*, edited by P. D. Sutherland, pp. 57–80. Mercury Series, Archaeology Paper 167. Gatineau, Quebec: Canadian Museum of Civilization.

Renouf, M. A. P., 2011. On the Headland: Dorset Seal Harvesting at Phillip's Garden, Port au Choix. In *The Cultural Landscape of Port au Choix*, edited by M. A. P. Renouf, pp. 131–160. New York: Springer.

Renouf, M. A. P., Trevor Bell, and Michael Teal, 2000. Making Contact: Recent Indians and Palaeoeskimos on the Island of Newfoundland. In *Identities and Cultural Contacts in the Arctic*, edited by Martin Appelt, Joel Berglund, and Hans-Christian Gulløv, pp. 106–119. Copenhagen: Danish Polar Center.

Rice, Glen E., 1998. War and Water: An Ecological Perspective on Hohokam Irrigation. *Kiva* 63(3):263–301.

Rice, Glen E., 2000. Hohokam and Salado Segmentary Organization: The Evidence from the Roosevelt Platform Mound Study. In *Salado*, edited by J. S. Dean, pp. 143–166. Albuquerque: University of New Mexico Press.

Rice, Prudence M., 1987. *Pottery Analysis: A Sourcebook*. Chicago: University of Chicago Press.

Richter, Bryce, 2008. Ancient Mounds Make UW-Madison a Unique Landscape. *University of Wisconsin-Madison News* (November 10, www.news.wisc.edu/15910).

Ritchie, William A., 1969. *The Archaeology of New York State* (revised edition). Garden City, NY: Natural History Press.

Ritzenthaler, Robert, 1972. The Pope Site: A Scottsbluff Cremation in Waupaca County. *Wisconsin Archaeologist* 53:15–19.

Robb, John E., and Timothy R. Pauketat, 2013. From Moments to Millennia: Theorizing Scale and Change in Human History. In *Big Histories, Human Lives: Tackling Problems of Scale in Archaeology*, edited by J. E. Robb and T. R. Pauketat, pp. 1–34. Santa Fe, NM: School for Advanced Research Press.

Robinson, Brian S., 2006. Burial Ritual, Technology, and Cultural Landscape in the Far Northeast: 8600–3700 BP. In *The Archaic of the Far Northeast*, edited by David Sanger and M. A. P. Renouf, pp. 341–381. Orono: University of Maine Press.

Robinson, Brian S., Jennifer C. Ort, William A. Eldridge, Adrian L. Burke, and Bernard G. Pelletier, 2009. Paleoindian Aggregation and Social Context at Bull Brook. *American Antiquity* 74:424–447.

Rodning, Christopher B., 2014. Cherokee Towns and Calumet Ceremonialism in Eastern North America. *American Antiquity* 79:425–443.

Rolingson, Martha Ann, 1998. *Toltec Mounds and Plum Bayou Culture: Mound D Excavations*. Arkansas Archeological Survey Research Series 54. Fayetteville: Arkansas Archeological Survey.

Romain, William F., 2000. *Mysteries of the Hopewell: Astronomers, Geometers, and Magicians of the Eastern Woodlands*. Akron, OH: University of Akron Press.

Romain, William F., 2009. *Shamans of the Lost World: A Cognitive Approach to the Prehistoric Religion of the Ohio Hopewell*. Lanham, MD: AltaMira Press.

Romain, William F., 2015. Moonwatchers of Cahokia. In *Medieval Mississippians: The Cahokian World*, edited by T. R. Pauketat and S. M. Alt, pp. 33–42. Santa Fe, NM: School for Advanced Research Press.

Romain, William F., 2016. The Milky Way Paths of Souls and Adena-Hopewell Earthworks. Paper presented at the 81st Annual Meeting of the Society for American Archaeology, Orlando, Florida.

Romain, William F., and Norm L. Davis, 2013. Astronomy and Geometry at Poverty Point. Website article, Louisiana Archaeological Society. www.laarchaeology.org/articles.html, accessed October 21, 2013.

Roper, Donna C., and Elizabeth P. Pauls, 2005. What, Where, and When is an Earthlodge? In *Plains Earthlodges: Ethnographic and Archaeological Perspectives*, edited by D. C. Roper and E. P. Pauls, pp. 1–31. Tuscaloosa: University of Alabama Press.

Rosenthal, Jeffrey S., Gregory G. White, and Mark Q. Sutton, 2007. The Central Valley: A View from the Catbird's Seat. In *California Prehistory: Colonization, Culture, and Complexity*, edited by Terry L. Jones and Kathryn A. Klar, pp. 147–163. Lanham, MD: AltaMira Press.

Ruddiman, William F., 2005. *Plows, Plagues and Petroleum: How Humans Took Control of Climate*. Princeton: Princeton University Press.

Russo, Michael, 1996. Southeastern Preceramic Archaic Ceremonial Mounds. In *Archaeology of the Mid-Holocene Southeast*, edited by Kenneth E. Sassaman and David G. Anderson, pp. 259–287. Gainesville: University Press of Florida.

Russo, Michael, 2004. Measuring Shell Rings for Social Inequality. In *Signs of Power: The Rise of Cultural Complexity in the Southeast*, edited by Jon L. Gibson and Philip J. Carr, pp. 26–70. Tuscaloosa: University of Alabama Press.

Russo, Michael, and Gregory Heide, 2001. Shell Rings of the Southeast US. *Antiquity* 75(289):491–492.

Rust, Horatio N., 1905. The Obsidian Blades of California. *American Anthropologist* new ser. 7:688–695.

Salwen, Bert, 1978. Indians of Southern New England and Long Island: Early Period. In *Handbook of North American Indians, vol. XV: Northeast*, edited by B. G. Trigger, pp. 160–176. Washington, DC: Smithsonian Institution.

Sanger, David, 1973. *Cow Point: An Archaic Cemetery in New Brunswick.* Mercury Series, Archaeological Survey of Canada Paper 12. Ottawa: National Museum of Man.

Sanger, David, and M. A. P. Renouf (eds.), 2006. *The Archaic of the Far Northeast.* Orono: University of Maine Press.

Sanger, Matthew C., 2015. Life in the Round: Shell Rings of the Georgia Bight. Ph.D. dissertation, Department of Anthropology, Columbia University, New York.

Sanger, Matthew C., and David Hurst Thomas, 2010. The Two Rings of St. Catherines Island: Some Preliminary Results from the St. Catherines and McQueen Shell Rings. In *Trend, Tradition, and Turmoil: What Happened to the Southeastern Archaic?*, edited by David Hurst Thomas and Matthew C. Sanger, pp. 45–69. Anthropological Papers 93. New York: American Museum of Natural History.

Sassaman, Kenneth E., 1993. *Early Pottery in the Southeast: Tradition and Innovation in Cooking Technology.* Tuscaloosa: University of Alabama Press.

Sassaman, Kenneth E., 2005. Poverty Point as Structure, Event, Process. *Journal of Archaeological Method and Theory* 12:335–364.

Sassaman, Kenneth E., 2006. *People of the Shoals: Stallings Culture of the Savannah River Valley.* Gainesville: University Press of Florida.

Sassaman, Kenneth E., 2010. *The Eastern Archaic: Historicized.* Lanham, MD: AltaMira Press.

Sassaman, Kenneth E., 2012. Drowning out the Past: How Humans Historicize Water as Water Historicizes Them. In *Big Histories, Human Lives: Tackling Problems of Scale in Archaeology*, edited by John E. Robb and Timothy R. Pauketat, pp. 171–191. Santa Fe, NM: School for Advanced Research.

Sassaman, Kenneth E., and Michael Heckenberger, 2004. Crossing the Symbolic Rubicon in the Southeast. In *Signs of Power: The Rise of Cultural Complexity in the Southeast*, edited by Jon L. Gibson and Philip J. Carr, pp. 214–233. Tuscaloosa: University of Alabama Press.

Sassaman, Kenneth E., and Asa R. Randall, 2012. Shell Mounds of the Middle St. Johns Basin, Northeast Florida. In *Early New World Monumentality*, edited by Richard L. Burger and Robert M. Rosenswig, pp. 53–72. Gainesville: University Press of Florida.

Sassaman, Kenneth E., and Wictoria Rudolphi, 2001. Communities of Practice in the Early Ceramic Traditions of the American Southeast. *Journal of Anthropological Research* 57:407–425.

Sassaman, Kenneth E., I. Randolph Daniel, Jr., and Christopher R. Moore, 2002. *G. S. Lewis-East: Early and Late Archaic Occupations along the Savannah River, Aiken County, South Carolina.* Occasional Papers of the Savannah River Archaeological Research Program,

South Carolina Institute of Archaeology and Anthropology. Columbia: University of South Carolina.

Sauer, Carl Ortwin, and Donald D. Brand, 1932. *Aztatlan: Prehistoric Mexican Frontier on the Pacific Coast.* Berkeley: University of California Press.

Saunders, Joe W., 2004. Are we Fixing to Make the Same Mistake Again? In *Signs of Power: The Rise of Cultural Complexity in the Southeast*, edited by Jon L. Gibson and Philip J. Carr, pp. 146–161. Tuscaloosa: University of Alabama Press.

Saunders, Joe W., 2010. Middle Archaic and Watson Brake. In *Archaeology of Louisiana*, edited by Mark A. Rees, pp. 63–76. Baton Rouge: Louisiana State University Press.

Saunders, Joe W., Rolfe D. Mandel, Roger T. Saucier et al., 1997. A Mound Complex in Louisiana at 5400–5000 Years before the Present. *Science* 277:1796–1799.

Saunders, Joe W., Thurman Allen, Dennis LaBatt, Reca Jones, and David Griffing, 2001. An Assessment of the Antiquity of the Lower Jackson Mound. *Southeastern Archaeology* 20:67–77.

Saunders, Rebecca, 1994. The Case for Archaic Mound Sites in Southeastern Louisiana. *Southeastern Archaeology* 13:118–134.

Saunders, Rebecca, 2004. Stratigraphy at the Rollins Shell Ring Site: Implications for Ring Function. *Florida Anthropologist* 57(4):249–270.

Schaafsma, Polly, 2008. Shamans, Shields, and Stories on Stone. In *The Great Basin: People and Place in Ancient Times*, edited by C. S. Fowler and D. D. Fowler, pp. 144–151. Santa Fe, NM: School for Advanced Research Press.

Scheiber, Laura L., 1993. Prehistoric Domestic Architecture on the Northwestern High Plains: A Temporal Analysis of Stone Circles in Wyoming. Unpublished Master's thesis, Department of Anthropology, University of Wyoming.

Scheiber, Laura L., and Judson Byrd Finley, 2011. Mobility as Resistance: Colonialism among Nomadic Hunter-Gatherers in the American West. In *Hunter-Gatherer Archaeology as Historical Process*, edited by Kenneth E. Sassaman and Donald H. Holly, Jr., pp. 167–183. Tucson: University of Arizona Press.

Scheiber, Laura L., and Judson Byrd Finley, 2012. Situating (Proto) History on the Northwestern Plains and Rocky Mountains. In *The Oxford Handbook of North American Archaeology*, edited by Timothy R. Pauketat, pp. 347–358. Oxford: Oxford University Press.

Schmidt, Christopher W., Rachel Lockhart Sharkey, Christopher Newman, Anna Serrano, Melissa Zolnierz, Jeffrey A. Plunkett, and Anne Bader, 2010. Skeletal Evidence of Cultural Variation: Mutilation Related to Warfare and Mortuary Treatment. In *Human Variation in the Americas: The Integration of Archaeology and Biological Anthropology*, edited by Benjamin M. Auerbach, pp. 215–237. Center for Archaeological Investigations, Occasional Paper 38. Carbondale: Southern Illinois University.

Schwadron, Margo, 2010. Prehistoric Landscapes of Complexity: Archaic and Woodland Period Shell Works, Shell Rings, and Tree Islands of the Everglades, South Florida. In *Trend, Tradition, and Turmoil: What Happened to the Southeastern Archaic?*, edited by David Hurst Thomas and Matthew C. Sanger, pp. 113–148. Anthropological Papers 93. New York: American Museum of Natural History.

Schwitalla, A. W., and Terry L. Jones, 2012. A Land of Many Seasons: Bioarchaeology and the Medieval Climatic Anomaly Hypothesis in Central California. In *Contemporary Issues in California Archaeology*, edited by T. L. Jones and J. E. Perry, pp. 93–114. Walnut Creek, CA: Left Coast Press.

Sears, William H., 1982. *Fort Center: An Archaeological Site in the Lake Okeechobee Basin*. Gainesville: University Press of Florida.

Seeman, Mark F., 1979. *The Hopewell Interaction Sphere: The Evidence for Interregional Trade and Structural Complexity*. Indianapolis: Indiana Historical Society.

Seeman, Mark F., 1994. Intercluster Lithic Patterning at Nobles Pond: A Case for "Disembedded" Procurement among Early Paleoindian Societies. *American Antiquity* 59:273–288.

Seeman, Mark F., 1995. When Words are not Enough: Hopewell Interregionalism and the Use of Material Symbols in the GE Mound. In *Native American Interaction: Multiscalar Analyses and Interpretations in the Eastern Woodlands*, edited by Michael S. Nassaney and Kenneth E. Sassaman, pp. 122–143. Knoxville: University of Tennessee Press.

Seeman, Mark F., and James L. Branch, 2006. The Mounded Landscapes of Ohio: Hopewell Patterns and Placements. In *Recreating Hopewell*, edited by D. K. Charles and J. E. Buikstra, pp. 106–121. Gainesville: University of Florida Press.

Service, Elman R., 1962. *Primitive Social Organization: An Evolutionary Perspective*. New York: Random House.

Shafer, Harry J., 1999. The Mimbres Classic and Postclassic: A Case for Discontinuity. In *The Casas Grandes World*, edited by C. F. Schaafsma and C. L. Riley, pp. 121–133. Salt Lake City: University of Utah Press.

Shafer, Harry J., 2003. *Mimbres Archaeology at the NAN Ranch Ruin*. Albuquerque: University of New Mexico Press.

Sharer, Robert J., 2003. Tikal and the Copan Dynastic Founding. In *Tikal: Dynasties, Foreigners, and Affairs of State: Advancing Maya Archaeology*, edited by J. A. Sabloff, pp. 319–353. Santa Fe, NM: School of American Research.

Shaul, David L., 2014. *A Prehistory of Western North America: The Impact of Uto-Aztecan Languages*. Albuquerque: University of New Mexico Press.

Sherwood, Sarah C., Boyce N. Driscoll, Asa R. Randall, and Scott C. Meeks, 2004. Chronology and Stratigraphy at Dust Cave, Alabama. *American Antiquity* 69:533–554.

Shipley, William F., 1978. Native Languages of California. In *Handbook of North American Indians, vol. VIII: California*, edited by R. F. Heizer, pp. 80–90. Washington, DC: Smithsonian Institution.

Shott, Michael J., 2005. Representativity of the Midwestern Paleoindian Site Sample. *North American Archaeologist* 25:189–212.

Silliman, Stephen W., 2004. *Lost Laborers in Colonial California: Native Americans and the Archaeology of Rancho Petaluma.* Tucson: University of Arizona Press.

Silliman, Stephen W., 2005. Culture Contact or Colonialism? Challenges in the Archaeology of Native North America. *American Antiquity* 70(1):55–74.

Silliman, Stephen W. (ed.), 2008. *Collaborating at the Trowel's Edge: Teaching and Learning in Indigenous Archaeology.* Tucson: University of Arizona Press.

Silliman, Stephen W., 2012. Colonial Reduction and Cultural Production in Native Northern California. In *The Oxford Handbook of North American Archaeology*, edited by T. R. Pauketat, pp. 235–245. Oxford: Oxford University Press.

Simmons, William S., 1978. Narragansett. In *Handbook of North American Indians, Northeast*, vol. XV, edited by B. G. Trigger, pp. 190–197. Washington, DC: Smithsonian Institution.

Simms, Steven R., 2008. *Ancient Peoples of the Great Basin and the Colorado Plateau.* Walnut Creek, CA: Left Coast Press.

Simms, Steven R., James F. O'Connell, and Kevin T. Jones, 2014. Some Thoughts on Evolution, Ecology, and Archaeology in the Great Basin. In *Archaeology in the Great Basin and Southwest: Papers in Honor of Don D. Fowler*, edited by Nancy J. Parezo and Joel T. Janetski, pp. 177–188. Salt Lake City: University of Utah Press.

Simon, Mary L., 2017. Reevaluating the Evidence for Middle Woodland Maize from the Holding Site. *American Antiquity* 82(1):140–150.

Skibo, J. M., and Michael B. Schiffer, 1995. The Clay Cooking Pot: An Exploration of Women's Technology. In *Expanding Archaeology*, edited by James M. Skibo, Axel Nielsen, and William Walker, pp. 80–91. Salt Lake City: University of Utah Press.

Smith, Bruce D., 1987. Independent Domestication of Indigenous Seed-Bearing Plants in Eastern North America. In *Emergent Horticultural Economies of the Eastern Woodlands*, edited by William F. Keegan, pp. 3–47. Center for Archaeological Investigations, Occasional Paper 7. Carbondale: Southern Illinois University.

Smith, Bruce D., 1992. *Rivers of Change: Essays on Early Agriculture in Eastern North America.* Washington, DC: Smithsonian Institution Press.

Smith, Bruce D., 2001. Low-Level Food Production. *Journal of Archaeological Research* 9:1–43.

Smith, Bruce D., and Richard A. Yarnell, 2009. Initial Formation of an Indigenous Crop Complex in Eastern North America at 3800 BP. *Proceedings of the National Academy of Sciences USA* 106:6561–6566.

Smith, Maria O., 1996. Biocultural Inquiry into Archaic Period Populations of the Southeast: Trauma and Occupational Stress. In *Archaeology of the Mid-Holocene Southeast*, edited by Kenneth E. Sassaman and David G. Anderson, pp. 134–154. Gainesville: University Press of Florida.

Snead, James E., 2008. History, Place, and Social Power in the Galisteo Basin, AD 1250–1325. In *The Social Construction of Communities: Agency, Structure, and Identity in the Prehispanic Southwest*, edited by M. D. Varien and J. M. Potter, pp. 155–167. Walnut Creek, CA: AltaMira Press.

Snow, Dean R., 1978. Late Prehistory of the East Coast. In *Handbook of North American Indians, vol. XV: Northeast*, edited by B. G. Trigger, pp. 58–69. Washington, DC: Smithsonian Institution.

Snow, Dean R., 1995. Migration in Prehistory: The Northern Iroquoian Case. *American Antiquity* 60:59–79.

Snow, Dean R., 2010. *Archaeology of Native North America*. New York: Prentice-Hall.

Sofaer, Anna, 2008. *Chaco Astronomy: An Ancient American Cosmology*. Santa Fe, NM: Ocean Tree Books.

Spielmann, Katherine A., 2002. Feasting, Craft Specialization, and the Ritual Mode of Production in Small-Scale Societies. *American Anthropologist* 104:195–207.

Spielmann, Katherine A., 2013. The Materiality of Spiritual Engagement: Art and the End of the Ohio Hopewell. *World Art* 3:141–162. http://dx.doi.org/10.1080/21500894.2013.773936.

Squier, Ephraim G., and Edwin H. Davis, 1848. *Ancient Monuments of the Mississippi Valley*. Smithsonian Contributions to Knowledge 1. Washington, DC: Smithsonian Institution.

Stahle, David W., Malcolm K. Cleaveland, Dennis B. Blanton, Matthew D. Therrell, and David A. Gay, 1998. The Lost Colony and Jamestown Droughts. *Science* 280:564–567.

Stanford, D. J., 1978. The Jones-Miller Site: An Example of Hell Gap Bison Procurement Strategy. In *Bison Procurement and Utilization: A Symposium*, edited by L. Davis and M. Wilson, pp. 90–97. Memoir 14. Lincoln, NE: Plains Anthropologist.

Stanford, Dennis J., and Bruce A. Bradley, 2012. *Across Atlantic Ice: The Origin of America's Clovis Culture*. Berkeley: University of California Press.

Stanislawski, M. B., 1978. If Pots Were Mortal. In *Explorations in Ethnoarchaeology*, edited by R. A. Gould, pp. 201–228. Albuquerque: University of New Mexico Press.

Stein, John R., Dabney Ford, and Richard Friedman, 2003. Reconstructing Pueblo Bonito. In *Pueblo Bonito: Center of the Chacoan World*, edited by J. E. Neitzel, pp. 33–60. Washington, DC: Smithsonian Institution Press.

Steinacher, Terry L., and Gayle F. Carlson, 1998. The Central Plains Tradition. In *Archaeology on the Great Plains*, edited by W. R. Wood, pp. 235–268. Lawrence: University Press of Kansas.

Stephens, Hiram B., 1890. *Jacques Cartier and his Four Voyages to Canada: An Essay, with Historical, Explanatory and Philological Notes*. Montreal: W. Drysdale and Company.

Steponaitis, Vincas P., Megan C. Kassabaum, and John W. O'Hear, 2015. Cahokia's Coles Creek Predecessors. In *Medieval Mississippians: The Cahokian World*, edited by T. R. Pauketat and S. M. Alt, pp. 13–19. Santa Fe, NM: School for Advanced Research Press.

Steward, Julian, 1955. *Theory of Culture Change*. Urbana: University of Illinois Press.

Stewart, Hilary, 1973. *Artifacts of the Northwest Coast Indians*. Victoria, BC: Hancock House.

Stewart, Omer C., 1987. *Peyote Religion: A History*. Norman: University of Oklahoma Press.

Stone, Connie L., 1987. *People of the Desert, Canyons, and Pines: Prehistory of the Patayan Country in West Central Arizona*. Phoenix: Arizona State Office of the Bureau of Land Management.

Storck, Peter L., 1997. *The Fisher Site: Archaeological, Geological, and Paleobotanical Studies at an Early Paleo-Indian Site in Southern Ontario, Canada*. Memoirs of the Museum of Anthropology 30. Ann Arbor: University of Michigan.

Storck, Peter L., and A. E. Spiess, 1994. The Significance of New Faunal Identifications Attributed to an Early Paleoindian (Gainey Complex) Occupation at the Udora Site, Ontario, Canada. *American Antiquity* 59:121–142.

Storey, Rebecca, 2012. Population Decline during and after Conquest. In *The Oxford Handbook of Mesoamerican Archaeology*, edited by D. L. Nichols and C. A. Pool, pp. 908–915. Oxford: Oxford University Press.

Stothers, David M., 1975. The Emergence and Development of the Younge and Ontario Iroquois Traditions. *Ontario Archaeology* 25:21–30.

Stothers, David M., and James R. Graves, 1983. Cultural Continuity and Change: The Western Basin, Ontario Iroquois, and Sandusky Traditions – A 1982 Perspective. *Archaeology of Eastern North America* 11:109–142.

Straus, Lawrence G., 2000. Solutrean Settlement of North America? A Review of Reality. *American Antiquity* 65:219–226.

Struever, Stuart, 1964. The Hopewellian Interaction Sphere in Riverine Western Great Lakes Culture History. In *Hopewell Studies*, edited by J. R. Caldwell and Robert Hall, pp. 85–106. Scientific Papers No. 12. Springfield: Illinois State Museum.

Styles, Bonnie W., Steven R. Ahler, and Melvin D. Fowler, 1983. Modoc Rock Shelter Revisited. In *Archaic Hunter-Gatherers in the American Midwest*, edited by J. L. Phillips and J. A. Brown, pp. 261–298. New York: Academic Press.

Sugden, John, 1997. *Tecumseh: A Life*. New York: Henry Holt and Company.

Sugiyama, Saburo, 2012. Ideology, Polity, and Social History of the Teotihuacan State. In *The Oxford Handbook of Mesoamerican Archaeology*, edited by D. L. Nichols and C. A. Pool, pp. 215–229. Oxford: Oxford University Press.

Sullivan, Lynne P., and Christopher B. Rodning, 2001. Gender, Tradition, and the Negotiation of Power Relationships in Southern Appalachian Chiefdoms. In *The Archaeology of Traditions: Agency and History before and after Columbus*, edited by T. R. Pauketat, pp. 107–120. Gainesville: University Press of Florida.

Sullivan, Lynne P., Bobby R. Braly, Michaelyn S. Harle, and Shannon D. Koerner, 2011. Remembering New Deal Archaeology in the Southeast: A Legacy in Museum Collections. In *Museums and Memory*, edited by Margaret Williamson Huber, pp. 64–107. Knoxville: Newfound Press, University of Tennessee Libraries.

Surovell, T. A., 2003. Simulating Coastal Migration in New World Colonization. *Current Anthropology* 484:580–591.

Sutton, Mark Q., Mark E. Basgall, Jill K. Gardner, and Mark W. Allen, 2007. Advances in Understanding Mohave Desert Prehistory. In *California Prehistory: Colonization, Culture, and Complexity*, edited by Terry L. Jones and Kathryn A. Klar, pp. 229–245. Lanham, MD: AltaMira Press.

Swanton, John R. 1922. *Early History of the Creek Indians and their Neighbors*. Bureau of American Ethnology Bulletin 73. Washington, DC: Government Printing Office.

Sweeney, Kara Bridgman, 2013. A Complex Web of History and Artifact Types in the Early Archaic Southeast. Ph.D. dissertation, Department of Anthropology, University of Florida, Gainesville.

Swentzell, Rina, 2004. A Pueblo Woman's Perspective on Chaco Canyon. In *In Search of Chaco: New Approaches to an Archaeological Enigma*, edited by D. G. Noble. Santa Fe, NM: School of American Research Press.

Talbot, Richard K., and Lane D. Richens, 2004. *Fremont Farming and Mobility on the Far Northern Colorado Plateau: The Steinaker Lake Project*. Museum of Peoples and Cultures, Occasional Paper 10. Provo, UT: Brigham Young University.

Tankersley, Kenneth B., 1996. Prehistoric Salt Mining in the Mammoth Cave System. In *Of Caves and Shell Mounds*, edited by Kenneth Carstens and Patty Jo Watson, pp. 33–39. Tuscaloosa: University of Alabama Press.

Tanner, Adrian, 1979. *Bringing Home Animals: Religious Ideology and Mode of Production of the Mistassini Cree Hunters*. Social and Economic Studies 23. St. John's, Newfoundland: Institute of Social and Economic Research, Memorial University.

Taube, Karl A., 2012. Creation and Cosmology: Gods and Mythic Origins in Ancient Mesoamerica. In *The Oxford Handbook of Mesoamerican Archaeology*, edited by D. L. Nichols and C. A. Pool, pp. 741–751. Oxford: Oxford University Press.

Taylor, Walter, 1948. *A Study in Archaeology*. Memoir of the American Anthropological Association 69. New York: American Anthropological Association.

Thakar, Heather B., and Lynn H. Gamble, 2015. Religions and Rituals of Native Coastal California. In *First Coastal Californians*, edited by L.

H. Gamble, pp. 74–81. Santa Fe, NM: School for Advanced Research Press.

Thomas, Cyrus, 1894. *Report of the Mound Explorations of the Bureau of Ethnology.* 12th Annual Report, Bureau of Ethnology. Washington, DC: Smithsonian Institution.

Thomas, David H., 1973. An Empirical Test for Steward's Model of Great Basin Settlement Patterns. *American Antiquity* 38:155–176.

Thomas, David H., 1982. *The 1981 Alta Toquima Village Project: A Preliminary Report.* Social Sciences and Humanities Publication 27. Reno: Desert Research Institute.

Thomas, David H., 1983. *The Archaeology of Monitor Valley: 2. Gatecliff Shelter.* Anthropological Papers of the American Museum of Natural History 59, pt. 1. New York: American Museum of Natural History.

Thomas, David H., 1985. *The Archaeology of Hidden Cave, Nevada.* Anthropological Papers of the American Museum of Natural History 61. New York: American Museum of Natural History.

Thomas, David H., 2010. *Skull Wars: Kennewick Man, Archaeology, and the Battle for Native American Identity.* New York: Basic Books.

Thomas, David H., 2012. Historical Archaeology and Native Agency across the Spanish Borderlands. In *The Oxford Handbook of North American Archaeology*, edited by T. Pauketat, pp. 39–51. Oxford: Oxford University Press.

Thomas, P. M., Jr., and L. J. Campbell, 1991. The Elliott's Point Complex: New Data Regarding the Localized Poverty Point Expression on the Northwest Florida Gulf Coast, 2000 BC–500 BC. In *The Poverty Point Culture: Local Manifestations, Subsistence Practices, and Trade Networks*, edited by K. M. Byrd, pp. 103–120. Geoscience and Man 29. Baton Rouge: Louisiana State University.

Thompson, Victor D., 2007. Articulating Activity Areas and Formation Processes at the Sapelo Island Shell Ring Complex. *Southeastern Archaeology* 26:91–107.

Thompson, Victor D., M. D. Reynolds, B. Haley, Richard Jefferies, Jay K. Johnson, and L. Humphries, 2004. The Sapelo Shell Rings: Shallow Geophysics on a Georgia Sea Island. *Southeastern Archaeology* 23:192–201.

Thompson, Victor D., Kristen Gremillion, and Thomas J. Pluckhahn, 2013. Challenging the Evidence for Prehistoric Wetland Maize Agriculture at Fort Center, Florida. *American Antiquity* 78:181–193.

Thompson, Victor D., William H. Marquardt, and Karen J. Walker, 2014. A Remote Sensing Perspective on Shoreline Modification, Canal Construction, and Household Trajectories at Pineland along Florida's Southwestern Gulf Coast. *Archaeological Prospection* 21:59–73.

Thompson, Victor D., William H. Marquardt, Karen J. Walker, Amanda D. Roberts Thompson, and Lee A. Newsom, 2018. Collective Action, State Building, and the Rise of the Calusa, Southwest Florida. *Journal of Anthropological Archaeology* 51:28–44.

Thornton, Thomas F., 2008. *Being and Place among the Tlingit.* Seattle: University of Washington Press.

Thulman, David K., 2006. A Reconstruction of Paleoindian Social Organization in North Central Florida. Ph.D. dissertation, Department of Anthropology, Florida State University, Tallahassee.

Thulman, David K., 2009. Freshwater Availability as the Constraining Factor in the Middle Paleoindian Occupation of North-Central Florida. *Geoarchaeology* 24:243–276.

Thwaites, Ruben Gold, 1898. *The Jesuit Relations and Allied Documents* (73 volumes). Cleveland: The Burrows Brothers.

Tiffany, Joseph A., 1991. Modeling Mill Creek–Mississippian Interaction. In *New Perspectives on Cahokia: Views from the Periphery*, edited by J. B. Stoltman, pp. 319–347. Madison: Prehistory Press.

Tiffany, Joseph A., 2007. Examining the Origins of the Middle Missouri Tradition. In *Plains Village Archaeology: Bison-Hunting Farmers in the Central and Northern Plains*, edited by S. A. Ahler and M. Kay, pp. 3–14. Salt Lake City: University of Utah Press.

Tiffany, Joseph A., and L. M. Alex, 2001. *Great Oasis Archaeology: New Perspectives from the DeCamp and West Des Moines Burial Sites in Central Iowa*. Plains Anthropolgist Memoir 33, 46(178). Lincoln, NE: Plains Anthropologist.

Todd, Lawrence C., Jr., 1983. The Horner Site: Taphonomy of an Early Holocene Bonebed. Ph.D. dissertation, Department of Anthropology, University of New Mexico, Albuquerque.

Todd, Lawrence C., David C. Jones, Robert S. Walker, Paul Burnett, and Jeffrey Eighmy, 2001. Late Archaic Bison Hunters in Northern Colorado: 1997–1999 Excavations at the Kaplan-Hoover Bonebed (5LR3953). *Plains Anthropologist* 46:125–147.

Tomka, Steven A., 2013. The Adoption of the Bow and Arrow: A Model Based on Experimental Performance Characteristics. *American Antiquity* 78(3):553–569.

Trigger, Bruce G., 2007. *A History of Archaeological Thought* (second edition). Cambridge, UK: Cambridge University Press.

Trimble, Donald E., 1980. *The Geological Story of the Great Plains*. United States Geological Survey Bulletin 1493. Washington, DC: United States Geological Survey.

Trouillot, Michel-Rolph, 1991. Anthropology and the Savage Slot: The Poetics and Politics of Otherness. In *Recapturing Anthropology*, edited by Richard G. Fox, pp. 17–44. Santa Fe, NM: School of American Research.

Tuck, James A., 1976. *Ancient People of Port au Choix: The Excavations of an Archaic Indian Cemetery*. Social and Economic Studies 17. St. John's, Newfoundland: Institute of Social and Economic Research, Memorial University.

Tuck, James A., 1978. Northern Iroquoian Prehistory. In *Handbook of North American Indians, vol. XV: Northeast*, edited by B. G. Trigger, pp. 322–333. Washington, DC: Smithsonian Institution.

Tuohy, Donald R., and L. Kyle Napton, 1986. Duck Decoys from Lovelock Cave, Nevada, Dated by 14 C Accelerator Mass Spectrometry. *American Antiquity* 51:813–816.

Ure, Scott, and Michael T. Searcy, 2016. Mapping the Ancient City of Paquimé: Harnessing the Power of Pix4Dmapper Unmanned Aerial Systems. White paper for Pix4D SA.

Van Dyke, Ruth M., 2004. Memory, Meaning, and Masonry: The Late Bonito Chacoan Landscape. *American Antiquity* 69:413–431.

Van Dyke, Ruth M., 2007a. *The Chaco Experience: Landscape and Ideology at the Center Place*. Santa Fe, NM: School for Advanced Research Press.

Van Dyke, Ruth M., 2007b. Great Kivas in Time, Space, and Society. In *The Architecture of Chaco Canyon, New Mexico*, edited by S. H. Lekson, pp. 93–126. Salt Lake City: University of Utah Press.

Van Dyke, Ruth M., 2008. Chaco Reloaded. *Journal of Social Archaeology* 9(2):220–248.

Van Nest, Julie, Douglas K. Charles, Jane E. Buikstra, and David L. Asch, 2001. Sod Blocks in Illinois Hopewell Mounds. *American Antiquity* 66:633–650.

Vanderpot, Rein (ed.), 2017. *The Mescal Wash Site: A Persistent Place along Cienega Creek, Southeastern Arizona: Archaeological Investigations at the Marsh Station Traffic Interchange and Pantano Railroad Overpass, Interstate 10, Pima County, Arizona*. Technical Series 96(1). Tucson: Statistical Research.

VanPool, Christine S., and Todd L. VanPool, 2007. *Signs of Casas Grandes Shamans*. Salt Lake City: University of Utah Press.

Vennum, Thomas, Jr., 1994. *American Indian Lacrosse: Little Brother of War*. Washington, DC: Smithsonian Institution Press.

Vivian, R. Gwinn, 2004. Puebloan Farmers of the Chacoan World. In *In Search of Chaco: New Approaches to an Archaeological Enigma*, edited by David G. Noble, pp. 7–13. Santa Fe, NM: School for Advanced Research Press.

Wagner, Gail, 2000. Tobacco in Prehistoric Eastern North America. In *Tobacco Use by Native North Americans: Sacred Smoke and Silent Killer*, edited by J. C. Winter, pp. 171–184. Norman: University of Oklahoma Press.

Wagner, Henry R., 1941. *Juan Rodríguez Cabrillo: Discoverer of the Coast of California*. San Francisco: California Historical Society.

Waguespack, Nicole M., 2012. Early Paleoindians, from Colonization to Folsom. In *The Oxford Handbook of North American Archaeology*, edited by T. Pauketat, pp. 86–96. Oxford: Oxford University Press.

Waguespack, Nicole M., and Todd A. Surovell, 2003. Clovis Hunting Strategies, or How to Make Out on Plentiful Resources. *American Antiquity* 68:333–352.

Walker, Renee B., 2007. Hunting in the Late Paleoindian Period: Faunal Remains from Dust Cave. In *Foragers of the Terminal Pleistocene in North America*, edited by Renee B. Walker and Boyce N. Driskell, pp. 99–115. Lincoln: University of Nebraska Press.

Walker, William H., 2008. Practice and Nonhuman Social Actors: The Afterlife Histories of Witches and Dogs in the American Southwest. In *Memory Work: Archaeologies of Material Practices*, edited by B. J. Mills and W. H. Walker, pp. 137–158. Santa Fe, NM: School for Advanced Research Press.

Wallace, Anthony F. C., 1956. Revitalization Movements. *American Anthropologist* 58(2):264–281.

Wallace, Henry D., 2007. Hohokam Beginnings. In *The Hohokam Millennium*, edited by S. K. Fish and P. R. Fish, pp. 13–21. Santa Fe, NM: School for Advanced Research Press.

Wallis, Neill J., 2011. *The Swift Creek Gift: Vessel Exchange on the Atlantic Coast*. Tuscaloosa: University of Alabama Press.

Wallis, Neill J., and Meggan E. Blessing, 2015. Ritual Deposition and Feasting Pits: Bundling of Animal Remains in Mississippi Period Florida. *Cambridge Archaeological Journal* 25:79–98.

Walthall, John A., 1998. Rockshelters and Hunter-Gatherer Adaptation to the Pleistocene/Holocene Transition. *American Antiquity* 63:223–238.

Walthall, John A., and Brad Koldehoff, 1998. Hunter-Gatherer Interaction and Alliance Formation: Dalton and the Cult of the Long Blade. *Plains Anthropologist* 43:257–273.

Ward, Albert E., 1976. Black Mesa to the Colorado River: An Archaeological Traverse. In *Papers on the Archaeology of Black Mesa, Arizona*, edited by George J. Gumerman and Robert C. Euler, pp. 3–105. Carbondale: Southern Illinois University Press.

Ware, John A., 2014. *A Pueblo Social History: Kinship, Sodality, and Community in the Northern Southwest*. Santa Fe, NM: School for Advanced Research Press.

Waring, Antonio J., Jr., and Preston Holder, 1945. A Prehistoric Ceremonial Complex in the Southeastern United States. *American Anthropologist* 47(1):1–34.

Washburn, Wilcomb E., 1978. Seventeenth-Century Indian Wars. In *Handbook of North American Indians, vol. XV: Northeast*, edited by B. G. Trigger, pp. 89–100. Washington, DC: Smithsonian Institution.

Waters, M. R., S. L. Forman, T. A. Jennings et al., 2011. The Buttermilk Creek Complex and the Origins of Clovis at the Debra L. Friedkin Site, Texas. *Science* 331:1599–1603.

Waters, Michael R., and Stafford, Thomas W., 2007. Redefining the Age of Clovis: Implications for the Peopling of the Americas. *Science* 315:1122–1126.

Watkins, Joe, 2012. Bone Lickers, Grave Diggers, and Other Unsavory Characters: Archaeologists, Archaeological Cultures, and the Disconnect from Native Peoples. In *Oxford Handbook of North American Archaeology*, edited by Timothy R. Pauketat, pp. 29–35. Oxford: Oxford University Press.

Watson, Patty Jo, 1969. *The Prehistory of Salts Cave, Kentucky*. Report of Investigations 16. Springfield: Illinois State Museum.

Watson, Patty Jo, 1974. *Archaeology of the Mammoth Cave Area*. New York: Academic Press.

Watson, Patty Jo, 2005. WPA Excavations in the Middle Green River Region: A Comparative Account. In *Archaeology of the Middle*

Green River Region, Kentucky, edited by William H. Marquardt and Patty Jo Watson, pp. 515–628. Institute of Archaeology and Paleoenvironmental Studies Monograph 5. Gainesville: University Press of Florida.

Webb, Clarence H., 1944. Stone Vessels from a Northeast Louisiana Site. *American Antiquity* 9:386–394.

Webb, S. David (ed.), 2006. *First Floridians and Last Mastodons: The Page Ladson Site in the Aucilla River.* Dordrecht, Netherlands: Springer.

Webb, William S., 1938. *An Archaeological Survey of the Norris Basin in Eastern Tennessee.* Smithsonian Institution. Bureau of American Ethnology Bulletin 118. Washington, DC: Government Printing Office.

Webb, William S., 1939. *An Archaeological Survey of the Wheeler Basin on the Tennessee River in Northern Alabama.* Smithsonian Institution. Bureau of American Ethnology Bulletin 122. Washington, DC: Government Printing Office.

Webb, William S., 1974. *Indian Knoll.* Knoxville: University of Tennessee Press.

Webb, William S., and David L. DeJarnette, 1942. *An Archeological Survey of Pickwick Basin in the Adjacent Portions of the States of Alabama, Mississippi and Tennessee.* Smithsonian Institution. Bureau of American Ethnology Bulletin 129. Washington, DC: Government Printing Office.

Webb, William S., and Raymond S. Baby, 1957. *The Adena People #2.* Columbus: Ohio Historical Society.

Webmoor, Timothy, 2007. What about "One More Turn after the Social" in Archaeological Reasoning? Taking Things Seriously. *World Archaeology* 39(4):563–578.

Wedel, Waldo R., 1994. Coronado and Quivira. In *Spain and the Plains: Myths and Realities of Spanish Exploration and Settlement on the Great Plains*, edited by R. H. Vigil, F. W. Kaye, and J. R. Wunder, pp. 45–66. Boulder: University Press of Colorado.

Weeks, Rex, 2012. Mide Rock-Paintings: Archaeology by Formal and Informed Methods. *Cambridge Archaeological Journal* 22(2):187–207.

Weiner, Annette, 1992. *Inalienable Possessions: The Paradox of Keeping-While-Giving.* Berkeley: University of California Press.

Weinstein, Richard A., David B. Kelley, and Joe W. Saunders (eds.), 2003. *The Louisiana and Arkansas Expeditions of Clarence Bloomfield Moore.* Tuscaloosa: University of Alabama Press.

Wells, Douglas C., and Richard A. Weinstein, 2007. Extraregional Contact and Cultural Interaction at the Coles Creek–Plaquemine Transition: Recent Data from the Lake Providence Mounds, East Carroll Parish, Louisiana. In *Plaquemine Archaeology*, edited by M. A. Rees and P. C. Livingood, pp. 38–65. Tuscaloosa: University of Alabama Press.

Wengrow, David, and David Graeber, 2018. "Many Seasons Ago": Slavery and its Rejection among Foragers on the Pacific Coast of

North America. *American Anthropologist* 120(2). https://doi.org/10.1111/aman.12969.

Whalen, Michael E., and Paul E. Minnis, 2001. *Casas Grandes and its Hinterland: Prehistoric Political Organization in Northwest Mexico.* Tucson: University of Arizona Press.

Whalen, Michael E., and Paul E. Minnis, 2009. *The Neighbors of Casas Grandes: Excavating Medio Period Communities of Northwest Chihuahua, Mexico.* Tucson: University of Arizona Press.

Whalen, Michael E., and Paul E. Minnis, 2012. Ceramics and Polity in the Casas Grandes Area, Chihuahua, Mexico. *American Antiquity* 75: 527–551.

Wheat, Joe Ben, 1972. *The Olsen-Chubbuck Site: A Paleo-Indian Bison Kill.* Memoirs of the Society for American Archaeology 26. Washington, DC: Society for American Archaeology.

White, Leslie A., 1959. *The Evolution of Culture: The Development of Civilization to the Fall of Rome.* New York: McGraw-Hill.

White, Nancy M. (ed.), 2005. *Gulf Coast Archaeology: The Southeastern United States and Mexico.* Gainesville: University Press of Florida.

Whitley, David S., 2000. *The Art of the Shaman.* Salt Lake City: University of Utah Press.

Whitridge, Peter, 1998. The Construction of Social Difference in a Prehistoric Inuit Whaling Community. Ph.D. dissertation, Department of Anthropology, Arizona State University, Tempe.

Whitridge, Peter, 2002. Social and Ritual Determinants of Whale Bone Transport at a Classic Thule Winter Site in the Canadian Arctic. *International Journal of Osteoarchaeology* 12:65–75.

Whittlesey, Stephanie M., 2007. Hohokam Ceramics, Hohokam Beliefs. In *The Hohokam Millennium*, edited by S. K. Fish and P. R. Fish, pp. 65–73. Santa Fe, NM: School for Advanced Research Press.

Widmer, Randolph J., 1988. *The Evolution of the Calusa: A Nonagricultural Chiefdom on the Southwest Florida Coast.* Tuscaloosa: University of Alabama Press.

Wilcox, David R., 1999. A Preliminary Graph-Theoretic Analysis of Access Relationships at Casas Grandes. In *The Casas Grandes World*, edited by C. F. Schaafsma and C. L. Riley, pp. 93–104. Salt Lake City: University of Utah Press.

Wilcox, David R., Thomas R. McGuire, and Charles Sternberg, 1981. *Snaketown Revisited.* Arizona State Museum Archaeological Series 155. Tucson: Arizona State Museum.

Wilkerson, S. Jeffrey K., 2005. Rivers in the Sea: The Gulf of Mexico as a Cultural Corridor in Antiquity. In *Gulf Coast Archaeology: The Southeastern United States and Mexico*, edited by N. M. White, pp. 56–67. Gainesville: University Press of Florida.

Willey, Gordon R., and Philip Phillips, 1958. *Method and Theory in American Archaeology.* Chicago: University of Chicago Press.

Willey, P., and Thomas E. Emerson, 1993. The Osteology and Archaeology of the Crow Creek Massacre. *Plains Anthropologist* 38(145):227–269.

Williams, Mark, and D. T. Elliot (eds.), 1998. *A World Engraved: Archaeology of the Swift Creek Culture.* Tuscaloosa: University of Alabama Press.

Williams, Stephen, 1990. The Vacant Quarter and Other Late Events in the Lower Valley. In *Towns and Temples along the Mississippi*, edited by D. H. Dye, pp. 170–180. Tuscaloosa: University of Alabama Press.

Williamson, Ray A., 1984. *Living the Sky: The Cosmos of the American Indian.* Norman: University of Oklahoma Press.

Williamson, Ronald F., 2012. What Will Be Has Always Been: The Past and Present of Northern Iroquoians. In *The Oxford Handbook of North American Archaeology*, edited by T. R. Pauketat, pp. 273–284. Oxford: Oxford University Press.

Wilmsen, Edwin N., 1974. *Lindenmeier: A Pleistocene Hunting Society.* New York: Harper and Row.

Wilshusen, Richard H., 2006. The Genesis of Pueblos: Innovations between 500 and 900 CE. In *The Mesa Verde World: Explorations into Ancestral Pueblo Archaeology*, edited by D. G. Noble, pp. 19–27. Santa Fe, NM: School of American Research Press.

Wilson, Gilbert Livingstone, 1917. *Agriculture of the Hidatsa Indians: An Indian Interpretation.* Studies in the Social Sciences, Bulletin 9. Minneapolis: University of Minnesota.

Wilson, Samuel M., 1990. *Hispaniola: Caribbean Chiefdoms in the Age of Columbus.* Tuscaloosa: University of Alabama Press.

Windes, Thomas C., 2004. The Rise of Early Chacoan Great Houses. In *In Search of Chaco: New Approaches to an Archaeological Enigma*, edited by D. G. Noble, pp. 14–21. Santa Fe, NM: School of American Research Press.

Windes, Thomas C., 2007. Gearing Up and Piling On: Early Great Houses in the Interior San Juan Basin. In *The Architecture of Chaco Canyon, New Mexico*, edited by S. H. Lekson, pp. 45–92. Salt Lake City: University of Utah Press.

Winter, Joseph C., 2000. Introduction to the North American Tobacco Species. In *Tobacco Use by Native North Americans: Sacred Smoke and Silent Killer*, edited by J. C. Winter, pp. 3–8. Norman: University of Oklahoma Press.

Winters, Howard D., 1969. *The Riverton Culture.* Reports of Investigation 13. Springfield: Illinois State Museum.

Wissler, Clark, 1912. *Ceremonial Bundles of the Blackfoot Indians.* Anthropological Papers of the American Museum of Natural History 7, pt. 2. New York: American Museum of Natural History.

Wissler, Clark, and Herbert J. Spinden, 1916. The Pawnee Human Sacrifice to the Morning Star. *American Museum Journal* 16(January):49–55.

Witthoft, John, 1949. *Green Corn Ceremonialism in the Eastern Woodlands*. Museum of Anthropology, Occasional Contributions 13. Ann Arbor: University of Michigan.

Wolf, Eric, 1982. *Europe and the People without History*. Berkeley: University of California Press.

Wolfe, Cary, 2009. *What is Posthumanism?* Minneapolis: University of Minnesota Press.

Wolff, Christopher B., 2012. Fear and Loathing in the Eastern Subarctic Archaic Period. Paper presented at the 111th Annual Meeting of the American Anthropological Association, San Francisco, CA.

Wood, W. Raymond, 1961. *An Interpretation of Mandan Culture History*. Bureau of American Ethnology Bulletin 198. Washington, DC: Smithsonian Institution.

Woodburn, James, 1982. Egalitarian Societies. *Man* 17:431–451.

Wright, Alice P., and Edward R. Henry (eds.), 2013. *Early Woodland Landscapes of the Southeast*. Gainesville: University Press of Florida.

Wright, James V., 1966. *The Ontario Iroquois Tradition*. Anthropological Series 75, Bulletin 210. Ottawa: National Museum of Canada.

Wyckoff, Don G., and Robert Bartlett, 1995. Living on the Edge: Late Pleistocene–Early Holocene Cultural Interaction along Southeastern Woodlands–Plains Border. In *Native American Interactions: Multiscalar Analyses and Interpretations in the Eastern Woodlands*, edited by Michael S. Nassaney and Kenneth E. Sassaman, pp. 27–72. Knoxville: University of Tennessee Press.

Yarnell, Richard A., and M. Jean Black, 1985. Temporal Trends Indicated by a Survey of Archaic and Woodland Plant Remains from Southeastern North America. *Southeastern Archaeology* 4:93–106.

Yerkes, Richard, and Linda M. Gaertner, 1997. Microwear Analysis of Dalton Artifacts. In *Sloan: A Paleoindian Dalton Cemetery in Arkansas*, edited by Dan F. Morse, pp. 58–71. Washington, DC: Smithsonian Institution Press.

Young, Gloria A., 2001. Intertribal Religious Movements. In *Handbook of North American Indians, Plains, Part 2 of 2*, edited by R. J. DeMallie, pp. 996–1025. Washington, DC: Smithsonian Institution.

Zaragosa Ocaña, Diana, 2005. Characteristic Elements Shared by Northeastern Mexico and the Southeastern United States. In *Gulf Coast Archaeology: The Southeastern United States and Mexico*, edited by N. M. White, pp. 245–259. Gainesville: University Press of Florida.

Zavala, Bridget M., 2006. Elevated Spaces: Exploring the Symbolic at *Cerros de Trincheras*. In *Religion in the Prehispanic Southwest*, edited by C. S. VanPool, T. L. VanPool, and D. A. Phillips. Lanham, MD: AltaMira Press.

Zavala, Bridget M., 2012. Terraced Lives: *Cerros de Trincheras* in the Northwest/Southwest. In *The Oxford Handbook of North American Archaeology*, edited by T. R. Pauketat, pp. 585–596. Oxford: Oxford University Press.

Zedeño, Maria Nieves, 2008. Bundled Worlds: The Roles and Interactions of Complex Objects from the North American Plains. *Journal of Archaeological Method and Theory* 15:362–378.

Zedeño, Maria Nieves, Jesse A. M. Ballenger, and John R. Murray, 2014. Landscape Engineering and Organizational Complexity among Late Prehistoric Bison Hunters of the Northwestern Plains. *Current Anthropology* 55:23–58.

Zelen, Alexey, 2014. Ceramics. In *Late Woodland Communities in the American Bottom: The Fish Lake Site*, edited by A. C. Fortier, pp. 127–262. Illinois State Archaeological Survey, Technical Report 145. Urbana: University of Illinois.

Zimmerman, Larry J., 1985. *Peoples of Prehistoric South Dakota*. Lincoln: University of Nebraska Press.

Index